The
Oxford Book
of
Greek Verse in Translation

Edited by
T. F. Higham
and
C. M. Bowra

Oxford
At the Clarendon Press
1938

PRINTED IN GREAT BRITAIN

TO HELLENISTS ON
BOTH SIDES OF THE ATLANTIC
AND TO
FRIENDS OF ENGLAND
IN HELLAS

Greek History
Periods

I Homeric B.C. 1000 — 500
        Trojan war to end of Persian

II Classical BC 500 — 338
      Salamis — Chaeronea
           (Philip & Alexander)

III Alexandrian B.C. 338 — about 100
                   (Sulla)

IV Roman
        To coming of Vandals — abt
           300 yrs.

V Byzantine — 1453
               abt 1000 yrs

VI Turkish — 1827 x Navarino

VII . Modern

PREFACE

WHEN *The Oxford Book of Greek Verse* was published in 1930, some demand arose for a volume of English translations to accompany the Greek text. This book is an attempt to meet that demand, but is also adapted to the needs of the general reader. Every piece in *The Oxford Book of Greek Verse* is here translated, and the same arrangement of authors and numeration is followed, except for some minor differences which either explain themselves or are explained in the Notes.

Wherever possible, we have used existing translations, sometimes adapting those of less recent date to bring them nearer the Greek. All these sources are named in the list of References on pp. 768–81, which expresses in detail our indebtedness to well over a hundred authors and the publishers concerned. It is pleasant to record that these numerous permissions to print were all most willingly given.

Where no translations, or none that were suitable, existed, we have either made our own or profited by the generous help of friends. In particular we are grateful to Sir William Marris for help with Hesiod, Theocritus, and the epigrammatists; to Mr. Jack Lindsay, who has revised some pieces already published and written for us new versions of Hesiod, the Homeric Hymns, and Æschylus; to Dr. Gilbert Murray and Professor E. R. Dodds for some unpublished pieces; and to Mr. George Allen, Mr. Gilbert Highet, and Mr. Michael Balkwill—

contributors representing a generation younger than our own.

Grateful recognition is also due to many scholars, living and dead, whose commentaries on the Greek texts have eased the way of translation. As far as possible, 'conscious debts' to these sources, or to other translations, such as those in the Loeb series, have been separately acknowledged; but others remain, none the less real because imponderable.

Mr. E. A. Barber and Mr. D. L. Page have given valuable help in the Notes; Professor J. R. R. Tolkien and Mr. W. H. Shewring in the second part of the Introduction; Sir Paul Harvey in the Note on Proper Names. There has also been some collaboration between the Editors and their contributors, the details of which, by mutual consent, need not be specified.

Finally we wish to thank the Officials and Staff of the Clarendon Press for long patience and much good guidance. In reading the proofs it has not been easy to ensure that the Greek names are accented uniformly throughout, but the effort has been made. For obvious reasons we have kept the translators' spelling of these names, and hope that readers will not be unduly puzzled by the varieties to be found. Some help in these matters is given on pp. cix–cxii and in the Notes.

INTRODUCTION. PART I

The Character and Development of Greek Poetry

WE owe so much to the Greeks that we are liable to approach their poetry as if it were a contemporary art and to expect from it qualities familiar in our own. So far as the essential enjoyment of it is concerned, this is right and reasonable; for the Greek poets make their perennial appeal through the permanent claims of the human heart. But such an approach has its dangers, and because of it we may both misunderstand some vital elements in Greek art and expect from it something which it never claimed or tried to give. Before reading Greek poetry it is important to see that in some respects it is far removed from our own and that we must view it with different eyes. In the forms of its composition, in its language, in its choice of subjects, in its limitations and conventions, it followed lines which other literatures have not followed, and some acquaintance with its peculiarities is indispensable for all who would understand what it means. It is, moreover, fragmentary. The *Iliad* and the *Odyssey* survive intact, but of a large number of tragedies once written we have only a selection, and for the brilliant phase of lyric poetry we have to rely largely on scattered and incomplete quotations. Small fragments, that would be negligible enough in a complete literature, take on a considerable importance as evidence for what once existed, and any anthology must include them, even if their intrinsic merit is not equal to their historical interest. They help to complete the picture, to give an idea of what once was there.

The Greeks, unlike the moderns, owed nothing to earlier literatures. They were not interested in foreign languages, and even foreign civilizations made an inconsiderable appeal to their imagination. They drew the strength of their arts from their own traditions, and they remained faithful to their own rules and standards. This was particularly true of their poetry. Its origins lay far back in an irrecoverable past, but by the eighth century it had found itself, and its first achievements in metre and verse-structure lasted for centuries into the period of greatest vitality and survived even into the Christian culture of Byzantium. Time, of course, tended to obliterate the traces of these origins and to confound distinctions of kind, but in its greatest days Greek poetry was still determined by them and owed to them many of its special characteristics. The force of precedent was stronger with the Greeks than it is to-day, and their special success is that instead of being hampered or discouraged by their predecessors they made use of them and advanced on the lines which they had marked.

In its early stages and in its heyday Greek poetry was composed not to be read but to be heard. Originally it was either recited or sung, and books were, for all practical purposes, a late invention which came into their own when the great days of poetry were passed. When a Greek poet composed, he had in mind not the solitary reader in his study but the choir singing at some public festival, or the rhapsode reciting to a popular gathering, or the man of substance singing songs of his own composition to a circle of friends. For some centuries Greek poetry was an art for the many, and from this it drew much of its strength. The poet felt behind him the force of an appreciative company, whose ideas he shared and with whom he might be on terms of equality, even of intimacy. He had no need to apologize or to explain: he need not defend himself against misapprehension or decry the hostility of others to his art. In consequence, Greek poetry was truly representative of the Greek world. In that world it had its honoured place, and from this fact it drew confidence and power. It was seldom the reserved speciality of a clique, seldom the protest of a few cultivated souls against the prevalent Philistinism of their time. Later indeed, in the fourth and later centuries before Christ, the poets no longer felt so much at home, and the character of their work changed. But in its great days Greek poetry belonged to the societies in which it was born, and in these its own part was allotted to it.

This part seems from the beginning to have been twofold, and the two kinds of early Greek poetry determined much in its subsequent course. The earliest known forms are Epic and the Choral Ode. Each came from a different origin and developed on its own lines. Interaction was, of course, inevitable; but for centuries each kept its own character and answered a different social or spiritual need. The origins of the Epic must lie in the songs which soldiers sang on the march or over the camp-fire, but it exists for us in the *Iliad* and the *Odyssey*, the two poems which the Greeks attributed to Homer. In these supreme epics, composed probably in the eighth century, a long tradition reached its culmination, and a great creative genius built two single and harmonious works of art out of a welter of legends. From Homer we know what the Epic was. It was sung or recited to the lyre; and since its tone is predominantly aristocratic or even princely, it was certainly composed for the ruling classes, for men of lineage and position whose chief interest was in fighting. Its unit of composition is not the stanza but the single line, and throughout it uses the hexameter. It was, moreover, meant mainly to give pleasure: the poet had no explicit message, though his work shows that he had his own sensitive appreciation of right and wrong, and the times of his performance must have been dictated simply by his patrons' wishes. In the Epic the poet remains anonymous, even impersonal. He passes no judgements, and he gives no advice; he says nothing at all about himself; his home and even his name have been matters of long debate. Homer is as remote as Shakespeare, and we know him not from any statement of his opinions but entirely from his art and from its appeal to the imagination and the emotions. He speaks as the voice of the Muse, the divine power which tells him what to say, and behind him lies the authority of tradition. Therefore the Epic is full of conventions. Its standard epithets, its recurring lines for recurring themes, its similes, its vocabulary elaborated from many sources to be unlike any spoken tongue, all show that Homer's art was the product of a long succession of bards, and that, when he sang, he sang as one who knew the old stories and the right way to tell them.

From this traditional basis Homer built his two great poems. His themes had been used before, and most of his characters were known by name and had certain obvious characteristics. But in the *Iliad* he turned a crude story of revenge into the tragic tale of a great man's wrath and its evil consequences, and in the *Odyssey* he combined various mariners' yarns of monsters and hairbreadth escapes with an age-old story of a wanderer who returns after many years to find his house in the possession of blackguards who want to marry his wife. The structure of both poems is easy and elastic, as befits tales meant for piece-meal recitation, but in both there is a central idea and a unifying plan. The poet shows his skill in knitting the many threads together into a coherent whole. His characters, too, are transformed from shadowy names into real creatures of flesh and blood, sharply distinguished from each other and seen clearly by a poet who knows what men and women are. Over his material Homer has a complete mastery. He takes what the tradition gives and shapes it into something new, shedding over all the light of his creative vision in which all details are significant and all episodes are constructed by a master of narrative. Homer was truly Greek both in his indebtedness to his predecessors and in his free use of what he took from them.

The form of the Epic was not confined to narrative. Hesiod was perhaps a contemporary of Homer, and he, too, learned his technique in the Epic school. But he used it for a very different purpose. His *Works and Days* is a treatise on farming, written with a practical aim, and his *Theogony* is an attempt to systematize the ancient theology of Greece. But since he wrote for his brother and not for princely patrons, he is unashamedly personal, full of advice and homely wisdom. He is the poet of the struggling farmer, the man who sings of the difficulties, rather than of the glories, of life. If Homer lived with a splendid past, Hesiod lived with a hard present. His art, in spite of its Epic form, owes more to traditional maxims on the weather and the treatment of the gods than to stories of a Heroic Age. He wrote in Homer's style because no other was known to him, but his work is far removed from Homer's and shows how even at this early date Greek poetry was capable of covering widely different fields. The true successors of Homer are to be seen not in him but in the writers of the so-called Homeric Hymns. These were really preludes recited before the public recitations of the Epic, and they were usually concerned with some god or goddess at whose festival the recitations took place. They are short pieces of narrative, and they often tell some delightful story about the gods. In spite of their varying dates—and the *Hymn to Pan* may be as late as 490 B.C.—they are authentic products of the Homeric spirit. The men who composed them were so deeply versed in the Epic that they carried its style and spirit into their own work.

Quite different from the Epic, and equally ancient, was the Choral Ode. It was well established in Homer's day, and though our earliest example, Alcman's *Maiden-Song* (No. 114), comes from the seventh century, the form is certainly very old. It differs from the Epic in that it was sung by a choir and was accompanied by dancing. The dance had regular movements, and the structure of the Ode was suited to them: therefore it was composed in stanzas, and its metre was not the regular single line of the Epic but varied with almost every Ode until in its later stages it reached a high degree of complexity. Nor was its difference from the Epic confined to its form. Odes were written for special occasions, and their origins were religious. They were in the first place Hymns sung to the gods at their festivals, and they were more stately and more formal than the Epic. To the end of its career the Ode kept certain of its earliest features. It told some story about gods or heroes: it announced maxims or fundamental truths about the relation of man to the gods: in a way quite alien to the Epic it introduced personal remarks about those who took part in it or were concerned with the ceremony. Moreover, in it the poet himself had an important role. He spoke with authority and was allowed to give free expression to his thoughts because he was regarded as in some sense the mouthpiece of a god; he could say what others felt and had the power to interpret the meaning of the ceremony. The Choral Ode is in consequence more difficult and more intimate than the Epic. Its full understanding demands a knowledge of its circumstances which is too often unattainable. But its very concentration adds to its power. The Choral Ode tells what the Greeks felt on those solemn or happy occasions when they met together and sang of their relations to the gods and to each other.

Enough examples of the Choral Ode survive to show that, although it kept its traditional features for some three centuries, it was treated differently by different poets. Alcman's *Maiden-Song* began with a Myth on the sin of pride and then changed in the portion best preserved into verses of charming badinage between the girls who sung it. Although the occasion was a religious festival and ended with a rite, it was not unduly solemn. The girls could make jokes about each other and especially about their leaders Hâgêsichora and Agidô, whose beauty and gifts are contrasted with delightful imagery. In Alcman's day the Choral Ode was still religious, but in the sixth century it was partly secularized. Great men, like the tyrant Polycratês of Samos, employed poets to write Choral Odes in their honour; and from Ibycus' stanzas to Polycratês' son (No. 166) we can see how the old form took on a courtly aspect in which the old themes were dismissed for a new convention of love. In the following century Bacchylidês seems to have been content to avoid most religious or moral issues in his odes and to write what were brilliant lyrical tales (Nos. 308–9). This secularization was no doubt connected with that characteristically Greek form of poetry, the Epinîkian Ode, written for winners in the great games. But by a remarkable paradox our best examples of these come from Pindar, who was a deeply religious man and infused this comparatively new form with all the fervour of his mystical spirit. He saw the glory of victory as a divine thing which made the winner share for the moment some of the gods' blessedness. To convey his full feelings he used all the resources of the old religious ode, and in every one of his poems he gives a large part to the gods. Moreover, it was his sense of the importance of victory that made him tell brilliant and moving stories from the heroic past. By means of these he was able to relate his victor to the men of divine breed who had done great things long ago and through the implied comparison to point out the underlying moral of the present occasion.

If the twin arts of Epic and the Choral Ode were the fundamental types of Greek poetry, there existed also a popular art, not perhaps so ancient, which vied with them in the quality of its success. The solo-song or Monody was the nearest Greek equivalent to the modern lyric, in that it was composed by a poet for his own need or pleasure and did not demand a choir for its singing. It was, it is true, always a genuine song, but since it was concerned largely with private emotions it is more modern than the Ode. Moreover, the free circumstances of its composition meant that in the case of great writers like Sappho, Alcæus, and Anacreon, it covered a wide range of subjects and used or invented a great variety of metres. Its origins lay in folk-song, like the song which the women sang when grinding corn at Myti-lênê (No. 125 ii), but it was taken up by leisured men and women who, with a perfect sense of its possibilities, used it for the revelation of their inmost feelings. Such songs were usually sung to the lyre, and they found their place wherever men or women met together and entertained each other with music. There was, too, another type of monody which was sung to the flute, in which the metrical unit was a couplet. To this belongs the great class of elegiac poems, which is at least as old as the seventh century, and was to last for some fifteen hundred years to Comêtas (No. 706). The metre used originally for marching-songs by Tyrtæus (No. 97) and Callînus (No. 102), or for love-songs by Mimnermus (Nos. 118–19), soon extended its sphere, and the elegiac epigram passed by a curious process from being sung at banquets to being engraved on tombs. It reached perfection with Simonidês, whose sepulchral epigrams are a faultless form of art. In a few telling words he said something inevitably and unforgettably right.

In its early period Greek poetry was composed in many parts of Greece, and no single city held a marked predominance. But in the fifth century Athens became the centre of Greek civilization and of Greek poetry. Hitherto it could boast of little but the gnomic elegiacs of Solon (Nos. 158–60) and some aristocratic drinking-songs (Nos. 226–36). Now it developed a new form of its own. Attic tragedy has had so vast an influence on the world that it is hard to believe that it grew out of the Choral Ode. But this influence is marked in its early stages and persists until its end. Tragedy began when Thespis made the leader of his choir assume the part of a character, who formed the subject of a song, and development came as the number of actors was increased and the scope of dramatic action widened. But Attic Tragedy differs from Elizabethan precisely because of its choral origin. It kept all through its history, despite some obvious inconvenience, the Chorus which sings its odes at intervals and draws morals and reflections from the action. The number of its actors was never increased above four, and with Comedy it remained a special art of Dionŷsus, at whose festivals it was performed. The tragic poets, like the choral, were allowed a great measure of liberty in their treatment of plots and in their expression of opinions. But they were restricted by the conditions in which their plays were performed. The Greek stage allowed little change of scene, and the religious character of the occasion demanded that, superficially at least, the poet should observe the decencies of a sacred festival. Tragedy was expected to be serious, and poets who, like Euripidês, varied from the normal tone, were severely criticized for it.

The traditional character of Tragedy is easy to see. The rhetorical speeches, the stiff interchange of formal conversation, the splendid odes with their balanced verses and elaborate language, the avoidance of violent action on the stage and the convention by which the crisis is usually related by a Messenger, all betray the influence of an archaic convention. But into this form the great tragedians each poured the wealth of his imaginative thought. If Æschylus composed on a grander scale than his successors,

Sophoclês showed a greater dramatic sense and keener psychological insight, while Euripidês, always adventurous and inventive, had a keen eye for an unusual situation and a wonderful gift of melodious song. Greek Tragedy was not always tragic in the modern sense. Æschylus' *Persæ* is a historical drama, while Sophoclês' *Philoctêtês* and Euripidês' *Îphigenia in Tauris* are plays of character and situation. But among these plays are some which are deeply and truly tragic. There are few scenes ever written more painful than that in which Cassandra waits for her own death at Agamemnon's door (No. 252), or that in which Œdipus explains why he has blinded himself (No. 320). Euripidês fully grasped the tragic possibilities of his art, and when he makes Hêraclês realize that he has killed his children (No. 370), or describes the horrors of the sack of Troy (No. 374), we can see why he was called 'the most tragic of the poets'.

Parallel to Tragedy, and developed from origins not entirely dissimilar, grew Attic Comedy. If Tragedy was concerned with the problems of death and suffering, Comedy was concerned with the mysteries of birth and fertility, but it treated them in a totally different spirit. Comedy, as an art, grew out of rustic ribaldry and ithyphallic rites. Abuse, that might once have been meant to avert the evil eye, became with Aristophanês a pleasure in itself, and the jester's privilege of speaking the truth was transformed by him into a criticism of Athenian politics, morals, and literature. Keeping the old dances, dresses, and characters, the Attic comedians created an astonishing art which has little in common with any later comedy. The Comedies of Aristophanês are imaginative farces, constructed with absurdly improbable plots and extraordinary freedom of speech. Many of the jokes are topical, and the point of some is lost for ever. In these flights of comic fancy there is nothing awkward or archaic, and yet the whole form is undeniably primitive. Aristophanês has so fine a sense of his medium that he created a coherent world of his own, entirely alive and beautiful, in which the laws of nature yield to other laws of his own making.

Between Comedy and Tragedy lay a curious form known as the Satyric Drama, whose main characteristic seems to have been that it usually had a Chorus of Satyrs, the traditional followers of Dionŷsus. This was composed by Tragedians and performed after a set of three tragedies was finished. In practice it must have given some light relief after the strong emotions aroused by Tragedy, but in origin it seems simply to have been another form of Dionysiac choral song, rather different from those which led to Comedy and Tragedy. Of the specimens which survive neither the *Ichneutæ* of Sophoclês (No. 344) nor the *Cyclops* of Euripidês (No. 350) show anything resembling an Aristophanic spirit. They treat traditional stories in a light-hearted way, but there is no wild fancy in them and no satire on contemporary events. Indeed the *Alcêstis* of Euripidês (Nos. 351–4), which is said to have been acted as a Satyric Drama, has in it elements very close to Tragedy, although it certainly treats an old story in a somewhat critical spirit.

These were the main forms of Greek poetry in its

great days, and it is clear that they were fewer and more distinct from each other than the forms of modern poetry. Each had its own rules and characteristics, and to these the poets were expected to conform. And in practice they conformed. Their success was judged by their new interpretation of an old story or by some new turn they gave to it. Like the religious painters of the Italian Renaissance, they were limited in their choice of subjects and in the manner of their presentation, but just as the painter could win renown by his new handling of an old theme, so the poet was judged successful if he made a new story live again or turned an established convention to a new use. He was confined within recognized limits, but within them he could act with reasonable liberty. The public knew what it expected from a poet, and he had to provide it, but he must also add to what his predecessors had done and show that he too had something to say. The result is that both Attic Tragedy and Comedy show great skill in their construction and are tightly packed with meaning. A poet who deals with an unprecedented subject need not take the same pains to perfect his work as one who is traversing familiar ground. The repetition of themes meant on the whole that each new version added something, and the poet took care that his new view was worthy of its predecessors. Sophoclês saw the story of Êlectra quite differently from Æschylus, and since he saw it differently, he took great trouble to make his presentation convincing in its dramatic and psychological details. The remarkable speed with which Aristophanês introduces and concludes a new scene shows that he too understood the art of saying just what was wanted and then passing on to something else. The economy, which is so marked a feature of Greek dramatic art, was largely a result of traditionalism. The audience knew the story and required no introduction or explanation. So the poet plunged into what was the essential part of his plot.

In 404 B.C. Athens surrendered to Sparta, and the Athenian Empire came to an end. The change so caused was far more than political. The fourth century has none of the high confidence and established certainty of the fifth. It was a period of anxiety, poverty, and doubt. Its mental state is reflected in the paucity of its poetry, and when poetry came to life again, it was in new conditions at Alexandria. Here a few cultivated men, living under the rule of Greek despots in a foreign land, created a new and delicate art which differed in many ways from earlier poetry. It was written to be read rather than to be heard, and it played little part in the national life. The great occasions which demanded Tragedies and Choral Odes did not exist in Alexandria, and even in Athens the development of drama, responding to new conditions, swung away from the older forms. So poets wrote for their friends and for each other, and their poems were usually, like modern poems, meant to be read. In the main they drew their style from the great masters of the past. The most popular form was the Simonidean epigram which found a new grace with Callimachus (Nos. 513–21) and Asclê-piadês (Nos. 524–9). Apollonius, it is true, wrote his

Epic, the *Argonautica*, and owed something to Homer in his metre and style, but he lacked Homer's broad sweep and heroic temper. His gifts were more lyrical and idyllic than epic. He looked to the past, but some of his contemporaries looked for undiscovered beauties in the present. The greatest of them, Theocritus, found much of his inspiration among simple shepherds, and even among the busy townsfolk of Alexandria, while in Athens Menander developed, not without some precedent in Euripidês, a new type of comedy in which character and incident were reflected through his gentle, contemplative mind. Herôdas (No. 556) found in low life the matter for short vivid sketches for the stage. The Alexandrian Age drew its strength from its sense of personality. Lacking institutions and cut off from the full life of the city-state, it found its material in personal relations and idiosyncrasies. Its conservatism was more deliberate than instinctive. It used the old forms because they belonged to the past, not because they served any definite function. But it used them with taste and discernment, and the invention of the Idyll by Theocritus shows how well he understood the artistic needs of his time. The Alexandrian style of writing survived when the centre of Greek life was transferred to Byzantium, and for the first six centuries after Christ the epigram continued to be vigorous and skilful. Even the Epic had its revival, and though Nonnus and Quintus Smyrnaeus are usually poor performers, they occasionally caught some breath of life and achieved an unexpected moment of tension or pathos.

In the elegiac epigram the Hellenistic poets found their characteristic means of self-expression. Their poems differed from earlier epigrams in being composed not for use but for literary enjoyment. Simonidês had written his epitaphs to be recorded on tombs, while other elegiacs, like those of Mimnermus, were sung over the wine. But the Alexandrians adopted the old form and copied it, writing sepulchral epigrams for imaginary dead and extending the scope of the form to many uses of social life. So the later elegiac was not unlike the modern lyrical poem in being primarily meant to be read and in being often simply a record of something which had touched the poet's heart or imagination. The change may have begun before Alexandrian times, and all the signs of it are to be seen in the epigrams attributed to Plato, if indeed they are his. These newer epigrams fall roughly into two classes. The Dorian epigram, written by Ánytê (Nos. 487–90) and Leônidas (Nos. 545–8), treated of pastoral scenes and village life. Other poets treated of more various scenes and wrote of books or personal relations or public events, as did Antipater of Sidon (Nos. 566–9), or of love as did Meleâger (Nos. 578–88). But this distinction came to be obliterated, and the epigram was used for almost any purpose the poet wanted, until in Palladas (Nos. 633–45) it became the means for a pessimistic philosophy of life. The epigram kept its small scale and its concentrated art, and though its rules became stricter and its language was always being enriched, it remained in essentials one of the oldest forms of Greek poetry.

Throughout its history Greek poetry shows the marks of tradition and of discipline, and the marvel is that with these limitations it did what it did. Once the circumstances of its development are seen, its achievement can be fully appreciated, and we can turn to it as to something that still has importance for the world. Its chief writers soon become known to us, and their special characteristics are as familiar and lovable as if they had lived much nearer to our own time. Each is himself, and may be known for his own sake; but at this distance they may be seen to have certain qualities which belong distinctively to their world and separate them from other ages and other poets. The modern world has a wider range than the Greek, and new kinds of poetry have been born of which the Greeks never dreamed. They lacked the mystical poetry of love which was the notable invention of the Middle Ages. Nor had they that special poetry of nature which is almost a creation of the nineteenth century. Their drama has not the wide sweep of Shakespeare, and even their religious poetry, splendid as it often was, was deprived by its very origin of those agonies and exaltations which are the glory of some Christian verse. Humanity has enlarged its experience since their time, and new regions have been annexed for poetry. But such lacks do not count. The claims of Greek poetry are positive enough without them.

The Greeks regarded poetry as a craft, comparable not merely with painting and sculpture, but with carpentry and horsemanship. They were extremely interested in its technicalities, and their poetry bears

the marks of careful thought in its construction. This
is, for example, particularly clear in tragedy. A play
like the *Œdipus Tyrannus* is so built that almost
every word counts in the main plan, and half the
beauty is spoiled when excerpts are made from the
whole. The same is true even of Pindar's Odes,
where remarkable changes of thought and apparent
irrelevances are really dictated by the dominating
idea of the complete poem. The Greek poets did not,
like the romantics, follow wherever the creative
whim led them. They worked as careful craftsmen,
and their intelligences were always wide awake.
They had an excellent sense of what was and what
was not real. Behind careering fancies and driving
emotions there lay minds which marked the facts
and stated them rightly. It was this which enabled
men so emotional as Archílochus to be perfectly
frank and accurate about their feelings, and even in
their most powerful rages to state their views just as
they held them. It was this too that kept the tragedians true to their task. The plots, which they were
almost forced to use, had often improbable and fantastic elements, but by thinking out the problems
implicit in them and relating them to human experience the tragedians got rid of this awkward unreality
and presented something which appeals to the intellect as well as to the aesthetic sensibility. The wildest
fantasies of Aristophanês are built out of extremely
local and topical elements; and the learned men of
Alexandria stated truly and correctly just the particular experience which they wanted to record.
This fundamental quality not only saves Greek

poetry from exaggeration and the falseness which kills great art, but adds a positive strength to it. The poetry of Homer or of Æschylus is all the more insistent and memorable because it is the creation of a mind which is not easily deceived and reaches its conclusions by a prolonged exercise of serious thought.

This sense of reality is particularly obvious in the Greek concern with human beings. Homer's heroes may be the sons of gods and capable of incredible strength and endurance, but they are solid men, individual and four-square. The tragic figures of Æschylus may be the instruments or victims of divine justice, but they act from human motives and speak with living words. The bright farces of Aristophanês defy the laws of nature, but his heroes and heroines are men and women of rapacious appetites and abundant zest for life. The world presented by the Greek poets is remarkably solid. Its characters may be imaginary, but the springs of their actions can be understood by all. Nor was this feeling for reality limited to the epic and dramatic poets. Even Pindar, who grapples with deep metaphysical and religious problems, concentrates the essence of his message in stories which make the heroic past illumine and explain the hardly less heroic present. The Greeks were primarily concerned with men, and their poetry, like their sculpture, kept firmly to human subjects and an anthropocentric outlook. Even their gods were, after all, glorified human beings, who, being free from old age and death, enjoyed their existence in a way that men envied but could not share. So Greek poetry remained remarkably concrete. Its figures are usually human and easily understood. There is little abstraction or religious symbolism. The poet is concerned with men and women, and from them and through them he gives his message.

The natural way in which the Greeks regarded their poetry accounts for one notable aspect which is not entirely agreeable to modern taste. The Greeks were not in the least ashamed of being didactic. The elegiac poetry of Solon and Theognis consists largely of versified maxims. Pindar and even Bacchylidês proclaim majestic judgements on the dangers of pride or the shortness of life. The Choruses of Tragedy, both in their songs and their spoken comments, are only too eager to point a moral. Nor are these maxims often striking by their ingenuity or their wit. Their claim is their truth, and that is sometimes of an obvious kind. The Greeks felt that the poet's business was to tell the truth, and it did not matter if he repeated what had been said before, provided he said it well and sincerely. The maxims were wrung out of experience and used by poets because they were thought to be helpful and useful. It would, indeed, be impossible for modern poets to imitate the Greeks in this respect and to compose apophthegms of such simplicity and candour. The modern man does not feel as the Greeks felt on such matters, and to repeat such ancient truths would mean a lack of conviction and a failure of power. But the Greeks felt differently, and maxims were in their opinion by no means the least important part of poetry.

Nor was the didactic spirit confined to stray maxims. Much of Greek poetry is consciously didactic in its main purpose. Where Hesiod set an example, others followed. In the sixth century his metre and manner were used for the exposition of new scientific or philosophical ideas. Parménidês expounded in hexameters a stiff cosmology of the One to which he prefixed an allegory of the soul's passage from ignorance to knowledge in the guise of a chariot-journey from darkness to light (No. 270). Empédoclês wrote a poem on the nature of things and another, called Purifications, on the right observances for the good man and the destiny of the soul (Nos. 345–9). The Alexandrians followed in the same tradition, and Aratus' *Phænomena* was largely a poetical description of the constellations (Nos. 505–6), while at a later date Oppian's *Halieutica* was a careful account of different kinds of fish (No. 625). Advocates of 'pure poetry' will certainly be distressed by this unashamed determination to use verse as a means for instruction, and it is true that prose would perhaps have done the work with more thoroughness. But the Greeks had their reasons for choosing verse. In a time when books were not common, verse could be more easily remembered, and maxims more readily kept in circulation. Moreover, the subjects usually gain in dignity by being treated in the grand manner with the full resources of a poetic vocabulary. The result may not usually be great poetry, but it is at least poetry. What might seem a thoroughly dull theme is raised above a pedestrian level and presented with some degree of liveliness and even of majesty.

On such foundations Greek poetry rests, but of

course they do not account for its greatness. Nor indeed is its success to be explained; for the peculiar gifts of the poet still elude analysis. But the qualities of Greek poetry must force themselves on the attention of every one who knows what poetry is. The Greek world was not large. The whole extent of Greek lands is small, and most of the Greek poets passed their lives in narrow districts separated from neighbouring cities by high mountains or the sea. They had few books, and their culture was limited. But this only meant that what they saw, they saw the more clearly. What they lost in variety, they gained in concentration, and because they were not worried by the conflicts of different civilizations or the burdens of too heavy a past, they kept their outlook clear and their attention undivided. Their unspoiled senses helped them to bring into their verse the very sight of what they saw, the very sound of what they heard. Their strong and often noble emotions enabled them to understand things with the special insight that comes in moments of tension and excitement. Even their haunting sense of the shortness of life was a great asset to them; for it made them feel that pleasure and power were all the more worth possessing, and through a sense of irreparable loss they found the heights of tragic grandeur. Into their poetry they put most sides of their gifted spirits, and there is hardly a fundamental quality of human nature which is missing from it. It is true that they often present life in its simplest terms, that they lack elaboration and some kinds of subtlety. But this lack makes their poetry stronger. Stripped of unnecessary trappings, their verse shows its muscle and sinew. In the main they wrote because they had to, because they had those moments of exalted illumination when some thing is seen as a radiant and harmonious whole and the spirit is moved to tell what it has felt and known.

C. M. B.

INTRODUCTION. PART II

Greek Poetry in Translation

§ I

PREFATORY

A FEW words must first be said about the making of this book and the principles on which translations were chosen.

The task of making it was accepted with misgiving. Every one knows that translators are traitors, and that they show the wrong side of the tapestry. Some, too, may remember that two-horned question recorded by Robert Bridges,[1] 'If you really thought the original was like that, what can you have seen in it to make you think it was worth translating?'; or how to Bohn's translations the 'signal service' was once attributed[2] 'of having finally shown up the Classics'. But other arguments, less often heard, were more convincing. No disparagement can obscure the essential value of an art which alone can mediate between past and present, or between living men of different speech. In every school and college it is taught and practised; and if practice must be guided by example, a book of this kind, at least in its intention, has a plausible excuse.

Translators, it is true, often miss their objective and destroy what they would save; but their achievement, taken as a whole, has been great. In this

---

[1] *Ibant Obscuri*, p. 40.

[2] By Labouchere; cf. Gilbert Murray, *The Interpretation of Greek Literature*, 1909, pp. 16 ff.

country, from the sixteenth century or before, the best of them have been conscious of a vocation. They have worked with faith and enthusiasm not only to communicate the wisdom and beauty found in other languages, but also to enrich and justify the vernacular—few, perhaps, to better effect than Philemon Holland, who 'framed his pen not to any affected phrase, but to a mean and popular style' and hoped 'to do some good whiles he lived to his sweet native country'.[1]

Translations written in that spirit by men of ability have lived long beyond their time; and as a rule they have borne two distinguishing marks—the use of a living language, and a proper regard for the claims of the reader as well as the claims of the author translated. It seemed not unlikely that, if the search was thorough enough, sufficient translations belonging to this tradition could be found, at any rate to make a nucleus for the book; and there was, besides, the encouraging fact, easily verified from the Index on pp. 764 ff., that many poets, from Chapman to our own times, have not disdained to translate.

Translations from the epigrammatists were tested first. Sir Edward Cook, in *More Literary Recreations*, pp. 359 ff., provides a list of 62, covering the period 1577–1919. To these some 15 or more may be added; and subsequent years have brought the total to about 120. Almost all were examined, with results that seemed satisfactory. But as the search extended to other fields, defects of quality were soon discovered. Anacreontics, for example, had attracted

[1] *The Romane History of T. Livius*, translated, 1659, *To the Reader*, p. 5.

numerous versifiers, especially clergymen of the earlier nineteenth century. But long journeys through dusty volumes led back in the end to Thomas Stanley, who wrote in 1651.

Homer was in much the same case. Exploration confirmed the remark of Tennyson, that 'the benefit of most translations from poetry, except they be by true poets, seems mainly to rest with the translator'.[1] It was clear that readable versions must sometimes be borrowed from the older poets. Their idiom is not our own, but provokes a smile, not a frown, and can even be relished, like that of any good piece of period furniture. No doubt they distort their original; but certain aspects of it only a poet can reflect at all. Pope, and Cowper at his best, both succeed where versifiers fail: they give the impression that to read Homer is to read great poetry, and that Homer was an artist who moved with ease and mastery in his craft.

For such reasons it was soon decided to mix 'period pieces' with others of modern workmanship as good as could be found; and along with this decision went another—namely that choice need not be restricted to any single translation either of the same Greek author or even of passages from the same poem. Translations of anthologies, such as *The Oxford Book of Greek Verse*, must follow certain rules of their own. Each piece in the Greek has to stand on its merits, concentrated, very often, in some few lines or phrases. It is reasonable, therefore, to choose the translation most apt in the places concerned.

The result, to the general reader, may appear

[1] *A Memoir*, by his son, vol. ii, p. 349.

confusing. The same Greek metre is represented in various ways; and the same author or poem is credited (within narrower limits) with strange varieties of style. But even so, unless the discrepancies are very great, a composite notion may be formed which is probably less misleading than any single impression. For no agreement has been reached on the best way of representing Greek metres, even in their simplest forms; and no translation of any Greek poet has been regarded for any length of time as canonical.

In the rest of this Introduction the reasons for this anarchy will be stated; and some attempt will be made to classify the translations in this book and explain their intentions. To-day, as in the past, there are, roughly speaking, two main sects of translators. Their essential difference lies in this—that the one sect aims at transporting us back to the poetry of Greece, and the other at bringing Greek poetry closer to our own.[1] The former aim is deserving of respect, and deserving of representation. We may learn from those who profess it more, perhaps, of Greek thought and character than the other sect can teach us; and on the formal side of poetry, imitations, as close as our language allows, of Greek metrical schemes may still conceivably prove interesting and even fruitful. On the other hand, it is evident that such translators are praised more often than read; and that some at least of their number have mistaken the true nature of translation and perhaps the true nature of poetry itself.

[1] Cf. G. M. Cookson, 'On Translating Greek Tragedy', in *The Classical Review*, vol. xxxvii, 1923, pp. 146-8.

Most translations in this book either keep to a middle way, or else incline to the side of 'bringing Greek poetry nearer to our own'; but sometimes, where the interest or effect of the Greek depends on the metre, translations have been written on the opposite principle. Let scholars who are doubtful of their allegiance ask themselves two questions—What kind of translations do I prefer from tongues unknown to me, say from Chinese poetry, or Hungarian? and How, in that after-world which Socratês imagined when condemned to death, should I translate our English lyrics to the poets of ancient Greece?

§ 2

THE NATURE OF TRANSLATION

Poetry, indeed, cannot be translated; and therefore it is the poets that preserve languages. Samuel Johnson, in Boswell's *Life* (1776), ed. Hill, iii. 36.
I remember saying to Anatole France that translation was an impossible thing. . . . He replied: 'Precisely, my friend; the recognition of that truth is a necessary preliminary to success in the art.' J. Lewis May, 'Concerning Translation' in *The Edinburgh Review*, Jan. 1927, p. 117.

What *is* translation? In what sense can poetry be 'transferred' from one language to another? What is preserved and what is lost in the process? Do translations of Greek differ in any respects from those of languages spoken to-day?

The first three questions, which here may be treated as one, have been asked more often than answered. Translators themselves (who should know their own business) are strangely evasive in their replies. They discourse of 'spirit' and 'substance' without defining those ambiguous terms; or else take refuge in metaphor, with surgical talk of transfusing blood; or chemical talk of poetry as a volatile essence that evaporates in transference; or talk pictorial and musical of etching and colour and pitch and tone. Others are botanists, who offer a *hortus siccus* in place of gay and breathing flowers; and many more, being tailorish and mathematical, flourish the yard-stick of 'commensurateness', cut their cloth by the measure of the Greek to a syllable, and contend that the 'spirit' of their author will approve its English dress and enter in.

The best and shortest answer was given by A. C. Bradley in his lecture on *Poetry for Poetry's Sake*[1] at Oxford in 1901. His remarks on translation were incidental, but far-reaching. They are not easy to abstract from their proper context; but this bald summary will not, it is hoped, be misleading.

A poem, unless we think of it as so much ink and paper, is 'the succession of experiences—sounds, images, thoughts, emotions—through which we pass' when reading or listening impressionably and exerting our imaginations in the act of re-creation. In such poetic experience 'meaning' and 'form' are not apprehended separately, but operate together. There is 'a resonant meaning or a meaning resonance'— two expressions for one and the same thing. It is only in later reflection that the 'formal' aspect of true poetry can, by a fiction, be detached from the aspect

---

[1] Cf. especially pp. 7, 18, 23-4.

of 'meaning'. We adopt this fiction for purposes of criticism, discussing now the 'meaning' of a poem, i.e. its ideas and images; and now its 'formal' aspect, under headings such as versification; or 'musical' elements; or style, i.e. the order, ease, rapidity with which ideas are presented. But the 'meaning', in strictness, 'cannot be expressed in any but its own words, nor can the words be changed without changing the meaning'. It follows that any translation of such poetry *is not really the old meaning in a fresh dress. It is a new product, something like the poem, though, if one chooses to say so, more like it in the aspect of meaning than in the aspect of form.*

Happily for translators 'true poetry' is rarer than verse. But the same argument holds good of both. The illusion of likeness in translation varies simply in degree.

In the sections below leave must be taken to isolate 'meaning' and 'form' in their turns and consider separately the problems relevant to each.

§ 3

PROBLEMS OF MEANING

'Literal' or 'word for word' translation is only possible when the 'brute' or '*in*herent' meaning of words—their denotation—is alone important, and when equivalents in the two languages exist. Arithmetical tables lose nothing by translation—or nothing that matters. The same applies to many works of exact science, and others that are too impersonal to be classed as literature. Outside this circle the 'word for word' translator finds himself embarrassed. Often the commonest words have no true equivalent. The Greek word *polis* is a good example. Protests were raised when Jowett rendered it by 'state'. But 'city' or 'country' are also make-shifts, and 'city-state' is only tolerable in certain contexts. *Demokratia*, in the same way, does not mean what we now understand by 'democracy', but direct popular government within a *polis*. Modern examples of the same problem were given by Mr. Hilaire Belloc,[1] lecturing at Oxford in 1931: 'You can no more translate the word "cad" into French than you can translate the word "gentleman" into French, at least not by a single word'—for both are the products of an aristocratic society. 'Nor, for that matter, can you translate into English the French word "goujat" or the French word "frondeur".'

Such obstacles vary in number and quality as be-tween the pairs of languages concerned. Greek language and civilization bequeathed so much to Rome, and Rome (through Christendom) so much to the Western world, that translators of the Classics, in countries once romanized, suffer no great disadvantage; and less perhaps in this country than in many others. For the old tradition of Classical culture has permeated our own literature. A modicum of equivalents or approximations exists, and occasional notes are not forbidden. Often difficulties arise owing to the very fact that Greek came to us first through Latin, and for long was overshadowed by it. But lately, though students of Greek are fewer, popular

[1] The Taylorian Lecture, *On Translation*, pp. 18–19.

knowledge of things Hellenic has increased. There is no longer the need that Samuel Butler felt to 'translate' the names of Greek divinities (and falsify their character) by giving them Latin names; and the same may be said of Greek proper names in general. In Bland's *Collections from the Greek Anthology*, which reached its third edition about a century ago and has often been excerpted, Greek names were largely avoided. Zênophilê (cf. No. 583) there became 'Lesbia'.

To represent *ad*herent meaning, that is to say the 'atmosphere' and associations (sometimes called 'connotation') of a word, offers a much more serious problem. Any transference of the *same* effect is clearly impossible. Once again let Mr. Belloc speak: The French word *terre*, he says, 'is a long and powerful syllable, becoming two syllables on occasion. It can be given a mystical value to which the English word *earth* alone corresponds and no other of its supposed equivalents. It is a more profound word in a peasant society than in an urban society. There is more still; it connotes very vaguely but quite certainly in one language one type of landscape, in another another. And there is more; it has been used by the poets and the great prose writers in different ways in the two languages, and this historical difference marks its effect whenever it is used.'[1]

Mr. Belloc's illustration from French suggests a parallel from Greek. Homer, in a well-known passage, uses the phrase φυσίζοος αἶα. Helen, in Troy, has referred to her brothers as though they were still alive; and Homer explains that in fact '*earth, the*

[1] Ibid., p. 17.

life-giver, held them fast, away in Lakedaimôn, their dear native land' (*Iliad*, iii. 243). Ruskin observed: 'The poet has to speak of the earth in sadness; but he will not let that sadness affect or change his thought of it. No; though Castor and Pollux be dead, yet the earth is our mother still—fruitful, life-giving.' Matthew Arnold rebuked Ruskin for a false application of modern sentiment; but provoked a critic in his turn. For Gilbert Murray[1] has argued that the epithet φυσίζοος (which occurs only five times in Greek poetry) is very far from being merely ornamental, as Arnold may have thought. It 'is steeped in primitive mysticism', and Ruskin, not having this clue, did not go far enough—'he stopped short at sentiment, whereas the word really connoted religion'. In Latin the word *pius*, Vergil's chosen epithet for Æneas, provides an equally good example. A lecturer once informed undergraduates: 'We translate it "good", but we understand by it "Æneas, that trained liturgiologist".'

The use of words charged with adherent meaning, and their combination in rhythmical forms, belong to the very essence of poetry. Adherent meaning varies, no doubt, for every writer and every reader; and for both on successive occasions. We cannot step into the same river twice, nor can we read the same poem twice. But a measure of fixity remains, and great writers, it seems, are guided in their choice and arrangement of words by some intuitive sym-

[1] 'What English Poetry may still learn from Greek' in *Essays and Studies* by members of The English Association, vol. iii, 1912, pp. 8–10.

pathy with the true genius of their own language and people. Their writing carries and convinces and is unforgettable. We may reduce the problem, if we like, to the choice of single words and ask why one is 'better' than another. Sometimes reasons can be given, but ultimately we are faced with a mystery and can only suppose that certain sounds, in the beginning of language, were thought more expressive than others and still prevail over so-called synonyms. Foreigners can never fully appreciate such words; and the same is true of words in rhythmical combinations, operating in various ways upon the feelings, the imagination, and the intelligence. What foreigner could understand why 'six simple words of Milton'—

> Nymphs and shepherds dance no more

'can draw tears', as A. E. Housman attested,[1] 'to the eyes of more readers than one'? What is there in—

> Brightness falls from the air,
> Queens have died young and fair,
> Dust hath closed Helen's eye

—why did these lines convey to C. E. Montague's mind 'a state of passionately poignant exaltation?[2] Unless a man is truly bilingual (and such men are rare) all these effects must escape him.

What notion, then, can translators form of adherent meanings in ancient Greek? Can we say at all how any poet's use of words affected the audience for which he wrote?

[1] *The Name and Nature of Poetry*, 1933, p. 46.
[2] *A Writer's Notes on his Trade*, Phoenix Library ed., 1931, pp. 253-4.

No general answer can be given to these questions. Homer and most of the earlier poets must be set apart. We cannot tell how they struck their contemporaries. But we can tell (better than Matthew Arnold supposed) how Homer struck an Athenian of the later fifth century; and subsequent critics, such as Plato, Aristotle, Dionysius of Halicarnassus, or the author whom we call Longinus, all throw back some light on the pre-classical writers. Thanks to these critics and to the grammarians and lexicographers, a scholar can distinguish, with some precision, the different characters of words and style. He can feel some part of their effect, never quite as contemporaries felt, but as Greeks who were later-born agreed in feeling. For example, antiquity records, sometimes with reasons given, the lyrical power of Sappho; and even to-day, in the meagre fragments that survive, that power, concentrated in a few words, may still be appreciated; the main loss is on the formal side, not on the side of meaning. Translators of early works in other Western languages are probably not much better off.

Poets of the 'classical' period in Greece are known to us far more fully. Aristophanês and others often help us to estimate the effect of tragic and lyrical diction upon contemporaries, old and young. We know in general, and sometimes in points of detail, what the old men thought of Æschylus, and how their opinions differed from those of Euripidês and the younger generation. Ancient commentaries and modern research help the scholar still farther on his way. He is better placed than the layman might suppose. But scholars would be the first to repudiate any over-statement of the case. Extant remains from the classical period are a very small percentage of its whole output; and only too often the literary and other associations of a word remain in doubt. Thus, the restoration of the word *kopis* in a lyrical passage of Sophoclês is open to some dispute. A metaphorical sense is required, as when we speak of 'the scythe of Time'; but objection has been made that the humble associations of the word (a 'chopper' or 'cleaver' in No. 493) would make it, in such a context, ridiculous. This kind of problem does not occur in Greek alone. Dr. Johnson[1] objected to a line in *Macbeth*:

That my keen knife see not the wound it makes.

A 'knife' to him, like *kopis* in Greek, was 'an instrument used by butchers and cooks in the meanest employments'. But was it so to Shakespeare? Or was it merely the fashions of poetic diction that had changed and not the associations of the word?

These examples may serve to remind us that the choice of any one word or phrase (or sound or cadence) involves the avoidance of certain others.[2] When Ruskin, addressing his heart, wrote 'Thou little bounder, rest',[3] he was guiltless of offence—if the dictionaries are right; for the slang use of 'bounder' dates only from 1890. Before that time

[1] *The Rambler*, 26 Oct. 1751.

[2] Cf. Edwyn Bevan, *The Poems of Leonidas of Tarentum*, translated, Oxford 1931, p. xxxiii.

[3] Quoted in *The Stuffed Owl*, An Anthology of Bad Verse, selected by D. B. Wyndham Lewis and Charles Lee, J. M. Dent & Sons, Ltd., 1930, p. 14.

the word had not acquired new adherent meaning that made its serious use impossible. Still less could Thomas Stanley, writing in 1651, foresee objections to this translation of Bion's *Lament for Adônis* (No. 573, lines 7 ff.)—

> On barren mountains doth Adônis lie,
> A boar's white tusk hath gored his whiter thigh:
> His short pants Venus grieve. . . .

To discover the reasons that guided choice and avoidance in Greek is the province of verbal scholarship—perhaps the most deserving of the servants of poetry, yet often the least regarded. Many obscurities remain to perplex it; nor is it easy to distinguish, in our admiration for one Greek poem or another, the warrantable and permanent from the personal and adventitious. But setting aside such errors of valuation, it is reasonable to suppose that where practised scholars, with good warrant behind them, cannot help feeling the spell of a tongue that is not their own, contemporary audiences and readers were affected much more profoundly. It follows that translation can only hope to produce analogous results by means of true poetry or prose that is akin to poetry.

Objection has been raised that true poetry is something wholly personal, and that translations are not. But evidence is abundant, from the time of the Romans onwards, that poets of different speech can be 'as definitely inspired' by each other's work 'as by any other causes that provoke verse'.[1] Two points should

---

[1] Cf. Humbert Wolfe, *Signpost to Poetry*, Cassell & Co., Ltd., 1931, p. 209.

be added: first, that to demand 'a poem for a poem' does not sanction paraphrase or imitation, but only such liberty as the technique of English poetry requires; and second, that in dealing with adherent meaning an extreme case has been stated, because the poetry that is most difficult to translate is often the most deserving of translation.

§ 4

PROBLEMS OF FORM

Greek is one of the most fluid and musical of all languages. Latin cannot approach it in these respects; and in the Western world of to-day it is rivalled only by Italian. This fluidity is determined by the proportion of vowels to consonants, which in Latin is smaller. Within Greek itself fluidity varies with the period and with the author and dialect. Homer is more fluid than the Attic writers; and the Ionic prose of Herodotus is richer in vowels than Homer.

Generally speaking, 'short' vowels are more numerous than in Latin; so that the verse of Homer is more dactylic than that of Vergil—though Ovid went some way in redressing the balance. But perhaps the most striking difference between Greek and Latin, and also between Greek and English, lies in the nature of Greek final syllables. The only consonants which close them are *n* and *s*, with its compounds *x* and *ps*, or, more rarely, *r* and *k*; otherwise, a vowel-ending is invariable. It results from this fluid character that grace and ease come much more readily to Greek than massiveness and force. A line such as Ennius'

> rem repetunt, regnumque petunt, vadunt solida vi

is thoroughly un-Greek in sound, though the metre derives from Greek.

Another point of some importance is the character of Greek syllabation. Here the contrast is with English rather than with Latin. Take for example the Greek word *pe-ri-e-phe-re* and its Latin equivalent *cir-cum-fe-re-bat*. The principle of syllabation is the same in both, though it happens that only in Greek are all the five vowels pure and metrically 'short'. English syllabates differently. Except in singing, we say *dis-in-her-it*, where a Roman would say *di-si-nhe-rit*. If Postgate is right, to Greeks and Romans the metrical effect of our four closed syllables would have been something like four 'longs' (————).[1]

That rapidity which Matthew Arnold rightly counted as one of the four distinctive qualities in Homer, can now be understood; and *if* translation can and should suggest the language of origin, certainly translations of Homer, and of Greek in general as compared with Latin, should be as limpid as possible. But this quality should vary as the Greek authors vary; for though the language shapes the poetry, the poets also shape the language, and the texture of their work is often very different.

[1] Cf. J. P. Postgate, *Translation and Translations*, 1922, p. 86. General acknowledgements in this section are also due to M. Croiset, *Hist. de la Litt. Grecque*, 1899, vol. i, ch. i; and to E. A. Sonnenschein, *What is Rhythm?*, 1925, pp. 56–62, 206–8.

On the formal side of Greek poetry, we can still appreciate these differences of texture, even though our knowledge of the ancient pronunciation is inadequate; or, if adequate, which is nearer the truth, not applied until recent years with any uniformity. The situation amounts to this—that of the four elements of Greek utterance, alphabetical sounds, time (or 'quantity'), pitch, and stress, the first is well enough known to modern scholars, and the second very much better.

Our chief difficulty in recapturing the sound of Greek poetry lies in the nature of the Greek accent. Its places of incidence are known, but Englishmen cannot, as a rule, reproduce its effect, which depended (so Dionysius tells us) on a variation of pitch between accented and unaccented syllables equivalent, at the outside limit, to the musical interval of a fifth ($3\frac{1}{2}$ tones). Time and pitch seem to have been almost independent in 'classical' Greek; but the relation of pitch and stress (i.e. loudness, force, intensity) remains obscure. It was only in later times that the incidence of the Greek accent was regulated in such a way as to suggest that stress as well as pitch was required at certain parts of the line—see, for example, Nos. 562 and 617, where the accent in the Greek text will be noticed to fall in almost every line on the penultimate syllable.

Some scholars can reproduce the Greek pitch-accent without imparting an English stress and thereby obscuring the quantitative principle which distinguishes Greek metre from our own. But the very rarity of this accomplishment at once suggests a very difficult question——If meaning and form are two aspects of the same thing, how is it that we can appreciate Greek poetry when we cannot or will not recapture its proper sound? Mr. Maurice Baring,[1] himself beneath the spell of that poetry, has brought this question home in a forcible way. There are two lines of Racine's *Phèdre*——

> Ariane ma sœur, de quel amour blessée
> Vous mourûtes aux bords où vous fûtes laissée!

——'the two most musical lines Racine ever wrote'; and so effectual, it is said, when Rachel first spoke them on the stage, 'that Alfred de Musset fainted in his box'. Now suppose that a thousand years hence Racine were pronounced like this:

> Areéany masséwer, dee kwél amoór blessée
> Vouss moórutées awks boárds ow voúss futées lessée!

would that, Mr. Baring asks, be a parallel to our make-shift fashion of pronouncing Greek?

It would be a parody rather than a parallel. There are no silent consonants, as in the French words *vous* and *aux*, to trouble us in Greek; and after all, may we not ask, with almost equal relevance, how Sophoclês sounded as recited by an Æolian, or how much we can now recapture of the sound of Chaucer's verse, or even Shakespeare's, as spoken by those poets themselves? Perhaps our fashion of pronouncing Greek is a kind of translation in itself. Ideas and images, or style and the forms of words attract us.

---

[1] *Have you anything to declare?*, Wm. Heinemann Ltd., 1936, pp. 115, 143.

1

Sounds and metre we interpret in a manner suitable to English speech and not unpleasing.

Pitch-accent exists in English, and poets sometimes exploit it, e.g. Shakespeare in *Troilus and Cressida,*

A slave whose gall coins slanders like a mint.

This example, with some from Milton, is given by Mr. W. H. Shewring,[1] who says: 'One's voice will naturally rise on the word *coins,* and this indirectly throws the metaphor into relief.' In Greek spoken verse the pitch-accent must have counted for something—perhaps for more than we think—but its part was subordinate, and certainly the main contrast between Greek and English verse lies rather in their metrical principles. In Greek spoken verse the quantities of syllables were fixed: they were either 'long' or 'short'; and a 'long' was regarded as twice the length of a 'short', so that two 'shorts' could, under certain conditions, be substituted for it. Metre was based not, as in English, upon the relation of stress-accents, but, as in Latin, upon this principle of quantity, i.e. the relative duration or musical time of the syllables and silent intervals. This statement does not imply that stress-accent played no part at all in the spoken verse of the Greeks, or that quantity plays no part in ours.[2] In the best English verse quantity

---

[1] *The Ampleforth Journal,* vol. xli, 1935, p. 34.
[2] Both subjects are full of dispute. Cf. Egerton Smith, *The Principles of English Metre,* 1923, pp. 84 ff.; E. A. Sonnenschein, op. cit., ch. vii–ix, and pp. 207 ff.

is treated with respect and may even be regarded as a structural element side by side with stress. Yet even so, stress in English is the basic and dominant factor; and English syllables, owing partly to its effects and partly to the nature of our syllabation, cannot be sharply distinguished as 'long' or 'short'. Their quantities are much more various, and often very hard to determine. English, therefore, is not a material out of which metres on the Greek or Greco-Latin model can be constructed, except as the roughest approximations.[1] Further, it is 'choked with consonants' and prolific of monosyllables.

In spite of these drawbacks, imitations of classical metres continue to be written; and nothing else will serve (for readers ignorant of Latin) if translation is to 'bring us nearer to the Greek'. In practice these imitations depend on Latin models. For Roman speech, like our own, was chiefly marked by stress; and since the Greek pitch-accent is hard to reproduce, our way of reading Latin is commonly extended to our reading of Greek; that is to say, we counterpoint[2] the metrical pattern by using stress in the Latin manner—which is better, at any rate, than using no counterpoint at all. The barrel-organ music of 'English accentual hexameters' reflects the older and more barbarous habit of stressing only the metrical beats.

[1] Cf. A. E. Housman in *The Classical Review*, vol. xiii, 1899, pp. 317–19.

[2] A convenient way of saying that the ordinary speech-accent or stress which we give to the words does not coincide with the metrical beats; it cuts across the scansion-rhythm, as in any proper reading of English verse.

Two of the commonest ancient metres may be illustrated by means of the elegiac couplet, in which a dactylic six-foot line ('hexameter') is followed by a line roughly equivalent to five dactylic units—a 'pentameter'. Except in certain feet, a spondee $(- -)$ might replace a dactyl $(- \cup \cup)$, on the principle, already mentioned, that a long-timed syllable $(-)$ had the duration of two 'shorts' $(\cup \cup)$; so that the metrical scheme may be thus represented:

$$- \underset{\smile\smile}{} \mid - \underset{\smile\smile}{} \mid - \underset{\smile\smile}{} \mid - \underset{\smile\smile}{} \mid - \cup \cup \mid - \underset{\smile}{}$$
$$- \underset{\smile\smile}{} \mid - \underset{\smile\smile}{} \mid - \wedge \parallel - \cup \cup \mid - \cup \cup \mid \underset{\smile}{}$$

Or in musical notation:[1]

followed by:

This account must suffice, though one important feature should at least be mentioned—namely, the regulated use of caesura (i.e. a break between words within a foot), which secured that the hexameter, in contrast with the pentameter, should not appear to consist of two equal portions. Hexameters, written in a series by themselves, are the metre of all the epic and oracular poetry in *The Oxford Book of Greek*

[1] Cf. Egerton Smith, op. cit., pp. 85, 163, where further details are given.

Verse, and of almost all the didactic poems. Elegiac pieces (mainly epigrams) number over two hundred.

The Latin hexameter was finally perfected by Vergil, but only after a century or so of ruder experiments; and almost half that time was again required before the elegiac metre was given, by Ovid, its final character. In English sporadic attempts to naturalize both metres have been made from the sixteenth century onwards. A few modern examples have been chosen for this book and must now be explained.

Imitations of classical models are usually classed either as 'accentual' or 'quantitative'. But further distinctions[1] are necessary. Kingsley in his *Andromeda* wrote 'accentual' hexameters:

> . . . From afar, unknowing, I marked thee,
> Shining, a snow-white cross on the dark green walls of
> the sea-cliff;
> Carven in marble I deemed thee, a perfect work of the
> craftsman.

And William Watson's *Hymn to the Sea*[2] is written in 'accentual' elegiacs:

> Miser, whose coffered recesses the spoils of eternity
> cumber,
> Spendthrift foaming thy soul wildly in fury away,—
> We, self-amorous mortals, our own multitudinous image
> Seeking in all we behold, seek it and find it in thee.

In both examples accented ('stressed') syllables are

[1] These are adopted from E. A. Sonnenschein, op. cit., ch. x.
[2] In *The Father of the Forest and other Poems*, London, John Lane, 1895, p. 27.

used throughout to represent the 'longs' on which the metrical beats would fall in Greek or Latin; and that feature we must here regard as the distinguishing mark which justifies the title 'accentual'. If the verses are also truly timed, i.e. if the syllables that stand for longs and shorts do seem to bear that relation when pronounced, quantity, as judged by the English ear, is also present. But such verses are best described not as 'quantitative', but as 'true-timed' accentual hexameters or elegiacs; for the term 'quantitative' has in practice been reserved for verse of another kind. As 'true-timed' accentual metres we may contrast them, if we like, with specimens such as Longfellow's *Evangeline* or Clough's *Bothie*, which often substitute – ∪ for – –, or treat as a 'long' any syllable which happens to bear a stress.

Accentual hexameters were regarded by Matthew Arnold as the best medium for translating Homer; and his reasoning would apply (with reservations) to a corresponding treatment of Greek elegiacs in translation. But Tennyson and later critics including Robert Bridges[1] have agreed rather with F. W. Newman than with Arnold. As Newman saw, the traditional associations of trisyllabic feet, as used in the English accentual hexameter, make the metre far more suitable for light than for serious verse; and efforts, such as those of Arnold, to remedy this defect, usually end in obscuring the metrical pattern. Specimens of accentual hexameters are given in Nos. 44(ii), 163, 167, 300–2. These are not always true-timed, cf. 'Yester-e'en', p. 87, line 6. Accentual

[1] *Ibant Obscuri*, p. 145.

elegiacs are used in Nos. 224–5 as a means of solving a difficult problem; they have their value, as Newman would have said, 'as a matter of curiosity, as erudite sport', or 'for initiating schoolboys into the metre'.

In Tennyson's judgement even 'quantitative' English hexameters were, as a rule, 'only fit for comic subjects'. By 'quantitative' Tennyson meant hexameters based on the classical rules of prosody; and here it is best to abide by that meaning. Such hexameters are not merely 'true-timed' according to English notions of quantity, but also bind themselves, more or less, by the classical 'Rule of Position', i.e. when two adjacent syllables respectively end and begin with a consonant sound, the first of the two is regarded as 'long'. They also differ from true-timed accentual hexameters by counterpointing the metrical beats (ˈ) with stress-accent (ˊ). A simple example is Spedding's line, which provoked Arnold's defence of the accentual type. Lengthenings due to the Rule of Position are italicized:

Softly cometh slumb*er* clos*ing* th' o'er wearied eyelid.[1]

The same general principle is observed in No. 13 and in No. 36, but with variations, here and there, in the judgement of quantity. No. 621, which, like No. 36, is by Robert Bridges, provides a similar example of quantitative elegiacs.

In earlier experiments the 'Rule of Position' was transferred to English almost without limitation.

[1] The scansion is: $- \cup \cup \mid -- \mid -- \mid -- \mid - \cup \cup \mid --$

This was certainly a mistake. W. J. Stone[1] and Bridges (who continued Stone's researches) rightly perceived that in English a double consonant often marks the syllable which it ends as 'short', not as 'long'—hence we find in line 5 of No. 36 *Achilles* and *sitting*. They also rightly treated *ng* as a single consonant, except in certain words such as *anger*; and in many other ways increased our sensitiveness to quantity, e.g. by curing the delusion, fostered by accentual hexameters, that a stressed syllable was necessarily 'long'. Even so, it is doubtful, to say the least, whether the 'Rule of Position' has any proper place in English at all.

Another crucial problem (as the Romans found before us) is the amount of counterpointing that a quantitative metre will bear. Tennyson's parody[2] of a quantitative pentameter

$$\widehat{}\ \smile\ \widehat{}\ \acute{}\ \widehat{}\ \mid\ \acute{}\ \smile\ \acute{}\ \smile\ \acute{}\ \widehat{\smile\smile}$$

All men alike hate slops, particularly gruel

has been, and will be, to some minds a sufficient argument against such forms of verse. But Bridges's quatrain (No. 621) cannot be so lightly dismissed. It is 'memorable speech', and gives at the same time a very plausible impression of classical metre and prosody.

What, then, are the possibilities of quantitative verse? Has it a future as well as a past? Bridges's experiments (he did not call them more), and latterly

---

[1] *On the Use of Classical Metres in English*, 1899; discussed by A. E. Housman in *The Classical Review*, vol. xiii, 1899, pp. 317–19.　　[2] *A Memoir*, by his son, vol. ii, p. 12.

Mr. C. W. Brodribb's *Georgics*, have gone some way to vindicate its usefulness in translation. But though not over-difficult[1] to write, it is not easy; and observance of quantity restricts the choice of words more, perhaps, than rhyme. It is also doubtful how far non-classical readers can discern the metre intended. Even if they master the general principle, there are still many causes of bewilderment. For writers of quantitative verse are by no means uniform in their practice; and though phoneticians, with aid of the kymograph, have helped to settle some disputes, there is always room for controversy—especially in a matter so delicate as the effect of stress on the syllable of incidence and those adjacent to it.

In free composition the future of quantitative verse is even less assured. The Romans, in taking over Greek metres and prosody, were very differently placed from us to-day. They had not behind them, as we have, a great body of poetry based on a different principle: still less a body of *great* poetry. At this date in our history accent, not quantity, must prevail. We must assume that Bridges's hexameter

Lazy Summer's burning dial, the serenely solemn spells . . .

will suggest, even in its context, the metre of *Locksley Hall*, and that in *Locksley Hall* the line

In the Spring a fuller crimson comes upon the robin's breast

will never be read as a potential hexameter—

[1] Cf. *Ibant Obscuri*, p. 142. No. 36 in this book was written at the average rate of 12 lines a day.

lengthening *the* before *Sp*—by classical rules, and trusting to luck for *comes* as a 'short'.

Imitations of Greek lyrical metres are discussed later on (§ 10). In these the complex patterns of the Greek can only be shown, if at all, by means of accentual verse.

§ 5

TRANSLATION IN PRACTICE

The process of translating a single elegiac couplet (No. 212) will bring together all the problems already discussed and show their issue in practice.

Three hundred Spartans under Leônidas had been ordered to hold Thermopylæ at all costs. None survived. Simonidês composed the inscription for their tomb, which runs:

Ὦ ξεῖν’, ἀγγέλλειν Λακεδαιμονίοις ὅτι τῇδε
κείμεθα, τοῖς κείνων ῥήμασι πειθόμενοι.

A make-shift 'word for word' construe would be: 'O stranger, take-news to the Lacedæmonians that here we-are-lying, to their words obedient.' Cicero, using a slightly different text in the second line, translated:

Dic, hospes, Spartae nos te hic vidisse iacentis
dum sanctis patriae legibus obsequimur.

The first thing to notice is this—that by a fiction the dead are made to speak, and that their epitaph takes the form of a message from the field. As none survived, some one else must deliver that message. Hence the appeal in the first two words—a form of address found in many another Greek epitaph, but with less excuse.[1]

These first two words are the first difficulty. Cicero rendered them by 'hospes', a closer approximation than English allows. No single word in English has the same meanings, inherent and adherent, as the Greek. 'Stranger' is too remote, and tends to be American; 'friend' is too familiar. The compromise 'passer-by' has found, perhaps, most favour.

Next, the word ἀγγέλλειν. Here a problem of adherent meaning is raised not by the word itself but by the use of the infinitive to convey an injunction. This idiom was common in Dorian speech, and would therefore be appropriate on the lips of the Spartan dead, while to Greek readers in general, familiar with its use in Hesiod and other old poets, it would also have had a dignified, archaic ring.[2] If that were the whole truth, an archaizing translation, such as 'Take tiding(s)', might be defended. But the idiom is also military and not confined to the Dorians. In this dispatch from the field its military use is appropriate; and hence a very different suggestion, namely, that we should translate '*Report* to the Lacedæmonians . . .'.

Modern poetry is wholesomely inclusive in its diction; but even so *Report* would be out of keeping. For the diction of the epitaph as a whole has a conscious poetic colouring, as the forms ξεῖν' for

[1] Cf. R. Heinze, *Neue Jahrb. f. d. klass. Altertum*, 1915, p. 6.
[2] Cf. W. Rhys Roberts, *Eleven Words of Simonides*, Camb. Univ. Press, 1920.

ξέν' and κείνων for ἐκείνων attest. And after all, the idiom was archaic and poetical as well as military. Once again, then, we must compromise on some neutral expression such as 'Tell them in Lacedæmon . . .'.

Two further problems of meaning are set by the last two words. Some have argued that ῥήμασι bears much the same sense as ῥημάτων in No. 206—the poem written by Simonidês on Danaê. It would then mean not 'orders' or 'ordinances', but 'words' or 'sayings' such as Plutarch collected in his *Sayings of Laconian Women*, e.g. 'Come back with your shield —or upon it.' One may answer, of course, that the meaning 'orders' is better suited to a soldierly dispatch; but why demand one meaning and one only? A poet's economy, especially in epigram, is to say one thing and suggest much more. In English 'word' (rather than 'words') has some of the requisite associations, and also covers the possible alternatives most completely.

Finally, πειθόμενοι. It is often said that the use of the present participle implies continuity and demands the translation '*still* obeying'. But the temporal reference of the participle cannot be stressed; and '*still* obeying' is a sentimental, un-Greek idea, certainly out of place on the lips of Spartans.

The difficulties so far considered are partly those of exact interpretation, partly those of transference. A scholar, when he reads the Greek, is conscious that the inherent meaning of certain words and idioms is open to doubt, and conscious also that literary and

lxi

other associations cannot in any real sense be transferred at all. They can merely be suggested, in a rough and ready way, by using English words that carry some analogous association. So it happens that many scholars agree both in theory and practice with the dictum of Moriz Haupt—'Never translate, translation is the death of the understanding'.

So much is lost in translation of poetry that sceptics might question the value of what remains. But let us return to the epitaph and take stock of the present position. In prose the translation arrived at would run as follows: 'Passer-by, tell them in Lacedæmon that here we lie, obedient to their word.' At least the main conception of the lines has been translated; and that conception in itself is valuable if we try to think ourselves into the time and place of Simonidês as he composed. What should be said of these Spartans, and how best to say it with the brevity and force demanded by memorial inscriptions?

Simonidês was writing well after his seventieth year, in old age too serene for bitterness or vainglory, but not secure, at the first touch, from other artistic mistakes. He made, perhaps, a number of attempts, only to reject them. Then there came to him the true creative idea—the fiction of a last dispatch, in which the dead are yet speaking. They must give the essential facts as they saw them when they died—annihilation, implying that the Persian was through; and obedience, implying that their utmost had been done. These facts they should state with Spartan brevity and self-control. Let 'obedience' be the last word, not 'death'.

Such are the thoughts which a prose-translation may occasion. They are worth having, if we would know how poetry is made and learn to exercise a critical taste. But poetry is 'memorable speech' and a prose-translation, as compared with the Greek, is not memorable. How much can be reproduced on the side of 'form'?

The music of the couplet depends not only on its metre but on a chiming repetition of the sound ει, pronounced in the time of Simonidês somewhere between the English l*ay* and l*ie*. So marked an assonance (for the sound recurs five times) should at least be suggested. But how? For it does not follow that the same or a similar sound in English would carry the same effect, or that five repetitions of it could be endured, e.g. if we were to write:

> Take Lakedaimon tidings, passer-by,
> That here abiding by her word we lie.

The most we can hope is that rhyme will help us, with perhaps a little internal assonance as well.

And what of the metre? English imitations, accentual or quantitative, are out of the question. For English, at its best, is more concise than Greek; and here, as often, its best words are not the longest and will not fill the space of an elegiac couplet. We must choose instead some English metre corresponding to the Greek in its traditional use and associations.

The nearest equivalent is our rhymed heroic couplet. It is used for translating the longer elegiac poems, e.g. those of Theognis. But often both the tone and the structure of Greek elegiac epigram are far more suggestive of a light quatrain in English; and often, too, the transference of Greek proper names, or the lack of suitable rhymes, makes couplet-form impossible. In practice, therefore, translators indulge their own fancy, representing a single Greek metre in ways far too numerous to specify.

Lately experiments have been made in unrhymed couplets. Mr. Gilbert Highet has translated Latin elegiacs in the metre shown by the following lines:

The oriental tree distilling balsam,
   the last waft of a drooping saffron-bloom,
the scent of ripening apples in the cupboard,
   an orchard when its trees laugh with the spring.[1]

Translations of Nos. 97 and 102 in this book were made on the same principle, but quite independently. By the use of a feminine ending in the first line of each couplet both metres aim at suggesting the contrast between hexameter and pentameter; the only difference lies in the even-numbered lines, where Mr. Highet preserves iambic rhythm, whereas in Nos. 97 and 102 the rhythm is trochaic.

New metres, devised for translation, may help to solve old problems; and what is more, they cannot distort our notion of the Greek by recalling the manner of some English poet. That argument will be stated in the following section. Here a final word is required on the version of Simonidês' couplet chosen for this book.

[1] *Kulturgeschichte Roms*, &c., by Otto Kiefer, translated by Gilbert and Helen Highet, George Routledge & Sons, Ltd., 1934, p. 283 (from Martial, xi. 8).

Just over one hundred years ago[1] 'Christopher North' sat in judgement over five versions by other hands and twelve, selected from forty-eight, of his own making. In the end he gave his preference to William Lisle Bowles (1762–1850) who wrote:

> Go tell the Spartans, thou who passest by,
> That here obedient to their laws we lie.

These lines are the basis of a new couplet that some may think no better.

§ 6

The Two Main Sects of Translators

Since names are required, let the one sect be known as 'Hellenizers' and the other as 'Modernists'. Hellenizers are those who would bring us nearer to the Greek, preserving its more 'literal' sense and also, as far as possible, its idiom and metrical character. They win approval, one suspects, not from the wholly Greekless, but from readers who look for guidance rather than for poetry, and are well content if the English avoids offence.

'A poem for a poem' is the creed of the Modernists. English analogues govern their choice of metre, or, where none exist, they credit their author, if alive to-day, with a preference similar to their own. So, too, in transferring the sense they will use analogous terms, seeing the present in the past and vice versa—risking, for example, such a word as 'militarists' in translating a chorus from Æschylus. Their popu-

---

[1] *Blackwood's Magazine*, Dec. 1833, pp. 970 ff.

larity is more general than that of the Hellenizers, but varies with the fashions of poetic taste.

Within each sect there is much disputed doctrine; and both may sometimes modernize in their form, since few Greek metres admit of transference. There is not, therefore, a clear-cut division. But the fiction is useful, and sectarian differences will appear at many subsequent points. Four quotations, two on each side, will show clearly enough the grounds of dissent. First two Hellenizers:

'If, because of the immense fame of the following Tragedy, I wished to acquaint myself with it, and could only do so by the help of a translator, I should require him to be literal at every cost save that of absolute violence to our language. The use of certain allowable constructions which, happening to be out of daily favour, are all the more appropriate to archaic workmanship, is no violence: but I would be tolerant for once—in the case of so immensely famous an original—of even a clumsy attempt to furnish me with the very turn of each phrase in as Greek a fashion as English will bear.' (Robert Browning, in the Preface to his translation of Æschylus' *Agamemnon*, 1877.)

'It is, in my opinion, a mistake to think that the best translations of Greek verse are those which make it seem to be most like well written conventional English verse. If an English reader, who is unable to read Greek, is to get a glimpse of what Homer is like, he must read something which does *not* remind him of Milton or Pope or Tennyson or Swinburne, because Homer does not do this. A reader of Homer is like a man in a dream, who enters into a strange world of beauty unlike tha which every day besets him: he is far removed from the associations of modern art and civilization, and unless he is enthralled in that dreamlike charm, he has not entered within the magic circle.' (Robert Bridges, *Ibant Obscuri*, 1916, p. 142 f.)

Next, two Modernists:

'I suppose very few People have ever taken such pains with Translation as I have, though certainly not to be literal. But at all Cost, a Thing must *live*, with a transfusion of one's own worse life if one can't retain the Original's better. Better a live sparrow than a stuffed eagle.' (Edward Fitzgerald, *Letters*, Coll. works, 1859, vol. ii, p. 100.)[1]

'The genius of the language into which a translation is being made is the first thing to be considered; if the original was readable, the translation must be so also, or however good it may be as a construe, it is not a translation. It follows that a translation should depart hardly at all from the modes of speech current in the translator's own times, inasmuch as nothing is readable, for long, which affects any other diction than that of the age in which it is written. . . . A poem's prosperity is like a jest's—it is in the ear of him that hears it. It takes two people to say a thing—a sayee as well as a sayer—and by parity of reasoning a poem's original audience and environment are integral parts of the poem itself. . . .' Change either poem or audience, 'and some corresponding change, spiritual rather than literal, will be necessary in the other, if the original

---

[1] J. S. Phillimore used this quotation and also the one from Browning in his pamphlet *Some Remarks on Translation and Translators* (1919). He gave his verdict to Fitzgerald. Later J. P. Postgate denied the existence of any true dilemma and found in Headlam's *Agamemnon* (cf. Nos. 248, 250–1) the middle way between extremes (*Translation and Translations*, 1922, p. 10). But Headlam can hardly have written on Hellenizing principles so rigid as those of Postgate himself.

harmony between the two is to be preserved.' (Samuel Butler, Preface to *The Iliad of Homer rendered into English prose*, 1898, Reissue, 1921, pp. v, vii.)

So the argument goes to and fro. But before deciding which kind of translation is the better, it is well to ask, Can they rightly be compared at all?

In practice the word 'translation' is used without precision. It applies to almost any work that depends on constant reference to a foreign original; and the different species of translation are determined by their different aims, e.g. cribs, verse-translations, acting-versions. No true comparison is possible except when the aim of two translations is identical. We can say, for instance, 'this is a better crib, or a better acting-version than that'; but no one would think of comparing a crib with an acting-version. It follows that if the two sects deliberately aim at satisfying different tastes, no comparison can rightly be made. If, on the other hand, they differ only in *method* while pursuing a single aim, if they desire to reach the *same* public and to spread as widely as possible a taste for Greek poetry, then comparison is justified—and several good reasons suggest themselves for preferring the Modernists.

For why should English conform itself to Greek or to any other translated language? It is idle to suppose that Greekless readers can discern the foreign idiom lying behind, or that they are any the better for suspecting it. Are not most of us more puzzled than comforted by Hebraisms in the Bible? Or, to take a modern instance, should the French expression 'mon vieux' be translated 'my old', thus giving, as

Browning would have it, 'the very turn' of the original? Archaisms, too, have little in their favour. They cannot suggest, in any real sense, the corresponding language in the Greek. Unless they are used as a poet would use them, they merely suggest that one dead language is burying another.

Such is the answer to Browning—discounted, no doubt, by that saving clause—'in as Greek a fashion *as English will bear*'. To Bridges one can only answer that general readers have not, in the past, shared his own good taste, but preferred Greek poetry 'brought nearer to our own'.

But taste is changing, and there lies in the future some hope of compromise. It used to be argued by Modernists that English poetry, to be poetry at all, must be 'fuller, more coloured, more personal in the turn of its expression than the Greek'.[1] Cory's *Heraclitus* (No. 513) is a typical product of the old creed. It is full to excess. As Mr. F. W. Bateson[2] has noticed, '*Told* comes twice in the first line and *bitter* twice in the second; *they brought me news* is a repetition of *they told me*, and *I wept* of *tears to shed*; *tired the sun* implies *sent him down the sky*; and *ashes* are generally *a handful* and *grey*.' *Bitter* and *grey* both serve, in different ways, as colouring; and the personal restraint of Callimachus becomes, in the net result, a poem effuse in sentiment, or, as Walter Headlam put it, 'a *vin sec* turned into a sweet'.[3]

---

[1] Cf. J. A. K. Thomson, 'Some Thoughts on Translation', in *The Greek Tradition*, 1915, p. 235.

[2] *English Poetry and the English Language*, Oxford, 1934, p. 124.   [3] *A Book of Greek Verse*, 1907, p. 303.

Greek poetry, at times, is just as full and coloured as English. It can take 'an unsophisticated delight in the obvious qualities of things',[1] as when Æschylus tells us that milk is white and good to drink, that honey is shiny and made by bees from flowers, even that water is wet. But on the whole it prefers to be terse and precise and avoids that verbal and structural diffuseness that modern critics have called, rather loosely, 'Victorian'. So it was that the Imagists, who began in 1912 'a militant movement towards a new poetry' claimed not only to have 'cleared the air of musty artifice and shallow sentiment', but also to have 'revived the clarity and conciseness of the Greeks'.[2]

On the formal side recent poetry has shown some liking for free verse and a growing disuse of rhyme and traditional metres. The great offence, as Tîmotheus and Callimachus once felt (cf. Nos. 438, 519, 522, and notes), is to be either obvious or reminiscent—except by intention. It is early yet to prophesy how much of this poetry will endure. But one thing is clear—that it offers to translators possibilities that have never yet been fully exploited. Modernists, writing prose poetry or poetic prose, can give to readers like-minded with themselves 'a poem for a poem'; and yet, by discarding rhyme and the stricter pattern of old metrical verse, they can follow more closely the sense of the Greek and sometimes

[1] Cf. *The Way of the Greeks*, by F. R. Earp, Oxford, 1929, pp. 173–4 (on Æschylus, *Persæ*, 610 ff.).

[2] *An Imagist Anthology*, Chatto & Windus, 1930, Foreword by Glenn Hughes, p. xvii.

even its movement. One caution is necessary. Let it not be thought that the new poetry will avoid the fault of recalling English modes rather than suggesting something foreign and unfamiliar. Only such Modernists as 'hellenize' in metre can attain that end. Others, in course of time, will appear as mannered and distinctive as translators of any other generation and suggest not the Greek but themselves.

§ 7

THE LANGUAGE OF GREEK POETRY

T. E. Lawrence complained that 'Wardour Street Greek like the *Odyssey*'s defies honest rendering'. We must ask, In what sense, if any, can Homer's language be called 'Wardour Street'? How far does it resemble the language of other Greek poets? And finally, How, when differences exist, can we mark them in translation?

'Wardour Street', i.e. a pseudo-antique or archaizing diction, was dear to historical novelists of the nineteenth century. Their works, no doubt, gave countenance to archaisms used in translation; but translators of Greek poetry were tempted to archaize for reasons of their own; and some even now cannot abandon what was, among the novelists, a brief and unlovely passion. The style at its best may be seen in Butcher and Lang's *Odyssey*—cf. No. 40 (ii). At its worst it is seen in the following translation of a choric ode from Æschylus:

'Surely 'twas a soothsay of fate, by whatsoever wizardry of demon tongues she was luckily clept Helena—that froward queen of strife and bride of the spear. A snare hight she, and a snare she set for ships and warriors and warraid burgh, whenas from forth her dainty curtains she sailed with the soughing of giant Zephyrus.'[1]

Æschylus, then, no less than Homer, wrote 'Wardour Street Greek'—if translators may be trusted. But what are the facts? Why are translators tempted to write in such a fashion?

Homer received, developed, and transmitted a special poetic language, sharply distinguished from the language used later on in prose. His vocabulary —as copious as Shakespeare's—was full of apparent synonyms; and full also of alternative scansions, and of variants, differing in dialect, for one and the same word.[2] Doric forms, for special reasons, do not occur; but many other dialects—Old Ionic, Æolic, even Cypriot, Cretan, and Arcadian—are represented. This language can nowhere have been a spoken vernacular. It served, and was meant to serve, for common Hellenic occasions; and since such occasions were formal or religious, a style of diction highly elaborate and highly exalted was preferred. Greeks of various dialect not only understood it, but accepted it naturally as the way a poet should express himself, lifting them to a vision of things that was strange and wonderful and truer, perhaps, than their own. If we call it 'artificial' we must remember

---

[1] Quoted from the late Professor Warr's *Orestean Trilogy*, 1900, p. 20, by T. E. Page, on 'Greek Poetry in English Verse', in *The Quarterly Review*, No. 445, Oct. 1915, p. 313.

[2] For example, there are five forms of the infinitive of the verb 'to be'—εἶναι, ἔμμεναι, ἔμεναι, ἔμμεν, and ἔμεν.

that most poetical language is equally artificial, and that 'artificial', in this sense, is not opposed to 'sincere'. Further, that while the spell of such poetry is on us, we are not conscious of its artificiality. That only comes with later reflection.

This 'grand' epic style was the first to mature. It therefore moulded poetic fashion, giving its own character to later poetry of certain other kinds—notably to shorter narrative poems in epic metre, to didactic verse, and even to the flute-songs of elegy. In each of these kinds the epic language persisted, surviving, very often, a secular remodelling by the poets of Alexandria. In lyric poetry, on the other hand, a distinction was observed: choral odes adopted Homeric style, but monodies or 'personal lyric' did not. Pindar, a Bœotian, Simonidês and Bacchylidês from Ionia, differ, it is true, in the colour of their language. Doric and Æolic forms, which mark the local origins of choral lyric, occur with varying frequency; so do the borrowed Homeric forms, which Ionians regarded as their own ancestral speech and favoured more. But the language of all three poets is recognizably the same—a single type, largely Homeric, and splendid with high-sounding compound words. One great difference from Homer's language lies in this—that though his vocabulary is equally artificial, the ideas he expresses are simple in themselves. They are also simply co-ordinated and direct in their manner of expression. Choral lyric is far more involved, and in Pindar full of striking metaphor. Monodies, by contrast both with Homer and with choral lyric, were written in the poet's own vernacular. Sappho and Alcæus wrote in Æolic, Anacreon in Ionic, and Corinna in Bœotian. Their diction, too, was less elaborate. It was suited to occasions more friendly and less formal; and was neither the language of prose nor yet the language of common speech, though sometimes racy in its idiom. Alcæus admitted some Homeric forms—or so it seems; and Sappho adapted a few Homeric words to her own Æolic. But generally speaking echoes of the 'grand' style are uncommon.

In the language of drama there are two important distinctions: one between tragedy and comedy, and one—less marked in comedy—between the spoken and the choral parts. Comedy served religion on the side of release and merrymaking. In the spoken part its distance from tragedy varies slightly with the metre. Iambics reflect common speech and are written so loosely that any line of strict pattern implies burlesque of tragedy or direct quotation; trochaics, on the other hand, sometimes bring tragedy more close to the comic level. In choral odes the diction of comedy keeps touch with the dialogue and often makes free with ritual abuse. Yet sometimes pure lyric poetry occurs. Nos. 418 and 422 are among the best examples. There, as in Pindar and Bacchylidês, Epic and Doric forms and also compound-epithets are used.

Odes of this type, in language of the 'grand' style, are the regular usage of tragedy. Their convention was fixed, and all three tragedians move, in their different ways, within fixed limits. But tragic dialogue belongs to a different, more fluid, and also more informal tradition, going back, as far as we can tell, through other iambic writers to Archilochus. Perhaps it was Æschylus himself who raised the level of iambic speech. Many of his words are unknown in Attic prose, and many are rare even in Attic poetry. He mixed with his own dialect some Æolic and Ionic forms that carried rich associations or lent an air of strangeness and antiquity. Other archaisms, of a simpler kind, added to this effect; and most of all he taxed his own capacity, and that of Greek, to invent new words by compounding old. Six hundred words, previously unrecorded, occur in his choral odes; but five hundred others are found in the dialogue, showing clearly that he wished to lessen the distinction between the two.

This practice was accepted but modified by his successors. Sophoclês cared less for strangeness and more for depicting character in action. His innovations, like his archaisms, are fewer; and like his metaphors, they are also less bold. His language is not spacious, but economical; not vividly coloured, but brilliantly precise. The meaning opens inward rather than outward; and sometimes his brevities make him obscure. Euripidês was more revolutionary; but the level of his dialogue is varied and capricious. As a sophist, he delighted in verbal subtleties; as a rhetorician, in clarity and point. He can write in a manner so plain that critics once claimed for him a papyrus fragment belonging much more probably to New Comedy; and yet, when he wishes, he reverts to the grander style—as in Nos. 361, 384—and borrows or adapts Æschylean compounds in a way that Sophoclês avoided.

Such are the main facts,[1] stated with a dogmatism that only brevity can excuse. If we face them as a whole, and ask what corresponding set of facts can be found in English, the answer must be that little or no correspondence exists. Our epic and drama, in the comparable state of maturity, had no liturgical character. The diction of our poetry has rarely departed so far from the diction of prose, and certainly keeps no such interval to-day. Still less can any connexion be traced in English between the dialect used and the species of poetic composition. 'Wardour Street Greek' is therefore an obvious misnomer for the language of the *Odyssey*. That language, variously modified, was the language of major poetry throughout the classical period—a traditional mode accepted as 'the echo of sublimity of soul'; puzzling to the Greeks themselves on analysis, but thrilling to hear, and certainly never analysed in the hearing. How, then, has 'Wardour Street English', a freakish and transitory mode of the nineteenth century, found such favour with translators?

It was not sponsored by Matthew Arnold. For though he pointed out to Newman that Homer sounded as familiar to Greeks of the fifth century as the Bible sounded to English ears in 1861, his own translations from *Iliad VI*, if compared with

[1] See further A. Meillet, *Aperçu d'une histoire de la langue grecque*, Paris, 1920, to which general acknowledgements are due.

'Lang, Leaf, and Myers', are modern in diction. He does not say 'Yea, of a surety' or 'forbiddeth' or grievously entreated' as they do. Butcher and Lang in their *Odyssey* (the forerunner of 'Lang, Leaf, and Myers') were perhaps the main sponsors. They argued that 'the Greek Epic dialect, like the English of our Bible, was a thing of slow growth and composite nature'. Further, 'it was never a spoken language, nor, except for certain poetical purposes, a written language. Thus the Biblical English seems as nearly analogous to the Epic Greek as anything our tongue has to offer'. They then archaized, not like Newman with his *houndis* and *dancen*, but more like Newman than Matthew Arnold.

The analogy offered by the English Bible, though in some ways misleading, is accepted by 'moderates' of both translating sects. But its full application in the practice of translation is a very different matter. Many Biblical words are current in modern poetry and speech; many others are not. A mixture of the two makes 'Wardour Street English'; and by Butcher and Lang this mixture was deliberately preferred. It is here that sectarian disputes once more begin. Hellenizing translators mix their language on principle, and contend that the mixture brings us closer to the Greek. Let us examine this theory, assuming that the faked Jacobean which results is always as good as Butcher and Lang's, or even superior to it.

One objection has already been stated, namely that the 'grand' style in Greek is not comparable to 'Wardour Street English' at all. But another objection is equally relevant. It amounts to this—that distinctions of style cannot be marked unless the translator regards himself as contemporary with the author translated. Only so can he credit that author with so many words already recorded, so many new words attested or possible, and numerous other departures from earlier style. Now to Homer this principle cannot be applied, for earlier poetry is unknown. But no other principle can be justified. Newman applied (and Arnold suffered him) a scale of antiquity that worked *downwards*. That is to say, he represented, or tried to represent, the language of Homer as it sounded to Sophoclês. But how then is the style of Sophoclês to be represented? Presumably as it sounded to Lucian or Plutarch. And how does this principle work in practice? It not only obliterates stylistic differences but ends in futility. Newman decided that as the Homeric word ἐπασσύτερον sounded to Sophoclês, so might the old word *blore* be received in 1861. This procedure the reader is expected to reverse, saying to himself 'As *blore*, whatever it may mean, sounds to me, so some word in the Greek (not necessarily the word thus translated) sounded to Sophoclês'. Coldly comforted, he may rightly ask whether the Rule of Three, as applied by the translator, can ever be certified as correct, and with equal reason he may ask 'Why should Homer's language be represented to me as heard by Sophoclês, and not rather as heard in the days of Homer himself?'

The fiction of contemporaneousness is the only reasonable fiction to adopt. Having adopted it, translators may assume, if they wish, that Homer archaized as much or even more than Æschylus. That assumption is very probably correct. But archaizing English will not necessarily bring the reader into closer contact with the Greek. In matters of detail this is obvious; for no one can tell with any certainty which words in Homer are archaic and which are not. The most that can be done is to give a general colouring of archaism; and even then the dangers are great and the total result may prove misleading. It requires both knowledge and tact to archaize consistently.[1] We may archaize in Biblical style, or in the style of the *Morte d'Arthur*, or in Spenserian style as Mr. A. D. Knox has done in his prose translation of Herôdas. But a single discord will spoil a whole passage; and when there is none, the reader still may find himself bewildered rather than enlightened, and drawn more close not to Homer's world, but quite another. Émile Littré translated the *Iliad*, Book I, into French verse of the thirteenth century. He used both knowledge and tact; but as M. Paul Mazon observes: 'Un pastiche de ce genre est un jeu de lettré; mais, pour le grand public, il présente un réel danger. Un lecteur moins érudit n'entend pas ces mots du XIIIe siècle dans le même sens que le traducteur; la signification précise de chacun d'eux, celle qui permet au traducteur de le rapprocher du mot homérique qu'il veut rendre, échappe à la plupart des lecteurs. Ce qu'il évoquera dans l'esprit de ceux-ci, c'est tout un cortège d'images, c'est le rappel d'une civilisation qui n'est pas celle d'Homère et qui

---

[1] Cf. E. Stuart Bates, *Modern Translation*, Oxford, 1936, p. 119.

offre même avec elle beaucoup plus de différences
profondes que de ressemblances superficielles.'[1] M.
Mazon then explains the true dilemma with which
archaizing translators are faced. They must choose
between archaisms defaced and colourless—the kind
that poets would reject—and others which do not
suffer from these defects but carry with them the
wrong associations.

What, then, is the proper means of differentiating
styles? For Æschylus must differ in English from
Sophoclês, Pindar from the monodists, and so on.
The only suggestions that can be made are these:
Before a colouring of archaism is applied, two points
must be settled. First, whether old words were vivid
in the Greek, or dulled by long poetic usage; and
second, whether a poet's innovations were not, on the
whole, more important than his archaisms. The
archaizing translator may then proceed, mixing his
colours in a rough proportion, and remembering
above all else that the 'grand' style in Greek must
be matched by the same style in English. The rules
for that style cannot be prescribed. But one thing is
certain—that archaisms do not make the poetry. On
the contrary, it needs high poetry to carry the
archaisms.

§ 8

COMPOUND-WORDS IN GREEK AND ENGLISH

Leopardi, we are told, admired Greek as the
language suited beyond all others for poetry. It

[1] *Madame Dacier et les traducteurs d'Homère en France*,
Oxford, 1936, pp. 21 ff.

possessed, in his opinion, 'such a marvellous disposition and capacity for novelties of all kinds, that . . . scarcely was an idea however new conceived, than there, ready created, was the new word for expressing it'.[1] This 'productive faculty', as he called it, which continues to supply the technical terms of every new science, reveals itself most clearly in the effortless formation of compound-words. Even German has not the same power. Latin and English come far behind, and French still farther—or perhaps one should say that whatever powers these languages may once have possessed, they have spared in practice to indulge them.

Greek has a neat way of combining prepositions with a verb, not trailing them behind it, as in the English *to put up with*, but coupling them in front, e.g. *ant-ep-ex-ienai*, to march *out against* an *in*vader. English, at times, cannot match this neatness, or not as well as certain other languages. It is said, for example, that a famous line of Sophoclês, 'It is not in my nature to join-in-hating but in loving', finds neater poetic expression in Welsh—'Gnawd im gydgaru ac nid cydgasau'.[2] But our main source of difficulty lies elsewhere, namely, in matching composite nouns in Greek.

Long ago substantival compounds were made as freely in English as in German, a related tongue; and

[1] *The Poems of Leopardi*, edited with Introduction and Notes and a verse translation in the metres of the original by G. L. Bickersteth, Cambridge, 1923, p. 49.

[2] Translated by Professor W. J. Gruffydd of Cardiff. The Greek words are: οὔτοι συνέχθειν, ἀλλὰ συμφιλεῖν ἔφυν (*Antígonê*, 523).

even now our language can furnish a word such as *by-pass* as of old it furnished *thoroughfare*. But after impact with French, it preferred to follow the Latin way, i.e. to restrict itself to a fairly small variety of patterns, in which the elements that form a complex notion are felt to coalesce. *Impenetrability* made an easier word than *ungothroughsomeness*; and so too, when adjectives were required, *vital* and *solar* supplied the lack of derivatives from *life* and *sun*.

It is chiefly in poetry that the original bent of our language survives, giving us compounds of which the separate parts stand side by side, each with its imagery of things or facts. For smooth-faced abstractions rob poetry of its life. Participial compounds are numerous enough—from examples so unusual as Shakespeare's 'always-wind-obeying deep' to the commoner type of Shelley's 'wind-built tent' or the pseudo-participles 'azure-lidded sleep', 'rose-lipt maiden'. Sometimes, too, we can revert to earlier practice, writing 'light-foot boys' instead of 'light-footed'. But adjectival formations of a non-participial character do not come easily to English. William Morris wrote of 'the corn-kind earth', and A. S. Way, in translating the same Greek word, wrote 'corn-bounteous'. Neither is very convincing; and many other examples could be given which show that English, in spite of its bi-lingual resources, cannot in this respect meet the demands of Greek.

Many Greek compound adjectives of simpler form have passed into English speech, e.g. eu-genic, dys-peptic, mono-syllabic, poly-gamous. This fact in itself reveals some narrowness in our own resources.

It is not, therefore, surprising that the far more complex epithets which belong to the 'grand' style in Greek have caused translators continual embarrassment. Some of these are *hieratic*, i.e. affixed by religious tradition—'Zeus the cloud-gatherer', 'Apollo of the silver bow'. Others, affixed by poetic tradition, are known as *characteristic*—'A long-shadowed spear', 'Whole-hooved horses'. These two classes are usually grouped together under the title 'standard' or 'conventional' epithets. But however 'conventional' an epithet may be, its images gleam out at each recurrence. In Homer the plumes of Hector are fluttering still at the thirty-seventh reading of *koruth-aiolos*. Twenty-four times the goddess Hêra is called 'white-armed'; but always a picture lives both of whiteness and of dress that left the arms bare.

Greek proper-names are often themselves compounds and difficult enough to fit into English verse. 'Tîmênor's *s*on', for example, is not euphonious, yet metre may forbid '(The) son of Tîmênor.' What, then, can be done when compound-epithets accompany such names? A prose-construe mixes hyphenated English with relative clauses, e.g. 'There went the daughter of Zeus the ægis-holder, bright-eyed Athênê, and Artemis who delights in arrows, and Poseidon the Earth-holder who shakes the earth.' Even so there are often syntactical difficulties. In Greek the inflexions of gender and case explain the statement that 'Æschylus died at Gela rich in corn'; and similarly the statement that certain islanders 'possessed no red-prowed ships' is explained at sight by Greek poetic usage. But English must somehow make it clear that Gela, not Æschylus, was rich in corn, and that ships were conventionally known as 'red-prowed'—in other words, that the islanders had no ships at all. Relative clauses, in the same way, need careful handling; or else a simple 'who' may be taken as explanatory—the Latin *qui* with sub-junctive.

In facing these various difficulties translators divide themselves, as usual, into sects. Prose-translators such as Pater, Samuel Butler, and T. E. Lawrence omit the conventional epithets with some freedom. Verse-translators are more reluctant to do so; but Modernists, sharing with poets a distaste for epithets in general, often follow the prose-translators. On one point there is general agreement—that English verse will not allow the same Greek epithet to be rendered always in the same terms. But what are the proper terms?

A. S. Way affected such formations as 'Zeus Cloudrack-herder', 'The Thunder-lord', 'The Glorious Twin-right-armed', 'speech-dowered men'. These are the last fruits of the saga tradition inherited from William Morris. They are also the fruits of Browning's dictum, to write 'in as Greek a fashion as English will bear'. Modernists, in common with Matthew Arnold, have a different view of the tolerance of English; and Hellenizers, in common with Newman, object: 'Mr. Arnold forbids me to invent new compound adjectives, as "fair-throned", "rill-bestreamed"; because they strike us as new, though Homer's epithets (he says) did not so strike the Greeks . . . I hold this doctrine (conceding his fact for a moment) to be destructive of all translation whatever, into prose or poetry.'

No one would dispute that our language has enriched itself by naturalizing foreign words and idioms, and that translators have contributed very largely to that enrichment. To continue the process is a laudable wish; and not less laudable is the wish of all Hellenizers to bring their readers nearer to the Greek. But new formations are much like archaisms. They cannot be accepted (still less gain currency) unless the translator has poetry enough to carry them off. Further, new language must supply real needs, and supply them well, i.e. it must be both intelligible and attractive. Hellenizers often forget one or other of these requirements; and sometimes their creed will drive them to extremes even stranger than 'Zeus Cloudrack-herder' or 'The Glorious Twin-right-armed'. *Hydropot*, for example, has lately been written for 'water-drinker', *glucipicric* for 'bitter-sweet', and *glaucous* (less strangely) for 'grey-green'—all in the earnest desire to enrich our language and enable the general reader 'to smack the sound, if not the full sense of the Greek'.[1] But the sound and the sense are 'resonant meaning or a meaning resonance' —two aspects of one thing that lives only in its context; and the sense in itself is not simple but manifold. To the scholar, as he translates, the word 'glaucous' is full of associations—the light of Athênê's eyes, or the colour of her olive-trees; and 'glucipicric' recalls to

[1] Shane Leslie, *The Greek Anthology, selected and translated*, London, Ernest Benn Ltd., 1929, p. 10. 'Hydropot' and 'glucipicric' are explained by footnotes on pp. 111, 218.

him two vivid lines of Sappho (cf. No. 152). He must not present the reader, in place of these associations, with an empty sound. Mr. K. A. Matthews, in raising some of these objections, further observed: 'Poetry cannot be mechanically transferred from one language to another. As translation approaches completeness, it becomes re-creation.'[1] That touches the heart of the matter.

Some twenty years ago Walter Headlam[2] reaffirmed a point of Matthew Arnold's by stating that compound-epithets were the normal use in Greek, but exceptional in English. Εὔδενδρος in English is 'wooded', πολυστεφής 'garlanded'. To say 'well-wooded', 'many-garlanded' is a form of over-translation. This doctrine certainly applies to the commoner types of compound-epithet and is useful as far as it goes. But it leaves some serious difficulties untouched. The Greeks were particularly fond of compound-epithets relating to hair. 'Wooded' does well for εὔδενδρος, but 'hairy' will not do for εὐπλόκαμος or καλλίκομος, and 'fair-haired' is ambiguous. Words like πολύρρην(ος) 'rich in sheep' or πολύπυρος, πυροφόρος 'rich in corn' are also troublesome. These are not always 'conventional' epithets. To omit them (as is sometimes done) in translating epitaphs from the Anthology is a great mistake, because as often as not they are full of local colour. Macedonia has been described as 'a country of crocuses on the mountains and hawks hovering over the plains'; and so, too, a

[1] *The Cambridge Review*, May 24th, 1929, p. 480; cf. ibid., May 10th, p. 435; May 17th, p. 459. [2] Op. cit., p. xx.

Greek poet, by means of the chosen epithet, would give a visual image of some one's native land or place of burial. Usually it is best to avoid an epithet in English and to say 'the sheep-cotes of Tégëa' or 'the corn-fields of Gela'. The picture remains, and the epithet is not over-translated.

Enough has now been said to make the Greekless reader sympathize with translators and appreciate their subterfuges. It remains only to notice a type of lyric in which extravagance of compounds, and of diction in general, became a virtuosity. This was the dithyramb of the late fifth century. It is known to us only by scanty remains, but Aristophanês parodies the style, and a proverb 'You have less sense than a dithyramb' seems to have been the Greek equivalent for 'mad as a hatter'. Tîmotheus (Nos. 438–9), intent, like some modern writers, on novelty, and more musician than poet, carried the Greek 'productive faculty' to its limits in his poem 'The Persians'—a dithyramb in style, though not in name. Its translator (No. 439) has rightly kept as close to the Greek formations as possible, cf. especially the last nine lines:

> Men lost from their gripe
> the hillborn longnecked
> seafeet of the ship: and leapt
> from their mouths the argentgleaming
> brothers aclatter together.
> Bestarred with bodies
> lightleaving and breathbereft
> glittered the ocean,
> and laboured the shores.

The first five of these are Tîmotheus' way of saying

that the Persians lost both their oars and their teeth. Pindaric metaphor has here run wildly to seed; and the compound-words which carry the metaphors are formed no longer by a single adjective and substantive but by an adjective and double substantive. To say μακραύχην, 'long-necked' or simply 'long', is good Euripidean; but to say μακραυχενόπλους, i.e. 'long-(necked)' and 'long-voyaging' in a single word, is the last resource of innovation.

To Mr. Highet Timotheus' language has suggested (with obvious differences) the style of G. M. Hopkins, e.g. in the following lines from *The Wreck of the Deutschland*:

> For the infinite air is unkind
> And the sea flint-flake, black-backed in the regular blow,
> Sitting Eastnortheast, in cursed quarter, the wind;
> Wiry and white-fiery and whirlwind-swivelled snow
> Spins to the widow-making unchilding unfathering deeps.

It is more than possible that release from rhyme and from conventional English metres will enable future translators to deal more faithfully with the Greek compounds—if they are poets enough to use the eye and the ear of precision. But here, as always in translation, one advantage will probably be gained only by sacrifice of another.

§ 9

THE GREEK HEXAMETER IN ENGLISH VERSE

Many different metres are employed in this book to represent the Greek hexameter; and the aims of several translators have been explained in the Notes. Hellenizing translations, i.e. accentual or quantitative hexameters, will be found in Nos. 44 (ii), 163, 167, 300–2 and Nos. 13, 36 respectively. The other metres used cannot all be specified here, but attention may be drawn to some recent experiments. Among the rhymed metres are Mr. Jack Lindsay's translations from Hesiod and the Homeric Hymns, and Mr. George Allen's from Apollonius Rhodius and Bion. Nos. 67 (i), (v) and 79–81 were written to match Mr. Lindsay's versions, but with minor differences of technique. Unrhymed metres, other than blank verse, are used in ten pieces. No. 24 is in 'sprung rhythm'—cf. No. 504 (from Asclepiad metre); Nos. 500–1 revive a verse of seven accents from Blake; Nos. 16, 483, 630–2 are in the metre of Bridges's *Testament of Beauty*; and Nos. 624–5 are jeux d'esprit in alliterative verse, suggested by Oppian's revival, as late as A.D. 200, of didactic hexameters. All these experiments must be left to the judgement of others; but a few remarks on a question of principle are perhaps not out of place.

Any discussion 'On Translating Homer' should consider the uses of Homer's metre *throughout Greek literature*. In English there is no exactly corresponding medium; but, on the whole, blank verse comes nearest. It is true that to use blank verse for translating both epic and drama obscures a distinction which the Greeks observed; and further, that blank verse, at least in its stricter form, is not well suited for songs—such as those which Theocritus writes in hexameters. On these (among other) grounds the ballad metre written long, as by William Morris or in No. 29, still has its adherents. But the place which the ballad metre occupies in English poetry is very different from that of hexameters in Greek; and as compared with blank verse it is far less subtle an instrument. Within the scheme of blank verse there are more than sufficient varieties of technique to mark the distinction not only between epic and drama, but also between hexameter verse as written by Homer and by Callimachus, or, to take an extreme instance, by Homer and by Theocritus in *Idyll* xv. The 'two main systems of English blank verse, the strict syllabic system of Milton and the free system best known from Shakespeare's later plays', are discussed briefly and well by Mr. W. H. Shewring in *The Ampleforth Journal*, vol. xli, 1936, pp. 222–6. He adds a warning: 'There are still many persons who assume in blank verse a series of quite regular accents, force what they read into such a series, and complain of the result; whereas all that the poet asks the reader to do is to give his verse the natural accents and pauses of speech.'

§ 10

Greek Choral Lyric in English Verse

In the spoken-verse of the Greeks, as we have seen, one 'long' and two 'shorts' were equivalent, and interchange was allowed in certain parts of the line. Their sung-verse admitted some other equivalents, and interchange was more free. Sometimes we get, as in No. 430 (p. 449), a run of twelve 'short' syllables representing $- \cup$ four times repeated:

ἕνεκα δόνακος, ὃν ὑπολύριον.

And in No. 422 (ii), line 14, iambics are represented by a run of twenty:

τά τε κατ' ὄρεα τά τε κοτινοτράγα τά τε κομαροφάγα.

Sequences such as these cannot be imitated in English, or not with the same effect; and a sequence of 'longs' (as in No. 424) is equally unmanageable. Between these extremes 'come all the varied proportions and arrangements of "long" and "short" which are classed by some metricians under the names of Dorian, Ionian, Æolian, and Pæonic rhythms. A given choral lyric keeps a general rhythmical unity by the repetition of fundamental phrases which are characteristic of one rhythm; it adds variety by changing disposal of them and by various modifications of their primary forms'; so that 'the abstract possibilities of such a prosody seem illimitable in contrast with those of English or any modern prosody'.[1] Further, all this diversity is contained, very often, within the structural unities of ode and antode; and in each structural part there exists what Gilbert Murray has called 'an architectural quality'—for 'a good Greek lyric always builds up to the rhythm of its final lines'.[2]

[1] Cf. W. H. Shewring, The Ampleforth Journal, vol. xli, 1936, pp. 207 ff.

[2] 'What English Poetry may still learn from Greek', in Essays and Studies by members of The English Association, vol. iii (1912), p. 24.

Odes of elaborate structure are not over-common in English; but translators' difficulties do not end there. For English metres that correspond to the Greek in their rhythmical character have acquired associations that prevent their use. This difficulty is explained by Gilbert Murray[1] as follows:

'The whole essence of lyric is rhythm. It is the weaving of words into a song-pattern, so that the mere arrangement of the syllables produces a kind of dancing joy. . . . The older English lyric seems to associate this kind of marked rhythm with triviality. It has no feeling for the sublimity of song as such. Even at the present day our clearest lyrical measures are almost confined to the music halls. Many people feel sublimity or even seriousness to be incompatible with good lyric rhythm. Now Greek lyric is derived directly from the religious dance; that is, not merely the pattering of feet, but the yearning movement of the whole body, the ultimate expression of emotion that cannot be pressed into articulate speech, compact of intense rhythm and intense feeling. The two in Greek are not incompatible; on the contrary, they are intimately and essentially connected.'

A soldiers' song,[2] current during the years 1914–18, will show well enough our trivial use of 'the clearest lyrical measures':

> Oh, oh, oh, it's a lovely war!
> What do we want with eggs and ham
> When we have plum and apple jam?
>   Form fours, right turn!
> What shall we do with the money we earn?
> Oh, oh, oh, it's a lovely war!

[1] Ibid., pp. 23–4.
[2] This example is provided by Mr. Bowra.

There we have a *reductio ad absurdum* of the difficulty that arises when we try to represent Greek choral lyrics in English accentual verse. For Sappho or Simonidês might have used and combined the quantitative rhythms that correspond; and many of them could be found, either singly or in combination, among the choral lyrics of Greek tragedy.

One root of the trouble is this—that our stressmetric, until the nineteenth century, was not overpartial, in serious lyric, to trisyllabic feet. Later, Shelley, Tennyson, and especially Swinburne developed their serious use, but only at the cost of certain qualities in poetry which some critics will always value more. Translators very naturally turned to the new models, especially to Swinburne. A. E. Housman went this way, but without much conviction (cf. No. 332 and Notes). Far better known are the lyrical translations of Gilbert Murray, written in the full belief that Swinburnian methods of handling trisyllabic feet had made possible a modernizing style that could also give some notion of the structure and rhythm of the Greek—cf. Nos. 360, 373, 385, 387. These formal aspects of Greek lyric have never been better suggested; but the metres employed and the manner of the period seem to encourage expansion, e.g. there is nothing in the Greek to match line 18 of No. 385.

Recent years have brought about a great cleavage among the Modernists. This is partly due to mislike of expansion and of diction associated with Romantic or Pre-Raphaelite models. But another reason goes deeper still. Mr. W. H. Shewring has stated it effectively in the following way: 'The material of what we call modern lyric—narrative, descriptive, meditative or intellectual—often requires a precision in statement and sequence of thought which would be blunted or destroyed by a display of elaborate metrical variety. Modern lyric is normally meant to be read, and it would be irrational to compose it as if for a dance and music.'[1]

Many poets would agree with Mr. Shewring in saying that 'what Dr. Murray considers the first necessity of lyric verse—"the rudimentary swing that urges you in the direction of singing"—is in fact necessarily absent from the highest kind of English Lyric'.[2] This prefers, within a strict metrical framework, to exploit the variety of living speech by means of 'inversion of accent, elision, changing pauses', and other features less possible in anapaests, dactyls, or choriambs than in simpler patterns of lyric that go back to before the nineteenth century. In translation, Modernists who share these views abandon all attempt to give the effect of the Greek metres. They usually write a kind of free verse, and would sooner do anything than incur the charge of trying to 'sing'.[3]

Prose translations of choral lyrics are treated separately below (pp. ciii–cv). Among the others in

[1] *The Ampleforth Journal*, vol. xli, 1936, pp. 215–16.

[2] Ibid., p. 211.

[3] J. S. Phillimore (*Some Remarks on Translation and Translators*, 1919, p. 21) suggested that this division of choice as between *Speaking Verse* and *Singing Verse* goes back in the end to racial differences; but the theory is highly controversial.

this book, many, too numerous to specify, adopt rhymed metres different in rhythm from the Greek and not always matching its structural pattern, i.e. its use of ode and antode that are metrically almost the same—a feature called 'strophic correspondence'. No. 368 may be mentioned as respecting the movement and structure of the Greek without aiming at close reproduction. So too No. 523 (not from drama).

Several are written in unrhymed verse of strict pattern, preserving the strophic correspondence. Such are Nos. 314, 317, 318, 363, 366, 369, 382. Sometimes their movement carries more than a hint of the Greek rhythms, as in Nos. 317, 366.

The only attempts to match the Greek metre and structure in some detail are Nos. 418, 422, and 430, all from Comedy. In all three accentual verse is used, and wherever possible this verse is true-timed. But words are sometimes lacking in translation that fulfil the requirements both of sense and poetry and also provide a true 'long' syllable where one is needed. Hence, for example, in No. 418 'forested pinnacles' does duty for $-\cup\cup-\cup\cup$, though probably the actual quantities of the words are different. Nothing but stress-accent can show the intended metrical pattern, and therefore some sacrifice of true-timed scansion must be made to it. If we wish to get the effect of the Greek, there is no harm in letting the voice dwell a little on the accented syllables.

No. 306 (from Bacchylidês) has been written on much the same principles. Since 'long' unstressed syllables in English, however carefully used, often tend to retard and confuse the stress-rhythms, assonance and alliteration have been relied upon to counteract this effect and also to make the metrical pattern less ambiguous.

§ 11

TRANSLATIONS INTO PROSE AND PROSE-POETRY

Nearly fifty years ago[1] R. Y. Tyrrell reviewed the earlier volumes of Jebb's *Sophoclês* together with the edition by Verrall of Æschylus' *Seven against Thebes*. Both these scholars had coupled a prose translation with their text and commentary, and had shown, in Tyrrell's opinion, that 'half a page of talk about the meaning of a passage does not tell so much as one line of perfect rendering'. But the new style of editing was not admired by older critics, who complained that it 'gave offence to a man of scholarly habits' and described both editions as 'cribs'.

If Tyrrell is right,[2] the prose-translation of classical verse, 'treated as a fine art', does not go farther back than the eighteen-sixties; and even after the supersession, not long before, of Latin by English commentaries, translation, as a rule, aimed only at elucidating the literal meaning and construction of the editor's text. It was thought unscholarly to go beyond those limits—'a baseness to write fair'. Hence the memorable construe in Paley's note on Æschylus' *Eumenidës* 160 ff.: 'There is present for me to feel (or perhaps "one may feel" . . .) the severe, the very severe chill ("smart") of a hostile public

[1] *Hermathena*, vol. vi, 1888, pp. 147 ff.
[2] See, however, No. 437 in this book.

executioner.'[1] Scholars who wrote translations for the general public incurred the stigma of idleness. They adopted, so Mark Pattison wrote,[2] 'the laziest of all modes of dealing with the Classics'.

Ernest Myers was among the early prose-translators. His *Pindar*, published in 1874, still has its admirers, e.g. Mr. E. Stuart Bates (*Modern Translation*, 1936, p. 121). But the style, though not unrhythmical, was fashioned rather for amateurs of Greek than for connoisseurs of English, and obviously defers to a literal scholastic tradition. Far more printable to-day is Hallam Tennyson's version of the sixth *Iliad* (No. 8), revised, in point of rhythm, by his father. This was written 'not long after' 1877, when *Achilles over the Trench* (No. 26) first appeared. It seems, therefore, to have preceded the *Odyssey* of Butcher and Lang, published in 1879, and is certainly earlier than the *Iliad* of Lang, Leaf, and Myers, which dates from 1882. All these translations, together with those of Jebb and Verrall, are coloured with archaism, and set a fashion (discussed in § 7 above) which has lingered on into the present century.

Hallam Tennyson's prose differs from that of Lang, Leaf, and Myers in its rhythmical character,

---

[1] From the 2nd Edition, 1861. Cf. A. E. Housman, in *The Classical Review*, vol. xiv, 1900, p. 232: 'When Mr. Paley sings *It is present . . . executioner*, or Mr. Buckley *They cut off his ears with the sharp brass; but he, injured in his feelings, went about, enduring that calamity with frantic mind*, scholars are as grateful as other folk.' Buckley's construe represents Homer, *Iliad*, xxi. 300–2.

[2] Referring to John Conington, *Memoirs*, 1885, p. 251.

which is marked by quasi-Biblical verse-divisions. This contrast is quickly discerned by reading aloud— choosing first some part of No. 8, and then, for example, the second sentence of No. 19, or the last paragraph on p. 49 of No. 32. Another example of prose-translation marked by verse-divisions is No. 67 (iii). Here archaism is mostly avoided; and the rhythmical units, shorter than those in No. 8, reflect a difference between Homer and Hesiod.

Walter Pater's translations, unlike others of that time, cannot be described as 'scholastic' or 'hellenizing'. Perhaps one may call them the earliest manifestoes, in prose, of the opposite sect. His *Myth of Dêmêter and Persephonê* was first published in 1876, and revised two years later. It includes the *Hymn to Dêmêter* (cf. Nos. 77–8) in 'a somewhat abbreviated version'; and also the version of Theocritus here printed as No. 502 (a). Archaisms are few and inoffensive, and the style is fluent and refreshing. But much of the *Hymn to Dêmêter* is shortened beyond the limits proper to translation and should rather be classed as paraphrase. Lang's *Homeric Hymns* and *Theocritus* are correctives in this respect. The latter still makes pleasant reading, but lacks any special distinction of character.

Samuel Butler's *Iliad* (cf. No. 33) was published in 1898, and his *Odyssey* (Nos. 40 i, 48, 54) in 1900. These also abbreviate, but are not paraphrastic; and the same applies to his *Hesiod* (Nos. 67 iv, vi). In the Preface to his *Iliad* he states a 'modernizing' theory of translation (quoted p. lxvii above), and also the principles which govern his rendering of verse into prose. Prose, for example, 'does not permit that iteration of epithet and title, sometimes due merely to the requirements of metre and sometimes otiose, which abounds in the *Iliad* without in any way disfiguring it'. In this respect, and in the avoidance of archaic language—'larding a crib with Chaucerisms' —he is at one with Pater and at variance with Lang, Leaf, and Myers. Their work he regarded as 'the best prose-translation that has yet been made', but still a 'construe', not a readable specimen of English prose. More especially he regrets 'the abandonment (no doubt deliberate) by Dr. Leaf of all attempt at stately, and at the same time easy, musical, flow of language'. He thought, like Maurice Hewlett after him, that more was lost by the lack of this 'power to march' than was gained by adherence to the letter— which after all is illusory.

To be provocative was Butler's mission. It is therefore unwise to take his apparent lapses of taste too seriously. When he translates, 'The King at once rose and said "Aldermen and town councillors of the Phæacians, let Dêmódocus cease his song, for there are those present who do not seem to like it"' (*Odyssey*, viii. 535 ff.), one may suspect a deliberate intention to shock; and any one nurtured on 'Lang, Leaf, and Myers' or 'Butcher and Lang' will receive from Nos. 33, 40 i, and 48 minor shocks of a similar kind, due mainly to incongruous diction, e.g. 'he was now beyond the reach of baths' (No. 33); and, by contrast, 'remained without the gates' or 'in such wise'—phrases which remind us that 'Lang, Leaf, and Myers' was always at Butler's elbow. But with all their faults, his versions are notable in two particulars. Both his *Hesiod* and his *Homer* emphasized the difference, which even sensitive scholars are apt to miss, between the better 'translation English' and idiomatic modern prose;[1] and further, his *Homer* applied, in a striking way, the principle of analogy that governs one sect of translators. For the true assumption on which it is based is this—that modern readers will find in a prose-romance or something like it the proper and most readable equivalent to ancient epic. He writes in No. 54: ' "My dear," answered Penelope, "I have no wish to set myself up, nor to depreciate you; but I am not struck by your appearance." ' That is not a model of translation for schoolboys. But it shows in an interesting way the kinship between the *Odyssey* and a modern novel—at the usual risk of vulgarizing a Classic in the attempt to make it more popular.

T. E. Lawrence (Nos. 44 i, 45, 50, 52) was likewise concerned to provoke; but less in his rendering than in his remarks on 'Homer's' defects. In the omission of epithets and titles the liberties he takes are much the same as Butler's, and his style is as fluent and vigorous. It differs from Butler's in response to his own conception of 'Homer' as a 'bookish' and 'house-bred' man, whose work 'smells

---

[1] It is worth comparing his *Hesiod* with other versions, such as A. W. Mair's or Evelyn-White's, and noticing the finer points of modern idiom. For example, he usually avoids that insidious word *lest*, which belongs far more to the language of the schoolroom than to current speech. Much, too, may be learnt by trying to emulate Butler on his own lines.

of the literary coterie' and 'of a writing tradition';
a man 'whose pages are steeped in a queer naïvety',
difficult to assess; who 'yet has a dignity which
compels respect'. To match this conception, Lawrence's prose is the more elaborate in details of workmanship. It is also less homely than Butler's in
diction, despite occasional touches of racy idiom or
something less commendable. He writes in his Preface: 'Wherever choice offered between a poor and
a rich word, richness had it, to raise the colour'; but
finds that his English 'is not plain enough'. His
complaint that 'Wardour Street Greek like the
Odyssey's defies honest rendering' is discussed elsewhere (§ 7 above).

This survey of Greek hexameter verse in prose-
translation reveals a fact of some importance. Translators whose names are familiar beyond the scholastic
world—Walter Pater, Samuel Butler, T. E. Lawrence—are all modernizers, and careful to regard the
genius of the language into which they translate.
One may group them roughly together under the
title 'men of letters' as opposed to 'scholastics'. In
'Butcher and Lang' and in 'Lang, Leaf, and Myers'
the two groups unite, but the scales tip down on the
more scholastic side. Their work had success partly
because of this union, but also for other reasons. It
was based on a plausible analogy[1] hardly questioned
at the time. As Walter Headlam puts it: 'The
nearest congeners of Homer in our language are the
Bible and the Morte d'Arthur and, what have now
become familiar to us, the prose sagas of the Norse.

[1] Cf. p. lxxvii *supra*.

An English reader recognizes a prose Homer and is ready to adopt him into the family' (*A Book of Greek Verse*, p. x). Further, these translators were assured of their public—a public interested in sagas and wanting to know 'the simple truth about the matter of the poems' (cf. 'Butcher and Lang', preface). For such readers, and for classical students, they provided, to the main of their intent, an accurate construe; and as such their work remains supreme. But the men of letters are right in trying to improve on the character of its prose, and also right in revolting towards a more living language. Or is it true that 'Biblical language suggests a world other than that of every day, an ideal world or dream-world whose glamour is the essence of poetry'?[1]

Greek tragedy in prose-translation has little history before the time of Jebb and Verrall. By Tyrrell (op. cit., p. 148) Jebb's translations were regarded as 'perfect models'; and grateful examinees still accept them as canonic. When Tyrrell adds, 'Though not in metrical language, they are really genuine poetry', even grateful examinees are seized with doubts. Individual turns of phrase are often excellent, but few continuous passages read convincingly. Jebb writes, in fact, an antiquated but superior kind of 'translation English'; and if the later history of Greek tragedy in prose-translation is briefly told, it is because his successors, for the most part, have followed suit. Little blame attaches to them. For

---

[1] Edwyn Bevan, *The Poems of Leônidas of Tarentum*, translated, Oxford, 1931, p. xxxvii. (The reference is not to 'Butcher and Lang' but to Swinburne's language.)

tragic dialogue, it seems, is difficult to render in honest prose. Walter Pater himself, whose essay on *The Bacchanals of Euripidês*[1] contains a prose translation of No. 384, here moves with less than his usual ease; and what is true of tragic dialogue applies with still more force to the lyrics. Gilbert Murray's version of No. 327 is the only prose-translation in this book of a choral ode from tragedy; and from comedy there is none. No. 327, as compared with his rhymed versions, recalls a pencil-study for a canvas in romantic colouring.

Other translators have taken refuge in a form of free verse that is hardly distinguishable from the cadenced prose of No. 327 except in the manner of presentation upon the page. This method of translation seems to have begun with the Imagists, notably 'H. D.', about the period 1912–16 (cf. p. lxx above). Their work was experimental, and often spoilt by apparent misunderstandings of the Greek; but by contrast with scholastic traditions of prose, and faded traditions of verse, it was lively and refreshing. No. 351 represents the Imagists from within; and Nos. 324 and 383 are exercises in the same manner, which sometimes, as in 383, departs from prose in allowing a touch of rhyme. Among translations of choral lyrics from tragedy, the only other example of free verse is No. 321. This differs from cadenced prose in its rhythms and word-order; but not by much. Nos. 371–2 are monodies from tragedy; and No. 386 a dialogue, mainly anapaestic. In all three, as trans-

[1] In *Greek Studies*. It was written about 1876, but not published till 1889.

lated, the Greek metre tends to assert itself, and the verse, to that extent, is no longer free.

Cadenced prose, spaced out like free verse, is also used in No. 459 (from Aristotle) and in five translations from Pindar—Nos. 274, 278, 281–2, 284. These latter, if compared with the work of Ernest Myers, or of Sandys and Farnell (an intermediate generation), will show, as well as anything else, the possibilities of the new method. By sacrificing structural pattern and recurrence of rhythm, and by carrying no suggestion of music or dance or song, something is lost which verse-translations, such as those of Gilbert Murray from tragedy, or C. J. Billson from Pindar, have tried to represent. But after all, any formal correspondence between Greek and English lyric verse is illusory; and if prose-poetry cannot convey the same intensity of feeling as verse (which is doubtful), it has, at any rate, compensating advantages in the sharpness of its images, in 'literal' fidelity, and in freedom from irrelevant associations. The definition of its frontiers, i.e. its distinction from free verse, is an old subject of dispute that can only receive the briefest attention here. Certainly, when a passage from Pater's *La Gioconda* or from Conrad is presented as free verse by the spacing-out of its rhythmical units, the distinction becomes obscure. If none exists, one may ask: Why use two names for the same thing? And what is gained by the spacing-out? Is the practice defensible except as enabling 'plumb-fools' to read better aloud?

One form of defence is suggested by Simonidês in lines 7–8 of No. 204—which, by the way, is another specimen of prose-poetry. But other pleas can be found—at least to defend the practice in certain translations. For example, it can serve to reproduce Pindar's *enjambements*, as in Nos. 278 (p. 299) and 284 (p. 316); and sometimes it allows, as in verse, a rapid sequence of images without any use of logical connectives—cf. No. 278, p. 299. Elsewhere, and especially in prose-translations of Greek tragedy, the problem becomes more acute. If the non-choric parts are written in cadenced prose, how are the lyrics to be distinguished? Merely by spacing-out? Or by giving the prose some different character? These questions are raised only to be left unanswered. But one thing may be noticed in passing—that Mr. W. B. Yeats, who printed Pater's *La Gioconda* as free verse,[1] rejected that medium in his acting-version of Sophoclês' *King Œdipus*. There the non-choric parts are in prose and the lyrics in rhymed verse.

Acting-versions of Greek drama must no doubt have rules of their own. Of his *Œdipus*,[2] composed for Dublin players and Dublin liturgical singers, Mr. Yeats writes: 'The one thing I kept in mind was that a word unfitted for living speech, out of its natural order, or unnecessary to our modern technique, would check emotion and tire attention.' So, too, some thirteen years before, Isadora Duncan had requested a version of Euripidês[3] 'as human as the

[1] In *The Oxford Book of Modern Verse*, 1937, p. 1.

[2] Macmillan & Co., Ltd., 1928, with a musical score appended. The quotation comes from the Preface.

[3] The *Íphigenîa in Tauris*, by Witter Bynner, New York, Mitchell Kennedy, 1915. See Preface. The non-choric parts are in blank verse, the lyrics in iambic metre of regular pattern.

Greek, no rhymes, no inversions, no loss of meaning in the sound'. Some would deny to acting-versions the title of 'translations'. Others would argue, on Samuel Butler's lines, that just as Homer is best 'translated' in the form of a prose-romance, so Greek tragedy, in any true 'translation', must suit the requirements of the modern stage and a modern audience. Here it is idle to discuss the proper term (cf. p. lxviii *supra*). It must suffice to say that for present purposes acting-versions of Greek tragedy are mostly[1] too abbreviated or paraphrastic; and so are the modern adaptations of Greek comedy, such as those of the *Lysistrata* by Laurence Housman or by Gilbert Seldes.

Greek epigrams in prose-translation have been excluded on more debatable grounds. There is much to be said in favour of prose, and Dr. Mackail's[2] well-known book has long occupied in this field much the same place as 'Butcher and Lang' or its companion volume in the field of translation from Homer. It is arguable that in verse-translation the Greek simplicity of image and statement is distorted. For the English metres used depend very largely on rhyme for their effect, and so an awkward dilemma is presented. If the rhymes are too obvious they make the translation unreadable; and if they are not, they read like protests against the Greek lack of 'point'.

[1] See, however, No. 252 and note.

[2] His successors, like those of Butcher and Lang, have concentrated mainly on prose-technique and modernization of diction, e.g. Mr. Richard Aldington (*The Poems of Meleâger*, translated, London, The Egoist Press, 1920); and Mr. Shane Leslie (*The Greek Anthology, selected and translated*, London, Ernest Benn Ltd., 1929).

There is force in this argument, but it neglects the attraction which exists in the more formal side of Greek epigram. Greek is a language very rich in long words, and their quantities are fixed. The skilful arrangement of such words within the expected metrical scheme is certainly a source of aesthetic satisfaction,[1] no less than the Greek simplicity of image and statement. English provides analogous pleasure by the skilful use of rhyme. Further, the Greek inflexions give an effect of assonance that is sometimes deliberately exploited, especially in the pentameter, e.g. in No. 450. Rhyme, after all, is only a kind of assonance disposed in regular places of incidence.

§ 12

CONCLUSIONS

What then is the sum and end of the argument? Briefly this: All translation is a kind of illusion, more or less perfect according to circumstances, and varying also with the skill of the translator. Greek, in its syllabation, its metric, its word-formation, and in the language and conventions of its poetry, differs so profoundly from English that illusions of likeness are rare and hard to achieve. Where there exists in English a corresponding form and manner, e.g. in dramatic dialogue of the more colloquial kind, a high degree of illusion is possible. Those translations are always best in which the illusion is most complete and

---

[1] Cf. Edwyn Bevan, *The Poems of Leônidas of Tarentum*, translated into English verse, Oxford, 1931, p. xxxv f.

the idiom least suggestive of translation. A scholar who reads them will say, 'Of course, I see through this; the verbal and metrical equivalents are far from exact. But so Euripidês, or so Menander might speak in our own age and tongue.' And the Greekless reader will say, 'I should never have guessed that this was a translation.'

Where no correspondence exists, the best translations are those which match the Greek most perfectly in its images and ideas, and also in the intensity and character of its appeal. The methods of attaining these ends cannot be prescribed. Swinburnian lyrics, unrhymed verse, prose-poetry, and imitations of Greek metre vary in their appeal to different tastes; and in each of these one kind of illusion is achieved only by sacrifice of another. As well write an Art of Poetry as an Art of Translation.

T. F. H.

PROPER NAMES
AND THEIR PRONUNCIATION

1. **Latinizations.** In some few translations (cf. p. xli) the names of Greek gods and heroes are latinized. Thus Saturn is written for Kronos or Cronus; Jupiter or Jove or The Saturnian for Zeus; Neptune for Poseidon; Mars for Arês; Mercury for Hermês; Vulcan for Hêphæstus; Minerva for Athênê; Venus for Aphrodîtê; Ulysses for Odysseus.

2. **Spelling.** Here too some translators latinize, or anglicize, and some do not. Typical variations are illustrated by the following examples:

Greek form	Latinized or anglicized form
Zênophil*ê*	Zênophil*a*
*K*ronos	*C*ronus
Pang*aios*	Pang*æus*
Atr*ei*dês	Atr*í*dês
*K*adm*ei*an	*C*adm*êa*n
Pho*i*bos	Ph*æb*us

All translators except Browning, an ardent hellenizer (cf. p.lxvi), write *y* for the Greek *v*.[1] He preferred the forms *K*upris, Electr*u*on (better Ele*k*tr*u*on), and even Tir*u*ns (Nos. 352–3). Shelley, by contrast, latinized Maias to Maia, and further anglicized it to May (No. 82). On similar principles Veronica might be written for Beronîkê, but modernization is not usually carried so far.

3. **Accentuation.** Not all scholars could say off-hand how certain Greek names, e.g. Cercidas, should be pronounced;

---

[1] Not in the diphthongs *av*, *ev*, *ov*.

and the need for guidance felt by other readers is very much greater. Symbols or accents have therefore been used to mark off the division of syllables when this is ambiguous; and also to show their metrical length or 'quantity' and the incidence of stress in our English pronunciation.

To be consistent (which is the main difficulty) would be possible if all proper names were marked with their true Greek quantities. But some of these names have been anglicized for centuries, and often the quantities they bear in English and in Greek do not correspond. In English, for example, the second syllable of Arcadia is long, but in Greek it is short. First of all, then, let it be said that names familiar through English usage have been treated as a class apart. Some are not accented at all, e.g. Achilles, Ajax, Penelope, Bellerophon, Pegasus, Orion, Solon, Apollonius, Ægina, Arcadia, Delos, Hesiod. Others have been accented only on the last syllable, e.g. Simonidês, Periclês, Sophoclês, Euripidês, Aristophanês. The Greek quantities of some of these names are mentioned below.

Apart from the grave accent, which serves its ordinary purpose, e.g. in marking the word *agèd* as disyllabic, the following are the only symbols used:

Diæresis marks off a 'short' syllable that might otherwise be thought to coalesce with what precedes, as in Pleiadës, Nêreïd, Pîrithoüs; or with what follows, as in Gêryön; or with either alternative, as in Orëads.

A circumflex marks a vowel as 'long'. All other vowels are 'short' except (i) final *o*, as in Chariclo, which is always 'long' and therefore not worth distinguishing; (ii) final *-on* in names such as Telamon or Bellerophon, where English, as a rule, shortens the *o*, making a circumflex necessary only when the Greek quantity is preserved; (iii) some other vowels which English pronounces inconsistently or without regard to the Greek. For example, we say Atreus with a long A, but tend to shorten the A in Atreidæ ('sons of Atreus'). We also say Dêmêter for Dêmêtér; Penelopê for Pênelopê; Pegasus for Pégasus; Sôlon for Solôn; Darîus for Dârîus; Símonidês and Euripidês for Simônidês and Euripidês.

Note that a circumflex serves instead of diæresis when the syllable to be distinguished is 'long', e.g. Laêrtes, Danaî, Laîus, Menelaûs, Alpheûs, Achelôus. When two adjacent vowels are not distinguished either by diæresis or circumflex, they coalesce and form a diphthong, e.g. Pangaius, Naiad, Atreidæ, Haleis, Atreus, Tyndareus, Zagreus. In Eileithyîa (p. 296) and Orîthyîa (p. 385) *yi* is a diphthong representing the Greek *υι*.

An acute accent marks the incidence of our English stress, when that stress falls on a 'short'. If it falls on a 'long', nothing is added to the circumflex. A good illustration is the word Salonica, which occurs in No. 698 and is written Salonîca. This means that the last two syllables are pronounced *eeka*. If the word rhymed with Veronica or japonica, it would be written Salónica.

4. **Pronunciation.** This is becoming more consistent, but most translators of past generations used the older fashion of pronunciation and many living translators have not abandoned it. Therefore it is best to show the alternatives in two columns, 'Modern' and 'Older'. The equivalents in the 'Modern' column are mostly taken from *The Restored Pronunciation of Greek and Latin*, by E. V.

Arnold and R. S. Conway, 4th and revised edition, Cambridge, 1908, pp. 6–9. Only selections from their list are necessary here.

Letter	Modern as in	Older as in
a	foot*p*ath	foot*p*ath or nearer *may*
â	f*a*ther	m*ay*
e	g*e*t	g*e*t
ê	nearer to b*ea*r than to t*a*ke	qu*ee*n
i	h*i*t	h*i*t
î	qu*ee*n	p*i*ke
c	always as in *c*at	soft before e, i, y, as in *c*ertain
k	*k*it	*k*it
ch	lo*ch*	*ch*aracter
o	cann*o*t, c*o*nsist	nearer to c*o*ke
ô	nearer to *o*re than to c*o*ke	c*o*ke
s	always as in *s*alt, mou*s*e, except that sb, sg, sm are as in ha*s* *b*een, ha*s* *g*one, ha*s* *m*ade	*s*alt, mou*s*e
u	French d*u* pain, l*u*tte	st*u*d or nearer *yu*le
û	French p*u*r	*yu*le

There are also differences between the Modern and the Older pronunciations of the diphthongs *ai, oi, ui, au, eu, ou*, and the aspirates *th, ph*.

HOMER
(Date unknown)

THE ILIAD

I

The Beginning of the Wrath

WHO of the gods set on those two to strife?
The son of Zeus and Lêto. He was angered
Against the king and stirred an evil plague
Upon the army, and the people perished,
Because Atrîdês had disdained his priest
Chrŷsês: for he had come to the quick ships
Of the Achæans to redeem his daughter,
Uncounted ransom bringing; and he carried
The fillets of the Archer-god Apollo
Upon a golden sceptre, and made prayer
To all the Achæans, but in chiefest place
To both the Atrîdæ, marshals of the host:

'Atrîdæ, and ye other armed Achæans,
Now may the gods in their Olympian houses
Grant you to ravage Priam's town and come
In honour home! But give me back my child
And take her ransom, showing deference
To Phœbus son of Zeus, who smites afar.'

Then all the other Achæans shouted 'Ay!
Respect the priest: and take the noble price.'
Only Atrîdês Agamemnon's heart
Disliked it, and he sent the priest away
Rudely, and laid on him a harsh command:

'Let not me find thee by the hollow ships
Or loitering now, or coming back anon,
Old man, lest possibly thou have no profit

From either wand or chaplet of thy god!
Her will I not let go; not till old age
Comes on her in my house in Argos, far
From home, where she shall ply the loom and share
My bed. No, get thee hence: provoke me not,
That thou mayest go the safer.'
   So said he, and the terrified old man
Obeyed his order: and he walked in silence
Along the beach of the loud-sounding sea;
Where in a lone place he made earnest prayer
To King Apollo, fair-haired Lêto's son:
'Lord of the silver bow, give ear! that hast
Chrŷsê and holy Cilla in thy keeping
And guardest Ténedos with thy strong arm;
O God of Plague, if ever I have roofed
One temple to thy heart, if ever I have
Burned unto thee fat thighs of bulls or goats,
Fulfil this prayer for me, and let the Dánaî
Pay by thine arrows for these tears of mine.'
   So said he praying, and Apollo heard.
Down from Olympus' peaks he came, enraged
At heart; and from his shoulders hung his bow
And lidded quiver, and upon his shoulders
The arrows rattled as he walked in wrath;
And like the night he came. Then down he sat
Far off the ships and let an arrow fly;
And a grim clang came from the silver bow.
At first he reached the mules and the quick dogs,
And then he turned and loosed his pointed bolt
Upon the troops; and all the time the pyres
Of dead were burning thickly.

SIR WILLIAM MARRIS   (I. 8–52)

2

2   *Thersîtês*

                                Now all sat down
And kept their seats, save one, Thersîtês. He,
A babbler, rattled on, stuffed full of words
Disorderly and random, which he flung
Against his chiefs, vainly, without a plan
Save this, to stir the Argives' laughter. He,
The ugliest man that ever looked on Troy,
Was bandy-legged and halt, curved in the back,
Pigeon-breasted, cone-pated, scanty-cropt
With hair. Him of all men Achilles loathed,
So did Odysseus, for he railed at them.
But now on Agamemnon he let loose
His shrill revilings, which the Greeks sore vext
Must hear with indignation. Yet on he ran
Girding at Agamemnon. 'What d'ye lack,
King Atreus' son? What next? Are not your huts
Heapt up with bronze, have you not plenty women
Pickt out for you, for you first, by us Greeks
Whatever town we sack? D'ye need gold too,
Such as some Trojan horseman brings to buy
His son withal, my prize or another man's?
Or need you another girl to keep shut up
And take your joy of? Unseemly is the Chief
Who brings his Greeks to shame! O shameful fools,
O you Greek women, who are men no more,
Come, let us ship off home, and leave him here
Glutting himself with honour, till he see
Whether our help avail him, yes or no—
Him who has put to shame a better man,
Achilles, snatching his prize to keep himself.

                                            3

But there! Achilles is mild and lets all go—
Else, son of Atreus, that flout had been your last!'

MAURICE HEWLETT   (II. 211–42)

3   *The Advance of the Trojans*

NOW marshall'd all beneath their several chiefs,
    With deafening shouts, and with the clang of arms,
The host of Troy advanced. Such clang is heard
Along the skies, when from incessant showers
Escaping, and from winter's cold, the cranes
Take wing, and over Ocean speed away;
Woe to the land of dwarfs! prepared, they fly
For slaughter of the small Pygmæan race.
Not so the Greeks; they breathing valour came,
But silent all, and all with faithful hearts
On succour mutual to the last, resolved.
As when the south wind wraps the mountain top
In mist, the shepherd's dread, but to the thief
Than night itself more welcome, and the eye
Is bounded in its ken to a stone's cast,
Such from beneath their footsteps dun and dense
Uprose the dust, for swift they cross the plain.

WILLIAM COWPER   (III. 1–14)

4   *Helen*

SO saying, the Goddess into Helen's soul
  Sweetest desire infused to see again
Her former Lord, her parents, and her home.
At once o'ermantled with her snowy veil
She started forth, and as she went let fall

4

A tender tear; not unaccompanied
She went, but by two maidens of her train
Attended, Æthra, Pittheus' daughter fair,
And soft-eyed Clýmenê. Their hasty steps
Convey'd them quickly to the Scæan gate.
There Priam, Pánthoüs, Clýtius, Lampus sat,
Thymœtês, Hicetâon, branch of Mars,
Antênor and Ucálegon the wise,
All, elders of the people; warriors erst,
But idle now through age, yet of a voice
Still indefatigable as the fly's,[1]
Which perch'd among the boughs sends forth at noon
Through all the grove his slender ditty sweet.
Such sat those Trojan leaders on the tower,
Who, soon as Helen on the steps they saw,
In accents quick, but whisper'd, thus remark'd:
'Trojans and Grecians wage, with fair excuse,
Long war for so much beauty. Oh, how like
In feature to the Goddesses above!
Pernicious loveliness! Ah, hence away,
Resistless as thou art and all divine,
Nor leave a curse to us and to our sons.'

So they among themselves; but Priam call'd
Fair Helen to his side. 'My daughter dear!
Come, sit beside me. Thou shalt hence discern
Thy former Lord, thy kindred and thy friends.
I charge no blame on thee. The Gods have caused,
Not thou, this lamentable war to Troy.
Name to me yon Achaian Chief for bulk
Conspicuous, and for port. Taller indeed
I may perceive than he; but with these eyes

_____
[1] The cicála.

5

Saw never yet such dignity, and grace.
Declare his name. Some royal Chief he seems.'
   To whom thus Helen, loveliest of her sex:
'My other Sire! by me for ever held
In reverence, and with filial fear beloved!
Oh that some cruel death had been my choice,
Rather than to abandon, as I did,
All joys domestic, matrimonial bliss,
Brethren, dear daughter, and companions dear,
A wanderer with thy son. Yet I alas!
Died not, and therefore now live but to weep.
But I resolve thee. Thou behold'st the son
Of Atreus, Agamemnon, mighty king,
In arms heroic, gracious in the throne,
And, (though it shame me now to call him such,)
By nuptial ties a brother once to me.'

WILLIAM COWPER   (III. 139–80)

5   *Menelâus and Odysseus*

THEN answer thus Antênor sage return'd:
   'Princess, thou hast described him: hither once
The noble Ithacan, on thy behalf
Embassador with Menelâus, came,
And at my board I entertain'd them both.
The person and the intellect of each
I noted; and remark'd, that when they stood
Surrounded by the Senators of Troy,
Atrîdês by the shoulders overtopp'd
The prince of Ithaca; but when they sat,
Ulysses had the more majestic air.
In his address to our assembled chiefs,

6

Sweet to the ear, but brief, was the harangue
Of Menelâus, neither loosely vague,
Nor wordy, though he were the younger man.
But when Ulysses rose, his downcast eyes
He riveted so fast, his sceptre held
So still, as if a stranger to its use,
That had'st thou seen him, thou had'st thought him, sure,
Some chafed and angry idiot, passion-fixt.
Yet, when at length, the clear and mellow base
Of his deep voice brake forth, and he let fall
His chosen words like flakes of feather'd snow,
None then might match Ulysses; leisure, then,
Found none, to wonder at his noble form.'

WILLIAM COWPER   (III. 203-24)

6   *The Two Hosts*

AS when the billow gathers fast
    With slow and sullen roar
Beneath the keen north-western blast
    Against the sounding shore:
First far at sea it rears its crest,
    Then bursts upon the beach,
Or with proud arch and swelling breast,
    Where headlands outward reach,
It smites their strength, and bellowing flings
    Its silver from afar;
So, stern and thick, the Danaän kings
    And soldiers marched to war.
Each leader gave his men the word,
Each warrior deep in silence heard;

So mute they marched, thou could'st not ken
They were a mass of speaking men;
And as they strode, in martial might,
Their flickering arms shot back the light.

But, as at even the folded sheep
    Of some rich master stand,
Ten thousand thick their place they keep,
    And bide the milkman's hand,
And more and more they bleat, the more
    They hear their lamblings cry;
So from the Trojan host, uproar
    And din rose loud and high.
They were a many-voicèd throng;
    Discordant accents there,
That sound from many a differing tongue,
    Their differing race declare.
These, Mars had kindled for the fight;
Those, starry-eyed Athênê's might,
And savage Terror, and Affright,
And Strife, insatiate of wars,
The sister and the mate of Mars;
Strife that, a pigmy at her birth,
    By gathering rumour fed,
Soon plants her feet upon the earth
    And in the heaven her head.
With hand impartial sowing now
    About the field she went,
That hatred in their hearts might grow
    And men the more lament.

W. E. GLADSTONE (to l. 443)   (IV. 422–45)

8

7   *The Rally*

SARPÊDON'S words bit deep in Hector's heart.
He flung himself in armour from the car
And shaking two keen spears he scoured the host
Calling to war, and raised the wild war-cry.
They rallied and they stood to face the Achæans,
While in a mass the Argives paused for them
And did not break. Just as the wind blows husks
Across the sacred threshing-floor where men
Are winnowing, when fair-haired Dêmêter sifts
With puff and puff of wind the grain and chaff,
And the chaff-heaps grow white; so now the Greeks
Grew white all over with the cloud of dust
Which in their midst the horses' hoofs beat up
To brazen heaven, as once again the fight
Joined, and the chariot-drivers swung them round.

SIR WILLIAM MARRIS   (V. 493–505)

8   *The Story of Bellérophon*

AND the glorious son of Hippólochus answered him:
Great-hearted son of Týdeus, wherefore dost thou
ask of my lineage? even as is the generation of leaves, such
is that of men.

The leaves—a wind streweth them on the ground, and
the forest flourisheth and produceth others, when the hour
of spring descendeth; so one generation of men produceth,
and another ceaseth altogether.

Yet if thou wouldst also learn of me these things,
hearken, that thou mayst know my lineage: many a man
there is that knoweth it.

9

There is a city of Éphyra, in a nook of horse-pastured Argos; and there dwelt Sîsyphus who was of all men the shrewdest; Sîsyphus, the son of Æolus, and he begat a son, even Glaucus; and Glaucus begat the princely Bellerophon.

And the gods bestowed on him the beauty of fair manhood, but Prœtus imagined evil in his heart against him; he drave him forth from among his people, since Prœtus was strongest among the Argives; for Zeus had subdued them unto his sceptre.

Now the fair Anteia, the wife of Prœtus, maddened to mingle with him privily in love's embracement; but in no way could she prevail over the noble nature and wise heart of Bellerophon.

And she with lying words spake unto King Prœtus: 'Mayst thou die, Prœtus, or mayst thou slay Bellerophon who would mingle in love's embracement with me altho' I would not.'

So she said, and wrath possessed the king when he heard thereof; yet he was loth to slay him, for his soul felt awe at the doing of it; so he sent him to Lycia, and gave him devices of doom, marking on a folded tablet many a deathful symbol.

And he bad him show them to his father-in-law, in hope that he might perish; but he went to Lycia under the gods' good guidance.

And when he had come to Lycia, and to the river Xanthus, the king of broad Lycia honoured him with all graciousness; nine days he entertained him, and nine bulls he sacrificed.

Yet when on the tenth day the rosy dawn appeared, then he questioned him, and asked to see the token; that which he had brought for his own behoof from Prœtus his son-in-law.

Now after he had received that evil token of his son-in-law, then indeed he first bad him slay the unconquerable Chimæra, which was of birth divine, not mortal; in front a lion, and behind a dragon, and a wild goat in the middle and breathing out the dreadful might of burning fire; and obeying the signs from heaven, he slew her.

Next he fought with the glorious Sólymi—of a truth the fiercest fight, he said, he ever underwent with warriors; and thirdly he smote down the manlike Amazons.

And another plot full of cunning the king wove for him returning—he chose from out broad Lycia the men that were bravest, and set an ambush; but those no more came homeward; for princely Bellerophon smote them all to the death.

So when now the king was aware that he was the strong offspring of a god, he kept him there with himself, and gave him to wife his own daughter, and bestowed on him half of all his kingly honours.

And the Lycians meted out unto him a richer portion of land than unto all the others; fair with tilth for corn and with plantations, so that he might dwell therein.

HALLAM TENNYSON, ALFRED TENNYSON

(VI. 144–95)

9   *Hektor and Andrómachê*

Hektor turn'd
Back from his house with speed, by the same way
Thro' the fair-builded streets, across the town,
And so to the Skaian Gates wherethro' he must go

Out to the plain; and there his fruitful wife
Came running to him, even Andrómachê
Daughter of Eëtion of the mighty heart,
Who under leafy Plakos used to dwell,
In Thêbê below Plakos: he was King
Of the Kilikians, and mail-clad Hektor had
His daughter to wife. She came to meet him now,
And with her came her woman, who on her breast
Had the young child, the tender innocent,
Hektor's belovèd, beautiful as a star,
Whom he had nam'd Skamander, but the rest
Called Ástyanax, seeing his father alone
Was saviour of Troy. And Hektor smiled and lookt,
Saying nothing; but Andrómachê stood
Close to him weeping, and took his hand in hers
And spake to him, saying, 'Lord, this might of thine
Destroys thee. Pity him, thy little child,
And me the unhappy, thy widow very soon.
For very soon the Greeks will set on thee
And slay thee; better then that I were laid
Under the earth if thou wert gone, for then
There would be no more joy, but only sorrow
For me, if thou should'st die. Father nor mother
Have I now. Great Achilles slew my father
When he laid waste the many-peopled town,
High-gated Thêbê of the Kilikians.
And there he slew Eëtion, but forebore
To spoil him, for of that he was ashamed,
So burn'd him in his wrought harness, and rais'd
A barrow over him where all about
The Orëads, children of Zeus, made elm-trees grow.
I had seven brothers within our house,

And these too on that same day were sent down
To the house of Hell, when Achilles the swift-footed
Slew all of them among the shambling kine
And woolly flocks. Then with the other spoil
He brought my mother here, my mother, a queen
Once under leafy Plakos, but let her go
Presently for great ransom. And then she fell
Struck in her father's house by Artemis
The Huntress. Hektor, so it is thou art
Father, mother, brother, as well as lord
And loving husband to me. Pity me now
And stay here on the tower for fear to make
The child an orphan and a widow of me!
And bid our people stand by the fig-tree,
There where the city may be entered best,
And where the wall lies weakest to assault.
Three times the best of them have made essay
At that point with the Aiantës and renown'd
Idómeneus, and Atreus's two sons,
And the great son of Tydeus, as if some man
Skill'd in soothsay had given word of it,
Or their own wit had led them find it out.'

　　Then said great Hektor of the gleaming mail,
'Wife, all these things are heavy on my soul,
But I have terrible fear to be ashamed
Before the Trojans and their long-robed wives
If I should be a coward and shirk the war.
That my heart will not suffer. I have learn'd
Nobility, ever to be the first
Fighting among the Trojans, for to win
Fame for my father and myself. And yet
I know this very well, the day shall come

When holy Troy shall fall, Priam shall fall,
And the people of Priam of the goodly spear;
But not the Trojans' grief that is to come
Afflicts me, nor yet Hékabê's, nor yet
King Priam's grief, not yet my brothers' grief,
The many and brave who must lie in the dust
Before their enemies, so much as thine
When some mail'd Greek shall take thee wailing away
And reive thy freedom from thee, and set thee down
In Argos, to some other woman's loom,
Or water-carrying from Messêis belike
Or Hypereía under harsh duress
Driven by heavy need. Then, seeing thy tears,
Some one may say, "This woman was the wife
Of Hektor, once the first man in the battle
Of the horse-taming Trojans when men fought
Round about Troy." So thou wilt hear them say,
And weep again for need of such a man
As I was to keep off the day of chains.
May I be dead and the earth heapt on me
Before I hear thee cry and know thee a slave.'

So saying, noble Hektor opened his arms
To take the child, but whimpering he held back
Upon the breast of his fair-girdled nurse,
Afraid to see his father look so grim,
Afraid of the mail and nodding dreadful crest
Topping his helm. His father and mother laught,
And then Hektor took off his helm and laid it
Shining upon the ground, and kist his son,
And lift him in his arms, praying the while
To Zeus and all the Gods, 'Zeus, all ye Gods,
Grant to this child of mine that he may be

14

Even as his father, excellent in Troy,
As brave as he, a mighty king in Troy,
So that men say who see him coming home
From battle-faring, "This was a better man
Than even his father was." Grant him the spoils
Of war, grant him to slay his enemy,
And make his mother glad because of him.'
So said, he put the child back in the arms
Of his dear wife who in her fragrant breast
Received him, smiling in the midst of tears;
Which pitying he saw, and stroked her cheek,
Speaking again to her. 'Let not thy heart
Be too much troubled, my love; there is no man
Shall drive me down to Hell against my fate.
But who shall avoid his fate, once he is born,
Coward or high of heart? Now hie thee home,
Set-to at loom or distaff, busy thyself,
And bid thy maids be busy. As for war,
That is the men's affair: and it is mine
Chiefest of all in Troy.'

     Having so said,
Great Hektor took his plumèd helm, and she,
His gentle wife, with many a backward look
Went home, shedding hot tears.

MAURICE HEWLETT   (VI. 392–496)

10   *The Scales of Zeus*

TILL sacred morn had brighten'd into noon,
The vollied weapons on both sides their task
Perform'd effectual, and the people fell.
But when the sun had climb'd the middle skies,

The Sire of all then took his golden scales;
Doom against doom he weighed, th'eternal fates
In counterpoise, of Trojans and of Greeks.
He rais'd the beam; low sank the heavier lot
Of the Achaians; the Achaian doom
Subsided, and the Trojan struck the skies.
Then roar'd his thunders from the summit hurl'd
Of Ida, and his vivid lightnings flew
Into Achaia's host. They at the sight
Astonish'd stood; fear whiten'd ev'ry cheek.

WILLIAM COWPER   (VIII. 66–77)

11   *The Trojan Camp-fires*

AND these all night upon the bridge of war
    Sat glorying; many a fire before them blazed:
As when in heaven the stars about the moon
Look beautiful, when all the winds are laid,
And every height comes out, and jutting peak
And valley, and the immeasurable heavens
Break open to their highest, and all the stars
Shine, and the shepherd gladdens in his heart:
So many a fire between the ships and stream
Of Xanthus blazed before the towers of Troy,
A thousand on the plain; and close by each
Sat fifty in the blaze of burning fire;
And eating hoary grain and pulse the steeds,
Fixt by their cars, waited the golden dawn.

ALFRED TENNYSON   (VIII. 553–65)

12   *Achilles' Reply to the Embassy*

THEN swift Achilles answer'd him, saying,
    'Lâertês' son, Odysseus, god-begot
And man of wiles, now I must speak plain truth
Of what I think and what must come to pass,
That you sit not beside and wheedle me
For this or that thing. Nay, I hate the man
Who thinking one thing, says another thing—
Even as the jaws of Death I hate him. Then
I will say this, which seems the best to me:
I am not to be won by Agamemnon,
That son of Atreus, nor by the other Greeks,
Seeing I had no thanks for battle done
Everlastingly on the foe. As good
The share of him that stays as his that fights,
And there is honour for the craven as well
As for the man of valour, while in death
Both share, the laggard and the man of deeds.
As for me, I gained nothing by my pains
Of heart, nor endless risking of my life
In battle. Like a hen-bird who brings home
To the fledglings of the nest what scraps she wins
And evil fares herself, so many a night
I watcht out sleepless, many a day of blood
Wore thro', striving with men for womenfolk.
Twelve cities of men I wasted with my ships,
Eleven on hard ground, as I make it, thro'
This goodly land of Troy; and from all these
Treasures I took, many and excellent,
And brought them in to Agamemnon and gave
To him, who, sitting back there by the ships,

Took them, and shared a little, and kept much.
Some deal he gave to chiefs and kings, to be
An honourable share, and those they keep
Untoucht. From me alone of all the Greeks
He took away, and has, my lovely dear—
Now let him keep her and get joy of her.
Why are the Argives making war on Troy?
Why called the son of Atreus on the Greeks
And led them hither? Was it not because
Of fair-tress'd Helen? Are the sons of Atreus
Alone of mortal men to have their wives?
Every good man sound-hearted loves his wife
And takes thought for her; and with all my heart
I loved mine, tho' a prize my spear had won.
But now he has her, now he has snatcht my prize
And cheated me. Let him not try again,
For now I know him well. He tempts me not. . . .

Nor will I deal with him in schemes or deeds
Who has cheated me and done me hurt. No more!
Never again with words to cozen me!
More than enough of him. Now let him go
Harmless, for Zeus hath robb'd him of his wits;
As for myself, I hate his gifts, and him
Reckon not at a hair's worth. Let him give
Ten times or twenty times what now he has,
Or what he may have; let him give the worth
Of Orchómenos, or Thebes of Egypt where
The treasuries are fullest—Thebes which has
A hundred gates, through each of which proceed
Two hundred men with chariots: nay, pile up
His gifts like sand or dust, not even so
Shall Agamemnon win me till he have paid

The shameful debt he owes me. As for his daughter,
I'll never wed her, nor would I, might she cope
With Aphrodîtê's beauty, or could vie
In craft-work with Athênê the Grey-eyed.
No, let him choose some other Greek, his peer,
A kinglier man than I; and if the Gods
Suffer me win safe home, Peleus himself
Will find me a wife; for many lords' daughters
Hellas and Phthîa hold, daughters of men
Who guard their cities. One of them shall be
My lady, as I choose her. Many a time
My soul urged me to wed a wife out there,
A mate with whom to pleasure in the gear
Old Pêleus has in house; but of what worth
Are all such things beside one's life? What worth
The store which Troy, they say, the peopled burgh,
Possest in days of peace, before the Greeks
Came hither, or the treasure fenced within
The stony threshold of Apollo's shrine
In rockbound Pŷtho? Flocks and cattle enough
There are for plunder, and a man can buy
Tripods and golden herds of mares—but life!
To fetch that back no reiving, nor no pence
Will serve, once it has slipt between your teeth.
Now thus the silver-footed Thetis saith,
My divine mother: two fates show me death;
For if I stay a-warring here by Troy
My homefare is cut off, tho' my fame lives
Imperishable; but if I go back
To my own land, then is my fame cut off
Albeit my days be long and death not swift
To fall. As for the rest of you, my rede

19

To you would be, Up sails and home again,
Since you shall never win sheer Îlios,
Whereover broad-brow'd Zeus has stretcht his hand,
Whose men are high of heart.'

MAURICE HEWLETT   (IX. 307–45 and 374–420)

13   *The Appeal of Phœnix*

'CONQUER the proud spirit in your breast, child,
   seeing it is not
Good to be implacable. The immortal deities are not,
Who have a pow'r and glory beyond our mortal attainment.
For we behold how savour of incense, vows of amendment,
Burnt offering, libation appease Gods, if we will only
Pray to them, however great our guilt is when we offend
     them.
Pray'rs, Áchileus, are daughters of high God. Could you
     behold them,
They would appear squint-eyed and lame and fearfully
     wrinkled.
They ever toil to follow where Sin may wander before
     them.
Sin's very swift and mighty—she leaves them limping a
     long way
After her as she travels God's world and causes abundant
Mischief among men in it. But Pray'rs come later to
     heal it.
He who receives them kindly, who gives God's daughters
     a welcome,
They never fail to bless him, they hear him calling upon
     them.

20

Woe to the man that drives them away and roughly denies
    them!
Calling upon Crónidês they pray their Father to send down
Sin to him and punish him for Sin's sake and to avenge
    them.
So, Áchileus, I pray you, be courteous unto the daughters
Of the divine Crónidês: respect wins over the wisest.'

GEORGE ERNLE   (IX. 496–514)

14   *Ajax in the Fight*

BUT the eternal father throned on high
    With fear fill'd Ajax; panic-fixt he stood,
His seven-fold shield behind his shoulder cast,
And, hemm'd by numbers, with an eye askant,
Watchful retreated. As a beast of prey
Retiring, turns and looks, so he his face
Turn'd oft, retiring slow, and step by step.
As when the watch-dogs and assembled swains
Have driv'n a tawny lion from the stalls,
Then, interdicting him his wished repast,
Watch all the night, he, famish'd, yet again
Comes furious on, but speeds not, kept aloof
By frequent spears from daring hands, but more
By flash of torches, which, though fierce, he dreads,
Till, at the dawn, sullen he stalks away;
So from before the Trojans Ajax stalk'd
Sullen, and with reluctance slow retir'd,
His brave heart trembling for the fleet of Greece.
As when (the boys o'erpower'd) a sluggish ass,
Whose tough sides erst have shiver'd many a staff,
Enters the harvest, and the spiry ears

21

Crops persevering; with their rods the boys
Still ply him hard, but all their puny might
Scarce drives him forth when he hath browzed his fill,
So, there, the Trojans and their foreign aids
With glitt'ring lances keen, huge Ajax urged
His broad shield's centre smiting. He, by turns,
With desp'rate force the Trojan phalanx dense
Facing, repulsed them, and by turns retired,
But still forbad all inroad on the fleet.
Trojans and Greeks between, alone, he stood
A bulwark. Spears from daring hands dismiss'd
Some, in his shield's thick folds unwilling stay'd,
While others, in the midway falling, spent
Their disappointed fury in the ground.

WILLIAM COWPER   (XI. 544–74)

15   *The Wall*

SO was Menœtius' valiant son employ'd
  Healing Eurýpylus. The Greeks, meantime,
And Trojans with tumultuous fury fought.
Nor was the foss ordain'd long time to exclude
The host of Troy, nor yet the rampart built
Beside it for protection of the fleet;
For hecatomb the Greeks had offer'd none,
Nor prayer to heaven, that it might keep secure
Their ships with all their spoils. The mighty work
As in defiance of the Immortal Powers
Had ris'n, and could not therefore long endure.
While Hector lived, and while Achilles held
His wrathful purpose; while the city yet

Of royal Priam was unsack'd,—so long
The massy structure stood. But when the best
And bravest of the Trojan host were slain,
And of the Grecian heroes, some had fallen
And some survived; when Priam's towers had blazed
In the tenth year, and to their native shores
The Grecians with their ships, at length, return'd—,
Then Neptune, with Apollo leagued, devised
Its ruin; every river that descends
From the Idæan heights into the sea
They brought against it, gathering all their force,
Rhêsus, Carêsus, Rhódius, the wide-branch'd
Heptáporus, Æsêpus, Grânicus,
Scamander's sacred current, and thy stream
Símoïs, whose banks with helmets and with shields
Were strew'd, and Chiefs of origin divine;
All these with refluent course Apollo drove
Nine days against the rampart, and Jove rain'd
Incessant, that the Grecian wall wave-whelm'd
Through all its length might sudden disappear.
Neptune with his tridental mace, himself,
Led them, and beam and buttress to the flood
Consigning, laid by the laborious Greeks,
Swept the foundation, and the level bank
Of the swift-rolling Hellespont restored.
The structure thus effaced, the spacious beach
He spread with sand as at the first; then bade
Subside the streams, and in their channels wind
With limpid course, and pleasant as before.

WILLIAM COWPER   (XII. 1–33)

16   *The Snow of Stones*

THUS shouting onward these twain roused the
    Achaian battle . . .
As on a winter's day the snowflakes thick and fast
Whirl down, when Zeus the Counsellor in storm begins
The revelation of these his arrows of the skies
To mortal men; in the silence of sleep the winds
Are stilled, and the unceasing fall of snow streams down
Until the high mountain peaks, the outermost headlands
Are hidden over, and the rich farmlands of men
With the clovered fields; only the lapping wave shakes off
This mantle strewn upon the harbours and the beaches
Along the wide grey sea—all else is shrouded over
Lying beneath this heaviness of the storm of Zeus;
So the stones hither and thither wing their crowded flight
From Trojan and Achaian, hurling both, and smitten,
Amid the tumult rising along the wall's whole length.

M. BALKWILL   (XII. 277–89)

17   *Sarpêdon and Glaucus*

                                    Not then
    Withal had doughty Hektor and his men
    Broke down the gates thereof and the long bar,
    If Counsellor Zeus had not sent forth his son
    Sarpêdon, like some lion at a herd
    Of crook-horn'd cattle. With his shield uplift,
    A fair round shield of hammer'd bronze, by smith
    Well hammer'd, and within of many hides
    Stitcht with gold wire about the rim; with this

24

Upheld before, and shaking in his hand
Two spears, he went his way out, like a lion
Bred in the hills which by long lack of meat
Urges his lordly spirit to assay
The flock or fall upon the guarded bield;
Nor if he find the shepherds there on watch,
Keeping with dogs and spears their flocks, not so
Will he be headed off without a rush
Upon the steading; with a bound he'll snatch
A prey, or with a dart from ready hand
Himself be smitten in front. Thus did his heart
Urge good Sarpêdon to assail the wall
And break the parapet. Thereon he spake
Glaukos, son of Hippólochos, saying, 'Why,
Glaukos, have we most honour among men
In Lykia, the chief seats, best portions, cups
Fullest, with all men taking us for Gods?
Why should we hold so goodly a demesne
Upon the banks of Xanthos, orchard-ground,
And plowland heavy in corn? On all these counts
It lies on us to take our stand the first
Of Lykians, and meet the burning brunt
Of battle, so some Lykian man may say,
"Not without glory go our native lords,
What though they feed full fat and drink full sweet—
Nay, they are mighty men, who hold the van
Of our array!" Comrade, if you and I,
Safe out of this, should live, and never die,
Nor yet grow old, then would I lead the van
No more, nor send you out to win renown
In battle. Yet tho' death in thousand shapes
Stand over us, 'tis not for us to avoid

25

Nor yet to flee. Let us go on, we two,
And yield renown, or win it for ourselves.'
    He said that, nor did Glaukos turn away,
Nor disregard.

MAURICE HEWLETT   (XII. 290–329)

18   *Apollo destroys the Wall*

HE said: and on his horses' shoulder-point
    Let fall the lash, and loudly through the ranks
Called on the Trojans; they with answering shout
And noise unspeakable, urged on with him
Their harnessed steeds; Apollo, in the van,
Trod down with ease the embankment of the ditch,
And filled it in; and o'er it bridged a way
Level and wide, far as a javelin's flight
Hurled by an arm that proves its utmost strength.
O'er this the columns passed; Apollo bore
His ægis o'er them, and cast down the wall:
Easy, as when a child upon the beach,
In wanton play, with hands and feet o'erthrows
The mould of sand which late in play he raised;
So, Phœbus, thou, the Grecian toil and pains
Confounding, sentest panic through their souls.

EDWARD, EARL OF DERBY   (XV. 352–66)

19   *Ajax on the Decks*

NOR yet did it please the spirit of high-hearted Aias,
    to stand in the place whereto the other sons of the
Achaians had withdrawn, but he kept faring with long
strides, up and down the decks of the ships, and he wielded

26

in his hands a great pike for sea-battles, jointed with rings,
two and twenty cubits in length. And even as a man right
well skilled in horsemanship that couples four horses out
of many, and hurrying them from the plain towards a great
city, drives along the public way, many men and women
marvelling on him, and firmly ever he leaps, and changes
his stand from horse to horse, while they fly along, even
so Aias went with long strides, over many a deck of the
swift ships, and his voice went up to heaven. And always
with terrible cries he summoned the Danaans to defend
the ships and the huts. Nor did Hector abide in the throng
of well-armed Trojans, but even as a tawny eagle rushes
on a flock of winged fowl, that are feeding by a riverside,
a flock of geese, or cranes, or long-necked swans, even so
Hector made straight for a black-beaked ship, rushing right
on it, and mightily Zeus urged him on from behind with
his strong hand, and roused on the host along with him.

ANDREW LANG, WALTER LEAF, ERNEST MYERS

(XV. 674–95)

20   *Achilles and Patroclus*

SO round that sturdy ship the battle raged.
    But to Achilles, shepherd of the host,
Patroclus came, and like a sunless spring
That spills its sombre stream down a steep rock
He wept hot tears. And at the sight of him
Divine swift-foot Achilles had compassion,
And spoke and said to him with wingèd words:
'Why all in tears, Patroclus, like a child,
A baby girl, who trots beside her mother
And begs to be picked up, and plucks her skirt,

27

And drags upon her movements, gazing up
All tears, until her mother takes her up?
Thy tears, Patroclus, are as round as hers!
Hast thou bad news to tell the Myrmidons,
Or me myself, or can it be thou hast
Private intelligence from Phthîa? They say
That Actor's son Menœtius still lives;
Still Pêleus, son of Æacus, is living
Among the Myrmidons; for both of whom,
So they were dead, we might be grieved indeed.
Or art thou troubled for the Greeks, to see
How they are perishing by the hollow ships
Thanks to their own transgression? Speak, nor hide it
Within thy mind, so that we both may know.'

With a deep groan the knight Patroclus said:
'Achilles, son of Pêleus, far the best
Of all the Achæans, do not blame me; for
Such great misfortune has o'erwhelmed the Achæans.
In fact all those that were of old the best
Are lying, shot or stabbed, aboard the ships.
Stricken is Tŷdeus' son, strong Diomed,
Odysseus, famous with the spear, is stabbed,
And Agamemnon; and Eurýpylus
Has had his thigh shot through. And busy round them
Are surgeons with their herbs to heal their wounds;
But nothing can be done with thee, Achilles!
Now God deliver me from the grip of anger
Such as thou nursest, vicious-valiant man!
What profit shall posterity have of thee,
Unless thou save the Argives from foul harm?
So then thy father was not knightly Pêleus,
Nor Thetis was thy mother! iron heart,

28

Grey sea and beetling rocks begot thee, that
Thy soul is so unbending. But if thou
Art thinking to avoid some oracle,
Some premonition which thy goddess mother
Hath given thee from Zeus, then send me out
And with me all the corps of Myrmidons
At once, if I perchance may prove a light
Unto the Dánaï. Give me thine own gear
To buckle on my shoulders; it may be
That, taking me for thee, the Trojans will
Desist from war and give a breathing-time
To our brave wearied sons of the Achæans;
For battle grants men little time for breath:
Then we fresh men should easily repel
Foes spent with fighting from the ships and huts
Back to the city.'
    So in his folly he besought him, for
The thing he prayed for was to be his own
Dark death and fate.

SIR WILLIAM MARRIS   (XVI. 1–47)

21   *Achilles' Prayer*

ACHILLES then within his tent withdrew,
    And of a gorgeous coffer raised the lid,
Well-wrought, by silver-footed Thetis placed
On board his ship, and filled with rich attire,
With store of wind-proof cloaks, and carpets soft.
There lay a goblet, richly chased, whence none,
But he alone, might drink the ruddy wine,
Nor might libations thence to other Gods
Be made, save only Jove; this brought he forth

29

And first with sulphur purified, and next
Washed with pure water; then his hands he washed,
And drew the ruddy wine; then standing forth
Made in the centre of the court his prayer,
And as he poured the wine, looked up to Heaven,
Not unbeheld of Jove, the lightning's Lord:

'Great King, Dôdôna's Lord, Pelasgian Jove,
Who dwell'st on high, and rul'st with sovereign sway
Dôdôna's wintry heights; where dwell around
Thy Sellian priests, men of unwashen feet,
That on the bare ground sleep; thou once before
Hast heard my prayer, and me with honour crowned,
And on the Greeks inflicted all thy plagues;
Hear yet again, and this my boon accord.
I 'mid the throng of ships myself remain;
But with a numerous force of Myrmidons
I send my comrade in my stead to fight:
On him, all-seeing Jove, thy favour pour;
Strengthen his heart, that Hector's self may learn
If, e'en alone, my follower knows to fight,
Or only then resistless power displays,
When I myself the toil of battle share.
And from our vessels when the foe is driven,
Grant that with all his arms and comrades true
He may in safety to the ships return.'

Thus prayed he: Jove, the Lord of Counsel, heard,
And half his prayer he granted, half denied:
For from the ships the battle to repel
He granted; but denied his safe return.

EDWARD, EARL OF DERBY   (XVI. 220–52)

22   *The Death of Patroclus*

BUT Hector, when he saw great-heart Patroclus
  Retiring wounded by the pointed bronze,
Came near him through the ranks, and plunged a spear
Into his groin, and ran the head clean through.
Thundering he fell, and on the Achæan host
Brought huge dismay. And as a lion in fight
O'ercomes a strenuous boar, when both of them
Fight in their pride upon the mountain peaks
Over a scanty water whereat both
Are bent on drinking, and the panting boar
Is mastered by the lion in his strength;
So from Menœtius' valiant son, when he
Had slaughtered many, Hector, Priam's son,
Took life away, with a close thrust of spear.
And boasting over him spoke wingèd words:
'Patroclus, thou didst think to sack my city,
And rob the Trojan dames of freedom's day,
And bear them off in ships to thine own land.
Fool! for in front of them the galloping steeds
Of Hector strain to war, and I myself
Am the best spear among the fighting Trojans
To keep from them the day of servitude.
But thee, the vultures shall devour thee here,
O luckless man! Achilles in his valour
Avails thee not, who, when thou camest and he
Remained behind, must have adjured thee straitly:
"Come not, Patroclus, master of the horse,
Back to the hollow ships, I bid thee, till
Thou gash the bloody tunic on the breast

31

Of murderous Hector." So, for sure, said he,
And he beguiled thee in thy foolishness.'

Then feebly, knight Patroclus, didst thou say:
'Now boast thy biggest, Hector, for to thee
Have Zeus Croníôn and Apollo given
The triumph, and have slain me without effort,
For they it was who took my armour from me.
But if a score of men like thee had met me,
Here should they all have perished by my spear.
No! deadly Fate and Lêto's son have killed me,
And then, of men, Euphorbus; in my slaying
Thou art but third. And one thing more have I
To say, and do thou lay it to thy heart.
I say thou hast not long to live thyself,
But death and potent fate stand close beside thee,
And thou art doomed to be subdued before
Achilles, matchless son of Æacus.'
    The end of death enclosed him as he spoke,
And fleeting from his limbs his spirit was gone
To Hades' house, bewailing what befell it
And leaving manliness and youth behind.
    Dead as he was to him said glorious Hector:
'Patroclus, why dost thou presage to me
A sudden end? who knows but that Achilles,
The son of fine-haired Thetis, may not first
Be stricken by my spear and lose his life?'

So saying upon the dead he set his foot,
And pulled the point of bronze out of the wound,
And thrust him backward from the spear. Anon
Taking the spear he chased Autómedon

The godlike squire of swift Æácidês,
For he was keen to smite him; but away
Those swift immortal horses bore him, which
The gods gave Pêleus as a glorious gift.

SIR WILLIAM MARRIS   (XVI. 818–67)

23   *The Horses of Achilles*

AND thus they fought; the iron clangour pierced
    The empty air, and brazen vault of Heaven.
But from the fight withdrawn, Achilles' steeds
Wept, as they heard how in the dust was laid
Their charioteer, by Hector's murderous hand.
Autómedon, Diôrês' valiant son,
Essayed in vain to rouse them with the lash,
In vain with honeyed words, in vain with threats;
Nor to the ships would they return again
By the broad Hellespont, nor join the fray;
But as a column stands, which marks the tomb
Of man or woman, so immovable
Beneath the splendid car they stood, their heads
Down-drooping to the ground, while scalding tears
Dropped earthward from their eyelids, as they mourned
Their charioteer; and, o'er the yoke-band shed,
Down streamed their ample manes, with dust defiled.
The son of Saturn pitying saw their grief,
And sorrowing shook his head, as thus he mused:

    'Ah, hapless horses! wherefore gave we you
To royal Pêleus, to a mortal man,
You that from age and death are both exempt!
Was it that you the miseries might share

3816   D   33

Of wretched mortals? for of all that breathe,
And walk upon the earth, or creep, is nought
More wretched than the unhappy race of man.
Yet shall not ye, nor shall your well-wrought car,
By Hector, son of Priam, be controlled;
I will not suffer it; enough for him
To hold, with vaunting boast, Achilles' arms;
But to your limbs and spirits will I impart
Such strength, that from the battle to the ships
Ye shall in safety bear Autómedon;
For yet I will the Trojans shall prevail,
And slay, until they reach the well-manned ships,
Till sets the sun, and darkness shrouds the earth.'
    He said, and in their breasts fresh spirit infused;
They, shaking from their manes the dust, the car
Amid the Greeks and Trojans lightly bore.

EDWARD, EARL OF DERBY   (XVII. 424-58)

24   *Patroclus' Body Saved*

SO they carried the dead man out of the fighting
    With passionate effort towards the hollow ships.
But the fight dragged at them angrily, like a fire
That springs with a sudden leap on a human city
And flares till the houses vanish in a great light
When the hurricane's strength sets it roaring. So
Unintermitting, a clatter of horses
And of men with spears pressed on them as they
        moved.
They were like mules strung to the pitch of effort,
Who from a fell-side drag by a rocky track

34

House-rafter or big ship's timber, though sweat and
    fatigue
Wear down the courage in their tugging bodies.
With such effort they carried the dead man, while
Behind them the two Aiantës held the pressure
As a wooded spur holds back a head of water,
Sprawling across the lowland: even the dangerous
Torrent waters of strong rivers it holds;
Diverting instantly across the levels
Every current, it stands in the swirl unbroken.
So the Aiantës still held up the forward
Surge of the Trojans pressing close—in the van of them
Anchîses' son Ænêas and glittering Hector.
But the Greeks—as a cloud of daws or starlings passes
Screaming for life, the hawk once sighted,
To lesser birds a messenger of murder,
So before Ænêas and Hector the young
Men of Achæa rushed screaming for life,
Forgetting battle-gaiety: round the trench
Dropped from the runaway Danaans many a handsome
Piece of gear—and still no pause in the fighting.

E. R. Dodds   (XVII. 735–61)

25   *Achilles and Thetis*

THEREWITH she left the cave, and with her went
    The weeping nymphs, and round them was the wave
Broken; and when they came to fertile Troia,
They went in sequence up the shore to where
The Myrmidonian ships were drawn up close
Round swift Achilles. He was groaning deeply,

35

And to his side his queenly mother came
And with a cry she clasped the head of her son,
And sadly spoke to him with wingèd words:

'My child, why weepest thou? what grief is come
Upon thy soul? speak out and hide it not.
Surely thy purpose has been brought to pass
By Zeus, according to the prayer thou madest
With hands outstretched, that the Achæans' sons
Should one and all be huddling by their ships
In need of thee, and suffer hideous things.'

But groaning deeply swift Achilles said:
'Mother of mine, that prayer the Olympian hath
Fulfilled; but what delight have I in that,
Since my dear friend is lost to me, Patroclus,
The man I honoured above all my friends
As mine own self? Him have I killed, and Hector
Hath slain and stripped him of his gallant arms,
Those giant arms, wondrous to look on, which
The gods gave Pêleus for a glorious gift
The day they cast thee in a mortal's bed.
O would that thou hadst sojourned where thou wert
Amid the immortal maidens of the sea
And Pêleus taken home a mortal bride!
But so it was—that thou too shouldst endure
Infinite pangs of heart for thy lost son,
Whom never thou wilt welcome home again,
Because my soul will no more let me live
Nor mix with men, if Hector has not first
Been smitten by my spear and lost his life
And paid the blood-price for Patroclus' spoils.'

But weeping Thetis answered him again:
'Short-lived wilt thou be then, my child, by what

36

Thou sayst; for after Hector has been killed
Thy death is close at hand.'
   Then, deeply moved, swift-foot Achilles said:
'O let me die at once, for that I was not
To help my comrade, in his hour of need!
Far from his home he died, and looked in vain
For me to ward off hurt from him. Now, since
I am not to return to mine own land,
And since I wholly failed to save Patroclus
And all my other friends who have been slain
By goodly Hector, but beside the ships
I sit, a useless cumberer of the ground—
I, who among the mailed Achæans have
No peer in war, though in the meeting-place
Others are better . . . perish all debate
From midst of gods and men! and perish hatred
That stirs to anger even the wise, and tastes
Sweeter than dripping honey, and that swells
Like rising smoke in human breasts, such hate
As lately Agamemnon king of men
Aroused in me! Ah well, for all our pain,
Let us bury what is past, and, as we must,
Master our feelings. Now let me go forth
And search out Hector who has killed the man
I loved: that done, I will accept my fate
Whenever Zeus and all the immortal gods
Wish to fulfil it.'

SIR WILLIAM MARRIS   (XVIII. 65–116)

Achilles on the Rampart

SO saying, light-foot Iris pass'd away.
Then rose Achilles dear to Zeus; and round
The warrior's puissant shoulders Pallas flung
Her fringèd ægis, and around his head
The glorious goddess wreath'd a golden cloud,
And from it lighted an all-shining flame.
As when a smoke from a city goes to heaven
Far off from out an island girt by foes,
All day the men contend in grievous war
From their own city, but with set of sun
Their fires flame thickly, and aloft the glare
Flies streaming, if perchance the neighbours round
May see, and sail to help them in the war;
So from his head the splendour went to heaven.
From wall to dyke he stept, he stood, nor join'd
The Achæans—honouring his wise mother's word—
There standing, shouted, and Pallas far away
Call'd; and a boundless panic shook the foe.
For like the clear voice when a trumpet shrills,
Blown by the fierce beleaguerers of a town,
So rang the clear voice of Æákidês:
But when the brazen cry of Æákidês
Was heard among the Trojans, all their hearts
Were troubled, and the full-maned horses whirl'd
The chariots backward, knowing griefs at hand;
And sheer-astounded were the charioteers
To see the dread, unweariable fire
That always o'er the great Pêleion's head
Burn'd, for the bright-eyed goddess made it burn.
Thrice from the dyke he sent his mighty shout,

Thrice backward reel'd the Trojans and allies:
And then and there twelve of their noblest died
Among their spears and chariots.

                              The Achæans
Eagerly dragg'd Patroclus from the fight
And laid him on a bier. His friends stood round
Weeping, and with them swift Achilles went
And shed hot tears, seeing his faithful friend
Laid on the litter, pierc'd with sharp-edg'd bronze;—
Him had he sent with chariots and horses
To war, but never welcomed his return.

ALFRED TENNYSON (to l. 231)   (XVIII. 202–38)

27   *Thetis and Hêphæstus*

SHE called the famous smith Hêphæstus, saying
    'Come here, Hêphæstus; Thetis needeth thee.'
Whereat the famous crippled god replied:
'Then 'tis a goddess I respect and honour
That is within! She saved me when I was
In pain by reason of my fearful fall,
Thanks to my shameless mother, and she offered
To hide me in my lameness. Then it had
Gone badly with me, had Eurýnomê
And Thetis not received me to their breast—
Eurýnomê, the child of Ocean who
Flows backward on himself. Nine years with them
I fashioned many curious works in bronze,
Brooches and spiral bracelets and rosettes
And necklaces, inside their hollow cave
About which Ocean's stream unending ran
With murmurous foam. And no one knew thereof

Neither of gods nor mortal men, but they
Who saved me, Thetis and Eurýnomê;
And now is Thetis come unto my house!
Therefore most bound am I to pay full price
To fair-haired Thetis, since she saved my life.
But set before her noble entertainment
While I lay by my bellows, tools and all.'

    He spoke, and rose up limping from the anvil,
A mighty bulk; yet his lean shanks were quick.
He moved the bellows from the fire, and packed
Into a silver box the set of tools
With which he worked; then with a sponge he wiped
His face and both his hands and muscled neck
And hairy chest: he put his tunic on,
And took up a stout stick and with a limp
Walked out of doors; and women servants wrought
In gold, the effigies of living maidens, moved
To help their master: they have active brains
And speech and strength, and from the deathless gods
Have learned their duties.

SIR WILLIAM MARRIS   (XVIII. 391–420)

28   *The Shield of Achilles*

(*i*)

THEN first he form'd the immense and solid shield;
   Rich various artifice emblazed the field;
Its utmost verge a threefold circle bound;
A silver chain suspends the massy round;
Five ample plates the broad expanse compose,
And godlike labours on the surface rose.

There shone the image of the master-mind:
There earth, there heaven, there ocean he design'd;
Th' unwearied sun, the moon completely round;
The starry lights that heaven's high convex crown'd;
The Pleiads, Hyads, with the northern team;
And great Orion's more refulgent beam;
To which, around the axle of the sky,
The Bear, revolving, points his golden eye,
Still shines exalted on th' ethereal plain,
Nor bathes his blazing forehead in the main.

 Two cities radiant on the shield appear,
The image one of peace, and one of war.
Here sacred pomp and genial feast delight,
And solemn dance and hymeneal rite;
Along the street the new-made brides are led,
With torches flaming, to the nuptial bed:
The youthful dancers in a circle bound
To the soft flute and cittern's silver sound:
Through the fair streets the matrons in a row
Stand in their porches, and enjoy the show.

          (XVIII. 478–96)

(ii)

Another part (a prospect differing far)
Glow'd with refulgent arms, and horrid war.
Two mighty hosts a leaguer'd town embrace,
And one would pillage, one would burn, the place.
Meantime the townsmen, arm'd with silent care,
A secret ambush on the foe prepare:
Their wives, their children, and the watchful band
Of trembling parents, on the turrets stand.

They march, by Pallas and by Mars made bold;
Gold were the gods, their radiant garments gold,
And gold their armour; these the squadron led,
August, divine, superior by the head!

(XVIII. 509–19)

(iii)

Next, ripe in yellow gold, a vineyard shines,
Bent with the ponderous harvest of its vines;
A deeper dye the dangling clusters show,
And, curl'd on silver props, in order glow:
A darker metal mix'd, intrench'd the place;
And pales of glittering tin th' enclosure grace.
To this, one pathway gently winding leads,
Where march a train with baskets on their heads,
(Fair maids and blooming youths) that smiling bear
The purple product of th' autumnal year.
To these a youth awakes the warbling strings,
Whose tender lay the fate of Linus sings;
In measured dance behind him move the train,
Tune soft the voice, and answer to the strain.
    Here, herds of oxen march, erect and bold,
Rear high their horns, and seem to low in gold,
And speed to meadows on whose sounding shores
A rapid torrent through the rushes roars:
Four golden herdsmen as their guardians stand,
And nine sour dogs complete the rustic band.
Two lions rushing from the wood appear'd;
And seized a bull, the master of the herd;
He roar'd: in vain the dogs, the men, withstood;
They tore his flesh, and drank the sable blood.

The dogs (oft cheer'd in vain) desert the prey,
Dread the grim terrors, and at distance bay.

Next this, the eye the art of Vulcan leads
Deep through fair forests, and a length of meads,
And stalls, and folds, and scatter'd cots between;
And fleecy flocks, that whiten all the scene.

A figured dance succeeds: such once was seen
In lofty Gnossus, for the Cretan queen,
Form'd by Dædalean art; a comely band
Of youths and maidens, bounding hand in hand;
The maids in soft cymars of linen dress'd;
The youths all graceful in the glossy vest;
Of those the locks with flowery wreaths inroll'd;
Of these the sides adorn'd with swords of gold,
That, glittering gay, from silver belts depend.
Now all at once they rise, at once descend,
With well-taught feet: now shape, in oblique ways,
Confus'dly regular, the moving maze:
Now forth at once, too swift for sight, they spring,
And undistinguish'd blend the flying ring:
So whirls a wheel, in giddy circle toss'd,
And, rapid as it runs, the single spokes are lost.
The gazing multitudes admire around;
Two active tumblers in the centre bound;
Now high, now low, their pliant limbs they bend:
And general songs the sprightly revel end.

Thus the broad shield complete the artist crown'd
With his last hand, and pour'd the ocean round:
In living silver seem'd the waves to roll,
And beat the buckler's verge, and bound the whole.

ALEXANDER POPE   (XVIII. 561–608)

29   *Achilles and Lycâon*

S O did the son of Priam, the princely, speak his word,
And begged and besought his life, but a pitiless voice
he heard:

'Fool, speak to me not of ransom nor waste in words your
breath;

Of old, before Patroclus came to his day of death,

Then to spare the Trojans it delighted the heart in me,

And many alive I captured and sold into slavery.

But now there is no man living who shall escape from
death

If before Troy to my hands a god him delivereth,

Even of all the Trojans, and most among Priam's breed.

Come, my friend, you must die. What tears can help your
need?

Patroclus also is dead, a better man far than you.

See what a man am I, strong of body and fair to view;

A kingly father begat me, I was born from a goddess'
womb,

But over me too stand death and overmastering doom.

A dawn there shall be, or an evening, or maybe a midday,

When a man shall delight the War God and take my life
away,

Smiting me down with his spear or shooting a shaft from
his bow.'

He spoke, and Lycâon's knees were shaken, his heart sank
low;

He dropped his sword on the ground, and with both his
hands he made

Entreaty, but then Achilles drew out his sharp sword-blade

And smote his neck by the collar. The two-edged falchion found

Its way straight through, and head-first he fell and lay on the ground

Outstretched, and the earth was soaked with the streaming of his black blood.

By his feet then Achilles dragged him to cast him into the flood,

And winged were the words he uttered, and over him spoke a pray'r:

'Lie there now among the fishes, and they with never a care

Shall lick up the blood from your wounds, nor shall your mother set

Your corpse on a bier and lament for you; Scamánder shall fret

Your bones and carry you whirling to hidden depths of the sea.

From under the black ripples along the wave maybe

A fish shall dart up and leap and your gleaming flesh shall eat.

So perish you all, until by holy Troy we meet;

Then shall you flee before and I shall lay waste behind,

Nor shall you in your river any salvation find,

With its fine-flowing silver eddies, to which you have offering made

Of numberless bulls, and hoovèd horses alive have paid.

Even so shall ye perish foully, till not a man remain

To pay for Patroclus' death and for Greeks in battle slain,

When you fought by the light-sped ships and I turned not to fight again.

C. M. BOWRA   (XXI. 97–135)

30   *Achilles and the Scamander*

Round Achilles rose
The boiling wave tremendous, and the flood
Beat on his shield and swept him, nor could he
Stand firm upon his feet: he clutched an elm,
Well-grown and lofty, but it fell uprooted
And tore off all the bank, and reached across
The pleasant waters with its matted boughs,
And falling wholly in the channel, made
A dam across it. Struggling from the swirl
Achilles in alarm set out to fly
Across the plain with all his speed: but yet
The great god would not cease; he rose at him
In a black crest, and chased divine Achilles
To make him hold his hand, and to preserve
The Trojans from destruction. Pêleus' son
Rushed back a spear-throw length with all the speed
Of a black eagle, that great hunter which
Has strength and pace above all things that fly.
Like him he sped, and on his breast the bronze
Rang grimly, as he swerved to dodge the River
And ran, while on his trail the River came
With a loud roar. And as a channel-maker
Guides from a sunless spring the flow of water
Among his crops and beds, and pick in hand
Clears barriers from the conduit; as it runs,
Before it all the pebbles roll away,
And with a gurgle down the slope apace
It slips, outrunning even him that guides it;
So did the River's deluge still o'ertake

46

Achilles, racer though he was: the gods
Are forceful beyond men.

SIR WILLIAM MARRIS   (XXI. 240–64)

31   *The Pursuit round the Walls*

THUS pondering he stood; meantime approach'd
  Achilles, terrible as fiery Mars,
Crest-tossing God, and brandish'd as he came
O'er his right shoulder high the Pêlian spear.
Like lightning, or like flame, or like the sun
Ascending, beam'd his armour. At that sight
Trembled the Trojan Chief, nor dared expect
His nearer step, but flying left the gates
Far distant, and Achilles swift pursued.
As in the mountains, fleetest fowl of air,
The hawk darts eager at the dove; she scuds
Aslant, he, screaming, springs and springs again
To seize her, all impatient for the prey,
So flew Achilles constant to the track
Of Hector, who with dreadful haste beneath
The Trojan bulwarks plied his agile limbs.
Passing the prospect-mount where high in air
The wild-fig waved, they rush'd along the road,
Declining never from the wall of Troy.
And now they reach'd the running rivulets clear,
Where from Scamander's dizzy flood arise
Two fountains, tepid one, from which a smoke
Issues voluminous as from a fire,
The other, even in summer heats, like hail
For cold, or snow, or chrystal-stream frost-bound.
Beside them may be seen the broad canals

47

Of marble scoop'd, in which the wives of Troy
And all her daughters fair were wont to lave
Their costly raiment, while the land had rest,
And ere the warlike sons of Greece arrived.
By these they ran, one fleeing, one in chase.
Valiant was he who fled, but valiant far
Beyond him He who urged the swift pursuit;
Nor ran they for a vulgar prize, a beast
For sacrifice, or for the hide of such,
The swift foot-racer's customary meed,
But for the noble Hector's life they ran.
As when two steeds, oft conquerors, trim the goal
For some illustrious prize, a tripod bright
Or beauteous virgin, at a funeral game,
So they with nimble feet the city thrice
Of Priam compass'd. All the Gods looked on.

WILLIAM COWPER   (XXII. 131–66)

32   *The Last Fight*

AND Achilles made at him, for his heart was filled with
wild fierceness, and before his breast he made a
covering with his fair graven shield, and tossed his bright
four-plated helm; and round it waved fair golden plumes
that Hêphaistos had set thick about the crest. As a star
goeth among stars in the darkness of night, Hesperos,
fairest of all stars set in heaven, so flashed there forth a light
from the keen spear Achilles poised in his right hand, devising mischief against noble Hector, eyeing his fair flesh
to find the fittest place. Now for the rest of him his flesh
was covered by the fair bronze armour he stripped from
strong Patroklos when he slew him, but there was an open-

48

ing where the collar bones coming from the shoulders clasp the neck, even at the gullet, where destruction of life cometh quickliest; there, as he came on, noble Achilles drave at him with his spear, and right through the tender neck went the point. Yet the bronze-weighted ashen spear clave not the wind-pipe, so that he might yet speak words of answer to his foe. And he fell down in the dust, and noble Achilles spake exultingly: 'Hector, thou thoughtest, whilst thou wert spoiling Patroklos, that thou wouldst be safe, and didst reck nothing of me who was afar, thou fool. But away among the hollow ships his comrade, a mightier far, even I, was left behind, who now have unstrung thy knees. Thee shall dogs and birds tear foully, but his funeral shall the Achaians make.'

Then with faint breath spake unto him Hector of the glancing helm: 'I pray thee by thy life and knees and parents leave me not for the dogs of the Achaians to devour by the ships, but take good store of bronze and gold, gifts that my father and lady mother shall give to thee, and give them home my body back again, that the Trojans and Trojans' wives give me my due of fire after my death.'

But unto him with grim gaze spake Achilles fleet of foot: 'Entreat me not, dog, by knees or parents. Would that my heart's desire could so bid me myself to carve and eat raw thy flesh, for the evil thou hast wrought me, as surely is there none that shall keep the dogs from thee, not even should they bring ten or twenty fold ransom and here weigh it out, and promise even more, not even were Priam Dardanos' son to bid pay thy weight in gold, not even so shall thy lady mother lay thee on a bed to mourn her son, but dogs and birds shall devour thee utterly.'

Then dying spake unto him Hector of the glancing

helm: 'Verily I know thee and behold thee as thou art, nor was I destined to persuade thee; truly thy heart is iron in thy breast. Take heed now lest I draw upon thee wrath of gods, in the day when Paris and Phœbus Apollo slay thee, for all thy valour, at the Skaian gate.'

He ended, and the shadow of death came down upon him, and his soul flew forth of his limbs and was gone to the house of Hades, wailing her fate, leaving her vigour and youth. Then to the dead man spake noble Achilles: 'Die: for my death, I will accept it whensoever Zeus and the other immortal gods are minded to accomplish it.'

ANDREW LANG, WALTER LEAF, ERNEST MYERS

(XXII. 312–66)

33   *Andrómachê*

HECTOR'S wife had as yet heard nothing, for no one had come to tell her that her husband had remained without the gates. She was at her loom in an inner part of the house, weaving a double purple web, and embroidering it with many flowers. She told her maids to set a large tripod on the fire, so as to have a warm bath ready for Hector when he came out of battle; poor woman, she knew not that he was now beyond the reach of baths, and that Minerva had laid him low by the hands of Achilles. She heard the cry coming as from the wall, and trembled in every limb; the shuttle fell from her hands, and again she spoke to her waiting-women. 'Two of you,' she said, 'come with me that I may learn what it is that has befallen; I heard the voice of my husband's honoured mother; my own heart beats as though it would come into my mouth and my limbs refuse to carry me; some great misfortune for Priam's children must be at hand. May I never live to hear it, but I greatly fear that Achilles has cut off the retreat of brave Hector and has chased him on to the plain where he was single-handed; I fear he may have put an end to the reckless daring which possessed my husband, who would never remain with the body of his men, but would dash on far in front, foremost of them all in valour.'

Her heart beat fast, and as she spoke she flew from the house like a maniac, with her waiting-women following after. When she reached the battlements and the crowd of people, she stood looking out upon the wall, and saw Hector being borne away in front of the city—the horses dragging him without heed or care over the ground towards the ships of the Achæans. Her eyes were then shrouded as with the darkness of night and she fell fainting backwards. She tore the tiring from her head and flung it from her, the frontlet and net with its plaited band, and the veil which golden Venus had given her on the day when Hector took her with him from the house of Eëtion, after having given countless gifts of wooing for her sake. Her husband's sisters and the wives of his brothers crowded round and supported her, for she was fain to die in her distraction; when she again presently breathed and came to herself, she sobbed and made lament among the Trojans saying, 'Woe is me, O Hector; woe, indeed, that to share a common lot we were born, you at Troy in the house of Priam, and I at Thebes under the wooded mountain of Placus in the house of Eëtion who brought me up when I was a child—ill-starred sire of an ill-starred daughter— would that he had never begotten me. You are now going into the house of Hades under the secret places of the earth, and you leave me a sorrowing widow in your house. The child, of whom you and I are the unhappy parents, is as yet a mere infant. Now that you are gone, O Hector, you can do nothing for him nor he for you. Even though he escape the horrors of this woful war with the Achæans, yet shall his life henceforth be one of labour and sorrow, for others will seize his lands. The day that robs a child of his parents severs him from his own kind; his head is bowed, his cheeks are wet with tears, and he will go about destitute among the friends of his father, plucking one by the coat and another by the shirt. Some one or other of these may so far pity him as to hold the cup for a moment towards him and let him moisten his lips, but he must not drink enough to wet the roof of his mouth; then one whose parents are alive will drive him from the table with blows and angry words. "Out with you," he will say, "you have no father here," and the child will go crying back to his widowed mother—he, Ástyanax, who erewhile would sit upon his father's knees, and have none but the daintiest and choicest morsels set before him. When he had played till he was tired and went to sleep, he would lie in a bed, in the arms of his nurse, on a soft couch, knowing neither want nor care, whereas now that he has lost his father his lot will be full of hardship—he, whom the Trojans name Ástyanax, because you, O Hector, were the only defence of their gates and battlements. The wriggling writhing worms will now eat you at the ships, far from your parents, when the dogs have glutted themselves upon you. You will lie naked, although in your house you have fine and goodly raiment made by the hands of women. This will I now burn; it is of no use to you, for you can never again wear it, and thus you will have respect shown you by the Trojans both men and women.'

In such wise did she cry aloud amid her tears, and the
women joined in her lament.

SAMUEL BUTLER   (XXII. 437–515)

34   *The Ghost of Patroclus*

THE soul came to him of his hapless friend,
     In bulk resembling, in expressive eyes
And voice Patroclus, and so clad as he.
Him, hovering o'er his head, the form address'd:
   'Sleep'st thou, Achilles! of thy friend become
Heedless? Him living thou didst not neglect
Whom thou neglectest dead. Give me a tomb
Instant, that I may pass the infernal gates.
For now, the shades and spirits of the dead
Drive me afar, denying me my wish
To mingle with them on the farthest shore,
And in wide-portal'd Ades sole I roam.
Give me thine hand, I pray thee, for the earth
I visit never more, once burnt with fire;
We never shall again close council hold
As we were wont, for me my fate severe,
Mine even from my birth, hath deep absorb'd.
And oh Achilles, semblance of the Gods!
Thou too predestined art beneath the wall
To perish of the high-born Trojan race.
But hear my last injunction! ah, my friend!
My bones sepulchre not from thine apart,
But as, together we were nourish'd both
Beneath thy roof, (what time from Opœïs
Menœtius led me to thy father's house,
Although a child, yet fugitive for blood,

                                              53

Which, in a quarrel at the dice, I spilt,
Killing my playmate by a casual blow,
The offspring of Amphídamas, when, like
A father, Pêleus with all tenderness
Received and cherish'd me, and call'd me thine),
So, let one vase inclose, at last, our bones,
The golden vase, thy Goddess mother's gift.'

To whom Achilles, matchless in the race:
'Ah, loved and honour'd! wherefore hast thou come?
Why thus enjoin'd me? I will all perform
With diligence that thou hast now desired.
But nearer stand, that we may mutual clasp
Each other, though but with a short embrace,
And sad satiety of grief enjoy.'

He said, and stretch'd his arms toward the shade,
But him seized not; shrill-clamouring and light
As smoke, the spirit pass'd into the earth.
Amazed, upsprang Achilles, clash'd aloud
His palms together, and thus, sad, exclaim'd:

'Ah then, ye Gods! there doubtless are below
The soul and semblance both, but empty forms;
For all night long, mourning, disconsolate,
The soul of my Patroclus, hapless friend!
Hath hover'd o'er me, giving me in charge
His last requests, just image of himself.'

WILLIAM COWPER   (XXIII. 65–107)

35   *After the Chariot-Race*

THE prudent chief with calm attention heard;
    Then mildly thus: 'Excuse, if youth have err'd;
Superior as thou art, forgive the offence,
Nor I thy equal, or in years, or sense.

54

Thou know'st the errors of unripen'd age,
Weak are its counsels, headlong is its rage.
The prize I quit, if thou thy wrath resign;
The mare, or aught thou ask'st, be freely thine
Ere I become (from thy dear friendship torn)
Hateful to thee, and to the gods forsworn.'
   So spoke Antílochus; and at the word
The mare contested to the king restor'd.
Joy swells his soul, as when the vernal grain
Lifts the green ear above the springing plain,
The fields their vegetable life renew,
And laugh and glitter with the morning dew:
Such joy the Spartan's shining face o'erspread.

ALEXANDER POPE   (XXIII. 586–600)

36   *Priam and Achilles*

WITH these words Hermês sped away for lofty
    Olympos:
And Priam all fearlessly from off his chariot alighted,
Ordering Îdæus to remain i' the entry to keep watch
Over the beasts: th' old king meanwhile strode doughtily
    onward,
Where Achilles was then most wont to be, and sitting
    indoors
Found he him; all his men sat apart; for his only attendance
His squire Autómedon and Álkimos in battle upgrown
Mov'd busilie to 'an fro serving, for late he had eaten,
And the supper-table disfurnish'd yet stood anigh him.
And Priam entering unperceiv'd til he well was among
    them,
Clasp'd his knees and seized his hands all humbly to kiss
    them,

Those dread murderous hands which his sons so many had
 slain.
 As when a man whom spite of fate hath curs'd in his
  own land
For homicide, that he fleeeth abroad and seeketh asylum
With some lord, and they that see^him are fill'd with
 amazement,
Ev'n so now Achilles was amaz'd as he saw Priam enter,
And the men all wer' amaz'd, and lookt upon each other
 in turn.
But Priam (as Hermês had bade) bow'd down to beseech
 him.

 'O God-like Achilles, thy father call to remembrance,
How he is halting as I, i' the dark'ning doorway of old age,
And desolately liveth, while all they that dwell about him
Véx him, nor hath he one from their violence to defend
 him:
Yet but an heareth he aught of thee, thy wellbeing in life,
Then he rejoiceth an' all his days are glad with a good hope
Soon to behold thee again, his son safe home from the
 warfare.
But most hapless am I, for I had sons numerous and brave
In wide Troy; where bē they now? scarce is one o' them
 left.
They were fifty the day ye arriv'd hither out of Achaia,
Nineteen royally born princes from one mother only,
While the others women of my house had borne me; of
 all these
Truly the greater part hath Arês in grim battle unstrung.
But hé, who was alone the city's lov'd guardian and stay,
Few days since thou slew'st him alas! his country defend-
 ing,

Hector, for whose sake am I come to the ships of Achaia
His body dear to redeem, offering thee a ransom abundant.
O God-like Achilles, have fear o' the gods, pity him too,
Thy sire also remember, having yet more pity on mé,
Who now stoop me beneath what dread deed mortal ever
      dar'd,
Raising the hand that slew his son pitiably to kiss it.'

    Then did Achilles yearn for thought of his ancient
      father,
And from th' old king's seizure his own hand gently dis-
      engag'd.
And each brooded apart; Priam o'er victorious Hector
Groan'd, low faln to the ground unnerved at feet of
      Achilles,
Who sat mourning awhile his sire, then turn'd to bewailing
Patroclus; while loudly the house with their sobbing
      outrang.

    But when Achilles now had sooth'd his soul in affection,
And all his bosom had disburden'd of passion extreme,
Swiftly from off his seat he arose, and old Priam uprais'd,
In pity and reverence for his age and silvery-blancht head,
And making full answer addrest him in airywingèd words.
    'Unhappy man! what mighty sorrows must thy spirit
      endure!
Nay, how durst thou come thus alone to the ships of
      Achaia,
Into the sight of him who thy sons so many and good
Spoil'd and sent to the grave? Verilie thy heart is of iron.
But come, sit thee beside me upon my couch; let us alwise
Now put away our griefs, sore tho' we be plagued with
      affliction.
Truly there is no gain in distressful lamentation,

Since the eternal gods have assign'd to us unhappy mortals
Hardship enough, while they enjoy bliss idly without end.
  Two jars, say they, await God's hand at th' entry of
    his court,
Stor'd ready with free gifts, of good things one, one of evil.
If mingling from both heav'n's thunderer equaly dispense,
Then will a man's fortune be chequer'd with both sorrow
    and joy;
But to' whom Zeus giveth only of evil that man is outcast,
Hunger houndeth him on disconsolate over the brave
    earth,
Unrespected alike whether of mortals or immortals.
So my sire Pêleus was dow'r'd with favour abounding,
And, from birth and cradle honour'd, all men living out-
    shone
In wealth and happiness, king o'er his Myrmidon armies:
And tho' he was but a man, Zeus made him a fair goddess
    espouse.
But yet an' ev'n to him was an ill thrown in, that he hath
    not
Sons born into his house to retain its empery,—one son
Only he gat, one doom'd to a fate untimely, nor evn he
Comforts th' old man at home, since exiled far from him I
    bide
Here in Troy, thy sons' destruction compassing and thine.
Thou too, sir, we have heard enjoy'd'st good fortune
    aforetime;
From Mytilênê in Lesbos away to the boundary eastward
Of Phrygia's highlands, and north to the briny Hellespont,
Thou, sir, didst all men for wealth and progeny excel:
But when once th' high gods let loose this mischief anigh
    thee,

The city was compass with nought but fierce battle and
    blood.
Bear up, allow thy temper awhile some respite of
    anguish:
Thou wilt not benefit thy dear son vainly bewailing,
Nor restore him alive ere thou taste further affliction.'
    Him then in answer addrest god-like Priam, Îlyon's old
    king.
'Bid me not, O heav'n born, to be seated, while ever Hector
Lẏeth i' the camp dishonour'd, nay rather quickly with all
    speed
Fetch him here to my eyes; and this great ransom appor-
    tion'd
Unto^his worth accept: may^it serve thy good pleasure,
    and thou
Safely return to thy home and sire, since now thou allow'st
    me
Still to renew my days i' the light o' the sun to behold it.'
    Then glancing full dourly bespake him swift-foot
    Achilles.
'O sir, vex me no more: myself I am already minded
Now to restore him. Awhile Zeus sent one here to com-
    mand me,
My mother,—and the wizard who hometh in Ocean is
    her sire.
Yea, an' I⁻know, Priam, also^of thee,—think not to
    deceive me——
That 'twas a god who brought⁻thee hither to the ships of
    Achaia,
Since no mortal alive would dare, nay not one in his prime,
Here to' intrude, neither cᵈ he pass our senteries unseen,
Nor the resistant bars of my doors easily undo.

Spare then again to provoke my soul o'erstrain'd in
    affliction,
Lest, old king, I do thee a wrong in thine enemy's camp,
Lest I in anger offend mine own honour and sin against
    God.'

ROBERT BRIDGES   (XXIV. 468–570)

37   *The Lamentations*

O F their lament white-armed Andrómachê
    Was leader, holding in her hands the while
The head of slaughterous Hector: 'O my man,
Thou art gone young from life, and leavest me
A widow in thy house! Thy son is yet
Only a babe, whom we two luckless ones
Begot; nor can I hope for him to come
To manhood, for ere that this city must
Be wasted root and branch. For thou art gone,
Who didst watch over it and keep it safe
And guard its noble wives and little ones.
And they will doubtless soon go riding on
The hollow ships, and I along with them;
And thither thou, my child, wilt follow me,
Where thou wilt labour at unseemly tasks,
Toiling before a brutal master's eyes;
Or else some Greek will seize thee by the arm
And hurl thee from the wall, a ghastly death,
Some rancorous man whose brother Hector killed
Or else his son or father, since full many
Achæans bit vast earth at Hector's hands;
For in distressful war thy father's touch
Was not caressing: therefore through the city

The people mourn him. Hector, grief untold
And desolation hast thou brought thy parents;
But the extremity of sorrow will
Be left to me, for in thy death thou didst not
Stretch out thy hands towards me from thy bed,
Nor speak to me one pregnant word, whereon
I might have wept and pondered night and day.'

And so she mourned; the women joined her wail.
Then Hécuba took up the throbbing dirge:
'Hector, of all my sons the best beloved,
Thou in thy life wert dear unto the gods,
And even in the doom of death they have
Shown care for thee. For other sons of mine
Swift-foot Achilles, when he took them, sold
Across the sterile sea to Samos' isle,
Imbros, or Lemnos hid in steam. But when
He took thy life with the long-bladed bronze,
He dragged thee many a time around the barrow
Of his own friend Patroclus, whom thou slewest;
Yet for all that he could not raise him up.
And now I see thee lying here at home
All dewy fresh, new-slain, like some one whom
Apollo of the silver bow hath reached
With painless darts and killed.'

And so she mourned and stirred the hopeless wail
Once more. But third to lead the dirge for them
Was Helen: 'Hector, whom I loved the best
Of all my husband's brothers; being the wife
Of godlike Alexander, him, who brought me
To Troy—and would that I had died ere that!
For this is now the twentieth year since I
Came thence and left my native land behind;

Yet never have I heard from thee one word
Of harshness or discourtesy; nay, more,
If any one else attacked me in the palace,
Brother of thine or brother's well-dressed wife,
Or else thy sister or thy mother (but
Thy father is as kindly with me always
As if he were mine own), then thou wouldst speak
Appeasing words to them, and check them with
Thy gentle-mindedness and gentle words.
Therefore with broken heart I weep for thee
And for my wretched self; for in wide Troia
No longer have I one to be a friend
Or kind to me, but all men shudder at me.'
She wept, and from the infinite people broke
A cry.

SIR WILLIAM MARRIS   (XXIV. 723–76)

THE ODYSSEY

38   *The Web*

INDIGNANTLY he spoke, and dashed to earth
The staff, and burst out crying. Pity took
The whole assembly; then the rest kept silence,
And no man had the heart to answer him
With angry words: alone Antínoüs answered:
     'Têlémachus, ungovernable spirit,
Thou boaster! what is this that thou hast said
To shame us, and wouldst hang reproach on us?
I tell thee, not with the Achæan suitors
But with thy mother lies the fault, for she
Is cunning above women. Why, 'tis now

The third year, and the fourth is passing swiftly,
Since she began to cheat the Achæans' hearts
Within them. Hope she gives to all, and makes
Each man a promise, and sends messages,
Although her mind is set on other things.
And in her heart she planned this trick besides:
She set up in her halls a mighty web,
And fell a-weaving; fine of thread it was
And very wide; whereon she said to us:

   ' "My princely suitors, now that good Odysseus
Is dead, though ye would speed my marriage on,
Have patience yet, till I complete my robe;
I would not that my spinning should be wasted;
'Tis prince Lâertês' shroud, against the day
When the fell doom of death that lays men low
Shall strike him down, that of Achæan women
Throughout the land no one may count it blame
In me, that he should sleep without a shroud,
Who in his life had gotten great possessions."

   'So said she, and our haughty hearts assented.
So then by day she wove at that great web,
And in the night she bade them set beside her
The torches, and unpicked it; thus by craft
She fooled the Achæans, and eluded them
A three years' space: but when the fourth year came
With the returning seasons, then it was
One of her women who knew all told us,
And her we caught undoing the fine web.
And so perforce and sore against her will
She finished it. To thee therefore the suitors
Return this answer, that thyself mayst know it,
And all the Achæans know it. Send away

63

Thy mother, and enjoin her that she marry
Whomso her father bids and she approves.
But if she still persistently affronts
The sons of Achæans, counting on
The gifts Athênê gave her beyond women—
Skill in fine handiwork, and clever wit
And craft—whereof we never heard the like,
Not even in fair-haired Achæan women,
Lost ladies of old years, Alcmênê, Tŷro,
Or comely-crowned Mycênê; none of these
Was like Penelope in shrewdness; yet
In this one thing her scheming is not sound,
For men shall eat thy substance and possessions
So long as she continues in this mind
Which now the gods suggest to her. She wins
Herself great glory, but for thee regret
For thy much substance. We will neither go
To our own lands, nor otherwhere, until
She marries of the Achæans whom she will.'

    Then wise Têlémachus replied to him:
'Turn out of doors against her will the one
Who bore and nursed me? No, Antínoüs,
I cannot do it! And, alive or dead,
My father is abroad. It would come hard
On me to pay Îcárius a big sum
As needs I must, if of mine own free will
I send her back; for I shall suffer evil
From him, her father, and the gods will send
Still more; for as she leaves the house, my mother
Will call the dread Avengers down, and men
Will blame me. I will never speak this word!
But if your heart mislikes it, quit my halls;

Make ready other feasts; eat up your own
Possessions, gadding round from house to house;
Or, if ye think it likelier and better
That one man's goods be spoiled without atonement,
Well, waste ye them! but I will call upon
The everlasting gods, if haply Zeus
May grant that deeds of recompense be wrought.
Then in this hall should ye die unavenged.'

    So spoke Têlémachus; and Zeus, whose voice
Is heard afar, in answer sent two eagles
High flying from the mountain top.

Sir William Marris   (II. 80–147)

39   *At Pylos*

     (i) Memories of Troy

AND Nestor, the Gerênian knight, replied:
    'O friend, to memory you recall the tide
Of miseries that encompassed in that land
The Achæan host in all their strength and pride:

'The woes we suffered on the misty sea
Cruising for plunder, our long ships and we,
Whereso Achilles led us, and the strife
That round King Priam's city mightily

'We waged in battle: there our bravest shed
Their life-blood, there lies valiant Aias dead,
There fell Achilles, there Patroclus fell,
Who with Gods' wisdom all our counsels led.

'And there among them lies mine own dear son,
A warrior brave and fleet of foot to run,
Antílochus, the fighter without fault;
And other ills we suffered many an one;

'What man of mortals all of them might tell?
Not if five years or six you here should dwell
Might you by asking all the sorrows learn,
That there the bright Achæan host befell:

'But sooner would you go in woeful mood
Back to your home. For nine years' space we stood
Devising many sleights against the foe,
That hardly Cronus' son at last made good.

'And in those days to bright Odysseus none
Might be compared in counsel, for he won
Far the first place by manifold device;
Your father, if indeed you are his son.

'While I behold you, wonder is on me.
For such you are in speechcraft as was he;
Nor would one say that of well-ordered words
So young a man might have such mastery.'

(III. 102–25)

(ii) A False Wife

But wise Têlémachus returned reply:
'Mentor, of this our grief discourse would I
No longer: a false tale is his return.
Surely on him the Gods that do not die

'Death and the phantom black ere this have sent.
But now another question am I bent
To ask of Nestor, since beyond all men
Righteous is he, and full of wise intent:

'And reigning here has witnessed, so say men,
Three generations rise and fall again;
And like a deathless God methinks is he.
O Nestor, son of Nêleus, tell me then,

'How Atreus' son, the lord of many a land,
Great Agamemnon, fell by violent hand.
Where then was Menelâus? In what wise
Was wrought the treason that Ægisthus planned,

One mightier than himself in death to lay?
Out of Achæan Argos far away
Belike he wandered among unknown men,
So that the slayer plucked up heart to slay.'

And Nestor, the Gerênian knight, replied:
'Look you, my son, the truth I will not hide.
Even as you deem, so was it: for if he
Had found Ægisthus living at that tide

'Within his halls, when home from Troy he won,
The fair-haired Menelâus, Atreus' son,
Not even on his body had men cast
The mound of earth, as for the dead is done,

'But dogs and birds had torn him for their prey
Cast out beyond the city where he lay,
And no Achæan woman wept for him;
So dreadful was the deed he did that day.

'For we sat down in leaguer overseas
Doing great feats of arms, while he at ease
Deep in horse-pasturing Argos won the soul
Of Agamemnon's wife with flatteries.

'And glorious Clytemnestra first for long
Rejected utterly the deed of wrong:
For her own mind was right; and by her side
She had for guardian a man skilled in song,

'Into whose keeping Atreus' son had lent
His wife, when to the Trojan land he went,
Charging him well to guard her: but when fate
Ordained her fall and her entanglement,

'He to an island not inhabited
Bore off the minstrel, and there left him dead,
A prey to birds, and to his house the Queen,
Her will consenting to his will, he led.

'And many beasts he burned on the divine
Altars, and offerings hung on many a shrine
Of woven cloths and gold; for he had done
A mighty deed, exceeding his design. . . .

'And for seven years he held beneath his reign
Golden Mycênæ, after he had slain
The son of Atreus, and the people bore
His yoke: but in the eighth year came his bane,

'When bright Orestes from the Athenian town
Returning struck his father's murderer down,
Ægisthus guileful-hearted, at whose hand
His sire had perished, dead in his renown.

'And while the funeral feast the slayer spread
　　Among the Argives for the twain laid dead,
　　The cursed woman and the faint-heart man,
　　The same day thither Menelâus led

'His ships freight-laden full as they could hold.'

J. W. MACKAIL　　　　　　　　(III. 239–75 and 304–12)

40　　　　　　　　　*At Sparta*

(*i*) *Helen and Menelâus*

THEN Jove's daughter Helen bethought her of
another matter. She drugged the wine with an herb
that banishes all care, sorrow, and ill humour. Whoever
drinks wine thus drugged cannot shed a single tear all the
rest of the day, not even though his father and mother both
of them drop down dead, or he sees a brother or a son hewn
in pieces before his very eyes. This drug, of such sovereign
power and virtue, had been given to Helen by Polydamna
wife of Thôn, a woman of Egypt, where there grow all
sorts of herbs, some good to put into the mixing bowl and
others poisonous. Moreover, every one in the whole
country is a skilled physician, for they are of the race of
Pæêon. When Helen had put this drug in the bowl, and
had told the servants to serve the wine round, she said:

'Menelâus, son of Atreus, and you my good friends,
sons of honourable men (which is as Jove wills, for he
is the giver both of good and evil, and can do what he
chooses), feast here as you will, and listen while I tell you
a tale in season. I cannot indeed name every single one of
the exploits of Ulysses, but I can say what he did when he

was before Troy, and you Achæans were in all sorts of
difficulties. He covered himself with wounds and bruises,
dressed himself all in rags, and entered the enemy's city
looking like a menial or a beggar, and quite different from
what he did when he was among his own people. In this
disguise he entered the city of Troy, and no one said anything to him. I alone recognized him and began to question him, but he was too cunning for me. When, however,
I had washed and anointed him and had given him clothes,
and after I had sworn a solemn oath not to betray him to
the Trojans till he had got safely back to his own camp and
to the ships, he told me all that the Achæans meant to do.
He killed many Trojans and got much information before
he reached the Argive camp, for all which things the
Trojan women made lamentation, but for my own part I
was glad, for my heart was beginning to yearn after my
home, and I was unhappy about the wrong that Venus
had done me in taking me over there, away from my
country, my little girl, and my lawful wedded husband,
who is indeed by no means deficient either in person or
understanding.'

Then Menelâus said: 'All that you have been saying, my
dear wife, is true. I have travelled much, and have had
much to do with heroes, but I have never seen such another
man as Ulysses. What endurance too, and what courage
he displayed within the wooden horse, wherein all the
bravest of the Argives were lying in wait to bring death and
destruction upon the Trojans. At that moment you came
up to us; some god who wished well to the Trojans must
have set you onto it and you had Dêíphobus with you.
Three times did you go all round our hiding place and pat
it; you called our chiefs each by his own name, and

mimicked all our wives—Diomed, Ulysses, and I from
our seats inside heard what a noise you made. Diomed and
I could not make up our minds whether to spring out then
and there, or to answer you from inside, but Ulysses held
us all in check.'

SAMUEL BUTLER   (IV. 219–84)

(*ii*) *Menelâus and Prôteus*

SO spake I, and straightway the fair goddess made
answer: 'Yea, now, sir, I will plainly tell thee all. So
often as the sun in his course stands high in mid heaven,
then forth from the brine comes the ancient one of the sea,
whose speech is sooth, before the breath of the West Wind
he comes and the sea's dark ripple covers him. And when
he is got forth, he lies down to sleep in the hollow of the
caves. And around him the seals, the brood of the fair
daughter of the brine, sleep all in a flock, stolen forth from
the grey sea water, and bitter is the scent they breathe of
the salt sea. There will I lead thee at the breaking of the
day, and couch you all orderly; so do thou choose diligently
three of thy company, the best thou hast in thy decked
ships. And I will tell thee all the magic arts of that old
man. First, he will number the seals and go over them; but
when he has told their tale and beheld them, he will lay
him down in their midst, as a shepherd mid the sheep of
his flock. So soon as ever ye shall see him couched, even
then mind you of your might and strength, and hold him
there, despite his eagerness and striving to be free. And
he will make assay, and take all manner of shapes of things
that creep upon the earth, of water likewise, and of fierce
fire burning. But do ye grasp him steadfastly, and press

71

him yet the more, and at length when he questions thee in his proper shape, as he was when first ye saw him laid to rest, then, hero, hold thy strong hands, and let the ancient one go free, and ask him which of the gods is hard upon thee, and as touching thy returning, how thou mayest go over the teeming deep.'

Therewith she dived beneath the heaving sea, but I betook me to the ships where they stood in the sand, and my heart was darkly troubled as I went. But after I had come down to the ship and to the sea, and we had made ready our supper and immortal night had come on, then did we lay us to rest upon the sea-beach. So soon as early Dawn shone forth, the rosy-fingered, in that hour I walked by the shore of the wide-wayed sea, praying instantly to the gods; and I took with me three of my company, in whom I trusted most for every enterprise.

Meanwhile, so it was that she had plunged into the broad bosom of the sea, and had brought from the deep the skins of four sea-calves, and all were newly flayed, for she was minded to lay a snare for her father. She scooped lairs in the sea-sand, and sat awaiting us, and we drew very nigh her, and she made us all lie down in order, and cast a skin over each. There would our ambush have been most terrible, for the deadly stench of the sea-bred seals distressed us sore: nay, who would lay him down by a beast of the sea? But herself she wrought deliverance, and devised a great comfort. She took ambrosia of a very sweet savour, and set it beneath each man's nostril, and did away with the stench of the beast. So all the morning we waited with steadfast heart, and the seals came forth in troops from the brine, and then they couched them all orderly by the sea-beach. And at high day the ancient one came

forth from out of the brine, and found his fatted seals, yea
and he went along their line and told their tale; and first
among the sea-beasts he reckoned us, and guessed not that
there was guile, and afterward he too laid him down. Then
we rushed upon him with a cry, and cast our hands about
him, nor did that ancient one forget his cunning. Now
behold, at the first he turned into a bearded lion, and
thereafter into a snake, and a pard, and a huge boar; then
he took the shape of running water, and of a tall flowering
tree. We the while held him close with steadfast heart.

S. H. BUTCHER, ANDREW LANG   (IV. 398–459)

41   *Penelope Forlorn*

AND Medon answer made, the man of skill:
  'Yea, Queen, if this now were the worst of ill!
But greater and more grievous far they plan,
Which may the son of Cronus not fulfil!

'With the sword's edge they plot your son to slay
Returning homeward; if some word he may
Hear of his sire, to lordly Pylos he
And to bright Lacedæmon takes his way.'

So spake he, and her heart with grief he stirred,
And shook her knees beneath her as she heard.
Long she sat speechless, and her eyes with tears
Brimmed over, and she said not any word.

Yet utterance at last she found, and slow
She spake: 'O herald, wherefore is it so
My child is gone from me? No need there was
For him upon swift-sailing ships to go!

'Which are the horses that men yoke to swim
Over the sea, and cross from brim to brim
The fields of water: oh, among mankind
Shall there not even a name be left of him?'

And Medon answered her, the man of skill:
'I know not whether by some God his will
Was roused within him, or his own heart planned
This voyage forth to Pylos to fulfil,

'If tidings of his father he may know,
Whether he comes, or by what fate laid low
He even now has perished.' Thus he said,
And turned him from Odysseus' house to go.

But bitter anguish at her heartstrings tore,
And on a seat she brooked to sit no more,
Of many that the house was furnished with;
But on the richly fashioned chamber's floor

Moaning in lamentable wise she clung,
While round her wailed the women, old and young,
All of her household: and Penelope
Bitterly sighing spake her maids among:

'Hearken, my women! for upon my head
Surely the Lord Olympian grief has shed
Exceeding great, beyond the lot of all
The women whom this age has born and bred.

'For I long since my noble husband lost,
The lion-hearted, in the Danaän host
Renowned for all achievement, and his fame
All over Hellas and mid-Argos crossed.

'And now again my own belovèd son
The winds have snatched from home, and tidings none
Had I, nor knew I of his setting forth.'

J. W. MACKAIL　　　　　　　　　　　　(IV. 696–728)

42　　　　　　　*Calypso's Island*

He stoopt *Piérea*, and thence
Glid through the aire; and *Neptune's* Confluence
Kist as he flew, and checkt the waves as light
As any Sea-mew, in her fishing flight,
Her thicke wings soucing in the savorie seas.
Like her, he pass'd a world of wildernesse;
But when the far-off Ile he toucht, he went
Up from the blue sea, to the Continent,
And reacht the ample Caverne of the Queene;
Whom he within found, without, seldome seene.
A Sun-like fire upon the harth did flame;
The matter precious, and divine the frame,
Of Cedar cleft, and Incense was the Pile,
That breath'd an odour round about the Ile.
Her selfe was seated in an inner roome,
Whom sweetly sing he heard; and at her loome,
About a curious web, whose yarne she threw
In, with a golden shittle.[1] A Grove grew
In endlesse spring about her Caverne round,
With odorous Cypresse, Pines, and Poplars crownd.
Where Haulks, Sea-owles, and long-tongu'd Bittours bred,
And other birds their shadie pinions spred.
All Fowles maritimall; none roosted there,
But those whose labours in the waters were.

　　　　　　　　　[1] Shuttle.

A Vine did all the hollow Cave embrace;
Still greene, yet still ripe bunches gave it grace.
Four Fountaines, one against another powr'd
Their silver streames; and medowes all enflowrd
With sweete Balme-gentle, and blue Violets hid,
That deckt the soft brests of each fragrant Mead.
Should any one (though he immortall were)
Arrive and see the sacred objects there;
He would admire them, and be over-joyd;
And so stood *Hermês* ravisht powres employd.

   But having all admir'd, he enterd on
The ample Cave; nor could be seene unknowne
Of great *Calypso* (for all Deities are
Prompt in each others knowledge; though so farre
Severd in dwellings) but he could not see
Ulysses there within. Without was he
Set sad ashore; where 'twas his use to view
Th' unquiet sea; sigh'd, wept, and emptie drew
His heart of comfort.

GEORGE CHAPMAN   (V. 51–83)

43   *Odysseus puts to Sea*
          (i) *Wreck of the Raft*

SO spake he, and the clouds at his command
  Gathered, and with the trident in his hand
He stirred the sea and roused the hurricane
Of all the winds, and blotted sea and land

With clouds: night swept across the firmament:
East wind and south, and west athwart them sent,
Clashed, and the crystal-cradled northern blast
Rolling a mighty wave before him went.

Trembled Odysseus then in heart and knee,
And to his mighty spirit inwardly
Grieving he spoke: 'O miserable man!
Is this the end? what shall become of me?

'I fear lest all was true the Goddess said,
How on the deep, ere yet my land I tread,
I must fill up the measure of my woes:
Now to the word is all accomplishèd.

'With such enveloping clouds the breadth of sky
Zeus covers, and the sea runs mountains high,
And all the hurricanes of all the winds
Burst round me: now as good as dead am I.

'Thrice of our host and four times happy they
Who in wide Troy of old were cast away,
Serving the sons of Atreus! Would to God
I too had died then and fulfilled my day,

'When the bronze spears of Trojans many an one
Struck nigh me round the corpse of Pêleus' son!
Then fame and funeral I had earned, nor here
Had perished by this dismal death undone.'

Even as he spoke, a monstrous wave abaft
Came towering up, and crashed into the raft:
And the raft heeled, and off it far he fell,
And from his hand shot out the rudder-shaft.

And in one whirling gust the hurricane
Snapped the mast midway; far into the main
Fell top and rigging: and beneath the surge
He sank, nor for a while his head again

Out of the overwhelming wave could lift:
For now the raiment, bright Calypso's gift,
Weighed heavy on him: but at last he rose,
And with abundant-streaming head made shift

Out of his mouth to spit the salt sea-spray.
Yet withal marking where the wrecked raft lay,
He plunged amid the waves and caught at it,
And crouched amidships, keeping death at bay:

While the raft helpless on the tideway spun,
As down the plain when Autumn is begun,
Before the North wind tufts of thistledown
Entangled close together twirling run;

So him across the sea in furious race
Hither and thither the winds bore apace:
And now south wind to north its plaything tossed,
And now east wind to west gave up the chase.

(V. 291–332)

(ii) The Swimming

Two days and nights upon the long smooth swell
He drifted on, nor could his heart foretell
Aught but destruction; but when fair-tressed Morn
Brought the third day to birth, the tempest fell,

And windless grew the calm; and now anigh
He saw the land, with keen and forward eye
Gazing, as lifted on the swell he rose:
And with such joy as children may descry

Hope for a father's life who long has lain
Wasted by sickness, bearing grievous pain
Beneath some grim God's hand, and gladly they
See him by kinder Heaven restored again:

So joyfully Odysseus saw appear
Forest and shore, and strongly swam to near
The mainland: but when now no farther off
Than a man's voice will carry, he could hear

Upon the reefs the thunder of the sea,
Where the great wave on dry land horribly
Belched roaring, and in spindrift all the coast
Was wrapped, nor any landing-place saw he,

Nor harbourage where ships might find relief,
But all was jutting fang of rock and reef.
Thereat Odysseus trembled, heart and limb,
And to his mighty soul he spoke in grief:

'Woe's me! when now beyond my hope to-day
Zeus grants me sight of land, and all this way
Throughout the sea-gulf I at last have pierced,
I see no issue from the ocean grey.

'For sharp rocks rise far out, and all around
Welters the breaker with a roaring sound,
And the cliff runs up sheer, and under it
The sea is deep, nor may I take the ground

'Or foothold find among the waves, lest one
Might catch and hurl me on a ridge of stone
As forth I climb: poor work were that: and yet
If I swim farther up to light upon

79

'Some shoaling beach or haven of the main,
I fear lest yet once more the hurricane
May sweep me out on the fish-pasturing sea,
And all my heavy woe begin again:

'Or lest heaven loose on me some monster dread,
Such as in Amphitrîtê's halls are bred
Full many: for I know how sore the great
Shaker of earth with me is angerèd.'

While he debated thus his heart within,
A great wave lifted him and bore him in
Upon a jagged rock, that there and then
Had shattered all his bones and stripped his skin,

But that the Goddess with the eyes of grey,
Athêna, put it in his heart to lay
Both hands tight-clutched upon the rock, and there
Cling gasping till the great wave passed away.

Over his head it went, but backward whirled
Bore down on him and struck him full and hurled
Far out to sea: as when a cuttlefish
Out of its hole is dragged with suckers curled

And clinging round the pebbles of its bed,
So from his mighty hands the skin was shred
Against the rocks; and in the whelming wave
Quite hidden, then Odysseus had been dead

Before his day, in grievous wise and grim,
But that grey-eyed Athêna put in him
Counsel, uprising from beneath the flood
That burst upon the land, far out to swim,

Still keeping on the land a sidelong eye,
Some shoaling beach or haven to descry:
Until he, swimming onward, to the mouth
Of a fair-flowing river drew anigh.

And there he chose what seemed the likeliest place,
Being clear of rocks and sheltered for a space.

J. W. MACKAIL   (V. 388–443)

44   *Nausicaä*

(*i*)

HAVING thus fulfilled her purpose Athênê went away to Olympus where evermore they say the seat of the gods stays sure: for the winds shake it not, nor is it wetted by rain, nor approached by any snow. All around stretches the cloudless firmament, and a white glory of sunlight is diffused about its walls. There the blessed gods are happy all their days: and thither, accordingly, repaired the grey-eyed One after clearly imparting her message to the maiden.

High-throned Dawn came to rouse Nausícaä of the goodly robe. She, waking, wondered at her dream and went straight through the house to tell her dear father and mother. She found them within. Her mother sat by the hearth with her serving women, twirling on the distaff yarn which had been dipped in sea-purple dye: while her father she crossed in the doorway as he went out to consult with the illustrious princes of the people—a council to which the noblest of the Phæacians had summoned them. She went near to this father she loved, that she might softly say:

'Dear father, will you not let me have the deep easy-wheeled waggon, that I may take all the good soiled clothes that lie by me to the river for washing? It is only right that you, whenever you go to sit in council with the leaders, should have clean linen to wear next your skin: while of your five sons begotten in the house only two have taken wives: and the three merry bachelors are always wanting clothes newly washed when they go out to dances. Thinking about all these things is one of my mind's cares.'

So much she said, too shy to name to her dear father the near prospect of her marriage: but he saw everything and answered in a word: 'My child, I do not grudge you mules, or anything. Go: the bondsmen will get you the tall, light waggon with the high tilt.'

As he spoke, he called his men, who obeyed.

T. E. SHAW (T. E. LAWRENCE) (VI. 47–71)

(ii)

NOW when at last they arrived at the beautiful stream of the river,

Here the perennial basins they found where waters abundant

Welled up brightly enough for the cleansing of dirtiest raiment.

So their mules they unloosened from under the yoke of the wagon,

Letting them wander at will on the bank of the eddying river,

Browsing on clover as sweet as the honey, and then from the carriage

Bearing within their arms to the deep dark water the garments,

Cast them in trenches and trod them in rivalry one with
　　another.

So, when the raiment was washed and was thoroughly
　　cleansed of the dirt-stains,

All on the shore of the ocean in order they spread on the
　　shingle

Where it is washed by the tides of the sea as they sweep to
　　the dry land.

There did they bathe and anointing themselves with the
　　oil of the olive

Set them adown to the mid-day meal on the bank of the
　　river,

Leaving the garments to dry on the beach in the glare of
　　the sunlight.

Now when in food they had fully delighted, both she and
　　her maidens,

Casting aside their scarfs with a ball they betook them to
　　playing,

White-armed Nausícaä with the choral melody leading.

E'en as descending a height moves Artemis, darter of
　　arrows,

Either on Tâÿgetus long-ridged or on huge Erymanthus,

Taking delight in the chase of the boar and of timorous
　　roe-deer,

Whilst all round her the daughters of Zeus who beareth
　　the ægis,

Nymphs of the woodland play—and Lêto sees it rejoicing;

Even as over the rest uplifting her brows and her forehead

Easily known in her beauty she stands, though fair be the
　　others,

Thus shone forth in her beauty the maiden amidst her
　　attendants.

Now when at last it was come to the moment of home-
        ward returning,
After the mules were yoked and folded the beautiful gar-
        ments,
Other was then the device of the grey-eyed goddess Athênê,
E'en that Odysseus awaking and seeing the fair-faced
        maiden
Her might follow as guide and reach Phæacia's city.
Seizing the ball, at a maiden among her attendants the
        princess
Flung it, but missing the maiden it fell in a bottomless eddy.
Piercingly all of them shrieked; and godlike Odysseus,
        awakened,
Sat straight up and pondered thereon in his heart and his
        spirit:
'Ah me! what is the folk whose country I now am arrived
        at?
Dwell here savages wanton and wild, despisers of justice?
Have they a love for the stranger and hearts that revere
        the immortals?
Lo, how piercing a cry as of maidens ringeth around me,
Nymphs peradventure that dwell on precipitous summits
        of mountains,
Or by the fountain springs of the rivers and leas of the
        lowlands;
Else, maybe, I am near to a folk of articulate language.
Nay, go to, I will test for myself this matter and view it.'

These words uttered, from under the bushes the godlike
        Odysseus
Issued, and breaking a branch with his powerful hand from
        the thicket

84

Girdled his body with leaves, its nakedness striving to
    cover.

Thus in the pride of his strength from his lair in the moun-
    tain a lion

Stalks forth soaked with the rain and battered with wind,
    and his two eyes

Flame as he prowleth abroad midst droves of the sheep and
    the oxen

Or on the track of the deer, and often his belly will bid him

Making assay on the flocks e'en strong-built granges to
    enter;

So to the fair-tressed maidens Odysseus was fain to betake
    him,

Though all naked his body—on such distress was he fallen.

Sight terrific he seemed to the maidens, disfigured with
    sea-brine.

Hastily hither and thither in panic they fled to the sand-
    spits.

Sole stood firmly the daughter of Alcínoüs: for Athênê

Gave to her courage of heart and took from her limbs all
    trembling;

Facing him calmly she stood; and Odysseus pondered
    within him

Whether as suppliant clasping the knees of the beautiful
    maiden,

Or as he was, at a distance, to speak soft words of entreaty,

Begging her show him the city and grant him the gift of a
    garment.

Thus as he pondered thereon, this plan seemed surely the
    better,

Holding apart, from a distance, to speak soft words of
    entreaty,

Since that by clasping her knees he was fearful to anger
    the maiden.

Straightway therefore a word both gentle and cunning he
    uttered:

'Thee, O queen, I implore. O . . . whether a goddess or
    mortal!

Art thou a goddess—of those who inhabit the infinite
    heaven—

Then it is Artemis surely, the daughter of Zeus the Al-
    mighty,

Both in thy form and thy stature and beauty to whom thou
    art likest.

Art thou a daughter of man, and dwellest on earth as a
    mortal,

Happy I deem, yea three times happy, thy mother and
    father,

Happy and three times happy thy brothers; for surely
    exultant

Gloweth in gladness the spirit within them, whene'er they
    behold thee

Entering into the dance, so lovely a flower of girlhood.

Yet, ah, how in his heart more happy than every other

He that with gifts shall prevail and homeward lead thee
    as lover!

Never till now have seen mine eyes such beauty in mortal,

Man nor woman: amazement possesseth me while I be-
    hold it.

Suchlike wonder indeed by Apollo's altar in Delos

Once I beheld—uprearing its column a sapling of date-
    palm;

(Yea, e'en thither I came, and was followed by many a
    fighter,

Holding a course whereon sore sorrow was fated to meet
 us).

Even as then this wonder beholding I marvelled in spirit,

Long time gazing—for ne'er such shaft from the earth
 shot upward—

Thus, O lady, I marvel at thee and am greatly astonished,

Fearing thy knees to approach, though sorrow hath fallen
 upon me.

Yester-e'en to the shore I escaped from the wine-dark
 ocean.

Nineteen days from the isle Ōgýgia billows and storm-
 blasts

Ceaselessly bore me, and hither at last some deity cast me,

Planning, meseemeth, that still I shall suffer; for never, I
 fear me,

All of my travail shall end till the Gods much more shall
 accomplish.

Nay, O queen, have pity! To thee, outworn with my
 labours,

Lo, as a suppliant first I am come, and of others I know not

Any, of all of the folk that inhabit the town or the
 country.

Show me the city, and give me a garment, to cast it about
 me,

Even a rag, or the wrapper perchance that thou broughtst
 for the linen!

So shall the gods all blessings bestow that thy soul desireth—

Husband and home; and oneness of heart may heaven
 vouchsafe thee,

Blessing supreme—since naught can be wished that is
 greater and better

While united in heart and in mind are dwelling together

Husband and wife. 'Tis a sight brings sorrow to wishers
   of evil,
Joy to the wishers of good; but the joy in their hearts is the
   loudest.'

H. B. COTTERILL   (VI. 85–185)

45 *Phæacian Nights—Dêmódocus*

WHEN the hero had made an end of speaking, the
herald bore his meat in hand to Dêmódocus who
received it and rejoiced. All stretched out and helped
themselves to the ready cheer; and when they were filled
with drink and food then Odysseus addressed Dêmódocus:
'Dêmódocus, I laud you above all mortal men: I know not
if it was the Muse, daughter of Zeus, that taught you, or
Apollo himself. Anyhow you have sung the real history
of the mishaps of the Achæans, their deeds, their sufferings,
their griefs, as if you had been there or had heard it from
eye witnesses. But now change your theme and sing of how
Epeius with the help of Athênê carpentered together that
great timber horse, the crafty device, which wise Odysseus
got taken into the citadel after packing it with the men who
were to lay Troy waste. Tell me all this in order, and then
I will maintain everywhere that the God's grace had conferred the bounty of inspiration on your singing.'

   So he said; and the minstrel, fired by the God, gave
proof of his mastery. He took up his tale where the main
body of the Argives embarked on their well-decked ships
after setting fire to their hutments, and sailed away; leaving
the remnant, the companions of famous Odysseus, enclosed
in the heart of Troy-town, in the meeting-place, hidden
within the horse which the Trojans themselves had
dragged up to their citadel. There the horse stood while

the people hung about it arguing this way and that uncertainly. They were of three minds:—either to prize open its wooden womb with their pitiless blades; or to drag it to the cliff's edge and roll it down among the rocks; or to leave it there dedicated as a mighty peace offering to the Gods. In the end this last counsel had it, for it was fated that they should perish when their city gave lodgement to the monstrous beast in which crouched all the flower of the Argives with their seeds of death and doom for Troy. He sang how the sons of the Argives quitted their hollow den, and poured out from the horse, and made an end of Troy. He sang the share of each warrior in the wasting of the stately town, and how Odysseus, Arês-like attacked the house of Dêîphobus with great Menelâus. There, he said, Odysseus braved terrible odds but conquered in the end, by help of resolute Athênê.

Thus ran the famous singer's song: but Odysseus melted and tears from his eyelids bedewed his cheeks. So it is when a loving wife flings herself, wailing, about the body of her man who has fallen before his township and fellow-citizens, defending the town and his children from their cruel day of sack and rapine. The sight of him labouring his last breath and dying makes her wail aloud and wind herself about him. Yet do the enemy from behind beat her with their spear-shafts across her bowed shoulders and lead her into servitude, to her fate of toil and grief. Just as that woman's cheeks are ravaged with despair, just so piteously did the tears fall from Odysseus' brows. Yet this time, too, his falling tears were missed by all the company, save only Alcinoüs who sat by him and marked his grief, unable not to hear the moaning deep within his breast.

T. E. SHAW (T. E. LAWRENCE)   (VIII. 482–534)

46 *Phæacian Nights—Odysseus' Tale*

(i) *Of Noman and Cyclops*

SO I spake, and he took it and drank, and became ex-
    ceeding fain

Of that sweet drink that I gave him, and besought me of
    drink again:

'Come give me the drink and be blythe, and straightway
    tell me thy name,

That a guest-gift I may give thee to gladden thine heart
    with the same,

Since verily for the Cyclops the corn-kind earth doth shed

The wine in plenteous bunches by the rain of Zeus full-fed:

But this indeed is handsel of the meat and drink divine.'

    So he spake, and again I gave him of the dark-red glow-
    ing wine,

And thrice I bore and gave it, and the fool thrice drank it
    out.

But when the heart of the Cyclops the wine had encom-
    passed about,

Then honied words I uttered, and to speaking thus befel:

'Cyclops, my name renownèd thou askest, the which I will
    tell,

But the guest-gift thou wouldst give me, now give me it
    I pray.

My name is Noman: Noman they called me on a day,

My father and my mother, and all my folk of old.'

    So I spake, but straight he answered from cruel heart
    and cold:

'Noman shall I eat the latest of all his fellows here,

And all the others before him; lo, a guest-gift good and
    dear!'

Therewith he fell a backward, and there he lay along,
His thick neck wryed and twisted, and Sleep, the tamer
    strong,
Held him, and forth from his gullet gushed wine with
    man's flesh blent,
And with the wine all heavy a belching forth he sent.
So then mid the plenteous ashes the olive bar I laid
Until all warm it was waxen, and words to my fellows I
    said,
And heartened them all, lest any should fear and shrink
    away.

But now when the spar of olive in the fire as there it lay
'Gan kindle for all its greenness, and brightly glowed the
    wood,
I fetched it up from the fire, and about my fellows stood,
And a stark and mighty courage the God on us did send;
And they took up the shaft of olive, sharp-pointed at the end,
And into his eye they thrust it, while I, raised up aloft,
Kept turning, e'en as a craftsman the ship-beam boreth oft
With the wimble, and on both sides his men still ply the
    thong
To each side fixed and steady, and it runneth around for
    long;
E'en so that shaft fire-hardened we took, and the eye of him
We bored, and about it glowing straightway the blood 'gan
    swim,
And his eyelid and his eyebrow were singed with the
    breath that came
From the burning ball as the eye-roots all cracked in the
    heat of the flame:
As when the smith of an hatchet or great axe taketh hold
And dippeth it, hissing loudly, amidst the water cold,

For its tempering; since thus only and thereby the steel is
  good—

So hissed the eye of the Cyclops around the olive wood.

But his mighty yells were fearful, and the den rang
  horribly.

Till we shrank away in terror. Then he tore from out his
  eye

The shaft of sharpened olive all dabbled about with
  blood,

And raging, aloof he cast it with his hands from where he
  stood.

Then he whooped out loud to the Cyclops, they who on
  either side,

Amid the rocky places of the windy bents abide;

And they heard his cry, and flocking from about there did
  they stand

Around the den, and were asking what harm was come to
  hand:

'Polyphêmus, what thing grieves thee, that through the
  deathless night

Thou criest aloud, and hast made us but sleepless folk
  outright?

Is some one of mortals driving thy flocks against thy
  will?

Or thyself is some man quelling with might or crafty
  skill?'

But the stark strong Polyphêmus thus answered them
  again:

'O friends, Noman me slayeth by guile and not by main!'

Then with wingèd words they bespake him, and answered
  presently:

'If alone thou art abiding, and no man enforceth thee,

The ill that great Zeus sendeth, no wight may shun the
    thing.
But put up the prayer to thy father, Poseidon the mighty
    king.'
And with that word they departed, and my dear heart
    laughed aloud
At my name that had so beguiled him and my worthy rede
    and proud.

(IX. 353–414)

(ii) *Of Cyclops and the Ram*

But when the Mother of Morning, Rose-fingered Day-
    Dawn, shone,
Then all the rams of the cattle fared out to the field to
    begone,
While the ewes unmilked and bleating about the folds
    must go,
For their udders were swollen to bursting. But their King,
    all worn with woe,
With his hand was ever groping the backs of all the sheep
As they stood up there before him; but the fool no heed did
    keep
How under the breasts of the fleecy-fair sheep were bound
    the men.
But the last of the flock, the ram, came forth from the door
    of the den,
With his plenteous wool encumbered, and with me and
    my wily thought:
So to him spake the stark Polyphemus, as a hold of him he
    caught:

'Dear ram, why then I prithee of the flock art thou the
last

To come forth from the den? aforetime ne'er left behind
thou wast,

But first of all to be cropping the tender flower of the grass,

Still striding big; and foremost to the river wouldst thou
pass.

And, first of all wert thou yearning in the eventide to hie

To the fold: but now art thou latest. Is it so that thou
mournest the eye

Of thy Master, which he the losel a while ago did blind

With his miserable fellows, when with wine he had van-
quished my mind?

That Noman, who, I swear it, hath not yet 'scaped his
bane.

Oh, if but as me thou wert minded, and a voice of speech
mightest gain

To tell me where in the wide-world the man my might
doth shun,

Then here and there o'er the rock-den his blood and brains
should run

As against the ground I dashed him, and some solace
should I have

For all the heap of evil which the nought-worth Noman
gave.'

So saying, away without doors the ram from his hand
he sent,

And a little way from the rock-den and the garth thereof
we went;

And then first from the ram I loosed me, and my fellows
presently.

WILLIAM MORRIS   (IX. 437-63)

94

(iii) Of the Læstrýgonës

                              Thither when we came
To the fair haven, where about there runs
On either side unbroken a high scarp,
And at its mouth facing each other stretch
Two jutting cliffs and make the entrance strait—
Then all the others steered their curved ships in,
And they were moored inside the hollow haven
Close-packed, for in it never swelled a wave,
Little or big, but bright calm lay on all.
But I alone moored my black ship outside
At the land's end, and roped her to a rock;
And climbed and stood upon a craggy hill,
A look-out place; and there appeared no sign
Of men's or cattle's labour; only smoke
We saw up-curling from the land. So then
Some of my crew I sent to go and learn
What kind of men were these who lived by bread
On earth. Two men I picked and with them sent
A third as herald. And being gone ashore
They followed a smooth road, whereby the carts
Were wont to bring down fire-wood to the city
From the high hills. Outside the town they met
A damsel drawing water, the tall daughter
Of Læstrygonian Antíphatês.
To the fair-flowing spring, Artácia,
Whence people carried water to the city,
She had come down. So up to her they went,
And spoke and asked her who was king of the land
And over whom he ruled: and she at once
Showed them the high-roofed dwelling of her father.

Now when they stepped within the noble house,
Therein they found his wife, as huge of bulk
As a hill-top, and were appalled at her:
And she forthwith called from the meeting-place
Renowned Antíphatês, her mate, who planned
A ghastly death for them. Straightway he seized
One of my men, and made his breakfast ready.
The other two sprang up and fled to the ships;
Thereon he raised the war-cry through the city,
And at the sound from this side and from that
The mighty Læstrygonians came thronging
Past number, not like men but like the Giants.
With boulders heavy as a man could carry
They stoned us from the cliffs, and through the fleet
Arose a dismal din of dying men
And shattered ships as well; and spearing them
Like fishes, they bore off their loathsome feast.
Now while they went on killing those within
The harbour gulf, my keen sword from my side
I pulled, and with it cut the ropes that moored
My blue-prowed ship, and called on my men quick
To dig their oars in, that we might escape
Our evil case. They all tore up the brine
In fear of death; and from the beetling rocks
My ship shot gladly out to sea; but all
Those other ships were lost there in a pack.

SIR WILLIAM MARRIS   (X. 87–132)

(iv) Of Circê

THEN my well-greaved fellows I numbered into two
    companies,
And a leader I appointed to be o'er each of these;

96

And I led the one, and the other godlike Eurýlochus led.

Then in a brazen helmet the shuffled lots we sped,

And therefrom the lot of Eurýlochus the great of heart
    did go.

So he went his ways, and with him were fellows twenty
    and two;

And they wept as they went and left us, and sorrow sore
    we made.

Now they came on the house of Circê well builded
    down in a glade,

And all of smooth stone fashioned in a place seen far and
    near:

And about it were wolves of the mountain, and lions
    haunted there;

And she herself had tamed them with the help of herbs
    of ill:

Nor fell they upon our fellows, though they thronged
    about them still,

But fawning there upon them their long tails wagged withal.

And as dogs will fawn on their master when he comes from
    the feastful hall,

Because he is wont to bring them things that their hearts
    deem good,

Round these the wolves the strong-clawed, and the lions
    fawning stood,

And they feared when they beheld them, the creatures
    fierce and great.

But there was the house of the Goddess, and there they
    stood in the gate,

And Circê heard they singing in a lovely voice within,

As she wove on the web undying, such works as the God-
    folk win,

Such works as are all-glorious, and delicate and fair.

Then the chief of men, Polîtês, bespake his fellows there,

A man who to me was dearest, and the heedfullest of all:

'O friends, there is some wight weaving a great web there in the hall,

And singing so fair that the pavement is echoing all about.

A goddess or a woman? but to her let us haste to cry out.'

So he spake, and they cried aloud, and their voices toward her cast,

And she, straight coming outwards, through the shining doorway passed,

And called them, and they followed, so witless was their mood;

But Eurýlochus dreaded treason, and without the door abode.

So she led them in and set them on bench and lordly seat,

And a mess of cheese, and meal and honey pale and sweet

With Pramnian wine she mingled; and she blended therewithal

Ill herbs, that the land of their fathers might clean from their memories fall.

But when she had given thereof, and they had drunk of the wine,

With a staff she smote them, and shut them within the sty of the swine;

And swine-shape they had, and the voice and the bristles and head of the boar:

But ever their minds abided e'en such as they were before.

So there were they styed up weeping, and Circê presently
Cast to them mast, and acorns, and nuts of the cornel tree,
Whereof the swine earth-wallowing are wont to make
    their meat.

WILLIAM MORRIS   (X. 203–43)

(v) Of his Mother's Shade

So saying back to the Dark House the ghost
  Of prince Tîrésias retreating sank,
  His soothsay uttered: but upon the bank
Abode I still, until my mother next
Came nigh the pit and of the dark blood drank.

Straightway she knew me then, and grieving sore
  A wingèd word she spake: 'O child I bore,
  How came you here beneath the misty West
Alive? for living men this dusky shore

'Hardly may see, which mighty floods enclose
  And awful rivers, and before it flows
  The Ocean-stream, that none afoot may cross,
Except in a well-builded ship he goes.

'Is it but now that while long time you roam
  Hither from Troy with ship and crew you come?
  And have you won not yet to Ithaca
Nor seen your wife who waits for you at home?'

So spake she, but I answering said: 'Alas,
  My mother, strong constraint has made me pass
  Down into darkness, to the ghost to seek
That was the Theban seer Tîrésias.

'Not yet have I come nigh Achæan land,
Nor set my foot upon my native strand,
But ever have been wandering wearily
Since with bright Agamemnon in one band

'To Ilion nurse of steeds I took my way,
Against the Trojans battle to array;
Now tell me this thing plainly: by what fate
Did Death the Leveller bring you to decay?

'Did a long sickness waste from you the bliss
Of life or arrow-showering Artemis
With shafts that hurt not strike you down and slay?
And of my father likewise tell me this;

'And of the son I left behind me then:
Do they yet keep my honour among men?
Or has it fallen into strangers' hands
Who say that I return not home again?

And of my wedded wife declare to me
The mind and counsel: with our child stays she
Still steadfast, or has some Achæan prince
Already taken her his wife to be?'

So said I: and the Queen returned reply,
My mother: 'Sure within your palace high
Abides she steadfast-hearted, and the days
And nights wear through with many a tear and sigh.

'Nor does a stranger hold your honour fair;
But still Têlémachus untroubled there
Keeps the domain that is his heritage,
And in the banquets has an equal share

'That for the lawgiver are duly spread;
For all men bid him. But in lonelihead

Your father keeps his farm, nor to the town
Goes in at all, nor covered is his bed

'With rugs and broidered blankets; by the fire
Where they that in the household serve for hire
Among the ashes lie, in wintertide
He sleeps, his body clad in mean attire;

'But when the summer comes and fruits abound
In autumn, then his lowly bed is found
Where all about his terraced vineyard-plot
The fallen leaves lie thick upon the ground.

'There lies he mourning, and his heart is sore,
Day after day, that you return no more,
While grievous eld comes over him: for thus
I likewise perished and my life outwore.

'For neither me where in my halls I lay
Did the keen-sighted Arrow-showerer slay
With shafts that pain not, nor was I assailed
By any sickness, such as takes away

'The life out of the limbs with wasting sad;
But died of longing that for you I had,
And for your wisdom and kind-heartedness,
Noble Odysseus, that my life made glad.'

So said she: but I inly for a space
Mused and was full of longing to embrace
The ghost of my dead mother. Thrice I sprang
Toward her, fain to clasp her face to face;

And thrice from out my hands to clasp her spread
Like to a shadow or a dream she fled.
And grief waxed ever keener at my heart.

J. W. MACKAIL　　　　　　　　　　(XI. 150–208)

(vi) Of the Shade of Achilles

HE spake, to whom I, answ'ring, thus replied:
'O Pêleus' son! Achilles! bravest far
Of all Achaia's race! I here arrived
Seeking Tîrésias, from his lips to learn,
Perchance, how I might safe regain the coast
Of craggy Ithaca; for tempest-toss'd
Perpetual, I have neither yet approach'd
Achaia's shore, or landed on my own.
But as for thee, Achilles! never man
Hath known felicity like thine, or shall,
Whom living we all honour'd as a God,
And who maintain'st, here resident, supreme
Controul among the dead; indulge not then,
Achilles, causeless grief that thou hast died.'

I ceased, and answer thus instant received:
'Renown'd Ulysses! think not death a theme
Of consolation; I had rather live
The servile hind for hire, and eat the bread
Of some man scantily himself sustain'd,
Than sov'reign empire hold o'er all the shades.'

WILLIAM COWPER (XI. 477-91)

(vii) Of the Shade of Ajax

SO I: when swift Achilles' long-limbed ghost
Made off, through meadow of the asphodel
Stalking in glory of his son's renown.

Now other wraiths, the souls of men outworn,
Stood by with heavy hearts for news of home;
Ajax the son of Télamôn alone

Kept far away, still angry in the ghost
To lose Achilles' armour, set for prize
By lady Thetis, when beside the ships
Pallas Athênê and the sons of Troy
Heard our pretensions, and the vote was mine.
O would to heaven that victory were unwon!
Denied those arms so brave a head went down,—
Ajax, in stature and in war supreme
Of all the Greeks, save Pêleus' noble son.

    Then said I to him with a smooth address:
'Ajax, son of noble Télamôn,
Must you then bear me rancour, even in death,
For that pernicious mail? Surely the gods
To Argos' injury set up that prize,
So strong a tower in your overthrow
Is fallen! All Achaia mourns for you
As for the son of Pêleus when he died,—
Achilles ever-wept. There's none to blame
But Zeus, whose hate for Danaän men-at-arms
Passing imagination, brought your doom.
Do but approach, great Ajax, and give ear,
Listen to word and speech of mine, control
The stubborn humour of your lordly soul.'

    So I: but he, no answer given, withdrew
To darkness, with the souls of men outworn.

T. F. HIGHAM   (XI. 538–64)

47   *Home-coming*

NOW at the hour when brightest shone on high
   The star that comes to herald up the sky
The Dawning of the Morning, even then
The ship sea-travelling to the isle drew nigh.

The fields of Ithaca a haven hold
Called after Phorcys' name, the Sea-God old.
Two jutting headlands breaking sheer in cliff
Stretch seaward, and the harbour-mouth enfold.

These from without keep back the surge and din
Of the great wind-blown billows, and within
May goodly-benchèd galleys all unmoored
Ride, when the chosen anchorage they win.

But at the haven head an olive tree's
Wide-stretching boughs outspread, and nigh to these
A cavern dim and lovely, to the nymphs
Held hallowed that are called the Naïadës.

In it are mixing-bowls and jars of stone
Where the bees build their combs, and high upgrown
Stone looms, whereon the nymphs their marvellous
Raiment of deep sea-purple weave alone.

And in it waters failing not in drouth
Well forth; and twofold is the cavern mouth:
One toward the north accessible to men,
And one diviner facing to the south:

Nor do men enter through it, but that door
Is for immortals. Thither they, of yore
Knowing it well, rowed in the ship full speed
To land, that half her keel's length lay ashore:

So swift she sped beneath the oarsmen's hand;
And from the benchèd ship upon dry land
They leapt and from the ship's hold lifted out
Odysseus first and laid him on the sand,

In linen sheet and broidered blanket gay
Still wrapped, as fast in slumber deep he lay.

J. W. MACKAIL   (XIII. 93–119)

48   *Eumæus the Swineherd*
(*i*) *His Cloak*

NOW the night came on stormy and very dark, for
there was no moon. It poured without ceasing, and
the wind blew strong from the West, which is a wet
quarter, so Ulysses thought he would see whether Eumæus,
in the excellent care he took of him, would take off his own
cloak and give it him, or make one of his men give him
one. 'Listen to me,' said he, 'Eumæus and the rest of you;
when I have said a prayer I will tell you something. It is
the wine that makes me talk in this way; wine will make
even a wise man fall to singing; it will make him chuckle
and dance and say many a word that he had better leave
unspoken; still, as I have begun, I will go on. Would that
I were still young and strong as when we got up an ambuscade before Troy. Menelâus and Ulysses were the leaders,
but I was in command also, for the other two would have
it so. When we had come up to the wall of the city we
crouched down beneath our armour and lay there under
cover of the reeds and thick brushwood that grew about
the swamp. It came on to freeze with a North wind blowing; the snow fell small and fine like hoar frost, and our
shields were coated thick with rime. The others had all
got cloaks and shirts, and slept comfortably enough with
their shields about their shoulders, but I had carelessly left
my cloak behind me, not thinking that I should be too
cold, and had gone off in nothing but my shirt and shield.

When the night was two-thirds through and the stars had shifted their places, I nudged Ulysses who was close to me with my elbow, and he at once gave me his ear.

'"Ulysses," said I, "this cold will be the death of me, for I have no cloak; some god fooled me into setting off with nothing on but my shirt, and I do not know what to do."

'Ulysses, who was as crafty as he was valiant, hit upon the following plan:

'"Keep still," said he in a low voice, "or the others will hear you." Then he raised his head on his elbow. "My friends," said he, "I have had a dream from heaven in my sleep. We are a long way from the ships; I wish some one would go down and tell Agamemnon to send us up more men at once."

'On this Thoäs son of Andræmon threw off his cloak and set out running to the ships, whereon I took the cloak and lay in it comfortably enough till morning. Would that I were still young and strong as I was in those days, for then some one of you swineherds would give me a cloak both out of good will and for the respect due to a brave soldier; but now people look down upon me because my clothes are shabby.'

And Eumæus answered, 'Old man, you have told us an excellent story, and have said nothing so far but what is quite satisfactory; for the present, therefore, you shall want neither clothing nor anything else that a stranger in distress may reasonably expect, but to-morrow morning you will have to shake your own old rags about your body again, for we have not many spare cloaks nor shirts up here, but every man has only one. When Ulysses' son comes home again he will give you both cloak and shirt, and send you wherever you may want to go.'

With this he got up and made a bed for Ulysses by throwing some goatskins and sheepskins on the ground in front of the fire. Here Ulysses lay down, and Eumæus covered him over with a great heavy cloak that he kept for a change in case of extraordinarily bad weather.

Thus did Ulysses sleep, and the young men slept beside him. But the swineherd did not like sleeping away from his pigs, so he got ready to go outside, and Ulysses was glad to see that he looked after his property during his master's absence. First he slung his sword over his brawny shoulders and put on a thick cloak to keep out the wind. He also took the skin of a large and well-fed goat, and a javelin in case of attack from men or dogs. Thus equipped he went to his rest where the pigs were camping under an overhanging rock that gave them shelter from the North wind.

(XIV. 457–533)

(ii) His Story

You may have heard of an island called Syra that lies over above Ortygia, where the land begins to turn round and look in another direction.[1] It is not very thickly peopled, but the soil is good, with much pasture fit for cattle and sheep, and it abounds with wine and wheat. Dearth never comes there, nor are the people plagued by any sickness, but when they grow old Apollo comes with Diana and kills them with his painless shafts. It contains two communities, and the whole country is divided between these two. My father Ctêsius son of Ormenus, a man comparable to the gods, reigned over both.

Now to this place there came some cunning traders from Phœnicia (for the Phœnicians are great mariners) in

[1] Literally: 'where are the turnings of the Sun.' See Notes.

a ship which they had freighted with gewgaws of all kinds. There happened to be a Phœnician woman in my father's house, very tall and comely, and an excellent servant; these scoundrels got hold of her one day when she was washing near the ship, seduced her, and cajoled her in ways that no woman can resist, no matter how good she may be by nature. The man who had seduced her asked her who she was and where she came from, and on this she told him her father's name. 'I come from Sidon,' said she, 'and am daughter to Árybas, a man rolling in wealth. One day as I was coming into the town from the country, some Taphian pirates seized me and took me from here over the sea, where they sold me to the man who owns this house, and he gave them their price for me.'

The man who had seduced her then said, 'Would you like to come along with us to see the house of your parents and your parents themselves? They are both alive and are said to be well off.' 'I will do so gladly,' answered she, 'if you men will first swear me a solemn oath that you will do me no harm by the way.'

They all swore as she told them, and when they had completed their oath the woman said, 'Hush; and if any of your men meets me in the street or at the well, do not let him speak to me, for fear some one should go and tell my master, in which case he would suspect something. He would put me in prison, and would have all of you murdered; keep your own counsel therefore; buy your merchandise as fast as you can, and send me word when you have done loading. I will bring as much gold as I can lay my hands on, and there is something else also that I can do towards paying my fare. I am nurse to the son of the good man of the house, a funny little fellow just able to run about. I will carry him off to your ship, and you will get a great deal of money for him if you take him and sell him in foreign parts.'

On this she went back to the house. The Phœnicians stayed a whole year till they had loaded their ship with much precious merchandise, and then, when they had got freight enough, they sent to tell the woman. Their messenger, a very cunning fellow, came to my father's house bringing a necklace of gold with amber beads strung among it; and while my mother and the servants had it in their hands admiring it and bargaining about it, he made a sign quietly to the woman and then went back to the ship, whereon she took me by the hand and led me out of the house. In the forepart of the house she saw the tables set with the cups of guests who had been feasting with my father, as being in attendance on him; these were now all gone to a meeting of the public assembly, so she snatched up three cups and carried them off in the bosom of her dress, while I followed her, for I knew no better. The sun was now set, and darkness was over all the land, so we hurried on as fast as we could till we reached the harbour, where the Phœnician ship was lying. When they had got on board they sailed their ways over the sea, taking us with them, and Jove sent them a fair wind; six days did we sail both night and day, but on the seventh day Diana struck the woman and she fell heavily down into the ship's hold as though she were a sea gull alighting on the water; so they threw her overboard to the seals and fishes, and I was left all sorrowful and alone. Presently the winds and waves took the ship to Ithaca, where Lâertês gave sundry of his chattels for me, and thus it was that ever I came to set eyes upon this country.

SAMUEL BUTLER   (XV. 403–84)

HE said, and urged him forth, who binding on
    His sandals, to the city bent his way.
Nor went Eumæus from his home unmark'd
By Pallas, who in semblance of a fair
Damsel, accomplish'd in domestic arts,
Approaching to the cottage entrance, stood
Opposite, by Ulysses plain discern'd,
But to his son invisible; for the Gods
Appear not manifest alike to all.
The mastiffs saw her also, and with tone
Querulous hid themselves, yet bark'd they not.
She beckon'd him abroad. Ulysses saw
The sign, and issuing through the outer court,
Approach'd her, whom the Goddess thus bespake:
    'Lâertês' progeny, for wiles renown'd!
Disclose thyself to thy own son, that, death
Concerting and destruction to your foes,
Ye may the royal city seek, nor long
Shall ye my presence there desire in vain,
For I am ardent to begin the fight.'
    Minerva spake, and with her rod of gold
Touch'd him; his mantle, first, and vest she made
Pure as new-blanch'd; dilating, next, his form,
She gave dimensions ampler to his limbs;
Swarthy again his manly hue became,
Round his full face, and black his bushy chin.
The change perform'd, Minerva disappear'd,
And the illustrious Hero turn'd again
Into the cottage; wonder at that sight
Seiz'd on Têlémachus, askance he look'd,

Awe-struck, not unsuspicious of a God,
And in wing'd accents eager thus began:
'Thou art no longer, whom I lately saw,
Nor are thy cloaths, nor is thy port the same.
Thou art a God, I know, and dwell'st in heav'n.
Oh, smile on us, that we may yield thee rites
Acceptable, and present thee golden gifts
Elaborate; ah, spare us, Pow'r divine!'
　　To whom Ulysses, Hero toil-inured:
'I am no God. Why deem'st thou me divine?
I am thy father, for whose sake thou lead'st
A life of woe, by violence oppress'd.'
So saying, he kiss'd his son, while from his cheeks
Tears trickled, tears till then perforce restrained.
Têlémachus (for he believed him not
His father yet) thus, wond'ring, spake again:
'My father, said'st thou? no. Thou art not He,
But some divinity beguiles my soul
With mockeries, to afflict me still the more;
For never mortal man could have so wrought
By his own pow'r; some interposing God
Alone could render thee both young and old,
For old thou wast of late, and foully clad,
But wear'st the semblance, now, of those in heav'n!
　　To whom Ulysses, ever-wise, replied:
'Têlémachus! it is not well, my son!
That thou should'st greet thy father with a face
Of wild astonishment, and stand aghast.
Ulysses, save myself, none comes, be sure.
Such as thou seest, after ten thousand woes
Which I have borne, I visit once again
My native country in the twentieth year.

This wonder Athênæan Pallas wrought,
She cloathed me even with what form she would,
For so she can. Now poor I seem and old,
Now young again, and clad in fresh attire.
The Gods who dwell in yonder heav'n, with ease
Dignify or debase a mortal man.'

    So saying, he sat. Then threw Têlémachus
His arms around his father's neck, and wept.
Desire intense of lamentation seized
On both; soft murmurs uttering, each indulged
His grief, more frequent wailing than the bird,
(Eagle or hook-nail'd vulture) from whose nest
Some swain hath stol'n her yet unfeather'd young.
So from their eyelids they big drops distill'd
Of tenderest grief.

WILLIAM COWPER   (XVI. 154–219)

50   *The Dog Argos*

AS they talked a dog lying there lifted head and pricked
his ears. This was Argos whom Odysseus had bred
but never worked, because he left for Ilium too soon. On
a time the young fellows used to take him out to course the
wild goats, the deer, the hares: but now he lay derelict and
masterless on the dung-heap before the gates, on the deep
bed of mule-droppings and cow-dung which collected
there till the serfs of Odysseus had time to carry it off for
manuring his broad acres. So lay Argos the hound, all
shivering with dog-ticks. Yet the instant Odysseus approached, the beast knew him. He thumped his tail and
drooped his ears forward, but lacked power to drag him-

self ever so little towards his master. However, Odysseus saw him out of the corner of his eye and brushed away a tear, which he covered by quickly saying to Eumæus in an off-hand way:

'Strange, that they let such a hound lie on the dung-hill! What a beauty to look at! though of course I cannot tell if he has speed to match, or is merely one of those show-dogs men prize for their points.' Eumæus answered: 'That is the hound of a man who died far from home. If only he could recover the fire and life that were his when Odysseus left for Troy, how your eyes would open at see-ing such speed and power. Put him on the trail and no quarry ever escaped him, not even in the densest thickets, so keen he was of scent. Now he has fallen low, his master having perished abroad and the heartless women caring for him not at all. Slaves, when their master's control is loosed, do not even wish to work well. Ah, the day a man's enslaved, Zeus robs him of half his virtue!' With this word he plunged into the house, going straight along the hall amidst the suitors; but Argos the dog went down into the blackness of death, that moment he saw Odysseus again after twenty years.

T. E. SHAW (T. E. LAWRENCE)   (XVII. 290–327)

51   *Penelope dreams*

(*i*)

SO said he, and the crone went down the hall
   To fetch fresh water for the bath; for all
The first was spilt; and then her master she
Washed, and with oil anointed therewithal.

Again Odysseus to the hearth drew nigher
His chair, that he might warm him at the fire,
Hiding the scar beneath his rags; and wise
Penelope broke silence to enquire:

'O stranger, yet a little more will I
Make question of you; for the hour is nigh
Of rest, that pleasant is for everyone
Whose sleep is sweet in spite of misery.

'But by God's ordinance my sorrows know
No measure; daylong I pass to and fro
With tears and sighs, while to the house I see
And to my handmaids in the house that go.

'But when night comes and all to bed are gone,
Then sleepless in my bed I lie alone,
And round my full-fraught heart thick-coming cares
Sting me full sharply as I make my moan.

'Even as when the maid of Pandarus,
The greenwood nightingale melodious,
Amid the thickened leafage sits and sings
When the young spring is waxing over us:

'And she with many a note and hurrying trill
Pours forth her liquid voice, lamenting still
Her own son Itylus, King Zêthus' child,
Whom long ago her folly made her kill:

'So alternating makes my mind alway
Division, whether by my child to stay,
And keep the thralls and the inheritance
And the great high-roofed house untouched to-day.

'Holding in reverence my marriage vow
And public honour, or to follow now
Among the Achæan suitors in my halls
Him who is best and will most gifts allow.

'Now for my son, while yet a child was he
And lightly-minded, it might nowise be
That I should wed and leave my husband's house;
But now that he is grown to man's degree,

'Surely he prays that I the house would quit,
Being vexed at heart to see how every whit
The Achæans eat up his inheritance.
Hear this my dream now, and interpret it.

'A score of geese within my house are bred
That come up from the water to be fed
With grain, and I take joy in watching them:
On these an eagle from the mountain-head,

'Huge, crooked-taloned, swooping from on high
Brake all their necks and left them there to lie
Dead in a heap within the house, while he
Soared up again into the shining sky.

'But in my dream I wept and wailed, and then
Came flocking round my fair-tressed townswomen,
As piteously I sorrowed for my geese
Killed by the eagle; until he again

'Returned, and on the jutting roof-beam lit,
And thus with human voice he stayed my fit:
Take courage, far-renowned Îcárius' child,
This is a vision good, no dream is it.

'Hereof a sure fulfilment shall befall:
These geese the wooers are, and I withal,
Who was the eagle, am your lord returned
To deal disastrous death upon them all.

'So spake he, and the sweet sleep rose from me;
And round the palace looking narrowly
I saw the geese there, feeding on their corn
Beside the trough where they were wont to be.'

And subtle-souled Odysseus answering spake:
'Lady, one may not vary nor mistake
The dream's interpretation, that himself
Odysseus told, and good his word will make.

'And on the suitors is foreshown to be
Destruction, nor shall one among them flee
Death and the weird appointed.' Then once more
Spake and made answer wise Penelope:

'O guest, of dreams may no man living know
The true interpretation, or foreshow
Their issue, nor do all of them come true:
For bodiless dreams through double gateways go,

'Of horn and ivory, from night's realm forlorn;
And those that through the ivory gate are borne
Deceive, and what they tell is unfulfilled;
But those that issue through the polished horn

'Fulfil themselves for mortals to whose sight
They issue; but not thence, I deem, that night
Issued that dream of boding, though to me
And to my son it were a dear delight.

116

'And this besides I tell, for you to lay
To heart and ponder: the disastrous day
That from Odysseus' house shall sunder me
Is even now at hand upon its way.

'I now the suitors to that feat will call
Of axes, that he used to set in hall
Twelve in a row, like a ship-stays, and far back
Standing would shoot an arrow through them all.

'Now therefore to the suitors I will show
This feat; and whoso in his hands the bow
Shall bend most easily, and down the line
Of the twelve axes make the arrow go,

'Him will I follow, putting far from me
This house of my espousals, fair to see
And full of substance, that I think in dreams
I shall remember through the days to be.'

And subtle-souled Odysseus thus begun:
'O wedded lady of Lâertês' son
Odysseus, now delay no more to set
This feat within the palace to be done.

'For subtle-souled Odysseus shall again
Come to this house ere one of these attain
Handling that polished bow, to stretch the cord
And send an arrow down the iron lane.'

J. W. MACKAIL   (XIX. 503–87)

117

(ii)

BUT when her heart had had its fill of weeping,
  To Artemis first that star of women prayed:
   'Dread goddess Artemis, thou maid of Zeus,
Would that this very hour thou mightest fix
Thine arrow in my breast and take my life!
Or else I would a storm might snatch me up
And sweep me headlong down the murky ways,
And cast me forth into the outgoings
Of backward-flowing Ocean; as when once
The storm-winds bore Pandareus' daughters off.
The gods had slain their parents, and at home
Were they left orphaned; Aphrodîtê fair
Stayed them with curds and honey and sweet wine,
And Hêrê gave them over all their kind
Wisdom and beauty, and white Artemis
Made them grow stately, and Athênê trained them
To mastery of noble crafts. But while
Fair Aphrodîtê was upon her way
To high Olympus to implore the crown
Of happy marriage for the maids (she went
To Zeus the thunder-lord, for well he knows
All things—the happiness and haplessness
Alike of mortal men), in that same hour
The spirits of the storm bore off the girls
And gave them to the horrible Avengers
To serve them. Even so I would that they
Who have Olympus for their habitation
Would blot me out, or fair-haired Artemis
Would smite me, so that dreaming on Odysseus
I might depart, yea, 'neath the hateful earth,

Nor ever make a meaner man's heart glad!
Ah well, a tolerable woe hath he,
Whoever weeps all day with heart sore vexed,
But falls asleep o' nights; for sleep makes us
Forget all things, both good and bad, when once
It folds the eyelids. But to me the god
Sends evil dreams as well: for this same night
I dreamt there lay beside me one like him,
Such as he was when with the host he went;
And then my heart rejoiced, because I thought it
A gleam of truth at last, and not a dream.'

E'en as she spoke, came Dawn the golden-throned.
But good Odysseus heard her as she wept.

SIR WILLIAM MARRIS   (XX. 59–92)

52   *The Vision of Theoclýmenus*

UPON these words of Télémachus, Pallas Athênê fired
the suitors to a laughter that ran on and on till it
crazed them out of their wits. Now they were laughing
with mouths that were not their own, while blood oozed
from the flesh they ate. Their eyes filled with tears and
their souls were racked in agony. Godlike Theoclýmenus
wailed aloud, 'O unhappy men, what is this horror come
upon you? A night shrouds your heads, your faces: it
creeps down to your knees. Weeping and wailing flash
back and forth. Cheeks stream with tears and a dew of
blood beads over the smooth wall-panels. Ghostly forms
throng the entrance and pack the hall itself, shuffling in
long file through the murk towards hell. The sun is lost
out of heaven and a dire gloom prevails.'

Laughter rang loud from the company as he unburdened himself, and Eurýmachus son of Pólybus rose to say, 'Our new-come visitor from alien parts has lost his senses. Quick, young men, escort him out and to the market-place. He fancies it is black night here.' Theoclýmenus retorted, 'Eurýmachus, I want none of your guiding. Eyes I have and ears, my two feet and a spirit not of the meanest. In their power will I pass the threshold, for I feel that evil—evil not to be shunned or avoided—looms over each single one of you suitors whose brutal and perverse imaginings pollute the house of Odysseus.' He quitted the hall, to receive honest welcome from Peiræus in his house.

T. E. SHAW (T. E. LAWRENCE)   (XX. 345-72)

53   *The Slaying*

(i)

SO he spake, and all the Wooers laughed on him pleasantly,
And their bitter wrath against him they laid aside withal.
And in that while the swineherd bare the bow adown the hall,
And drawing anear to Odysseus in his hands the weapons laid.
Then he called forth the nurse, Euryclêa, and spake to her and said:
'Euryclêa, thou the heart-wise, Têlémachus biddeth thee
That the hall-doors closely-fitting thou shut and lock with a key;
And if any hear a groaning, or the noise of men and the din
Amidst our walls, in nowise go ye outdoors from within,

But there abide in silence beside the work ye speed.'

So he spake; and his word was wingless and abode with her
    for her heed,

And she locked with a key the doors of the halls of the
    lovely stead.

And silently forth from the house meanwhile had Philœtius
    sped,

And therewith he bolted the gate of the well-walled fore-
    court there;

But there lay beneath the cloister a curved ship's mooring-
    gear,

A flax-wrought rope, and therewith he bound o'er the gate
    of the close,

And then gat him aback and sat down on the bench whence
    he erewhile arose,

And set his eyes on Odysseus, who as now the great bow
    bare,

And was turning it over on all sides, and trying it here and
    there,

Lest the worms its horn should have eaten while long was
    its master away,

And one would be eyeing his neighbour, and thuswise
    would he say:

'Lo here, a lover of bows, one cunning in archery!

Or belike in his house at home e'en such-like gear doth lie;

Or e'en such an one is he minded to fashion, since handling
    it still,

He turneth it o'er, this gangrel, this crafty one of ill!'

And then would another be saying of those younglings
    haughty and high:

'E'en so soon and so great a measure of gain may he
    come by

As he may now accomplish the bending of the bow.'

So the Wooers spake; but Odysseus, that many a rede did
    know,

When the great bow he had handled, and eyed it about and
    along,

Then straight, as a man well learnèd in the lyre and the song,

On a new pin lightly stretcheth the cord, and maketh fast,

From side to side the sheep-gut well-twined and overcast:

So the mighty bow he bended with no whit of labouring,

And caught it up in his right hand, and fell to try the string,

That 'neath his hand sang lovely as a swallow's voice is fair.

But great grief fell on the Wooers, and their skin changed
    colour there,

And mightily Zeus thundered, and made manifest a sign;

And thereat rejoiced Odysseus, the toil-stout man divine,

At that sign of the Son of Cronus, the crookèd-counselled
    Lord;

And he caught up a swift arrow that lay bare upon the
    board,

Since in the hollow quiver as yet the others lay,

Which those men of the Achæans should taste ere long that
    day,

And he laid it on the bow-bridge, and the nock and the
    string he drew,

And thence from his seat on the settle he shot a shaft that
    flew

Straight-aimed, and of all the axes missed not a single head,

From the first ring: through and through them, and out at
    the last it sped

The brass-shod shaft; and therewith to Têlémachus spake
    he:

'The guest in thine halls a-sitting in nowise shameth thee,

Têlémachus. I missed not thy mark, nor overlong

Toiled I the bow a-bending; stark yet am I and strong.

Forsooth, the Wooers that shamed me no more may make
    me scorn!

But now for these Achæans is the hour and the season
    born

To dight the feast in the daylight, and otherwise to be fain

With the song and the harp thereafter that crown the
    banquet's gain.'

So he spake; and with bent brow nodded, and Têlémachus
    the lord,

Dear son of the godlike Odysseus, girt on his whetted
    sword;

His dear hand gripped the spear-shaft, and his father's side
    anear,

He stood by the high-seat crested with the gleaming brazen
    gear.

But Odysseus of many a rede of his rags he stripped him
    bare,

And on the great threshold he leapt, and the bow, and the
    quiver fair

Fulfilled of arrows he handled, and all the shafts to the
    ground

Before his feet then poured he, and spake to those Wooers
    around:

'Thuswise then is accomplished the strife so hard to do;

Now another mark will I loose at that no man hath hit
    hitherto,

If I perchance may attain it, and so fame of Apollo be
    earned.'

So spake, and the bitter shaft on Antinoüs then he turned.

                                        (XXI. 376—XXII. 8)

(ii)

But about his house peered Odysseus, if yet a man
there were
Who shunning the black doom-day was left a-lurking
there;
But adown in the dust and the blood he beheld them all
lying about
Yea, as many as the fishes which the fishers have drawn out
With a net of many meshes from out the hoary sea
Up on to the hollow sea-beach; there heaped up all they be
Cast up upon the sea-sand, desiring the waves of the brine;
But the sun their life is taking with the glory of his shine.
Thus then in heaps the Wooers on one another lay.

Then at last into Têlémachus did all-wise Odysseus say:
'Têlémachus, go and call thou the nurse Euryclêa here,
That somewhat I may tell her which on my mind I bear.'
So he spake, and Têlémachus straightway his lovèd father
obeyed,
And smote on the door and a word to the nurse Euryclêa
said:
'Up hither, O ancient of days, who over the women-
thralls
Art ever the ward and the watcher within our house and
halls;
Come! for my father calls thee, and hath a word to tell.'
So he spake; and the word was wingless, and by her yet
did dwell,
And therewith she opened the doors of the hall of the
pleasant place,
And went her ways; but the youngling led on before her
face.

And there she found Odysseus amidst the men dead slain,
With blood and gore bedabbled, as a lion stalketh amain,
Who cometh from devouring an ox of the meadowy place,
And all his breast is bloody and either side his face,
And fearful is he fashioned to look upon with eyes:
So befouled were the feet of Odysseus and his hands in
  e'en such wise.
But she, when she saw the corpses and that abundant
  blood,
Was setting up a joy-shout, so great seemed the work and
  so good;
But Odysseus refrained and withheld her, though yearning
  sore indeed,
And sent his voice out toward her, and this winged word
  fell to speed:
'Rejoice in thy soul, O goodwife, and thy shout of joy
  refrain,
For nowise is it righteous to boast above the slain.
But these men the Fate of the Gods and their wanton
  deeds did quell,
Whereas they honoured no man of men on the earth that
  dwell,
Were he good or were he evil, whosoever came their way.
So through their wanton folly met they loathly end to-day.'

WILLIAM MORRIS   (XXII. 381–416)

54 *Penelope makes Trial of Odysseus*

HE sat down opposite his wife on the seat he had left.
'My dear,' said he, 'heaven has endowed you with a
heart more unyielding than woman ever yet had. No other
woman could bear to keep away from her husband when

he had come back to her after twenty years of absence, and after having gone through so much. But come, nurse, get a bed ready for me; I will sleep alone, for this woman has a heart as hard as iron.'

'My dear,' answered Penelope, 'I have no wish to set myself up, nor to depreciate you; but I am not struck by your appearance, for I very well remember what kind of a man you were when you set sail from Ithaca. Nevertheless, Euryclêa, take his bed outside the bed-chamber that he himself built. Bring the bed outside this room, and put bedding upon it with fleeces, good coverlets, and blankets.'

She said this to try him, but Ulysses was very angry and said, 'Wife I am much displeased at what you have just been saying. Who has been taking my bed from the place in which I left it? He must have found it a hard task, no matter how skilled a workman he was, unless some god came and helped him to shift it. There is no man living, however strong and in his prime, who could move it from its place, for it is a marvellous curiosity which I made with my very own hands. There was a young olive growing within the precincts of the house, in full vigour, and about as thick as a bearing-post. I built my room round this with strong walls of stone and a roof to cover them, and I made the doors strong and well-fitting. Then I cut off the top boughs of the olive tree and left the stump standing. This I dressed roughly from the root upwards and then worked with carpenter's tools well and skilfully, straightening my work by drawing a line on the wood, and making it into a bed-prop. I then bored a hole down the middle, and made it the centre-post of my bed, at which I worked till I had finished it, inlaying it with gold and silver; after this I stretched a hide of crimson leather from one side of it to the other. So you see I know all about it, and I desire to learn whether it is still there, or whether anyone has been removing it by cutting down the olive tree at its roots.'

When she heard the sure proofs Ulysses now gave her, she fairly broke down. She flew weeping to his side, flung her arms about his neck, and kissed him. 'Do not be angry with me, Ulysses,' she cried, 'you, who are the wisest of mankind. We have suffered, both of us. Heaven has denied us the happiness of spending our youth, and of growing old, together; do not then be aggrieved or take it amiss that I did not embrace you thus as soon as I saw you. I have been shuddering all the time through fear that some one might come here and deceive me with a lying story; for there are many very wicked people going about. Jove's daughter Helen would never have yielded herself to a man from a foreign country, if she had known that the sons of Achæans would come after her and bring her back. Heaven put it in her heart to do wrong, and she gave no thought to that sin, which has been the source of all our sorrows. Now, however, that you have convinced me by showing that you know all about our bed (which no human being has ever seen but you and I and a single maidservant, the daughter of Actor, who was given me by my father on my marriage, and who keeps the doors of our room) hard of belief though I have been I can mistrust no longer.'

Then Ulysses in his turn melted, and wept as he clasped his dear and faithful wife to his bosom. As the sight of land is welcome to men who are swimming towards the shore, when Neptune has wrecked their ship with the fury of his winds and waves; a few alone reach the land, and these, covered with brine, are thankful when they find them-

selves on firm ground and out of danger—even so was
her husband welcome to her as she looked upon him, and
she could not tear her two fair arms from about his neck.

SAMUEL BUTLER   (XXIII. 164–240)

55   *The Last Journey of the Wooers*

AND now Cyllênian Hermês summon'd forth
    The spirits of the suitors; waving wide
The golden wand of power to seal all eyes
In slumber, and to ope them wide again,
He drove them gibbering down into the shades,
As when the bats within some hallow'd cave
Flit squeaking all around, for if but one
Fall from the rock, the rest all follow him,
In such connexion mutual they adhere;
So, after bounteous Mercury, the ghosts
Troop'd downward gibbering all the dreary way.
The Ocean's flood and the Leucadian rock,
The Sun's gate also and the land of Dreams
They pass'd, whence next into the meads they came
Of Asphodel, by shadowy forms possess'd,
Simulars of the dead.

WILLIAM COWPER   (XXIV. 1–14)

56   *Lâertês*

(*i*)

WITH that he gave the thralls his battle-gear.
      Then quickly to the house they went, while he
Drew near the fruitful vineyard on his quest.
He found not Dólius there, as he went down

128

Through the big plot, nor any of his sons
Or slaves. It chanced that they had gone to gather
Stones for the vineyard wall, and the old man
Was at their head. And so he found his father
Alone, in the well-ordered vineyard, digging
About a plant, clad in a filthy coat
Patched and unseemly; and around his shins
Were laced a pair of mended ox-hide leggings
To save him from the scratches; and he wore
Gloves on his hands by reason of the thorns,
And on his head he had a goat-skin cap;
And so he nursed his grief. But when Odysseus,
That sore-tried goodly man, saw him with age
So worn, and in such grief of heart, he stood
Beneath a pear-tree tall and shed a tear.

(XXIV. 219–34)

(ii)

Thereat Lâertês answered him and said:
'If thou art verily my son Odysseus,
Come home again, now tell me of some sign
Infallible, so that I may be sure.'
　　Then deep Odysseus answered him and said:
'Look first on this scar and consider it,
Where the boar ripped me with his gleaming tusk,
Upon Parnassus, whither I had gone.
Thou and my honoured mother, ye had sent me
Unto Autólycus, my mother's father,
To get the gifts which on his coming hither
He promised and agreed to give me. But
Come, I will tell thee also of the trees

Through all this ordered garden, which of old
Thou gavest me when I was but a child
Begging for this and that, and following thee
All through the garden. 'Twas these very trees
That we were passing, and thou toldest me
The name and kind of each, and gavest me
Thirteen pear-trees, ten apple-trees, and figs
Two score; and fifty rows of vines as well
Thou namedst as the ones which I should have,
Whereof each row ripened successively,
Bearing all sorts of clusters, whensoe'er
Zeus' seasons from above weighed down on them.'
    E'en as he spoke, his father's knees and heart
Were loosed, to recognize the certain signs
Odysseus told him; and he cast his arms
Round his dear son, and steadfast good Odysseus
Caught up his father fainting unto him.

SIR WILLIAM MARRIS   (XXIV. 327–48)

HESIOD

(Date unknown)

57   *Pandôra*

FROM men the source of life has been hidden well.
  Else you would lightly do enough work in a day
to keep you the rest of the year while you lounged at
    play.
Over the smoke you'd store your rudder in haste,
no oxen or sturdy mules would reclaim the waste.
But the source was hidden by Zeus, in the rage of his
    heart,
because Promêtheus tricked him with cunning art.

Therefore he planned for men a grief and a bane.
Fire he concealed. But the good Promêtheus again
stole it from counsellor Zeus in a hollow reed—
stole it for men while the Thunderer paid no heed.

Then Zeus, who gathers the clouds, in anger cried:
'Son of Îápetos, craftiest one, in your pride
you rejoice at your theft, you have made me a thing of
			your scorn,
and won a plague for yourself and for men yet unborn.
For I shall give men an evil as price of fire:
they will clasp destruction with laughter of desire.'

So cried the Father of gods and men, and laughed.
He bade Hêphaistos to mingle clay with craft,
giving it power of limb and speech, and to trace
the tender and darling shape of a girl with the face
of a goddess. Athênê he bade to add to the mould
all skill with the needle and loom; Aphrodîtê the Gold
to shed on the image, along with the gifts that please,
cruel lust, and shattering anxieties.
And Hermês, the Guide, the Slayer of Argos, he bade
to fix a deceitful heart in the shameless maid.

So the son of Kronos spoke, and they turned to obey.
At once the famous Lame-god moulded the clay
till the shape of a modest maiden was duly shown.
Bright-eyed Athênê draped her and fastened the zone.
The Graces and lady Persuasion laced her with gold,
and the Hours, who came with their lovely tresses, were
			told
to deck her with flowers of the spring as a garlanded bride.
And the Herald of gods, the Slayer of Argos, the Guide,

put lies and intricate cunning and lack of shame
deep in her heart, and gave her *Pandôra* for name,
for all the Olympian gods had their bounty shed—
a dower of plagues for mortals, eaters of bread.

When the image was made, a sheer inescapable snare,
the Father sent Hermês (who swiftly wings through the
    air,
the Argos-slayer) to offer the maid thus adorned
to Epimêtheus, who forgot what his brother had warned:
'Accept no gift from Zeus. Be sure to refuse,
for something harmful to mortals may lurk in the ruse.'

O he took the gift, and through suffering learned what
    he'd done.
Till now in peace all the days of the earth had run;
the tribes of men had been saved from the toil that
    drives,
and disease that flings the swarming Fates on our lives.
But Pandôra lifted the jar's great lid, and then
its plagues were scattered abroad, with mischief for men.

Only Hope remained, entrapped for evermore,
under the rim of the jar; through the open door
she'd failed to escape; and now she's imprisoned fast.
All else, a numberless plague, on the world were cast,
and earth is full of evil, and full is the sea,
by day diseases are here, and the night's not free—
countless, assailing our lives, forever they come
in silence; for Zeus in his wisdom left them dumb.

JACK LINDSAY   (*Works and Days*, 42–104)

58   *The Five Ages*

THE gods who own Olympus as dwelling-place,
   deathless, made first of mortals a Golden Race,
(this was the time when Kronos in heaven dwelt),
and they lived like gods and no sorrow of heart they felt.
Nothing for toil or pitiful age they cared,
but in strength of hand and foot still unimpaired
they feasted gaily, undarkened by sufferings.
They died as if falling asleep; and all good things
were theirs, for the fruitful earth unstintingly bore
unforced her plenty, and they, amid their store
enjoyed their landed ease which nothing stirred,
loved by the gods and rich in many a herd.

But in time the earth received and hid them away,
and now the pure spirits, haunting earth, are they,
kindly deliverers, watchers, by whom men live
in wealth, for that royal gift is theirs to give.

Next the immortals, who dwell on Olympus, made
a second race, of Silver, greatly decayed.
Neither in body nor thoughts were they like the Gold.
On his mother's skirt each frolicking child would hold,
a fatuous oaf, till a hundred years were past.
But when they had grown and attained their prime at last,
their lives were brief, yet wretched with folly; for still
they could not desist from sinning with cankered will
and wronging each other. Aye, scorn for the heavens they
      showed
and refused to the holy altars what victims were owed.
(Such service is owed by each race wherever they dwell.)
So Zeus was wroth, and the Race of Silver fell

for scorning the gods who hold Olympus in sway,
and in time the earth received and hid them away,
and under the earth they are blessèd shades, and there,
though second in rank, a kind of honour they share.

Then Zeus the Father again made humankind,
a breed of Bronze, far differently designed,
a breed from the Ash-tree sprung, huge-limbed and
      dread,
lovers of battle and horror, no eaters of bread.
Their hearts were hard, their adamant hearts: none stood
to meet their power of limb and their hardihood
and the swing of the terrible arms their shoulders bore.
Bronze were their homes, bronze the armour they wore,
and their tools; for no dark iron supplied their needs.
And they murdered one another with violent deeds
and down to the house of dank chill Hades they went
and left no name. In black Death's grasp they spent
their turbulence, and lost the land of day,
and in time the earth received and hid them away.

Again on the bountiful earth by heaven was sent
a worthier race; on righteous deeds they were bent,
divine, heroic—as demigods they are known,
and the boundless earth had their race before our own.
Some of them met grim war and its battle-fates:
in the land of Kadmos at Thebes with seven gates
they fought for Œdipus' flocks disastrously,
or were drawn to cross the gulf of mighty sea
for sake of Helen tossing her beautiful hair,
and death was the sudden shroud that wrapped them
      there.

But for some by grace of Zeus a fertile ground
apart from men, at the ends of the earth was found;
and there they dwell with never a care distressed,
by deep-swirled Ocean, safe in isles of the blest:
delighted heroes for whom in the fields of corn
honey-fruit thrice in the year is lusciously born.

Fifth is the race that I call my own and abhor.
O to die, or be later born, or born before!
This is the Race of Iron. Dark is their plight.
Toil and sorrow by day are theirs, and by night
the anguish of death; and the gods afflict them and kill,
though there's yet a trifle of good amid manifold ill.
And Zeus will smash them in turn on his chosen day,
when children at birth show heads already grown grey.

Father and child will quarrel and bring the end,
guest with host will quarrel, and friend with friend.
No brother will claim from brother the love once claimed,
and parents will quickly age, dishonoured and shamed,
and men will scorn them and bitter words they'll say,
hard-hearted, no longer god-fearing. They'll not repay
the cost of their nurture, but might their right they'll call,
and ravaging men will break through a city-wall.
No favour will then be found for the true or the just
or the good, but men will praise the creature of lust
and violence. Might will rule while decency dies.
Giving false witness and swearing to any lies,
the wicked will trick the worthy and strike them down.
Envy, that's foul of the mouth and dark with a frown,
will dog all mortals, for evil is his delight.
Down the broad paths of the earth for Olympus-height,

135

forsaking the human race for the gods, in flight
with beautiful bodies veiled in their robes of white,
Forbearance and Righteous Wrath will depart, and leave
evil too great to resist, and mortals who grieve.

JACK LINDSAY   (*Works and Days*, 109–23, 126–201)

59   *Wholesome Strife*

POTTER'S at odds with potter,
    Builder at builder fleers;
There's strife among the beggars
    And bards are by the ears.

SIR WILLIAM MARRIS   (*Works and Days*, 25–6)

60   *Plain Living*

FOOLS, to ignore how much the more
        the half is than the whole;
How greatly kail and leek avail
        to profit a man's soul.

SIR WILLIAM MARRIS   (*Works and Days*, 40–1)

61   *Might and Right*

                         (*i*)

NOW shall I tell a tale to kings
    Who know themselves the truth of things.
Thus said a falcon, who had caught
A nightingale of speckled throat

136

Fast in his claws, and borne his prey
High up among the clouds away,
While on his crooked claws impaled
Most piteously she wept and wailed;
To her said he in haughty tone:
'Unreasonable wretch, why moan?
Your captor is the stronger far,
And therefore, songstress though you are,
Where'er I take you, must you go:
And I shall eat, or set you free
Just as I choose. Insane is he
Who with his betters tries a throw.
He cannot win, and suffers woe
Besides dishonour.' So averred
The darting hawk, that long-winged bird.

(Works and Days, 202–12)

(*ii*)

O Princes, take ye also thought
Of wrath laid up: the gods are close
To men, and mark how they abuse
Each other with perverse awards,
And hold the wrath of heaven as nought.
For on the bounteous earth doth Zeus
Keep thrice ten thousand spirit guards
To watch o'er mortal men, and these
Invisible in a cloak of mist,
Patrolling earth, where'er they list,
Requite harsh doings and decrees.

(Works and Days, 248–55)

(iii)

He hurts himself who aims
His fellow-man to gall:
For wicked plotting maims
The plotter most of all.

SIR WILLIAM MARRIS (*Works and Days*, 265–6)

62 *Shame*

NOW shame can hurt men mightily
and help them too;
But shame that goes with poverty
is all to rue.

SIR WILLIAM MARRIS (*Works and Days*, 317–18)

63 *Neighbours and Kinsfolk*

CALL him who loves you to your feast;
Leave out a foe. By no means least
Invite a man whose house is near;
For if upon a place comes hurt,
The neighbours hurry out ungirt
But kinsmen dawdle o'er their gear.

SIR WILLIAM MARRIS (*Works and Days*, 342–5)

64 *Giving and Taking*

BEFRIEND the friends you have, and go
To him who comes to you. Bestow
Your gifts on whoso gives: to him
Who grudges, give not. Men endow

Munificent, not niggard, palms.
Bounty is excellent, but grim
Is theft, and bringeth death as alms.

SIR WILLIAM MARRIS   (*Works and Days*, 353–6)

65   *Spending and Sparing*

WHEN the jar is just begun,
    When the jar is nearly done,
       Drink at ease;
Halfway down it, drink with care;
'Tis poor husbandry to spare
       Of the lees.

SIR WILLIAM MARRIS   (*Works and Days*, 368–9)

66   *Marriage*

BRING not a wife to your home too soon or too late.
Wait till you're thirty, but don't thereafter wait;
thirty's the age. And give her, as rightly you should,
four ripening years, her first of womanhood.
Choose out a virgin, and then you will be obeyed,
teaching her thrift. Make sure with a neighbouring
    maid,
but watch if people grin when you name her for wife.
She's best of all prizes, or worst of all horrors in life—
a sly greedy-guts, a woman who'll drag you down
and need no fire at all to be roasting you brown;
strong you may be, but unripe you'll shrivel away.

JACK LINDSAY   (*Works and Days*, 695–705)

67   *The Farmer's Year*

(i) The Sign of the Pleiads

WHEN first the Pleiads, children of Atlas, arise,
    begin your harvest: plough, when they quit the
    skies.
For two score days they are hidden, and nights two score,
and soon as the sickle is sharpened appear once more.
Here's a rule of the plains, a rule that the farmer obeys
who dwells by the coast, or in winding valley ways
far from the heaving sea, where the soil is deep:
'Strip you to sow and to plough, and strip to reap.'
So do, if a timely harvest be your care
of fruits by Dêmêter given. For each prepare
a timely increase against your hour of need,—
or beg at another's door, and none shall heed.

T. F. HIGHAM   (*Works and Days,* 383–95)

(ii) When the Crane flies South

MARK, when you hear aloft in the clouds of the sky,
    crying her yearly cry of warning, the crane!
She gives the signal for ploughing and heralds the rain
of winter, but makes the oxless farmer mourn.
Go then and feed in the byre your crumple-horn.

'Lend me your oxen and waggon,' it's easy to say.
It's easy to answer, 'I've work for my oxen to-day.'
The dreamer thinks that his waggon is built, but his wits
betray him. A waggon needs timber, a hundred bits!
See that you have them prepared, each one, in your store.

As soon as the time of ploughing's announced once more,
make haste, yourself and your slaves, in wet and in dry,
to plough the land ere the time for ploughing goes by.
Early to work! and thick will your harvest be found.
Plough in the spring, or in summer break fallow-ground.
The fallow ought to be sown while the soil is light,
the fallow puts children to sleep and troubles to flight.

And pray to Zeus of the Earth and Dêmêter the Pure
that the holy grain of Dêmêter's crop may be sure,
when first you plough, when you grasp the handle and
        wield
your stick on the backs of the oxen that draw down the field
the pole of the plough by the yoke-straps; and, as you go,
let a slave make trouble for birds in your rear with a hoe
by hiding the seeds. Good husbandry still is the first
of blessings: of evils bad husbandry still is the worst.

   Then the fat ears of the corn will bow to the soil
if but the Olympian smiles and completes your toil.
You'll clear your bins of cobwebs; I make no doubt,
your heart will be glad as you serve your substance out.
In ease you'll await grey spring, with unenvious eyes,
and it's others will come and be begging with thriftless
        sighs.

But if at the solstice you furrow the trusty land,
sitting you'll reap, and grasp all your grain in your hand;
dusty, with criss-cross sheaves, a figure of woe,
one basket-load on your back, unregarded you'll go.

Yet Zeus of the Buckler at times varies his will,
and mortal men with their guess can misread it still.

One chance there is of redemption for late-ploughing folk.
When first the cuckoo calls from the leaves of the oak
and over the boundless earth spreads merry hours,
if three days later Zeus will send you showers
to fill the print of an ox-hoof and then to stop,
the late-sown fields as well as the early will crop.
Keep all these facts in your mind. Be ready again
for the coming of grey-husked spring and the season of
    ráin.

JACK LINDSAY   (*Works and Days*, 448–92)

(*iii*) *Winter*

BEWARE the month of Lênaion—foul days, all of
them, of sharp air that would flay an ox; beware the
cruel hoar-frosts that Bóreas brings when he blows upon
the face of the earth.

Over Thrace the land of horses he blows, and breathes
upon the wide sea and lifts it up. Earth also and her
forests bellow aloud.

On many a high-crested oak he falls, and on many a
thick-set fir. In hollows of the hills he lays them low; they
are brought to the earth's rich lap, and the huge wood is
all in uproar.

Wild beasts shiver and set their tails between their legs.
Some have pelts that are thick with fur; but even so the
cold wind pierces their shaggy breasts.

Through hide of ox he goes, it does not stay him; and
through the fine hairs of the goat, but not through fleeces
of sheep. Because their wool is abundant, Bóreas, that
mighty wind, pierces them not at all. But the old man is
bent before him, like a wheel.

Neither does he pierce the tender skin of a girl, while yet she keeps to the house at her mother's side, unschooled by golden Aphrodîtê.

Carefully she bathes her gentle body and anoints it with olive oil; and so will go to her bed in a room withdrawn.

For then is the season of winter, when the Boneless One[1] gnaws his foot in a fireless home and habitations of sorry comfort; nor does the sun beckon him forth where he may feed, but wheels about over land and city of the Black Men and shines less readily upon the Hellene race.

Then too wild creatures of the woods, horned and hornless, whimper for misery as they flee through the forest dales. No thought is theirs but to find shelter in thick coverts or the hollow of a rock.

Feeble then as a three-legged mortal,[2] as one back-broken and staring towards the ground, they go about to escape the white snow.

Then wrap yourself up, as I bid you, in a soft cloak and a tunic of body-length; and look to the making, that the weft be thick and the warp spare.

This take, and clothe yourself, that the hairs of your body may lie at rest and not start up on end.

And bind sandals upon your feet, cut to measure from the hide of a slaughtered ox, and stuffed with a lining of felt.

Take also, when the cold season comes, the skins of firstling kids, and stitch them together with ox-sinew, to shield your back against the rain.

And wear on your head a hat made up of felt, to keep your ears dry.

For morning strikes cold, once Bóreas is upon us; and

---

[1] The Polypus.　　　　[2] One who walks with a stick.

at morning also a mist comes down from the heaven of
stars.

Upon the fields of the rich it is spread, and nurtures the
corn.

Sucked from the ever flowing rivers and raised high
aloft by the stormy wind, sometimes it turns to rain towards evening; and sometimes to wind, when Thracian
Bóreas packs cloud upon cloud.

T. F. HIGHAM   (*Works and Days*, 504–53)

(iv) *When the Snail climbs*

WHEN the snail quits the earth and gets up into the
plants, flying before the Pleiads, this will be no
season for hoeing vines; you should then be sharpening
your sickles and bidding your servants bestir themselves.
Let there be no sitting in the shade nor lying abed in the
morning during harvest time, when the sun is scorching
hot; you should then be busy getting your harvest in, and
should rise at dawn if you would have plenty, for the third
part of the day's work should be got through in the small
hours of the morning, for Dawn speeds a man on his way
and in his work; many a man does she start on a journey,
and on the neck of many an ox does she set the yoke.

SAMUEL BUTLER   (*Works and Days*, 571–81)

(v) *Cicada Days*

WHEN the cardoon flowers, and the loud cicada sings
perched on a tree, pouring from under his wings
a flood of shrillest music time and again:
when summer is ripe, and the heat a burden of pain,

144

then are the she-goats fattest, and wine is best,
and women most fain; but men are languidest,
for Sîrius parches the heads and the knees of men
and burns their bodies with drouth. O give me then
the shade of a rock, with Biblis' wine set by,
and bread of the best, and the milk of goats drained dry!
Then be that heifer chosen to make my meat
that has not calved but feeds in the greenwood yet,
and firstling kids! Bright wine for my plenishment
I'd drink, in the shade, when food has brought content;
and there, as I sit, briskly the West should blow
meeting my brow; and from the unsullied flow
of some spring-water for ever running past
three cups to the gods I'd pour: of wine a last.

T. F. Higham   (*Works and Days,* 582–96)

(vi) Sailing Weather

THE best time for making a voyage is during the fifty
days that follow upon the solstice, when summer is
drawing to a close. You will not wreck your ship at that
season, nor will the sea drown your men, unless Neptune
lord of the earthquake sets himself to wreck you, or Jove
king of the immortals compasses your destruction, for the
issues of good or evil are in their hands. At that season the
winds are steady and the sea safe; you can therefore draw
your ship into the water in confidence, relying upon the
winds, and get your cargo duly within her, but come home
again as fast as you can; do not wait for the new wine, nor
for the autumn rain and the beginning of winter with the
great gales that the South wind raises when it begins
to blow after heavy rain in autumn, and makes the sea

dangerous. There is also a time in spring when men make
voyages; as soon as the buds begin to show on the twigs
of a fig-tree about as large as the print of a crow's foot, the
sea is fit for sailing, but a voyage at this season is dangerous;
I do not advise it, I do not approve of it, for the voyage
will be a snatched one, and you will hardly escape trouble
of some sort. Nevertheless, men are foolish enough to go
voyages even then, for money is the life and soul of us poor
mortals, but drowning is a horrible death; I bid you,
therefore, think well over all that I have been saying to
you. And again, do not put all your substance on to a single
ship; leave the greater part behind, and put the smaller
half on board. It is a sad thing for a man to meet with a
mishap on the high seas; and it is a sad thing if you have
overloaded your waggon, so that the axle breaks and your
load is damaged; use moderation in all things and let
everything be done in due season.

SAMUEL BUTLER   (*Works and Days*, 663–94)

68   *Good Days and Bad*

(i)

RECKON the days that Zeus ordains, and in due array
   Point them out to your slaves: show how the thirtieth
     day
    For the o'erlooking of work and dealing out stores is
     best.

These be the days that come from the master-mind of Zeus,
While men have eyes to see and apply the truth to use.
    Chief of the hallowed days are the first and fourth
     and seventh,

146

(Seventh when Lêto bore Apollo with sword of gold)
Eighth and ninth as well, these two, as the moon grows
       old,
    For helping the works of man have a worth above the
       rest.

Yet the eleventh and twelfth are also of good repute
Whether for shearing sheep or garnering kindly fruit;
    Only the twelfth herein is better far than the eleventh,

For on the twelfth the Spider swinging in air doth spin
Webs in full day, and the Wise One[1] gets her harvest in:
That is the time for a wife to set up her loom and begin.

                 (*Works and Days*, 765–79)

(ii)

Such are the stated days that bring great profit to men;
All the others are shifty, unpredestinate, thin:
    Men have favourite days, but few men know aright;
One step-motherly day will come like a mother again:
Blest in his days and rich he is, who has in his ken
    All these things, as he toils blameless in heaven's sight,
    Judging the omens of birds, shunning the paths of sin.

SIR WILLIAM MARRIS   (*Works and Days*, 822–8)

69   *Length of Life*

NINE times the span of an old old man
   Is the life of the cawing crow;
But four crows' days a stag outstays,
    And the stag's life thrice will go

       [1] The ant.

While a raven thrives, and a phœnix lives
    Nine times the raven's share;
Yet the phœnix' hours are a tenth of ours;
For Zeus in his might brought us to light,
    The Nymphs of the shining hair.

SIR WILLIAM MARRIS   (*Precepts of Chîron*)

70   *The Muses' Gift*

(*i*)

LET our song begin with the choir of Muses that own
    the great and sacred mountain of Helicôn.
They dance round a spring as dark as violets, round
the altar of mighty Zeus, softly treading the ground.

Hesiod one day they taught a beautiful song
while under their mountain to pasture his lambs he led—
and I listened, and thus the heavenly Muses said,
daughters of Zeus of the Buckler, Olympians born:
'Shepherds of the wild, mere bellies, creatures of scorn,
we can make false things seem true, so great is our skill,
but we know how to utter the truth, when that is our will.'

So sang the ready-voiced daughters of highest god,
and they plucked from the sturdy bay-tree a wonderful rod
for me, and they breathed in my frame a voice divine,
and the power to tell of the past or future was mine,
and they bade me sing of the gods who never may die,
and ever, the first and the last, on themselves to cry—
But why this wandering tale of a tree or stone?

(*Theogony*, 1-4, 22-35)

148

(ii)

When the watching daughters of Zeus attend with their
      grace
the honoured birth of a prince of god-nurtured race,
down on his tongue they let a honeydew fall
and his lips pour eloquence out. To him one and all
look reverently, as he in righteousness
interprets the law, and with serene address
swiftly resolves the bitterest brawls that arise.
Therefore so blest a ruler is counted wise:
when the people assembled are erring, his words have
      force
with gentle ease to persuade the better course.
Godlike he moves; with modest mien all men greet
his presence, and still he outstands where the elders meet.

Such are the gifts of the Muses, and holy they are.
From the Muses and lord Apollo who shoots from afar
come the singers and harpers of earth; but from Zeus, the
      kings.
Happy is he that the Muses love. When he sings,
sweetly speech from his lips forever flows.
Aye, though fresh troubles have crazed a man till he knows
nothing but dread and despair, should a singer praise,
as the Muses' servant, the glory of ancient days,
the heroes and blessed gods of Olympus-crest,
the man will forget that he ever was darkly distressed,
such powers of healing to gifts of the Muses belong.

JACK LINDSAY   (*Theogony*, 81–103)

71   *Zeus and the Titans*

THEN Zeus no longer held back his power. On the
      height
his heart was swarming with fury, and all his might
he uttered forth. From Heaven and Olympus he swung,
tossing his lightning-darts. The bolts he flung
were fierce with thunder and lightning, and thickly they
      came
out of his strong right hand with a sacred flame
rolling: the life-giving earth with a shudder of sound
took fire, and measureless forest crackled around.
All land was seething and heaving, and Ocean-stream,
and the barren sea. Lapped round with a fiery steam
stood the earthborn Titans. Numberless flames were blown
to the brightening æther. Glare of the thunderstone
and lightning blinded the eyes of the strongest there.
A marvellous heat grasped Chaos. Everywhere
tumult burst on the ear and smote on the eye,
till Earth seemed wrestling for life with the broad-backed
      sky
collapsing. Loud was the fall of the thunderbolt blasting,
as if Earth to the pit was cast and the Heavens were
      casting.
Such was the shock of the gods when they met embattled,
while winds brought storms of dust and the earth rattled,
while winds swept lightning and lurid bolts through the
      skies,
the shafts of almighty Zeus, with clatter and cries
tossed to the midmost air, as the battle-field
rang without end, and the might of their hands was re-
      vealed.

      150

The battle broke: till then they grappled and tore,
still merged in war's remorseless scrimmage and roar.
Cottus, Bríareus, and Gyês bore the brunt,
unquenchable fighters, they raised fierce war in the front,
hundreds of stones in thick shower with strong hands they
       hurled;
and the Titans stood under the shower in a darkening
       world
and beneath the wide-wayed earth they were all of them
       cast
and bound in grievous chains imprisoned at last,
for despite their great spirits the strength of the others
       prevailed.

JACK LINDSAY   (*Theogony*, 687–719)

72   *Combat of Hêraclês and Cycnus*

THEN from the well-laced cars leapt down the twain
       to earth apace,
The son of King Enŷalus, the son of mighty Zeus.
    And even as in a mountain glen a fanged boar ill to face
Resolves to fight his hunters—and his head he sideways
       slews
And whets his gleaming tushes, and his gnashing jaws drip
       froth;
His eyes are like a flame of fire, and on his mane and nape
His hackles bristle: from his car so leapt the son of Zeus.
What time the loud cicada perched, black-winged, on a
       green spray,
Whose food and drink is dainty dew, begins his summer lay
For men, and through the livelong day and at the dawn
       renews

151

His utterance in the fiercest heat, when Sîrius sears the
skin,
When millets sown in summer grow a beard, and the crude
grape
Which Dionŷsus gave, to be a joy and sorrow both,
Is turning colour: in that hour they fought: loud rose the din.

And as with crooked beaks and claws two vultures
screaming shrill
Fight on a lofty rock about a chamois of the hill
Or fat wild deer disabled by some nimble archer's shot,
Who following up his quarry goes astray and finds it not—
And quick the vultures are to mark, and over the spoil
array
Grim battle: even so they cried, and at each other sprang.

Then Cycnus smote the son of Zeus in eagerness to slay
With brazen spear hurled on his shield; but could not
break the bronze.
God-given gift, it saved him, and strong Hêraclês at once,
Amphítryon's son, with his long spear dealt him a lusty
stroke
Below the chin 'twixt shield and helm, where bare the
gullet lay.
Full-force came down the hero's might on him: through
both the thews
That deadly spear of ash-wood cut. He fell as falls an oak
Or soaring pine-tree stricken by the smoking bolt of Zeus.
Even so he fell, and over him his wrought bronze
armour rang.

Sir William Marris

(*Shield of Hêraclês*, 370–1, 386–401, 405–23)

73   *A Visitation*

DOWN from the stately trees amain
   The lovely petals fell like rain,
And fruits came dropping on the earth
As Bóreas sent his fury forth
At Zeus' behest: the ocean boiled,
And all things from his wrath recoiled.
Men's strength became a whining wail,
And early spring saw fruitage fail,
What time the Hairless One[1] betakes
Herself to breed, among the brakes,
In each three years, three little snakes.

SIR WILLIAM MARRIS   (*Eoiæ*)

74   *Light-footed Îphiclus*

OVER the spikes of the ripened corn
   Would he run, and they not wilt:
Over the wheaten ears would he race
   And never a grain be spilt.

SIR WILLIAM MARRIS   (*Eoiæ*)

75   *The Spring called Parthénius*

AS unconcernedly it flows
   As on her way a soft maid goes.

SIR WILLIAM MARRIS

76   *The Ages of Man*

SWEAT, thought, and prayer—engage
   Youth, middle years, and age.

SIR WILLIAM MARRIS

          [1] The Snake.

HOMERIC HYMNS

(Date unknown)

77   *The Rape of Persephonê*

OF great Dêmêter here begins my lay,
    The bright-haired goddess: and in one accord
I sing her light-foot daughter, stolen away
From rich Dêmêter of the golden sword;
For Zeus the thunderer, lord of wide survey,
To Aïdôneus yielding, gave his word
That he might take her, from her playmates torn,
Maidens deep-bosomed to old Ocean born.

She gathered flowers along a grassy green,
The rose, the saffron, and the violet fair,
Or flag, or hyacinth. There too was seen
Narcissus, that the Earth was made to bear
By will of Zeus, who set for that young queen
Fresh as the opening buds, a fatal snare,
With kindly thought to make that god's delight
Who houses many in the halls of Night.

Alike to mortal and immortal eyes
It rose a marvel. From one root had birth
A hundred blossoming crowns, that took the skies
With fragrance, and they laughed, and all the earth
Laughed, and the salty sea. Upon that prize
She gazed in wonder, then both hands put forth
And bent towards it, with desire to take
The lovely plaything for its beauty's sake.

But spacious earth, the path of many feet,
Yawned, and a chasm cleft all the Nŷsian plain;
And he, the Ready Host, whom mortals greet
As son by Kronos gotten, he, whose reign

Is many-titled, from his dark retreat
Leapt with the coursers of immortal strain
And seized her, loth to go; then wheeled about
His golden chariot, while her cry rang out

Bidding her father, son of Kronos, hear,
Of gods the highest and most excellent.
But deaf were mortal and immortal ear;
And not the wood-nymphs caught her sharp lament,
That dwelt in berried olives shimmering near.

W. M. W. CALL, T. F. HIGHAM   (II. 1–23)

78   *Dêmêter at Eleusis*

                              She, with heavy heart
Sat by a wayside fountain in the shade,
The Maiden Spring, from which the townsfolk drew,
Where overhead a branching olive grew.

The likeness of some ancient one she wore
Whose bearing-time is past, of one to whom
Wreath'd Aphrodîtê lends her gifts no more,—
Kings, who in judgement sit and give their doom,
Take such to nurse their sons, or mind the store,
Going about from echoing room to room.
And soon there came and marked her in that place
Daughters of Keleus, of Eleusis' race.

They came to dip their brazen urns and bear
Spring-waters home, a godlike company,
Wearing their youth as flowers their spring-time wear,—
Kallídikê, and Dêmo, dear as she;

                              155

With whom Kleisídikê appears, and there
The eldest of the four, Kallíthoê.
Yet goddess saw they none: to men below
The faces of the gods are hard to know.

Close by they stood, and words came winging forth:
'Pray tell us who you are, and whence you come,
Old mother, from the ancient ones of earth?
And why so far from town? Seek you no home
In shadowy halls where women keep the hearth
Grown old as you are old? There too are some
Of younger age and charity no less
In word and deed to comfort your distress.'

To them the heavenly queen her answer gave:
'Welcome, dear girls, whoever you may be.
Listen, and I will tell you all you crave,
For surely you should hear the truth from me.
Doris the name my mother bade me have.
From Crete I come, over the broad-ridg'd sea;
By force compelled, reluctantly I sailed;
For pirates seized me and their will prevailed.

'Swiftly they ran to Thôricos for trade,
And put ashore the women, every one;
Then by the cables to the stern belayed
Sweet food prepared: but I had heart for none.
Over the dark mainland by stealth I made
From those proud masters ere the meal begun,
That they might nothing get who nothing gave
But looked for profit from a stolen slave.

156

'And so I wandered and am here arriven,
And nothing of your land or people know.
But O I pray that gods in highest heaven
May give you each a husband, and bestow
Children upon you,—and to them be given
What gifts a parent will! Pity me now,
Young maids, and of your kindness, children dear,
Tell me some house of man or woman here

'Where I may go and serve with ready will,
Doing such tasks as one grown old may do;
A baby I could nurse and dandle still,
Or mind the house, or for my master strew
His bed, in timbered chamber joined with skill,
And teach the serving-maids their housework too.'
So spake the goddess. Then Kleisídikê,
The loveliest of that virgin company:—

'Mother, we suffer as the gods ordain,
For we are men, and gods are mightier far.
Now will I tell you truly and explain
Who the great chieftains, high in honour, are,—
The overlords, whose counsel sovereign
And honest ruling at the judgement-bar
Uphold the State, keeping this land of ours,
And this our city with its crown of towers.

'Know first Triptólemos, in counsel shrewd,
Then Díoklos, and Polyxeinos then;
And three besides,—Eumolpos, called the good;
Dólichos; and our father, best of men.

157

Whose ladies all, that mind their livelihood,
Would think no scorn, nor bid you forth again.
To win their hearts enough one look would be,
For like the holy gods you seem to me.

'But wait on our return, till we go tell
Deep-girdled Metaneira all you say;
For she's our mother, and may bid you dwell
With us, and spare your search a longer way.
A son of many prayers, late-born, loved well,
In our good home she nurses, and would pay,
To see him fully grown, so rich a prize
As would bring envy to a woman's eyes.'

She bowed assent. Each one her gleaming urn
Dipped, and rejoicing to the great house sped;
And Metaneira, soon as she could learn
How looked that ancient one and what she said,
A great wage bade them offer, and return.
Then light as fawn or heifer meadow-fed
In spring-time skips, along the rutted track
Lifting their pretty skirts, they darted back.

Like flower of the saffron as they ran
Rippled their hair, over their shoulders playing;
Quickly they found the Power Olympian
Beside the road, where late they left her, staying,
Then, going first, their homeward way began.
And she with covered head and heart dismaying
In robe of sable went, whose hem below
About her slender feet tossed to and fro.

Through pillared porch they ran, their journey done,
Into the house of Keleus heaven-blest,
And soon, beside a column set, whereon
The roof-beams lay of timber finely drest,
They found the queen, their mother, and her son
Fresh as a young bud growing at her breast.
Then stepped the goddess in: her head she bore
Roof-high: a glory of heaven filled the door.

The other looked, and shrank before her face,
Compelled by awe and worship. Pale for fear
She left her seat and gave the goddess place.

W. M. W. CALL, T. F. HIGHAM   (II. 98–191)

79   *Iônian Holiday*

BUT Delos is pleasant, O Phœbus, above the rest.
  Long-robed Iônians there gather in to thy feast
with children and gentle wives, a holiday throng
who look to thy pleasure in boxing and dance and song,
and ever, when games are appointed, make trial of skill
remembering thee, and the joy of thy heart fulfil.
Wherever Iônians meet, a stranger attending
would match them with gods everlasting, of vigour un
      ending;
with joy he would gaze on the beauty of men and the dress
of beautiful women, girdled in loveliness,
and the speed of their ships and the plentiful treasure they
      own.
There too are the Maidens, a wonder of endless renown:
all magic of song thy Delian votaries know,
praising Apollo, their lord, and the strength of his bow,

with Lêto the next, and the arrows of Artemis then;
and sweetly they sing of the old generations of men.
The tongues of all people they mimic; all patter, all singing
they match to the life, with a clatter of castanets ringing.
So truly they fashion the numbers and echo the tone,
all men are deceived: each hears in that music his own.

T. F. HIGHAM (III. 146–64)

80 *The Blind Old Man*

NOW Apollo have mercy, and Artemis be thou kind:
and so farewell to you all. Yet bear me in mind,
maidens, whenever there comes in after-days
a son of this earth, inured to pain, and says:
'Tell me, maidens, of poets that visit here
who sings you the sweetest, whom do you hold most dear?'
Remember me then, one answer, one only, giving:
'A man that is blind, in scarry Chios living,
supreme in song both now and in times to come.'
And I to you shall give honour, wherever I roam
among fine cities of men, telling ever of you;
and all shall believe, for the thing that I speak is true.

Apollo be praised, whom rich-haired Lêto bore,
and the strength of his silver bow, for evermore.

T. F. HIGHAM (III. 165–78)

81 *The Choirs of Heaven*

NOW glorious Lêto's child goes up with the sound
of his hollowed harp to Pŷtho's rocky ground.
His raiment is breathing of heaven, sweet melodies thrill
with dirling note to the touch of his golden quill;

and thence to Olympus, swift as a thought, he towers,
to the home of Zeus, and joins the assembled Powers.
   Then cithern and song employ the gods undying.
The Muses together, with choir to choir replying,
tell of immortal gifts, the riches of heaven,
and of sorrowful dooms to men by Immortals given,—
improvident, powerless men, unable to stay
the plague of death, or keep old age away.
Now dance the genial Hours and the long-haired Graces;
Harmónia now and Hêbê take their places
with heaven-born Aphrodîtê, all in a ring
joined hand to wrist, and merrily round they swing.
And one nor plain nor lowly is choiring there,
mighty in stature, fair among the fair,
Artemis, shooter of arrows, Apollo's twin.
There makes the War-god merry; and following in,
the watchful Slayer of Argus takes his pleasure.
But Phœbus Apollo treads the loftiest measure,
harping the while, in a dazzle of glory thrown
by the flash of his feet and the flirt of his damask gown.
Then golden Lêto and Zeus the god all-wise
rejoice, large-hearted, and watch with loving eyes
their son at play with the gods in paradise.

T. F. HIGHAM   (III. 182–206)

82   *The Tortoise-shell*

OUT of the lofty cavern wandering
     He found a tortoise, and cried out—'A treasure!'
(For Mercury first made the tortoise sing)
   The beast before the portal at his leisure

The flowery herbage was depasturing,
    Moving his feet in a deliberate measure
Over the turf. Jove's profitable son
Eying him laughed, and laughing thus begun:—

'A useful godsend are you to me now,
    King of the dance, companion of the feast,
Lovely in all your nature! Welcome, you
    Excellent plaything! Where, sweet mountain-beast,
Got you that speckled shell? Thus much I know,
    You must come home with me and be my guest;
You will give joy to me, and I will do
All that is in my power to honour you.

'Better to be at home than out of door,
    So come with me; and though it has been said
That you alive defend from magic power,
    I know you will sing sweetly when you're dead.'
Thus having spoken, the quaint infant bore,
    Lifting it from the grass on which it fed
And grasping it in his delighted hold,
His treasured prize into the cavern old.

Then scooping with a chisel of gray steel,
    He bored the life and soul out of the beast.—
Not swifter a swift thought of woe or weal
    Darts through the tumult of a human breast
Which thronging cares annoy—not swifter wheel
    The flashes of its torture and unrest
Out of the dizzy eyes—than Maia's son
All that he did devise hath featly done.

And through the tortoise's hard stony skin
At proper distances small holes he made,
　　And fastened the cut stems of reeds within,
And with a piece of leather overlaid
　　The open space and fixed the cubits in,
Fitting the bridge to both, and stretched o'er all
Symphonious cords of sheep-gut rhythmical.

When he had wrought the lovely instrument,
　　He tried the chords, and made division meet,
Preluding with the plectrum, and there went
　　Up from beneath his hand a tumult sweet
Of mighty sounds, and from his lips he sent
　　A strain of unpremeditated wit
Joyous and wild and wanton—such you may
Hear among revellers on a holiday.

He sung how Jove and May of the bright sandal
　　Dallied in love not quite legitimate;
And his own birth, still scoffing at the scandal,
　　And naming his own name, did celebrate;
His mother's cave and servant maids he planned all
　　In plastic verse, her household stuff and state,
Perennial pot, trippet, and brazen pan,—
But singing, he conceived another plan.

　　Seized with a sudden fancy for fresh meat,
He in his sacred crib deposited
　　The hollow lyre, and from the cavern sweet

Rushed with great leaps up to the mountain's head,
   Revolving in his mind some subtle feat
Of thievish craft, such as a swindler might
Devise in the lone season of dun night.

P. B. SHELLEY   (IV. 25–67)

83   *The Cattle-thief*

APOLLO hearing this, passed quickly on—
   No wingèd omen could have shown more clear
That the deceiver was his father's son.

   So the God wraps a purple atmosphere
Around his shoulders, and like fire is gone

   To famous Pylos, seeking his kine there,
And found their track and his, yet hardly cold,
And cried—'What wonder do mine eyes behold!

'Here are the footsteps of the hornèd herd
   Turned back towards their fields of asphodel;—
But *these* are not the tracks of beast or bird,
   Gray wolf, or bear, or lion of the dell,
Or manèd Centaur—sand was never stirred
   By man or woman thus! Inexplicable!
Who with unwearied feet could e'er impress
The sand with such enormous vestiges?

'That was most strange—but this is stranger still!'
   Thus having said, Phœbus impetuously
Sought high Cyllênê's forest-cinctured hill,
   And the deep cavern where dark shadows lie,
And where the ambrosial nymph with happy will
   Bore the Saturnian's love-child, Mercury—
And a delightful odour from the dew
Of the hill pastures, at his coming, flew.

And Phœbus stooped under the craggy roof
    Arched over the dark cavern:—Maia's child
Perceived that he came angry, far aloof,
    About the cows of which he had been beguiled;
And over him the fine and fragrant woof
    Of his ambrosial swaddling-clothes he piled—
As among fire-brands lies a burning spark
Covered, beneath the ashes cold and dark.

There, like an infant who had sucked his fill
    And now was newly washed and put to bed,
Awake, but courting sleep with weary will,
    And gathered in a lump, hands, feet, and head,
He lay, and his belovèd tortoise still
    He grasped and held under his shoulder-blade.
Phœbus the lovely mountain-goddess knew,
Not less her subtle, swindling baby, who

Lay swathed in his sly wiles. Round every crook
    Of the ample cavern, for his kine, Apollo
Looked sharp; and when he saw them not, he took
    The glittering key, and opened three great hollow
Recesses in the rock—where many a nook
    Was filled with the sweet food immortals swallow,
And mighty heaps of silver and of gold
Were piled within—a wonder to behold!

And white and silver robes, all overwrought
    With cunning workmanship of tracery sweet—
Except among the Gods there can be nought
    In the wide world to be compared with it.

165

Lâtôna's offspring, after having sought
   His herds in every corner, thus did greet
Great Hermês:—'Little cradled rogue, declare
Of my illustrious heifers, where they are!

'Speak quickly! or a quarrel between us
   Must rise, and the event will be, that I
Shall hurl you into dismal Tartarus,
   In fiery gloom to dwell eternally;
Nor shall your father nor your mother loose
   The bars of that black dungeon—utterly
You shall be cast out from the light of day,
To rule the ghosts of men, unblessed as they.'

To whom thus Hermês slily answered:—'Son
   Of great Lâtôna, what a speech is this!
Why come you here to ask me what is done
   With the wild oxen which it seems you miss?
I have not seen them, nor from any one
   Have heard a word of the whole business;
If you should promise an immense reward,
I could not tell more than you now have heard.

'An ox-stealer should be both tall and strong,
   And I am but a little new-born thing,
Who, yet at least, can think of nothing wrong:—
   My business is to suck, and sleep, and fling
The cradle-clothes about me all day long,—
   Or half asleep, hear my sweet mother sing,
And to be washed in water clean and warm,
And hushed and kissed and kept secure from harm.

166

'O, let not e'er this quarrel be averred!
   The astounded Gods would laugh at you, if e'er
You should allege a story so absurd
   As that a new-born infant forth could fare
Out of his home after a savage herd.
   I was born yesterday—my small feet are
Too tender for the roads so hard and rough:—
And if you think that this is not enough,

'I swear a great oath, by my father's head,
   That I stole not your cows, and that I know
Of no one else, who might, or could, or did.—
   Whatever things cows are, I do not know,
For I have only heard the name.'—This said,
   He winked as fast as could be, and his brow
Was wrinkled, and a whistle loud gave he,
Like one who hears some strange absurdity.

P. B. SHELLEY   (IV. 212–80)

84   *The Power of Music*

THESE words were wingèd with his swift delight:
   'You heifer-stealing schemer, well do you
Deserve that fifty oxen should requite
   Such minstrelsies as I have heard even now.
Comrade of feasts, little contriving wight,
   One of your secrets I would gladly know,
Whether the glorious power you now show forth
Was folded up within you at your birth,

'Or whether mortal taught or God inspired
   The power of unpremeditated song?
Many divinest sounds have I admired,
   The Olympian Gods and mortal men among;

But such a strain of wondrous, strange, untired,
    And soul-awakening music, sweet and strong,
Yet did I never hear except from thee,
Offspring of May, impostor Mercury!

'What Muse, what skill, what unimagined use,
    What exercise of subtlest art, has given
Thy songs such power?—for those who hear may choose
    From three, the choicest of the gifts of Heaven,
Delight, and love, and sleep,—sweet sleep, whose dews
    Are sweeter than the balmy tears of even:—
And I, who speak this praise, am that Apollo
Whom the Olympian Muses ever follow:

'And their delight is dance, and the blithe noise
    Of song and overflowing poesy;
And sweet, even as desire, the liquid voice
    Of pipes, that fills the clear air thrillingly;
But never did my inmost soul rejoice
    In this dear work of youthful revelry
As now. I wonder at thee, son of Jove;
Thy harpings and thy song are soft as love.

'Now since thou hast, although so very small,
    Science of arts so glorious, thus I swear,—
And let this cornel javelin, keen and tall,
    Witness between us what I promise here,—
That I will lead thee to the Olympian Hall,
    Honoured and mighty, with thy mother dear,
And many glorious gifts in joy will give thee,
And even at the end will ne'er deceive thee.'

168

To whom thus Mercury with prudent speech:—
   'Wisely hast thou inquirèd of my skill:
I envy thee no thing I know to teach
   Even this day:—for both in word and will
I would be gentle with thee; thou canst reach
   All things in thy wise spirit, and thy sill
Is highest in Heaven among the sons of Jove,
Who loves thee in the fulness of his love.

'The Counsellor Supreme has given to thee
   Divinest gifts, out of the amplitude
Of his profuse exhaustless treasury;
   By thee, 'tis said, the depths are understood
Of his far voice; by thee the mystery
   Of all oracular fates,—and the dread mood
Of the diviner is breathed up; even I—
A child—perceive thy might and majesty.

'Thou canst seek out and compass all that wit
   Can find or teach;—yet since thou wilt, come take
The lyre—be mine the glory giving it—
   Strike the sweet chords, and sing aloud, and wake
Thy joyous pleasure out of many a fit
   Of trancèd sound—and with fleet fingers make
Thy liquid-voicèd comrade talk with thee,—
It can talk measured music eloquently.

'Then bear it boldly to the revel loud,
   Love-wakening dance, or feast of solemn state,
A joy by night or day—for those endowed
   With art and wisdom who interrogate

169

It teaches, babbling in delightful mood
    All things which make the spirit most elate,
Soothing the mind with sweet familiar play,
Chasing the heavy shadows of dismay.

'To those who are unskilled in its sweet tongue,
    Though they should question most impetuously
Its hidden soul, it gossips something wrong—
    Some senseless and impertinent reply.
But thou who art as wise as thou art strong
    Canst compass all that thou desirest. I
Present thee with this music-flowing shell,
Knowing thou canst interrogate it well.

'And let us two henceforth together feed,
    On this green mountain-slope and pastoral plain,
The herds in litigation.'

P. B. SHELLEY   (IV. 434–92)

85   *Aphroditê on Ida*

THEN Aphroditê, the lover of laughter, was clad
    richly and decked with gold. She left all the scent
of Cypros Isle, and Troyward swiftly she went,
hurrying through gliding clouds high overhead.
To many-fountained Ida, mother of beasts, she sped,
straight to the homestead on the mountain-side.
Fawning came grey wolves and lions grimly-eyed,
bears and quick leopards ravenous for deer.
She rejoiced to see them coming from far and near,
and cast desire in their hearts, and at once they lay
coupling along the shadowy valley-way.

She came to the shelters, neatly built out of wood,
where, formed like a god, the hero Anchîses stood.
No one else had stayed in the mountain-home;
over the pasture the others had gone to roam
with the hungry herds, and alone in the steading he stayed,
stroking a lyre till it thrilled with the music he made.

Then Aphrodîtê, the daughter of Zeus, came in sight.
Like a maiden she seemed in her gracious ways and her
    height,
having no wish to scare him with what he saw.
Anchîses beheld her and marked with wondering awe
her gracious ways and her height and her dress that seemed
a haze of fire as it warmly rippled and gleamed,
an embroidered robe that shimmered a moon of gold
over her breasts—a marvellous thing to behold.

JACK LINDSAY   (V. 64–90)

86   *Afterthoughts*

'BUT this may not be. Age is shrouding you down into
  death,
pitiless age that on all men someday will come,
loathed by the very gods, crushing and wearisome.
Henceforth among the immortal gods I must bend,
because of you, in a shame that knows no end.
Till now my beguiling jests and laughter they dreaded,
and one and all with women of earth I bedded;
for though they struggled, yet my will was stronger.
But now my mouth will possess this power no longer
in heaven, for I have been mad. I have fallen the prey
of a mastering magick, which drove my wits astray.

Under my girdle a man and his seed I have taken.
But when the time comes for the child in the light to
     awaken,
the Nymphs will rear him suckled at their deep breasts,
the Nymphs of the mountain, that haunt these holy crests.
Neither gods, wholly, are they, nor of mortal breed,
but long with the earth they live and on heaven they feed,
and with the immortals the dances of beauty they trace,
and the Sîlêni hug them in warm embrace,
and quick-eyed Hermês, in caverns of cool surprise;
and when they are born, from the childing earth arise
pinetrees or oaks that spread out their branches on high,
beautiful mountain-trees that mix with the sky,—
the abode of immortal spirits (so all men declare)
unscathed by the woodman; for none brings iron there.
But when the fate of death looms close at hand,
the beautiful trees must shrivel away where they stand;
the bark is scabby, on earth all the foliage lies,
and out of the sunlight a tree and a spirit dies.

'These Nymphs will rear up our baby, and when at length
he gains the loveliness of boyhood's strength,
the goddesses will bring him that you may see;
and then, to tell you my thoughts of destiny,
in the fifth year I'll return and fetch the boy;
and that bough of our grafted flesh will give you joy
when you see how godlike he is. Then I'll bid you begone
away at once to windy Îlion.
But if you should ever be asked by a man of earth
under whose girdle your son was brought to birth,
answer as I bid you, recall my power.
Say he was got on a Nymph with a body like a flower,

a Nymph who dwells in a covert of the mountain-side.
But if you answer, mad in your boastful pride,
that you lay in bed and the crowned Cythereia lay under,
Zeus will slash you with a bolt of smoking thunder.
Now you have heard me. Remember well each word.
Speak not my name, or wrath of gods will be stirred.'

JACK LINDSAY   (V. 244–90)

87   *To Dionŷsus*

I SING of Dionŷsus, an old story,—
  How showed the son of noble Sémelê
Like a young lad, beside a promontory
Where ran the breakers of the barren sea.
With mop of floating hair, an ebon glory,
And purple cloak on shoulders broad went he,
When pirates drove their gallant ship in sight,
Over the wine-dark waters running light.

Tuscans they were, by evil fortune guided.
With nods consenting, quickly on the beach
They leapt, and stole him, and his worth decided,—
'A son of kings,' they gloried, each to each,
'One born to fatness by the Lord provided.'
Unkindly then to tie his limbs they reach,
But all in vain they fasten legs and hands;
Far off, by magic, fall their withy-bands.

He sat with laughter in his sloe-black eyes.
The helmsman seeing, cries 'Poor fools, let go.
What god, what mighty one, make you your prize?
Shipmates, there's one aboard no ship can stow.

Yonder is Zeus himself, as I surmise,
Or lord Apollo of the silver bow,
Or else Poseidon. His no mortal station;
A god he seems, of heavenly habitation.

'Come, on the dark mainland with no delays
We'll set him, if your helmsman may prevail.
Unhand him, mates, lest he in anger raise
Strong winds upon us and call up a gale.'
He ceased. Then spitefully the captain says:
'Look to the wind, fool! Help me hoist the sail,
And catch the sheets together. As for him,
This is no matter for your woman's whim—

'To Egypt sailing, (if the cruise fulfil
My present hope,) or Cyprus, or the ends
Of the far North, or on, and farther still,
He shall speak out at last, and name his friends,
His wealth and brothers. For by god's good will
The man's our prisoner.' Up the mast he sends,
And hoists the sail. The canvas bellying goes.
The crew pull both sheets tight, and wring them close.

The dark ship ran. And what bedevilment
About her decks appeared! First, wine abounding
With fragrance paradisal wimpling went,
A stream delicious, every eye astounding;
Then sprung a vine, with swaying clusters bent,
This way and that the square-sail top surrounding;
Dark ivy bloomed, and rich with berries clung
About the mast; the tholes were garland-hung.

Too late, too late they bid the helmsman shore her,
  For now the god, in lion's fearful shape
Bestrides the fo'c'sle-top, a lusty roarer,
  Then makes amidships, murderously agape
A rough-necked bear, her ramping claws before her,
  While he from fore-peak scowls. To find escape
They ring their prudent helmsman, in a daze;
But the god leaps, and on the captain preys.

Into the bright sea tumble all the rest
  To fly that fate, and dolphins there become.
The helmsman Dionŷsus saved, and blest,
  Saying, 'Take courage, noble sir, in whom
My heart delights! And know, you are addrest
  By Dionŷsus, loud and frolicsome,
Whom Sémelê, the child of Kadmos (won
By Zeus in love consenting) had for son.'

Hail, son of loveliest Sémelê! None makes
Sweet song run truly who thy name forsakes.

T. F. HIGHAM   (VII. 1–59)

88   *To Pan*

MUSE, tell of Pan, the dear seed of Hermês, that shows
goat-hooves and horns, the lover of noise, as he goes
through wooded glades with Nymphs who dance all the
    way:
sheer on the edge of the cliff they entwine and sway,
calling on Pan, the god of the shepherds, whose hair
is long and unkempt, who owns for his mountain-lair

175

ridges and scarps of rock and crests of snow.
Through tangled thickets he wanders to and fro.
Now by the murmuring stream englamoured he lags,
and now climbs up and away through towering crags,
for the topmost rocks, to look down on the pasturing
  flocks.

Often up glistening mountains his wandering leads;
often on shouldered hills in the chase he speeds
with arrowy eyes; and only at dusk, as he strays
home from the hunting, sweetly and lowly he plays
on his pipes of reed. No song so lovely is heard
even when spring has heaped the flowers and the bird
of sorrow among the leaves pours honey of song.
Then round him clear-voiced Nymphs of the mountain
  throng;
nimbly they circle about the dark-bubbling spring,
and Echo sobs above in the crags as they sing.

Pan moves around the choirs, then sidles in
and dances sprightly amid them. The tawny skin
of a lynx he wears on his back, and he loves the cry
of soaring song in soft meadows where hyacinths lie
fragrantly mingled in grass with the crocus-flowers.

They sing of the gods and their blessed Olympian hours.
Of Hermês they chiefly tell. All luck he brings
and carries the word of the gods by speed of his wings.
To Arcadia, mother of flocks, a fountaining land,
he came, to Cyllênê's close, where his altars stand.
There, though a god, a farmer's curly-fleeced sheep
he tended. For love in his heart grew lush and deep;

176

the rich-haired daughter of Dryops he longed to enjoy,
and so they were merrily wedded; a darling boy
she bore him—a boy who from birth was a marvellous
　　　sight
with his hooves and his horns, his chuckling noise and
　　　delight.
When the nurse beheld him, she leaped to her feet and
　　　feared;
she fled away from his face uncouth with its beard.
Then Hermês, the bringer of luck, accepted and raised
the boy from the ground, and was filled with joy as he
　　　gazed.
Straight to the home of the gods he carried with care
his son wrapped snug in pelts of the mountain-hare.
He set him down near Zeus and the others, who smiled
with pleasure to see the ways of the marvellous child,
and Dionŷsus in chief. They decided to call
the newcomer *Pan* because he had charmed them *All.*

I sing for your favour, Lord. All hail, I say.
I'll remember you with a song another day.

JACK LINDSAY　　　　　　　　　　　　(XIX. 1–49)

89　　*To Apollo*

THE clear-toned swan, to the beating of his wings
　　　alighting where Pênêus eddies past,
sings of you, Phœbus. The sweet-voiced poet sings,
to his shrilling lyre, of you, both first and last.

So hail to you, Lord. For your grace this poet sings.

JACK LINDSAY　　　　　　　　　　　　(XXI. 1–5)

90   *The Goddess of the Hearth*

HESTIA, wherever homes shelter, raised to the sky,
   men going on earth or gods who never may die,
the foremost honour you've gained, and a lasting place.
Noble your portion and right. For, lacking your grace,
no mortal would dare to eat. First, he must bend,
pouring sweet wine to you, and again at the end.

JACK LINDSAY   (XXIX. 1–6)

91   *Earth the Mother of All*

O UNIVERSAL Mother, who dost keep
   From everlasting thy foundations deep,
Eldest of things, Great Earth, I sing of thee!
All shapes that have their dwelling in the sea,
All things that fly, or on the ground divine
Live, move, and there are nourished—these are thine;
These from thy wealth thou dost sustain; from thee
Fair babes are born, and fruits on every tree
Hang ripe and large, revered Divinity!

   The life of mortal men beneath thy sway
Is held; thy power both gives and takes away!
Happy are they whom thy mild favours nourish;
All things unstinted round them grow and flourish.
For them, endures the life-sustaining field
Its load of harvest, and their cattle yield
Large increase, and their house with wealth is filled
Such honoured dwell in cities fair and free,
The homes of lovely women, prosperously;

   178

Their sons exult in youth's new budding gladness,
And their fresh daughters free from care or sadness,
With bloom-inwoven dance and happy song,
On the soft flowers the meadow-grass among,
Leap round them sporting—such delights by thee
Are given, rich Power, revered Divinity.

Mother of gods, thou Wife of starry Heaven,
Farewell! be thou propitious, and be given
A happy life for this brief melody,
Nor thou nor other songs shall unremembered be.

P. B. SHELLEY   (XXX. 1–16)

HOMERIC EPIGRAM
(Date unknown)

92   *Mîdas' Tomb*

ON Mîdas' grave, a maid of bronze, I lie.
   While water flows and while the tall trees bloom,
And sun and radiant moon arise and shine,
And rivers run and ocean breaks in brine,
Abiding on this mournful mound shall I
Tell passers-by that this is Mîdas' tomb.

SIR WILLIAM MARRIS

MARGÎTÊS
(Date unknown)

93   *Master of None*

(*i*)

A Jack of all trades, he was master of none.

179

(ii)

He dug not, he ploughed not: those arts were denied;
God sent him a fool in whatever he tried.

T. F. HIGHAM

TÎTÂNOMÁCHIA

(Date unknown)

94 *Golden Fish*

MUTE fishes, too, with eyes of gold inlaid,
Through paradisal water swum and played.

T. F. HIGHAM

95 *Zeus dances*

HIMSELF, the sire of men, of gods the sire,
The centre took, and led the dancing quire.

T. F. HIGHAM

CYPRIA

(Date unknown)

96 *Flowery Garments*

SHE wrapped her flesh in raiment which the Hours
And Graces made and dipped in springtime flowers,
All that the Hours bring forth. Crocus they bring,
Bluebell and violet brave-blossoming,
Roses with lovely buds and nectarous scent,
Ambrosial petals of the jonquil blent
With lily-cups. So Aphrodîtê wore
Clothes that the scent of every season bore.

C. M. BOWRA

TYRTÆUS

(fl. 685–68 B.C.)

97 *How can Man die better*

NOBLE is he who falls in front of battle
  bravely fighting for his native land;
and wretchedest the man who begs, a recreant,
  citiless, from fertile acres fled.

Dear mother, ageing father, little children
  drift beside him, and his wedded wife;
unwelcome he shall be, wherever turning,
  press'd by want and hateful penury;
he shames his folk and cheats his glorious manhood;
  all disgrace attends him, all despite.

Come then,—if beggars go unheard, uncared for,
  spurn'd in life and in their children spurn'd—
with courage let us battle for our country,
  freely spending life to save our sons.

Young men, stand firm and fight, stand one by other;
  base retreat and rout let none begin.

Be high of heart, be strong in pride of combat;
  grapple, self-forgetting, man to man.

Forbear to fly, deserting men grown older—
  stiff about the knees, in honour old.

O foul reproach, when fallen with the foremost
  lies an elder, hindermost the young—
a man whose head is white, whose beard is hoary,
  breathing out his strong soul in the dust,

In nakedness his blood-wet members clutching—
  foul reproach, a sight no gods condone!
Naked he lies where youth were better lying—
  sweet-flow'rd youth, that nothing misbecomes.

181

Grown men regard the young, women desire them—
  fair in life, in noble death still fair.
Be steadfast then, be strong and firmly rooted,
  grip the ground astride, press teeth to lip.

T. F. HIGHAM

98   *Marching Song*

U P, in free-born hardihood,
    Soldiers born of Spartan blood!
Guard your left with shields a-swinging;
High the gallant spear-shafts flinging.
Hoard not life nor stint to pay:
Such was never Sparta's way.

C. M. BOWRA

TERPANDER
                                            (fl. 676 B.C.)

99   *To Zeus*

Z EUS, beginning of all things,
    Of all things the leader,
Zeus, to thee a libation
I pour, of hymns the beginning.

C. M. BOWRA

100   *To Apollo and the Muses*

L ET us pour a libation
    To Memory's daughters,
The Muses, and to the Muses'
Leader, Lêto's son.

C. M. BOWRA

101   *Sparta*

SPEAR-POINTS of young men blossom there:
   Clear-voiced the Muse's songs arise:
Justice is done in open air,
   The help of gallant enterprise.
C. M. BOWRA

CALLÎNUS

(fl. 660 B.C.)

102   *A Call to Action*

HOW long, young men, unsoldiered, disregarding,
   laze you, scorned by neighbours round about?
Slack to the bone, on peace resolved, supinely
   careless in a land where all is war?

   .   .   .   .   .

   hurl in death your javelins once again.
For great and glorious is a man defending
   home and children and his wedded wife
against the enemy. At Fate's own moment
   snaps his thread of life. So forward all
with spear in poise, crouching to shields that cover
   hearts courageous, soon as battle's joined.
There's no escaping death: that destination
   men must face—ev'n of immortal seed.
Many from war and ringing lance have sheltered,
   homeward fled: at home death finds them out.
But these the people love not, none regrets them:
   brave men fallen great and small lament.
The whole land mourns a man of heart heroic
   dead: in life a demigod he seems.
His strength is as a tower to all beholders—
   work for many hands he does alone.
T. F. HIGHAM

ARCHILOCHUS

(fl. 648 B.C.)

103   *The Poet's Spear*

MY spear wins bread, my spear wins Thracian wine:
To drink it, on my spear-head I recline.

C. M. BOWRA

104   *The Poet's Shield*

A PERFECT shield bedecks some Thracian now;
I had no choice: I left it in a wood.
Ah, well, I saved my skin, so let it go!
     A new one's just as good.

SIR WILLIAM MARRIS

105   *Thasos*

       Like a donkey's back
It stands, the summit crowned with savage woods.
It is no pretty place, nor stirs my love
And longing like the land by Sîris' pools.

C. M. BOWRA

106   *Simple Tastes*

I DO not care for Gygês' store of gold,
Nor envy it, nor gaze with jealousy
On what the gods have. For proud tyranny
I have no love. It lies far from my eyes.

C. M. BOWRA

184

107   *A Girl*

HOLDING a myrtle-rod she blithely moved,
    And a fair blossoming rose; the flowing tresses
Shadowed her shoulders, falling to her girdle.

J. A. SYMONDS

108   *Rough Sea*

GLAUCUS, look! at sea already splashing waves are
    swelling high,
And above the Cape of Gýræ pillared clouds mount up the
    sky,
Sign of storm to come, and panic comes upon us suddenly.

C. M. BOWRA

109   *The Ideal General*

NOT for me the general renowned nor the well-
    groomed dandy,
Nor he who is proud of his curls or is shaven in part;
But give me a man that is small and whose legs are bandy,
Provided he's firm on his feet and is valiant in heart.

A. WATSON BAIN

110   *Be still, my Soul*

HEART, my heart, with griefs confounded whence you
    no deliv'rance find,
Up against them! guard yourself and show the foe a
    gallant breast;

Take your stand among the foremost where the spears of
    battle fly
Gallantly. Nor when you conquer make your pleasure
    manifest,
Nor in turn, if you are conquered, lie down in your home
    and cry.
Take your joy when life is joyful, and in sorrow do not
    mind
Overmuch, but know what ups and downs belong to
    humankind.

C. M. BOWRA

III   *There is Nothing Strange*

NEVER man again may swear, things shall be as once
    they were;
Never more in wonder stare, since the Olympian thunderer
Bade the Sun's meridian splendour hide in shade of murky
    night;
While affrighted nations started, trembling at the sudden
    sight.
Who shall dare to doubt hereafter, whatsoever man may
    say?
Who refuse with stupid laughter credence to the wildest
    lay?
Though for pasture dolphins ranging leap the hills and
    scour the wood,
And fierce wolves, their nature changing, dive beneath
    th' astonished flood.

After J. H. MERIVALE

112   *God punishes*

Z EUS, father Zeus, the sky owns thy command:
    Thou overseest what men do
Both right and lawless, and in wild beasts too
    Pride and right doing feel thy hand.

C. M. Bowra

113   *Knowledge*

F EW tricks there are a fox won't learn:
    Hedge-hogs have one—a master-turn.

Anon.

ALCMAN

(fl. 630 B.C.)

114   *Hâgêsíchora*

V ENGEANCE is God's: he will repay.
    Lucky who, without a tear,
fills the pattern of one day
    with gaiety.

                        And now, give ear!
Of radiant Ágido my lay
shall be—her radiance as clear
as the sun, whose morning ray
she conjures to appear.

                        I hear,
but any praise or any blame of her
is silenced by our fair chief-chorister
    whose beauty seems as high and rare
    as if with brutes one should compare
a sturdy thundering horse, a champion,
    of wingèd dreams the son.

There's the likeness, plain to see:
steed of proud Enétic race,
and my cousin—fair is she
and her tresses have the grace
of a golden filigree;
beneath the gold, a silver face—
shall I say whose it must be?

It is Hâgêsíchora's.
In beauty they shall be competitors—
a Lydian horse to pace a Scythian horse.
For while we make our offering
the Pleiadës arise and sing
in rivalry, like Sîrius burning bright
in the ambrosial night.

Not the wealth of crimson dress
makes our choir victorious,
nor do golden snakes that press
wrist and neck embolden us;
Lydian coif brings not success—
veiling our luxurious
maiden-eyes—nor Nanno's tress
nor Áretê the beauteous.
Sýlakis, or Kleêsisêra? nay—
Nor at the school of Ainêsimbrotê
can you say 'My saviour is
Philylla, or Ástaphis,
lovely Viánthemis, Dâmáreta—'
'tis Hâgêsíchora!

Look, beside me sings my friend,
my cousin, of the ankles small:
Ágido and she commend
alike our ceremonial.
Immortals, who possess the end
of every action, hear their call
with favour, as their voices blend!
For my own singing is the squall
which the owl screeches foolishly above
the rooftree; though my heart would dearly love
   to please the goddess Dawn who brings
   comfort for our sufferings.
Yet Hâgêsíchora leads us with song
    to peace, for which we long.

The chariot obediently
follows the outrunning steed;
men obey the helmsman's cry,
when on shipboard, with all speed.
Our own leader's melody
though it surpasses not, indeed,
the Sirens—they are gods—will vie
with ten or more of mortal breed.
Her voice is like a swan upon the streams
of Xanthus river; and the golden gleams
   in her companion's hair. . . .

GILBERT HIGHET

115 *The Halcyons*

NO more, O maiden voices, sweet as honey, soft as
love is,
No more my limbs sustain me.—A halcyon on the wing
Flying o'er the foam-flowers, in the halcyon coveys,
Would I were, and knew not care, the sea-blue bird of
spring!

H. T. WADE-GERY

116 *On the Mountains*

WHERE, on the mountain peaks high up,
Their torch-lit feasts the gods amuse,
Often you took a great gold cup,
A vessel such as shepherds use,
And milked a lioness with your hands, to make
A round of silver-bright cheese-cake.

C. M. BOWRA

117 *Night*

THE far peaks sleep, the great ravines,
The foot-hills, and the streams.
Asleep are trees, and hivèd bees,
The mountain beasts, and all that dark earth teems,
The glooming seas, the monsters in their deeps:
And every bird, its wide wings folded, sleeps.

H. T. WADE-GERY

MIMNERMUS

(fl. 630 B.C.)

118   *Sine amore nil est jucundum*

O GOLDEN Love, what life, what joy but thine?
  Come death when thou art gone and make an end!
When gifts and tokens are no longer mine,
  Nor the sweet intimacies of a friend.
These are the flowers of youth. But painful age,
  The bane of beauty, following swiftly on,
Wearies the heart of man with sad presage
  And takes away his pleasure in the sun.
Hateful is he to maiden and to boy,
And fashioned by the gods for our annoy.

G. LOWES DICKINSON

119   *We all do fail as a Leaf*

WE are as leaves in jewelled springtime growing
  That open to the sunlight's quickening rays;
So joy we in our span of youth, unknowing
  If God shall bring us good or evil days.

Two fates beside thee stand; the one hath sorrow,
  Dull age's fruit, that other gives the boon
Of Death, for youth's fair flower hath no to-morrow,
  And lives but as a sunlit afternoon.

And when thine hour is spent, and passeth by thee,
  Surely to die were better than to live,
Ere grief or evil fortune come anigh thee,
  And penury that hath but ill to give.

Who longs for children's love, for all his yearning
    Shall haply pass to death anhungered still;
Or pain shall come, his life to anguish turning,
    Zeus hath for all an endless store of ill.

J. A. POTT

120   *The Never-resting Sun*

SURELY the Sun has labour all his days,
    And never any respite, steeds nor god,
Since Eôs first, whose hands are rosy rays,
    Ocean forsook, and Heaven's high pathway trod;
At night across the sea that wondrous bed
    Shell-hollow, beaten by Hêphaistos' hand,
Of wingèd gold and gorgeous, bears his head
    Half-waking on the wave, from eve's red strand
To the Ethiop shore, where steeds and chariot are,
Keen-mettled, waiting for the morning star.

GILBERT MURRAY

SÊMÔNIDÊS

(fl. 630 B.C.)

121   *The Dead*

OF souls departed, if our minds were strong,
    We'd think no longer than a day is long.

ANON.

122   *Some Women*

AT the creation God made women's natures
    various. One he made from a bristly sow:
and all her household welters in confusion,
    lying aground in miscellaneous muck,

while she unwashen in unlaundered clothes
reposes in her pigsty, fattening.

God made another from a canny vixen,
the woman who knows all—nothing escapes her,
evil and good, she knows it all alike.
Many a time she says an evil thing,
but often good: such is her shifty nature.

The dog's own image for activity,
eager to hear and find out everything,
runs peering everywhere, casting about,
and even without finding still gives tongue.
Her husband's threats will not avail to stop her,
not even anger and a stone to smash
her teeth, nor yet a kindly word and a pat:
even if she's a guest in another home,
the bitch persists in her incessant yapping.

The Heavenly Ones moulded a woman of earth
and gave her to a husband, incomplete.
She lacks the knowledge of both good and evil:
the only work she understands is eating;
not even when she's chilled by wintry weather
does she bestir herself to move to the fire.

Another is the sea, and double natured.
One day she is all laughter and radiance:
a stranger, seeing her at home, would praise her—
'There is no finer woman in existence
anywhere in the earth, nor lovelier.'
Another day she cannot be approached
or looked upon—she is a maniac,
berserk, like mother-dog above her whelps;
implacable she is to all alike,
a stumbling-block to enemies and friends.

She is the sea: it lies in kindly calm,
often in summertime, a boundless joy
to sailors; yet it often turns to madness,
sweeping along in thundershouting billows.
This woman has a kindred temperament:
she has a nature like the fickle deep.

And one, a bee: fortunate man who gets her!
In her alone blame finds no resting place:
she makes a life fertile and prosperous;
bearing a noble and illustrious stock
she reaches age in the love of a dear spouse.
She grows in good repute among all women
and is invested with a heavenly grace.
Her pleasure is not sitting among women
when they tell tales of love and venery.
Such a woman is a bounty given to man
by God—she is the best and wisest wife.

GILBERT HIGHET

ARÎON?

(fl. 620 B.C.)

123   *Hymn to Poseidon*

MIGHTY God Poseidon, thee I sing,
   Girder of the Earth, of Ocean king,
   Golden trident brandishing.

Round thee sport in joyous rout
      Lightly leaping, gleaming, glancing,
      Tossing in their finny dancing
Bristly mane and flattened snout,
Dolphins, whom the Muse enthrals—
      Playmates 'neath the briny waters
      Chasing Amphitrîtê's daughters
         In the Nêreïds' halls.

These bore me to the coast of Pelops' isle
    On their curvèd backs uplifted,
Cleaving the furrows of a pathless plain,
    On a perilous voyage I drifted,
Cast by treacherous seamen's guile
    Into the darkling main.

HERBERT KYNASTON

ANONYMOUS
                                        (7th and 6th cent. B.C.)

124   *Country Lore*

            (*i*) *Sowing Days*

SOW your wheat in muddy weather;
    In the dust your barley sow.

            (*ii*) *Wind and Weather*

Sou'west blows the cloud together,
    And as quickly clears again;
Nor'west makes the rainy weather,
    Every cloud is in his train.

T. F. HIGHAM

125   *Songs of Work*

            (*i*) *For the Sheaf*

    A sheaf, a sheaf, send, send a great sheaf.

J. M. EDMONDS

(*ii*) *At the Mill*

GRIND, mill, grind,
Even as Pittacus grinds,
Master of great Mytilênê.

R. SYME

126 *Songs of Play*

(*i*) *Here we go gathering . . .*

—Where are my roses, where are my violets,
And where is my fine parsley?
—Here are your roses, here are your violets,
And here is your fine parsley.

(*ii*) *Blind Man's Buff*

—I go a-hunting a Copper Fly.
—Hunt you may, but you'll never come nigh.

(*iii*) *Tortoise in the Ring*

—Turtle-tortle, what dost thou there?
—I'm weaving a weft of Milêsian rare.
—And how comes thy bantling a corpse for to be?
—He drove a white horse and went splash in the sea.

J. M. EDMONDS

127   *A Love Song*

UP, for mercy, and be going,—
  O will nothing rouse my dear?
These delays are my undoing;
  Up, or *he* will find us here.

What a mischief's in the making!
  Misery me, we're both undone!
See, the window,—dawn is breaking;
  Up, dear lover, and begone.

T. F. HIGHAM

128   *Spartan Three-choir Festival*

CHOIR OF OLD MEN: Time was, our hearts were young and
                   stout.
  MEN FULL-GROWN: Like ours to-day,—look round about!
   CHOIR OF BOYS: And we'll be better men, out and out!

T. F. HIGHAM

129   *Línos*

O LÍNOS, pure music was given
  To thee of all mortals alone,—
Thy gift, by the grace of all heaven,
  Or ever a singer was known.
Phœbus in anger strikes thee dead,
And tears of the Muses for thee are shed.

T. F. HIGHAM

130   *Swallow Song*

THE swallow comes winging
   Her way to us here;
Fair weather she's bringing,
And a happy new year.
White is her breast,
And black all the rest.

Roll us out a plum-cake,
For the swallow's sake,
From the house of your plenty;
And wine in a flasket,
And cheese in a basket;
Or a bakie she'll eat
Of your pease or your wheat,
She's not over-dainty!

Will you give us? Or shall we go?
If you will,—why, rest you so;
But and if you shall say us nay,
Then we will carry the door away,
Or the lintel above it, or, easiest of all,
Your wife within, for she is but small.
Give us our need
And take God speed.
Open the door to the swallow, then,
For we are children and not old men.

(VARIOUS HANDS)

ALCÆUS

(fl. 600? B.C.)

131   *To Athêna*

QUEEN ATHÊNA, strong in war,
   Sentinel of that demesne
Where the water-meadows are
And Côrálius rolls between
   Corônêa's banks of green.

T. F. HIGHAM

132   *An Armoury*

SPLENDID burns the huge house with bronze; rich is
   the ample roof
with radiant helmets; overhead each helmet lets a horsehair plume
droop, the warrior's ornament. Plates of armour hang on
   the pin,
greaves of radiant bronze, defence against the sturdy javelin.
Curved shields and cuirasses of new linen bestrew the room;
here are blades from Chalcis; here is many a cincture and
   kilt of proof.
These are things we must remember now our duty shall
   begin.

GILBERT HIGHET

133   *Storm at Sea*

(*i*)

THE quarrelling winds perplex me. On this side
   One wave rolls up, on that a different tide,
And the black ship, whereon we sail,
Shifts with the shifting of the gale.

We are exhausted by the fearful blast:
Round the mast's foot the bilge is rising fast.
　　And all the sail is thin and worn,
　　With great holes gaping, rent and torn.

(ii)

On top of all the rest comes on a new
Wave up, and that will give us much to do . . .
　　Patch up with haste the gaping side
　　And into a safe harbour ride!

Let no soft fear lay hold of anyone;
Before us lies a great task to be done.
　　Remembering the past and how
　　We suffered, prove our manhood now!

C. M. Bowra

134 *Antiménidas*

FRIEND, you have come from the world's end home
　With an ivory hilt to your blade
Gold-inlaid; for you fought
Among Babylon's ranks and you wrought
In their need, a great deed,
When you slew in the fight
A redoubtable man
Who was five royal cubits in height
Save a span.

Sir William Marris

135 *Drinking Songs*

(i)

ZEUS rains; a storm comes in its might
From heav'n, and freezes rivers tight . . .

Put down the storm! Pile up the fire,
Mix the sweet wine to your desire,
  And round your forehead set
  A dainty coronet.

To woe the heart must not give in.
In grief's no help. One medicine,
  My friend, alone is fit—
  Wine—, and get drunk on it.

(ii)

Now bind the woven necklaces
Of dill about your throat
And let the smell of frankincense
Into your bosom float.

(iii)

Drink! Why wait for lamps? The day
Has not another inch to fall.
Fetch the biggest beakers—they
Hang on pegs along the wall.

Bacchus, son of Sémelê
And of Zeus, discovered wine
Giving it to man to be
Care's oblivious anodyne.

Pour in water two to one,
Fill them full to overflowing;
When the first is drained and done,
Set another cup a-going!

(iv)

Soak your lungs with wine, for now
The Dog Star's at the turn.
How the summer wounds, and how
All must thirst and burn.

In the bushes, strong and clear
Now the cricket sings,
And sweet music fills the air
From beneath his wings.

Now is all the earth at song
In the summer's fire,
And the girasole is strong.
Now does wild desire

Make the girls most amorous.
But the men won't please;
For the fire of Sîrius
Withers heads and knees.

(v)

On my long-suffering head let the sweet myrrh flow,
Let it flow on my breast where the white hairs show.
C. M. BOWRA

136   *To Sappho*

    Violet-haired, holy, sweetly-smiling Sappho!

ANON.

137   *Immortalia ne speres*

DRINK, Melanippus, and be drunk with me.
   How can you think that you will ever see,

Once over Ácheron, the pure bright day
Again? Come, throw such proud desires away.

Sîsyphus, wisest of men, thought he could find
An artifice that should leave death behind,

But fate decreed his wisdom should not save
Him from twice crossing Ácheron's rough wave,

And Cronus' son gave him great sufferings
Below the dark earth. Hope not for such things,

While we are young. Now is the moment, now,
To take what happiness the gods allow.

C. M. BOWRA

138   *Helen and Thetis*

NOT thee, O world's desire
   Did Pêleus bear away
As bride from her sea-sire;
   When on his wedding-day
He bade the immortals come
And feast in Cheiron's home.

No; but a maiden chaste
Was she whom he embraced,
    A princess of the sea;
And when a year had passed
    She bare a son, and he
    Of demigods was best,
Driving his chestnut yoke,
    A charioteer of pride;
But Troy, and all her folk,
    Because of Helen, died.

SIR WILLIAM MARRIS

139   *Castor and Polydeucês*

COME, sons of Zeus, from Pelops' isle,
    Lêda's children valorous,—
Castor and Polydeucês, smile
    With gentle hearts on us.

O'er earth's broad lands and every sea
    Your racing horses' reins you hold,
And men you rescue easily
    From death in freezing cold,

When on trim ships astern you spring
    And climb the thwarts, a far-seen light:
A lantern to black ships you bring
    In the despairing night.

C. M. BOWRA

SAPPHO

To Aphrodîtê

(fl. 600? B.C.)

IMMORTAL on thy many-splendoured throne
  Hear, Aphrodîtê Queen, that art
Zeus' witching daughter; and with pain and moan
  Break not my heart!

But come, if ever thou hast caught of old
  My distant cry and heard my plea,
And left thy father's palaces of gold
  To visit me;

And yoked thy chariot, and from heaven forth
  Driven thy sparrows fleet and fair
With whirr of wings above the swarthy earth
  Through middle air.

How fast they came! Then, Blessèd One, didst thou
  With lips divinely smiling ask:
'What new mischance is come upon thee now?
  Unto what task

'Have I been called? what is the dearest aim
  Of thy mad heart? who is to be
Persuaded to thy passion? Sappho, name
  Thine enemy!

'For whoso flies thee now shall soon pursue;
  Who spurns thy gifts shall give anon;
And whoso loves thee not, whate'er she do,
  Shall love thee soon.'

205

Ah, come then, and release me from alarms
          That crush me: all I long to see
Fulfilled, fulfil! A very mate-in-arms
          Be thou to me.

SIR WILLIAM MARRIS

141   *To a Bride*

BLEST beyond earth's bliss, with heaven I deem him
    Blest, the man that in thy presence near thee
Face to face may sit, and while thou speakest,
    Listening may hear thee,

And thy sweet-voiced laughter:—In my bosom
    The rapt heart so troubleth, wildly stirred:
Let me see thee, but a glimpse—and straightway
    Utterance of word

Fails me; no voice comes; my tongue is palsied;
    Thrilling fire through all my flesh hath run;
Mine eyes cannot see, mine ears make dinning
    Noises that stun;

The sweat streameth down,—my whole frame seized with
    Shivering,—and wan paleness o'er me spread,
Greener than the grass; I seem with faintness
    Almost as dead.

WALTER HEADLAM

142   *The Moon*

BRIGHT stars, around the fair Selênê peering,
    No more their beauty to the night discover
When she, at full, her silver light ensphering,
          Floods the world over.

T. F. HIGHAM

143   *Forgotten*

D EAD shalt thou lie; and nought
   Be told of thee or thought,
For thou hast plucked not of the Muses' tree:
     And even in Hades' halls
     Amidst thy fellow-thralls
No friendly shade thy shade shall company!

THOMAS HARDY

144   *Flowers for the Graces*

W EAVE garlands, maiden, from the strands
   Of dill, and with soft gentle hands
Set the delicious leafage round your head.
     The Goddess and the happy Graces
     Love to look on flower-crown'd faces,
But turn aside from the ungarlanded.

C. M. BOWRA

145   *An Absent Friend*

A GLORIOUS goddess in her eyes
   Were you, her comrade, and your songs
Above all other songs she'd prize.

With Lydian women now she dwells
Surpassing them, as when day dies
The rosy-fingered moon excels

The host of stars, and light illumes
The salt sea and the cornland glows
With light upon its thousand blooms.

In loveliness the dew spills over
And with new strength revives the rose,
Slim grasses and the flowering clover.

But sadly up and down she goes,
Remembering Atthis, once her lover,
And in her heart sick longing grows.

C. M. Bowra

146   *Evening*

THOU, Hesper, bringest homeward all
    That radiant dawn sped far and wide,
The sheep to fold, the goat to stall,
    The children to their mother's side.

Sir Rennell Rodd

147   *Parting*

Truly I want to die.
Such was her weeping when she said Good-bye.

These words she said to me:
'What sad calamity!
Sappho, I leave you most unwillingly.'

To her I made reply:
'Go with good heart, but try
Not to forget our love in days gone by.

'Else let me call to mind,
If your heart proves unkind,
The soft delightful ways you leave behind.

'Many a coronet
　　Of rose and violet,
Crocus and dill upon your brow you set:

'Many a necklace too
　　Round your soft throat you threw,
Woven with me from buds of ravishing hue,

'And often balm you spread
　　Of myrrh upon my head,
And royal ointment on my hair you shed.'

C. M. Bowra

148　　　　　　*A Young Bride*

(*i*)

LIKE the sweet apple which reddens upon the topmost
　　bough,
A-top on the topmost twig,—which the pluckers forgot
　　somehow,—
Forgot it not, nay, but got it not, for none could get it
　　till now.

(*ii*)

Like the wild hyacinth flower, which on the hills is
　　found,
Which the passing feet of the shepherds for ever tear and
　　wound,
Until the purple blossom is trodden into the ground.

D. G. Rossetti

149   *Mother, I cannot mind my Wheel*

SWEET mother, let the weaving be,
My hand is faint to move.
Frail Aphrodîtê masters me;
   I long for my young love.

T. F. HIGHAM

150   *Wedding Songs*

(*i*)

BRIDE.   Maidenhood, O Maidenhood
               Where art thou flown away from me?
MAIDENHOOD.   Never again shall I come back,
               Never again back to thee.

C. M. BOWRA

(*ii*)

BRIDEGROOM dear, to what shall I compare thee?
To a slim green rod best do I compare thee.

ANON.

151   *Garden of the Nymphs*

COOL waters tumble, singing as they go
Through appled boughs. Softly the leaves are
      dancing.
Down streams a slumber on the drowsy flow,
      My soul entrancing.

T. F. HIGHAM

152   *Love*

LOVE has unbound my limbs and set me shaking,
  A monster bitter-sweet and my unmaking.

C. M. BOWRA

153   *A Girl*

I HAVE a child; so fair
  As golden flowers is she,
My Cleïs, all my care.
I'd not give her away
For Lydia's wide sway
Nor lands men long to see.

C. M. BOWRA

154   *To Atthis*

I LOVED you, Atthis, once, long, long ago . . .
  You seemed to me a small, ungainly child.

C. M. BOWRA

155   *The Nightingale*

THE dear good angel of the spring
  The nightingale.

BEN JONSON

156   *Night*

THE Moon is gone
  And the Pleiads set,
  Midnight is nigh;
Time passes on,
And passes, yet
  Alone I lie.

J. M. EDMONDS

211

157 *Andrómachê's Wedding*

'HECTOR and his men bring the girl, her eyes
     gleaming,
From Thêbê the Holy, from Plácia fount unfailing,
Andrómachê the beautiful, over the salt sea sailing
With whorls and roundlets golden, with robes for her
     arraying
Purple embroidered daintily, away on the wind streaming;
And silver cups uncountable and carven ivory.'
   This was the herald's story.
And Hector's father heard it, and gay he rose, and the
     saying
Went the round of Troy Town for all friends' knowing.
Then the men of Troy put their mules into harnessing
Back against the chariots, and then mounted pressing
The rout of young women, and of lightfoot girls going,
Then Priam's daughters apart; and then the soldiers
Were harnessing their horses under the chariot rim,
The young men in their prime. . . .

And the sweet piping with lyreplay was blending,
With castanets clashing; and the maidens high singing
Sang the holy song to heaven ascending
With strange din ringing. . . .

There were myrrh and cassia with frankincense smoking;
There the elder women their chant were choiring;
There all the men sang their high song invoking
The God far-darting, Pæan of the lyring,
Singing for Hector and for Andrómachê divine.

GEORGE ALLEN

212

SOLON

(fl. 594 B.C.)

158 *The Protectress of Athens*

OUR city, by the immortal gods' intent
     and Zeus' decree, shall never come to harm:
for our bold champion, of proud descent,
     Pallas of Athens shields us with her arm.

GILBERT HIGHET

159 *The Lawgiver's Boast*

I GAVE the commons their sufficient meed
     of strength, nor let them lack, nor yet exceed.
Those who were mighty and magnificent,
I bade them have their due and be content.
My strong shield guarded both sides equally
and gave to neither unjust victory.

GILBERT HIGHET

160 *Diversity of Gifts*

THEIR several ends pursuing, one will roam
     The teeming sea, hard-driven by obstinate gales;
And hoping still to ship some profit home
     The prodigal of his own life he sails.
Some know the curving plough, and score therewith
     Earth's timbered fields, in yearlong bondage led.
Athênê and Hêphæstus, that great smith,
     Grant skill of hand: so others win their bread.
Another man the Olympian Muses teach
     By whose dear cunning measured numbers flow;
And lord Apollo, archer of long reach,
     Makes prophets, who foresee the impending blow

If god be with them: but the appointed doom
  No sign of bird or victim can prevent.
Pæôn, the god of medicine, gives to some
  That other art of slow accomplishment;
Now agony from a trifling hurt may spring,
  Nor any salve untie the knot of pain,
Now men distraught by desperate suffering
  At a mere touch are won to health again.

T. F. HIGHAM

STÊSÍCHORUS

(c. 630–c. 553 B.C.)

161　　　　　*The Setting Sun*

BUT now the Sun, great Hyperîon's child,
  Embark'd again upon his golden chalice,
And westward steer'd, where far o'er ocean wild
  Sleeps the dim night in solitary valleys;
Where dwell his mother, and his consort mild,
  And infant sons in his sequestered palace;
Whilst onward through the laurel-shaded grove
Mov'd with firm steps the hero son of Jove.

H. M.

162　　　　　*Palinode on Helen*

IT is not true, this tale:
  You never once set sail
On well-benched ships, nor went
To Troy's tall battlement.

C. M. BOWRA

DELPHIC ORACLE

(c. 580? B.C.)

163   *The Power of an Oath*

HEAR, Epicŷdês' son: 'twere much to thy present
  advantage
Could'st thou prevail by an oath and ravish the stranger's
  possessions:
Swear, an thou wilt; death waits for the just no less than
  the unjust.
Ay—but an oath hath a son, a nameless avenger of evil:
Hands hath he none, nor feet; yet swiftly he runneth
  pursuing,
Grippeth his man at the last and maketh an end of his
  offspring.
Better endureth the line of the man that sweareth not
  falsely.

A. D. GODLEY

IBYCUS

(fl. 560 B.C.)

164   *In the Spring*

IN the season of Spring is the season of growing;
  Where lies the inviolate orchard-meadow,
    The apple-garden where Maidens dwell,
There, watered freshly with runnels flowing,
  The quince-trees blossom, and safe in shadow
    The vine-buds under the vine-leaf swell
In the season of Spring. But in my heart passion
  At no tide ever asleep is laid:
From the Lady of Love as a blast of the North,
When a blaze of lightning flashes it forth,

215

With a rush, with a burst,
In a dark storm parching and maddening with thirst,
   Unabashed, unafraid,
It shoots to my bosom, gripping it still
   In the same rude fashion,
And shakes and shatters at will.

WALTER HEADLAM

165   *Love*

LO, Love again with glancing eyes
   That melt from under lids of jet
Drives me with manifold sorceries
Into the Cyprian's boundless net.
Ah, how I tremble when he comes on,
Like an old champion chariot-horse,
Who drags the light car, when youth is gone,
Unwillingly to the course.

C. M. BOWRA

166   *An Epilogue to Polýcratês*

THEY sailed from Argos, and brought down
   Dardanian Priam's happy town,
     Far-famed. Its doom fulfilled
     What mighty Zeus had willed.

For bright-haired Helen's beauty, long
Came war and tears,—'tis told in song,—
     A curse on patient Troy
     Sent Cypris, to destroy.

No trickster Paris suits my lay,
Nought of Cassandra shall I say,
    The slender-ankled, nor
    Of Priam's sons of yore,

Nought of the day which none may name
When Troy's tall towers passed in flame.
    No deeds shall I repeat
    Of those the well-built fleet

Of hollow warships brought to Troy,
Fine heroes banded to destroy:
    Them Agamemnon led,
    A prince of princes bred.

Them might the subtle muses tell,
The Helicônian sisters, well:
    No mortal man may trace
    Each vessel in its place,

How Menelâus set his sail
From Grecian Aulis to prevail
    In Dardan pasture-land
    With his bronze-shielded band,

Achæans all! First in the fight
Achilles showed his fleet-foot might,
    And Ajax, mighty one,
    Strong son of Télamon . . .

And one there was surpassing fair,
Whom golden-girdled Hyllis bare.
    But Greeks and Trojans less
    Admired his loveliness,

When set by Trôilus, side by side;
Like virgin gold thrice purified
    Compared with common brass
    His grace of body was.

Loveliness still belongs to these;
And with them you, Polýcratês,
    Shall have an endless name
    With my song and my fame.

C. M. BOWRA

ORACLE

(c. 546 B.C.)

167   *The Capture of Athens*

NOW hath the cast been made, and the net wide-
    spread is awaiting:
Tunnies come with the night, slipping on through the
    moon-lit water.

T. F. HIGHAM

PHOCÝLIDÊS

(fl. 544 B.C.)

168   *The Exception*

THIS also said Phocýlidês:
    'There's not an honest man
In Leros, but for Prócleês,
    And he's . . . a Lerian.'

T. F. HIGHAM

169   *A Small City on a Rock*

THIS also said Phocýlidês:
    A tiny rock-built citadel
Is finer far, if ordered well,
Than all your frantic Ninevehs.

C. M. Bowra

DÊMÓDOCUS
(fl. 537 B.C.)

170   *The Snake it was that died*

A VIPER stung a Cappadocian's hide,
    And poisoned by his blood that instant died.

J. H. Merivale

ANACREON
(c. 563–478 B.C.)

171   *To Artemis*

TO Artemis I kneel, whose bow
    Finds the stag and lays him low,
      The Queen whom beasts obey—
O child of Zeus, his golden daughter,
From Lêthæus whirling water
Thine eyes on men brave-hearted rest
With joy; for these thou shepherdest
      Have learnt the gentler way.

T. F. Higham

172 *To Dionŷsus*

ROVING god, whose playfellows
  Over the mountains' airy brows
    In happy chase are led;
Where Love, who breaks the heart of pride,
Or Nymphs amuse thee, violet-eyed,
Or Aphrodîtê keeps thy side,
    The goddess rosy-red—
Lord Dionyse, I kneel to thee;
Stoop to me of thy charity
    And this my prayer receive:
Dear Lord, thy best persuasion use,
Bid Cleobûlus not refuse
    The gift of love I give.

T. F. HIGHAM

173 *To Cleobûlus*

SOFT-EYED, a girl's, your face is . . .
  Unheard I plead: unknown
My soul takes on the traces
  And moves by you alone.

T. F. HIGHAM

174 *Love*

ONCE more the Lad with golden hair
  His purple ball across the air
    Flings at me, true to aim;
And light her broidered slippers go,
That Lesbian lass,—my playfellow
    As Love would set the game.

O Lesbos isle is tight and trim . . .
She's not the breed to pleasure him,
          Another game she plays;
My hair mislikes her, grown so white;
There's someone lovelier in her sight
          Who draws that callow gaze.

T. F. HIGHAM

175 (a)   *The Golden Mean*

NO Amalthéa's horn for me!
          Riches I disdain;
Nor in Tarshish would I be,
To king it for a century
          And half as long again.

175 (b)   *Old Age*

Sweet Youth no more will tarry,
          My friend a while ago;
Now white's the head I carry,
          And grey my temples grow,
          My teeth—a ragged row.

To taste the joy of living
          But little space have I,
And torn with sick misgiving
          I can but sob and sigh,
          So deep the dead men lie.

So deep their place and dismal,
  All means, be sure, they lack
Down in the murk abysmal
  To scale the upward track
  And win their journey back.

T. F. HIGHAM

176   *Nunc est bibendum*

WATER bring, and bring me wine,
  Bring the wreaths where flowers entwine;
Hasten, lad; our fists we try,
Matched together, Love and I.

Come, a wassail I would keep,
Drinking pledges flagon-deep.
Pour me wine, five measures, lad;
Measures ten of water add;
So good manners shall remain
In your Bacchant, foxed again.

Drink, good fellows, drink no more
With a clutter and uproar;
Thus, when Scythians hold a bout,
Wine goes in and tongues let out.
Gentlemen observe a mean,
Tippling with good songs between.

T. F. HIGHAM

177   *Take her, break her*

AH tell me why you turn and fly,
  My little Thracian filly shy?
    Why turn askance
    That cruel glance,
And think that such a dunce am I?

O I am blest with ample wit
To fix the bridle and the bit,
    And make thee bend
    Each turning-end
In harness all the course of it.

But now 'tis yet the meadow free
And frisking it with merry glee;
    The master yet
    Has not been met
To mount the car and manage thee.

WALTER HEADLAM

ANACREONTEA

(Date unknown)

178   *To the Swallow*

GENTLE Swallow, thou we know
    Every year dost come and go,
In the Spring thy nest thou mak'st;
In the Winter it forsak'st,
And divert'st thy self awhile
Near the Memphian Towers, or Nile;
But Love in my suff'ring breast
Builds, and never quits his nest;
First one Love's hatcht; when that flies,
In the shell another lies;
Then a third is half expos'd;
Then a whole brood is disclos'd,
Which for meat still peeping cry,
Whilst the others that can fly
Do their callow brethren feed,
And grown up, they young ones breed.

223

What then will become of me,
Bound to pain incessantly,
Whilst so many Loves conspire
On my heart by turns to tire?

THOMAS STANLEY

179   *At the Mid Hour of Night*

DOWNWARD was the wheeling Bear
    Driven by the Waggoner:
Men by powerful sleep opprest,
Gave their busie troubles rest:
Love, in this still depth of night,
Lately at my house did light;
Where perceiving all fast lockt,
At the door he boldly knockt.
'Who's that,' said I, 'that does keep
Such a noise, and breaks my sleep?'
'Ope,' saith Love, 'for pity hear;
'Tis a childe, thou need'st not fear,
Wet and weary, from his way
Led by this dark night astray.'
With compassion this I heard;
Light I struck; the door unbarr'd:
Where a little Boy appears,
Who wings, bow, and quiver bears;
Near the fire I made him stand,
With my own I chaft his hand;
And with kindly busie care
Wrung the chill drops from his hair:
When well warm'd he was, and dry,
'Now,' saith he, ''tis time to try

If my bow no hurt did get,
For me thinks the string is wet.'
With that, drawing it, a dart
He let fly that pierc'd my heart:
Leaping then, and laughing said,
'Come, my friend, with me be glad;
For my Bow thou see'st is sound,
Since thy heart hath got a wound.'

THOMAS STANLEY

180   *Cicada*

WE bless you, cicada,
    When out of the tree-tops
Having sipped of the dew
Like a king you are singing:
And indeed you are king of
These meadows around us,
And the woodland's all yours.
Man's dear little neighbour,
And midsummer's envoy,
The Muses all love you,
And Apollo himself does—
He gave you your music.
Age cannot wither you,
Tiny philosopher,
Earth-child, musician;
The world, flesh and devil
Accost you so little,
That you might be a god.

EDMUND BLUNDEN

HIPPÔNAX

(fl. 542 B.C.)

181   *A Visit from Wealth*

B UT never came there Plutus, the blind one,
   Unto my house, nor spake thus: 'Hippônax,
Minas of silver give I thee thirty.'

A. D. KNOX

PSEUDO-HIPPÔNAX

182   *Best Days*

T WO days are the best of a man's wedded life,
   The days when he marries and buries his wife.

J. M. EDMONDS

183   *Marriage*

T HAT Wife is best (as prudent men have found)
   Who brings for dower a Character that's sound.
No Marriage Portion serves a man instead
To stave Domestick Ruin from his head.
He'll find no Shrew to task him, but a Friend,—
A Fellow-worker faithful to the end.

ANON.

XENÓPHANÊS

(570–479 B.C.)

184   *Pythágoras and the Dog*

O NCE he was passing by an ill-used pup,
   And pitied it, and said (or so they tell)
'Stop, do not thrash it! 'tis a dear friend's soul:
   I recognized it when I heard it yell.'

SIR WILLIAM MARRIS

THEOGNIS

(fl. 520 B.C.)

185 *Choosing Friends*

WITH base men, boy, do not communicate;
  I tell you, cleave to men of high estate;
Eat you and drink with those, and sit with those,
And study those to pleasure that are great.

'Good rank, good sense.' Low company, no less,
Shall rob whatever wisdom you possess.

A. E. CRAWLEY (to l. 34)   (31–6)

186 *Reproach no Man for Poverty*

RAIL not at grinding Poverty, nor curse
  A man hard-driven for his empty purse;
As dips the balance, Zeus from day to day
Gives great possessions, or takes all away.

T. F. HIGHAM   (155–8)

187 *The Bane of Poverty*

POVERTY, Kyrnos, breaks a gallant man
  More than white hairs or shivering fevers can.
To flee it, Kyrnos, in the deep sea drown,
Or from a towering precipice leap down;
Broken by poverty, a man's denied
All power of speech and act: his tongue is tied.

T. F. HIGHAM   (173–8)

188   *Eugenics*

RAM, ass, and horse, my Kyrnos, we look over
.   With care, and seek good stock for good to cover;
And yet the best men make no argument,
But wed, for money, runts of poor descent.
So too a woman will demean her state
And spurn the better for the richer mate.
Money's the cry. Good stock to bad is wed
And bad to good, till all the world's cross-bred.
No wonder if the country's breed declines,—
Mixed metal, Kyrnos, that but dimly shines.

T. F. HIGHAM   (183–92)

189   *All Things to All Men*

BE versatile, my Kyrnos; make a blend
.   Of tone and temper suited to each friend.
Study the writhen cuttle where he lies
Toned to his fellow rock, and cheats our eyes.
Match every colour, follow every move,—
Wisdom is supple: folly keeps a groove.

T. F. HIGHAM   (213–18)

190   *Immortality conferred in vain*

I'VE given thee wings shall waft thee forth with ease
.   High o'er the land, high o'er the boundless seas;
No feast shall ever be but thou'lt be there
Couch'd on men's lips, for oft the young and fair
With ordered sweetness clear shall sing thy praise
To the clear flute; and when in after-days

To the dark and dolorous land thou com'st below,
Ne'er even in death shalt thou thy fame forgo,
But men will keep in memory unchanging
The name of Cyrnus, who shalt, all Greece ranging,
Mainland and island, pass the unharvested
Home of the fish, not Pegasus-wise, but sped
By the grand gifts of Them of the Violet Crown,
To all that ope their doors, and up and down
While Sun and Earth endure, world without end,
Shalt live a song to men;—yet I, sweet friend,
I have no honour small or great with thee,
But, like a child, with words thou cheatest me.

J. M. EDMONDS   (237–54)

191 *May I drink the Blood of my Enemies*

OLYMPIAN Zeus, a timely prayer fulfil
And grant good fortune may reprieve me still.
Come death, if I from ill find no relief
And vex not those that vex me, grief for grief.
There lies just measure. Now, in vain I wait
To smite the spoilers, lords of my estate,
Who stript me,—like a dog I scrambled past
The rain-swol'n torrent and shook free at last!
O let me drink their dark blood down! Take heed
Some kindly Spirit, and fulfil my need.

T. F. HIGHAM   (341–50)

192   *Refined Gold*

S O dress me down and douse me as you will,
   From head to foot shall flow clear water still.
In all I do assay me: you shall find
Pure gold, in red upon the touchstone sign'd,—
A grain no rust can foul, nor any trace
Of soiling mould its perfect bloom deface.

T. F. HIGHAM   (447–52)

193   *A Faithless Friend*

Y OU stole my friend, a sneakthief manifest,
   Driving the old road that you still have driven
With that cold spotted snake claspt to your breast,—
O damned,—by man a knave, a fiend by heaven!

T. F. HIGHAM   (599–602)

194   *An Oath*

L ET the brass dome of heaven, wide and great,
   Fall on me, and man's terrors consummate,
   If I be not a true friend to my friends,
And a true grief and pain to those I hate.

A. E. CRAWLEY   (869–72)

195   *Put Money in thy Purse*

S AVE up. Your very death won't dim an eye
   If none perceive a heritage put by.

T. F. HIGHAM   (931–2)

230

196   *Weep for Youth's Passing*

WHAT fools men are to weep the dead and gone!
　　Unwept, youth drops its petals one by one.

T. F. HIGHAM   (1069–70)

197   *Pride of the Flesh*

PRIDE it was that laid Magnêsia low,
　　And Kólophôn and Smyrna. Well I know,
Kyrnos, the way that you and yours shall go.

T. F. HIGHAM   (1103–4)

198   *The Dead feel not*

THAT my dead bones should lie in royal state
　　I wish not, but would live more fortunate.
Lie hard, lie soft, all's one: when we are dead
Rugs are no richer than a quick-thorn bed.

T. F. HIGHAM   (1191–4)

199   *The Crane's Message*

I HEARD the crane cry unto men his greeting,
　　To tell them it was time to drive the plough:
Ah, friend! he set my sorry heart a-beating,
　　For others have my fertile acres now.

SIR WILLIAM MARRIS   (1197–1200)

231

ANONYMOUS

200   *Kicking against the Pricks*

Said horse to ass, 'Why kick against the pricks?'
ANON.

201   *Belly and Mind*

A fat paunch never bred a subtle mind.
ANON.

202   *A Mite*

This trifle rates my wealth, not my esteem.
ANON.

SIMONIDÊS
(556–467 B.C.)

203   *The Greek Dead at Thermopylæ*

GREAT are the fallen of Thermopylæ,
Nobly they ended, high their destination—
Beneath an altar laid, no more a tomb,
Where none with pity comes or lamentation,
            But praise and memory—
            A splendour of oblation
No rust shall blot nor wreckful Time consume.

The ground is holy: here the brave are resting,
And here Greek Honour keeps her chosen shrine.
Here too is one the worth of all attesting—
Leónidas, of Sparta's royal line,
Who left behind a gem-like heritage
            Of courage and renown,
            A name that shall go down
            From age to age.

T. F. HIGHAM

232

204   *Human Imperfection*

HARD it is wholly to win worthy manhood,
with hand and foot and heart alike to be foursquare,
an ashlar cut without a flaw.
Who is not bad, not all a niddering, who knows
the right that makes the city stand—
a sound man he: not I indeed
will ever fault him, for of fools
the generation's endless. All, all is fair
that is not mingled with the base.

Harmony sings not in Píttacus' proverb,
nay, not for me, although a wight of wisdom spake
the word, that *to excel is hard*.
A god alone could have such privilege: a man
undone by a resistless fate
must needs be bad. Yes: every man
is worthy if his luck is good,
and bad if it goes badly. They most excel
who are belovèd by the gods.

Therefore I seek no impossible being,
I squander not my life's allotted term, in vain,
on an impracticable hope—
faultless humanity—beyond their power who win
the bread of life from spacious earth;
when 'tis discovered, I shall tell.
Honour and love to every man
who wills to do no baseness; but not the gods
themselves oppose necessity.
GILBERT HIGHET

233

205 *The Turn of a Dragonfly's Wing*

BEING but man, forbear to say
    Beyond to-night what thing shall be,
And date no man's felicity.
        For know, all things
        Make briefer stay
Than dragonflies, whose slender wings
        Hover, and whip away.

T. F. HIGHAM

206 *Dánaê*

THE wind blew fresh and seaward made,
    The water stirred and lifted;
She, in carven coffer laid,
Rode the sea, and drifted.

Stolen upon her cheek tear-wet
Fear in that hour came preying;
But Perseus in her arm she set
And held him to her, saying:

'Child, my heart is faint with care ...
You lie quiet, unaware,
    Drowsing still, dream-possest,
All the world a mother's breast.

In this vessel brute and bare,
Brazen-clamped and timbered tight,
    Stark your bed, wrapt about
With the darkness of our night
And the raven gloom without.

234

Spindrift comes and then is gone
Dashing your hair with deepening brine,
And the wind howls—all in vain.
        Safe you rest, sleeping on
In your cloak of purple stain,
Cheek laid up to cheek of mine.

Child, if fear to you were fear,
Soon would turn that dainty ear
To my words attending;
Now I bid you nothing hear—
        Sleep, my babe, sleep, O sea,
Sleep, my pain unending.

Father Zeus, I call to thee.
Lighten our adversity,
Turning evil into good.
Oh, forgive my hardihood
If I speak offending.'

T. F. Higham

207   *Orpheus*

                And over his head
Birds without number are flying. Fishes leap around
Out of the deep blue waters won by the tuneful sound.

J. Sterling

208 *Stillness and Sound*

NO breath of a wind rose then
      To stir the leaves of the trees,
Nor any quivering breeze
To stay the sweet note of his song
From travelling straight along
To be fixed to the ears of men.

C. M. BOWRA

209 *Monuments perish*

THOUGHTFUL men their praise withhold
      From Lindian Cleobûlus. He defied
Running rivers, spring flowers, burning gold
Of sun and moon, and swirling ocean pools
In strength to outbide
A stone.
The gods are strong alone.
Marble our hands can break to bits.
Those Lindian wits
Are but a fool's.

T. F. HIGHAM

210 *The Climb to Virtue*

VIRTUE dwells, so runs the tale,
      On precipices hard to scale.
Swift holy Nymphs attend her place;
No mortal eyes may see her face,
But only he, who with distress
Of soul and sweating heart can press
On to the height in manliness.

C. M. BOWRA

211   *The Athenian Dead*

O N Dirphys' wrinkled side we fell;
   And where the Narrow Waters drift
Our countrymen, to mark us well,
   Raised up this cairn, their gift.

A gift deserved; for youth is sweet,
   And youth we gave, nor turned away,
Though sharp the storm of battle beat
   That darkened all our day.

T. F. HIGHAM

212   *At Thermopylæ*

T ELL them in Lakëdaimôn, passer-by,
   That here obedient to their word we lie.

(VARIOUS HANDS)

213   *The Poet's Friend*

T HIS is the grave of famed Megistias, whom
   Beside Spercheius' stream the Persian slew:
A seer he, who dared to share the doom
   Of Sparta's leaders, though that doom he knew.

G. B. GRUNDY

214   *Platæa*
   (i) *The Spartan Monument*

I NTO the dark death cloud they passed, to set
   Fame on their own dear land for fadeless wreath,
And dying died not. Valour lifts them yet
   Into the splendour from the night beneath.

H. MACNAGHTEN

(ii) *The Athenian Monument*

IF Valour's best be gallantly to die,
Fortune to us of all men grants it now.
We to set Freedom's crown on Hellas' brow
Laboured, and here in ageless honour lie.

W. C. LAWTON

215   *Tégëa*

(i) *A Cenotaph*

NO cloud of smoke, from Tégëa thrown
In blaze of ruin, smote the sky;
Such men were these, she holds her own,
And wide her acres lie.

As counting freedom hard to lose,
To sons they left her prime unspent;
Themselves the battle's front they chose,
And went to death content.

T. F. HIGHAM

(ii) *A Grave*

HERE let them lie, remembered well,
Who died for Tégëa, spear in hand,
The guardians of her citadel
And flocks that graze her land.

With Hellas' freedom for their crown
In battle onward still they thrust,
That she might live, nor tumble down
Her garland in the dust.

T. F. HIGHAM

216   *Archédikê*

THE child of Hippias, foremost captain once
  In Hellas' land, lies here, Archédikê.
With lords for father, husband, brethren, sons,
  She lifted not her heart to vanity.

W. LEAF

217   *Lost at Sea*

                        (*i*)

FROM Sparta to Apollo we
  Sailed with the first-fruits of the year;
But one night wrecked us in one sea,
  And in one grave men laid us here.

G. ARUNDELL ESDAILE

                        (*ii*)

GO, topless Geraneia, and gaze, foul precipice,
  On Ister far, or reaches of Scythian Tánaïs,
Neighbour no more to Scîron, whose maddened sea
      consumes
Its rage around Molûrias, storming the mountain combes.
A cold corpse now you leave him: these empty stones
      bewail
The heaviness of shipwreck, the unreturning sail.

T. F. HIGHAM

(iii)

A STRANGE land holds thy bones; the Euxine sea
   Has brought thee, roving Cleisthenês, thy doom.
No honey-sweet returning was for thee,
   Nor sight of thy sea-girdled Chian home.

W. LEAF

218   *Tîmómachus*

W HEN in his father's arms he lay
    And breathed the joy of youth away,
Tîmómachus for good-bye said,—
'Son of Tîmênor, mourn your son.
Look not for such another one,
    A heart so brave, so cool a head.'

T. F. HIGHAM

219   *A Friend's Grave*

C RUEL disease, to grudge the soul of man
  Its sojourn with sweet youth a little span!
Before the lad had looked upon a wife,
You spoiled Tîmarchus of his happy life.

SIR WILLIAM MARRIS

220   *A Cretan Merchant*

H ERE Brótachus from Cretan Gortyn lies:
  He did not come for this, but merchandise.

C. M. BOWRA

240

221   *A Hound*

ALTHOUGH beneath this grave-mound thy white
   bones now are lying,
  Surely, my huntress Lycas, the wild things dread thee
    still.
The memory of thy worth tall Pêlion keeps undying,
   And the looming peak of Ossa, and Cithæron's lonely
    hill.

F. L. LUCAS

222   *Timócreon*

AFTER much eating, drinking, speaking ill
   Of others, here Timócreon lies still.

C. M. BOWRA

223   *Dedication for a Spear*

TO pillar's height reach up, and rest thee now,
   Tall ashen beam, with Zeus the Oracular.
Outworn and old thy head of bronze and thou,
   A spear long shaken in the blaze of war.

T. F. HIGHAM

224   *A Winner of the Pentathlon*

PHÎLO begat Díophôn, who was crowned at the
   Isthmus and Delphi,
  winning the race and the leap, wrestle and discus and
   spear.

GILBERT HIGHET

225   *A Boxer*

WHAT is your name? and your father's? your
country? and where was your prowess?
Kásmylos: Euágoras: Pythian boxer: from Rhodes.

GILBERT HIGHET

ANONYMOUS

(6th–5th cents. B.C.)

226   *To Athêna*

PALLAS, born by Trîton side,
  Guide our State, our people guide;
   Queen Athêna, hear us.
Pain and strife keep far away,
And deaths that come before their day;
   Zeus thy father hear us.

T. F. HIGHAM

227   *To Pan*

PAN, who hast to thy command
  Arcady, that famous land,
Pan the dancer, borne along
With the nymphs of Bacchus' throng,
Smile upon me, Pan, for pleasure
At a merry heart and measure.

T. F. HIGHAM

228   *A Window in the Breast*

COULD we but see men as they are!
      Could bare the breast, unpin it,
Hold it apart, and view the heart,
      And read what lies within it;
Then close it fast again, and call
A friend a friend for all in all!

W. HEADLAM

229   *The Four Best Things*

HEALTH is the first good lent to men;
      A gentle disposition then:
Next, to be rich by no by-wayes;
Lastly, with friends t'enjoy our dayes.

ROBERT HERRICK

230   *Harmódius and Arístogeiton*

The blade I bear
A myrtle spray shall wear;
Harmódius and Arístogeiton so
      Enwreathed the brand
That laid the tyrant low
And liberated our Athenian land.

Not dead thou art,
Harmódius, dear heart,
But gone, men say, to islands of the blest,—
      For all his speed
Achilles there finds rest,
And Týdeus' child, the gallant Diomede.

243

The blade I bear
A myrtle spray shall wear;
Harmódius and Arístogeiton drest
The brand even so,
When at Athêna's feast
They laid Hipparchus, that great tyrant, low.

Dear hearts, your worth
Has deathless fame on earth,—
Harmódius and Arístogeiton, ye
Who blade in hand
Dealt death to tyranny
And liberated our Athenian land.

GILBERT HIGHET, T. F. HIGHAM

231   *Leipsýdrion*

AH, Leipsýdrion, thou hast betrayed them,
These thy comrades. What men were they!
They showed of what their fathers made them,
Stout fighters of no common clay.

C. M. BOWRA

232   *The Crab and the Snake*

SAID the Crab unto the Serpent,
As he held him fairly caught:
*Straightforward, sir, a mate should go,
And have no crooked thought.*

WALTER HEADLAM

233   *Wishes*

O THAT a lovely lyre were I,
   Fashioned all of ivory,
And lovely youths would bear me by
   To the Bacchic revelry!

O that a lovely cup were I,
   Virgin-gold made perfectly,
That a lovely dame might lift me high
   To shrive her soul to purity!

F. E. GARRETT

234   *What makes a Friend*

W HEN I am drinking, drink with me,
   With me spend youth's gay hours:
My lover equal-hearted be,
   Go crowned, like me, with flowers.
When I am merry and mad,
   Merry and mad be you:
When I am sober and sad,
   Be sad and sober too.

After H. H. MILMAN

235   *A Scorpion under Every Stone*

B EWARE the lurking scorpion, friend;
   There 's one to every stone;
All dangers on the dark attend,—
   Leave mysteries alone.

T. F. HIGHAM

236   *Wayward Desire*

THE sow one acorn has,
    Another fancy takes her;
And mine's a pretty lass,
    But fancy still forsakes her.

T. F. HIGHAM

HYBRIAS

(Date uncertain)

237   *A Soldier's Riches*

MY wealth's a burly spear and brand,
    And a right good shield of hides untann'd,
        Which on my arm I buckle:
With these I plough, I reap, I sow,
With these I make sweet vintage flow,
        And all around me truckle.

But your wights that take no pride to wield
A massy spear and well-made shield,
        Nor joy to draw the sword;
Oh, I bring those heartless, hapless drones
Down in a trice on their marrow-bones,
        To call me king and lord.

THOMAS CAMPBELL

ÆSCHYLUS

(525–456 B.C.)

Io

CHORUS

OUR steps again are homed
  Where once our Mother roamed
The guarded meadow of her flowery feeding;
  Hence, from the soil we tread,
  The sore-teased Io fled,
Through many a tribe of men so madly speeding;
  Then to fulfil her destined fate,
Held for the far shore, sundering the opposèd strait.

  Through Asia then she flew,
  The Phrygian pastures through,
By Teuthras' town among the Mysians lying,
  O'er Lydian lowlands wide
  And many a mountain-side
Alike Pamphylian and Cilician flying,
  Perennial river, golden plain,
And corn-abounding region, Aphrodîtê's reign.

  Still by the wingèd herd
  With sharp goad's pricking spurred,
She won at last that fair divine green isle,
  God's pasture fed with snows,
  Where met the eternal foes,
Harsh Tŷpho and the pure diseaseless Nile;
  There, maddening with despiteful shame
And stings of Hêra's malice, all distraught she came.

247

The folk then dwelling near
Paled with sickly fear,
Trembling amazed before the uncouth sight,—
A creature twinned, half-human,
Part heifer and part woman,—
Monstrous, a thing for marvelling and affright:—
Then who was he that gave her peace
And made the long-tormented Io's pain to cease?

Lord through all time's unending length,
O Zeus, the act was thine!
By force of thine unhurtful strength
And by thy breath divine
Her pain was healed, the spring unsealed
Of sorrowing tears and shameful ruth:
Zeus-laden then in very sooth,
A perfect Son she bare to thee.

A Son throughout all ages blest;
Whence every land doth cry:
'Here is the seed of Zeus confessed,
Life-giving Lord on high:
Those plagues that Hêra's wrath designed
Whose power but His had strength to cure?
This was His doing; these, for sure,
The ancient race of Épaphus.'

Where have I cause in equal deed
To call on such another's name?
He with his hand hath sown our seed,
In wisdom hath designed our frame;
Lord Zeus, before whose favouring air
Move all things to an issue fair.

248

And is there none with prouder might
   He waits on in the lower place?
None is there underneath whose right
   He bows, abiding soveran grace:
Whate'er his counsel, it may run;
He speaks it,—and the act is done.

WALTER HEADLAM   (*Supplices*, 538–99)

239   *Prayer for Deliverance*

CHORUS

O BOSOMED Earth, O altar of my prayer,
   What is upon us? Whither can I fly?
In all this Âpian land is there no lair
   Hid deep from every eye?
I'd be a wisp of smoke, up-curled
To the soft clouds above the world,
   Up, without wings, in the bright day,
Like dust, in dying streamers whirled
   To pass in nothingness away.

The heart within my breast is passion-tossed
   And will not sleep; mine eyes see nothing clear.
That sight my father saw has left me lost,
   And my strength gone with fear.
O better toward my doom to hie
In a rope's strangling agony,
   Than lay this body down beside
The man I loathe. Oh, best to die!
   Let Hades take his bride!

Some skyey throne—Oh, thither I would go,
Where the wet clouds, back-beaten, freeze to snow:
    Some unbestridden, undescried,
    Smooth vulture-crag, in lonely pride
    Hanging; there to stand and leap
    Alone, alone to the great deep,
    Rather than face that forcèd Love
    And the heart-stabbing shame thereof.

I fear not then a prey for dogs to lie,
A feast for all the vultures of the sky.
    Once to be dead sets woman free
    From every wrong and misery.
    God give me to the grave instead
    Of that polluting marriage-bed.
    What outlet can I hew, what path
    To save us from this lust and wrath?

GILBERT MURRAY   (*Supplices*, 776–807)

240   *Salamis*

MESSENGER

PRINCESS, the first beginner of all the woes
    That afterwards ensued, though whence he came
None knoweth, was some genius of wrath,
Some wicked spirit such as lures men on
To their destruction. There came a man,
A Hellene, from the Athenian host, and he
On this wise spake unto Xerxês, thy son—
'If there shall come a dusk and darksome night
The Hellenes will not tarry; leaping down

250

Upon their rowers' benches they will pull
For safety, hither, thither scattering
In secret flight.' And when thy son heard that,
He instantly—perceiving not the guile
Of the Hellene nor the spite of jealous gods,—
Made known to all the captains of his ships
That when the burning sun should cease to beam
Across the world, and glimmering twilight took
The court and curtilage of serene air,
The main armada must disperse and form
Three squadrons line abreast, blocking the exits
And narrow channels where the salt waves churn:
The residue to compass Ajax' isle.
Then, if the Hellenes turned to flee from doom
By privily withdrawing in the dark,
Not one could get away, but their whole fleet
Must fall into our hands. So spake the king
In sanguine mood, with not the least surmise
Of the divine purpose, presently fulfilled.
And not at all in any disarray
But with a disciplined obedience,
They made their dinner ready, every seaman
Lashing his oar-shank to the well-turned thole;
And when the sun waxed dim and night came on,
Each master oarsman went aboard his ship
And every captain of the fighting crews,
And down the long lines of those ships of war
Squadron to squadron spake right cheerily,
Hailing each other; not a ship of them
Lost her allotted station; and all night
The captains kept them cruising to and fro.
And night passed, and the Hellenic armament

Made no attempt to steal away unseen.
But when with her white horses day shone fair
And overspread the broad and ample earth,
There rose and rang from the Hellenic host
A roar of voices musical with psalms,
And loudly from the island precipices
Echo gave back an answering cheer. Thereat
Seeing their judgement grievously at fault,
Fear fell on the barbarians. Not for flight
Did the Hellenes then chant that inspiring hymn,
But resolutely going into battle,
Whereto the trumpet set all hearts on fire.
The word was given, and, instantaneously,
Oars smote the roaring waves in unison
And churned the foam up. Soon their whole fleet appeared;
The port division thrown out like a horn
In precise order; then the main of them
Put out against us. We could plainly hear
The thunder of their shouting as they came.
'Forth, sons of Hellas! free your land, and free
Your children and your wives, the native seats
Of gods your fathers worshipped and their graves.
This is a bout that hazards all ye have.'
And verily from us in the Persian tongue
There rose an answering roar; the long suspense
Was ended. In an instant, ship smote ship,
With thrust of armoured prow. The first to ram
Was a Greek; that impact carried clean away
A tall Phœnician's poop. Then all came on,
Each steering forthright for a ship of ours.
At first the encountering tide of Persians held;
But caught in the narrows, crowded without sea-room,

None could help other; nay, they fell aboard
Their own ships, crashing in with beak of bronze,
Till all their oars were smashed. But the Hellenes
Rowed round and round, and with sure seamanship
Struck where they chose. Many of ours capsized,
Until the very sea was hid from sight
Choked up with drifting wreckage and drowning men.
The beaches and low rocks were stacked with corpses:
The few barbarian vessels still afloat,
Fouling each other fled in headlong rout.
But they with broken oars and splintered spars
Beat us like tunnies or a draught of fish,
Yea, smote men's backs asunder; and all the while
Shrieking and wailing hushed the ocean surge,
Till night looked down and they were rapt away.
But, truly, if I should discourse the length
Of ten long days, I could not sum our woes.
There never yet 'twixt sunrise and sunset
Perished so vast a multitude of men.

G. M. COOKSON   (*Persæ*, 353–432)

241   *Xerxes defeated*

CHORUS

THIS earth, this Asia, wide as east from west,
    Mourns—empty,—of her manhood dispossessed.
Xerxês the King led forth his war-array!
Xerxês the King hath cast his host away!
Xerxês the King (O King unwise!)
Steered in the wake of doom his orient argosies!

How fell it that Darîus, lord of the bow,
     In Susa long ago,
Fair fortune had? That then
He who ruled Persia won the hearts of men?

The ships, the swarthy ships, with brow of gloom
And wide wings woven on the weary loom,
Landsmen and mariners haled to that far shore!
The ships, the black ships whelmed them evermore!
They struck, they split, they filled,
They sank: and, oh, death's throes Ionian vengeance filled.
And now by plain and pass, rude, wild and bare,
     In the frore Thracian air,
After long wandering,
Scarce 'scaped with life, comes home our lord the King.

     But they on that wild water,
     Firstlings of death and slaughter,
Roam, where the long waves lash Kychrêan sands;
     Roam, but no wave shall lift them,
     Nor ebb nor flood-tide drift them
To this dear earth beloved above all lands.
     Wide as the sky, and deep
     As those dark waters sweep,
Wail! let grief gnaw your heart, and wring your hands!

     Combed with no tender combing,
     Where angry waves break foaming,
Children of Ocean's unpolluted tide
     Flesh their dumb mouths, and tear
     The dead men once so fair:

Old eyes are wet whose tears Time long since dried;
    The sire weeps his lost son,
    The home its goodman gone,
And all the woeful tale is bruited far and wide.

They pay no more tribute; they bow them no more!
    The word of power is not spoken
By the princes of Persia; their day is o'er,
    And the laws of the Medes are broken
Through Asia's myriad-peopled land;
For the staff is snapped in the King's right hand.

And a watch is not set on the free, frank tongue,
    Yea, liberty's voice speaks loud;
And the yoke is loosed from the neck that was wrung
    And the back to dominion bowed:
For the earth of Ajax' isle is red
With the blood of Persia's noble dead.

G. M. Cookson   (*Persæ*, 548–96)

242   *News of War*

MESSENGER. ÉTEOCLÊS

MESS. King of this people, good lord Éteoclês,
    Lo, I bear back to thee the very shape
    Of things wrought yonder in the host: mine eyes
    Have seen them and my lips shall utter them.
    Seven men there were, chief-captains, fiery-proud,
    These same did slay a bull: the bason was
    A shield, black-bounden: and each man his hand
    Dipp'd in the dark stream of hot bestial life,
    And sware, crying dread names, the Lord of War,

255

The Battle-Maiden and blood-ravening Fear,
That either he would sack by strength of hand
The town Cadmêan and unbuild her towers,
Or, slain, make bloody clay of this land's dust.
And each did bind the chariot of the king
Adrastus with such token as might keep
His memory in far days with those at home
Who bare him, not without some fall of tears,
But, for their mouth, nought weak was found therein:
Those hearts were iron-proof: there burn'd the clear
Spirit of war unquenchable: they seem'd
Lions, whose eyes are even as gleaming swords.
And look, no lag-foot post is this I bring;
Even as I went from them, they cast the lot,
How each must launch his battle at the gates.
Wherefore let chosen men, the city's best,
Be set by thy ordainment presently
To keep the issuing of the gates: for near—
The Argive host, full-harness'd, draweth near,
With trampling and with whirl of dust: the fields
Be fleck'd with flying white from the hot breath
Of horses. But do thou, O king, this ship's
Good rudderman, make strong her civic wall
Or ever lighten on us the hurricane
Immense of war, the roaring of the sea
That is of men, not waters. Nay, dispose
As shall be swiftest in the act, and I
Shall do my daylight office with as true
Curious an eye, that thou by clear report
May'st look beyond the doors and take no harm.

ÉT. O Zeus and Earth and gods that dwell with us,
    O dark and strong Destroyer, my father's Curse,

I cry to you, break not us utterly!
Make not this city as a tree pluck'd up
By the roots, abolish'd, broken of battles, one
That speaketh the sweet speech of Hellas, homes
Where the old fire burneth; this free land, this town
Of Cadmus, bind it never in bonds of shame.
Be strong to save. Surely ye too are grieved
In all our grieving, for that city's gods
Do get most honour, which most prospereth.

E. R. BEVAN   (*Septem contra Thebas*, 39–77)

243   *Promêtheus Bound*

PROMÊTHEUS

O DIVINE air! Breezes on swift bird-wings,
  Ye river fountains, and of ocean-waves
The multitudinous laughter! Mother earth!
And thou all-seeing circle of the sun,
Behold what I, a God, from Gods endure!
        Look down upon my shame,
        The cruel wrong that racks my frame,
    The grinding anguish that shall waste my strength,
Till time's ten thousand years have measured out their
        length!

    He hath devised these chains,
The new throned potentate who reigns,
Chief of the chieftains of the Blest. Ah me!
The woe which is and that which yet shall be
I wail; and question make of these wide skies
When shall the star of my deliverance rise.

And yet—and yet—exactly I foresee
All that shall come to pass; no sharp surprise
Of pain shall overtake me; what 's determined
Bear, as I can, I must, knowing the might
Of strong Necessity is unconquerable.
But touching my fate silence and speech alike
Are unsupportable. For boons bestowed
On mortal men I am straitened in these bonds.
I sought the fount of fire in hollow reed
Hid privily, a measureless resource
For man, and mighty teacher of all arts.
This is the crime that I must expiate
Hung here in chains, nailed 'neath the open sky.

G. M. COOKSON   (*Prométheus Vinctus*, 87–113)

244   *Prométheus the Teacher of Men*

PROMÊTHEUS

THINK not that I for pride and stubbornness
    Am silent: rather is my heart the prey
Of gnawing thoughts, both for the past, and now
Seeing myself by vengeance buffeted.
For to these younger Gods their precedence
Who severally determined if not I?
No more of that: I should but weary you
With things ye know; but listen to the tale
Of human sufferings, and how at first
Senseless as beasts I gave men sense, possessed them
Of mind. I speak not in contempt of man;
I do but tell of good gifts I conferred.
In the beginning, seeing they saw amiss,

And hearing heard not, but, like phantoms huddled
In dreams, the perplexed story of their days
Confounded; knowing neither timber-work
Nor brick-built dwellings basking in the light,
But dug for themselves holes, wherein like ants,
That hardly may contend against a breath,
They dwelt in burrows of their unsunned caves.
Neither of winter's cold had they fix'd sign,
Nor of the spring when she comes decked with flowers,
Nor yet of summer's heat with melting fruits'
Sure token: but utterly without knowledge
Moiled, until I the rising of the stars
Showed them, and when they set, though much obscure.
Moreover, number, the most excellent
Of all inventions, I devised for them,
And gave them writing that retaineth all,
The serviceable mother of the Muse.
I was the first that yoked unmanaged beasts,
To serve as slaves with collar and with pack,
And take upon themselves, to man's relief,
The heaviest labour of his hands: and I
Tamed to the rein and drove in wheelèd cars
The horse, the ornament of sumptuous pride.
And those sea-wanderers with the wings of cloth,
The shipman's waggons, none conceived but I.
These manifold inventions for mankind
I perfected, who, out upon 't, have none,—
No, not one shift—to rid me of this shame.

G. M. Cookson   (*Promêtheus Vinctus*, 436–71)

245   *The Overthrow of Zeus*

PROMÊTHEUS

I TELL thee that the self-willed pride of Zeus
  Shall surely be abased; that even now
He plots a marriage that shall hurl him forth
Far out of sight of his imperial throne
And kingly dignity. Then, in that hour,
Shall be fulfilled, nor in one tittle fail,
The curse wherewith his father Cronos cursed him,
What time he fell from his majestic place
Established from of old. And such a stroke
None of the Gods save me could turn aside.
I know these things shall be and on what wise.
Therefore let him secure him in his seat,
And put his trust in airy noise, and swing
His bright, two-handed, blazing thunderbolt,
For these shall nothing stead him, nor avert
Fall insupportable and glory humbled.
A wrestler of such might he maketh ready
For his own ruin; yea, a wonder, strong
In strength unmatchable; and he shall find
Fire that shall set at naught the burning bolt
And blasts more dreadful that o'er-crow the thunder.
The pestilence that scourgeth the deep seas
And shaketh solid earth, the three-pronged mace,
Poseidon's spear, a mightier shall scatter;
And when he stumbleth striking there his foot,
Fallen on evil days, the tyrant's pride
Shall measure all the miserable length
That parts rule absolute from servitude.

G. M. COOKSON   (*Promêtheus Vinctus*, 907–27)

246   *Promêtheus in the Earthquake*

PROMÊTHEUS. HERMÊS. CHORUS

PROMÊTHEUS

THESE are stale tidings I foreknew ;
    Therefore, since suffering is the due
A foe must pay his foes,
Let curlèd lightnings clasp and clash
And close upon my limbs: loud crash
    The thunder, and fierce throes
Of savage winds convulse calm air:
The embowelled blast earth's roots uptear
    And toss beyond its bars
The rough surge, till the roaring deep
In one devouring deluge sweep
    The pathway of the stars !
Finally, let him fling my form
Down whirling gulfs, the central storm
    Of being; let me lie
Plunged in the black Tartárean gloom;
Yet—yet—his sentence shall not doom
    This deathless self to die !

HERMÊS

These are the workings of a brain
More than a little touched; the vein
    Of voluble ecstasy !
Surely he wandereth from the way,
His reason lost, who thus can pray !
    A mouthing madman he !

261

Therefore, O ye who court his fate,
Rash mourners,—ere it be too late
      And ye indeed are sad
For vengeance spurring hither fast,—
Hence! lest the bellowing thunderblast
      Like him should strike you mad!

CHORUS

Words which might work persuasion speak
If thou must counsel me; nor seek
      Thus, like a stream in spate,
To uproot mine honour. Dost thou dare
Urge me to baseness! I will bear
      With him all blows of fate;
For false forsakers I despise;
At treachery my gorge doth rise:—
      I spew it forth with hate!

HERMÊS

Only,—with ruin on your track,—
Rail not at fortune; but look back
      And these my words recall;
Neither blame Zeus that he hath sent
Sorrow no warning word forewent!
      Ye labour for your fall
With your own hands! Not by surprise
Nor yet by stealth, but with clear eyes,
      Knowing the thing ye do,
Ye walk into the yawning net
That for the feet of fools is set
      And Ruin spreads for you.

PROMÊTHEUS

The time is past for words; earth quakes
Sensibly; hark! pent thunder rakes
    The depths, with bellowing din
Of echoes rolling ever nigher:
Lightnings shake out their locks of fire:
    The dust cones dance and spin;
The skipping winds, as if possessed
By faction—north, south, east and west,
    Puff at each other; sea
And sky are shook together: Lo!
The swing and fury of the blow
    Wherewith Zeus smiteth me
Sweepeth apace, and, visibly,
To strike my heart with fear. See, see
    Earth, awful mother! Air,
That shedd'st from the revolving sky
On all the light they see thee by,
    What bitter wrongs I bear!

G. M. COOKSON   (*Promêtheus Vinctus*, 1040–94)

247   *The Sacrifice of Îphigenîa*

CHORUS

I CALL on Zeus, whoever Zeus may be.
  If thus he wishes to be known,
I call him Zeus obediently.
He, the unequalled, reigns alone.
I've weighed all things from first to last
and see in Zeus my only stay,
if from my mind I'm yet to cast
these shadowy crushing fears away.

There was another mighty one of old
sapful of high defiant strength:
now in one word his tale is told.
The next god measured out his length
and took the final wrestler's fall.
One course alone is never wrong,
one course brings wisdom: gladly call
on Zeus and sing his Triumph Song!

He guides us on the road of right,
stating for law this one sure thing:
Knowledge is won by suffering.
O, pain can drip before the heart in sleep,
anguish of memory; and men can reap
much wisdom in their own despite.
The gods who sit on glorious thrones above
at times chastise us with their love.

The elder king who led the host
was mute. No word of blame he said.
He bowed his unavailing head.
He floated with the tides of destiny.
The army, scourged by the forbidding sea,
lay hunger-pinched on Aulis' coast,
across from Calchis where the surges roar
and eddy back along the shore.

Winds from the Strŷmôn baffled ship and crew,
making a starved and ruinous holiday,
drifting the men away,
rotting the timbers and the cables through;
and time, twice-told, with gnawing of delay

raked off the Argive youth. So at the last
Calchas gave bitter counsel—to assuage
the bitter wintry blast
sent by the goddess in her rage;
and both the kings, hearing the prophet's cries,
dashed staff to earth, and tears stood in their eyes.

The elder brother rose to make reply:
'Hard is my lot if now I disobey,
and harder yet if I
agree upon the altar-block to slay
my darling girl, my house's pride: to dye
my hands with blood of hers and do her hurt . . .
Both acts are wrong. Which may I choose?
Yet how can I desert
my gathered friends and break our cruise?
They're clamorous, desiring righteously
the wind-appeasing victim. Let it be.'

He took the yoke of claimed necessity
and in his head the bad winds changed again.
His tugging conflicts ceased to veer,
he set one course for bold-faced villainy.
For frenzy with base reasoning will sear
the conscience, prodigal of after-pain.
He dared to take his daughter's life
in sacrificial infamy,
to battle for a stolen wife
and gain his fleet good luck at sea.

Her sobs of *Father* passed the judges by.
They met her virgin youth with ruthless frown.
Their thought was war. The father prayed,
then bade the attendants stoutly swing her high
above the altar like a kid. Dismayed
she drooped, her raiment flowing loosely down.
And while they lifted her and dragged,
he bade them tie some ragged strips
with muffling might, until they gagged
the curses on her lovely lips.

Down to the ground her yellow raiment poured.
To each and all, before they bared the steel,
shot forth her arrows of appeal,
and *pity pity* her wild eyes implored:
bright as a picture, fain to speak, but dumb—
not as at home, when friends were come,
beside her father she would take her place
and sing, or at his loving invitation
would virginally grace
his luck-chant given at the third libation.

And then—I saw no more. No more I say.
But Calchas deals in no deceptive fates.
We suffer. Justice compensates
with knowledge. We'll unveil the future day
when it arrives. Till then, give it goodbye!
We meet pangs half-way when we pry.
Clear truth will meet us with dawn's clearing rays.

JACK LINDSAY   (*Agamemnon*, 160–254)

248 *The Beacons*

ELDER. CLYTÆMÊSTRA

ELDER. What courier could arrive thus rapidly?
CLYT. Hêphæstus; his bright flame from Ida sprang,
    And fast in fiery post the beacons flew,
    As one dispatched another: Ida first
    To Hermês' hill in Lemnos; third the mount
    Of Zeus in Athos caught the mighty brand
    From the island thrown in turn. Then towering high
    To clear the broad sea's back, the travelling torch
    Shot up to the very sky the courier flame,
    In golden glory, like another sun,
    Fame to the far Mâkistos messaging:
    Whose fiery office no defaulting sleep
    Or tarrying sloth let fail; his ensign flying
    Over the Sound Eurîpos made aware
    Messâpion's watchmen of his advent; they
    With answering countersign, a kindled stack
    Of old gray heather, passed the word along:
    Which vigorous lamp with unabated force
    Did shining as the bright Moon overleap
    Asôpos even to Cithæron's ridge,
    There to wake new dispatch; nor being aroused
    That watch denied the far-sent missioner;
    They burned above their bidding, and their light
    Went sailing far beyond Gorgôpis' lake
    To the heights of Ægiplanctus, urging still
    No dallying in the breathless ordinance.
    Whereat with liberal heart aloft they sent
    Flame in a great beard streaming, that his flight
    Should clean beyond the foreland pass, that looks

267

O'er the Sarônic gulf; nor ever stooped
His pinion ere he gained our neighbouring height,
Arachnæ's vigilant peak: alighting thence
Upon the Atrîdæ's roof a gleam there came,
That Ida's fire his ancestor may claim.

This was the ordering of my torchmen's race,
One from another in succession still
Supplied and plenishèd; and he that won
Was he *ran first*, though last in all this run.

WALTER HEADLAM   (*Agamemnon*, 280–314)

249 *Helen*

CHORUS

THE bow of Zeus has twanged. All must confess
his power is put to angry proof,
his will has measured out their due distress.
One said *the high gods stand aloof*
and men may tread the holy things in dust.
Who spoke it was a godless man,
for here we all may clearly see
that Zeus demands a penalty.
He curbs the reckless leaders who began
a war to please their panting lust,
though wealth had crammed their store-rooms to excess.
O let me live unscathed by guilt!
So will the wise folk pray;
since gold has no defence
for him that spurns away
in trampling insolence
the shrine that Justice built.

268

Temptation leads him forward wretchedly,
the child of his deliberate curse.
Nothing can save him. Sin burns plain to see,
mad in his eyes; no glare is worse.
For if you rub and buffet worthless brass
you find the dark and blotchy grain;
and thus we learn the man's true face.
'A boy goes on a sparrow-chase,'
but light-winged hopes bring heavy hurt to pass,
and Troy has felt the shock of pain.
The gods are deaf to every moaning plea;
they let the prayer-wise sinner pray.
Then retribution falls.
A guest, young Paris came
into these friendly halls:
he stained the hearth with shame
and filched a wife away.

Helen has gone, and left us for our share
spear clang, shield clang,
and clatter as the docks awaken.
Sure Ruin for her dowry she has taken
while passing lightly through the gate,
daring what no one well may dare;
and thus the home's lamenting prophets sang:
'Woe for the home, the man left desolate,
her yielding body dinted on the bed!
Behold the silence scorned yet uncomplaining
of him that sits apart with care.
He yearns, but still the sundering sea denies—
Queen of his house, a ghost is reigning.

269

He looks with grudging hate
on graceful statues there,
and in his cheated eyes
all love is dead.

'O, shapes appear in flattering dreams and sway
across his night,
bringing a vain delirium;
for vain it is when limbs desired will come
yet through the clutching fingers drain,
plucked in an ebbing flash away,
flurrying the paths of sleep with wings of flight.'
His hearth is thus embittered with his pain,
he's sadder still whichever way he turns . . .
But every Grecian home sent volunteers,
though brooding thoughts of misery stay.
And time has many a thrust to shatter strength,
piercing the heart that waits and fears.
They sent out lads to fight
with faces known and gay;
and they get back at length
ashes in urns.

The war-god is a broker, flesh his gold.
He holds his scale above the wavering spears.
Instead of men, burnt from Scamandros' banks
a little pinch of dust he sends
to unconsoled and weeping friends:
a row of vases for the warrior-ranks.
Men sigh, 'This lad was young and bold,
and he had trained for years;

and nobly in the shambles that one died
to fetch another's gadding bride.'
Hoarsely the men complain beneath their breath;
and wrath against the Atrîdæ, sadly stern,
shrugs through the town on every side.
But many comely lads in death
lie under walls of Trojan stone.
The enemy-earth now takes in turn
the lads that took it as their own.

A heavy thing is rumour fiercely spread,
a curse denounced by the exacting town.
Inward my hopes and fears are straining hard
to catch some tidings from the dark.
The gods have set a murder-mark
on all who make the earth a slaughter-yard;
and dark-stoled Furies, by the heavens led,
in time bring tumbling down
the man unrighteously entitled great.
With sad eclipse of shining state
forsaken quite, among the unknown he lies.
The noise of glory hems a man with hate:
down on his eyes Zeus' bolts will blaze.
The unenvied life delights the wise.
No city-sacker would I be,
nor do I wish to end my days
a war-slave herded cruelly.

JACK LINDSAY   (*Agamemnon*, 367–474)

250   *Welcome to Agamemnon*

CLYTÆMÊSTRA

CLYT. My reverend Elders, worthy citizens,
I shall not blush now to confess before you
My amorous fondness; fear and diffidence
Fade from us all in time. O 'tis not from
Instruction I can tell
The story of my own unhappy life
All the long while my lord lay under Îlium.
First for a woman 'tis a passing trial
To sit forlorn at home with no man present,
Always malignant rumours in her ears,
One bawler tumbling on another's heels
With cruel blows each heavier than the last:——
Wounds! if my lord had got as many wounds
As rumour channelling to us homeward gave him,
He had been more riddled than a net with holes.
Or had his deaths but tallied with all tales!
He might have been a second Gêrÿon,
Three-bodied, with a triple coverture
Of earth above——one for each several corpse.

    By reason of
These cross malignant rumours, other hands
Full many a time have set my desperate neck
Free from the hanging noose, recovering me
Against my dearest will.——Hence too it is
We see not present by our side this day
The child, Orestês, in whose person dwell
The pledges of our love; nor wonder at it:
He rests in keeping of our trusty cousin,
Stróphius the Phôcian, my forewarner oft

Of danger on two scores,—thy jeopardy
At Troy, and fear of popular tumult hatching
Plots in the lack of master, as 'tis common
When the man's down the more to trample on him:
Under which showing lies not trace of guile.

    For me, the gushing fountains of my tears
Are e'en dried up, there's not a drop now left;
And my late-rested eyes have suffered hurt
From weeping o'er the lanterns lit for thee
That still were unregarded. If I slept,
The puniest whining of a pulsing gnat
Would rouse me from beholding in my dreams
More accidents to thee than could befall
Within the time that was my bedfellow.

    Now, after all this borne, with heart unpined
I hail my lord, safe watchdog of the fold,
Main forestay of the ship, firm-footed pillar
Bearing the roof up, sole-born child vouchsafed
To father, to the wave-tossed seaman land,
Bright day that greets the eyesight after storm,
Well-water to the thirsty wayfarer!
Sweet is escape from every harsh constraint.

WALTER HEADLAM (to l. 900)   (*Agamemnon*, 855–902)

251   *The Purple Carpet*

CLYTÆMÊSTRA

CLYT. There is the sea—shall any stanch it up?—
    Still breeding, for its worth of silver weight,
    Abundant stain, freshly renewable,
    For purpling robes withal: nay, Heaven be praised,

The house, my lord, affords us plenty such;
'Tis not acquainted yet with penury.
I had vowed the trampling of a thousand robes,
Had the oracles enjoined it when I sought
Means for recovery of a life so precious!
Still from the living root the mantling green
Against the Dog-star spreads a leafy screen,—
So thou returning to thy hearth and home,
Warmth as in winter cries *Behold me come!*
Aye and when mellowing Zeus makes ripe and sweet
Wine from the young grape's bitter, cool in heat
Reigns within walls where moves the man complete;—

> *[As Agamemnon goes in.*

O Zeus completer, now complete my prayer,
Completion of thy plans be now thy care!

WALTER HEADLAM   (*Agamemnon*, 958–74)

252 *Cassandra prepares to die*

CHORUS. CASSANDRA

LEADER OF CHORUS: O woman very unhappy and very wise,
　　　　Your speech was long. But if in sober truth
　　　　You know your fate, why like an ox that the gods
　　　　Drive, do you walk so bravely to the altar?
CASS. There is no escape, strangers. No; not by postpone-
　　　　ment.
LEADER. But the last moment has the privilege of hope.
CASS. The day is here. Little should I gain by flight.
LEADER. This patience of yours comes from a brave soul.
CASS. A happy man is never paid that compliment.

LEADER. But to die with credit graces a mortal man.

CASS. O my father! You and your noble sons!

　　　　(She approaches the door, then suddenly recoils.)

LEADER. What is it? What is the fear that drives you back?

CASS. Faugh.

LEADER. Why faugh? Or is this some hallucination?

CASS. These walls breathe out a death that drips with
　　　blood.

LEADER. Not so. It is only the smell of the sacrifice.

CASS. It is like a breath out of a charnel-house.

LEADER. You think our palace burns odd incense then!

CASS. But I will go to lament among the dead
　　　My lot and Agamemnon's. Enough of life!
　　　Strangers,
　　　I am not afraid like a bird afraid of a bush,
　　　But witness you my words after my death,
　　　When a woman dies in return for me a woman
　　　And a man falls for a man with a wicked wife.
　　　I ask this service, being about to die.

LEADER. Alas, I pity you for the death you have foretold.

CASS. One more speech I have; I do not wish to raise
　　　The dirge for my own self. But to the sun I pray
　　　In face of his last light that my avengers
　　　May make my murderers pay for this my death,
　　　Death of a woman slave, an easy victim.

　　　　　　　　　(She enters the palace.)

LEADER. Ah the fortunes of men! When they go well
　　　A shadow sketch would match them, and in ill-
　　　fortune
　　　The dab of a wet sponge destroys the drawing.
　　　It is not myself but the life of man I pity.

LOUIS MACNEICE　　　　　　　*(Agamemnon, 1295–1330)*

253 *Invocation of Agamemnon's Ghost*

ORESTÊS. CHORUS. ÊLECTRA

OR.　　O father, father of our woe!
　　　How can I serve thee now by word or deed?
　　　From this far world what homing wind shall blow
　　　Where the Eternal Anchors hold thee fast?
　　　　　There thy long day is night:
　　　And at this gate of death where thou hast passed,
　　　Our grief that are of Atreus' royal seed
　　　Is all thou hast of glory and delight.

CHO.　　Child, the proud spirit of the dead
　　　Succumbs not to the ravening tooth of fire.
　　　Their passions work, when life is fled:
　　　　　The mourner's wail
　　　Discovers him that did the wrong.
　　　And lamentation for a murdered sire
　　　A hunter is, that rallies to the trail
　　　　　All dogs that e'er gave tongue.

OR.　　Hearken then, father, our lament,
　　　While at thy mounded tomb our salt tears flow;
　　　An alternating song, of sad concent,
　　　Dirged by thy children; suppliants that crave
　　　Access to thee; banned, both, from thy high hall,
　　　Met at the common refuge of thy grave.
　　　What's here of good? Where's aught that is not
　　　　　woe?
　　　And is not Doom the master of us all?

276

CHO.   But God can touch the broken strings
         To melody divine;
And for this unrejoicing round,
The burden of sepulchral ground,
In the high banquet-hall of kings
      Blithe song bring in new wine.

OR.   Oh, if 'neath Îlium's wall,
Gashed by some Lycian spear,
Father, thou hadst fall'n in fight,
Then hadst thou left thy house great praise,
And to thy children in the public ways
Honour in the eyes of all.
Then thine had been a sepulchre
Builded of many hands beyond the sea,
And easy would our burden be,
And all its weight of earth how light!

CHO.   And in the Kingdom of the Dark,
Welcome wert thou to souls that nobly died;
      A lord of majesty and mark,
         The cupbearer
Of Hell's vast Thrones; for while thou yet hadst
      breath
Thou wast a King; and, in that Kingdom wide,
Next them that the huge orb of Fate upbear,
      Their rod and sceptre Death!

ÊLEC.   No, not on Troy's far plain
Would I have thee lie, interred,
Where Scamander's waters flow,
With meaner men that fell to the spear,
But none, oh, none, that was thy peer.

277

Death should have first thy murderers slain;
And, haply, we had heard
Some far-off rumour of their dying,
And never ate the bread of sighing
Nor tasted of this cup of Woe.

G. M. COOKSON   (*Choêphoræ*, 315–71)

254   *Orestês goes Mad*

ORESTÊS. CHORUS

OR. Behold the tyrants that oppressed your land,
Slayers of fathers, plunderers of kings' houses.
But now they kept great state, seated on thrones;
Yea, and, methinks, they yet lie lovingly
In death, true honourers of their oath and bond.
They sware that they would kill my father, sware
To die together, and were not forsworn.
Behold, ye judges of their heinous crimes,
The thing they wrought, the links that bound my
        father,
Gyves for his wrists and fetters for his feet.
Shake it abroad, stand round me in a ring,
Hang out these trappings, that a father's eye,
Not mine, but he that watcheth all the world,
Hêlios, may view my mother's handiwork;
Ay, and hereafter testify for me
That justly I pursued even to the death
My mother: I reck not Ægisthus' end;
For by the law the adulterer shall die.
But she that hatched this horror for her lord,
By whom she went with child, carried the load

278

Of sometime love,—but this tells you 'twas hate—!
What? Had she conger's teeth or adder's fangs,
She had corrupted where her tooth not bit,
So absolute was she in iniquity.
How shall I name this right and use fair words?
Trap for a beast? Clout for a dead man's feet?
A towel is 't? Fore God, a trapper's toil;
A noose; a gown that trips the wearer up;
Some rascal publican might get one like it,
That robs his guests for a living; ay, with this,
Put scores away and feel no cold fit after.
I pray God one like her may never house
With me,—I'd liefer go childless to my grave.

CH. Aiai! thy woeful work! This hideous death
Ends thee; thy pride and all thy passions cold;
For him that yet must draw this lethal breath
The flower of suffering begins to unfold.

OR. Was this her work or not? This proves it, this
Robe, sullied with Ægisthus' dagger-plunge.
The tinct of murder, not the touch of Time
Alone, hath—here and here—spoiled its rich brede.
I'll praise and mourn him now, I was not by
To mourn and praise with his death-robe before me.
Sad act, sad end, thrice-wretched race, triumph
No man need envy, soilure of my soul.

CH. Time grants not our so perishable clay
Bliss that endures or glory that shall last;
Heaviness wears the instant hour away,
Or it will come before the next be passed.

OR. Mark this; for I know not where it will end,
Dragged like a driver of hot, headlong horses
Quite from the track; beaten and borne afar

279

By break-neck thoughts; fear at my heart, at stretch
To strike up the grim tune, whereto 'twill dance.
While I am in my senses, I protest
I slew not, friends, my mother save with cause,
My father's blood upon her and Heaven's hate.
I lay it on the charm that made me bold;
On Pŷtho's prophet, Loxias, that charged
Me do the deed, and sware to hold me guiltless
If done; if not,—I sink the consequence:
No bolt ere shot can hit the height of suffering.
And now behold and see how I am furnished
With branch and wreath, and, thus apparelled, go
To earth's great nombril-precincts, Loxias' ground,
And that famed fount of indestructible fire,
Kin-murder's outlaw; at no hearth but His
Did Loxias bid me look for sanctuary.
Hereafter let all Argives bear me out
Not without strong compunction did I deal
So ruefully with her that gave me life.
I am a wanderer now, I have no friends,
But, live or die, this shall be told of me.

CH. Thou hast done well; let words of evil note
Be far from thy lips: give not ill fancies speech.
Thou hast delivered all the land of Argos;
Sawn off with one sword-sweep two dragon-heads.

OR. Ha! Ha!
Women, they come about me,—Gorgon shapes,
Sheeted in gray,—clasped round with scaly folds
Of intertwisted snakes,—away! away!

CH. True son to thy father, what fantastic thoughts
Are these? Stand fast! thou hast triumphed; fear for
        nought,

OR. These fearful torments are no phantasies;
    These are the leashed sleuth-hounds my mother slips!

CH. Because the blood is fresh upon thy hands,
    Therefore this sudden frenzy rocks thy soul.

OR. Apollo! Prince! Look, look!—They come in crowds,—
    And from their eyeballs blood drips horribly!

CH. Haste thee where cleansing is! To Loxias!
    Hold fast to him and find deliverance!

OR. Ye see them not, but I see them; they turn
    Upon me! Hunt me forth! Away! Away!

G. M. COOKSON   (*Choêphoræ*, 973–1062)

255   *The Furies' Prayer*

CHORUS

COME, dance and song, in linkèd round!
    More deep than blithe Muse can
We'll make these groaning chanters sound
    Our governance over man!
No parley! Give us judgement swift!
We vex not in our wrath who spread
White hands to Heaven uplift.
Not unto such; he journeyeth
Unharmed, a happy traveller
Through life to the last pause of Death:
But to the froward soul, that seeks,
Like *him*, to cloak up, if he could,
Plague-spotted hands, with murder red,
To such our apparition speaks,
The faithful witness for the dead,
Plenipotentiary of Blood
And Slaughter's sovran minister.

281

Hear me, my mother! Hark,
  Night, in whose womb I lay,
Born to punish dead souls in the dark
  And the living souls in the day!
Lo, Lêto's Lion-cub
  My right denies;
He would take my slinking beast of the field,
Mine, mine by mother-murder sealed,
  My lawful sacrifice.

But this is the song for the victim slain,
To blight his heart and blast his brain,
Wilder and wilder and whirl him along;
This is the song, the Furies' song,
  Not sung to harp or lyre,
To bind men's souls in links of brass
And over their bodies to mutter and pass
  A withering fire!

Long the thread Fate spun
  And gave us to have and hold
For ever, through all Time's texture run,
  Our portion from of old.
Who walks with murder wood,
  With him walk we
On to the grave, the deep-dug pit;
And when he's dead, he shall have no whit
  Too large a liberty!

Oh! this is the song for the victim slain,
To blight his heart and blast his brain,

    Wilder and wilder and whirl him along!
    This is the song, the Furies' song,
       Not sung to harp or lyre,
    To bind men's souls in links of brass
    And over their bodies to mutter and pass
       A withering fire!

G. M. Cookson   *(Euménidês,* 307–46)

256   *The Euménidês*

CHORUS

PALLAS' home contenteth me:
  Honour to the strong citie
Zeus Almighty made his own
And Arês' armèd strength sustains;
A fortress for the Gods of Greece,
A jewel flashing forth anew,
When ravished were her costly fanes
And her high altars overthrown.
Breathe on her blessings, breathe the dew
Of prayer; Earth, yield her thine increase;
Shine, thou rejoicing Sun, and speed
All nature sends and mortals need!

I will have nor storm nor flood
Scathe her vines and olive-bowers;
No scorching wind shall blind the bud
In the waking-time of flowers.
By my grace all airs that blow
Their appointed bounds shall know.

283

No distemper blast her clime
With perpetual barrenness;
Flocks and herds in yeaning time
Pan shall with twin offspring bless;
And Earth's wombèd wealth, God-sealed,
All its lucky ingots yield.

Untoward and untimely Doom
Bring not strong Youth to his death-bed:
Ye maidens, in your beauty bloom,
Live not unloved, nor die unwed.
You, Heavenly Pair, this good gift grant.
Grant it, ye Elder Destinies,
Our Sisters, whom one Mother bare,
Spirits whose governance is law,
Of every home participant,
And at all seasons, foul or fair,
Just Inmates, Righteous Presences,
Shadows of an Unseen Awe;
Over the wide earth and the deep seas
Honoured above all Deities.

Tiger-throated Faction fed
On the meat of human woe,
Filled but never surfeited,
Come not hither growling low,
Nor wake Athens with thy roar.
Never be this thirsty ground
Drunk with fratricidal blood,
Nor lust of Power insatiate
Snatch at vengeance evermore.

In one fellowship of Good
Each be to his neighbour bound,
One in love and one in hate;
For such grace, where'er 'tis found,
Lays the balm to many a wound.

Joy to you, joy and all good things!
Joy to the fortunate city that lies
With Zeus about her and above:
Vowed to the Unmarried Maiden's love
And in the dawn of Time made wise,
Whom Pallas covers with her wings
And the Father sanctifies!

Joy, joy to Athens! Oh, twice blest
Be all that in her borders dwell,
Or be they men of mortal mould
Or deathless Deities that hold
Pallas' rock-built citadel!
Love me that am your Sacred Guest
And bid to Grief a long farewell!

G. M. COOKSON   (*Euménidês*, 916–26, 938–48, 956–67,
                          976–87, 996–1002, 1014–20)

257 *The Marriage of Heaven and Earth*

THE holy Heaven longs to thrust the Earth,
    And Earth, for love, would make her marriage-bed.
Rain-showers falling from the bridegroom Heaven
Impregnate Earth, who brings to birth for men
Grass for the flocks and the Earth-mother's corn.
And from the shining stream of rain the trees
Perfect their fruits. Joint cause of all am I.

C. M. BOWRA   (*Danáidês*)

258   *The Worship of Cotys*

KOTŶTTO'S ritual feast they keep.
    One handles the chiselled wood that hums
Its droning music full and deep
To work on the soul till frenzy comes;
The brasses clash as a second sings;
Another howls to the twang of strings;
And the roar of a terrible bull-like note
Keeps time, from some invisible throat,
While tom-tom beats with a fearful sound
Like the voice of a thunderclap underground.
ANON.   (*Êdôni*)

259   *Zeus*

ZEUS is the air, Zeus earth, and Zeus the sky,
    Zeus everything, and all that's more than these.
C. M. BOWRA   (*Hêliadës*)

260   *The Wounded Eagle*

THIS is the story told in Libyan tales:
    An eagle, struck with arrow from a bow,
Said, when he saw the crafty wingèd thing,
'So not by others but by our own plumes
We're taken.'
C. M. BOWRA   (*Myrmidonës*)

286

261   *Inexorable Death*

ALONE of gods Death has no love for gifts,
Libation helps you not, nor sacrifice.
He has no altar, and he hears no hymns;
From him alone Persuasion stands apart.

C. M. BOWRA   (*Niobê*)

262   *The Gods' Children*

     Nearest in blood to gods,
Zeus' kinsmen they, who have on Ida's mount
An altar to their sire beneath the sky;
Nor has the blood of gods yet failed in them.

C. M. BOWRA   (*Niobê*)

263   *The Red Sea*

TO the scarlet plain and the holy place
Shall you come, where the Red Sea flows apace,
And the mere where the brazen thunders roar,
And the Ethiops live by the Ocean shore,
Where even the all-discerning sun
Comforts himself when his work is done,
Refreshing himself and his weary team
With soft warm drafts from the gentle stream.

C. M. BOWRA   (*Promêtheus Liberatus*)

264   *Philoctêtês calls for Death*

O HEALER Death, spurn not to come to me;
For you alone of woes incurable
Are doctor, and a dead man feels no pain.

C. M. BOWRA   (*Philoctêtês*)

265   *Justice protects the Dead*

IF you would do a kindness to the dead,
   Or do an ill, it matters not that men
Are neither pleased nor grieved at what you do.
Yet Nemesis is mightier than we,
And Justice wreaks their vengeance for the dead.

C. M. BOWRA   (*Phrygës*)

266   *The Daughters of Atlas*

AND Atlas' seven daughters, named from him,
   Wept for their father's mighty punishment
Of holding up the sky, where, doves unwinged,
Their shapes are visitations of the night.

C. M. BOWRA

267   *Thetis*

HE praised the greatness of the child I bore,
   As free from sickness, gifted with long days;
And when he had said all, to comfort me
About my heavenly fortune sang a hymn.
And I then hoped that Phœbus' holy lips
Could never lie in their prophetic art.
But he who sang, who stood there at the feast,
Who said these words, he is the very one
Who slew my son.

C. M. BOWRA

288

268   *A Grave on Ossa*

H ERE too were steadfast men and brave
    By dark fate overcome;
Against the spears they stood, to save
    The flocks and fields of home.

In fame they live, immortal dead
    Who found their rest that day,
Enswathed in sorry dust for bed
    On Ossa's mountain way.

T. F. HIGHAM

269   *His Own Epitaph*

O NE Æschylus, Athenian born,
    Son of Euphórìon,
Lies under this memorial stone
    In Gela's fields of corn.

At Marathon a sacred wood
    His courage will declare,
Or ask the Medes, with braided hair,
    Who tried and found it good.

T. F. HIGHAM

PARMÉNIDÊS

(fl. 502 B.C.)

270   *The Way of Knowledge*

F AR as the utmost reach of heart's desire
    They sped my chariot, these that draw me now,
And set me on that roadway known to fame,—
Way of the Goddess, leading by one route
Through every city,—if a man but know.

Borne wisely onward by the straining pair
That road I took: and Maidens led the way.
    Then piped the burning axle loud and shrill,
Spun in the sockets by the racing wheels
At either end revolving: such our haste
When Daughters of the Sun from Night's abode
Conveyed me, leading on towards the light,
And plucked from off their heads the veils obscure.
    There stands the gate whereby both Night and Day
Their paths determine; high as heaven it rises,
With lintelled top and threshold built of stone,
A bolted portal blocked by mighty doors.
Avenging Justice holds the double key.

T. F. HIGHAM

CORINNA

(fl. 500 B.C.)

271   *Pindarum quisquis ...*

SWEET-VOICED Myrtis too I blame.
    Though a woman born, she came
Striving after Pindar's fame.

C. M. BOWRA

272   *Helicon and Cithæron*

THE Muses took the vote and told
    The Blessed Ones to cast their stones
In vessels made of gleaming gold,
    And all stood upright from their thrones.

Cithæron got the greater part.
Then Hermês, crying out aloud,
Proclaimed the victory that his heart
Desired. Above Cithæron's eyes
The Blessed Ones then set the prize
Of laurel, and his heart was proud.

But Helicon in bitter woe
Tore from its bed a large smooth rock,—
The mountain yielded to the shock.—
And with a loud and piteous cry
He flung the great stone from on high,
And it broke in countless bits below.

C. M. BOWRA

273   *The Daughters of Asôpus*

'SHE shall attend the gods and be
Blessed in her felicity.

'Thy daughters all are wedded, three
To Zeus, the lord of everything,
And three are wedded to the King
Poseidon, ruler of the sea,
And two is Phœbus honouring.

'One is the bride of Maia's son,
Good Hermês. So did Love design
With Aphrodîtê, when they won
The gods to secret union
In thy house with thy daughters nine.

'In time shall they a progeny
Of demigods and heroes breed,
And with a multitudinous seed
Shall keep unending youth—To me
The oracular tripod spoke its rede.

'This sacred privilege is mine.
My fifty brothers share it not,
For all their strength. It is my lot
To tell of mysteries divine—
I, true Akraiphen—at the shrine.

'The son of Lâto first had planned
That Euônymus should tell
The tripod's mystic oracle.
But Hýrieus cast him from the land.
To Hýrieus next the task befell,

'Son of Poseidon. Time passed by.
Orion came, whose son am I,
And took his own back lawfully.
Now he is dwelling in the sky,
And this high duty fell to me.

'Therefore I tell you what I find
In oracles to help mankind.
Yield, friend, to the Immortals' need
And putting hatred from your mind
Find kinsmen born of heavenly breed.'
So spake the prophet full of grace.

C. M. BOWRA

PINDAR
(522–448? B.C.)

274   *Pelops*

WHEN he came to the sweet flower of his growth
    And down covered his darkening chin,
He lifted his thoughts to a bridal awaiting him,

To have far-famed Hippodameia
From her Pîsan father.
He went down beside the grey sea
In the darkness alone,
And cried to the loud-bellowing Lord of the Trident.
And the God was with him
Close beside his feet: and Pelops said:
'If the dear love you had of me, Poseidon,
Can turn, I pray, to good,
Keep fast now the brazen spear of Oinomáos,
And on the swiftest chariots carry me
To Êlis, and bring me to victory;
For he has slain thirteen men that wooed her,
And puts back the bridal day

Of his daughter. The danger is great,
And calls not the coward: but of us who must die,
Why should a man sit in darkness
And cherish to no end
An old age without a name,
Letting go all lovely things?
For me this ordeal waits: and you
Give me the issue I desire.'
So he spoke, and the prayer he made was not unanswered.
The God glorified him, and gave him a chariot of gold,
And wing'd horses that never tired.

So he brought down the strength of Oinomáos,
And the maiden to share his bed.
She bore him princes,
Six sons eager in nobleness.
And now, by the ford of Alpheios,
He is drenched with the glorious blood-offerings,
With a busy tomb beside that altar
Where strangers come past number.

H. T. Wade-Gery, C. M. Bowry   (*Olympian*, i. 67–93)

275   *The Island of the Blest*

B UT in sunshine ever fair
   Abide the Good, and all their nights and days
      An equal splendour wear.
And never as of old with thankless toil
For their poor empty needs they vex the soil,
      And plough the watery seas,
But dwelling with the glorious gods in ease
      A tearless life they pass
      Whose joy on earth it was
To keep their plighted word; but far from these
Torments the rest sustain too dark for human gaze.

      Whosoe'er can thrice endure
In either biding-place their souls to save
      From all transgression pure,
These tread the Heavenly Way to Cronus' Tower,
Where round the Happy Islands hour on hour
      The ocean breezes blow;
And there are blossoms of clear gold that grow

On shining trees, or rest
On the fond water's breast,
And wreaths thereof they twine round arm and brow.
Thus Rhadamanthus wise his all-just mandate gave,

Who sits in judgement by the side
Of world-throned Rhéa's lord most high.
Pêleus and Cadmus both abide
Among that blessed company;
And thither too his mother bore
Achilles, when her pleading sore
The heart of Zeus to mercy wore.

Cycnus he to death had done
And foremost Hector, Troy's unshaken tower,
And Morning's Æthiop son.

C. J. BILLSON   (*Olympian*, ii. 61–83)

276   *Evadnê and Her Son*

BY Cronus' son Poseidon loved and won
    Was Pítanê, to whom a child she bare,
    The dusky-haired Evadnê; but men say
With flowing robes she hid her maiden care
    Till the due moon, then sent her babe away
        To Eilatus' wise son
Who o'er Arcadians at Phæsânê reigned
    Beside Alphêus' streams, and nurtured there
    His tender charge grew up a damsel fair,
Whose virginal sweet love Apollo gained.

From Æpytus she could not hide for aye
   Her Heavenly burden, and the king reined tight
     His wordless wrath, and went to ask for aid
   From Pŷtho's prophet in his grievous plight;
      While she beneath the brake's deep purple shade
       Her crimson zone laid by,
And put her silver pitcher down, and bare
   A godlike-minded son, for at her side
   The bright-haired god had set the Fates to bide,
And sent her Eileithŷia's gentle care.

And Íamus came forth with pleasing pain
   Into the sun's clear light. But on the ground
     She needs must leave him in her hapless mood,
When lo! two grey-eyed snakes the infant found,
     By God's design, and nursed him with the food
      Of bees' unharmful bane.
But when the king came driving with all speed
   From rocky Pŷtho home, he asked each one
   Through all his household for Evadnê's son,
Proclaiming him Apollo's very seed;

And thus the boy's fair fortune he revealed,
   That far beyond all mortals he should prove
     A prophet of mankind of fadeless race.
But all declared that none beneath that roof
     Had heard the five-day babe, nor seen his face;
      For he, in reeds concealed,
Lay mid the trackless brake, his tender frame
   Suffused with pansies' gold and purple rays;
   Wherefore his mother vowed him all his days
To bear the pansy's death-denying name.

And when his golden youth was blooming fair
   Deep in Alphêus' stream the stripling stood,
     And called his grandsire, the wide-ruling king
   Poseidon, and blest Delos' Archer-god,
     Praying that honour for his head might spring,
       And a great people's care.
'Neath the bare heavens he stood in utter night;
   And thus his father's faultless words came back:
   'Arise, my son, pursue my voice's track,
And hither come where all men meet in light.'

To Cronus' steep and lofty hill they came.
   There was he given a twofold prophet-boon:
     To hear that night the voice that cannot lie,
   And,—after Hêraclês, the Alcîdæ's son,
     The brave-thewed hero reverenced for aye,
       In his dread Father's name
An all-embracing festival had planned
   And wrought the Games' great code,—then should he
     found,
   On the top tier of Zeus's altar-mound,
A new prophetic shrine by God's command.

C. J. BILLSON   (*Olympian*, vi. 29–70)

277   *Bellerophon*

AND long it irked his father when he tried
    To capture Pegasus, the Gorgon's son,
   Hard by Pîrênê's spring, until it seemed
That Pallas, with a gold-chased bridle, shone
    Before him—and 'twas even as he dreamed—
     And thus the Virgin cried:

'Sleepest thou still, Æolian king? Arise!
   Take to thy father this horse-amulet,
    —He is the Steed-Subduer—nor forget
A bull all-white shall be thy sacrifice.'

So spake the Maid of the grey-glimmering Shield
   As he lay sleeping in the shades of night.
    Then up he sprang, and taking in his hand
   The wondrous gift, he showed it with delight
    To Coiranus' son, the prophet of the land,
     And all the tale revealed,
How at her altar—as his mandate ran—
   He laid him down at nightfall to repose,
   When She, the Child of thundering Zeus, uprose,
And gave to him that golden talisman.

And the seer bade him with all haste obey
   The Vision's rede, and, after he had killed
    For Earth's Enfolder the strong-footed beast,
   Then for Athênê's self an altar build,
    Where the pure Goddess of the Steed might feast.
     Now that which seems to-day
A desperate thing that no man dare foretell
   God's power will lightly do, so that winged horse
   Bellerophon o'ermastered not by force
But placing in his mouth the gentle spell.

Then in his bronze armour mounting high
   On that swift steed he made his weapons play,
    And from the cold air's bosom waste and wide
   He smote the Amazonian array
    Of women archers in their warlike pride,
     And slew the Sólymi,

And quenched the fierce Chimæra's breath of fire.
   Of his own fate no word my song shall tell,
   But that immortal horse doth ever dwell
In age-old stables of Olympus' Sire.

C. J. BILLSON   (*Olympian*, xiii. 63–92)

278   *The Power of Music*

O LYRE of gold, Apollo's
   Treasure, shared with the violet-wreathed Muses,
The light foot hears you, and the brightness begins:
Your notes compel the singer
When to lead out the dance
The prelude is sounded on your trembling strings.
You quench the warrior Thunderbolt's everlasting flame:
On God's sceptre the Eagle sleeps,
Drooping his swift wings on either side,

The King of Birds.
You have poured a cloud on his beak and head,
   and darkened his face:
His eyelids are shut with a sweet seal.
He sleeps, his lithe back heaves:
Your quivering song has conquered him.
Even Arês the violent
Leaving aside his harsh and pointed spears
Comforts his heart in drowsiness.
Your shafts enchant the souls even of the Gods
Through the wisdom of Lâto's son
   and the deep-bosomed Muses.

And things that God loves not
Hear the voice of the maids of Pieria: they shudder
On earth and in the furious sea.
And He is afraid who lies in the horrors of Hell,
God's enemy,
　　　Tŷphôs the hundred-headed,
Nursed once in the famed Cilician Cave.
But now above Kŷmê the foam-fronting heights,
And the land of Sicily, lie
Heavily on his shaggy chest.
The Pillar of Heaven holds him fast,
White *Etna*, which all year round
Suckles its biting snows.

Pure founts of unapproachable fire
Belch from its depths.
In the day-time its rivers
Pour forth a glowing stream of smoke:
But in the darkness red flame rolls
And into the deep level sea
　　　throws the rocks roaring.
And that huge Worm
Spouts dreadful fountains of flame,—
A marvel and wonder to see it, a marvel even
　　　to hear from those who are there,
What a monster is held down
Under Etna's dark-leaved peaks, and under the plain.
The bed he lies on
Driving furrows up and down his back
Goads him.

H. T. WADE-GERY, C. M. BOWRA　　　(*Pythian*, i. 1–28)

279   *Asclêpius*

O LET me breathe what all men pray !
   Would Chîron were alive, whom Phílyra bore
To Cronus, Heaven's own son, in years of yore,
   Long-vanished chief of widely-ruling sway.
      O that neath Pêlion's lofty brow
      His uncouth form were reigning now;
      For human pains his pity moved,
      And dearly all mankind he loved.
      He too the wise Asclêpius taught,
      Who many a balm in mercy sought
      The bruised and broken frame to stay,
And like a hero strove all suffering to allay.

      For lo ! before her babe was born
Proud Phlégyas' daughter, as Apollo bade,
By golden arrows of the Huntress Maid
   Fell stricken in her room, and passed forlorn
      Adown the grey and ghostly path;
   So stern is an Immortal's wrath,
      Which in her folly she defied,
      For she who once had been the bride
      Of flowing-haired Apollo's bed
      Without her father's knowledge wed
      Another spouse, of mortal earth,
While in her womb she bare the seed of heavenly birth.

She for no marriage banquetings would bide,
   Nor wait the chime of hymeneal lays,
Such as the girl companions of a bride
   With merry voices in the evening raise:

                                             301

For she like many others held most dear
 What lay beyond her own familiar ways,
As mortals oft who scorn their homely sphere
 On things far distant bend a foolish gaze,
Pursuing idle dreams and hopes unsatisfied.

  And richly-robed Corônis then
Such madness seized, who letting fancy rove
To some Arcadian stranger gave her love,
 Yet 'scaped not so the Loxian watcher's ken.
  For though at Pŷtho he abode
  The royal shrine's all-knowing god,
  By his unerring Father taught,
  Saw for himself the wrong she wrought;
  For one who scorns to use deceit
  On others, none may hope to cheat;
  Nor man nor god, in thought nor deed,
Apollo's guileless mind can e'er by guile mislead.

  But when her treachery he knew
And traffic base with one of strangers' blood,
Ischys, the son of Elatus,—the god
 Bade his own sister wreak the vengeance due.
  Then Artemis in awful might
  To Lacereia sped forthright,
  (For by the Bœbian mere she dwelt
  Whose lawless soul her ruin dealt),
  And there her shafts the sinner slew;
  And many with her perished too,
  As sometimes on a mountain's side
A single spark lays low great forests far and wide.

But when her kin had placed her on the pyre,
   And the fierce flames ran round, Apollo said:
'No more can I endure by cruel fire
   To burn my offspring with its mother dead.'
And with one stride he ripped the babe away,
   For cloven apart for him the burning bier
Left a clear path to where the body lay.
   To Chîron then he gave his child to rear,
And teach him how to heal all ills that men acquire.

    And all who came Asclêpius cured;
Those whom some taint of nature had laid low,
And those whose limbs were wounded by the blow
   Of far-flung stone or bronzen-gleaming sword,
     Whom summer suns too fiercely smite,
     And whom the freezing winters bite;
     Relieving each peculiar pain,
     And cleansing all from scar and blane.
     And one he healed with spells benign,
     And one with soothing anodyne.
     With simples too their flesh he bound,
Or with the keen-edged knife restored the festering wound.

    Yet wisdom too is thrall to gain;
And even he, beguiled by glittering gold,
To work forbidden arts his knowledge sold,
   And raised from death a man already slain.
     But Zeus with thunder-blast of fire
     Struck through them both in sudden ire,
     From both their bosoms drove the breath,
     And with bright lightning wrought their death.

O mortals, seek no more from Heaven
    Than God to mortal man hath given;
    Know what a course is ours to run,
And what we are, and how our destiny is spun!

C. J. BILLSON   (*Pythian*, iii. 1–60)

280   *The Quest of the Golden Fleece*

HOW first began their voyage? What sore strait
    Held them constrained by adamantine bands?
Of Pélias once an oracle had said
That Æolus' proud sons by their own hands
    Or through resistless craft should lay him dead.
        And fearful words of fate
Rose from the green Earth-Mother's central stone,
    Bidding him guard against a man who trod
    The hill-steads' pathway with one sandal shod
Down to the valley where Iolchos shone,

Stranger or friend. And so at last he came,
    Wielding two spears, a man of aspect dread,
        Twofold in garb, his shapely limbs revealed
    In their close country dress, while o'er it spread
        A leopard's skin, from shivering rains to shield,
            And like a wave of flame
His unshorn hair behind him floated bright.
    Swift to Iolchos' market-place he strode,
    And there to test his bold young heart he stood
Amidst the surging crowd in all men's sight.

They knew him not and marvelled to behold;
 And one would say: 'This stranger from afar
  Is not Apollo surely, nor the mate
 Of Aphrodîtê with his bronzen car.
  Îphimedeia's sons have found their fate,
   Both Ephialtês bold
And Ôtus, slain on shining Naxos' beach,
 And Tîtyus truly Artemis laid low
 With shafts of her unconquerable bow,
Lest men's desires should soar above their reach.'

Thus they together talked. But Pélias came
 Driving the mules in his bright car anon
  With headstrong haste, and shuddered when he spied
 One sandal on the man's right foot alone,
  A signal plain, yet hid his fear and cried:
   'What country dost thou claim
To be thy fatherland, thou man unknown?
 What rustic wife hath dropt thee on the earth
 With senile pangs? Now tell me of thy birth,
Nor shame it worse by falsehoods of thy own.'

Then soft but bold the other's voice was heard:
 'My speech shall show what Chîron taught me well,
  For from his cave am I, where Phílyra,
 Chariclo, and his virgin daughters dwell,
  My nurses, whom I lived with till this day,
   And ne'er by act or word
In twenty years have shamed. I come to claim
 My father's ancient realm, which others hold
 Unjustly, since to Æolus of old
Zeus gave in fee a reigning sovereign's name.

For lawless Pélias in his scorn of right,
    Thus was it told me, from my parents stole
      Their immemorial kingdom, and in dread
Of that proud chieftain's overweening soul
      They made a sound of mourning for the dead,
        When first I saw the light,
In shuttered rooms where women rent the air,
    While swathed in purple, with the night alone
    Around me, I was hurried forth unknown,
And left in godlike Chîron's fostering care.

Most of this tale ye know. Now, burghers brave,
    Show me the palace of my sires who rode
      Their proud white steeds, for Æson's son I am,
Born in this place, and 'tis no strange abode
      Methinks I come to. Jason is my name
        Which the good Centaur gave.'
So said, he entered; and his father's eyes
    Knew him, and tears from their old lids down rolled,
    And all his heart grew happy to behold
His son, of all men fairest and most wise.

Then both his uncles, when they heard the tale,
    Came hither, Pherês from the neighbouring spring,
      And Amythâon from Messênê's bay.
And quickly too Melampus and the king
      Admêtus to Iolchos made their way,
        To bid their cousin hail:
And Jason, when the common board was spread,
    Spake courtly words, and let the feast's delights
    Unstinted flow through five full days and nights,
Plucking life's bloom of joyance ere it fled.

  306

But grave of speech when the sixth morning shone
    From first to last he showed his kinsmen all.
      Then leaping from their tents with him they strode
    In full assent to Pélias' lofty hall,
      And entered in, and in the palace stood:
        And fair-haired Týro's son,
Pélias himself, on hearing them, drew near,
    And Jason gently thus began to build
    The words of wisdom through soft lips distilled:
'Son of Poseidon, the Rock-Cleaver, hear!

Too prone are men to choose ill gains in lieu
    Of righteousness, though sharp the awakening is;
      But thou and I must rule our hearts with care,
    To weave for future years our crown of bliss.
      No news I tell. The dam that Crêtheus bare
        Bare rash Salmôneus too,
And we, their grandsons, from one lineage came
    Who look this day upon the golden sun.
    If men fall out whom Nature joined in one,
The Fates shrink back, and hide their heads in shame.

Seemless it were for us with sword and spear
    To rend our sires' great heritage in twain.
      The flocks and fields and droves of russet kine
    Reft from our parents to increase thy gain,
      All these I leave thee, and no grudge is mine
        At thy abundant cheer.
But yield to me the sceptre and the throne
    On which the royal son of Crêtheus sat,
    Dealing just laws to his wild horse-proud state,
Lest some new ill should rise from thence anon.'

Thus Jason spake, and Pélias answered meek:
  'Such as thou wouldest I will be, but lo!
    To me already fall life's twilight hours,
  While thy bright youth is in its opening blow,
     And thou canst lull the wrath of ghostly powers;
      For Phrixus bids us seek
Aêtês' house, and bring away the fleece
  Of that great ram which erstwhile from the waves
  Saved him and from his stepdame's wicked glaives,
So shall his spirit rest at last in peace.

Strange visions taught me thus: then I appealed
  To pure Castália's oracle, to test
    If aught were toward, and the god bade speed
  To fit a ship for sailing on that quest.
     If thou wilt undertake the perilous deed
      To thee I then will yield
The crown and sovereignty. By mighty Zeus,
  Forefather of us twain, this oath I swear.'
  They then between them made agreement there,
And parted thence. And Jason spread the news

Of his own sailing over all the land;
  And quickly came three warriors to his side,
    Unwearied sons of Zeus, whom Lêda bore
  And dancing-eyed Alcmênê, and in pride
     Of conscious might, high-plumed, from Pylus' shore
      And far Tænárian stránd
Euphêmus came and Periclýmenus,
  Poseidon's sons, who won unfading fame;
  And from Apollo's side a minstrel came,
Great Orpheus, parent of the lyric muse.

And Hermês of the golden wand had sent
　　To that hard task his sons in manhood's bloom,
　　　Echîon brave and Eurytus, who made
　Beneath Pangaius' brow their distant home.
　　　And Bóreas, monarch of the winds, arrayed,
　　　　With heart of glad content,
Zêtês and Cálaïs, his children leal,
　Whose flame-hued wings from either shoulder fell.
On those half-gods Queen Hêra cast a spell
Of dear desire for Argo's plunging keel,

That none should linger by his mother's side
　　Through days undangered, but to death's last hour
　　　With others strive to grasp the skirts of fame.
　Then Jason cheerly marshalled all that flower
　　　Of seafarers that to Iolchos came;
　　　　And Mopsus prophesied
From lots and omens, and with gladsome heart
　Bade them God-speed to sea. And when at last
The anchors o'er the vessel's bows were cast
Their leader stood upon the stern apart,

And lifted up a golden cup and cried
　　To Zeus, the Sire of Heaven, the lightning's lord,
　　　To waves and winds and sea-ways of the night,
　Fair days and sweet returning to afford.
　　　Then pealing thunder from the clouded height
　　　　With favouring voice replied,
And bright the flashes of the lightning shone.
　Those Heavenly signs the faithful heroes heard,
　And took fresh courage as the prophet's word
Cheered them with hope and bade them hasten on,

Plying with rapid hands the unsated oar.
　　Thus wafted by the blowing South they came
　　　Beside the mouth of the Unfriendly Sea,
　　And there a hallowed precinct did they frame
　　　For sea Poseidon's hoar divinity,
　　　　Where on the desolate shore
A tawny herd of Thracian bulls they spied,
　　And the stone hollow on a new-built shrine,
　　But ere they cleft the deadly perilous brine
On him that guards the mariner they cried

To save them from the Clashing Rocks, those twain
　　Fierce living creatures that together drew
　　　Swifter than sallies of the roaring East.
　　But soon they perished when that godlike crew
　　　Came sailing there. And, from that bale released,
　　　　Aêtês' own domain,
Phâsis, they came to, and in battle mixed
　　With dusky Colchians. Then the Cyprian first
　　From high Olympus brought the bird accurst,
On four-spoked wheel immovably transfixed,

The speckled wryneck, to bewitch men's hearts.
　　'Twas she taught Jason with what magic charm
　　　To draw Mêdêa from her filial ways,
　　That she, sore stricken by Persuasion's arm,
　　　Might yearn for Hellas in her passion's blaze.
　　　　And soon with subtle arts
Mêdêa showed him how to do aright
　　Her father's tasks, and gave him balm and oil
　　To salve himself against his aching toil,
And with sweet vows their spousal troth was plight.

Then in their midst Aêtês set a plough
   Of adamant with oxen breathing fire
     From tawny nostrils, who at each step drove
Their brazen hoofs deep in the earth and mire.
      Himself he yoked and led them forth and clove
        Furrows in even row,
And fathom-deep each loamy ridge uprolled.
    'Now let your king,' quoth he, 'your captain brave,
     Perform this task for me, and he shall have
My glittering fleece of ever-during gold.'

He said; and Jason, trusting God, down cast
   His saffron mantle, and the work essayed.
     Nor flinched he at the fire who well had conned
The magic precepts of the stranger maid,
      But seized the plough, and with resistless bond
        The bullocks' necks held fast,
Thrust in their brawny flanks the tireless goad,
    And all his task fulfilled. And at the close
    A wordless outcry from the king arose,
For wonder at that strength a mortal showed.

Then all his comrades stretched their hands in glee
   With wreaths of grass the strong man's brows to bind,
     And hailed him with soft plaudits. But straightway
The Sun's great offspring told him where to find
      The shining fleece which Phrixus' knife did flay.
        'For verily,' thought he,
'This task at least will baffle all his zeal.'
    For in thick woods it lay, within the grip
    Of a fierce dragon larger than a ship
Of fifty oars long hammered by the steel.

'Twere long to keep the road, as time goes by;
　　But I a briefer byeway can pursue,
　　　Whose art to many is as a beacon's ray.
Know then, Arcésilas, that Jason slew
　　　The glaring speckled snake, and stole away
　　　　Mêdêa, his ally
And Pélias' death. To Ocean streams they came,
　　The Sea of Red, and where each Lemnian wife
　　Her husband slew; and there in sportive strife
They wrestled for the robe, their meed of fame.

C. J. Billson   (*Pythian*, iv. 70-253)

281   *Human Life*

WHO, in his tenderest years,
　　Finds some new lovely thing,
His hope is high, and he flies
On the wings of his manhood:
Better than riches are his thoughts.
—But man's pleasure is a short time growing
And it falls to the ground
As quickly, when an unlucky twist of thought
Loosens its roots.

Man's life is a day. What is he?
What is he not? A shadow in a dream
Is man: but when God sheds a brightness,
Shining light is on earth
And life is sweet as honey.
　　Ægina, dear mother,
Keep this city in her voyage of freedom:
You, with Zeus and lord Aiakos,
Pêleus, and noble Télamon, and Achilles.

H. T. Wade-Gery, C. M. Bowra   (*Pythian*, viii. 88-100)

282   *Cyrênê*

SHE loved not the walk to and fro before the loom
        Nor the delight of feasting with her companions
Who kept the house:
But with javelins of brass and a sword
She fought and slew wild beasts,
And gave great peace and quiet
To her father's herds: niggard was she,
Letting her sweet bedfellow,
Sleep, brush her eyes but briefly, towards the dawn.

The God of the Broad Quiver found her:
Whilst she was wrestling once
Alone with a strong lion, without her spears,
Far-shooting Apollo came on her.
Thereat with a shout
He called Cheiron out of his dwelling,
        'Leave your dread cave, son of Phílyra, and be
                amazed
At the courage and great strength of a woman.
Look what a fight she makes, her head unflinching,
Her maiden spirit high
Above the struggle:
Fear makes no winter in her heart.
What mortal begot her? From what stock was she torn

To dwell in the folds of the shadowy hills, and sound
Her unplumbed depths of valour?
Were it no sin to lay my mighty hand on her
And take the delicious pasture of her love?'

—With softened eyes, the huge Centaur
Dewily laughed: swift and wise was his answer:
  'They are secret keys
With which Persuasion knows how to unlock
The sanctuaries of love,
Phoibos: Gods and men are alike
Shy of it being said, when first they come
To some sweet maidenhead.

So you, whom untruth may not touch,
Were led in the honey-sweetness of your mood
To speak with guile.
You ask of what race the girl is—
You, Sire, you know
The appointed end of all, and all paths:
How many leaves in April the earth puts forth,
How many grains of sand
In the sea and in the rivers
Are troubled by the waves and the swirling winds,
And what shall be, and whence it shall come,
You see with clear eyes.
If I must match my own wisdom with that,

I will speak:—
You came to this glade to wed her,
And you will carry her over the sea
To the chosen garden of God.
You will make her there a Queen of Cities,
Gathering an island people
To a hill amidst a plain: but now
Among wide meadows the Lady *Libya*

314

Shall welcome her, your glorious bride,
In gold palaces gladly.
She shall give her at once, that she may dwell beside her,
A portion of land
To yield her fruit of all that grows,
And wild beasts shall be found there.

H. T. Wade-Gery, C. M. Bowra   (*Pythian*, ix. 18–58)

283   *The Hyperboreans*

YET in their midst the Muses too are found,
   For maidens gay are dancing everywhere,
While the loud notes of lyre and flute go round,
   And joyously they wreathe about their hair
With golden leaves which the sweet bay-tree bore.
   And no disease is theirs, and no sad eld
   Touches that holy race, who there are held
Aloof from toils and battles evermore,

And ransomed from the Avenging Goddess' ire.
   To that blest concourse by Athênê led
In days of old, breathing a soul of fire,
   Came Danaê's son, who smote the Gorgon dead,
And brought her head away, whose tresses shone
   With many-glinting serpents' baleful glare,
   And to Serîphus' island people bare
With that weird spectacle a death of stone.

C. J. Billson   (*Pythian*, x. 37–48)

284   *Orestês*

HIM Arsínoa, his nurse,
—After his father's murder at the strong hands
Of Klytaimêstra—
Saved from that grievous traitress, whose grey bronze
Made Kassandra, Dardanid Priam's child,
Bear company with Agamemnon's spirit
To Ácheron's shadowy shore,

Pitiless woman. Was it Îphigeneia,
Slain at Eurîpos far from her land,
Who stung her to uplift
The wrath of her heavy hand?
Or was she broken in to a paramour's bed
And the nightly loves
Turned her mind? That sin in young wives
None forgives,
And there is no way to hide it,

For others will talk
And foul speech runs in a city.
For bliss makes envy as big as itself;
And he who breathes the dust
Whispers, but is not known.
        And the son of Atreus himself, the hero,
Died, when with years he returned,
In famous Amyklai,

And brought death on the maiden prophetess, he
Who had burned for Helen's sake
The Trojans' houses, and made cease their delight.

And Orestês, the young child,
Came to a friend, old Stróphios, that dwelt
At the foot of Parnassos. Yet Arês at the last
Brought him to slay his mother, and lay Aigisthos in blood.

H. T. WADE-GERY, C. M. BOWRA   (*Pythian*, xi. 17–37)

285   *The Infant Hêraclês*

BUT fast in heart I hold the lofty fame
      Of greatly-labouring Hêraclês, and sing
    A tale of olden time; for once, men say,
That son of Zeus with his twin brother came
    Straight from his mother's womb of suffering
      Into the wonder of the radiant day,
And, while his limbs were swathed in crocus-hued array,

Great Hêra saw him from her throne of gold,
    And straightly, in the fury of her wrath,
      The Queen of gods two serpents thither sent,
    Which, when the doors were opened, took their path
      To the wide inner chamber, fiercely bent
          The children to enfold,
And with quick-darting fangs to strike them dead.
    But Hêraclês, on his first field of fight,
      Undaunted stood, and held his head upright,
And forth his two avoidless hands outspread,

And grappled by their necks the serpents twain;
    And so it was that all their life was shed
      By strangling moments from their dreadful hearts,
    While those who stood about Alcmênê's bed
      Were stricken through their women's souls by darts
          Of irresistless pain,

317

For even the mother from her couch uprose,
　　Leapt to her feet, all robeless as she lay,
　　And fain would set herself to drive away
The shameless outrage of those brutish foes.

C. J. BILLSON (*Nemean*, i. 33–51)

286 *The Childhood of Achilles*

BUT golden-haired Achilles, biding still
　　In Phílyra's dwelling-place, made all his play
Of manly deeds, and often as a child
Poising his tiny-headed darts would slay,
　　Wind-fleet in strife, the lions of the wild,
　　　　And mighty boars would kill,
And drag their bodies panting to the son
Of Cronus, Chîron, from six years of age
And ever after; and Athênê sage
And Artemis in wonderment looked on,

While, with no help of hound or meshy snare,
　　He brought down stags by speed of foot alone.
　　Oft too by men of yore this tale was told:
How Chîron wise beneath his roof of stone
Reared Jason, then Asclêpius of old,
　　　　Whose hands he taught the care
Of healing salves. He too to Pêleus gave
Nêreus' bright-bosomed daughter for his wife,
And nurtured their great son, and in the strife
Of manly exploits nursed his spirit brave,

318

That so, when strong sea-winds should blow him o'er
  To Troy, he might abide the battle-cry
    Of Lycians, Phrygians, and the oncoming
Dardanian host, and might in conflict sore
  With Æthiop spearmen fix his purpose high
    Never to let their chief, their prophet king,
Memnon, the kin of Hélenus, once more
Return alive to his own natal shore.

C. J. BILLSON   (*Nemean*, iii. 43–63)

287   *Castor and Polydeucês*

THEY with alternate change for one day keep
    By their dear father Zeus; the next they lie
Far-sunk beneath Therapnê's valleys deep
  In earth, fulfilling thus one destiny
For each alike; for Polydeucês chose
        To share the grave's repose
And not himself alone in Heaven to dwell
  In full eternity of life divine,
Since in the strife his brother Castor fell,
  When Îdas haply for his raided kine
Was angered sore, and through his body sheer
        Drove the bronze-pointed spear.

For gazing from Tâÿgetus' far height,
  Lynceus espied them where they lay reclined
Within an hollow oak, for keener sight
  Had he than all the rest of humankind;
And thither straight on lightning feet he hied
        With Îdas at his side,

319

And they together planned the monstrous deed.
  Yet dreadful retribution fell anon
On both Apháreus' sons, as Zeus decreed,
  When swiftly on their track came Lêda's son,
And face to face they stood, anigh the ground
        Of their sire's burial-mound.

    From thence a carven stone, that bore
    The glory of the dead, they tore,
        And flung it at the breast
    Of Polydeucês; but it failed
    To crush him, and he still assailed,
        And forward hotly pressed,
    And through the side of Lynceus sped
    His flying javelin's brazen head,
        While Zeus on Îdas threw
    His bolt of fire; and there the two
    Perished forlorn, for hard it is to fight
With those that be of stronger might.

Then quickly to his brother's manly frame
  Back Polydeucês went. Not yet had Death
Quite mastered him, but from his throat there came
  The shuddering gasps of his departing breath.
And while he moaned and the hot teardrops shed,
        He cried aloud and said:
'O Father, Son of Cronus, what can fall
    To save me from my grief? O let me die,
Let me too die with him, great Lord of All!
    The glory of life departeth utterly
When dear ones leave us, and of all mankind
        In sorrow we shall find

Few only we may trust to share our woe.'
 He spake; then Zeus himself before him stood
And uttered thus his voice: 'Full well I know
 Thou art my son, whereas thy brother's blood
Flowed through thy mother from her lord on earth
   After thy Heavenly birth.
But now, behold, this choice I offer thee.
 If thou thyself would'st never more be vowed
To death and hateful age, but dwell with me,
 And with Athênê, and with Arês proud,
The dark spear's lord, upon our Mount Divine,
   That portion shall be thine.

 But if for thy dear brother slain
 Thou pleadest, and thyself art fain
  To share with him thy doom,
 Then may'st thou draw the living breath
 For half thy time where after death
  He lies in nether gloom,
 And half thy time abide on high
 In golden mansions of the sky.'
  Then, hearing the god's voice,
 The other stayed not in his choice;
And straightway Zeus unsealed the lips and eyes
 Of Castor in his bronzen guise.

C. J. BILLSON   (*Nemean*, x. 55–90)

288   *The Sons of Æacus*

LONG since her warrior sons abroad did wend
  And won great glory, which through ages long
The lyre and voiceful flute shall spread.

Now by God's grace a theme
For holy hymns are they. The Ætôlian lights
   For Œneus' sons the blaze of offerings fair;
In Thebes hath Iolâus solemn rites,
   Perseus in Argos, and the Heavenly Pair
    Are honoured by Eurôtas' stream.

But in Œnônê Æacus and all
   His great-souled sons are famed, who twice did seize
   Troy's war-swept town, led once by Hêraclês,
And then with Atreus' sons they wrought her fall.
Lift me, O Muse, from earth to loftier song!
   Say who were they who laid fair Cycnus low,
   Who slew great Hector, and the undaunted foe,
Memnon bronze-mailed, who led the Æthiop throng?
And who was he who by Caîcus' shore
   Speared Têlephus of yore?
Men were they who for motherland could claim
   Ægina's isle of glorious name.

   A tower of old was there
Built for their climbing virtues, and my tongue
   Hath many a singing shaft to praise their might:
Yea, even now from Ajax' isle hath sprung
   The witness of her seamen's saving fight,
    When Salamis the tempest bare,

    The ruining blast of God,
And countless men as thick as hailstones fell.
   But let no boast be heard, for it is Zeus,
Zeus, Lord of All, who dealeth ill or well.
   Your honours too awaken the sweet muse,
    And crave the joyous triumph-ode.

C. J. BILLSON   *(Isthmian,* v. 26–54 *b)*
322

289　　　　*Strepsiadês of Thebes*

THE Muses weave a brightness for his head,
　　And with his uncle, who has borne his name,
　He shares their violet coronal, although
Bronze-bucklered Arês laid the warrior dead.
　For Honour watcheth o'er a brave man's fame;
　　And well may all the heroes know
Who in this cloud of war undaunted stand
And overthrow their foes, from their dear land

Warding the storm of blood, that it is they,
　　Living or dead, who for their native state
　Sow glory's seed. And foremost in the fray,
　Son of Diódotus, thou found'st thy fate,
With Hector, Meleâger, and the seer
Amphiarâus, by the hostile spear.

There didst thou breathe thy rosy youth away
　　Where warriors bold the battle's brunt upbore
　　In hope forlorn, and speechless grief was mine.
But lo! the Holder of the Earth to-day
　A calm hath sent me, and the storm is o'er.
　　Now will I raise the song, and twine
My hair with wreaths: O may the Immortals spare
For any grudge to vex this peaceful air!

Whate'er the sweetness of the passing hours
　　I shall abide content, and free from care
　　Pass to grey age and life's allotted end.
Death takes us all, whatever fate be ours,

323

And if a man should gaze on things afar
    Too puny is he to ascend
The brazen heavens, as once Bellerophon
By Pegasus, the winging horse, was thrown,

When he would fain have soared to Heaven's own Gates,
    And joined the conclave of Almighty Zeus.
For lawless joys a bitter ending waits.
    But unto us O may'st thou not refuse
To grant, Apollo of the golden hair,
From thine own Pythian Games a garland fresh and fair!
C. J. Billson   (*Isthmian*, vii. 23–51)

290   *The Marriage of Thetis*
        Nor were the courts divine
Unmindful of their worth, when highest Zeus
    With glorious bright Poseidon strove,
    Since both were captured by the love
Of beauteous Thetis; yet did they refuse,
In their immortal wisdom, to fulfil
Her marriage with a god, but bowed to Fate's own will,

When Themis in their midst with counsel fair
    Uttered these words of doom: 'The Fates require
This goddess of the sea to bear
    A prince more potent than his sire;
And if her love to Zeus she yield
Or to his brethren, then her son will wield
A weapon to outbrave the thunder's might
    Or the dread Trident. Put your purpose by,
And rather let her wed a mortal wight,
    And see her son in mortal battle die,

    324

A son strong-armed as Arês, and with feet
  That match the fiery lightning swift.
 I pray you, grant the Heavenly gift
To Pêleus, son of Æacus. 'Tis meet
This marriage should be his, whom all maintain
The most God-fearing man reared on Iolchos' plain.

'These tidings speed to Chîron's holy cave
  Forthwith, and let not Nêreus' child again
Lay in our palms this issue grave,
  These leaves of strife, but, ere the wane
Of this full moon, for him alone
At evening's hour unloose her maiden zone.'
These words to Cronus' Sons the goddess said,
 And they with brows immortal bowed assent;
Nor did the fruit of her wise utterance fade,
  For Zeus with such a marriage waxed content,
Nor have the lips of poets sung in vain
  To men unversed, in mellow rhyme,
  The glory of Achilles' prime,
Who once imbrued the vine-clad Mysian plain
With the black blood of Têlephus, and gave
The Atreidæ safe return across the late-bridged wave.

And he delivered Helen, when his spear
  Cut Troy's strong sinews that had stayed his toil
Of deadly carnage many a year
  On Îlion's plain, till on the soil
He laid the might of Memnon low,
Stout Hector, and the foremost of the foe.

           325

To them that champion of the Æacid name
    Revealed Persephonê's dim dwelling-place,
And lifted to the starry heights of fame
    Ægina's isle and his own glorious race.
Nor did sweet songs forsake him after death,
        For Helicon's own maiden choir
        Stood by his tomb and funeral pyre,
Hymning his dirge with many a tuneful breath;
For thus it was the Immortal Gods' desire
To crown a brave man dead with strains of Heavenly fire.

C. J. BILLSON   (*Isthmian*, viii. 26–60)

291 *To Athens*

SHED o'er our choir, Olympian dominations,
    The glory of your grace,
O ye who hallow with your visitations
    The curious-carven place,
The heart of Athens, steaming with oblations,
    Wide-thronged with many a face.
Come, take your due of garlands violet-woven,
Of songs that burst forth when the buds are cloven.

Look on me—linked with music's heaven-born glamour
    Again have I drawn nigh
The Ivy-wreathed, on earth named Lord of Clamour,
    Of the soul-thrilling cry.
We hymn the babe that of the maid Kadmeian
Sprang to the sire throned in the empyrean.

By surest tokens is he manifested:—
    What time the bridal bowers
Of Earth and Sun are by their crimson-vested
    Warders flung wide, the Hours.
Then Spring, led on by flowers nectar-breathing,
    O'er Earth the deathless flings
Violet and rose their love-locks interwreathing:
    The voice of song outrings
An echo to the flutes; the dance his story
Echoes and circlet-crowned Sémelê's glory.

ARTHUR S. WAY   *(Dithyramb)*

292   *An Eclipse*

WHEN God reveals his plans to men,
    Straight is the way to glory then
    And good the end for all;
And God can from the murky night
Create inviolable light
Or hide the stainless day from sight
    Beneath a black cloud's pall.

C. M. BOWRA   *(Hyporchême)*

293   *Theóxenus*

THERE'S a season in life's spring,
    Heart, to gather up love's prize.
Theóxenus has eyes
Whence the rays fly glittering.
He who sees and is not swayed
On the flood-wave of desire,
His black heart on a dead fire
Out of steel or brass was made.

327

Aphrodîtê glancing-eyed
Scorns him, and he toils in vain
Violently wealth to gain,
Or with woman's desperate pride
Many ways he treads upon,
Slavish ways of life and chill;
While I, at the Goddess' will,
Like wax bitten by the sun,

Stored by bees in honey-cells,
Melt, when I turn eyes on him,
Strong in youth and fine of limb.
Beauty lives in Ténedos,
And with her Persuasion dwells;
There they bore Theóxenus!

C. M. Bowra   (*Skólion*)

294   *Thrasybûlus*

SONG, the chariot of delight,
Thrasybûlus, here I send.
When the feasters make an end,
Song shall rouse them, and invite
To speed the Vine-god on his way
In the cups of Attica.

Then our weary cares are gone,
Hearts within are free and bold;
Breaking on the seas of gold
There we sail where all are one;
Wealth fantastic lures our eyes
Onward to a shore of lies.

      Who was penniless before
        Holds a fortune in his hands;
        Who was rich, in power expands,
     Dreaming still of wealth the more.
        So our vanquished hearts incline,
        Shot by arrows of the vine.

T. F. HIGHAM   (*Skólion*)

295   *Life after Death*

FOR them the sun shines ever in full might
   Throughout our earthly night;
There, reddening with the rose, their paradise,
A fair green pleasance, lies,
Cool beneath shade of incense-bearing trees,
And rich with golden fruit:
And there they take their pleasure as they will,
In chariot-race, or young-limbed exercise
In wrestling, at the game of tables these,
And those with harp or lute:
And blissful where they dwell, beside them still
Dwells at full bloom perfect felicity:
And spreading delicately
Over the lovely region everywhere
Fragrance in the air
Floats from high altars where the fire is dense
With perfumed frankincense
Burned for the glory of Heaven continually.

WALTER HEADLAM   (*Thrênos*)

296   *The Power of Custom*

CUSTOM is lord of everything,
  Of mortals and immortals king.
High violence it justifies,
With hand uplifted plundering.
For this my testimony lies
In Hêraclês. He sacked the stalls
Of Gêrÿon, and his cattle brought
And stood them by Eurystheus' halls
Cyclopean,—loot unasked, unbought.

C. M. BOWRA

297   *Delos*

DELIAN Apollo, save!
  Scattered islets breeding sheep
Were their portion, and they keep
Delos, which Apollo gave,
Master golden-haired, that they
On Astéria might stay.

Delian Apollo, hail!
Lêto's Children, welcome me,
Your attendant, graciously.
Loudly let my song prevail,
While the honeyed voices sing
And the glorious pæans ring.

C. M. BOWRA   (*Pæan*, v)

330

CRATÎNUS

(520–422 B.C.)

298 *Periclês*

HERE'S Periclês, our own squill-headed Zeus.
Where *did* he buy that hat? With what excuse?
It's new head-cover in *Ôdêum* style—
Late storms of censure hardly left a Tile.

T. F. HIGHAM

299 *The Poet's Inspiration*

IF with water you fill up your glasses
You'll never write anything wise;
For wine is the horse of Parnassus,
Which hurries a bard to the skies.

THOMAS MOORE

DELPHIC ORACLE

(480 B.C.)

300 *The Army of Xerxês*

WRETCHES, why tarry ye thus? Nay, flee from
your houses and city,
Flee to the ends of the earth from the circle embattled of
Athens!
Body and head are alike, nor one is stable nor other,
Hands and feet wax faint, and whatso lieth between them
Wasteth in darkness and gloom; for flame destroyeth the
city,
Flame and the fierce War-god, swift driver of Syrian
horses.
Many a fortress too, not thine alone, shall he shatter;
Many a shrine of the gods he'll give to the flame for de-
vouring;

Sweating for fear they stand, and quaking for dread of the
    foeman,
Running with gore are their roofs, foreseeing the stress of
    their sorrow;
Wherefore I bid you begone! Have courage to lighten
    your evil.

A. D. GODLEY

301   *The Wooden Walls of Athens*

VAINLY doth Pallas strive to appease great Zeus of
    Olympus;
Words of entreaty are vain, and cunning counsels of wisdom.
Nathless a rede I will give thee again, of strength adaman-
    tine.
All shall be taken and lost that the sacred border of
    Cecrops
Holds in keeping to-day, and the dales divine of Cithæron;
Yet shall a wood-built wall by Zeus all-seeing be granted
Unto the Trîton born, a stronghold for thee and thy
    children.
Bide not still in thy place for the host that cometh from
    landward,
Cometh with horsemen and foot; but rather withdraw at
    his coming,
Turning thy back to the foe; thou yet shalt meet him in
    battle.
Salamis, isle divine! 'tis writ that children of women
Thou shalt destroy one day, in the season of seed-time or
    harvest.

A. D. GODLEY

302   *Neutral Argos*

HATED of dwellers around, by the gods immortal
   belovèd,
Couch with a lance in rest, like a warrior fenced in his
   armour,
Guarding thy head from the blow; and the head shall
   shelter the body.

A. D. GODLEY

LAMPROCLÊS

(fl. 480? B.C.)

303   *A National Anthem*

WRECKER of the city's wall,
   Pallas, awful power, I call:
Waker of the battle's din,
Trusty bulwark, undefiled
Maiden, who breaks horses in,
Mighty Zeus' belovèd child.

C. M. BOWRA

TÎMÓCREON

(fl. 480 B.C.)

304   *The God of Wealth*

BLIND god Plutus, better far
   Had you hidden, never seen
On island or peninsular,
Seas, or continents between!
Better had you kept your place
Down in depths of Ácheron—
Who but you has brought our race
All its miseries, every one!

T. F. HIGHAM

305   *Themistoclês*

PAUSANIAS you may praise,
  Or Xanthippus' noble ways,
Or Leutýchidas; but I
Rank Aristîdês high
  From Athens' holy town.
Him best of all I rate,
Since now, from Lêto's hate,
  Themistoclês is down.

Cheat, blackguard, traitor, he
From crookèd bribery
Refused to take his friend
Timócreon, or send
  Him to his island home.
He pocketed the pay,
And then he sailed away
  To the devil and to doom.

Some wrongly home he brought,
Some he murdered, some out-fought;
Then gorged with vicious gains
At the Isthmus entertains,
  But his cold meats did not please.
They ate, and swore that they
Would no attention pay
  To Themistoclês.

C. M. BOWRA

BACCHYLIDÊS

306   *Crœsus*

SHRINES fill with festival and with sacrificing,
    And full of carousing and feasts the alleys;
    And here with the beautiful work of tripods
High before the temple erected shining

Gold glitters, and the assembled priests of Delphi
        By fountain of Castaly praising Phœbus
        Proceed through his ground so immense—to god be
Praise! to god! in praising is best of treasures.

And so with the Lydian monarch
        In the land the horseman loves:—
        There, when doom of Zeus was due
For Sardis at the time Fate decreed,
Persia stormed the town and laid it desolate;
        But for Crœsus help was found.

Apollo of the gold sword was found to help him,
        When, falling on days never dreamed of, Crœsus
        In slavery longer to live disdaining
Built a pyre in front of his bronze-walled palace.

And sadly he ascended it, his wife ascended,
        And all of his daughters, their long hair flowing.
        They cried without ceasing, he held both hands up
To highest heaven, and his voice he lifted:

335

'O arrogant Deity,' crying,
          'Where do gods reward man's grace?
          Where is Lêto's child, our lord?
     For falling are the proud palaces
That Alyáttês built: what will Pŷtho pay me back
          For the many gifts I gave?

'My city has been mastered by the Medes, they sack it.
          The gold in the swirls of Pactôlus river
          Is reddened and bloody, the women rudely
     Forth from my magnificent palace carried.

'And dear is what I formerly have hated; dying
          Is sweetest.' He signed for a footman lighting
          The tower of timber; his daughters shrieking
     Held their clasped hands high to their mother pleading;

For hardest of deaths to a mortal
          Is the death he sees ahead.
          But when shining might of fire
     Appallingly the pyre darted through,
Zeus put down a cloud of darkness over it,
          Orange flame extinguishing.

Incredible is nothing that the care of heaven
          Causes, for Apollo of Delos carried
          The old man, the lightfooted daughters also,
     To the Hyperboréans; home they found there,

Because of piety and because he offered
     The best gifts of all men to holy Pŷtho.

GEORGE ALLEN   (III. 15–62)

336

The Eagle of Song

LO, now to a song thy heart incline;
    The girdled Graces wove it so,
They, and a bard of the Isle Divine,
    Whose fame to meet your own shall go.
By a friend shall Híero's praise be told;
    My heart is ready, my voice shall flow.
        The lady of heaven
        Her charge has given,
      The Muse brow-bound with gold.

Angel of Zeus, on sweeping pinion
    The brown bright eagle heavenward soars,
Serving the lord of wide dominion
    Whose voice in thunder roars.
Across the sky through gulfs profound
    Great strength conveys him undismayed,
While smaller fowl with piping sound
    Shrink back to earth afraid.
No peak that the giant earth upheaves,
    No rough sea-wave unwearying
Can stay him: the fathomless air he cleaves
    And so will veer and lean his wing
To the west wind's breath as he sails in sight
    On plume of delicate pencilling
        That every eye
        Must testify
      The bird of sovran flight.

By thousand ways I too may sail
    And praise of Híero's house declare,
While Arês goes in coat of mail
    And Victory shakes her raven hair.

T. F. HIGHAM   (V. 8–34)

308   *Hêraclês and Meleâger*

HE, who could sack a gated town,
    The Shining Thunderer's son, went down
To halls of tall Persephonê.
To bring from Hades' house sought he
The sharp-toothed dog, the spawn of Her
Whom living man may not draw near.
He saw the souls of luckless men
There by Côcýtus' flood, as when
There dance on Ida's gleaming rocks
The leaves among the pasturing flocks;
And there, the noblest ghost, stood one—
Brave spearman and Porthâon's son.

Alcmêna's first-born, child divine,
Then saw him in his armour shine;
And opening his quiver's lid
Out a bronze-tipped arrow slid,
And fixed the bow's clear-sounding string
Upon the tip. Encountering
His gaze, stood Melcâger's shade,
Who knew him well, and spoke, and said:
'Son of great Zeus, stand where thou art
And pacify thy lusty heart,

338

'Nor shoot thy angry shaft in vain
Against the spirits of the slain.
No need for fear!' His speech was done,
And wonder seized Amphítryon's son,
'What mortal or immortal hand
Reared such a shoot, and in what land?
Who was his slayer? Soon shall *he*
Be sent by Hêra to slay me.
But that's in golden Pallas' keeping.'
Then Meleâger answered weeping:
'No living man can turn away
The purpose which the gods display.

'My sire, horse-tamer, Œneus, could
Not turn aside the angry mood
Of holy white-armed Artemis,
Queen crowned with flowers, begging this
With sacrifice of many goats
And cutting red-backed oxen's throats.
Relenting not, the goddess sent
A shameless-battling boar, that rent
With ravening tusk, in strength's full tide,
Broad Cálydon's fair countryside;
All flocks he slew and living men
Who thought to face his onslaught then.

'The flower of Greece, without respite
Six days we fought a murderous fight,
And when a god the victory gave
To us Ætolians, a grave
We made for all the boar had slain
In onslaught loud with might and main,—

339

Anchæus, and Agelâus
Best of my brothers valorous—
My mother was their mother too
In Œneus' halls which all men knew.

'More yet were slain by cruel Fate.
Wild Artemis stayed not her hate;
With the Cûrêtës, battle's pride,
We fought to win the brindled hide.
Midst many others I slew these,
Îphiclus and brave Apharês,
My mother's brothers, swift of speed.
Bold-hearted Arês takes no heed
Of friends in war, but blindly flies
His shaft against all enemies;
Death is the gift he brings to all
Whose fated hour it is to fall.

'Fierce Théstius' daughter reckoned not
—My mother—in her evil lot
Of this, but planned a death for me,
A woman deaf to pity's plea.
Weeping, from out a carven chest
She took, swift ending and unblest,
A brand and kindled it, which fate
Decreed should mark my life's full date.
Strong Clýmenus I meant to slay
And make his flawless limbs my prey;
Before the walls I tracked him down,
In rout toward the ancient town

340

'Of Pleurôn with its well-built wall—
But then I felt my strength grow small
And life grow short. I breathed my last
And wept that glorious youth was past.'
They say that then and then alone
Tears welled up in Amphítryon's son
In pity for man's destiny,
And thus to him he made reply:

'''Tis best for man not to be born,
Never to see the light of morn.
But since by tears is nothing won,
A man must say what may be done.
In warrior Œneus' halls maybe
A maiden daughter, like to thee
In beauty, lives? Her would I take
Gladly, my brilliant bride to make.'
Then spake brave Meleâger's shade:
'At home I left a soft-necked maid,
Dêianîra, stranger still
To golden Cypris' magic will.'

C. M. BOWRA   (V. 56–175)

309   *Thêseus*

                   (*i*)

SO said the valiant master of the lance:
   Fear fell on all the crew,

Fear for the overboldness of the man.
   Then in his soul the son-in-law of the Sun
Was angry, and he schemed an evil plan,
   And prayed, 'Most Mighty One,

'Hear, Father Zeus! If thou'rt my sire indeed,
  Of the white-wristed Tyrian's child true sire,
Give me a visible sign! Send down with speed
  The lightning's tress of fire!

(Turning to Thêseus.)

'Prince, if Trœzênian Æthra mothered thee
  Got by Poseidon, Shaker of the Earth,
Cast thyself boldly down into the sea,
  His home who gave thee birth!

'Fetch me this golden jewel from my hand
  Out of the deep! Soon shalt thou be aware
Whether the Lord of Thunder, whose command
  Rules all, will hear my prayer.'

Zeus to that high request his ear inclined,
  And with peculiar praise to magnify
His son, and give a sign to all mankind,
  Did lighten in the sky.

Then at the welcome sign the warrior-King
  Spreading his palms to hallowed heaven wide,
'Thêseus, the grace of God is in this thing
  Made manifest,' he cried.

'Go, get thee down into the sounding swell!
  Surely the God thy father shall upraise
In all the wooded earth for thee as well
  Exceeding glory and praise.'

But Thêseus at the word, no whit unmanned,
    Turnèd not back in spirit; on deck he stood
Poised for a leap, and passed within the bland
    Sanctuary of the flood.

The son of Zeus was merry in his mind;
    The tight ship to the breeze he bade them lay;
Fast flew the keel, the strong North drove behind;
    But Fate ruled not that way.

All the Athenians trembled when the first
    Knight of their number seaward sprang, the tear
Ran down smooth faces, waiting for the worst
    In heavy hopeless fear.

But quick the dolphin-people of the deep
    Down to his father's vasty dwelling steered;
He saw the state the Gods of Ocean keep,
    And at the sight he feared.

The daughters of the blessed Nêreus there
    Beamed from their radiant limbs a fiery blaze,
Ribbons of golden web reeled round their hair,
    All dancing in a maze

Of fluent feet for pleasure; and he saw
    His father's wife the lady Amphitrite,
Eyed like an ox,—a Goddess throned for awe
    In chambers of delight.

343

She flung about him purple raiment brave,
    Over his curls a perfect wreath she laid,
The wedding-gift that cozening Venus gave,
    Thick roses in a braid.

The thing God wills, the wise man never deems
    Beyond belief. Close by the slender stern
The prince appeared, and O the world of schemes
    He slit by that return,

Miraculous from the deep! Bright maids arow
    Sang for surprise and joy—Upon his limbs
Shone gifts of Gods!—laud sang the lads also—
    The sea was loud with hymns.

J. S. PHILLIMORE   (XVI. 47–129)

(ii)

CHORUS. Lord of Athens' holy ground,
            Delicate Ionia's king,
        Hear the brass-belled clarion sound,
            To the battle summoning!
        Are the boundaries of our land
        Circled by an evil foe,
        With whom bands of soldiers go?
        Does some crafty robber-band
        Drive the flocks and herds away,
        Though the shepherds say them nay?
        What is it that frights you so?
        For, methinks, if any one,
        You have young men to give aid,
        Mighty men and unafraid,
        Pandîon's and Creûsa's son.

ÆGEUS. From the Isthmus far away
Lately came a message here—
Prowess more than man can say,
And a warrior without peer!
Mighty Sinis has he slain—
Stronger mortal was there none,
Cronus' seed, Poseidon's son—
And the sow that murdered men
Found its death in Cremmÿon's vales,
And proud Scîron tells no tales!
Down is wrestling Cercÿon;
From Procoptês' hand he cast
His great hammer easily,
Giving him his match at last—
Ah! but what the end will be!

CHORUS. Who and whence can this man be?
What the raiment he has on?
Does he lead a company
In warlike caparison?
Does he with his guards alone
Like a merchant-traveller come
To another people's home—
Strength's and valour's paragon?
Such his courage who has thrust
These men's powers to the dust.
Some god spurs him on to bring
Punishment to the unjust.
Else he could not easily
Find so often victory.
Time will show us everything.

ÆGEUS. With two men alone comes he;
Round his neck a sword he wears
With a hilt of ivory,
In his hands two javelins bears,
And a fine Laconian cap
Covers up his golden head;
While his chest a coat of red
And Thessalian mantle wrap.
From his eyes a tawny fire
Flashes with volcanic ire.
Proud with youth's first years his tread,
Thoughts of fighting fill his soul,
Where the War God likes to play,—
War and battle's loud array—
Glorious Athens is his goal!

C. M. BOWRA   (XVII. 1–60)

310   *Peace*

Peace upon earth
Brings Wealth and blossom of dulcet Song to birth;
To the Gods on carven altars makes thighs of oxen burn,
And sheep in the yellow flame,
And bids the young men's thoughts to the wrestling-game
And revel and hautboy turn.

Webs of the spider brown in the iron shield are made,
And rust grows over the edge of the sword and the lance's
    blade;
The sound of the brazen trumpet is not heard,
Nor the still air stirred

And the sweet of slumber torn
From the eyelid heavy at morn:
Banquet and blithe carousal throng the ways,
And the amorous hymn like fire in the air breaks forth in
    praise.

WALTER HEADLAM

311   *Fecundi calices*

LUTE, no longer hang upon your peg unstirred,
   Silencing your liquid voice of seven strings!
To my hands! for I would send a golden word
To Alexander from the Muses' wings,

Joy to those who sit and drink in groups of twenty,
When the soul warms with compulsion soft and sweet,
And the cups go jostling round the board in plenty;
Hopes of love then make the young hearts beat.

Dionŷsus mingles in the wine new powers,
Sending high adventure to the thoughts of men;
This man thinks he sacks a city's crown of towers,
That man dreams himself a monarch then.

Here with gold and ivory the halls are burning;
Bringing wheat and wealth across the gleaming brine
Back from Egypt come the merchantmen returning—
So is each man's spirit stirred by wine.

C. M. BOWRA

347

SOPHOCLÊS

(495–406 B.C.)

312   *Universal Change*

AJAX

ALL strangest things the multitudinous years
    Bring forth, and shadow from us all we know.
Falter alike great oath and steeled resolve;
And none shall say of aught, 'This may not be.'
Lo! I myself, but yesterday so strong,
As new-dipt steel am weak and all unsexed
By yonder woman: yea I mourn for them,
Widow and orphan, left amid their foes.
But I will journey seaward—where the shore
Lies meadow-fringed—so haply wash away
My sin, and flee that wrath that weighs me down.
And, lighting somewhere on an untrodden way,
I will bury this my lance, this hateful thing,
Deep in some earth-hole where no eye shall see—
Night and Hell keep it in the underworld!
For never to this day, since first I grasped
The gift that Hector gave, my bitterest foe,
Have I reaped aught of honour from the Greeks.
So true that byword in the mouths of men,
'A foeman's gifts are no gifts, but a curse.'
    Wherefore henceforward shall I know that God
Is great; and strive to honour Atreus' sons.
Princes they are, and should be obeyed. How else?
Do not all terrible and most puissant things
Yet bow to loftier majesties? The Winter,
Who walks forth scattering snows, gives place anon
To fruitage-laden Summer; and the orb
Of weary Night doth in her turn stand by,

348

And let shine out, with her white steeds, the Day:
Stern tempest-blasts at last sing lullaby
To groaning seas: even the arch-tyrant, Sleep,
Doth loose his slaves, not hold them chained for ever.
And shall not mankind too learn discipline?
I know, of late experience taught, that him
Who is my foe I must but hate as one
Whom I may yet call Friend: and him who loves me
Will I but serve and cherish as a man
Whose love is not abiding. Few be they
Who, reaching Friendship's port, have there found rest.
    But, for these things, they shall be well. Go thou
Lady, within, and there pray that the Gods
May fill unto the full my heart's desire.
And ye, my mates, do unto me with her
Like honour; bid young Teucer, if he come,
To care for me, but to be *your* friend still.
For where my way leads, thither I shall go:
Do ye my bidding; haply ye may hear,
Though now is my dark hour, that I have peace.

C. S. CALVERLEY   (*Ajax*, 646–92)

313   *Before Death*

                    AJAX

SO stands my cut-throat fitliest for its work—
    Give me but time to think this matter out—
First, as 'tis Hector's gift, of all my friends
Worst foeman, and most hateful in my sight;
Then, as 'tis planted in Troy's hostile soil,
New-whet on whetstone hungry for the steel:

But delicately, with care, I planted it,
With best good will to give me speedy death.
So all is ready, and so, my part being done,
Thou, Zeus, be first to help me, as is fit.
'Tis no great boon of thee that I shall ask:
Send now some messenger and let him bear
The ill-news to Teucer, that no hand ere his
May lift me fallen about this reeking sword:
And let no enemy behold me first
And fling me forth, to dogs and birds a prey.
Zeus, unto thee my prayer is said: but thou,
Hermês, good guide to deathward, give me good sleep—
With unconvulsive and with sudden bound,
Leaping upon this sword to pierce my heart.
Moreover, I call to aid the virgins ever,
Whose eyes fail never of seeing wrong done on earth,
Far-striding, dread Erînyës—to see
How by the Atreidæ, hapless, I am undone:
And with a swift perdition sweep them off,
An evil portion for their evil deeds—
As by this fatal and unnatural hand
They see me die, grant them to perish so,
Unnaturally, by their own children slain.
Come vengeful Furies, swift Erînyës,
Spare not, but glut your will on all the host.
And thou that chariotest the steeps of heaven,
When on my native land falls next thy gaze,
Awhile, O Sun-god, draw thy golden rein,
And tell the old man my father—let him know,
And my sad mother, my sufferings and my death.
Poor soul, I think that, when she hears the tale,
Loud weeping through the city she will send.

350

But now what use lamenting, all in vain?
Quick as I may, let me begin this deed.
O death, death, death, come now and look on me!
Nay rather—for I shall commune *there* with thee—
This present radiance of the shining day,
Now I invoke, and Hêlios, charioteer,
Thee with my latest breath, and never more.
O light, O sacred soil of Salamis
My home, and firm-set hearth of my father's house,
And glorious Athens, and the kindred race,
Founts and these rivers, and ye plains of Troy—
All ye have nursed my life—to all farewell!
His latest word to you thus Ajax speaks:
To ghosts in Hades shall the rest be said.

R. WHITELAW   (*Ajax*, 815-65)

314   *Dreams come True*

CHORUS

IF I am not a fool in prophecy
   And destitute of wisdom utterly,
Justice by this dream reveals her purpose.
Justice comes, with victory
For the good cause, hunting the evil down,
Very soon, my child:
Yea, I am well assur'd;
Breathing a spirit of joy from the tale of a dream.
The lord of Greece, thy father,
Hath not forgotten.
Nor hath that brazen two-edg'd axe forgotten
Through all the waste of years,
Which slew him shamefully

Yea, with the clash of many swords, the noise
Of many trampling feet, forth from the lair
Vengeance, brazen-footed Fury, ambush'd
Now in darkness, cometh soon
To the light—Sin tainted the bridal bed
Of the twain that slew.
Therefore my soul knows well,
Sure is the presage of evil, the sign of the doom;
It cannot, may not fail us.
They needs must suffer,
Or else there is no truth in mortal dreaming,
And vain is prophecy,
Unless this dream comes true.

J. T. Sheppard   (*Êlectra*, 473–502)

315   *A Chariot-race*

SERVANT

To Delphi, to Apollo's festal games,
    The pride and glory of assembled Greece,
He came. He heard the herald's thrilling cry
Summon the runners: for the race came first.
He rose in beauty, radiant: all the throng
Was hush'd in wonder: so he ran the course
From first to last victorious, crowned at length
With perfect honour. Oh, the tale were long
If I should tell you all. I have not known
A man so valiant, so victorious,
Fast as the judges order'd each event,
Winning, and winning yet again. At last
He was acclaim'd by all, an Argive born,

His name Orestês, son of that great prince
Who gather'd Greece for war, King Agamemnon.
　So fell these things. But when a god intends
Destruction, even the strong may not escape.
Next day at sunrise, when the lists were set
For the racing of swift-footed steeds and cars,
In a throng of charioteers he also enter'd.
One was Achæan: one from Sparta: two
From Africa, well-skilled in horsemanship:
And he was fifth, driving a team of mares
From Thessaly: then an Ætolian
With chestnut steeds: next a Magnêsian,
And after him an Ænian, with white horses,
The eighth: from god-built Athens came the ninth,
And from Bœotia the tenth and last.
They took their places where the judges, set
To do that office, by the lot assign'd them.
The trumpet sounds! They start, with a shake of the reins
And a shout to the horses. All the course is fill'd
With noise of rattling cars and rising clouds
Of dust and racers struggling in close pack—
No stinting of the goad—on, on, to pass
The hurrying rival wheels, the flying foam
Of panting steeds, whose labour'd breath bedews
The track of the car, the back of the charioteer.
Boldly he drove close by the stone that marks
The turning, to the trace-horse on his right
Giving free rein, but pulling on the left;
And all the cars drove safely on and on
For six completed courses. Suddenly,
At the seventh course, just as they made the turn,
The Ænian's colts refused the curb, and bolted,

Colliding with a car from Africa,
And from that first mishap, car after car
Crash'd and was overturn'd, and filled the plain
Of Crîsa with confusion and with wreckage.
The man of Athens understood. He wrench'd
His horses from their course, and cunningly
Drove clear of all that surging sea of trouble.
Last came Orestês, holding back his team,
And trusting for the victory to the end.
Now, now he saw no rivals left but one!
He rous'd his horses with a sharp shrill cry,
Hotly pursuing. Neck and neck they drove,
First one and then the other, as the cars
Sped on together, leading by a head,
Course after course: and all this while the youth
Unfortunate drove safely and drove well.
At last the moment came when thoughtlessly
He slack'd his left rein as he took the corner,
And struck the pillar, and his axle snapp'd:
He fell back from the car, a prisoner,
Caught in the leathern reins, and, as he fell,
His horses left the track and bolted madly:
Upon which sight, the assembled multitude
With one great shout of wonder and of grief
Acclaim'd a youth, so nobly valiant,
So greatly suffering. High in the air
His madden'd horses flung him, then to earth
Dash'd him again and yet again. At last
His comrades brought the horses to a stand
And loos'd the blood-stain'd body, now so changed
That those who loved him best would not have known
          him.

They gave him to the fire. Their messengers
Are on their way to bring you what is left
Of all that greatness, ashes and an urn,
For the last honours in his father's realm.

    This is my tale, and it is pitiful,
Even to tell. For us who witness'd all,
It was a sight sadder than I have seen.

J. T. SHEPPARD   (*Êlectra*, 681–763)

316   *A Burial-urn*

ÊLECTRA

O SAD memorial of the life I priz'd
   Beyond all other lives, my lov'd Orestês,
How much this welcome home belies the hope
With which I sent you forth, so young, so bright—
O child! and now this nothing, which I hold
So lightly in my hand. Would I had died
Before I sent you out, stolen from death,
Retriev'd from murder, sav'd, to dwell far off
With strangers. Better had you died that day
And shared your father's grave than perish'd so,
Miserably in helpless homeless banishment,
Far from my care. Alas! these hands of mine
Which should have dress'd and bathed you lovingly,
Then from the hungry flames have gather'd in
Grief's precious load for burial—not so!
Some stranger did my office—all I have
Is this— a little dust, a paltry urn.

    Alas for all my care, my loving care,
Prov'd useless now! The labour was so sweet,
Because it was for you, but all in vain.

Your mother never loved you as I loved you;
And you would call me, 'Sister', always, 'Sister'.
One day you died, and in that one day all
Has vanish'd, all. You gather'd up my life
And, like a whirlwind left me. Everything
Vanish'd. Our father's dead, and it is death
To me that you are gone. Our enemies
Laugh, and our mother, most unmotherly
Runs mad for joy. How often you would send
Your secret messages. You would come, you said,
And punish her yourself. The luckless chance
That haunts us both has stolen hope away,
And sent me for the bright form that I lov'd
These ashes and a shade that cannot help.

    Ah me, alas!
    O pitiful and strange!
    Ah me, alas, alas!

O dearest, by what strange and terrible ways
You travell'd, to destroy me utterly,
Yes, brother, to destroy! Come, welcome me
To this same narrow room, which houses you,
My nothing to your nothing. Let me dwell
With you below for ever. Here in life
We shared and shared alike. Now I would share
Your grave, and never part from you again.
I see, only the dead can feel no pain.

J. T. SHEPPARD   (*Êlectra*, 1126-70)

SOPHOCLÊS

In Time of Pestilence

CHORUS

I

Glad Message of the voice of Zeus,
From golden Pŷtho travelling to splendid Thebes, what
burden bringest thou?
Eager, am I, afraid, heart-shaken with fear of thee—
(Healer, Apollo of Delos, God of the Cry, give ear!)
Shaken with reverent fear. Is it some new task to be
done?
Or is it some ancient debt thou wilt sweep in the fulness
of time to the payment?
Tell me thy secret, Oracle deathless, Daughter of golden
Hope!
First call we on the child of Zeus,
Deathless Athênê; then on her that guards our land, her
Sister, Artemis,
Lady of Good Report, whose throne is our market
place;
Aye, and Apollo! I cry thee, Shooter of Arrows, hear!
Three that are strong to deliver, appear! Great
fighters of Death,
Now, if in ancient times, when calamity threatened, ye
came to help us,
Sweeping afar the flame of affliction,—strike, as of old,
to-day!

II

Alas! Alas! Beyond all reckoning
My myriad sorrows!
All my people sick to death, yet in my mind
No shaft of wit, no weapon to fight the death.
The fruits of the mighty mother Earth increase not.

Women from their tempest of cries and travail-
    pangs
    Struggle in vain . . . no birth-joy followeth.
As a bird on the wing, to the west, to the coast of
    the sunset god
Look ! 'tis the soul of the dead that flies to the dark, nay,
    soul upon soul,
Rushing, rushing, swifter and stronger in flight than the
    race of implacable fire,
        Myriads, alas, beyond all reckoning,—
        A city dying !
None has pity. On the ground they lie, unwept,
    Spreading contagious death ; and among them wives
    That wail, but not for them, aye, and grey mothers
    Flocking the altar with cries, now here, now there,
    Shrilling their scream of prayer . . . for their own
        lives.
    And a shout goeth up to the Healer ; and, cleaving
    the air like fire,
Flashes the Pæan, above those voices that wail in a
    piping tune.
Rescue ! Rescue ! Golden One ! Send us the light of thy
    rescuing, Daughter of Zeus !

III

Turn to flight that savage War-God, warring not with
    shield and spear,
    But with fire he burneth when his battlecry is loud,
    Turn him back and drive him with a rushing into
    flight,
    Far away, to exile, far, far away from Thebes,
        To the great sea-palace of Amphitrite,

Perchance to the waves of the Thracian sea and his own
    barbaric shore.
      He spareth us not. Is there aught that the night
      has left?
        Lo! Day cometh up to destroy.
    King and Lord, O Zeus, of the lightning fires,
Father of all! Thine is the Might. Take up the bolt
    and slay!
Phœbus, King Lycêan, I would see thee string thy golden
    bow,
    Raining on the monster for our succour and defence
    Shafts unconquered. I would see the flashing of the
    fires
    From the torch of Artemis, that blazeth on the hills
      When she scours her mountains of Lycia.
And another I call, the Golden-Crowned, and his name
    is a name of Thebes;
    He is ruddy with wine, and his cry is the triumph cry,
    And his train are the Mænadës;—
    Come, great Bacchus, come! With a splendour of
    light,
    Blazing for us, strike at the god cursed among gods, and
    save!

J. T. SHEPPARD   (*Œdipus Tyrannus*, 151–215)

318   *God and Man*

CHORUS

O MAY my constant feet not fail,
  Walking in paths of righteousness,
Sinless in word and deed—
True to those eternal laws

That scale for ever the high steep
Of heaven's pure ether, whence they sprang:
For only in Olympus is their home,
Nor mortal wisdom gave them birth,
And howsoe'er men may forget,
They will not sleep;
For the might of the god within them grows not old.

Rooted in pride, the tyrant grows;
But pride that with its own too-much
Is rashly surfeited,
Heeding not the prudent mean,
Down the inevitable gulf
From its high pinnacle is hurled,
Where use of foothold there is none.
But, O kind gods, the noble strength,
That struggles for the city's good,
Unbend not yet:
In the gods have I put my trust—I will not fear.

But whoso walks disdainfully,
In act or word,
And fears not justice, nor reveres
The thronèd gods,
Him let misfortune slay
For his ill-starred wantoning,
Should he heap unrighteous gains,
Nor from unhallowed paths withhold his feet,
Or reach rash hands to pluck forbidden fruit.
Who shall do this, and boast
That yet his soul is proof
Against the arrows of offended Heaven?

360

If honour crowns such deeds as those,
No song, but silence, then for me!

To Earth's dread centre, unprofaned
By mortal touch,
No more with awe will I repair,
Nor Abæ's shrine,
Nor the Olympian plain,
If the truth stands not confessed,
Pointed at by all the world.
O Zeus supreme, if rightly thou art called—
Lord over all—let not these things escape
Thee and thy timeless sway!
For now men set at nought
Apollo's word, and cry 'Behold, it fails!'
His praise is darkened with a doubt;
And faith is sapped, and Heaven defied.

R. WHITELAW   (*Œdipus Tyrannus*, 863–910)

319   *Jocasta's Death*

MESSENGER. CHORUS

MESS. Great Lords, that keep the dignities of Thebes,
     What doings must ye hear, what sights must see,
     And oh! what grief must bear, if ye are true
     To Cadmus and the breed of Labdacus!
     Can Ister or can Phâsis wash this house—
     I trow not—, with their waters, from the guilt
     It hides. . . . Yet soon shall publish to the light
     Fresh, not unpurposed evil. 'Tis the woe
     That we ourselves have compassed hurts the most.

CHOR. That which we knew already, was enough
      For lamentation. What have you besides?
MESS. This is the briefest tale for me to tell,
      For you to hear:—your queen Jocasta's dead.
CHOR. Alas! Poor lady! Dead! What was the cause?
MESS. She died by her own hand. Of what befell
      The worst is not for you, who saw it not.
      Yet shall you hear, so much as memory
      Remains in me, the sad Queen's tragedy.

      When in her passionate agony she passed
      Beyond these portals, straight to her bridal-room
      She ran, and ever tore her hair the while;
      Clashed fast the doors behind her; and within,
      Cried to her husband Lâius in the grave,
      With mention of that seed whereby he sowed
      Death for himself, and left to her a son
      To get on her fresh children, shamefully.
      So wept she for her bridal's double woe,
      Husband of husband got, and child of child.
      And after that—I know not how—she died.

      We could not mark her sorrows to the end,
      For with a shout, Œdipus broke on us,
      And all had eyes for him. Hither he rushed
      And thither. For a sword he begged, and cried:
      'Where is that wife that mothered in one womb
      Her husband and his children! Show her me!
      No wife of mine!' As thus he raged, some god—
      'Twas none of us—guided him where she lay.
      And he, as guided, with a terrible shout,
      Leapt at her double door; free of the bolts
      Burst back the yielding bar,—and was within.
      And there we saw Jocasta. By a noose

362

Of swaying cords, caught and entwined, she hung.
   He too has seen her—with a moaning cry
Looses the hanging trap, and on the ground
Has laid her. Then—Oh sight most terrible!—
He snatched the golden brooches from the Queen,
With which her robe was fastened, lifted them,
And struck. Deep to the very founts of sight
He smote, and vowed those eyes no more should see
The wrongs he suffered, and the wrong he did.
'Henceforth,' he cried, 'be dark!—since ye have seen
Whom ye should ne'er have seen, and never knew
Them that I longed to find.' So chanted he,
And raised the pins again, and yet again,
And every time struck home. Blood from the eyes
Sprinkled his beard, and still fresh clammy drops
Welled in a shower unceasing, nay, a storm
With blood for rain, and hail of clotting gore.
   So from these twain hath evil broken; so
Are wife and husband mingled in one woe.
Justly their ancient happiness was known
For happiness indeed; and lo! to-day—
Tears and Disasters, Death and Shame, and all
The ills the world hath names for—all are here.

J. T. SHEPPARD   (*Œdipus Tyrannus*, 1223–85)

320   *Blindness*

ŒDIPUS

NAY, give me no more counsel. Bid me not
   Believe my deed, thus done, is not well done.
I know 'tis well. When I had passed the grave,
How could those eyes have met my father's gaze,

Or my unhappy mother's—since on both
I have done wrongs beyond all other wrong?
Or live and see my children?—Children born
As they were born! What pleasure in that sight?
None for these eyes of mine, for ever, none.
Nor in the sight of Thebes, her castles, shrines
And images of the gods, whereof, alas!
I robbed myself—myself, I spoke that word,
I that she bred and nurtured, I her prince,
And bade her thrust the sinner out, the man
Proved of the gods polluted—Lâius' son.
When such a stain by my own evidence
Was on me, could I raise my eyes to them?
No! Had I means to stop my ears, and choke
The wells of sound, I had not held my hand,
But closed my body like a prison-house
To hearing as to sight. Sweet for the mind
To dwell withdrawn, where troubles could not come.

Cithæron! Ah, why didst thou welcome me?
Why, when thou hadst me there, didst thou not kill.
Never to show the world myself—my birth!

O Pólybus, and Corinth, and the home
Men called my father's ancient house, what sores
Festered beneath that beauty that ye reared,
Discovered now, sin out of sin begot.

O ye three roads, O secret mountain-glen,
Trees, and a pathway narrowed to the place
Where met the three, do you remember me?
I gave you blood to drink, my father's blood,
And so my own! Do you remember that?
The deed I wrought for you? Then, how I passed
Hither to other deeds?

                                    O Marriage-bed
That gave me birth, and, having borne me, gave
Fresh children to your seed, and showed the world
Father, son, brother, mingled and confused,
Bride, mother, wife in one, and all the shame
Of deeds the foulest ever known to man.
    No. Silence for a deed so ill to do
Is better. Therefore lead me hence away!
To hide me or to kill. Or to the sea
Cast me, where you shall look on me no more.
Come! Deign to touch me, though I am a man
Accursèd. Yield! Fear nothing! Mine are woes
That no man else, but I alone, must bear.

J. T. SHEPPARD   (*Œdipus Tyrannus*, 1369–1415)

321   *What a Piece of Work is a Man*

CHORUS

WONDERS are many, but there is no wonder
        Wilder than Man—
Man who makes the winds of winter bear him,
Through the trough of waves that tower about him,
Across grey wastes of sea;
Man who wearies the Untiring, the Immortal—
Earth, eldest of the Gods, as year by year,
His plough-teams come and go.
The care-free bands of birds,
Beasts of the wild, tribes of the sea,
In netted toils he takes,
The Subtle One.
Creatures that haunt the hills, the desert-dwellers,

His cunning snares; he lays his mastering yoke
On the horse's shaggy mane,
On the tireless mountain-bull.
Speech, too, and wind-swift thought
And the soul of the ruler of cities
He hath learned, untaught of any.
To shun the bitter arrows of the roofless frost,
The bitter shafts of rain,
He knows, the all-deviser; for without device
No morrow finds him. Only against Death
He shall call for help in vain,
Yet many a mortal sickness he hath mastered.

Thus with his wisdom,
Subtle past foretelling,
Man wins to joy, or sorrow.
Does he keep his native laws
And the justice sworn by heaven?—
High stands his city. But all citiless
Wanders the wretch that dares make sin his fellow.
May never such transgressor
Share hearth, nor heart, of mine!

F. L. Lucas   (*Antigonê*, 332–75)

322   *The Undying Law*
                    ANTÍGONÊ

IT was not Zeus, I think, made this decree,
   Nor Justice, dweller with the Gods below,
Who made appointment of such laws to men.
Nor did I think your edicts were so strong

366

That any mortal man should override
The Gods' unwritten and undying laws.
Their life is not to-day and yesterday
But always, and none knoweth whence they came.
I would not pay the price before the Gods
Of breaking these for fear of any man.
I knew that I should die; and why not so?
Though you had not ordained it. If I die
Before my time, I count it something gained.
For whoso lives with many miseries
As I live, is not death a gain to him?
Therefore I count the coming of this doom
No grief at all. Rather,—if I had left
Unburied mine own mother's son in death,—
That would have grieved me. This can bring no grief.
If what I do seems foolishness to you,
A foolish judgement reckons me a fool.

C. M. BOWRA   (*Antigonê*, 450–70)

323   *Unconquerable Love*

CHORUS

WHEN Love disputes
      He carries his battles!
Love he loots
      The rich of their chattels!
By delicate cheeks
      On maiden's pillow
            Watches he all the night-time long;
His prey he seeks
      Over the billow,
            Pastoral haunts he preys among.

Gods are deathless, and they
    Cannot elude his whim;
And oh! amid us whose life's a day
    Mad is the heart that broodeth him!

And Love can splay
    Uprightest of virtue;
Lead astray,
    Better to hurt you!
'Tis he did the wrong,
    'Tis he beguilèd
        Father and son to feud so dire.
Desire's too strong!
    —Out of the eyelid
        Peeped of a lovely bride, Desire!
He with Law has a court,
    Sovran in might with her.
Divine Aphrodîtê wreaks her sport;
    Who will be bold to fight with her?

J. S. PHILLIMORE   (*Antígonê*, 781–801)

324   *The Last Journey*

                    ANTIGONE

LOOK, my countrymen,
    as I go my last road,
and see my last of the sunlight
    now and for ever.
Death, who puts all to their sleep,
    leads my living body
to his dark lakeside.
    For me were no choristers

to sing the bride home;
no song of the wedding night
they sang for me.
I shall lie with the waters of Death.

Tales of doom I have heard,
and hers most pitiful
who wed here, out of Phrygia,
—a daughter of Tantalus—
and died on Sípylus top.
Taut as ivy
the hardness of stone crept up
and held her fast.
She wastes away, so they tell,
in everlasting rain
and falls of snow;
from under her weeping brows
scarped rocks run wet.
    Most like her
I am borne by destiny
to the bed of my rest.

T. F. HIGHAM   (*Antígonê*, 806–16, 823–33)

325   *Buried alive*
                 ANTÍGONÊ

O TOMB! O nuptial chamber! O house deep-delved
   In earth, safe-guarded ever! To thee I come,
And to my kin in thee, who many an one
Are with Persephonê, dead among the dead:
And last of all, most miserably by far,
I thither am going, ere my life's term be done.

But a good hope I cherish, that, come there,
My father's love will greet me, yea and thine,
My mother—and thy welcome, brother dear:
Since, when ye died, I with mine own hands laved
And dressed your limbs, and poured upon your graves
Libations; and like service done to thee
Hath brought me, Polyneicês, now to this.
But, if these things are pleasing to the gods,
I'll freely own I suffered for my fault;
If theirs the fault, who doomed me, may to them
No worse befall than they unjustly do.

R. WHITELAW   (*Antigonê*, 891–903, 925–8)

326   *Hêraclês*

DÊIANÎRA. CHORUS. LICHAS

DÊI. By Zeus I charge thee, whose clear lightnings shine
Down the high glens of Œta, keep back nought.
To one not evil-natured wilt thou speak,
One who knows well, 'tis human to rejoice
Not in the same delight continually.
I know, they are not wise, who set themselves
To fight with Love, challenging him to blows.
For even gods he governs as he will;
And me—why not another, weak like me?
Oh, if I blame my husband that he suffers
This madness, mad indeed am I myself;
Or blame this maiden, cause with him of that
Which causes me no shame, does me no wrong.
I cannot blame. But now, if taught of him
You lie, no noble lesson have you learned;

370

Or, if you school yourself, take heed lest then
You be found cruel, when you would be kind.
Nay, tell me all the truth. To be called false
Is for free men no honourable lot.
That you should 'scape discovery, cannot be:
Many there are who heard you, and will speak.
And if you are afraid, you fear amiss:
For, not to know—this would afflict me; but
Fear not my knowing: hath not Hêraclês
Loved many another—most of all men he?
And never any of them bore from me
Harsh word or gibe; nor shall, howe'er she be
Consumed with love, this maiden; nay, for her
Most of them all I pity, having seen
That 'twas her beauty that made waste her life—
Poor soul, who sacked, unwitting, and enslaved
The city of her home. But now I charge thee—
Heed not what winds blow whither—but be false
To others, if thou wilt, to me speak truth.

CHO.   Obey good counsel. Cause thou shalt not find
To blame this lady, and shalt have thanks of me.

LICH.   Nay then, dear mistress, since I see, being human,
Thou hast a human heart, that knows to feel,
I will keep nothing back, but tell thee all.
For so indeed it is, as this man says.
Huge passion for this maid smote through and
        through
My lord, and for her sake the ruined town,
Her home Œchália, fell beneath his spear.
And this—so much for him I needs must say—
He nor himself denied nor bade conceal;
But I, O lady, who feared to grieve thy heart

371

With telling of these tidings, I alone
Have sinned, if sin thou holdest it, in this.
But, now that all the story thou hast heard,
Both for his sake and for thine own no less,
Suffer the maiden, and let concerning her
The words that thou hast spoken bind thee still.
For, as no triumph he hath not won save this,
So for her love no bondage he'd not bear.

R. WHITELAW   (*Trâchîniæ*, 436–89)

327   *Dêianîra's Wooing*
CHORUS

GREAT and strong is the Cyprian alway to win her
will. I pass the doings of the gods, I tell not how she
beguiled the Son of Cronos and nocturnal Hades and
Poseidon, Shaker of the Earth; but when this bride was
to be won, what far-reaching arms spread out to possess
her, what beings went forth to that ordeal of battle—
blows everywhere, and everywhere blinding dust? Here
the strength of a River, towering horns, crashing hooves,
and a vision of a Bull, Achelôus from Œniadæ; and there
the Zeus-begotten from Bacchic Thebes, bent bow and
spear and club sweeping the air. Crashing they met together, mad for a bride; and none save the couchèd
Cyprian was near, holding her wand above them.

Thud of fists and rush of arrows and crash of wild-bull
horns in confusion; close-wound grapples and deadly
shocks of brow on brow and groaning from both; while
a girl tender and sweet-faced sate on the side of a wide-
looking hill, awaiting the master that should be hers.

I speak as one that hath borne a child. The bride's face for
which they rage waits piteous-eyed for the end; and suddenly she is gone from her mother, like a heifer left alone.

GILBERT MURRAY   (*Trâchîniæ*, 497–530)

328   *Philoctêtês deserted*

PHILOCTÊTÊS

GLADLY they saw me sleeping on the shore,
   Worn with long hours at sea; in a deep cave
They left me and went off, and by my side
Set some few rags fit for a luckless man
And scanty food-scraps. May they have the like!
Think of the manner of my waking then
When I woke up from sleep and found them gone,
What tears were mine, what injuries to weep.
I saw the ships which had been mine at sea
All gone, no living being in the place,
None to give help, none to relieve my pains
In sickness. Though I looked on every side
I could find nothing but calamity,
But that in great abundance, O my son.
   Time followed in the footsteps of time past,
And in this narrow dwelling I must sate
My wants. My belly's need this bow would find,
Shooting the doves that darted on the wing,
And everything my bow-sped arrow shot
Myself would in great anguish creep to it,
Dragging my miserable foot to it.
At times there would be need of drink, at times
In winter when the frost was spread abroad

373

Wood must be broken. I would creep in pain
And manage it. Then there would be no fire,
But rubbing with great labour stone on stone
I struck a phantom flame. This saves my life.
This roof which gives me shelter and my fire
Give all I need, save freedom from disease.

C. M. BOWRA   (*Philoctêtês*, 271–99)

329   *The Stolen Bow*
                          PHILOCTÊTÊS

O FLAME and horror, masterpiece of evil
    And hate and craftiness, what have you done,
What treachery? Can you look unashamed,
Hard-hearted, on this kneeling suppliant?
You take my bow, and with it goes my life.
Give it back, I beg, I pray you, give it back.
In Heaven's name take not my life away.
Alas, he does not even speak to me,
He looks away. He will not give it back.

    O bays and promontories, companies
Of beasts who haunt the hills and rugged cliffs,
To you—I have no other friends to call—
I tell with tears, to you, my constant friends,
What wrongs Achilles' son has done to me.
He swore to take me home, and now to Troy
He takes me. Though he swore with his right hand,
He keeps the holy bow of Hêraclês
And wants to show his booty to the Greeks.
He drags me off, as if my strength were great,
And knows not that he kills a corpse, a shade

374

Of smoke, a phantom. If I had been strong,
He'd not have taken me. Nor had he now
Made me his prisoner but for treachery.

      Twin-gated rock of mine, to you I come
Unarmed for ever, with no means of life.
But I shall wither in this cave alone.
My arrows will not slay the wingèd birds
Or mountain-haunting beasts. Myself, poor wretch,
Shall make a feast for those on whom I fed,
And beasts I hunted once will hunt me now;
And blood for blood in payment shall I give
Because of one who seemed to know no wrong.

      Death take you,—no, not yet, till I have learned
If you will change. If not, an evil death.

C. M. BOWRA   (*Philoctêtês*, 927–62)

330   *Everything decays*
ŒDIPUS

DEAR son of Ægeus, to the gods alone
   Belongs immunity from death and age:
All else doth all-controlling time confound.
Earth's strength decays, the body's strength decays,
Faith dies, and faithlessness bursts into flower,
And never does the same wind blow for long
Steadfast from friend to friend, from town to town.
For this man now, and that man afterwards,
Likes what he liked not, loathes what once he loved.
Though now with Thebes and thee all promise fair,
Yet Time in his unreckonable track
Brings days and nights unreckoned to the birth,

In which our present pledges of good will
Shall fade in fighting from an idle word;
When my cold body, sleeping secretly,
Shall drink the warm blood of my enemies,
If Zeus is Zeus and his son, Phœbus, true.

C. M. BOWRA   (*Œdipus Colônêus*, 607–23)

331   *The Grove of Colônus*

CHORUS

STRANGER, where thy feet now rest
 In this land of horse and rider,
Here is earth all earth excelling,
White Colônus here doth shine!
Oftenest here and homing best
Where the close green coverts hide her,
Warbling her sweet mournful tale
Sings the melodious nightingale,
Myriad-berried woods her dwelling,
And the wine-hued ivy, where
Through the sacred leafage lonely
No sun pierces, or rude air
Stirs from outer storm, and only
Those divine feet walk the region—
Thine, O Reveller, thine,
Bacchus, following still that legion
Dear, thy nursing Nymphs divine.

Fresh with heavenly dews, and crowned
With earliest white in shining cluster,
Each new morn the young narcissus
Blooms, that antique use of old

376

Bids the Great Queens bind around
Their twain brows; in golden lustre
Here the crocus beams; and here
Spring, nor minish all the year,
Cool deep wells that feed Cephissus:
Rich with balm of speedy birth
Day by day the sleepless river
Issuing o'er the breasted Earth
Wandereth in pure streams to give her
Ease and life. Nor frown the Muses
Or their quires withhold;
Nay, nor sweet Love's Queen refuses
Her bright chariot-reins of gold.

And a marvellous herb of the soil grows here,
   Whose match I never have heard it sung
In the Dorian isle of Pelops near
   Or in Asia far hath sprung.
'Tis a plant that flourishes unsubdued,
Self-engendering, self-renewed,
   To her armed foes' dismay:
That never so fair but in this land bloomed,—
With the grey-blue silvery leaf soft-plumed,
   Her nurturing Olive-spray.
No force, no ravaging hand shall raze it,
   In youth so rash, or in age so wise,
For the orb of Zeus in heaven surveys it,
   And blue-grey light of Athêna's eyes.

Yet again my song shall arise and tell
   Of the proudest jewel the region wears;
To her Mother's portion of old it fell,
   And the Child her birth-right shares:—

377

Blest in gift of the horse is she,
Gift of the young horse, gift of the sea,
   Twice-blest in a two-fold dower:
Thy gift, O Lord of the waves, her throne,
For in her streets first upon earth was shown
   Thy chastening bridle's power;
And here most wonderful over the waters
   Slender and shapely the trimmed oar fleet
In the sea-dance following Nêreus' daughters
   Leaps to the foam of a hundred feet.

WALTER HEADLAM   (*Œdipus Colônêus*, 668–719)

332   *Old Age*

WHAT man is he that yearneth
   For length unmeasured of days?
Folly mine eye discerneth
   Encompassing all his ways.
For years over-running the measure
   Shall change thee in evil wise:
Grief draweth nigh thee; and pleasure,
   Behold, it is hid from thine eyes.
   This to their wage have they
   Which overlive their day.
And He that looseth from labour
   Doth one with other befriend,
   Whom bride nor bridesmen attend,
Song, nor sound of the tabor,
   Death, that maketh an end.

Thy portion esteem I highest,
　　Who wast not ever begot;
Thine next, being born who diest
　　And straightway again art not.
With follies light as the feather
　　Doth Youth to man befall;
Then evils gather together,
　　There wants not one of them all—
　　　Wrath, envy, discord, strife,
　　　The sword that seeketh life.
And sealing the sum of trouble
　　Doth tottering Age draw nigh,
　　Whom friends and kinsfolk fly,
Age, upon whom redouble
　　All sorrows under the sky.

This man, as me, even so,
　　Have the evil days overtaken;
And like as a cape sea-shaken
With tempest at earth's last verges
And shock of all winds that blow,
His head the seas of woe,
　　The thunders of awful surges
　　Ruining overflow;
Blown from the fall of even,
　　Blown from the dayspring forth,
Blown from the noon in heaven,
　　Blown from night and the North.

A. E. HOUSMAN   (*Œdipus Colônêus,* 1211–48)

379

333   *The Passing of Œdipus*

MESSENGER

HOW he departed hence, you who stood by
   Know well; he had no friend to guide his steps
But was himself the guide to all of us.
And when to that steep threshold he had come,
Rooted by brass foundations to the earth,
He stood in one of the dividing ways,
Near to the hollow urn, where deathless lie
The pledges Thêseus and Pîrithoüs made.
He stopped midway between the hollow pear-tree
And the Thorícian rock. On that stone tomb
He sat and took his stained apparel off;
Then called he to his children, bade them bring
Libation water from the running brook;
To green Dêmêter's overlooking hill
They went and in short space of time did all
Their father's bidding, washed his body clean
And gave him raiment as the rite demands.
But when he was content with all things done
And nought was undone that he wanted, then
Zeus thundered underground, and, when they heard,
The maidens shuddered. At their father's knees
They fell and wept, nor ceased to beat their breasts
Nor stopped their long and lamentable cries.
But when he heard the sudden bitter voice,
He spread his hands above them, saying: 'Children,
You have no more a father in this world;
For all my life is ended, and no more
Shall you have trouble looking after me:

380

'Twas hard, I know, my children, but one word
Alone redeems our sum of sufferings.
From no man living have you had such love
As you have had from me; deprived of me
Shall you now pass all your remaining days.'

Together folded in each other's arms
They mingled sobs and sighing. When the end
Came to their weeping and no more cries came,
There was a silence. Suddenly a voice
Called summoning him, and straightway all in fear
Were shaken and their hair stood up on end.
The god was calling him and called again:
'Œdipus, Œdipus, why dost delay
To go? Too long hast thou been lingering.'
And when he saw that the god summoned him,
He called to Thêseus, ruler of the land,
And when he came, addressed him: 'O my friend,
Give to my children—children, give to him—
Your hands in faithful oath, and promise me
That you will never willingly betray them,
But do your best in kindness for their sakes.'
And he, the noble Thêseus, not with tears
Consented upon oath to help his friend.
And when he did this, straightway Œdipus
Feeling with sightless hands his children, said:
'Now must you go, my children, patiently
Enduring it and nobly, nor perceive
What it is wrong to see, nor hear the voices.
Go with all speed from here, but let the king,
Thêseus, remain to see what comes to pass.'
Obediently we listened to his words
Together, and, not holding back our tears,

Accompanied the maidens. On our way
We turned a little later, and we saw
Œdipus nowhere in that neighbourhood,
And Thêseus with his hand above his head
Shading his eyes, as if some awful thing
Had happened that no eyes could look upon.
We saw him do obeisance to the earth
And to Olympus in a single prayer.
What fate took Œdipus no living soul
On earth, save only Thêseus, can declare.
No fiery-flashing thunderbolt of God
Encompassed his destruction, and no wind
Came whirling from the ocean in that hour,
But either the gods took him, or the earth
In good will opened up its lightless caves.
For with no lamentations was his passing,
Nor sad with painful sickness, but most like
A miracle. And if my words seem mad,
I ask no grace of those who think them so.

C. M. Bowra   (*Œdipus Colônêus*, 1587–1666)

334   *Wind in the Poplars*

AS in the boughs of a tall poplar-tree,
   If nothing else, at least her shivering top
Moves 'neath the breeze, and waves her leafy pinions.

J. A. Symonds   (*Ægeus*)

335   *Night Fears*

TAKE courage, lady: many fearful things
   That breathed dark dreams in night, by day are
     solaced.

J. A. Symonds   (*Âcrísius*)

336   *Hécatê*

SUN, Lord and Master, and sacred flame,
    Sword that Hécatê shakes in her hands,
Whether among the streets she stands,
Or through the sky on her chariot rides,
Or shrined on earth takes her holy name
From the crossways where the road divides,
Crowned with leaves from the oaken brake
Or with twisting coils of a savage snake.

C. M. BOWRA   (*Rhizotomi*)

337   *Womankind*

AWAY from home I am nothing. Oftentimes
    Have I considered what is womankind
And seen that we are nothing. In girlhood's days
Ours is the sweetest of all lives at home,—
For thoughtlessness is a kind nurse to children.
But when we reach maturity and wisdom,
We are driven abroad and made a traffic of,
Far from our parents and our country's gods,
Some to strange men and some to foreigners,
Some to true homes and some to contumely,
And just because a single night has joined us,
We must give praise and think that all is well.

C. M. BOWRA   (*Têreus*)

338   *Suave mari magno*

Ah, what joy
Can out-joy this—to reach the land—and then
Safe lodged, with happy drowsing sense to hear
The raindrops pattering on the roof outside!

WALTER HEADLAM   (*Tympanistæ*)

339   *The God of War*

ARÊS is blind, and with unseeing eyes
    Set in a swine's face stirs up all to evil.

C. M. BOWRA

340   *Fortune is like the Moon*

BUT my fate, on some throbbing wheel of God,
    Always must rise and fall, and change its being:
As the moon's image never two nights long
May in one station rest: out of the dark
The young face grows, still lovelier, still more perfect,
Then at the noblest of her shining, back
She melts and comes again to nothingness.

GILBERT MURRAY

341   *Melting Ice*

LOVE is a pain with purest joy combined:
    No bad comparison to Love I'll find—
Boys when the heavens are frosty, in a trice
Will take a handful of hard-frozen ice;
And first it's all delight and wonder, then
The lump no more will be let go again,
Nor yet be pretty treasure to retain.
Even so with lovers, when their hearts require
To love and not-love by the same desire.

After J. S. PHILLIMORE   (*Achillis Amatores*)

342   *The Power of Love*

MY children, know Love is not Love alone,
    But in her name lie many names concealed:
For she is Death, imperishable Force,
Desire unmixed, wild Frenzy, Lamentation;
In her are summed all impulses that drive
To Violence, Energy, Tranquillity.
Deep in each living breast the Goddess sinks,
And all become her prey; the tribes that swim,
The fourfoot tribes that pace upon the earth,
Harbour her; and in birds her wing is sovereign,
In beasts, in mortal men, in gods above.
What god but wrestles with her and is thrown?
If I may tell—and truth is right to tell—
She rules the heart of Zeus without a spear,
Without a sword. Truly the Cyprian
Shatters all purposes of men and gods.

SIR RICHARD LIVINGSTONE (to l. 13)

343   *The Edge of the World*

LAST peaks of the world, beyond all seas,
    Wellsprings of night, and gleams of opened heaven,
The old garden of the sun.

GILBERT MURRAY   (*Orîthyîa*)

344 *A Riddle*

CYLLÊNÊ, CHORUS

CYLL. Though the goddess made you wonder, do believe the things she said.

CHO. How can I believe such thunder comes from any creature dead?

CYLL. Do believe,—when dead, the creature talks: alive, its mouth is shut.

CHO. How explain its form and feature? Tall, or arched, or sharply cut?

CYLL. It is very short and pot-like, shrivelled, and with chequers barred.

CHO. Is it like a cat, or not like?... Or more nearly like a pard?

CYLL. Half and half. You see it grew monotonously fat and squab.

CHO. Why, it sounds like an ichneumon,—or perhaps it is a crab?

CYLL. No, it's not like that to meet. Alas, you'd better try again.

CHO. Isn't it a horny beetle of the old Ætnêan strain?

CYLL. Much the nearest—that is clever—to the beast I talk about.

CHO. Tell me, tell me, then, wherever is its voice,—inside or out?

CYLL. .... Sinister and dark of hide, to the shell-back near allied.

CHO. Then its name you might report us, if you know what we desire.

CYLL. Boy Hermês calls it 'tortoise': and its voice he calls 'the lyre'.

GEORGE ALLEN   (*Ichneutæ*, 291–305)

386

EMPÉDOCLÊS

(494–434 B.C.)

345   *The Limitations of Knowledge*

FOR Knowledge must make shift by narrow ways
   To enter, here or there; and pains abound
Whose sudden visitation blunts our thought.
Each man, with eye particular beholding
Some corner of his momentary world,
Soon, like a wisp of smoke, flits up and away.
His chance experience fashions all his faith;
And, driven upon that random round, each boasts
The Universe laid bare! How hardly, then,
Shall eye or ear perceive or the grasp of mind
Reach out to wisdom! Therefore, here secluded,
You'll learn what springs from mortal wits,—not more.
T. F. HIGHAM

346   *Nature the Artist*

AS painters, men of knowledge in their art,
   Tint votive-tablets to a rich design,
And blend the various colours, quick to hand,
In harmonizing hues, now more, now less,
A mimic world, born at their touch appearing—
Trees in their likeness, man and womankind,
Beasts and birds, fish in the waters living,
And long-enduring gods, more great than all—
So too,—let not deceit but truth prevail—
The generation of all mortal things
Born visible, a countless host, sprang forth
From elements compounded, less and more.
   So be assured: the Muse declared my tale.
T. F. HIGHAM

347   *The Divine Philosopher*

YE friends, who in the mighty city dwell
    Along the yellow Ácragas hard by
The Acropolis, ye stewards of good works,
The stranger's refuge venerable and kind,
All hail, O friends! But unto ye I walk
As god immortal now, no more as man,
On all sides honoured fittingly and well,
Crowned both with fillets and with flowering wreaths.
When with my throngs of men and women I come
To thriving cities, I am sought by prayers,
And thousands follow me that they may ask
Where lies advantage and the better way.

W. E. LEONARD (to l. 8)

348   *The Blood-guilty*

THERE is a law of stern Necessity,
    The immemorial ordinance of the gods
Made fast for ever, bravely sworn and sealed:—
Should any Spirit, born to enduring life,
Be fouled with sin of slaughter, or transgress
By disputation, perjured and forsworn,
Three times ten thousand years that soul shall wander
An outcast from Felicity, condemned
To mortal being, and in diverse shapes
With interchange of hardship go his ways.
The Heavens force him headlong to the Sea;
And vomited from the Sea, dry land receives him,
But flings unwanted to the burning Sun;
From there, to the heavenly vortex backward thrown,
He makes from host to host, by all abhorred.

T. F. HIGHAM

349   *Transmigration*

FOR I have been, ere now, a girl and a boy,
   A bush, a bird, and a dumb fish in the sea.

FRANCES CORNFORD

EURIPIDÊS
                                    (480–406 B.C.)
350   *A Cyclops' Philosophy*

CYCLOPS

WEALTH, my good fellow, is the wise man's God,
   All other things are a pretence and boast.
What are my father's ocean promontories,
The sacred rocks whereon he dwells, to me?
Stranger, I laugh to scorn Jove's thunderbolt,
I know not that his strength is more than mine.
As to the rest I care not:—when he pours
Rain from above, I have a close pavilion
Under this rock in which I lie supine,
Feasting on a roast calf or some wild beast,
And drinking pans of milk, and gloriously
Emulating the thunder of high Heaven.
And when the Thracian wind pours down the snow,
I wrap my body in the skins of beasts,
Kindle a fire, and bid the snow whirl on.
The earth, by force, whether it will or no,
Bringing forth grass, fattens my flocks and herds,
Which, to what other God but to myself
And this great belly, first of deities,
Shall I be bound to sacrifice? I well know
The wise man's only Jupiter is this,

389

To eat and drink during his little day,
And give himself no care. And as for those
Who complicate with laws the life of man,
I freely give them tears for their reward.
I will not cheat my soul of its delight,
Or hesitate in dining upon you:—
And that I may be quit of all demands,
These are my hospitable gifts;—fierce fire
And yon ancestral cauldron, which o'er-bubbling
Shall finely cook your miserable flesh.
Enter: and for the inner god's delight
Stand round the altar, fill my belly full.

P. B. SHELLEY (to l. 344)   (*Cyclops*, 316–46)

351   *To Alcêstis*

CHORUS

O DAUGHTER of Pélias,
  Hail to you in the house of Hades,
In the sunless home where you shall dwell!
Let Hades, the dark-haired God,
Let the old man, Leader of the Dead,
Who sits at the oar and helm,
Know you:
Far, far off is the best of women[1]
Borne beyond the flood of Ácheron
In the two-oared boat!

Often shall the Muses' servants
Sing of you to the seven-toned
Lyre-shell of the mountain-tortoise,
And praise you with mourning songs at Sparta

[1] See Notes.

When the circling season
Brings back the month Carneius
Under the nightlong upraised moon
And in bright glad Athens.
Such a theme do you leave by your death
For the music of singers!

Ah! That I had the power
To bring you back to the light
From the dark halls of Hades,
And from the waves of Côcŷtus
With the oar of the river of hell!
O, you only,
O dearest of women,
You only dared give your life
For the life of your lord in Hades!
Light rest the earth above you,
O woman.
If your lord choose another bridal-bed
He shall be hateful to me
As to your own children.

RICHARD ALDINGTON   (*Alcêstis*, 435–65)

352   *Hospitality*

HÊRACLÊS

WHY look'st so solemn and so thought-absorbed?
    To guests a servant should not sour-faced be,
But do the honours with a mind urbane.
While thou, contrariwise, beholding here
Arrive thy master's comrade, hast for him
A churlish visage, all one beetle-brow—

Having regard to grief that's out-of-door!
Come hither, and so get to grow more wise!
Things mortal—know'st the nature that they have?
No, I imagine! whence could knowledge spring?
Give ear to me, then! For all flesh to die
Is nature's due; nor is there any one
Of mortals with assurance he shall last
The coming morrow: for, what's born of chance
Invisibly proceeds the way it will,
Not to be learned, no fortune-teller's prize.
This, therefore, having heard and known through me,
Gladden thyself! Drink! Count the day-by-day
Existence thine, and all the other—chance!
Ay, and pay homage also to by far
The sweetest of divinities for man,
Kupris! Benignant goddess will she prove!
But as for aught else, leave and let things be!
And trust my counsel, if I seem to speak
To purpose—as I do, apparently.
Wilt not thou, then,—discarding overmuch
Mournfulness, do away with this shut door,
Come drink along with me, be-garlanded
This fashion? Do so, and—I well know what—
From this stern mood, this shrunk-up state of mind,
The pit-pat fall o' the flagon-juice down throat
Soon will dislodge thee from bad harbourage!
Men being mortal should think mortal-like!
Since to your solemn, brow-contracting sort,
All of them,—so I lay down law at least,—
Life is not truly life but misery.

ROBERT BROWNING   (*Alcêstis*, 773–802)

353   *Death the Enemy*

HÊRACLÊS

O MUCH-ENDURING heart and hand of mine!
  Now show what sort of son she bore to Zeus,
That daughter of Electruon, 'Tiruns' child,
Alkmênê! for that son must needs save now
The just-dead lady: ay, establish here
I' the house again Alkêstis, bring about
Comfort and succour to Admêtos so!
I will go lie in wait for Death, black-stoled
King of the corpses! I shall find him, sure,
Drinking, beside the tomb, o' the sacrifice:
And if I lie in ambuscade, and leap
Out of my lair, and seize—encircle him
Till one hand join the other round about—
There lives not who shall pull him out from me,
Rib-mauled, before he let the woman go!
But even say I miss the booty,—say
Death comes not to the boltered blood,—why then,
Down go I, to the unsunned dwelling-place
Of Korê and the king there,—make demand,
Confident I shall bring Alkêstis back,
So as to put her in the hands of him
My host, that housed me, never drove me off:
Though stricken with sore sorrow, hid the stroke,
Being a noble heart and honouring me!

ROBERT BROWNING   (*Alcêstis*, 837–57)

393

354 *Bereavement*

CHORUS

I HAD a kinsman; he
  Lost in his home a son,—
True tears were his to shed,—
His child, his only one.
He bore his misery,
His lonely doom.
White hair was on his head,
His long life, nearly sped,
Drooped to the tomb.

Your luck was good before.
To you, untouched by ill,
This sorrow came, but you
Are quick and breathing still.
Your wife is dead. No more
That love abides.
What grief is here that's new?
From many others too
Death robs their brides.

C. M. BOWRA   (*Alcêstis*, 903–10, 926–33)

355 *Shifting Fortune*

CHORUS

NOW backward the founts of the sacred streams are
    driven,
  All's o'erturned and Justice becomes but as Wrong.
Crook'd grow man's counsels, and Faith in God's sight
    given
  Fails that aforetime was strong.

394

But of us now songs shall be other, new fame shall crown
 our days,
Yea for Woman also comes her hour of praise,
 Woman no more shall be made a thing of shame in song.

And *they* shall be silenced, the bards of old that chide us,
 Harping still their stories of false bride that fell.
Well that the Singer, Apollo, hath denied us
 Song and the lyre's magic spell!
Else our tongues had given Man answer, and loud our lips
 had rolled
Strains to challenge his. Ay, well the years of old
 Many a tale of the deeds 'twixt us and Man could tell!

F. L. LUCAS   (*Mêdêa*, 410–30)

356   *Vengeance*

MÊDÊA

O ZEUS, O Zeus-born Justice, O bright Sun,
 Now shall I triumph over mine enemies;
Now on the road, dear friends, my feet are planted,
Now I shall see my haters pay the price.
This Ægeus stands revealed—my sorest need—
A haven of refuge now for all my councils;
Ay, and from him the cable of my hopes
Shall be made fast when I come safe within
Athêna's town and tower. Hark, all my plot
I'll tell thee—listen, bitter though it be.
One of my household I shall send to Jason
Asking to see him once more face to face;
And when he comes I'll make him honeyed speeches,
Saying that his will is mine—all's well and fair
In this royal marriage he betrays me for—

All for our good and wisely planned of him.——
I shall but pray him let my children stay;
Not that I would abandon child of mine
In a hostile land to be flouted by my foes;
But that I may spin death for Creon's daughter.
For I shall send them carrying gifts from me
To the bride, that she may save them banishment——
A fine-wrought robe, a golden diadem;
And once she takes those gauds and puts them on,
A dreadful death is hers and any man's.

But I will say no more—yet Oh, my heart
Cries at the thought of what a deed I must
Do after that. For I must kill my children,
Mine own. There lives not who shall rescue them.
And having thus confounded all the house
Of Jason, I will go hence and flee afar
My sweet babes' blood and my own bitter sin.
For bitterer yet, my friends, the laugh of foes.

So be it! What good is life? I have no land,
No home, no shelter for my misery.
Fool that I was, the day I ever quitted
My father's house confiding in the tongue
Of a Greek—ay him, God willing, I'll repay.
For never shall he see alive again
The sons I bore him, nor any other sons
Shall his new bride bring forth, since by my magic
She shall find an end as evil as herself.
Let no man think of me as mean or weak
Or a quiet soul,—nay very far from it!——
As dangerous a foe as loyal friend.
For such are they that live most honourable.

F. L. Lucas   (*Mêdêa*, 764–810)

396

357   *Mêdêa's Resolve*

MÊDÊA

My friends, the deed's resolved—that with all haste
I will kill my children and set forth from Corinth,
Not, hesitating here, yield up my sons
For other and less loving hands to murder.
Die they must, either way; and since they must,
Then I will slay them that did bring them forth.
Come steel thyself, my heart. What help to linger
Shrinking to do that dreadful thing thou must?
The sword, O miserable hand, the sword—
Take it and onward to that bitter race
Thy feet must run! No weakening now, no thought
Of thy sons, how dear they are, how thou didst once
Give life to them. For this one little day
Forget thy babes, and, after, weep for them.
For though thou slay them, yet dear-loved were they,
Thine own,—and I a miserable woman.

F. L. LUCAS   (*Mêdêa*, 1236–50)

358   *Macária and Iolâus*

MACÁRIA. IOLÂUS. DÊMOPHÔN

MAC.   Now fear no more the enemy spear of Argos,
        For I myself, before they order me,
        Am ready, old man, to die and meet the knife:
        For what shall we say, if for the sakes of us
        The city shall accept and run great risk,
        While we, imposing trouble on other men,
        Now we could save them run away from dying?
        It is not to be thought; and laughably

397

Idle before the gods we should wail and pray
And, being the children of our father born,
Show coward! how should this be a noble part?
O better I'll say—but never be it so!—
If with our city taken, I should fall
In the enemy's hands, a noble father's child,
Shame to endure and look no less on death.
Or exiled from this land shall I wander away?
How shall I not be shamed, suppose men taunt?

  'Why come you here with suppliant symbols
    crowned,
Lovers of your own lives? out of our country!
Begone! not cowards we in this land assist.'

  And yet, with these once dead, I would have no
    hope,
Not even myself being saved, of good success—
And many there are who have their friends betrayed
Long before this—for who would want a maiden
Forlorn for a wife, or to have sons of me?
Is it not better to die than be so shamed,
Dishonourable? that fits another more,
A maiden not so known as I am known.

  So lead me where this body of mine must die,
Wreathe me, and take the first fruits as you will;
Vanquish the enemy, for here my life
Willing and not unwilling is yours to have.
You'll say for brethren and myself I perished,
Because, no slave to life, I still have found
This my best finding, decently to die.

IOL.   My child, from no mean source your blood derives,
But you are born of the true Hêraclês,
A divine seed; nor have I any shame

Hearing your word; it is your fate that shames me.
But now I'll tell you of a juster way;
Bring all her sisters here, and for her race
Let her then die, whoever draws the lot;
But with no lot for you to die is wrong.

MAC. I would not die by choice of casting lots,
For that's ungracious; bid me not, old man,
But follow me, sir, for by your hand I'll die.
Be with me, cover my body with a cloak!

IOL. I could not ever at your death stand by.

MAC. (*turning to Dêmophôn*) Yet grant me this, that not in
hands of men
But in the hands of women I may expire.

DÊM. It shall be so, poor maiden, and for me
Base would it be to have you meanly arrayed,
For many a cause, for sake of your good spirit
And for the right. A fate it is you bear
Sadder than of all women I have seen.
But come; and if you will, to these around
And this old man utter your latest words.

MAC. Old man, farewell, farewell, and teach I pray you
These children to be such,—in all things wise
As you, no more, for then they'll have enough.
And try to keep them from dying, as you wish;
For we are your children, by your hand bred up,
And here you see me for the sake of them
Giving away the age of marriage, and dying.
And you, my many brethren that stand here,
Farewell, receive all that for cost of which
My life must first be sacrificed away;
And honour the old man and in the house
The old Alcmênê, mother of our father,

399

And these we love; and if an end of troubles
You find and a safe homecoming from the gods,
Forget not then to bury me who saved you,
Giving me my due honour of burial—
I did not fail you, dying for my people.
And this for children and for virginity
Shall be my treasure, if there be aught in death—
Yet be there nothing! for if we mortals die,
And still must have our troubles in the grave,
I know not where to turn to, since in dying
Is thought to be best remedy for hurts.

GEORGE ALLEN (*Hêraclîdæ*, 500–34, 539–48, 560–1, 564–96)

359   *The Garland*

HIPPÓLYTUS

FOR thee this woven garland have I braided
   And bring it, lady, from a virgin field,
Where never shepherd dares to feed his flocks
Nor ever comes the scythe; unsullied, it
Is traversed only by the vernal bee,
Tended with river-dew by Modesty.
But those who need no teaching—for their hearts
Belong to shamefastness in everything—
Those have the right to reap it, not the evil.
Do thou, belovèd lady, take this garland
From reverent hands to bind thy golden hair.
Alone of men I have this privilege;
To you I speak, with you keep company,
Your voice I hear, but may not see your face.
May my last course be as my life began.

C. M. BOWRA   (*Hippólytus*, 73–87)

400

360   *The Birds of God*

CHORUS

COULD I take me to some cavern for mine hiding,
    In the hill-tops where the Sun scarce hath trod;
Or a cloud make the home of mine abiding,
    As a bird among the bird-droves of God!
        Could I wing me to my rest amid the roar
        Of the deep Adriatic on the shore,
Where the waters of Êrídanus are clear,
    And Phaëthon's sad sisters by his grave
Weep into the river, and each tear
    Gleams, a drop of amber, in the wave.

To the strand of the Daughters of the Sunset,
    The Apple-tree, the singing and the gold;
Where the mariner must stay him from his onset,
    And the red wave is tranquil as of old;
        Yea, beyond that Pillar of the End
        That Atlas guardeth, would I wend;
Where a voice of living waters never ceaseth
    In God's quiet garden by the sea,
And Earth, the ancient life-giver, increaseth
    Joy among the meadows, like a tree.

GILBERT MURRAY   (*Hippólytus*, 732–51)

361   *The Doom of Hippólytus*

MESSENGER

SO we, no distance from the sea-wet shore,
    Were smoothing out with combs our horses' manes,
And weeping. For a courier came to say

That in this land Hippólytus should no more
Set foot, condemned to sad exile by you.
Himself then came to us upon the shore
With tears to that same tune. A countless host
Of friends and comrades followed in his train,
And, when the lamentation ceased, he spoke:
'Why am I thus distraught? I must obey
My father's words. Slaves, yoke my horses up.
This city now no more belongs to me.'

    Then straightway every man bestirred himself,
And, quicker than a man could speak, we set
His horses ready at our master's side.
He caught the reins up from the chariot-rail
And firmly on the foot-board set his feet:
Then first with outspread hands he called the gods:
'Zeus, let me die if I am base of heart.
And let my father know he does me wrong,
Whether I die or still look on the light.'

    With this he took the goad in hand and urged
His horses on together. We, his men,
Followed our master's lead, beside the reins,
For Argos on the Epidaurian road.
And when we struck into a desolate place,—
There lies beyond the frontier of this land
A shore that faces the Sarônic Sea,—
There came a sound, as if within the earth
Zeus' hollow thunder boomed, awful to hear.
The horses lifted heads towards the sky
And pricked their ears; while strange fear fell on us,
Whence came the voice. To the sea-beaten shore
We looked, and saw a monstrous wave that soared
Into the sky, so lofty that my eyes

Were robbed of seeing the Scîrônian cliffs.
It hid the Isthmus and Asclêpius' rock.
Then seething up and bubbling all about
With foaming flood and breath from the deep sea,
Shoreward it came to where the chariot stood.
And with the billow at the third wave's break
The sea gave up a bull, a monstrous brute.
His bellowing filled the land, whose answering voice
Set all a-shuddering, for we saw a sight
That seemed too horrible for human gaze.
At once a fearful panic took the team.
Our master, long conversant with the ways
Of horses, snatched the reins up in his hands,
And pulled, as pulls a sailor at the oar,
Fast'ning the leather reins behind his back.
They took the fire-made bits between their teeth
And bolted, with no heed of steering hands,
No heed of harness or the jointed car.
But, if towards the smooth part of the ground
He held his course and steered a passage straight,
Before him It was there, and turned him back,—
The bull,—and drove his horses mad with fear.
And if he swept in frenzy to the rocks,
Silent it followed by the chariot-wheel,
Until he struck his axle on a crag
And tripped and overturned his chariot.
Then all was ruin. Up the wheel-naves shot
Above the wheels, and out the linch-pins fell.
Himself, poor wretch, entangled in the reins
Was dragged, fast in the indissoluble bonds;
His dear head thudding down upon the rocks,
His flesh all torn, his cries most pitiful:

'My horses, stop, whom my own mangers fed,
You smash me.... O my father's fatal curse!
Who here will save a man most innocent?'
    Though many wished, our steps were slow, and we
Were far behind. Some way, I know not how,
He slipped the bondage of the shapen reins
And fell, still breathing with a little life.
The horses disappeared, and the fell bull
Is hidden, I know not where, among the rocks.

C. M. BOWRA   (*Hippólytus*, 1173–1248)

362   *His Death*

ARTEMIS. HIPPÓLYTUS. THÊSEUS

AR.   Poor wretch with what calamity art thou joined:
       It is thy noble heart that hath laid thee low.

HIPP. (*dimly aware of Artemis, but not seeing*). O heaven
       This is thy breath of fragrance, known to me
       Even in my hurts; now easier lies my body,
       For Artemis from her heaven is in this place.

AR.   Poor wretch, she is, and thy best friend in heaven.

HIPP. O queen dost thou behold me in this plight?

AR.   I do, but from my eyes may drop no tear.

HIPP. Thy huntsman and thy servant lives no more.

AR.   No more, but thou art dear to me though dying.

HIPP. No more to drive thy steeds, to guard thy shrines.

AR.   Cypris the jade was plotter of all this.

HIPP. Woe's me, I mark the goddess murdering me.

AR.   Thy prudence marred her honour and angered her.

HIPP. Victims, I see, the three of us to Cypris.

AR.   Yea, both thy father, thou, and third his wife.

404

HIPP. Let me lament the thing my father has done.

AR. Deceived was he by schemes a goddess laid.

HIPP. O father, wretched in this calamity!

THÊS. I'm lost, my child, nor have I joy in life.

HIPP. For you more than for me I rue the offence.

THÊS. My child, if only I were dead for you!

HIPP. O bitter the gifts your sire Poseidon gave!

THÊS. They should have never come upon my lips.

HIPP. Why? Would you have killed me in that furious
    rage?

THÊS. My judgement met a stumbling block divine.

HIPP.   Woe's me,
    If mortals could but curse the race of gods!

AR. Be still, for not unvisited by me
    Shall Cypris in her anger divine drive down
    Thee to the darkness under the earth, thy body
    Smiting for piety and goodness of heart;
    For I shall another with this hand of mine—
    Whoever be her darling of mortal men—
    Requite with arrows that he shall not escape.
    And thou, unfortunate, for these thy woes
    The highest honours Trœzên city can give
    Shalt win from me: before their wedding rites,
    Virgins shall cut a tress for thee, and always
    Thou shalt be reaping the sad fruit of tears;
    To thee shall ever come the maiden song
    Caring for thee, nor Phædra's love for thee
    Into the silence of no name shall fall.

      But take thy son, thou child of Ægeus old,
    And in thy arms gather him to thyself;
    Unwilling wast thou his death; when gods permit,
    Then it is natural for men to err.

And, thee I bid, hate not, Hippólytus,
Thy father, knowing the doom that lays thee low.
   And fare ye well; for me it is not lawful
Mortals to see, nor sully eyes with breath
Of dying men; I see thee near death's pain.

HIPP.   O fare thee well and go most blissful maiden.
Long was I with thee, and easily thou leavest!
As thou dost bid, my quarrel with my father
I end, for always to thy word I listened.

   Alas, already darkness is over my eyes;
Take me father, and lay my body straight.

THÊS. Woe's me my son, what do you to me unhappy?
HIPP. I die, already the nether gates I see.
THÊS. And do you go leaving my hand still foul?
HIPP. No, for I free you from this murder's taint.
THÊS. How do you say? Do you set me free from blood?
HIPP. Bear witness Artemis whose bolt subdues!
THÊS. Dear son, what goodness to your father shown!
HIPP. Pray that the sons you get be not less good.
THÊS. Alas, the virtue of your heart devout!
HIPP. Fare well, I bid you a long farewell, my father.
THÊS. O fail me not my son, but be you strong.
HIPP. My strength is over; I am lost, my father,
Make speed and with the mantles cover my face.

GEORGE ALLEN   (*Hippólytus*, 1389–1458)

363   *The Kings of Troy*

CHORUS

O PHŒBUS embattling the high wall of Îlium,
  And thou of ocean, guiding behind black horses
        Thy chariot on salt water,
              Why have ye, in what wrath,
              Given the work of your hands—
            A fine work scorned, to the spear
        Of war, deserting unhappy
                    Unhappy Troy?

Many on Símoïs banks were the quick chariots
Inspanned, and bloody the ungarlanded racing
        That ye for mortals made there:
              Dead and gone are the kings
              Of Îlium, and no fire
              On altar-hearth now burns,
            There is no more incense smoking
                    In Troy for Gods.

Gone is the son of Atreus, wifely hands
Killed him, and she, requited by her children,
        Suffered God's anger, dying.
The word of God prophetic turned on her,
When, out of Argos, Agamemnon's son
Trod the rich temple floors and went to be
        The killer of his mother.
    O God, can I trust thy word, O Phœbus?

                                    407

Troy's women all through the Grecian market places
Sang lamentations for their unlucky children,
      And wives must home abandon
To follow another man; it is not you
Alone on whom fell difficult grief, it is not
Your friends alone. A plague, a plague held Greece;
      And to deep fields in Phrygia
   Crossed over a storm, and rained down murder.

GEORGE ALLEN   (*Andrómachê*, 1009–46)

364   *Polýxena*

POL. I see you, Odysseus, with your hand in hiding
   Beneath your cloak, and face averted, fearing
   My supplication upon your cheek; fear not.
   You have escaped the god who pleads for me:
   For now I'll follow you, as follow I must,
   And I long for death; because if I hold back,
   A coward of a woman I shall appear,
   My own life loving; and why live? My father
   Was king of all the Phrygians; this my life
   Was well begun, and, nursed in happy hopes,
   I was a bride for kings, and no poor match
   For him whose palace and hearth I was to come to.
   Princess—unlucky too—have I been in Ida,
   Where women and girls alike to me would look,—
   Equalled with gods in everything but dying;
   But now I'm slave, a word that most of all
   Enamours me of death, being strange to me;
   For well may I find a master hard of heart,
   Whoever with his wealth be purchaser
   Of me, sister of Hector and his brothers.

Corn in his house he well may force me to grind,
Or sweep the floor, or at the shuttle stand,
Leading a bitter life of enforced days.
Me in the marriage bed some slave will taint,
Bought heaven knows where, though I was fit for
    princes.
Not now! this day, bright only for free eyes,
I now renounce and give my body to death.
Take me, Odysseus, take me and kill me now,
Because with us I see no hope or comfort,
No inkling of the honourable state
That I should find. Then, mother, thwart me not
In word or deed, but rather counsel dying
Before indignities are mine to endure.
When trouble smacks unwonted, one can bear it,
But yet the neck is winced into the yoke;
And dying would be greater joy than living;
To live so poor a life would be mere sorrow.

GEORGE ALLEN   (*Hécuba*, 342–78)

365   *Whither away?*
              CHORUS

WIND on the waters blowing,
    Sea wind, borne on by thee
Run ships of sail light-going
    Over the heaving sea—
        Ay me,
Whither, O whither driven
    Shall I with sorrow come,
A captive woman, given
    In bondage—and to whom?
At Dorian port arriven,

Or some Thessalian home
Where shine the fabled waters,
Apídanus' fair daughters,
That feed the level loam.

Shall blade of oar go sweeping
To island harbour bound?
Waits now the house of weeping
In Delos' holy ground?
Ay me,
Laurel and palm-tree plaited
Latôna's bower of old,
The green leaf new-created
That holy birth extolled;
There I, so it be fated,
Sad festival shall hold
In choirs that sing a Maiden
With bow and quiver laden,
And diadem of gold.

T. F. HIGHAM   (*Hécuba*, 444–65)

366   *Troy*

CHORUS

My fatherland, O my Troy!
None shall hail thee now, the impregnable city,
Shrouded, compassed round by the host of Hellas,
By the spear of the spoiler.
They have shorn from thy brow the beauty,
Thy towers. We have seen thy ways
Ravaged, smirched by the smoke of ruin,
Alas! Ways that are mine no longer.

In the night was my sorrow born,
When the feast was done, at the hour when the weary
Turn to sleep. Ah sweet! when the song and the dancing
    And the worship were over,
    And my lord in the bower was waiting;
    His spear on the wall, at rest;
    No more watch at the ships, no longer
        Trampling feet in the Trojan city;

    And I in ribands and laces caught
    And twined the tresses of my hair,
      And read the dim glad secret
        The haze of my mirror told,
Of a bride and a happy lover, waiting . . .
    A stir in the city, and a noise,
A shout that rang in the streets of Troy,
        Crying 'Up,
Sons of Grecian sires, it is time, it is time!
    Will ye not ravage and sack
      Troy's tower and turn you homeward?'

    I left the bed of my lord, I ran,
    In the shift of a Dorian maid, ungirt;
      I sought thy shrine, in vain;
        Goddess, Artemis! All in vain!
For they took me, they slew my lord, I saw him,
    My lord, and they dragged me to the sea
Still gazing back to Troy. . . . The ship
        Homeward bound
Strained her tackling eagerly, bearing me on
    Far from the land of my love,
      Ah grief! my spirit left me,

And, fainting, cried my curse upon Helen, my curse on
    fatal Paris—
  Herdsman of Ida, and sister of the sons of Zeus.
        Torn from that ruined fatherland,
Outcast from home, I curse her, the bride who was not a
    bride, but a fiend, a fury,
And pray that the waves of the sea may not carry her again
    safe home,
        Never more
     Home, to her father's country.

J. T. SHEPPARD   (*Hécuba*, 905–52)

367   *Chivalry*

THÊSEUS. ÆTHRA

THÊS. Why weeping, mother? and why veil your eyes
     In your soft dress? Is it because you hear
     These cries of sorrow? I too feel this pang.
     Lift your white head again, and do not weep
     When sitting by Dêmêter's solemn hearth.

ÆTH. Alas!

THÊS. These women's troubles do not ask our tears.

ÆTH. Unhappy women!

THÊS.   You are not among them.

ÆTH. Grant me a word to help you and the city.

THÊS. The words that women say are often wise.

ÆTH. The speech I leave unspoken brings me fear.

THÊS. A sorry speech to hide good words from friends.

ÆTH. Speak then I shall, nor later find reproach
     That I have now kept silence wrongfully.
     Nor, fearing that a woman's words are idle,

Shall I in fear withhold an honest thought.
First, son, I bid you look to holy things,
Lest from dishonouring the gods you fall:
In all else right, in this alone you failed.
Next, if we should not rightly give our help
To injured men, I should have held my tongue:
Now see what honour this will bring to you—
I do not fear to counsel you, my son—
That violent men who try to rob the dead
Of funeral rites and their last offices
Should to the like constraint be brought by you
And stopped from ruining the laws that reign
Through Hellas. What unites the towns of men
Is this—that laws are honourably kept.
Some one will say that out of cowardice,
When you might win a crown of fame for Athens,
You feared and stood aside,—who made light sport
Of fighting with the wild and angry boar—
But when you should have stood against the spear-points
And helmets, then you proved yourself afraid.

　　My son, for you are mine, do not this thing.
You see your country, helpless and reviled,
Lift up its glittering eye against all those
Revilers? In its sorrows it finds strength.
Cities, which work in twilight silently,
Have twilit looks, for all their careful plans.
These dead men and these weeping women need
Your help, my son. Will you not give it them?

C. M. BOWRA   (*Supplices*, 286–327)

413

368   *Dirge*

SONS. CHORUS

SONS.   I bring from funeral,
        Sad mother, I bring the ashes of my father,
        A burden burdened with woe; my all in all
                  Compact I gather.
CHO.   O let me weep, let weep:
          How could you bring such tears to shed
          For loving mother of men dead,
        Once in Mycênæ gloriously embodied,
                  Now ashes, a small heap?

SONS.   Childless, childless your doom;
        But dead my luckless father, and I'll stand
        Forlorn an orphan in a lonely room,
                  Not held in father's hand.
CHO.   O let me weep, let weep:
          Where are my sons for whom so hard
          I worked, and where my pangs' reward,
        And mother's milk, and sallies of meeting kisses,
                  When eyes would watch, not sleep?

SONS.   All dead, none lives, dear father, alas,
         All dead.
CHO.   The thin air them now has,
                Ashes crumbled in flame,
                Winged way to death they came.
SONS.   Father, your sons' grief hear you yet?
        Shall ever I fight with shield on, that your dying,
                Please God, may other deaths beget?

SONS.   Your father's vengeance, if God will,
             May yet come.

CHO.   Not yet sleeps this ill.
             Alas, enough of fate
             Is mine, grief amply great.

SONS.   Will bright Asôpus ever again
        Welcome me leading Greeks in golden chariots,
             The avenger of my father slain?

SONS. Father, my eyes yet seem to see you whole—
CHO.   Kissing a kiss on your dear cheek.
SONS.   The counsel you could speak
             Is gone away upon wind.
CHO.   Both weep—mother is left her dole,
             And father mourned shall haunt son's mind.

SONS. The heavy sorrow I have did me destroy.
CHO.   O this dear Ash to breast I'll hold.
SONS.   I wept to hear this told
             Most cruel, my heart was moved.
CHO.   Son you are gone, your mother's joy,
             I shall not see you, loving and loved.

GEORGE ALLEN   (*Supplices*, 1123–64)

369   *Youth*

                       CHORUS

I COUNT it always a joy to be young,
        But age a burden
    Oppressiver than the Ætna rocks
    To thrust upon head, a mantle thrown
Enfolding darkly away the light from eyes.

O never would I desire to be wealthy
    With Asian sovereignty
    And households full of gold
       Exchanged for my prime:
    So lovely in wealth it is,
    So lovely poor, to be young.
But Age, woebegone, murderous,
I do detest. I wish it were gone
To the deep of the sea. Better by far
Never had Age approached the homes of men
Or cities: better on wings in air
    For ever and ever to fly.

If Reason and all that's wise with men
    Held good in heaven,
Then there would be second youth to win,
A signal of honour marking all
Possessing honour: and then coming to die
    These again would be off to the light
    Of day, their course renewing.
    But one span only of life
      The mean would enjoy:
    And that would enable us
    To tell the bad from the good,
Just as sailors among the clouds
Find a small number of stars to steer by.
But there's no heaven-sent frontier now
Distinguishing the good men from bad;
Riches alone as times roll on,
    Gather, for this man or that.

I will not ever abate my joining
    Of Graces and Muses,
Sweetest of all yokefellowships—
O let me never with folly live,
But still be found where the garlands are;
For you know the singer, old as he is,
Sings of Remembrance even now:
      And still of Hêraclês
        I sing the victory song
By side of Brómios, vintage god,
To the note of lyreshell seven-strung
      And the African pipe:
I shall never abate my Muses, for they
      Their mystery taught me.

Pæans sing the Dêlian maidens
      Around the gateways;
There to the glory of Lêto's child
They the beautiful dance revolve.
Pæans I also within your house
Old as I am, a swan melodious
From the grey down of cheeks do sing,
      Because my melodies
        Have dear occasion—
This child is of Zeus; by virtue he
Outshining even his lineage
      Rendered the life of men
      Serene for them, destroying
      The beasts of their fear.

GEORGE ALLEN   (*Hercules Furens*, 637–700)

Thou shalt not die

THÊSEUS. HÊRACLÊS

THÊS. Enough.
On you, who sit like one most miserable,
I call to lift your face up to your friends,
For there's no darkness has a cloud so black
To hide the sorrows that have fallen you.
Why wave your hand to show that murder's done?
Lest a pollution strike me from your speech?
Misfortune hurts me not if shared with you.
For I had joy once. Let's go back to that,
When from the dead to light you brought me safe.
I hate friends' gratitude when it grows old,
And him who likes to share prosperity
But will not sail with friends in troubled seas.
Stand up, uncover your unhappy head,
And look at us. The noble man endures
All pitfalls from the gods and does not shrink.

HÊR. Thêseus, you see this battle with my sons?

THÊS. I heard, and now I see the ills you show.

HÊR. Why have you made me show the sun my head?

THÊS. Why? Mortal you cannot defile the gods.

HÊR. Unhappy man, fly from my foul contagion.

THÊS. From friend to friend no Spirit of Vengeance comes.

HÊR. I thank you. And I helped you once, I know.

THÊS. And I, whom then you helped, now pity you.

HÊR. Pitiable am I, my children's murderer!

THÊS. I mourn for your sake in this altered fortune.

HÊR. Have you known others in still greater woe?

THÊS. From earth your sorrow reaches to the sky.

HÊR. Therefore have I prepared myself for death.

THÊS. Do you believe the gods care for your threats?

HÊR. Self-willed are gods, and to them self-willed I.

THÊS. Silence, lest big words bring a bigger woe.

HÊR. My cup is full—I have no room for more.

THÊS. What will you do? Where does wrath carry you?

HÊR. Dead I go whence I came—beneath the earth.

THÊS. The words you speak are those of lesser men.

HÊR. And you, being outside sorrow, give me warning!

THÊS. Does much-enduring Hêraclês say this?

HÊR. Endure I cannot—grief must have its bourne.

THÊS. This mankind's helper and its mighty friend?

HÊR. They do not help me; Hêra rules my life.

THÊS. Hellas forbids you foolishly to die.

C. M. BOWRA   (*Hercules Furens*, 1214–54)

371   *Dawn*

ION

SEE, already over the earth
    The Sun lights up his four-horsed team;
His flames put the stars to flight from the sky
Into holy night.
Parnassus' untrodden mountain-peaks
Are lit with his fires, and welcome for men
The chariot-wheels of day.
Smoke of rainless frankincense
Spreads over Apollo's roof;
The Delphian woman is taking her seat
On the holy tripod and sings to the Greeks
The dooms that ring from Apollo.
        Come, Apollo's Delphian servants,

419

Come to Castália's whirling waters
Silver-shining. Wash yourselves
In the pure spring and come to the shrine.
Seal your lips in reverent silence;
To all who would question the oracle
Nothing unseal
But holy words from your lips.

    And I, who from my childhood's days
Have done this task, will sanctify
With laurel branches and holy crowns
Apollo's doorway and cleanse the floor
With splash of water. Flocks of birds,
Who spoil the sacred offerings,
My bow and arrow shall put to flight.
For, since I have neither mother nor father,
I give my service
To Apollo's house which has nursed me.

C. M. Bowra   (*Ion*, 82–111)

372   *Apollo the Betrayer*

CREÛSA

HOW can I keep silence, soul?
And how betray that bed in the dark,
Stripping myself of shamefastness?

What can stop me and hold me back?
I seek no rival in innocence.
Has not my bridegroom betrayed me,
Who robbed me of home, robbed me of sons?

My hopes are gone, vain hopes I built
Guarding my honour: I who said
Nothing of wedlock,
Nothing of travail and all its tears.

No,—by the starry throne of Zeus,
By the goddess who watches the rocks of my home,
By the majestical shore
Of Lake Tritônis' water,
I'll speak and tell with whom I lay,
I'll lock in my breast no more
That load, but feel at peace.

My eyes drop tears, my soul
Is sick with the foul conspiracies
Of mortal men and immortal gods;
Them shall I prove
Ungrateful traitors against my love.

O chanter of melody
On the seven strings of the lyre,
Melody echoing
From the dead strips of rustic horn
Your musical hymns and loud,
Shame on you, Lâto's son,
Before the sunlight I shall cry.

You came to me, your hair
Burning with gold, when I
Was gathering yellow flowers
Into the folds of my bosom,
Gold cups of light for woven crowns:
You gripped me by my white wrists
And while I cried out 'Mother',

Dragged me to lie in a cave—
You, god, were my paramour,
Dragging me shamelessly,
Doing the Cyprian's will.

And I, poor maid,
Gave birth to a son,
And, fearful of my mother,
Flung him into that bed
Where you had forced me and wed me—
O cruelty! . . . Poor maid,
Most cruelly wed!

Ay me, ay me,
And now he is gone,
Snatched by the birds for their feast,
My son . . . and yours, O pitiless!
While you to the lyre's loud tones
Are chanting hymns of praise.

To you, son of Lâto, to you
I raise my cry,
To you who give forth oracles
From a golden throne
Seated at earth's centre,
In your ear I shall cry aloud.

Ah, wicked ravisher,
Owing no debt to my husband
You settle a son in his house:
But my son . . . and yours, O cruel-hearted,
Is gone, picked by the birds,
Robbed of the wrappings his mother gave him.

Delos hates you, the laurel hates you
Which grows by the palm-tree's delicate leaves,
Where Lâto in holiness
Gave you birth,
Fruit of the loins of Zeus.

C. M. BOWRA   (*Ion*, 859–922)

373   *Troy*

CHORUS

IN Salamis, filled with the foaming
   Of billows and murmur of bees,
Old Télamon stayed from his roaming,
   Long ago, on a throne of the seas;
Looking out on the hills olive-laden,
   Enchanted, where first from the earth
The grey-gleaming fruit of the Maiden
      Athêna had birth;
A soft grey crown for a city
   Belovèd, a City of Light:
Yet he rested not there, nor had pity,
      But went forth in his might,
Where Hêraclês wandered, the lonely
   Bow-bearer, and lent him his hands
For the wrecking of one land only,
Of Îlion, Îlion only,
      Most hated of lands!

Of the bravest of Hellas he made him
   A ship-folk, in wrath for the Steeds,
And sailed the wide waters, and stayed him
   At last amid Símoïs reeds;

And the oars beat slow in the river,
　　And the long ropes held in the strand,
And he felt for his bow and his quiver,
　　The wrath of his hand.
And the old king died; and the towers
　　That Phœbus had builded did fall,
And his wrath, as a flame that devours,
　　Ran red over all;
And the fields and the woodlands lay blasted,
　　Long ago. Yea, twice hath the Sire
Uplifted his hand and downcast it
On the wall of the Dardan, downcast it
　　As a sword and as fire.

In vain, all in vain,
　　O thou 'mid the wine-jars golden
　　　　That movest in delicate joy,
　　　　Ganymêdês, child of Troy,
The lips of the Highest drain
　　The cup in thine hand upholden:
And thy mother, thy mother that bore thee,
　　Is wasted with fire and torn;
　　　　And the voice of her shores is heard,
　　　　Wild, as the voice of a bird,
For lovers and children before thee
　　Crying, and mothers outworn.
And the pools of thy bathing are perished,
　　And the wind-strewn ways of thy feet:
Yet thy face as aforetime is cherished
　　Of Zeus, and the breath of it sweet;

Yea, the beauty of Calm is upon it
  In houses at rest and afar.
But thy land, He hath wrecked and o'erthrown it
  In the wailing of war.

O Love, ancient Love,
  Of old to the Dardan given;
    Love of the Lords of the Sky;
    How didst thou lift us high
In Îlion, yea, and above
  All cities, as wed with heaven!
For Zeus—O leave it unspoken:
  But alas for the love of the Morn;
    Morn of the milk-white wing,
    The gentle, the earth-loving,
That shineth on battlements broken
  In Troy, and a people forlorn!
And, lo, in her bowers Tîthônus,
  Our brother, yet sleeps as of old:
O, she too hath loved us and known us,
  And the Steeds of her star, flashing gold,
Stooped hither and bore him above us;
  Then blessed we the Gods in our joy.
But all that made them to love us
  Hath perished from Troy.

GILBERT MURRAY   (*Trôadës*, 799–859)

374 *The End of Troy*

HÉCUBA. TALTHÝBIUS. CHORUS

HEC.   Ah, me! and is it come, the end of all,
    The very crest and summit of my days?
    I go forth from my land, and all its ways

Are filled with fire! Bear me, O agèd feet,
A little nearer: I must gaze, and greet
My poor town ere she fall.

                Farewell, farewell!
O thou whose breath was mighty on the swell
Of orient winds, my Troy! Even thy name
Shall soon be taken from thee. Lo, the flame
Hath thee, and we, thy children, pass away
To slavery ... God! O God of mercy!... Nay:
Why call I on the Gods? They know, they know,
My prayers, and would not hear them long ago.

  Quick, to the flames! O, in thine agony,
My Troy, mine own, take me to die with thee!
          (*She springs toward the flames, but
           is seized and held by the Soldiers.*)

TAL. Back! Thou art drunken with thy miseries,
  Poor woman!—Hold her fast, men, till it please
Odysseus that she come. She was his lot
Chosen from all and portioned. Lose her not!
          (*He goes to watch over the burning of
           the City. The dusk deepens.*)

CHO.   Woe, woe, woe!
DIVERS WOMEN. Thou of the Ages, O wherefore fleëst thou,
      Lord of the Phrygian, Father that made us?
       'Tis we, thy children; shall no man aid us?
       'Tis we, thy children! Seëst thou, seëst thou?

OTHERS. He seëth, only his heart is pitiless;
       And the land dies: yea, she,
    She of the Mighty Cities perisheth citiless!
       Troy shall no more be!

426

OTHERS.　Woe, woe, woe!
　　　　　Îlion shineth afar!
　　　　Fire in the deeps thereof,
　　　　Fire in the heights above,
　　　　　And crested walls of War!

OTHERS.　As smoke on the wing of heaven
　　　　　Climbeth and scattereth,
　　　　Torn of the spear and driven,
　　　　　The land crieth for death:
　　　　O stormy battlements that red fire hath riven,
　　　　And the sword's angry breath!
　　　　　　(*A new thought comes to Hécuba; she kneels
　　　　　　and beats the earth with her hands.*)

HEC.　O Earth, Earth of my children; hearken! and O
　　　　mine own,
　　　　　Ye have hearts and forget not, ye in the dark-
　　　　　ness lying!

LEADER.　Now hast thou found thy prayer, crying to them
　　　　that are gone.

HEC.　Surely my knees are weary, but I kneel above
　　　　your head;
　　　　Hearken, O ye so silent! My hands beat your
　　　　bed!

LEADER.　I, I am near thee,
　　　　I kneel to thy dead to hear thee,
　　　　Kneel to mine own in the darkness; O husband,
　　　　hear my crying!

HEC.　Even as the beasts they drive, even as the loads
　　　　they bear,

LEADER.　(Pain; O pain!)

HEC.   We go to the house of bondage. Hear, ye dead,
          O hear!

LEADER.   (Go, and come not again!)

HEC.   Priam, mine own Priam,
             Lying so lowly,
          Thou in thy nothingness,
          Shelterless, comfortless,
          See'st thou the thing I am?
          Know'st thou my bitter stress?

LEADER.   Nay, thou art naught to him!
          Out of the strife there came,
          Out of the noise and shame,
          Making his eyelids dim,
             Death, the Most Holy!
                (The fire and smoke rise constantly higher.)

HEC.   O high houses of Gods, belovèd streets of my
             birth,
             Ye have found the way of the sword, the fiery
             and blood-red river!

LEADER.   Fall, and men shall forget you! Ye shall lie in the
             gentle earth.

HEC.   The dust as smoke riseth; it spreadeth wide its
             wing;
          It maketh me as a shadow, and my City a vanished
             thing!

LEADER.   Out on the smoke she goeth,
             And her name no man knoweth;
          And the cloud is northward, southward; Troy is
             gone for ever!
                      *(A great crash is heard, and the Wall
                      is lost in smoke and darkness.)*

428

HEC.   Ha! Marked ye? Heard ye? The crash of the
            towers that fall!

LEADER. All is gone!

HEC.   Wrath in the earth and quaking and a flood that
            sweepeth all,

LEADER. And passeth on!

(The Greek trumpet sounds.)

HEC.   Farewell!—O spirit grey,
              Whatso is coming,
            Fail not from under me.
            Weak limbs, why tremble ye?
            Forth where the new long day
            Dawneth to slavery!

CHO.   Farewell from parting lips,
            Farewell!—Come, I and thou,
            Whatso may wait us now,
            Forth to the long Greek ships
              And the sea's foaming.

*(The trumpet sounds again, and the
Women go out in the darkness.)*

GILBERT MURRAY   *(Trôadës, 1272–1332)*

375   *Êlectra and Orestês*

êL. So be it; you must bring the body inside.
       Cover it darkly, slaves, that when she comes,
       Our mother see no death before her own.

OR. O wait—let's break into another thought.

êL. Why? do I see the runners from Mycênæ?

OR. No, but the mother who has given me birth.

êL. She comes most fine and fairly into the net!
Resplendent too, with chariots and with pomp!

OR. What shall we do to our mother? murder her?

êL. Has pity come with seeing of your mother?

OR. O God!
How can I kill her, mother and nurse of me?

êL. Kill, as she killed the father of you and me.

OR. O Phœbus, utter folly was thy word, . . .

êL. Suppose Apollo to err, and who is right?

OR. To bid me kill my mother, it is wrong.

êL. Now you avenge your father can you trip?

OR. Now charged with a mother's murder, pure till now.

êL. But impious, if you fail your father now.

OR. My mother I—? to whom shall I pay for murder?

êL. To whom, if your father's vengeance you put off?

OR. Did a fiend speak, taking the form of god?

êL. Throned on Apollo's tripod? I think not.

OR. I cannot think his word was well vouchsafed.

êL. Beware of being daunted into a coward!

OR. But shall I lay the selfsame trap for her?

êL. The trap with which you killed her man Ægisthus.

OR. I'll go; an awful scheme I start, and awful
The deed I'll do; but if the Gods approve,
So be it: bitter and sweet in me contend.

GEORGE ALLEN   (*Êlectra*, 959–87)

376 *Agamemnon's Children*

îPHIGENîA. ORESTÊS

îPH. Say first . . . which is it men call Pyladês?

OR. 'Tis this man's name, if that will give thee ease.

îPH. From what walled town of Hellas cometh he?

OR. Enough!—How would the knowledge profit thee?

îph. Are ye two brethren of one mother born?

or. No, not in blood. In love we are brothers sworn.

îph. Thou also hast a name: tell me thereof.

or. Call me Unfortunate. 'Tis name enough.

îph. I asked not that. Let that with Fortune lie.

or. Fools cannot laugh at them that nameless die.

îph. Why grudge me this? Hast thou such mighty fame?

or. My body, if thou wilt, but not my name.

îph. Nor yet the land of Greece where thou wast bred?

or. What gain to have told it thee, when I am dead?

îph. Nay: why shouldst thou deny so small a grace?

or. Know then, great Argos was my native place.

îph. Stranger! The truth!... From Argos art thou come?

or. Mycênæ, once a rich land, was my home.

îph. 'Tis banishment that brings thee here—or what?

or. A kind of banishment, half forced, half sought.

îph. Wouldst thou but tell me all I need of thee!

or. 'Twere not much added to my misery.

îph. From Argos!... Oh, how sweet to see thee here!

or. Enjoy it, then. To me 'tis sorry cheer.

îph. Thou knowst the name of Troy? Far doth it flit.

or. Would God, I had not; nay, nor dreamed of it.

îph. Men fable it is fallen beneath the sword?

or. Fallen it is. Thou hast heard no idle word.

îph. Fallen! At last!—And Helen taken too?

or. Aye; on an evil day for one I knew.

îph. Where is she? I too have some anger stored. . . .

or. In Sparta! Once more happy with her Lord!

îph. Oh, hated of all Greece, not only me!

or. I too have tasted of her wizardry.

îph. And came the armies home, as the tales run?

or. To answer that were many tales in one.

îph.	Oh, give me this hour full! Thou wilt soon die.
or.	Ask, if such longing holds thee. I will try.
îph.	A seer called Calchas! Did he ever come . . .?
or.	Calchas is dead, as the news went at home.
îph.	Good news, ye gods!—Odysseus, what of him?
or.	Not home yet, but still living, as men deem.
îph.	Curse him! And may he see his home no more.
or.	Why curse him? All his house is stricken sore.
îph.	How hath the Nêreïd's son, Achilles, sped?
or.	Small help his bridal brought him! He is dead.
îph.	A false fierce bridal, so the sufferers tell!
or.	Who art thou, questioning of Greece so well?
îph.	I was Greek. Evil caught me long ago.
or.	Small wonder, then, thou hast such wish to know.
îph.	That war-lord, whom they call so high in bliss. . . .
or.	None such is known to me. What name was his?
îph.	They called him Agamemnon, Atreus' son.
or.	I know not. Cease.—My questioning is done.
îph.	'Twill be such joy to me! How fares he? Tell!
or.	Dead. And has wrecked another's life as well.
îph.	Dead? By what dreadful fortune? Woe is me!
or.	Why sighest thou? Had he any link with thee?
îph.	I did but think of his old joy and pride.
or.	His own wife foully stabbed him, and he died.
îph.	O God!
	I pity her that slew . . . and him that slew.
or.	Now cease thy questions. Add no word thereto.
îph.	But one word. Lives she still, that hapless wife?
or.	No. Her own son, her first-born, took her life.
îph.	O shipwrecked house! What thought was in his brain?
or.	Justice on her, to avenge his father slain.

432

ÎPH. Alas!
        A bad false duty bravely hath he wrought.
OR.   Yet God, for all his duty, helps him not.
ÎPH. And not one branch of Atreus' tree lives on?
OR.   Êlectra lives, unmated and alone.
ÎPH. The child they slaughtered . . . is there word of her?
OR.   Why, no, save that she died in Aulis there.
ÎPH. Poor child! Poor father, too, who killed and lied!
OR.   For a bad woman's worthless sake she died.
ÎPH. The dead king's son, lives he in Argos still?
OR.   He lives, now here, now nowhere, bent with ill.
ÎPH. O dreams, light dreams, farewell! Ye too were lies.
OR.   Aye; the gods too, whom mortals deem so wise,
        Are nothing clearer than some wingèd dream;
        And all their ways, like man's ways, but a stream
        Of turmoil. He who cares to suffer least,
        Not blind, as fools are blinded, by a priest,
        Goes straight . . . to what death, those who know
              him know.

GILBERT MURRAY   (*Îphigenîa in Tauris*, 492–575)

377   *Pyladês*

                    ORESTÊS. PYLADÊS

OR.   What? If thou hast need of me, let it be said.
PYL. I cannot live for shame if thou art dead.
        I sailed together with thee; let us die
        Together. What a coward slave were I,
        Creeping through Argos and from glen to glen
        Of wind-torn Phôcian hills! And most of men—
        For most are bad—will whisper how one day
        I left my friend to die and made my way

Home. They will say I watched the sinking breath
Of thy great house and plotted for thy death
To wed thy sister, climb into thy throne . . .
I dread, I loathe it.—Nay, all ways but one
Are shut. My last breath shall go forth with thine,
Thy bloody sword, thy gulf of fire be mine
Also. I love thee and I dread men's scorn.

OR. Peace from such thoughts! My burden can be borne;
But where one pain sufficeth, double pain
I will not bear. Nay, all that scorn and stain
That fright thee, on mine own head worse would be
If I brought death on him who toiled for me.
It is no bitter thing for such an one
As God will have me be, at last to have done
With living. Thou art happy; thy house lies
At peace with God, unstainèd in men's eyes;
Mine is all evil fate and evil life . . .
Nay, thou once safe, my sister for thy wife—
So we agreed:—in sons of hers and thine
My name will live, nor Agamemnon's line
Be blurred for ever like an evil scroll.
Back! Rule thy land! Let life be in thy soul!
And when thou art come to Hellas, and the plain
Of Argos where the horsemen ride, again—
Give me thy hand!—I charge thee, let there be
Some death-mound and a graven stone for me.
My sister will go weep thereat, and shear
A tress or two. Say how I ended here,
Slain by a maid of Argolis, beside
God's altar, in mine own blood purified.

  And fare thee well. I have no friend like thee
For truth and love, O boy that played with me,

434

And hunted on Greek hills, O thou on whom
Hath lain the hardest burden of my doom!
Farewell. The Prophet and the Lord of Lies
Hath done his worst. Far out from Grecian skies
With craft forethought he driveth me, to die
Where none may mark how ends his prophecy!
I trusted in his word. I gave him all
My heart. I slew my mother at his call;
For which things now he casts me here to die.

PYL. Thy tomb shall fail thee not. Thy sister I
Will guard for ever. I, O stricken sore,
Who loved thee living and shall love thee more
Dead. But for all thou standest on the brink,
God's promise hath not yet destroyed thee. Think!
How oft, how oft the darkest hour of ill
Breaks brightest into dawn, if Fate but will!

OR. Enough. Nor god nor man can any more
Aid me. The woman standeth at the door.

GILBERT MURRAY   (*Íphigenîa in Tauris*, 672–724)

378   *Bird of the Sea*

CHORUS

BIRD of the sea rocks, of the bursting spray,
    O halcyon bird,
That wheelest crying, crying, on thy way;
Who knoweth grief can read the tale of thee:
One love long lost, one song for ever heard
    And wings that sweep the sea.

Sister, I too beside the sea complain,
    A bird that hath no wing.
Oh, for a kind Greek market-place again,
For Artemis that healeth woman's pain;
    Here I stand hungering.
Give me the little hill above the sea,
The palm of Delos fringèd delicately,
The young sweet laurel and the olive-tree
    Grey-leaved and glimmering;
O Isle of Lêto, Isle of pain and love;
The Orbèd Water and the spell thereof;
Where still the Swan, minstrel of things to be,
    Doth serve the Muse and sing!

Ah, the old tears, the old and blinding tears
    I gave God then,
When my town fell, and noise was in mine ears
Of crashing towers, and forth they guided me
Through spears and lifted oars and angry men
    Out to an unknown sea.

They bought my flesh with gold, and sore afraid
    I came to this dark East
To serve, in thrall to Agamemnon's maid,
This Huntress Artemis, to whom is paid
    The blood of no slain beast;
Yet all is bloody where I dwell, Ah me!
Envying, envying that misery
That through all life hath endured changelessly.

For hard things borne from birth
Make iron of man's heart, and hurt the less.
'Tis change that paineth; and the bitterness
Of life's decay when joy hath ceased to be
    That makes dark all the earth.

        Behold,
    Two score and ten there be
    Rowers that row for thee,
And a wild hill air, as if Pan were there,
    Shall sound on the Argive sea,
    Piping to set thee free.

    Or is it the stricken string
    Of Apollo's lyre doth sing
Joyously, as he guideth thee
    To Athens, the land of spring;
    While I wait wearying?

    Oh, the wind and the oar,
    When the great sail swells before,
With sheets astrain, like a horse on the rein;
    And on, through the race and roar,
    She feels for the farther shore.

        Ah me,
    To rise upon wings and hold
    Straight on up the steeps of gold
Where the joyous Sun in fire doth run,
    Till the wings should faint and fold
    O'er the house that was mine of old:

437

> Or watch where the glade below
> With a marriage dance doth glow,
> And a child will glide from her mother's side
> Out, out, where the dancers flow:
> As I did, long ago.

> Oh, battles of gold and rare
> Raiment and starrèd hair,
> And bright veils crossed amid tresses tossed
> In a dusk of dancing air!
> O Youth and the days that were!

GILBERT MURRAY   (*Îphigenîa in Tauris*, 1089–1151)

379   *Siren-spirits*

HELEN. CHORUS

HEL. Siren-spirits, hover near,
Daughters of the earth appear.
  Winged and beautiful are ye,
  Swift in your virginity.
Come, for music with you bringing,
Fit response to my sad singing,
Egypt's lotus-flute and reeds,
Blending for the heart that bleeds
Tear with tear and pain with pain
In a desolate refrain;
So perchance the Muse may hear,
  And to Queen Persephonê
In the courts of darkness drear,
  Sing my dirge again, and she
May turn the bitter tears I shed
To sweet music for the dead.

438

CHO. I had washed my robes of red,
  And on fresh green rushes spread
  In the meadows by the cool
  Darkly gleaming waterpool
  For the golden sun to dry,
  When I hear a voice, a cry;
  Such a cry as ill would suit
  The happy music of my lute;
  And I wondered what might be
  The cause of that strange minstrelsy,
  So sad, and yet so wondrous clear,
 It might have been some Naiad flying,
  With a cry of sudden fear,
 Or in secret cavern lying
  Desolate, the ravished bride
  Of Pan upon the mountain-side.

J. T. SHEPPARD   (*Hélena*, 167–90)

380   *Éteoclês and Polynîcês*

JOCASTA. POLYNÎCÊS. CHORUS. ÉTEOCLÊS

JOC. My son Polynîcês, now you have first word,
For you at head of Grecian army are come,
Dealt meanly with, you say; but may some God
Decide this thing, and reconcile us of harm.

POL. O simple is the saying of the truth,
And what is just, itself being fit, requires
No clever gloss; it is the unjust cause
That sick within wants dose of sophistry.

 I have been thinking of my father's house
Both mine and my brother's, eager to escape
The curse that Œdipus called down on us.

          439

I freely left this land, giving it him
To rule there for the rounding of a year,
If I might then myself in turn receive it
And rule there, not in battle or bloodshed coming
To inflict and suffer hurt, as I now must.
And this he approved, and gave me his pledged word,
But carried out no pledge; and now the rule
My brother enjoys, and what is part my house.

And now I am ready what is mine to accept,—
Dismissing all my army from the land,
To dwell within my house, my own turn taking,
Leaving it for my brother as long again—
Rather than waste this country, bringing up
Ladders built for attack against the towers,
As, if I lack redress, I'll seek to do.
Bear witness all the spirits I now invoke,
That all I do is just, and justice failing
I shall be held most foully from my land.

Now mother I have said my say complete,
Not gathering twisted words, but what is just
For wise, I think, and simple men to approve.

CHO. For me, though Grecian soil was not our nurse,
Yet still for me your word has sense enough.

ET. If good and wise were but one thing for all,
Men would not have contention so, nor strife;
But, as it is, there is no equal or just—
Such things are found only in name, not fact.

Now mother I will speak and nothing hide;
I to the ultimate risings of the planets
And under the earth would go, could I do that,
If Sovranty, the queen of gods, be mine.
Therefore this treasure, mother, I will not

440

Pass on to another, but I'll hold it mine.
A cowardly thing to lose the greater part
And take the less; moreover I am ashamed
That he approaching armed, the country spoiling,
Should get his purpose—and for Thebes were shame
If I afraid of Mycênæan arms
Should give my brother this my sceptre to bear!
His reconciliation not with arms
He should have made, O mother; spoken word
Gets all that enemy steel could ever do.
Yet if no king he here consents to live,
Let live! but I will not relinquish rule.
Am I, if I can reign, to be his slave?
  Now therefore welcome fire and welcome sword,
The horses yoke, and with chariots fill the plain.
I will not yield him Sovranty; but if
I wrongly must do, then for my Sovranty
Let me do wrong, and elsewhere be devout!

GEORGE ALLEN   (*Phœnissæ*, 465–525)

381   *Orestês and Électra*

ORESTÊS. ÉLECTRA

OR. O soothing sleep, dear friend, best nurse of sickness!
How sweetly came you in my hour of need.
Best Lêthê of all woes, how wise you are,
How worthy of the prayers of wretched men!
Whence came I to this place? How journeyed I?
I cannot think: my former mind is vanished.

ÊL. O dearest, how hath your sleep gladdened me!
Say, can I help to soothe or raise your body?

441

OR. Yes, take me, take me: with your kind hands wipe
The foam of fever from my lips and eyes.

ÊL. Sweet is this service to me; I am glad
To soothe my brother with a sister's hand.

OR. Support me with your breast; the matted hair
Brush from my forehead. I can hardly see.

ÊL. Now listen to me, dearest brother mine,
While the Avengers leave you space to think.

OR. What have you new to say? Good news will cheer me;
But of what's bad I have enough already.

ÊL. Menelâus is here, your father's brother:
His ships are safely moored in Nauplia.

OR. What! Has he come to end your woes and mine?
He is our kinsman and our father's debtor.

ÊL. He has: and this is surety for my words—
Helen hath come with him from Troy, is here.

OR. If heaven had saved but him, he'd now be happier:
But with his wife he brings a huge curse home.

ÊL. Yea: Tyndareus begat a brood of daughters
Marked out for obloquy, a shame through Hellas.

OR. Be you then other than the bad; you can:
Make not fine speeches, but be rightly minded!

ÊL. Ah me, my brother! your eyes roll and tremble—
One moment sane, and now swift frenzy fires you!

(*Orestês speaks to phantoms in the air.*)

OR. Mother, I sue to thee: nay, mother, hound not
Those blood-faced, snake-encircled women on me!
There! There! See there—close by they bound
upon me!

ÊL. Stay, wretched brother; start not from the bed!
Things evident to your sick brain are nothings.

442

OR. O Phœbus, they will slay me, those dog-faced
    Fierce-eyed, infernal ministers, dread goddesses!

ÊL. I will not leave you—see, I twine my arms
    To stay your madness as you hurl and plunge.

                    (*Orestês throws Êlectra from him.*)

OR. Let go! Of my damned Furies you are one,
    That with your grip would hale me down to hell.

ÊL. Ah, woe is me! What succour shall I find,
    Seeing the very gods conspire against us?

OR. Give me my bow and arrows, Loxias' gift,
    Wherewith Apollo bade me fight the fiends,
    If they should scare me with wild-eyed delirium.
    Some god shall feel the fury of man's hand,
    Unless ye vanish forth from out my sight!

                    (*He threatens the phantoms.*)

    Hear ye not! See ye not the feathery wings
    Of swift, sure-striking shafts, ready to flutter?
    Ha! Ha!
    Why linger here? Go, sweep with outspread pinions
    The windy sky! Hence, and complain of Phœbus!

After J. A. SYMONDS   (*Orestês*, 211–24, 237–76)

382   *The Furies*

CHORUS

Terror!
O moving with the quickness of wings,
    Royallest goddesses,
      To revelling sent, not flushed with wine,
      But in tears and crying,
    Swart avengers that flail the sweep

Of air ascending, visiting blood
With vengeance, visiting murder.
You I beseech! you I beseech!
　　To Agamemnon's son
Concede oblivion of his rages
　　Of errant frenzy: alas, poor Orestês!
Undone, for fearful ends you are lost,
From Phœbus' tripod hearing his word uttered
　　Within the precinct that hides
The fabled innermost navel-stone.

O Zeus!
What pity is there? what struggle
　　Is bloodily moving now,
Besetting you, wretched one, for whom
　　A fiend avenging
Sorrow heaps on sorrow, and brings
Maddening indoors your mother's blood—
Great wealth not lingers with mortals:
Let me lament! let me lament!
　　Like mainsail on swift ship
Him some deity hath shattered,
　　And dashed in the violence of waves deadly,—
Of dreadful troubles as though of the sea.
Where is there another house than this
　　From heavenly seed derived,
From Tantalus, for me to revere?

GEORGE ALLEN　　　　　　　(*Orestês*, 316–47)

Bacchanal

CHORUS

O FOR Cyprus,
  island of Aphrodîtê!
There go the Loves
in fields familiar;
they who beguile
man's heart awhile
on his road to death.

O for Paphos,
thick with fruits
secretly watered
by far-off Nile!
Streaming from hundred mouths
he comes, a stranger,
stolen under the sea—
Nile, whom no rain feeds.

O for Pîeria,
home of Muses!
There, to the very heart
of beauty,
a holy place
on slant Olympus,
there, there
lead me, Brómios,
lead me, O swift runner,
Spirit attended
by cries ecstatic
ringing behind thee.

445

There are the Graces,
soul's desire is there;
there, in joy of worship,
with god's good will
thy servants go.

T. F. HIGHAM   (*Bacchæ*, 403–15)

384   *On Cithæron*
MESSENGER

OUR herded kine were moving in the dawn
Up to the peaks, the greyest, coldest time,
When the first rays steal earthward, and the rime
Yields, when I saw three bands of them. The one
Autonoê led, one Ino, one thine own
Mother, Agâvê. There beneath the trees
Sleeping they lay, like wild things flung at ease
In the forest; one half-sinking on a bed
Of deep pine greenery; one with careless head
Amid the fallen oak leaves; all most cold
In purity—not as thy tale was told
Of wine-cups and wild music and the chase
For love amid the forest's loneliness.
Then rose the Queen Agâvê suddenly
Amid her band, and gave the God's wild cry,
'Awake, ye Bacchanals! I hear the sound
Of hornèd kine. Awake ye!'—Then, all round,
Alert, the warm sleep fallen from their eyes,
A marvel of swift ranks I saw them rise,
Dames young and old, and gentle maids unwed
Among them. O'er their shoulders first they shed

446

Their tresses, and caught up the fallen fold
Of mantles where some clasp had loosened hold,
And girt the dappled fawn-skins in with long
Quick snakes that hissed and writhed with quivering tongue.
And one a young fawn held, and one a wild
Wolf cub, and fed them with white milk, and smiled
In love, young mothers with a mother's breast
And babes at home forgotten! Then they pressed
Wreathed ivy round their brows, and oaken sprays
And flowering bryony. And one would raise
Her wand and smite the rock, and straight a jet
Of quick bright water came. Another set
Her thyrsus in the bosomed earth, and there
Was red wine that the God sent up to her,
A darkling fountain. And if any lips
Sought whiter draughts, with dipping finger-tips
They pressed the sod, and gushing from the ground
Came springs of milk. And reed-wands ivy-crowned
Ran with sweet honey, drop by drop.—O King,
Hadst thou been there, as I, and seen this thing,
With prayer and most high wonder hadst thou gone
To adore this God whom now thou rail'st upon!

Howbeit, the kine-wardens and shepherds straight
Came to one place, amazed, and held debate;
And one being there who walked the streets and scanned
The ways of speech, took lead of them whose hand
Knew but the slow soil and the solemn hill,
And flattering spoke, and asked: 'Is it your will,
Masters, we stay the mother of the King,
Agâvê, from her lawless worshipping,
And win us royal thanks?'—And this seemed good
To all; and through the branching underwood

447

We hid us, cowering in the leaves. And there
Through the appointed hour they made their prayer
And worship of the Wand, with one accord
Of heart and cry—'Iacchos, Brómios, Lord,
God of God born!'—And all the mountain felt,
And worshipped with them; and the wild things knelt
And ramped and gloried, and the wilderness
Was filled with moving voices and dim stress.

Soon, as it chanced, beside my thicket-close
The Queen herself passed dancing, and I rose
And sprang to seize her. But she turned her face
Upon me: 'Ho, my rovers of the chase,
My wild White Hounds, we are hunted! Up, each rod
And follow, follow, for our Lord and God!'
Thereat, for fear they tear us, all we fled
Amazed; and on, with hand unweaponèd
They swept toward our herds that browsed the green
Hill grass. Great uddered kine then hadst thou seen
Bellowing in sword-like hands that cleave and tear,
A live steer riven asunder, and the air
Tossed with rent ribs or limbs of cloven tread,
And flesh upon the branches, and a red
Rain from the deep green pines. Yea, bulls of pride,
Horns swift to rage, were fronted and aside
Flung stumbling, by those multitudinous hands
Dragged pitilessly. And swifter were the bands
Of garbèd flesh and bone unbound withal
Than on thy royal eyes the lids may fall.

Then on like birds, by their own speed upborne,
They swept towards the plains of wavering corn
That lie beside Asôpus' banks, and bring
To Thebes the rich fruit of her harvesting.

On Hýsiæ and Erythræ that lie nursed
Amid Kithæron's bowering rocks, they burst
Destroying, as a foeman's army comes.
They caught up little children from their homes,
High on their shoulders, babes unheld, that swayed
And laughed and fell not; all a wreck they made;
Yea, bronze and iron did shatter, and in play
Struck hither and thither, yet no wound had they;
Caught fire from out the hearths, yea, carried hot
Flames in their tresses and were scorchèd not!

The village folk in wrath took spear and sword,
And turned upon the Bacchæ. Then, dread Lord,
The wonder was. For spear nor barbèd brand
Could scathe nor touch the damsels; but the Wand,
The soft and wreathèd wand their white hands sped,
Blasted those men and quelled them, and they fled
Dizzily. Sure some God was in these things!

And the holy women back to those strange springs
Returned, that God had sent them when the day
Dawned, on the upper heights; and washed away
The stain of battle. And those girdling snakes
Hissed out to lap the waterdrops from cheeks
And hair and breast.

     Therefore I counsel thee,
O King, receive this Spirit, whoe'er he be,
To Thebes in glory. Greatness manifold
Is all about him; and the tale is told
That this is he who first to man did give
The grief-assuaging vine. Oh, let him live;
For if he die, then Love herself is slain,
And nothing joyous in the world again!

GILBERT MURRAY   (*Bacchæ*, 677–774)

385   *Where shall Wisdom be found?*

CHORUS

(Some Maidens)

WILL they ever come to me, ever again,
    The long long dances,
On through the dark till the dawn-stars wane?
Shall I feel the dew on my throat, and the stream
Of wind in my hair? Shall our white feet gleam
    In the dim expanses?
Oh, feet of a fawn to the greenwood fled,
    Alone in the grass and the loveliness;
Leap of the hunted, no more in dread,
    Beyond the snares and the deadly press:
Yet a voice still in the distance sounds,
A voice and a fear and a haste of hounds;
O wildly labouring, fiercely fleet,
    Onward yet by river and glen . . .
Is it joy or terror, ye storm-swift feet? . . .
    To the dear lone lands untroubled of men,
Where no voice sounds, and amid the shadowy green
The little things of the woodland live unseen.

What else is Wisdom? What of man's endeavour
    Or God's high grace, so lovely and so great?
    To stand from fear set free, to breathe and wait;
    To hold a hand uplifted over Hate;
And shall not Loveliness be loved for ever?

    Happy he, on the weary sea
Who hath fled the tempest and won the haven.
    Happy whoso hath risen, free,
Above his striving. For strangely graven

450

Is the orb of life, that one and another
In gold and power may outpass his brother.
And men in their millions float and flow
And seethe with a million hopes as leaven;
And they win their Will, or they miss their Will,
And their hopes are dead or are pined for still;
But whoe'er can know,
As the long days go,
That To Live is happy, hath found his Heaven.

GILBERT MURRAY (*Bacchæ*, 863–76, 897–911)

386 *Watch before Dawn*

AGAMEMNON. OLD SERVANT

AG. Come out, old man, out from the tent to me!
SER. Coming, my lord!
What new plan is afoot,
King Agamemnon?
AG. O, make haste, make haste!
SER. All that you will, my lord.
I'm a light sleeper yet.
AG. What star is yonder, travelling in the sky?
SER. Sîrius;
Close to the sevenfold voyaging Pleiadës,
Still high overhead.
AG. No sound from the birds;
No sound from the sea.
The hush of the winds
Broods over Eurîpus.
SER. Why did you hasten out of the tent,
Lord Agamemnon?

451

No one is stirring in Aulis yet:
Nothing has roused
The guards on the ramparts.
Let us go in.

AG. O, you are fortunate,
Fortunate, all of you humble men,
Unknown, unhonoured, and free from fear!
Leaders may envy your lot.

SER. Ay, but glory is theirs.

AG. And in that glory lies their grief.
Suddenly, full in their pride of place
The wrath of the high gods shatters their life,
Or the quarrels of men
Mock them and thwart them.

SER. Are those the words of a chief? For shame!
You were not born for a life of ease,
Lord Agamemnon!
Joy and grief are a mortal's lot,
And the will of the high gods stronger than we.
But what has troubled you
All through the night? You kindled a torch,
Wrote on the tablet you hold in your hand,
Wrote and rewrote, sealed it, unsealed,
Dashed out the torch and burst into tears,
As though you were crazed.
Tell me, trust me, a faithful man,
Who came with your queen from her father's home,
One of the guard for the bride.

F. MELIAN STAWELL   (*Îphigenîa in Aulis*, 1–48)

387   *Night Watch*

CHORUS

SAY, whose is the watch? Who exchanges
   With us? The first planets to rise
Are setting; the Pleiadës seven
Move low on the margin of heaven,
And the Eagle is risen and ranges
   The mid-vault of the skies.
No sleeping yet! Up from your couches
   And watch on, the sluggards ye are!
The moon-maiden's lamp is yet burning.
Oh, the morning is near us, the morning!
Even now his fore-runner approaches,
   Yon dim-shining star.

Nay, hearken! Again she is crying
   Where death-laden Símoïs falls,
Of the face of dead Itys that stunned her,
Of grief grown to music and wonder:
Most changeful and old and undying
   The nightingale calls.
And on Ida the shepherds are waking
   Their flocks for the upland. I hear
The skirl of a pipe very distant.
And sleep it falls slow and insistent.
'Tis perilous sweet when the breaking
   Of dawn is so near.

GILBERT MURRAY   (*Rhêsus*, 527–37, 546–56)

The Death of Rhêsus

CHARIOTEER

DISASTER, yea: and with disaster shame,
  Which lights disaster to a twofold flame
Of evil. For to die in soldier's wise,
Since die we needs must . . . though the man who dies
Hath pain . . . to all his house 'tis praise and pride;
But we, like laggards and like fools we died!

  When Hector's hand had showed us where to rest
And told the watchword, down we lay, oppressed
With weariness of that long march, and slept
Just as we fell. No further watch was kept,
Our arms not laid beside us; by the horse
No yoke nor harness ordered. Hector's force
Had victory, so my master heard, and lay
Secure, just waiting for the dawn of day
To attack. So thought we all, and our lines broke
And slept. After a little time I woke,
Thinking about my horses, that the morn
Must see them yoked for war. I found the corn
And gave them plenteously. Then in the deep
Shadow I saw two men who seemed to creep
Close by our line, but swiftly, as I stirred,
Crouched and were seeking to make off unheard.
I shouted then, and bade them keep away:
Two thieves, I thought, from the great host that lay
Round us. They never answered, and, for me,
I said no more but turned and presently
Was sleeping. In my sleep there came a dream.
I seemed to see the horses—mine own team

I had trained long since and drove at Rhêsus' side—
But wolves were on their backs, wolves, couched astride,
Who drove and scourged; I saw the horses rear
And stagger with wide nostrils, stiff with fear,
And, starting up to drive the beasts away,
I woke.—A terror of great darkness lay
About me, but I lifted up my head
And listened. There was moaning, like the dead
That moan at night, and over me there flowed,
So soft, so warm—it was my master's blood,
Who writhed beside me, dying! With a bound
I sprang up, empty-handed, groping round
For spear or sword, when, lo, a young strong man
Was close to me and slashed, and the sword ran
Deep through my flank. I felt its passage well,
So deep, so wide, so spreading . . . then I fell.
And they, they got the bridles in their hand
And fled. . . . Ah! Ah! This pain. I cannot stand.
I know, I saw, thus much. But why or how
Those dead men went to death I cannot know,
Nor by whose work. But this I say; God send
'Tis not foul wrong wrought on us by a friend.

GILBERT MURRAY   (*Rhêsus*, 756–803)

389   *The Old Men*

ALAS, how right the ancient saying is:
We, who are old, are nothing else but noise
And shape. Like mimicries of dreams we go,
And have no wits, although we think us wise.

C. M. BOWRA   (*Æolus*)

Andrómeda

ANDRÓMEDA. PERSEUS

(*i*)

ANDR. Holy Night!
　　How long is the road of thy horses,
　　When thou drivest across the bright
　　Virginal spaces on high
　　Mid the starry courses
　　In the sacred expanse of sky.
　　And on thee, I call in thy cave,
　　Echo, to silence thy voice above me:
　　Ah, leave me alone to have
　　My fill of lament, and cry
　　With my maidens who love me.

(*ii*)

PERS. Maiden, I pity thee who hangest there.
ANDR. And who art thou who pitiest my sorrow?

(*iii*)

ANDR. Stranger, have pity on my misery
　　And loose me from my chains.

(*iv*)

PERS. Maid, if I save thee, wilt thou give me thanks?

(*v*)

ANDR. Do not by offering hopes force me to tears.
　　Much yet may chance of which we have no thought.
　　But lead me, stranger, to attend on thee,
　　If so it please, or as a wife, or slave.
C. M. BOWRA

(vi)

ANDR. O Love, our lord, of gods and men the king,
Either teach not how beauteous beauty is,
Or else, in troubles of thine own devising
Help lovers onward to a happy end.
Thus shalt thou gain high honour: otherwise
The loving lessons that men learn of thee
Will rob thee of their worship and goodwill.

When it befalls poor mortal men to love,
Should they find worthy objects for their loving,
There is no fuller joy on earth to long for.

After J. A. SYMONDS   (*Andrómeda*)

391   *There are no Gods*

DOTH some one say that there be gods above?
There are not; no, there are not. Let no fool,
Led by the old false fable, thus deceive you.
Look at the facts themselves, yielding my words
No undue credence: for I say that kings
Kill, rob, break oaths, lay cities waste by fraud,
And doing thus are happier than those
Who live calm pious lives day after day.
How many little States that serve the gods
Are subject to the godless but more strong,
Made slaves by might of a superior army!
And you, if any ceased from work and prayed
To gods, nor gathered in his livelihood,
Would learn gods are not. All Divinity
Is built up from our good and evil luck.

J. A. SYMONDS (to l. 11)   (*Bellerophon*)

392   *Children*

LADY, the sunlit hour is beautiful,
And beautiful, when winds blow soft, the sea,
And Earth in her spring flower, and affluent streams.
Of many beauties I could tell the praise,
But none there is beams on the eye so bright
As when the childless, heart-sore with desire,
See children like young buds about their house.

T. F. HIGHAM   (*Danaê*)

393   *Love is Idle*

LOVE is a sluggard, and for these things lives:
Mirrors he loves, and yellowed locks of hair,
But work he hates. One proof there is of this:
No man who seeks his bread has ever loved,
By wealthy men alone his power is felt.

C. M. BOWRA   (*Danaê*)

394   *Old Age*

LET my spear lie down for the spider to weave its
thread;
May Peace dwell with me at home when I grow old.
May I sing with garlands bound on my whitening head;
Let the pillared shrine of Pallas Athênê hold
My buckler from Thrace, while in books I unfold
Sweet words which the wise have said.

C. M. BOWRA   (*Erechtheus*)

395   *Six Letters*

LETTERS I cannot read, I have no skill;
   But I will tell their shapes and give clear signs.
A circle measured with the compasses—
And in the middle is a clear device.
The second sign is fashioned of two lines,
And these are parted by a third between.
The third is like a twisted lock of hair,
While in the fourth one line stands up erect,
And on it are three others propped askew.
The fifth is not so easy to describe:
Two lines there are that straddle off apart,
But run together to a single foot:
The last remaining one is like the third.

C. M. Bowra   (*Thêseus*)

396   *Pure Love*

BUT, truth to tell, men have another love,
   Love for an honest, sober, noble, heart.
And there should be a law for men, to love
All who are reverent and modest-minded,
And bid farewell to Cypris, child of Zeus.

C. M. Bowra   (*Thêseus*)

397   *Song of the Initiated*

LORD of Eurôpa's Tyrian line,
   Zeus-born, who holdest at thy feet
   The hundred citadels of Crete,
I seek to thee from that dim shrine,

Roofed by the quick and carven beam,
    By Chalyb steel and wild bull's blood
    In flawless joints of cypress wood
Made steadfast. There in one pure stream

My days have run, the servant I,
    Initiate, of Idæan Jove;
    Where midnight Zagreus roves, I rove;
I have endured his thunder-cry;

Fulfilled his red and bleeding feasts;
    Held the Great Mother's mountain flame;
    I am set free and named by name
A Bacchos of the Mailèd Priests.

GILBERT MURRAY   (*Crêtenses*)

398   *Vanity of Vanities*

TREAT well the living. Dead men are but dust
    And shadow: our nothingness to nothing goes.

ANON.   (*Meleâger*)

399   *What is Life?*

(i)

WHO knows if living after all is death,
    While death is counted life by those below?

C. M. BOWRA   (*Polyîdus*)

(ii)

WHO knows if that be life which we call death,
   And life be dying?—save alone that men
Living bear grief, but when they yield their breath
They grieve no more and have no sorrow then.

J. A. SYMONDS   (*Phrixus*)

400   *Take Life as it comes*

ACCEPT the counsel that I offer, lady.
   No mortal is born free from suffering:—
He buries children, and begets him new,
And also dies himself. And yet men grieve
At bringing earth to earth! It is Fate's will
To reap Life's harvest like the fruited ear,
That one should be, one not. Where is there cause
For grief, when only 'tis the path of Nature?
Nothing is dread that Fate makes necessary.

WALTER HEADLAM (from l. 2)   (*Hypsìpylê*)

401   *Earth and Sky*

O potent Earth, and Heaven god-built,—
   Of Heaven are god and man begot,
   And Earth brings forth to mortal lot
Fruits of the rain from Heaven spilt—

The grass she bears and wild things' breed:
   All-Mother rightly is her name.
   To Earth go back from Earth who came,
And what was born from skyey seed

461

Travels again to Heaven's field.
   There's nothing dies of all that's born;
   But one by other toss'd and torn
Old things are changed, and new revealed.

C. M. Bowra   (*Chrýsippus*)

402   *The Worst Horror*

DIRE is the violence of ocean waves,
   And dire the blast of rivers and hot fire,
And dire is want, and dire are countless things;
But nothing is so dire and dread as woman.
No painting could express her dreadfulness,
No words describe it. If a god made woman,
And fashioned her, he was for men the artist
Of woes unnumbered, and their deadly foe.

J. A. Symonds

403   *The Beginning of Day*

NOW the sweet-voiced nightingale
   In the woods takes up her tale,
Itys, *Itys* her refrain,
Waking grief to light again.
Shepherds on the hilly weald
Pipe their reeds to flocks afield;
Yellow foals in couples pass,
Roused from stall to eat their grass;
And the huntsman sets to work
Quartering where the wild beasts lurk.
Swans about the Ocean springs
Cry, and sweet their music rings;

Boats cast off and take the seas
Driven by oar and spanking breeze;
Sails, run up to catch the blow,
Bellying white to fore-stay go.

ANON.   (*Phaëthon*)

ANONYMOUS

404   *The Power of God*

DISTINGUISH god in your imaginings
    From men that die, think not of him as flesh.
You know him not. Sometimes he leaps in fire,
Swift, unapproachable; sometimes in water
Comes, or in the darkness clothed about,
And still is god in likeness of a beast,
In wind, cloud, lightning, thunder and rain.
The sea and all the rocks therein obey him;
Springs, rivers, tributaries all are his.
The mountains tremble, earth and the nethermost depths
Of monstrous ocean, earth and the mountain-tops
Tremble before the terrible eye of god,
A lord most powerful, in praise most high.

T. F. HIGHAM

405   *The Final Conflagration*

VERILY, verily that day shall come
    That rounds the sum of worldly destinies.
Then shall the gold-browed empyrean rend
His crammed repository. Flame, long-stored,
In fury shall consume the face of the earth

And the hung heavens; till, the whole being spent,
Deep-hollowed ocean shall be seen no more,
No more the earth, her last foundations fled,
And no bird float upon the burning air.
    This done, who shattered all, shall all restore.

T. F. HIGHAM

406   *Mais où est le preux Charlemagne?*

OLD pride and consequence, where lodge they now?
  Where's the great Lydian Crœsus? Xerxês where,
Whose yoke constrained the stiff-necked Hellespont?
One home, oblivion, in the pit they share.

T. F. HIGHAM

407   *Virtue*

POOR Virtue, she's but words,—a vain romance
  I took for truth; a slave of Circumstance.

T. F. HIGHAM

THUCYDIDÊS (?)

(471–401 B.C.)

408   *Euripidês*

ALL Greece is headstone to Euripidês;
  His bones let Macedon, his death-place, claim;
Athens his home, the very Greece of Greece;
  The world his Muse delighted owns his fame.

WALTER LEAF

464

PRAXILLA

(fl. 440 B.C.)

409 *The Lost World of Adonis*

I LOSE the sunlight, lovely above all else;
  Bright stars I loved the next, and the moon's face,
Ripe gourds, and fruit of apple-tree and pear.

T. F. HIGHAM

410 *At the Window*

LOOK to the lattice above
  For a pretty wonder,—
Down to the necklet—a girl,
  But a woman, under.

T. F. HIGHAM

ANONYMOUS

411 *Death*

THEN shall he lie in the earth
  Under the thick dark trees
Not hearing the lyre or the feasters' mirth
Or the flute's gay melodies.

C. M. BOWRA

ARISTOPHANÊS

412 *A Plea for the Enemy*

DICÆÓPOLIS

BEAR me no grudge, spectators, if, a beggar,
  I dare to speak before the Athenian people
About the city in a Comic Play.
For what is true even Comedy can tell.
And I shall utter startling things but true.

Nor now can Cleon slander me because,
With strangers present, I defame the State.
'Tis the Lênæa, and we're all alone;
No strangers yet have come; nor from the states
Have yet arrived the tribute and allies.
We're quite alone clean-winnowed: for I count
Our alien residents the civic bran.

  The Lacedæmonians I detest entirely;
And may Poseidon, Lord of Tænarum,
Shake all their houses down about their ears:
For I, like you, have had my vines cut down.
But after all—for none but friends are here—
Why the Laconians do we blame for this?
For men of ours, I do not say the State,
Remember this, I do not say the State,
But worthless fellows of a worthless stamp,
Ill-coined, ill-minted, spurious little chaps,
Kept on denouncing Mégara's little coats.
And if a cucumber or hare they saw,
Or sucking-pig, or garlic, or lump-salt,
All were Megarian, and were sold off-hand.
Still these were trifles, and our country's way.
But some young tipsy cottabus-players went
And stole from Mégara-town the fair Simætha.
Then the Megarians, garlicked with the smart,
Stole, in return, two of Aspásia's hussies.
From these three wantons o'er the Hellenic race
Burst forth the first beginnings of the War.
For then, in wrath, the Olympian Periclês
Thundered and lightened, and confounded Hellas,
Enacting laws which ran like drinking-songs,
That the Megarians presently depart

From earth and sea, the mainland, and the mart.
Then the Megarians, slowly famishing,
Besought their Spartan friends to get the Law
Of the three Wantons cancelled and withdrawn.
And oft they asked us, but we yielded not.
Then followed instantly the clash of shields.
Ye'll say *They should not*; but what should they, then?
Come now, had some Lacônian, sailing out,
Denounced and sold a small Serîphian dog,
Would you have sat unmoved? Far, far from that!
Ye would have launched three hundred ships of war,
And all the City had at once been full
Of shouting troops, of fuss with trierarchs,
Of paying wages, gilding Pallases,
Of rations measured, roaring colonnades,
Of wineskins, oar-loops, bargaining for casks,
Of nets of onions, olives, garlic-heads,
Of chaplets, pilchards, flute-girls, and black eyes.
And all the Arsenal had rung with noise
Of oar-spars planed, pegs hammered, oar-loops fitted,
Of boatswains' calls, and flutes, and trills, and whistles.
This had ye done; and shall not Têlephus,
Think we, do this? we've got no brains at all.

B. B. ROGERS   (*Acharnians*, 496–556)

413   *The Poet and the People*

CHORUS

SINCE first to exhibit his Plays he began,
   our Chorus-instructor has never
Come forth to confess in this public address
   how tactful he is and how clever.

But now that he knows he is slandered by foes
    before Athens so quick to assent,
Pretending he jeers our City and sneers
    at the People with evil intent,
He is ready and fain his cause to maintain
    before Athens so quick to repent.
Let honour and praise be the guerdon, he says,
    of the Poet whose satire has stayed you
From believing the orators' novel conceits
    wherewith they cajoled and betrayed you:
Who bids you despise adulation and lies,
    nor be citizens Vacant and Vain.
For before, when an embassy came from the states
    intriguing your favour to gain,
And called you the town of the VIOLET CROWN,
    so grand and exalted ye grew,
That at once on your tiptails erect ye would sit,
    those CROWNS were so pleasant to you.
And then, if they added the SHINY, they got
    whatever they asked for their praises,
Though apter, I ween, for an oily sardine
    than for you and your City the phrase is.
By this he's a true benefactor to you,
    and by showing with humour dramatic
The way that our wise democratic allies
    are ruled by our State democratic.
And therefore their people will come oversea,
    their tribute to bring to the City,
Consumed with desire to behold and admire
    the poet so fearless and witty,
Who dared in the presence of Athens to speak
    the thing that is rightful and true.

468

And truly the fame of his prowess, by this,
    has been bruited the universe through,
When the Sovereign of Persia, desiring to test
    what the end of our warfare will be,
Inquired of the Spartan ambassadors, first,
    which nation is queen of the sea,
And next, which the wonderful Poet has got,
    as its stern and unsparing adviser;
For those who are lashed by his satire, he said,
    must surely be better and wiser,
And they'll in the war be the stronger by far,
    enjoying his counsel and skill.
And therefore the Spartans approach you to-day
    with proffers of Peace and Goodwill,
Just asking indeed that Ægina ye cede;
    and nought do they care for the isle,
But you of the Poet who serves you so well
    they fain would despoil and beguile.
But be *you* on your guard nor surrender the bard;
    for his Art shall be righteous and true.
Rare blessings and great will he work for the State,
    rare happiness shower upon you;
Not fawning, or bribing, or striving to cheat
    with an empty unprincipled jest;
Not seeking your favour to curry or nurse,
    but teaching the things that are best.

B. B. ROGERS   (*Acharnians*, 628–58)

DEMOSTHENÊS

WITH reverence to your worships, 'tis our fate
  To have a testy, cross-grain'd, bilious, sour
Old fellow for our master; one much giv'n
To a bean-diet; somewhat hard of hearing:
Dêmos his name, sirs, of the parish Pnyx here.
Some three weeks back or so, this lord of ours
Brought home a lusty slave from Paphlagonia,
Fresh from the tan-yard, tight and yare, and with
As nimble fingers and as foul a mouth
As ever yet paid tribute to the gallows.
This tanner-Paphlagonian (for the fellow
Wanted not penetration) bow'd and scraped,
And fawn'd and wagg'd his ears and tail, dog-fashion:
And thus soon slipp'd into the old man's graces.
Occasional douceurs of leather-parings,
With speeches to this tune, made all his own.
'Good sir, the court is up,—you've judg'd one cause,
'Tis time to take the bath: allow me, sir,—
This cake is excellent—pray sup this broth—
This soup will not offend you, tho' cropfull—
You love an obolus: pray take these three—
Honour me, sir, with your commands for supper.'
Sad times meanwhile for us!—with prying looks,
Round comes my man of hides, and if he finds us
Cooking a little something for our master,
Incontinently lays his paw upon it,
And modestly in his own name presents it!
It was but t'other day these hands had mixt
A Spartan pudding for him: there—at Pylos:

Slily and craftily the knave stole on me,
Ravish'd the feast and to my master bore it.
Then none but he, forsooth, must wait at table:
(We dare not come in sight) but there he stands
All supper-time, and with a leathern fly-lap
Whisks off the advocates: anon the knave
Chants out his oracles, and when he sees
The old man plung'd in mysteries to the ears,
And scared from his few senses, marks his time,
And enters on his tricks. False accusations
Now come in troops; and at their heels the whip.
Meanwhile the rascal shuffles in among us,
And begs of one,—browbeats another,—cheats
A third, and frightens all. 'My honest friends,
These cords cut deep, you'll find it—I say nothing,—
Judge you between your purses and your backs:
I could perhaps'—We take the gentle hint,
And give him all: if not, the old man's foot
Plays such a tune upon our hinder parts,
That flogging is a jest to't, a mere flea-bite.

T. MITCHELL   (*Knights*, 40–70)

415   *The Poet and his Rivals*

CHORUS

IF one of the comedy-makers of old had attempted to
order the Knights
To come forward and speak to the House in his name,
    we'd have said he exceeded his rights,

But this man really merits our help. He has hated the
things we hate,

Defended the Right, and fronted the Storm, stood fast in
the roaring Spate.

Now he tells us that dozens of people have come, and asked
him, in some surprise,

Why he hasn't produced his plays himself, long ago, without any disguise.

Well, he wants us to say he has waited so long not for
nothing, but—so he insists—

Because the production of Comedy is the most ticklish
thing that exists.

Our fair Comic Muse is courted, he says, by hundreds,
but smiles upon few.

Besides he has read your natures of old; you were annual
plants, he knew,

You had never kept faith with the poets you loved; just
used them and thrown them away.

He thought of what Magnês suffered, as soon as his
temples began to be grey,

Though there never had been such a chorus as his, such
a winner of prize upon prize,

Though he uttered all manner of varying sounds with his
Lutes and his *Wings* and his *Flies*,

Though he talked like a *Lydian*, turned green like a *Frog*.
Not enough! In the valley of years,

Though never in youth, he was hissed off the stage. 'There
was not enough life in his jeers!'

Of Cratînus he thought, at the height of his power, like a
flood that burst through the level,

Till oaks, planes, enemies, up by the roots went flying, and
off to the Devil;

472

When never a song at a banquet was heard but *Slipper of Silvery Tips*,

Or *Songful Grafters of Glutinous Palms*; 'twas a glory that none could eclipse.

And now, when you see him doddering past, for shame! have you nothing to say,

When he walks in a maze, like Connas of old, his lyre far gone in decay,

With the pegs dropping out, and the strings out of tune, and the joints of the framework burst,

The flowers of his garland of victory dead, and the old boy dying of thirst?

Why, if men had their rights, he should drink at his ease at the Hearth of Athêna, and sit

Beside Dionŷsus here, clad in his best, in return for those glories of wit.

Then Cratês, too, what tempers of yours and buffetings *he* underwent!

Light lunches he gave you, at little expense, and dismissed you amused and content;

He made you the neatest confections of wit, well-phrased by the driest of lips;

He did—he only—hold out to the end, and stood—with occasional slips . . .

Their fate made him nervous and willing to wait; and besides he felt perfectly clear

That a sailor must first learn to manage his oar before he professes to steer;

And, next after that, take his stand at the prow and study the winds and the weather;

And then, last of all, rule the vessel himself. For all these reasons together,

473

And because he was modest, and didn't rush in and brawl
    with incompetence horrid,
Come, a shout like the sea, a salute with all oars!
A Lênêan salute till the theatre roars!
And so let your poet in triumph depart
    With a smile in his heart
And a gleaming expanse on his forehead.

GILBERT MURRAY   (*Knights*, 507–50)

416   *Dêmos Rejuvenated*

OFFAL-MONGER. CHORUS

o.m. Now peace, and be still! A seal on your lips! Let
    the witness-box echo no voices!

    Shut be the gates of the Jurors' Courts, wherein this
    people rejoices.

    Let the Theatre sing for the news I bring, and wel-
    come a wondrous tale!

cho. O star in the night to Athens the Blest, O help of the
    Islands, hail!

    Say what glad thing is this that you bring, and our
    altars shall smoke in the street.

o.m. I have boiled your Dêmos in magical herbs, and
    turned him from rotten to sweet!

cho. O worker of wonders! Where standeth he now, or
    where hath he laid him down?

o.m. He dwells in the Athens of ancient days, in Her of
    the violet crown.

cho. How can we look on him? How is he changed?
    What like in carriage and dress?

o.m. As he was when he sat at Miltíadês' side and with
    great Aristîdês at mess.

But soon ye shall see him. There, hearken, above us
    the Gates of the Rock unfold.

Uplift your voices and open your eyes on Athens,
    the Athens of old.

The wonderful City, the City of song, true home of
    our Dêmos! Behold!

CHO. O shining Athens, O violet-crowned, O blest all
    cities above,

Unveil to our eyes the Lord of the Greeks, the Lord
    of the Land we love!

O.M. It is he, in the clean grave raiment of old, the grass-
    hopper bright on his crown,

No longer he smells of balloting shells, but of Peace
    and myrrh running down.

CHO. All hail, O King over Hellas the Great, we rejoice
    in thy joy! For again

Thy life is worthy of Athens and true to the Trophy
    on Marathon plain.

GILBERT MURRAY   (*Knights*, 1316–34)

417   *Socrates' Experiments*

STREPSÍADÊS. DISCIPLE

STR. Well, I must go. Why keep on loitering here?
    Why don't I knock and enter?—Hoa! within
    there!—   (*Knocks violently at the door.*)

DIS. (*half-opening the door*) Go, hang yourself! and give
    the crows a dinner—
    What noisy fellow hammered at the door?

STR. Strepsíadês of Cicýnna, son of Pheidon.

DIS. However named, 'fore Heaven, you're a fool
    Not to respect these doors; battering so loud,

475

And kicking with such vengeance, you have marred
The ripe conception of my pregnant brain,
And brought on a miscarriage.

STR.   Oh! the pity!—
Pardon my ignorance: I'm country bred
And far afield am come: I pray you tell me
What curious thought my luckless din has strangled,
Just as your brain was hatching.

DIS.   These are things
We never speak of but amongst ourselves.

STR. Speak boldly then to me, for I am come
To be amongst you, and partake the secrets
Of your profound academy.

DIS.   Enough!
I will impart, but set it down in thought
Amongst our mysteries—This is the question,
As it was put but now to Chærophôn,
By our great master Socratês, to answer—
How many of his own lengths at one spring
A flea can hop—for we did see one vault
From brow of Chærophôn onto the head
Of the philosopher.

STR.   And how did t'other
Contrive to measure this?

DIS.   Most accurately:
He dipt the insect's feet in melted wax,
Which, hardening into sandals as it cooled,
Gave him the space by rule infallible.

STR. Imperial Zeus! what subtilty of thought!

T. MITCHELL   (*Clouds*, 131-53)

418   *Song of the Clouds*

CHORUS

Clouds, ever drifting in air,
Rise, O dewy anatomies, shine to the world in splendour.
   Upward from thundering Ocean who fathered us
   rise, make way to the forested pinnacles.
      There let us gaze upon
   summits aërial opening under us;
   Earth, most holy, and fruits of our watering;
   rivers melodious, rich in divinity;
   seas, deep-throated, of echo reverberant.
Rise, for his Eye, many-splendoured, unwearying,
      burns in the front of Heaven.
   Shake as a cloak from our heavenly essences
   vapour and rain, and at Earth in our purity
      with far-seeing eye let us wonder.

      Maidens that minister rain,
Come, gaze down on the city of Pallas, the land of Cecrops.
   O for the lustre, the manhood, the charm of her!
   There are the Rites unspoken, inviolate,—
      holy solemnities
   calling the faithful to Mysteries visible.
   Treasures of marble in high-roofed sanctuaries
   honour the Blessèd; and holy processionals,
   feast and blood-offering, wreathing of flower on
      flower
      praise everlasting give them.
   Merrily also the choirs of Brómios
   herald the Spring with a battle of melody
      and music of clarinet droning.

T. F. HIGHAM   (*Clouds*, 275–90, 299–313)

419   *The Old Education*

JUST ARGUMENT. UNJUST ARGUMENT

J.A. Now hear the old Rule,
      Of instruction at school,—
         I'll tell you the way it was done, sir;
      When, with morals at par,
      It still paid me to air
         The good and the right as a preacher.
      First of all, not a boy
      Was allowed to annoy
         With a sound from his mouth, never one, sir!
      But sober and solemn
      Our parish's column
         Of lads for the local lute-teacher
      Without coats on would go
      Through the streets, though the snow
         Might be snowing as thickly as bran there;
      And he'd see to each learning
      The song without turning
         His backside too near the next man there.
      They would learn simple ditties:
      'The sacker of cities,
         Great Pallas', or 'Echoed a far cry . . .'
      Some classic passed on
      From father to son,
         Pitched high as a Dorian war-cry.
      No play to the gallery!
      No Phrŷnis' fallalery
         Of twisting the tongue round a trill!

478

  For all such abuses
  That murder the Muses
   We'd beat them and beat with a will!

U.A. If you let him persuade you,
  My boy, I'm afraid you
   Will be—bear me out Dionŷsus!—
  Like Hippócratês' sons,—
  It's a sucker, a dunce,
   You'll be nicknamed, and that won't surprise us!

J.A. Well, I think, you'll be found
  On the Track or the Ground,
   And bright fit and busy all day, sir!
  Not like moderns be mouthing
  An ultra-sharp nothing
   Of wit on the boulevards paraded;
  Nor stand, brought to book
  By a slick-mannered crook
   Who quibbles your credit away, sir!
  No sir, you will go
  Where in Ácademe grow
   The worshipful trees colonnaded,
  Running lap after lap
  With some sensible chap
   Of your age, till you finish your measure;
  On your brow there will shine
  The rushes you twine,
   And a savour of let-live and leisure
  The catkins descending
  With bryony blending
   In fragrance around you be wreathing;

And you'll laugh in the prime
　　Of the fresh spring-time
　　　When the plane to the elm-tree is breathing.
GEORGE ALLEN, T. F. HIGHAM　　　(*Clouds*, 961–71, 1000–8)

420　　*The Trial of the Dog*

PHILOCLEON. BDELYCLEON. DOG. SÔSIAS

PH.　Defendant?

BD.　　　　　　Here he is.

PH.　　　　　　　　　　　He'll get it hot.

BD.　Now hear the charge:—A dog from Cydathên
　　　Accuses Labês of Aixônê here
　　　Of being sole consumer of the cheese
　　　Of our Sicilian branch. He thus incurs
　　　The grafter's collar, snapt about his neck.

PH.　He'll die a dog's death, if we find him guilty.

BD.　Here Labês stands, defendant in this case.

PH.　What a bounder! look, he's got a burglar's mug,
　　　Thinking he'll fix me with that toothy grin.
　　　But where is he who prosecutes the charge,
　　　The dog from Cydathên?

DOG.　　　　　　　　　　　Auw-wuff, auw-wuff.

BD.　He stands.

PH.　　　　　　But this is Labês' absolute double.

BD.　He's guaranteed to bark and lick the dishes.
　　　(*to dog*) Ssh, down sir! (*to Sôsias*) You there, rise
　　　　　　and bring your charge.

PH.　Give me a helping of the lentil-soup.

SÔ.　Gentlemen of the jury, you have listened
　　　Attentively to this the charge preferred

480

        Against the prisoner:—In the fo'c'sle mess
        He did the dirty by the boys and me;
        For running off to a corner in the dark
        He lined his person with Sicilian cheese—

PH. Yes, that he did; at any rate, just now
        He broke his nasty cheesy breath on me,
        The beast.

SÔ.   I said 'please pass the cheese,'—he wouldn't.

BD. For god's sake, father, don't prejudge the case
        Until you've heard both sides.

PH.   But don't you see
        The matter's obvious? it speaks for itself.

SÔ. And don't acquit him, either; of all dogs
        That man's the most unsociable at meals.
        And round and round he licked the platter clean,
        Scraping the cities even of their rind.

PH. I'm even out of paste to mend my pots.

SÔ. Then punish him. Two burglars of a feather
        Can't feed together on one currant bush.
        (*earnestly, to Philocleon*) I think my prosecution
            should not prove
        Useless; for if it does, from that day on
        I'll never bark again.

PH. (*really shocked*) Perish the thought!
        The crimes the prosecution charged him with!
        The man's a mass of theft. (*to his cock*) Hey, Cocka-
            doodle,
        Don't you agree? (*to the court*) You see, it's blinking
        'yes'.

BD. (*to Philocleon*) For a change you might stop being
            surly now
        And nasty, specially at defendants' heels.

Why *must* you fix your teeth in them? (*to Labês*)
    Get up,
And plead your case! Why are you dumb, sir?
    Speak!

PH. He doesn't seem to have a word to say.

BD. No, but the way it seems to be with him
Reminds me of Thucydidês' bad luck
In court. He got paralysis of the jaws
    Suddenly. (*to Labês*) Well, stand down. I'll plead
        myself.
    (*to the court*) It is not easy, gentlemen, to speak
Considering my client is a dog
With a bad name; but speak for him I will.
He's a good dog and scares the wolves away.

PH. A burglar's what he is, one of the gang.

BD. No, of contemporary dogs my client
Ranks first, considering the flocks he can guard.

PH. What is the use of that, if he eats cheese?

BD. What use? to fight for you and guard the door,
And good all round. And if he did take pickings,
Be kind; he's had no Higher Education.

PH. Tut, tut. What's this damned feeling making me
        soft?
    There's something coming over me, I'm yielding.

BD. O I beseech you, father, pity him
And do not drag him down! Where are his pups?
Get up, you poor little things, and whimper there,
Just supplicate and obsecrate and cry.

PH. (*overcome*) Down, down; you've won; down, down, sir!

BD.   I'll get down.
And yet that 'down, you've won' has up to date
Diddled a lot of us—but I'll get down.

PH. O hell! It isn't good to gulp like this.
   To think I've cried away my purpose, just
   Because of being full of lentil-soup.

BD. Is he Not Guilty then?

PH.   It's hard to say.

BD. My dearest Pa, to better courses turn;
   Just put your ballot in the second box
   And shut your eyes, slip through, and vote Not
   Guilty.

PH. Not me! I lack the Higher Education.

BD. Well, hurry. I'll take you round the quickest way.

PH. Is that box first, for 'Guilty'?

BD. (*ambiguously, his father pointing to the wrong box first*)
                                    That's the first.

PH. Well, there's my vote.

BD.   (*to himself*) Father's been taken in,
   Voting Not Guilty unawares. (*to the court*) Allow me
   To draw the votes.

PH.   How has the battle been?

BD. The event will tell. Not Guilty, Labês! Father!
   Father! What is the matter? Water, ho!
   Be very brave now.

PH.   Tell me then just this,
   Is he in actual fact Not Guilty?

BD.   Yes.
   He is Not Guilty.

PH.   Then am I laid low.

GEORGE ALLEN   (*Wasps*, 893–914, 919–34, 942–59, 973–97)

483

421 *To Heaven on a Beetle*

TRYGÆUS. SERVANT

TRY. (*to the beetle*) Easy, Ned, easy, go soft, an it
please 'ee,
Be patient, don't hustle in pride of your muscle
And zoom from the mark like a giddy young spark;
No, no, you must let yourself work to a sweat,
And, as you begin, you will supple the sinew
With a regular swing from the joints of the wing.
This too I must teach you:—Not a breath . . . I
beseech you!
If you're taken that way, it's at home you will stay,
For your wind is as foul as your diet.

SER. My poor lord and master! what crazy disaster . . .

TRY. Be quiet, I tell you, be quiet!

SER. O where and O where do you thresh through the air?

TRY. I fly for the sake of all Hellas, and take
To the perilous skies on a new enterprise.

SER. Must you *fly*? O it's vanity, hopeless insanity . . .

TRY. Not a sound should be heard of an ill-omened
word,—
Let nothing slip out but a jubilant shout!
Bid the whole human race be hushed and replace
Good brickwork again at midden and drain;
Stop up any crack, and every man jack
From the motions of nature refrain.

T. F. HIGHAM   (*Peace*, 82–101)

422   *The Hoopoe's Call*

HOOPOE

(i)

(To his wife Procnê, the nightingale)

DEAR comrade, arise, from slumber awake,
    let flow the sad rapture of hallowed song;
mindful of Itys, ever-wept, sing on,
tell again old tales of your sorrow and mine.
There's a throbbing in air as the heavenly cry
            of your brown bright throat
travels up, flung clear through the bryony-leaf
skyward to high-throned Zeus in his heaven.
To the sorrowful sound golden Apollo
gives ear, and a sweet response strikes out
on his ivoried lute. Ranged round to his will
celestial choirs in unison chant,
giving out from lips immortal a sound
loud-voiced, of all heaven acclaiming.

(A pipe-solo follows, representing the nightingale.)

(ii)

*(A general call to the birds. The bird-notes in italics are
    those of Procnê breaking in.)*

Epopoi
popo popo popo poi
Iô iô
itô itô itô itô

Come one, come all,
my feathered folk,
fly over!
The farm-lands forsake,
the rich fields of grain,
from barley-feast and seed-picking up and away
strong generations of birds
fluttering innumerable,
swift, and smoothly calling.
Up from the arable come you
smaller folk about the clods with pipe so slender
twittering for gladness.

tio tio tio tio
tio tio tio tio

Hurry over
from the ivied
city gardens,—
quick! from your forage begone!
From the hill hurry you
strippers of the bush-olive,
nibblers of the arbute,—
flit across the air to me,
hurry,
obey my call!
Marshy dyke
leave you now
all who snap
piercing gnats.
Water-fowl,
leave the moist
meadow-lands;

486

seek no more
heart's delight
deep in green
Marathon.
Hither come all,
hither come *you*
speckled and splashed
francolin
francolin!

Birds of all feather, the sea's generations,
over the billows with halcyons flying,
hasten you hither, await our intelligence.
Here at our summoning, flock upon flock of them,
All birds long-throated assemble.

T. F. HIGHAM   (*Birds*, 209–22, 227–54)

423   *The Hymn of the Birds*

CHORUS

COME on then, ye dwellers by nature in darkness,
and like to the leaves' generations,
That are little of might, that are moulded of mire,
unenduring and shadow-like nations,
Poor plumeless ephemerals, comfortless mortals,
as visions of shadows fast fleeing,
Lift up your mind unto us that are deathless,
and dateless the date of our being:
Us, children of heaven, us, ageless for aye,
us, all of whose thoughts are eternal;
That ye may from henceforth, having heard of us
all things aright as to matters supernal,

Of the being of birds, and beginning of gods,
    and of streams, and the dark beyond reaching,
Truthfully knowing aright, in my name
    bid Prodicus pack with his preaching.
  It was Chaos and Night at the first, and the black-
    ness of darkness, and Hell's broad border,
Earth was not, nor air, neither heav'n; when in depths
    of the womb of the dark without order
First thing first-born of the black-plumed Night
    was a wind-egg hatched in her bosom,
Whence timely with seasons revolving again
    sweet Love burst out as a blossom,
Gold wings gleaming forth of his back,
    like whirlwinds gustily turning.
He, after his wedlock with Chaos, whose wings
    are of darkness, in Hell broad-burning,
For his nestlings begat him the race of us first,
    and upraised us to light new-lighted,
And before this was not the race of the gods,
    until all things by Love were united:
And of kind united with kind in communion
    of nature the sky and the sea are
Brought forth, and the earth, and the race of the gods
    everlasting and blest. So that we are
Far away the most ancient of all things blest.
    And that we are of Love's generation
There are manifest manifold signs. We have wings,
    and with us have the Loves habitation. . . .
  All best good things that befall men come
    from us birds, as is plain to all reason;
For first we proclaim and make known to them spring,
    and the winter and autumn in season:

Bid sow, when the crane starts clanging for Afric,
    in shrill-voiced emigrant number,
And calls to the pilot to hang up his rudder
    again for the season, and slumber;
And then weave cloak for Orestês the thief,
    lest he strip men of theirs if it freezes.
And again thereafter the kite reappearing
    announces a change in the breezes,
And that here is the season for shearing your sheep
    of their spring wool. Then does the swallow
Give you notice to sell your greatcoat, and provide
    something light for the heat that's to follow.
Thus are we as Ammon or Delphi untò you,
    Dôdôna, nay, Phœbus Apollo.
For, as first ye come all to get auguries of birds,
    even such is in all things your carriage,
Be the matter a matter of trade or of earning
    your bread, or of any one's marriage.
And all things ye lay to the charge of a bird
    that belong to discerning prediction:
Winged fame is a bird, as you reckon: you sneeze,
    and the sign's as a bird for conviction:
All tokens are 'birds' with you—sounds too, and lackeys,
    and donkeys. Then must it not follow
That we ARE to you all as the manifest godhead
    that speaks in prophetic Apollo?

A. C. SWINBURNE   (*Birds*, 685–704, 708–22)

489

424   *The Birds' Life*

CHORUS

ALL the wide world now I sway
    And my subject realm survey;
Mortals all to me shall bring
Votive prayer and offering.
For the whole earth I defend,
All her thriving fruits I tend;
One and all I slay the brood
That preys on every ripening bud,
Sits on trees and sucks their fruit,
Or mining saps the secret root.
Through the damask gardens I
Seize the reptile, chase the fly,
Whoe'er with harmful power presume
To waste the sweets or soil the bloom;
    Crushed by my wing the felons lie.

    Happy race of birds, that wear
No fleece to fend the winter's air;
Nor can summer's beaming ray
Scorch us through the sultry day.
Bosomed deep in leafy green
Us the flowery meadows screen,
While the shrill cicala cries
Rapt in noontide ecstasies.
When the wintry time is come
In hollow caves I make my home
And with hill-top nymphs delight;

Then with spring the grounds invite
Of garden-plots the Graces till;
Browsing there we crop our fill
Of myrtle-berries maiden-white.

After H. F. CARY   (*Birds*, 1058–70, 1088–1100)

425   *The Building of Cloudcuckoocity*

MESSENGER. PISTHETAIROS

(*Enter a Messenger, breathlessly.*)

M. Wh-wh—wh-wh—wh-where's he, wh—wh-where's
the city-prefect Pisthetairos?   P. Here.

M. The building's done, your wall complete.   P. Good
news.

M. A perfect structure, on the grandest scale!
Along the top Proxenidês the Braggart
might meet Theógenês, his fellow, driving
horses, the pair of them, huge as the Trojan,
and pass—so wide the road is.   P. Hêraklês!

M. In height it measures (as I proved myself)
six hundred feet.   P. Poseidon! that's a height!
Who were the builders of a wall so big?

M. Birds, only birds. Brick-carriers from Egypt,
stone-masons, carpenters—not one was there!
Alone they built it,—a marvel of hand-labour!
Some thirty thousand cranes, from Libya flown,
disgorged foundation-stones they'd lifted over;
These same the rasping corn-crakes pecked to shape,
while storks, ten thousand strong, fetched up the bricks.
Water was carried skyward from below
by lapwings and the like, birds of the river.

491

p. And who served mortar to the builders? m. Herons,
in hods.   p. And how were hodfuls loaded in?

m. That, my dear fellow, was the cleverest touch!
Web-footed geese struck down into the mortar
and heaved them hodfuls up, like shovellers.

p. There's nothing to which we cannot turn our—feet.

m. And damme if the ducks, with aprons on,
weren't laying bricks! Behind, for hard cement
bearing their clay in bill (as little lads
will serve a mason) up the swallows flew.

p. What need to go on hiring hired labour?
But now, let's see . . . what birds about the wall
faced off the woodwork? m. Woodpeckers were there,
carpenters of the best, who used their beaks
to hack the gateways trim—with a knocking noise
tap-tap-tapping like shipwrights in a dockyard.
Now the last detail is complete—gates fitted,
bolted and barred,—sentry-posts in a ring,
guards visited, the bellman going round,
everywhere watchmen set and beacons ready
up on the barbicans.

T. F. Higham   (*Birds*, 1122–62)

426   *The Wedding Chant*

CHORUS

WHEN Olympian Hêra was given
In marriage, the Fates on a day
Led Zeus, in the height of his heaven,
To her bed, singing loud all the way,—
With a Hymen O!
Hymenaios,
Hymen O Hymenaios!

Love rode for good luck in the carriage,
　　　The child of a couple who throve;
Happy bride! with a groom to her marriage
　　　Gold-winged, pulling back as he drove,—
　　　　　With a Hymen O!
　　　　　　Hymenaios,
　　　　　　　Hymen O Hymenaios!

T. F. HIGHAM　　　　　　　　　　(*Birds*, 1731–43)

427　　　*How the Women will stop War*

MAGISTRATE. LŶSISTRATA

MAG.　You, I presume, could adroitly and gingerly
　　　　　settle this intricate, tangled concern:
　　　You in a trice could relieve our perplexities.

LYS.　　　Certainly.

MAG.　　　　　　　　How? Permit me to learn.

LYS.　Just as a woman, with nimble dexterity,
　　　　　thus with her hands disentangles a skein,
　　　Hither and thither her spindles unravel it,
　　　　　drawing it out, and pulling it plain.
　　　So would this weary Hellenic entanglement
　　　　　soon be resolved by our womanly care,
　　　So would our embassies neatly unravel it,
　　　　　drawing it here and pulling it there.

MAG.　Wonderful, marvellous feats, not a doubt of it,
　　　　　you with your skeins and your spindles can
　　　　　　show:
　　　Fools! do you really expect to unravel a
　　　　　terrible war like a bundle of tow?

LYS.　Ah, if you only could manage your politics
　　　　　just in the way that we deal with a fleece!

493

MAG. Tell us the recipe.

LYS.   First, in the washing-tub
      plunge it, and scour it, and cleanse it from
         grease,
Purging away all the filth and the nastiness;
      then on the table expand it and lay,
Beating out all that is worthless and mischievous,
      picking the burrs and the thistles away.
Next, for the clubs, the cabals, and the coteries,
      banding unrighteously, office to win,
Treat them as clots in the wool, and dissever them,
      lopping the heads that are forming therein.
Then you should card it, and comb it, and mingle it,
      all in one Basket of love and of unity,
Citizens, visitors, strangers, and sojourners,
      all the entire, undivided community.
Know you a fellow in debt to the Treasury?
      Mingle him merrily in with the rest.
Also remember the cities, our colonies,
      outlying states in the east and the west,
Scattered about to a distance surrounding us,
      these are our shreds and our fragments of wool;
These to one mighty political aggregate
      tenderly, carefully, gather and pull,
Twining them all in one thread of good fellowship;
      thence a magnificent bobbin to spin,
Weaving a garment of comfort and dignity,
      worthily wrapping the People therein.

MAG. Heard any ever the like of their impudence,
      those who have nothing to do with the war,
Preaching of bobbins, and beatings, and washing-
         tubs?

LYS.   Nothing to do with it, wretch that you are!
        We are the people who feel it the keenliest,
              doubly on us the affliction is cast;
        Where are the sons that we sent to your battle-fields?

MAG.   Silence! a truce to the ills that are past.

LYS.   Then in the glory and grace of our womanhood,
              all in the May and the morning of life,
        Lo, we are sitting forlorn and disconsolate,
              what has a soldier to do with a wife?
        We might endure it, but ah! for the younger ones,
              still in their maiden apartments they stay,
        Waiting the husband that never approaches them,
              watching the years that are gliding away.

MAG.   Men, I suppose, have their youth everlastingly.

LYS.   Nay, but it isn't the same with a man:
        Grey though he be when he comes from the battle-
                  field,
              still if he wishes to marry, he can.
        Brief is the spring and the flower of our womanhood,
              once let it slip, and it comes not again;
        Sit as we may with our spells and our auguries,
              never a husband will marry us then.

B. B. ROGERS   (*Lýsistrata*, 565–97)

428   *Hymn of Peace*
CHORUSES OF ATHENIANS AND SPARTANS

ATHENIANS. Now for the Chorus, the Graces, the
              minstrelsy,
        Call upon Artemis, queen of the glade:
        Call on her brother, the Lord of festivity,
        Holy and gentle one, mighty to aid.

Call upon Bacchus, afire with his Mænadës:
Call upon Zeus, in the lightning arrayed;
Call on his queen, ever blessèd, adorable;
Call on the holy, infallible Witnesses,
Call them to witness the peace and the harmony,
This which divine Aphrodîtê has made.
Allala! Lallala! Lallala, lallala!
Whoop for victory, Lallalalæ!
Evoi! Evoi! Lallala, Lallala!
Evæ! Evæ! Lallalalæ.

SPARTANS. Leave Tâÿgety, an' quickly
Hither, Muse Lacônian, come.
Hymn the Gude o' braw Amyclæ,
Hymn Athâna, Brassin-dome.
Hymn the Tyndarids, for ever
Sportin' by Eurôtas river.
Noo then, noo the step begin,
Twirlin' licht the fleecy skin;
Sae we'se join our blithesome voices,
Praisin' Sparta, loud an' lang,
Sparta wha of auld rejoices
In the Choral dance an' sang.
O to watch her bonnie dochters
Sport alang Eurôtas' waters!
Winsome feet for ever plyin',
Fleet as fillies, wild an' gay,
Winsome tresses tossin', flyin',
As o' Bacchanals at play.
Lêda's dochter, on before us,
Pure an' sprety, guides the Chorus.
         Onward go,
    Whilst your eager hand represses

496

A' the glory o' your tresses;
Whilst your eager foot is springin'
          Like the roe;
Whilst your eager voice is singin'
Praise to her in might excellin'
Goddess of the Brassin' dwellin'.

B. B. ROGERS   (*Lŷsistrata*, 1279–94, 1296–1321)

429   *Euripidês*

SCYTHIAN. MNÊSÍLOCHUS. EURIPIDÊS

(*The Scythian brings Mnêsílochus in, fastened to his plank, and sets it up on the stage.*)

SC. Dere now bemoany to de ouder air.

MN. O, I entreat you.

SC.   Nod endread me zu.

MN. Slack it a little.

SC.   Dat is vat I does.

MN. O mercy! mercy! O, you drive it tighter.

SC. Dighder zu wiss him?

MN.   Miserable me!
Out on you villain.

SC.   Zilence, bad ole man.
I'se fetch de mad, an vatch zu comfibly.

MN. These are the joys Euripidês has brought me!

(*Euripidês makes a momentary appearance as Perseus.*)

O Gods! O saviour Zeus! there's yet a hope.
Then he won't fail me! Out he flashed as Perseus.
I understand the signals, I'm to act
The fair Andrómeda in chains. Ah, well,

Here are the chains, worse luck, wherewith to act her.
He'll come and succour me; he's in the wings.

(*Euripidês enters singing.*)

EUR.   Now to peep, now to creep
           Soft and slily through.
        Maidens, pretty maidens,
           Tell me what I am to do.
        Tell me how to glide
        By the Scythian Argus-eyed,
        And to steal away my bride,
     Tell me, tell me, tell me, tell me, tell me, tell me,
           tell,
     Echo always lurking in the cavern and the dell. . . .
                                              (*Exit.*)

        (*Euripidês speaks in the voice of Echo from
        behind the scenes.*)

EUR.   O welcome, daughter; but the Gods destroy
        Thy father Cêpheus, who exposed thee thus!

MN.   O, who art thou that mournest for my woes?

EUR.   Echo, the vocal mocking-bird of song,
        I, who, last year, in these same lists contended,
        A faithful friend, beside Euripidês.
        And now, my child, for thou must play thy part,
        Make dolorous wails.

MN.   And you wail afterwards?

EUR.   I'll see to that; only begin at once.

MN.   O Night most holy,
        O'er dread Olympus, vast and far,
           In thy dark car
           Thou journeyest slowly
        Through Ether ridged with many a star.

498

EUR.   With many a star.

MN.   Why on Andrómeda ever must flow
       Sorrow and woe?

EUR.   Sorrow and woe?

MN.   Heavy of fate.

EUR.   Heavy of fate.

MN.   Old woman, you'll kill me, I know, with your prate.

EUR.   Know with your prate.

MN.   Why, how tiresome you are: you are going too far.

EUR.   You are going too far.

MN.   Good friend, if you kindly will leave me in peace,
       You'll do me a favour, O prithee, cease.

EUR.   Cease.

B. B. ROGERS   (*Thesmophoriazûsæ*, 1000–21, 1056–78)

430   *The Frogs' Song*

FROGS. DIONŶSUS

(*The* FROGS *call the time for* DIONŶSUS, *who is rowing*
CHARON'S *boat. Their first song is lenient in rhythm, but
its final croak sets a brisk pace.*)

FR.   Brékeke·kéx ko·áx ko·áx,
         brékeke·kéx ko·áx ko·áx—
           Uplift your voice
             children born
           of lake and stream!
           Pipes ring out;
         ring out my song
       Lord Dionŷsus praising,
           —ko·áx ko·áx—

499

O sweet refrain
sung of old
to Nŷsa's lord,
child of Zeus,—
our song of the fens
lifted loud
calling the folk who assemble
down at our Close in the Marshlands
and keep with a jolly carouse
High Feast of Pots.
Brékeke·kéx ko·áx ko·áx!

DI. (*slowly, with stroke to match*)
I have,—I find,—a spot—behind
that's tender (*wincing*)—Ow, ko·áx ko·áx!

FR. (*speeding him up*)
Brékeke·kéx ko·áx ko·áx.

DI. You're not—the kind,—it seems,—to mind.

FR.   Brékeke·kéx ko·áx ko·áx.

DI. To hell—with you—and ko·áx too!
The same—old song—the whole—day long!

FR. (*briskly*)
Song,—you clever busybody!—
learnt of the lyric Muses,
learnt of Pan, who loved me,
Pan, of the vocal reeds mellifluous,
Pan, the Goat-foot.
Pleasant am I no less to Apollo,
lord of lute-play—
Reeds, of a wood to re-echo his fingering,
down in our own ooze-garden grow.
Brékeke·kéx ko·áx ko·áx.

DI. (*as before*)
    From rub—of oar—my hands—grow sore—

FR.   Brékeke·kéx ko·áx ko·áx.

DI. (*sings*)   How long? how long?
              Sing no more
              O sons of song!

FR. (*still more briskly*)
              Sing we on,—
    louder, louder, now if ever!
    Sing, as when blue days have set us
    hopping in and out for pleasure
    through the galingale, through rushes,
    now for a dip, and now for a ditty.
    Sing, as when we bob for shelter
    out of the rain, and from our chorus
    giddy songs of the underwater
                swell
              hubble-bubble
               to the
               top.

DI. (*anticipates the croak, and spurts*)
        Brékeke·kéx ko·áx ko·áx
  (*relapsing*)
    You've met—your match:—I've caught—your catch.

FR.   How he'll wreck it there's no knowing!

DI. (*spurts*)
    You'll wreck *me*, if I go rowing
    till I crack my back in two.

FR.   Brékeke·kéx ko·áx ko·áx.

DI. (*relapses*)
    Be damned!—I don't—care what—you do!

FR.   No, we'll croak you to a finish,
       never a note shall we diminish
       open-throated all day long.

DI.   (*spurts and relapses*)
                 Brékeke·kéx ko·áx ko·áx.
       At least—I'll beat—you, song—for song.

FR.   *You* beat *us*? We can't conceive it!

DI.   (*frantic*)
                 You shall not put *me* to rout!
       I shall croak and never leave it,
          all day long, needs be, I'll shout
                 BRÉKEKE·KÉX KO·ÁX KO·ÁX
       (*relapsing*)
       till my—ko·áx—has croaked—you down—and out.
       (*defiantly, shooting the boat to shore*)
                 BRÉKEKE·KÉX KO·ÁX KO·ÁX!
       Silenced!—so there!—Who wins—our croaking-
                 bout?

T. F. HIGHAM   (*Frogs*, 209–69)

431   *Hymn of the Initiates*

                       CHORUS

HERE in thy home we await thy tread,
   O come Iacchus of high renown,
       Iacchus, Iacchus!
Dance o'er this meadow, shake on thy head
The berries that cluster, thy myrtle crown.
And lead with the beat of thy tireless feet
The holy bands in mystic rite,
The dance of wantonness and delight,

502

Where the Graces find their chiefest pleasure,
Thy hallowed worshippers' sacred measure.

> Bravely forward, mystic band,
> Beat upon this meadow-land;
> Jesting, laughing,
> Gaily chaffing,
> Visit every flowery dell,
> Now we've breakfasted so well.

> Onward! See ye nobly raise
> High the Saviour Maiden's praise.
> Sing aloud,
> She hath vowed
> To protect our country still,
> Though Thôrýcion wish us ill.

And now to her who gives earth fruit, Dêmêter, queen on
    high,
Sing a new song, adorning it with heavenly melody.

> Queen of sacred ritual,
> Save the choirs that praise thee;
> Stand Dêmêter by us all,
> Grant that safely all the day
> I may dance and I may play.
> Homage let me, much in jest,
> Much in earnest, raise thee;
> Sport and play be worthiest,
> So may I, thy revels run,
> Wear thy garlands truly won.

Call *him* too hither, call him in your song,
The god, young and lovely, to speed this dancing throng.

Iacchus high in glory, thou whose day
Of all is merriest, hither, help our play;
   Show, as we throne thee at thy Maiden's side,
How light to thee are our long leagues of way.
   Iacchus, happy dancer, be our guide.

Thyself, that poorest men thy joy should share,
Didst rend thy robe, thy royal sandal tear,
   That feet unshod might dance, and robes rent wide
Wave in thy revel with no after care.
   Iacchus, happy dancer, be our guide.

Lo there! but now across the dance apace
A maiden tripped, a maiden fair of face,
   Whose tattered smock and kerchief scarce could
     hide
The merry bosom peeping from its place.
   Iacchus, happy dancer, be our guide.

    On, to the fields of roses,
    The meadows gay with flowers;
    Old custom so disposes,
    Dance out the merry hours.
    Beside us go the Muses blest
    Uniting us in song and jest.

    The sun to us is giving
    Alone his happy ray,
    For holy was our living,
    And we have learnt the Way;
    Did citizen or stranger call,
    We had a welcome for them all.

(VARIOUS HANDS)   (*Frogs*, 324–36, 372–416, 449–59)

432   *The Rival Poets*

CHORUS

FIERCELY, methinks, will he rage in his heart and loud
     will he bellow,
When, as he glances aside, he espies this acid-tongued
     fellow
     Whetting his tusks. Then in furious frenzy of soul
     Round and round his eyes will roll.

O what a fight! How his phrases will charge, helm a-
     glancing, plume waving,
Down on the pin-pricking ranks of his foe, the splinter-
     and-shaving
     Troops that engage with poetic genius free,
     Prancing phraseology!

Here 'neath a crest all his own, the mane on his shaggy
     neck curling,
Brows drawn down in a terrible frown, he is roaring and
     whirling
     Riveted phrases, and baulk upon baulk follows fast,
     Tossed on the titanic blast.

Here the smooth tongue uncoiling, the prattler, all
     blemishes tracing
Sets with a shake of their bridle the steeds of her jealousy
     racing,
     Feasts on the phrases, and nibbles and nibbles to naught
     All the other's lungs have wrought.

MARSHALL MACGREGOR   (*Frogs*, 814–29)

433   *The Fatal Oil-flask*

ÆSCHYLUS. EURIPIDÊS. DIONŶSUS

ÆS.   Nay, I'll not chip and scratch them line by line,
       Phrase after phrase, but, an Heav'n help my task,
       Ruin your prologues with—a pocket-flask.
EUR.   Mine! with a pocket-flask!
ÆS.   But one I ask.
       They're so composed they'll suffer any tag,
       Eider-down, pocket-flask, or carpet-bag,
       In the line's structure. I'll soon show you how.
EUR.   O *you* will show me?
ÆS.   Yes.
DION.   Recite some now.
EUR.   'Ægyptus, this the tale sown far and wide,
       With fifty sons upon the oar did ride
       To Argos' shore and . . .'
ÆS.   Lost his pocket-flask.
DION. (*puzzled*) What *is* this flask? There's trouble still
           in store.
       Say him another, let me see once more.
EUR.   'With wand and fawnskin Dionŷsus dight
       Mid the pine torches o'er Parnassus' height
       Footed the dance and . . .'
ÆS.   Lost his pocket-flask.
DION. Gracious! The flask has scored another hit.
EUR.   O there's no need to trouble. Wait a bit,
       I have a prologue here his flask won't fit.
       'Bliss ne'er for man complete in all may be.
       Either he hath high birth with poverty,
       Or lowly blood and . . .'
ÆS.   Lost his pocket-flask.

DION. Euripidês—

EUR.   Yes?

DION.   I'm for lowering sail,
This pocket-flask will blow a heavy gale.

MARSHALL MACGREGOR   (*Frogs*, 1198–1221)

434   *An 'Æschylean' Chorus*

(*Euripidês sings, thrumming a lyre between the
monotonous dactylic rhythms.*)

        . . . How Hellas' youth,
liegemen Achæan of brothers embattled,

        tophlattothrat tophlattothrat

Foul as a Sphinx that apportioneth havoc, a hell-hound,

        tophlattothrat tophlattothrat

grasping the spears that avenge, bidden on by a bird of
ill-omen,

        tophlattothrat tophlattothrat

                were thrown to feed
hounds of the air ever eagerly questing;

        tophlattothrat tophlattothrat

how swords that bent on Ajax' breast . . .

        tophlattothrat tophlattothrat

T. F. HIGHAM   (*Frogs*, 1285–95)

435   *A 'Euripidean' Chorus*

ÆSCHYLUS

(With tragical foreboding.)

GLOOM of the night, gloom of the night,
  Light that is blackness, darkly bright,
What presage of ill, most horrible,
What Thing of the Mists beyond Surmise
On the windways of dream comes to mine eyes
        Upward from gulfs of Hell?
A living Spirit that yet lives not;
A phantom on Night's dark womb begot;
A vision of terror and tremblement
Gowned in darkness of deadman's veils,
With eyes on murder, murder bent
        And great big finger-nails!

(Brisker: a call to action.)

Handmaidens, a light! with your pitchers begone,
There's dewy-fresh water to draw from the stream;
I'll wash and be clean, when the kettle's put on,
And banish the taint of this god-driven dream.

(Frenzied.)

            Ay me,
        God of the Sea,
    Truth is out, truth foretold!
    Lodgers, wake! Come and behold
    Things of wonder, past belief!
    My rooster gone! Glykê's a thief!
    A raid, a rape, a roost left bare . . .
    And Glykê vanished—into thin air!

O Nymphs in your cradle of hills, give aid!
I cry to the Nymphs . . . and the poultry-maid!

(*Sadly, with 'droppings of warm tears'.*)

I worked—ah God!—at a flaxen skein
    Turning a loaded spindle,
    A spindle-indle-indle;
On through the dusk, as the dawn-stars wane
I'd take the road, with my flaxen load,
    To market on the morrow—
When airily, airily up he flew
    And left to me sorrow, sorrow!
O heart of a bird in the wild far blue,
    O wing-blades fleet and free . . .
        Nothing is here
        But tear upon tear,
          Drip-drop,
        O misery me!

(*In the manner of a tragical invocation.*)

Sons of Crete, on Ida bred,
Bows in hand your comfort bring;
Lithe and lofty be your tread,
Close the household in a ring.

Artemis, Fair Maiden, come!
Cast, O Huntress, to and fro;
About the house from room to room
Bid your pets, the Bitch-pack, go.

Come, O Hékatê, I pray,
Child of Zeus, and light me in;
With twin-torch of keenest ray
Show me Glykê, hot from Sin.

T. F. HIGHAM   (*Frogs*, 1331–63)

509

436   *Praxágora rehearses*

PRAXÁGORA.   WOMEN

PRAX.   You, too, retire and sit you down again,
For I myself will wear the chaplet now
Your cause to further: and I pray the gods
That I may haply prosper our design.

I have, my friends, an equal stake with you
In this our country, and I grieve to note
The sad condition of the state's affairs.
I see the state employing evermore
Unworthy ministers; if one do well
A single day, he'll act amiss for ten.
You trust another: he'll be ten times worse.
Hard, hard it is to counsel wayward men,
Always mistrusting those who love you best,
And paying court to those who love you not.
There was a time, my friends, we never came
To these Assemblies; then we knew full well
Agýrrhius was a rogue: we come here now,
And he who gets the cash applauds the man,
And he who gets it not, protests that they
Who come for payment ought to die the death.

1ST W.   By Aphrodîtê now, but that's well said!

PRAX.   Heavens! Aphrodîtê! 'Twere a pleasant jest,
If in the Assembly you should praise me so!

1ST W.   Ah, but I won't.

PRAX.   Then don't acquire the habit.
This League again, when first we talked it over,
It seemed the only thing to save the state.
Yet when they'd got it, they disliked it. He
Who pushed it through was forced to cut and run.

Ships must be launched; the poor men all approve,
The wealthy men and farmers disapprove. . . .

1ST W. Here's a shrewd man!

PRAX.   Ah, now you praise me rightly.
Ye are to blame for this, Athenian people,
Ye draw your wages from the public purse,
Yet each man seeks his private gain alone.
So the state reels, like any Æsimus.
Still, if ye trust me, ye shall yet be saved.
I move that now the womankind be asked
To rule the state. In our own homes, ye know,
They are the managers and rule the house.

1ST W. O good, good, good!

2ND W.   Speak on, speak on, dear man.

PRAX. That they are better in their ways than we
I'll soon convince you. First, they dye their wools
With boiling tinctures, in the ancient style.
You won't find *them*, I warrant, in a hurry
Trying new plans. And would it not have saved
The Athenian city had she let alone
Things that worked well, nor idly sought things
    new?

They roast their barley, sitting, as of old:
They on their heads bear burdens, as of old:
They keep their Thesmophória, as of old:
They bake their honied cheesecakes, as of old:
They victimize their husbands, as of old:
They still secrete their lovers, as of old:
They buy themselves sly dainties, as of old:
They love their wine unwatered, as of old:
They like a woman's pleasures, as of old:
Then let us, gentlemen, give up to them

The helm of state, and not concern ourselves,
Nor pry, nor question what they mean to do;
But let them really govern, knowing this,
The statesman-mothers never will neglect
Their soldier-sons. And then a soldier's rations,
Who will supply as well as she who bare him?
For ways and means none can excel a woman.
And there's no fear at all that they'll be cheated
When they're in power, for they're the cheats
    themselves.
Much I omit. But if you pass my motion,
You'll lead the happiest lives that e'er you
    dreamed of.

1ST W.   O, good! Praxágora. Well done, sweet wench.
    However did you learn to speak so finely?

PRAX.   I and my husband in the general flight
    Lodged in the Pnyx, and there I heard the
    speakers.

B. B. ROGERS   (*Ecclesiazûsæ*, 168–98, 204–44)

437   *The Gifts of Poverty*

CHRÉMYLUS (*addressing Poverty*): With what Good canst
thou supply Mankind, except Blisters on the Legs from the
public Bagnio-Fires, and the Cries of half-starved Children
and old Women! together with an Army of Lice, Gnats,
and Fleas, (too numerous to be muster'd) which humming
round our Heads, torment us, awakening us, and saying,
Rise, or Starve. Moreover, instead of Clothes we shall have
Rags; instead of a Bed of Down we shall have one of
Rushes full of Bugs, which will awaken us out of the
soundest Sleep; instead of a Carpet we shall have a rotten

Mat; and instead of a Pillow, we shall prop our Heads
with a Stone. As to our Food, we shall exchange Bread
for Mallow-Branches, and Furmety for the Leaves of
Radishes. Our Seats will not be Chairs, but the Head of
a broken Jar; and lastly, we shall be even compelled to use
one Side of a broken Crutch, instead of a Kneading-
Trough—Well, Madam, do not I demonstrate that you
are the Author of many Blessings to Mankind?

HENRY FIELDING. WILLIAM YOUNG   (*Plûtus*, 535-47)

TIMÓTHEÜS

(c. 447–357 B.C.)

438   *A Manifesto*

OLD songs I will not sing
    Now better songs are sung.
Zeus reigns now, and is young,
Where Kronos once was king.
Old Muse, your knell is rung.

GILBERT HIGHET

439   *A Sea-fight*

WHEN rebullient the brine
    outjetted his mouth,
with hoarse harsh howl
and maniac mind,
spiketeeth gnashing
with furious feigning
he threatened his body's
bane, the sea.

'Arrogant thing, yet heretofore
in shackles sewn of hemp
yoked was your neck for turbulence.
And anon will my lord, my
own, upwhirl you
with peakborn pinetree, and will
fast prison your watery meadows in peregrin shipwalls—
frenzymad ancient abhorrence,
perfidious minion
of combercoursing gales!'
Fordone and gasping, he spoke,
and forth flung a fearful foam,
as throat spewed back the brine
drawn from the deeps.
Now back in a rout the Persians,
back rushed the barbarous army precipitate.
Shoals here smashed them, and there.
Men lost from their gripe
the hillborn longnecked
seafeet of the ship: and leapt
from their mouths the argentgleaming
brothers aclatter together.
Bestarred with bodies
lightleaving and breathbereft,
glittered the ocean
and laboured the shores.

GILBERT HIGHET   (*Persæ*, 74–108)

514

EUPOLIS

(446– ? B.C.)

440   *Periclês*

A. In eloquence no man could equal him—
When Periclês arose and took the floor,
By ten good feet our common orators
As by an expert runner were outstript.

B. Not only voluble, but with persuasion
Sitting upon his lips. He bound a spell,
And had this power, alone of orators,—
To prick men's hearts and leave behind the sting.

T. F. HIGHAM

PHRŶNICHUS

(fl. 420 B.C.)

441   *Sophoclês*

HOW blessed Sophoclês, who, dying old,
Was old in happiness and skill of hand.
Beautiful were his Tragedies, and many;
And beautiful his end, who lived untroubled.

T. F. HIGHAM

PLATO

(429–347 B.C.)

442   *Laïs' Mirror*

LAÏS of the haughty smile,
The despair of Greece erewhile,
Whose doors fond gallants wont to crowd,
Hath her glass to Venus vowed:
'Since what I am I will not see,
And cannot what I used to be.'

F. E. GARRETT

443   *The Eretrian Dead*

(*i*)

FAR from the blue Ægean's boom and swell,
    here in Ecbátana's mid-plain lie we.
Farewell, thou famed Eretria, fare thee well,
    our neighbour Athens, and farewell, dear sea.

H. K. St. J. Sanderson

(*ii*)

EUBŒANS we, men of Eretria city,
    Here lying, overseen
By Persian Susa. O for pity,
    How long the road between!

T. F. Higham

444   *Take Thought*

GOD by land and sea defend you,
    Sailors all, who pass my grave;
Safe from wreck his mercy send you,—
    I am one he did not save.

T. F. Higham

445   *Aster*

(*i*)

THOU gazest on the stars:
    Would I might be,
O star of mine, the skies
    With myriad eyes
        To gaze on thee.

(Author uncertain)

516

(ii)

THOU wert the morning-star among the living,
　　Ere thy fair light had fled;
But now thou art as Hesperus, giving
　　New splendour to the dead.

P. B. SHELLEY

446　　　　　*Farmer and Sailor*

SHIPWRECKED I, a farmer he,—
　　Grave to grave lies vis-à-vis.
Go by land, by water go,
Death keeps open house below.

T. F. HIGHAM

447　　　　　*Dion of Syracuse*

FOR Priam's queen and daughters at their birth
　　The fates weaved tears into the web of life;
But for thee, Dion, in thy hour of mirth,
　　When triumph crowned thy honourable strife,
Thy gathering hopes were poured upon the sand:
　　Thee, still thy countrymen revere, and lay
In the broad precincts of thy native land,
　　Thee,—love for whom once took my wits away.

After CHARLES MERIVALE

448　　　　　*Time the Changer*

LIFE brings our all: long Time leaves nought abiding—
　　Name, form, or nature, good or evil tiding.

T. F. HIGHAM

449   *Country Gods*

SILENCE, Dryads' leafy keep;
    Rocky fountains, hush your spraying;
Hush your babble, bleating sheep,
    Pan is playing, Pan is playing.
O'er the clustered reed-pipe see
    How his mellow lips are glancing;
Nymphs of fountain, nymphs of tree
    Foot it round him, dancing, dancing.

WALTER LEAF

450   *Country Music*

COME sit aneath this pinetree, whose lofty tressèd
        crown
    Sighs as her tufty sprays stir to the west wind's kiss:
And with the babbling waters my flute thy care shall
        drown,
    And lull thy dreamy eyelids to sweet forgetful bliss.

ROBERT BRIDGES

ANTÍPHANÊS
(fl. 380 B.C.)

451   *Not Dead, but gone before*

MOURNING your dearest friends, be wise in grief.
    They are not dead, but on that single road
Which all are bound to travel, gone before.
We too, in after days, shall overtake them;
One road-house shall receive us, entered in
To lodge together for the rest of time.

T. F. HIGHAM

518

452   *The Profession of Flattery*

CONSIDER, then, the flatterer's profession:
    There is no jollier trade, nor like to be,
No easier money,—if you have the flair.
Your artists are laborious, touchy folk;
Your farmers never safe from speculation;
Everywhere it's the same,—care and hard work!
Ours is a merry, comfortable life;
There's nothing to it, all the work is play,—
A hearty laugh, a jibe or two, long drinks,—
Second to none, say I, unless you're rich.

T. F. HIGHAM

EUBÛLUS
                                    (fl. 376–373 B.C.)

453   *Love is not Winged*

WHO gave Love wings? Whose pencil drew the line
    Or fingers modelled wax to that design?
To sketch a swallow was his only art,
A man unschooled to know the god apart.
Love is no feather-weight: whom love attacks
Have pains to shift that burden from their backs,—
A load so plaguy where he sits and clings
The man's a fool who ever mentioned wings.

T. F. HIGHAM

MOSCHIÔN

(fl. 350 B.C.)

454   *Primitive Man*

FIRST I shall trace and show in argument
The origin and tenure of man's life.
A generation once upon a time
There lived of men like-mannered with the beasts,
Their homes making in caverns of the hills,
In chasms where the sun spared visitation,
With never yet a roof on house, nor wide
City built strong and the stone towers thereof;
Nor ever down black earth the twisted plough
Went cutting clods that give rich grain for harvest.
No iron worked upon exuberant rows
Of vines—the reveller's glory—carefully pruned;
The womb of Earth was barren of livelihood.
For food men ate the flesh of mutual slaughter,—
This gave them feasting. Law was nothing worth;
Might reigned coequal on the throne with Zeus.

    Then was the aspect of man's life reversed
By Time all things engendering, nurse of all;
Whether Promêtheus toiled for man, or whether
Necessity fore-doomed, or Time and Use
Made Nature's own book clear for all to read.
Then first by skill of careful husbandry
In gift of grain was pure Dêmêter known;
Then Bacchus first, in the grape's luscious flow;
And Earth, unsown before, was furrowed now
With harnessed oxen; now their towns men towered,
Their houses walled for shelter, savagery
Converting to a milder way of life.

520

So custom first appointed for dead men
A place of burial, and their due meed of dust
To give unburied bodies, with no relic
Left visible of older sin of feast.

GEORGE ALLEN

CHÆREMÔN

(fl. 350? B.C.)

455 *Maidens at Rest*

One lay lit by the moon, breast white and bare,
Her strap off shoulder fallen. There a dancer
From dancing showed her left flank naked in air
Visible, picture living to declare
Of dazzling white to shadow making answer.

And one her arms and dainty wrists revealed
Twining them round the neck of playmate fair;
One—for being torn the pleated dress must yield—
Her thigh: and love, for lover to despair,
Deep on her laughing summer time was sealed.

They fell in sleep on elecámpanon lying,
Or bruising the violets' plumage darkly flying,
And yellow crocus, by their robes concealed
Yet still the underweave with sun's grain dyeing,
As they leaned their necks upon the gentle field.

GEORGE ALLEN

ÊRINNA

(fl. 350 B.C.)

456 ### *A Distaff*

(*i*)

PILOT-FISH, who giv'st to sailors pleasant sailing,
  Grant my sweet companion escort from a-stern.

(*ii*)

Soft-voiced white-haired women, like old age's blossoms . . .

(*iii*)

Emptily from here to Hades floats the echo,
Hushed among the dead. My voice goes down the
    night.

C. M. BOWRA

457 ### *Baucis*

YE Columns and my Sirens, and thou funereal jar
  Holding the little ash that now is I,
To all who pass give greeting, no matter if they are
    My countrymen or from another sky:
'My father called me Baucis', say: say 'Têlos was my
      home.'
    And tell them I was buried here, a bride,
That all may know: and name the friend who thus in-
      scribed my tomb,
    Erinna; she was always at my side.

SIR WILLIAM MARRIS

ANONYMOUS

(4th cent. B.C.)

458   *Maidens' Song*

NINE are we who enter, each maiden votaress
   Come to great Dêmêter in a pretty dress;
A pretty dress, a necklet of clean-cut ivory
Gleaming like the star-shine, beautiful to see.

T. F. HIGHAM

ARISTOTLE

(384–322 B.C.)

459   *To Virtue*

VIRTUE, so hardly pursued by men,
   so glorious to possess,—
O Virgin Goddess,
to die for thy beauty's sake
or to endure,
ravaged by unending hardship,
in Greece is accounted great;
so strong is the love of thee,
subjecting the soul
and holding it always.
No gold is so precious,
no gems, nor the richness
of Sleep's melting eye.

For thy sake Hêraklês, son to Zeus,
for thy sake Lêda's pair
endured much labour, and in their deeds
proclaimed thy mastery.

523

For love of thee Achilles, Ajax,
went both to the House of Death;
and now for thee and thy beauty
the Man of Atarneus
has lost the sun's light.
Therefore singers shall praise his works,
and Muses, daughters of Memory,
lift him to immortal life.
They shall tell, with beauty of song,
how Zeus the god of Hospitage
was held in honour,
and friendship, nobly given,
stayed firm to the end.

T. F. HIGHAM

ALEXIS

(372–300? B.C.)

460   *The Confident Scientist*

DISCOVERY attends on every quest,
  Except for renegades who shirk the toil.
Now certain men have pushed discovery
Into the sphere of heaven. Some part they know,—
How planets rise and set and wheel about,
And of the sun's eclipse. If men have probed
Worlds far remote, can problems of this earth,
This common home to which we're born, defy them?

T. F. HIGHAM

524

ANÁXILAS

(fl. 330 B.C.)

461 *Human Worms*

FLATTERERS are the worms who prey upon
Men of rich substance. Into some innocent host
Insinuated, they sit down and eat;
And when, like corn-ears with no grain to show,
He's a mere husk, cleaned out, they gnaw another.

T. F. HIGHAM

462 *The Cautious Householder*

YOU'RE worse than snails, who vote the whole world
vicious
And hump their houses round, they're so suspicious.

T. F. HIGHAM

PHILÊMON

(361–263 B.C.)

463 *Who is Free?*

I SERVE my master: you, and countless others,
Are governed by convention. Some, again,
Obey a tyrant, ruled himself by fear.
Kings have their servants, but submit to gods:
God, to Necessity. Considered well,
All things in their degree give place, the small
By nature's law made subject to the greater.

T. F. HIGHAM

464 *The Greatest Tribute*

GRANT, in good sooth, our great dead, all the same
Retain their sense, as certain wise men say,
I'd hang myself to see Euripidês.

ROBERT BROWNING

AMPHIS

(fl. 322 B.C.)

465 *The Solace of Art*

THERE is no comfort in adversity
More sweet than Art affords. The studious mind
Poising in meditation, there is fixed,
And sails beyond its troubles unperceiving.

T. F. HIGHAM

MENANDER

(343?–293 B.C.)

466 *My Own, my Native Land*

DEAR land, I greet you after many years,
And take you to me. Not to every plot
I give such greeting, but to fields of home.
The ground that nursed me is to me divine.

C. M. BOWRA

467 *Whom the Gods love*

Whom the gods love die young.

LORD BYRON

468   *The Mutes in Life's Chorus*

NOT all the chorus sing: to swell their number
   Some two or three stand by, no utterance giving.
And so with men: the ground full many cumber:
   None live but those who have the means of living.

SIR WILLIAM MARRIS

469   *Evil Communications*

   Evil communications corrupt good manners.

ANGLO-RHEMISH NEW TESTAMENT

470   *This World is all a Fleeting Show*

           I count it happiness,
Ere we go quickly thither whence we came,
To gaze ungrieving on these majesties,
The world-wide sun, the stars, water and clouds,
And fire. Live, Pármeno, a hundred years
Or a few months, these you will always see,
And never, never, any greater things.
   Think of this lifetime as a festival
Or visit to a strange city, full of noise,
Buying and selling, thieving, dicing-stalls
And joy-parks. If you leave it early, friend,
Why, think you have gone to find a better inn;
You have paid your fare and leave no enemies.
The lingerer tires, loses his fare, grows old,
And lacks he knows not what: moons round and seeks
To find an enemy and a plotting world,
And no smooth passage when, in time, he goes!

GILBERT MURRAY

527

471 *The Common Lot*

IF, when your mother bore you, you were born
Alone of men, young sir, always to do
Your pleasure and live always happily,—
If some god promised you such privilege,
Then rightly are you angry. He has lied
And done you singular wrong. But if one law
Of Nature holds, and you breathed common air—
So let me phrase it in the tragic style—
Put on a better grace and use your reason.
To sum up what I mean, you are a man,
Than whom no creature suffers change more quickly,
Climbing up high, then falling back to the depths,—
It's logic. He, whom Nature made so weak,
Plays manager to all that is most great,
And when he falls, shatters so much that's good.

C. M. BOWRA

472 *Here are Sands, Ignoble Things*

IF you with your true self would be acquainted,
look at the grave-stones as you travel past.
Bones lie beneath and the light-drifting dust
of kings and despots, of the skilled and wise,
of men who gloried in their birth or riches
or reputation won or beauty of body—
then all was gone before the assault of Time.
One place of death men share, and share alike.
Look to the graves—and make your own acquaintance.

T. F. HIGHAM

473   *This defileth a Man*

                              My son, you do not see
        How everything that dies, dies by its own
        Corruption: all that injures is within.
        Rust is the poison of iron, moths of wool,
        And worms of wood; in you there is a poison
        Most deadly, which has made you sick to death
        And makes and shall make—envy.

GILBERT MURRAY

474   *Conscience doth make Cowards of us All*

T HE boldest man with something on his conscience
     Is turned by knowledge of it to a coward.

C. M. BOWRA

475   *Marriage—Two Views*
                         (*i*)

N O things, my Lachês, are so close akin,
     If you look carefully, as man and woman.

                         (*ii*)

        Marriage, if we look honestly at the truth,
        Is evil, but a necessary evil.

C. M. BOWRA

476   *Threats*

        No threat was ever yet sincerely made
        By son to father, lover to beloved.

C. M. BOWRA

477 *The Family Dinner-Party*

WHAT a thing to come upon relations sitting at their
food!
Father first will take the cup and tell you something for
your good,
Washing down a heavy humour. Mother then must do
her bit;
Next a nurse chips in with comment; a deep rumble
seconds it,
—That is grand-pa. Then some grannie calls the lad a
'pet'; and he
Nods assent to every speaker, too polite to disagree.
C. M. BOWRA

478 *Charîsius rebukes himself*

NOW I, the sinless saint, aiming at honour,
seeking to know the essence of good and evil,
living reproachless and immaculate—
now God has served me well and fittingly,
now I have proved my own humanity.
'Fool of all fools, you bluster and pretend:
you will not endure your wife's unwitting fault—
now I will show you caught in the same snare!
and she will treat you kindly then, while you
dishonour her. You will be pilloried
as a creature of ill luck, ill ways, ill breeding.
Her answer to her father—very like
what you intended!—"he is my life's partner,
and so I must not shirk the evil chance
fallen on him". But you were high and mighty!—'
GILBERT HIGHET   (*Epitrepontës*, 693–707)

479   *Advice to a Lover*

PATÆCUS. PÓLEMO

PAT. Now, Pólemo, if the matter really is
as you assert, and if your wedded wife—

PÓL. Why *if*, Patæcus? Where's the difference?
I took her for my wedded wife.

PAT.   Less noise.
Who gave her to you?

PÓL.   Why, she did.

PAT.   Very well.
She liked you once, maybe: she does not now:
and so, since you behaved improperly,
she is gone.

PÓL.   What's that? Improperly? Ah, there's
the hardest word of all you've said!

PAT.   You will
admit, I make no doubt, that what you are doing
is craziness. Where are you blundering? Whom
can you carry off? The woman's her own mistress.
One course is left for the unlucky lover—
persuasion.

PÓL.   And am I not wronged, by him
who has seduced her in my absence?

PAT.   Yes—
enough to summons him, if you come to words;
but if to force, you'll pay the penalty.
Your remedy is a lawsuit, not revenge.

PÓL. And so I cannot—?

PAT.   You can not.

PÓL.   Oh, God—
what am I to say—except—I'll kill myself!

My Glýkera has left me, she has left me,
my Glýkera, Patæcus!
                Still—if you do
believe this is my course—you know her well,
talked with her often: go you first, bespeak her,
be my envoy, I beg you.

PAT.   Yes, our course,
as you see, is that.

PÓL.   You're a good speaker, doubtless,
Patæcus?

PAT.   Fairly.

PÓL.   O my friend, you must be!
the matter turns on that, to make or mar.
Now, if I ever wronged her any how—
if I am not assiduously attentive—
now, you should only look here, at her wardrobe—

PAT. Thank you, no.

PÓL.   Please, please, Patæcus, look,
and pity me, much rather.

PAT.   Oh, good Lord . . .

PÓL. Come, see: what dresses! and how fine she looked
wearing them! Perhaps you never saw her.

PAT. Oh, yes.

PÓL.   You know, I think her stately figure
took every eye. But what's the use of this
pointless and crazy talk about her figure?

PAT. Why, none whatever.

PÓL.   None? Yet you must see
the dresses—please go on.

PAT.   You first.

PÓL.   This way, then.

GILBERT HIGHET   (*Perikeirómenê*, 363–402)

PHILÊTAS

(c. 340–285 B.C.)

480   *The Last Request*

WEEP me not long, but truly; speak me fair;
  And though we're parted, have a thought to spare.

T. F. HIGHAM

481   *Life's Medley*

REST friend, no tears for you: much good befell
  You living, and some ill, God's gift as well.

H. MACNAGHTEN

ORACLE OF SERÂPIS

(Date uncertain)

482   *The Living God*

LISTEN and learn what manner of god I am:
  My head the firmament, the sea my belly,
Earth for my feet, my ears in æther fixed,
And radiant sunlight my far-flashing eye.

T. F. HIGHAM

CLEANTHÊS

(331–232 B.C.)

483   *Hymn to Zeus*

MOST glorious of immortals, Zeus all powerful,
  Author of Nature, named by many names, all hail.
Thy law rules all; and the voice of the world may cry to
    thee,
For from thee we are born, and alone of living things
That move on earth are we created in God's image.

533

So will I praise thee, ever singing of thy might
By whom the whole wide firmament of heaven is swayed
And guided in its wheeling journey round this earth
In glad submission to thee: for in thine unconquered
    hands
Thou hast a mighty servant, the thunderbolt of heaven
Wrought with a double edge, and of never-dying fire,—
A pulse of life beating through all created things
That walk in thy ways; and with this thou dost direct
Thy Omnipresent Word that moves through all creation
And mingles with the sun and the company of the stars.
All things confess thee as their life that are on earth
Or in the sea or in the holy air of heaven,
Save what in foolishness is wrought by evil men:
But into harmony thou canst turn such discords
And make of chaos order; for hate with thee is love,
And thus by thee all things of good and evil are joined
To make thy eternal Word,—still unperceived by those
Who blindly shun this truth. Theirs is the bitterness
Of loss, who in their heart's desire of its own good,
As understanding not God's omnipresent law
Nor hearkening to his voice, forgo their happiness.
Self-willed, they seek in folly evil's many forms,
And some find suffering in the difficult race for fame,
And some in headlong chase for gain swerve from their
    course,
While to the senses' swoon of pleasure others turn
And to the body's delight,—fools all, who spending folly
In conflict striving with their own desire of good,
Hither and thither are borne in the wake of vanity.
    But Zeus that givest all, hear us and bring salvation,—
Dark in thy clouds and shining in thy lightning's flames —

534

Save men from all their ignorance and its distress,
Scatter it from their hearts, and in their quest for wisdom
Grant them success; for in wisdom thou art powerful
And rulest justly. So for our meed of honour
May we requite thee with the honour of our song,
And ever praise thee and thy works,—a glorious theme
For men; and not the gods themselves know higher honour
Than rendering thee due praise for thy Omnipresent Law.

MICHAEL BALKWILL

484   *God leads the Way*

LEAD me, O God, and thou my Destiny,
   To that one place which you will have me fill.
I follow gladly. Should I strive with Thee,—
A recreant, I needs must follow still.

C. C. MARTINDALE

PHANOCLÊS

(fl. c. 300 B.C.)

485   *Orpheus*

ORPHEUS, whom Œagrus begot in Thrace,
   Loved Cálaïs the child of Bóreas;
Often he sate him down in shadowy grove,
But found no peace in singing of his love;
Unsleeping cares that fret the heart were his,
Casting his eyes on youthful Cálaïs.
Him the Bistónian women, leagued for ill,
Surrounded with their whetted swords to kill;
Then off with sword of bronze his head they cut,
Nailing it fast upon his Thracian lute,

And flung them both into the sea to ride
Together on the wet and shining tide.
So lute and head reached on the waters grey
Lesbos divine; and sound as of lute-play
On sea and isles and oozy shores was come,
When the melodious head was laid in tomb,
And with it the clear shell whose note subdued
The voiceless crags and Phorcys' sullen flood.
Songs thence and tuneful lute-musics enthrall
The island of all isles most musical.

GEORGE ALLEN

THEÓPHILUS

(fl. 300? B.C.)

486 *Crabbed Age and Youth*

OLD husband and young wife never agree.
For, like a boat, she will not be controlled
by half a rudder—so she breaks her moorings
one night: day finds her in another harbour.

GILBERT HIGHET

ÁNYTÊ

(fl. 300 B.C.)

487 *The Goat*

RED reins, O Goat, these boys have set about
Thy neck, a muzzle on thy shaggy snout,
And round God's temple ply their mimic race,
That he may look on them with kindly face.

W. H. D. ROUSE

488   *Death the Leveller*

I N life this man was Mânês, and a slave;
  He's peer of great Darîus in the grave.

SIR WILLIAM MARRIS

489   *A Statue of Cypris*

H ERE Cypris dwells. Always it was her will
  To gaze from land upon the sparkling sea
And give the ships good sailing: ocean still
    Quivers to watch her radiant effigy.

SIR WILLIAM MARRIS

490   *Under a Laurel*

S IT all beneath fair leaves of spreading bay,
  And draw sweet water from a timely spring,
And let your breathless limbs, this summer day,
    Rest, in the west wind's airy buffeting.

R. A. FURNESS

SÎMIAS

(fl. 300 B.C.)

491   *Sophoclês' Tomb*

W IND gently, ivy, o'er the tomb,
    Gently, where Sophoclês is laid;
  Lend thy green tresses for a shade;
Rose-petals all about him bloom:

Twine thy lithe tendrils, gadding vine,
　To praise the cunning of his tongue,
　The notes in honeyed concert sung
With Graces and the Muses nine.

WALTER LEAF

492　　　　　*A Decoy Partridge*

NO more, poor partridge, taught to lure
　　And lurk in woodland glade,
No more thy tuneful note shall sound
　A-ringing through the shade,
There in the forest dell to tempt
　Thy dappled fellows on;
Thy last long road is travelled now,
　The road to Ácheron.

WALTER LEAF

ADDÆUS
(fl. 300 B.C.)
493　　　　*An Ox past Service*

WITH weight of years and yoke forspent,
　To no grim slaughter-house was sent
　　The ox from Alcôn's plough.
His grateful master gives him ease
At liberty in grassy leas
　　To graze and rest and low.

WALTER LEAF

ZENÓDOTUS (?)

(325–260? B.C.)

494 *A Statue of Love*

WHO sculptured Love beside this fountain?—Fool!
   To think with water such a flame to cool!

H. WELLESLEY

ANONYMOUS

495 *Chance*

CHANCE, in whom men start and end,
   Throned on high in Wisdom's place,
Glory to man's work you send.
More the good your presence brings
Than the evil; such a grace
Shines about your golden wings.
When your ruling balance swings,
What it gives endures most blest.
For the pathless and distressed
You have found a guiding way,
In the darkness bringing day,
Goddess excellent and best.

C. M. BOWRA

496 *Hymn of the Cûrêtës*

HAIL to thee, Boy, Mighty One!
   Glory to thee, Cronus' son!
Joy and strength, thou comest here,
Leading on thy spirit-throng;
Visit Diktê year by year,
Gladdened by our dance and song.

For we interweave for thee
Hymn on flute and string;
Round thy well-built altar we
Set our choir and sing.
> Hail to thee, Boy, Mighty One!
> Glory to thee, Cronus' son!
> Joy and strength, thou comest here,
> Leading on thy spirit-throng;
> Visit us another year,
> Gladdened by our dance and song.

Here thy shielded nurses took
Thee, immortal child,
From thy mother, and they shook
Earth with leapings wild.
> Hail to thee, Boy, Mighty One!
> Glory to thee, Cronus' son!
> Joy and strength, thou comest here,
> Leading on thy spirit-throng;
> Visit us another year,
> Gladdened by our dance and song.

Crops were bursting every year,
Justice governed men;
Peace, the giver of good cheer,
Ruled all creatures then.
> Hail to thee, Boy, Mighty One!
> Glory to thee, Cronus' son!
> Joy and strength, thou comest here,
> Leading on thy spirit-throng;
> Visit us another year,
> Gladdened by our dance and song.

Leap to fill our vats, and leap
For our crops of fruit;
Leap for herds of fleecy sheep,
Leap for swelling root.
>   Hail to thee, Boy, Mighty One!
>   Glory to thee, Cronus' son!
>   Joy and strength, thou comest here,
>   Leading on thy spirit-throng;
>   Visit us another year,
>   Gladdened by our dance and song.

Leap for cities of our men,
Leap for ships at sea;
Leap for each young citizen;
Let Right honoured be.
>   Hail to thee, Boy, Mighty One!
>   Glory to thee, Cronus' son!
>   Joy and strength, thou comest here,
>   Leading on thy spirit-throng;
>   Visit us another year,
>   Gladdened by our dance and song.

C. M. BOWRA

THEOCRITUS
(c. 316 c. 260 B.C.)

497
The Cup

ABOUT its lip winds ivy, ivy flecked
    With golden berries, which goes twisting round
In all the glory of its saffron fruit.
And carved within the bowl a woman stands,
As beautiful as if a god had graved her,
With snood and cloak; and either side of her

A man with fair long hair; and angrily
Each speaks in turn but cannot reach her heart.
For now she smiles at one of them, and now
She flings the other just a moment's thought;
The long fatigue of love is on their eyes;
They lose their labour. Next to these is wrought
An ancient fisher and a rugged rock,
On which the old man stands and gathers up
His big net for a sturdy cast, like one
Who labours stoutly. Every limb, you'd say,
Was putting all its might into the work,
So swollen are the muscles down his neck,
Grey-headed though he is—indeed his strength
Is as the strength of youth. And close beyond
The sea-worn veteran is a vineyard, bowed
With fire-red clusters, and a little lad
Perched up on a stone wall is watching them.
And near him are two vixens, and the one
Goes prowling down the rows of vines to steal
A bite of fruit. Against the urchin's scrip
The other concentrates her wiles, resolved
To dog him, till she sets him down to make
A barren breakfast. All the time the boy
Is plaiting a fine locust cage with stalks
Of asphodel, and fitting it with reeds,
And never minds his wallet or his vines,
So happy is he in his basket-work.
And all around the cup are climbing sprays
Of lithe acanthus. Goatherds think it is
A marvel, and your soul will be amazed.

SIR WILLIAM MARRIS   (*Idyll* i. 29–56)

542

498   *The Passing of Daphnis*

'O PAN, O Pan, where'er thou rangest now—
   Lycæus' hill-top or tall Mænalus—
Come to the isle of Sicily, and leave
The cairn of Hélicê, and the towering tomb,
Where Arcas lies, which even the gods admire.'

   Muses, forgo, forgo the pastoral song.

'Master, approach: take to thee this fair pipe
Bedded in wax that breathes of honey still,
Bound at the lip with twine. For Love has come
To hale me off unto the house of Death.'

   Muses, forgo, forgo the pastoral song.

'Now let the briar and the thistle flower
With violets; and the fair narcissus bloom
On junipers: let all things go awry,
And pines grow pears, since Daphnis is for death.
Let stags pursue the hounds, and from the hills
The screeching owls outsing the nightingales.'

   Muses, forgo, forgo the pastoral song.

So said he then—no more. And Aphrodîtê
Was fain to raise him; but the Destinies
Had spun his thread right out. So Daphnis went
Down-stream: the whirlpool closed above his head,
The head of him whom all the Muses loved,
Of him from whom the Nymphs were not estranged.

   Muses, forgo, forgo the pastoral song.

Sir William Marris   (*Idyll* i. 123–42)

499   *Sîmætha*

WHERE are the bay-leaves, Théstylis? where are the
     love-charms?
and wreath the bowl with the crimson flower of wool.
For I'll put the witch-knots on my cruel lover.
Twelve days he has not come to me, the wretch.
He does not know if I'm alive or dead.
He has not knocked at my door. His heart is giddy,
it is stolen by Erôs, stolen by Aphrodîtê.
To-morrow I'll go to Tîmâgêtos' School
to see him and ask why he's so hard with me;
but to-night I'll spell him with fire. Shine brightly, Moon,
this murmured spell is for you and Hékatê
dark of the earth, who scares the trembling whelps,
visiting the barrowed dead where blood rots blackly.
Hail, dreadful one, be with me till I've made
this magic fiercer than any made by Circê,
Mêdêa, or Perimêdê the yellow-haired.
Bird-wheel, hither wind him, wind home my lover.

First barley burns. Come, Théstylis, scatter the grain.
Where, fool, are your wits astray now? Do I matter
so little that a drab can mock my pain?
Throw more, and say: 'The bones of Delphis I scatter.'
Bird-wheel, hither wind him, wind home my lover.

Delphis has rent me. So I burn the bay
for Delphis. See, it crackles. In a flash
it burns away and leaves a ghost of ash.
Thus may the flesh of Delphis burn away.
Bird-wheel, hither wind him, wind home my lover.

The spirit aids, the mammet melts above.
May Myndian Delphis thus be drained by love.
Dizzy him, magic bronze, swung roaringly
by Aphrodîtê, twirl him home to me.
Bird-wheel, hither wind him, wind home my lover.

I burn the bran. O Artemis, adamant hell
you'd move, or anything immovable.
Across the town by barking dogs she's traced—
she's at the crossroads. Clang the gong in haste.
Bird-wheel, hither wind him, wind home my lover.

Now quiet is the wind, and quiet the sea,
but in my heart no quiet comes to me.
I'm burned to death, I'm wretched and betrayed
by him that left me neither wife nor maid.
Bird-wheel, hither wind him, wind home my lover.

Thrice with libations I beg, and thrice with prayer.
O may the girl or boy he takes to bed
desert him, as in Dîa Thêseus fled
from Ariadnê sad with lovely hair.
Bird-wheel, hither wind him, wind home my lover.

This herb, colt's-madness, with wild juices fills
stallions and mares that stamp Arcadian hills.
Hither to me O let my Delphis race,
mad, and oiled sleekly from the wrestling-place.
Bird-wheel, hither wind him, wind home my lover.

From Delphis' cloak this tattered fringe once came.
I shred it now on the consuming flame.
I feel my dark blood flowing out, O harsh
is Love, a leech come clinging from the marsh.
Bird-wheel, hither wind him, wind home my lover.

I'll bray an eft; I'll brew him, when it's day,
an evil drink; but while the night is here,
Take simples, Théstylis, secretly; spit, and say,
smearing his lintel, 'Delphis' bones I smear.'
Bird-wheel, hither wind him, wind home my lover.

Now I'm alone . . . but how bewail my shame
of love, and her that brought my suffering?
Euboulos' daughter, Ánaxo, once came
with basket for the Grove of Artemis
where beasts (a lioness one) marched in a ring.
Hear, Lady Moon, how into me came this love.

Next-door Theumáridas' Thracian nurse (now blest
in death) implored and coaxed me not to miss
the show, and out I went along the street;
poor fool, in a long dress of silk I'd dressed,
with Clëarista's cloak to make it neat.
Hear, Lady Moon, how into me came this love.

We met two youths at Lycon's house, half-way,
Delphis and Eudâmippus, striding free.
Their beards were golder than cassidony,
O Moon, their breasts shone broad as you at full,
for, lithe and fit, they came from wrestling-school.
Hear, Lady Moon, how into me came this love.

I saw and loved, my heart was struck with dread,
my beauty ebbed, I could not see the show,
and how I reached my home I do not know.
By parching fever ravaged on my bed
senseless for ten days and ten nights I lay.
Hear, Lady Moon, how into me came this love.

The hair was falling from my head; my skin
was paler far than boxwood; shrunken in,
my body sagged. What witch was left untried?
what spell-wise crone but drew my steps aside?
No salve was gained, and still time hurried by.
Hear, Lady Moon, how into me came this love.

At last I told my servant all my grief.
'Théstylis, one thing only will bring relief.
I am the Myndian's, utterly. Then go
at once to Tîmâgêtus' wrestling-ground
where most he lounges, there he'll now be found.'
Hear, Lady Moon, how into me came this love.

'When he's alone, sign gently with your head.
Tell him, "Sîmætha wants you."' So I spoke,
and she obeyed, and hither he was led,
sleek with his wrestler's oil; and when I woke
and heard him coming with his springy tread—
Hear, Lady Moon, how into me came this love—

a shudder clenched me into ice, and wet
damper than dew my brow with sudden sweat;
I could not even cry as children cry
wanting their mother in their frightened sleep.
I lay, a doll, with body stiffly set.
Hear, Lady Moon, how into me came this love.

547

He sat upon my bed with lowered eyes,
and spoke to me, this man for whom I weep.
'Sîmætha, though you took me by surprise,
you but outran my coming by as far
as I Philînos when I won the prize.'
Hear, Lady Moon, how into me came this love.

'I meant to come with comrades, three or four,
to come in love's name with the earliest star—
with Dionŷsos-apples for my vow,
and with the poplar-sprig of Hêraklês
entwined with purple ribbons round my brow.'
Hear, Lady Moon, how into me came this love.

'And they'd have smiled if you'd said "Enter now,"
for I in look and sprinting beat them all—
a kiss I would have claimed from you, no more—
sweet lips!—but if you'd bolted out my pleas,
with torch and axe I'd then have breached your door.'
Hear, Lady Moon, how into me came this love.

'But when I knew that you had deigned to call,
first, thanks I offered to the Cyprian
and then to you that plucked a dying man
from dangerous flames, for wilder burns Desire
than burns the Smith-god's Liparêan fire.'
Hear, Lady Moon, how into me came this love.

'The frenzy drives. It lures the chambered maid;
and brides, still warm from marriage-beds, have strayed
to lovers. . . .'
                    I then, credulously gay,
touched him and drew him down where soft I lay.

548

Limbs moved on limbs, our faces bloomed with heat,
and as we clasped our murmuring mouths were sweet.
Hear, Lady Moon, how into me came this love.

Moon, I'll not tell each kiss lest you be tired.
We did what lovers do; what we desired.

No fault in him I found, nor he in me;
we twined in love till yesterday. But when Dawn,
dripping from Ocean, charioted aloft
with flushing arms, Melixo's mother came
(Philista, once our flute-girl, is her child)
and in the midst of wandering gossip swore
that Delphis was in love. So much she knew,
but if with girl or boy she wasn't sure.
'He pours out wine to Love, and then he runs
to heap the garlands round his darling's door.'
That was her tale, and she's not one to lie.
Once three or four times a day he'd come to me,
and leave his Dorian oil-flask for excuse.
But now for twelve days I've not seen his face,
elsewhere his pleasure lies and I'm forgotten.

So with my magic I'll charm him. If he persists,
by the Fates, the door on which he'll knock is death's.
Mistress, in a chest I have evil drugs
whispered to me by an Assyrian.
But farewell, Lady, oceanwards whip your team,
and my desire I'll bear as best I can.
Farewell, sleek body of the Moon, farewell,
star-courtiers nodding after drowsy Night.

JACK LINDSAY   (*Idyll* ii)

500 *Serenade*

O BEAUTIFUL Amaryllis, why no longer from your
cave

Do you peep forth to greet me, your beloved? Do you
hate me then?

Can it be I appear snub-nosed, dear nymph, when seen
from close?

A jutting-bearded satyr? You will make me hang myself.

See here ten apples I have brought you, fetched down
from the tree

From which you bade me fetch them. I will bring ten
more to-morrow.

Look on my heart-tormenting grief. Would that I might
become

Yon booming bee, and enter to your cavern, steering
through

The ivy and the feathery fern, wherein you lie em-
bowered.

Now I know Love. A cruel god is he: a she-lion's breasts

He sucked, and in a forest his mother nurtured him,

Since with slow fire he burns me thus, smiting me to the
bone.

O beautifully glancing—but all stone! O dark-browed
Nymph!

Around me, your own goatherd, fling your arms, that I
may kiss you.

Even in empty kisses there is a sweet delight.

Soon you will make me tear this garland into little shreds,

This ivy wreath, dear Amaryllis, that I keep for you,

Twining it with rose-buds and sweet-smelling parsley-
leaves.

Oh misery! What will be my fate, poor wretch! Will you
    not answer?
I'll strip my cloak off and leap down to the waves from
    yonder cliff,
Whence Olpis, the fisherman, watches for tunny shoals:
And if I perish—well, at least that will be sweet to you.

R. C. TREVELYAN   (*Idyll* iii. 6–27)

501   *Coy Polyphêmus*

DAPHNIS began the singing, for the challenge came
    from him.
'See you not, Polyphêmus, how Galateia is pelting
Your flock with apples? Fool-in-love she calls you, a goat-
    herd clown,
Yet no glance will you give her, hard of heart, but still
    you sit
Piping so sweetly. There again, look how she pelts your
    dog,
The faithful guardian of your sheep. Into the sea he peers
And barks, while in the pretty waves, that plash so tran-
    quilly,
His image is reflected as he runs along the sand.
Take good care, or else he'll leap right at the maiden's legs,
As she comes from the sea, and rend her fair flesh with his
    teeth.
See how she stands coquetting there, light as the dry
    winged seeds
Blown from a thistle in the lovely summer's noonday heat.
If a man love, she flies him; if he love not, she pursues,

And moves her last piece from the line: for truly in Love's
    eyes
Often, O Polyphêmus, what is not fair seems fair.'

Then after him Dâmœtas struck a prelude and sang thus:
'I saw it, yes, by Pan, when she was pelting at my flock:
She escaped not me, nor this one beauty of mine, where-
    with to the end
I'll look at her. Let Têlemos, that evil-boding seer,
Carry his evil bodements home to keep them for his
    children.
Nay, 'tis to punish and torment her that I will not look,
Giving it out I love some other girl: this she has heard,
And pines with jealousy for me, by Paian, and from the
    deep
Comes in a frenzy forth to gaze upon my caves and herds.
I hissed to my dog to bark at her; for when I was in love,
He used to whine for joy and rub his muzzle on her knees.
Perchance, seeing me treat her thus time after time, she'll
    send
Some messenger: but I'll shut my doors, until she swear to
    make me
With her own hands upon this isle a lovely nuptial bed.
For truly not ill-favoured is my face, as they pretend.
Not long ago I looked into the sea, when it was calm,
And beautiful my beard seemed, beautiful my one eye,
If I have any judgment; and the gleaming of my teeth
Whiter than Parian marble was reflected in the sea.
Then, to avoid the evil eye, I spat thrice in my breast,
A charm once taught me by that ancient crone, Cotýttaris.'

R. C. TREVELYAN   (*Idyll* vi. 5–40)

502   *Bound for the Harvest-home*

O NCE in a season past we left the town,
     Friend Eucritus and I, and journeyed down,
The fair Amyntas with us, to the banks
Of Haleis river. There was harvest-thanks
A-making for Dêmêter's charities
With Phrasidâmus and Antígenês,—
Brothers, Lycôpeus' children, of the best
True noble ancestry and ancientest,
From Clýtia, from old Chalcon's very stock,
Who pressed his knee, and straightway from the rock
The fount Bûrîna sprang,—whereby a grove
Rose at the side, that elms and poplars wove
With green leaves in a shady roofing pleached.

    The half-way in our road was hardly reached,
The tomb of Brásilas not showing yet,
When travelling on the way a man we met,
A good Cydônian—bless the Muses' aid!
By name hight Lycidas, and by his trade
A goatherd; none had seen him and mistook,
For every inch a goatherd was his look.

    On the left shoulder was a leathern coat
Made from the rough skin of a tawny goat,
And savouring of fresh rennet; on his breast,
Girt with a plaited belt, an old worn vest;
And in his right hand was a crooked staff
Made of wild olive.

                                                553

With a quiet laugh
Eye twinkling, and with mirth around his lip,
'Simíchidas,' said he, 'pray whither trip
Your feet at noonday so? This hour intense
Even the lizard in the roadside fence
Is sleeping, and abroad no longer roam
The tombstone-crested larks, but drowse at home.
Is it a banquet and the bidden guest?
Or is some neighbour's vintage to be pressed?
Such eager haste you make, the boot in springing
Strikes against every stone and sets it ringing.'

'Friend Lycidas,' I answered, 'all men still
Call you the prince of pipers in your skill
Among the shepherds and the reapers both;
And glad it makes my heart: yet by my troth
I think that I might make a match with thee!
This road now is the road of harvestry:
Our friends to-day are keeping merrymake
And banquet for the robed Earth-Mother's sake
With first-fruit offering of the golden store
Piled in so bounteous measure on their floor.

What say you, friend, then? Common is the way
And common is the morn,—come let us play
In pastoral fashion, brother-bard with brother;
Haply the one may benefit the other.
For I too am the Muses' ringing voice,
In minstrelsy most exquisite and choice,
As all men speak of me—though I am not
So fond and credulous; not I, God wot!

I cannot outsing yet, in my compare,
Sîcélidas from Samos, or the rare
Philêtas; 'tis but as a frog I croak
Against cicalas.'

                With intent I spoke,
For ends.—The goatherd, with his pleasant laugh,
Said, 'Here then is a gift, my crooked staff;
Because thou art a shoot of Jove's own tree,
Moulded throughout in perfect verity.
I hate your builder that would build a shed
As towering as the sovran mountain's head,
And birds of poesy that fondly strain
Cackling against the Chian bard in vain.
But come, Sîmíchidas, let us now sing
The rustic song: I have a trifling thing—
See if it please you, friend, this little lay
I wrought out on the uplands yesterday.'

WALTER HEADLAM   (*Idyll* vii. 1–51)

502 (a)   *Late Summer in the Country*

HE went his way, leftward bent towards Pyxa. So
I, and Eucritus and the fair Amýntichus, turned
aside into the house of Phrasidâmus, and lay down with
delight in beds of sweet tamarisk and fresh cuttings from
the vines, strewn on the ground. Many poplars and elm-
trees were waving over our heads, and not far off the
running of the sacred water from the cave of the nymphs
warbled to us; in the shimmering branches the sun-burnt
grasshoppers were busy with their talk, and from afar the
little owl cried softly, out of the tangled thorns of the

blackberry; the larks were singing and the hedge-birds, and the turtle-dove moaned; the bees flew round and round the fountains, murmuring softly; the scent of late summer and of the fall of the year was everywhere; the pears fell from the trees at our feet, and apples in number rolled down at our sides, and the young plum-trees were bent to the earth with the weight of their fruit.

WALTER PATER   (*Idyll* vii. 130–46)

502 (*b*)   *In Praise of Bombŷca*
                    A CLOWNISH SONG

MUSES of Pîeria, join one and all to sing
    my sweetheart so slender—your touch gilds everything.

Pretty Bombŷca, in you the world may see
'an Arab, lean and swarthy'—you're 'honey-blonde' to me.

Dark blow the violets, and corn-flag's lettered crest;
and yet to make a garland they're plucked before the rest.

Nanny-goat loves clover, the wolf must her pursue,
stork attends the plough-tail—and mine's a craze for you.

O for the wealth of Crœsus, that famous king of old!
I'd give to Aphrodîtê our statues done in gold.

With pipes and rose or apple you'd strike a posture there,
and I in dandy costume, and brogues—a brand-new pair.

Your feet, pretty Bombŷca, are hucklebones[1] for grace,
your voice soother than nightshade, and O your pretty
    ways!

T. F. HIGHAM   (*Idyll* x. 24–37)

[1] Used for dicing.

556

502 (*c*)   *Reapers' Song*

DÊMÊTER, rich in harvest of fruit and corn, to thee
we pray to bless our field-work with ears as full can be.

Bind the sheaves, bandsters, and save the passing jest:
'These men are rotten lumber—another wage gone west.'

Northward set the sheaf-butts, or let the west-wind blow
to catch the haulms and dry them—the grain grows
fatter so.

Beware the sleep, threshers, that comes at noon of day;
for then's the best of all times to flail the chaff away.

The lark is early risen: reapers, begin as soon.
When she's to bed, give over, and slacken off at noon.

No butler for the frog, boys! he lives without a care;
the drink is at his elbow—enough and to spare.

Oh, bailiff, you're a miser: make thicker lentil-stew—
and mind your finger, splitting the cumin-seed in two.

T. F. HIGHAM   (*Idyll* x. 42–55)

502 (*d*)   *Polyphêmus to Galatêa*

O GALATÊA faire, why dost thou shun thy lover
true?
More tender than a Lambe, more white than cheese when
it is new,
More wanton than a calfe, more sharpe than grapes unripe
I finde.
You use to come, when pleasant sleepe my senses all doe
binde.

557

But you are gone againe, when pleasant sleepe dooth leave
    mine eie,

And as a sheep you run, that on the plaine a Woolfe doth spie.

I then began to love thee, Galatê, when first of all

You with my mother came, to gather leaves of Crowtoe
    small

Upon our hil, when I as usher, squirde you all the waie.

Nor when I saw thee first, nor afterward, nor at this daie,

Since then could I refraine; but you, by Jove, nought set
    thereby.

But well I knowe, fair Nimphe, the verie cause why you
    thus flie.

Because upon my front, one onlie brow, with bristles
    strong

From one eare to the other eare, is stretchèd al along.

Nethe which, one eie, and on my lips a hugie nose there
    standes.

Yet I, this such a one, a thousand sheep feed on these
    lands.

And pleasant milke I drinke, which from the strouting[1]
    bags is prest.

Nor want I cheese in summer, nor in Autumne of the best,

Nor yet in winter time. My cheese-rackes ever laden are,

And better can I pipe, than anie Cyclops maie compare.

O Apple, sweet, of thee, and of my selfe, I use to sing,

And that at midnight oft. For thee, aleavne[2] faunes up I
    bring,

All great with young, and foure beares whelps, I nourish
    up for thee.

But come thou hither first, and thou shalt have them all
    of me.

        [1] smelling.   [2] eleven.

And let the blewish colorde Sea beat on the shore so nie.

The night with me in cave, thou shalt consume more
  pleasantlie.

There are the shadie Baies, and there tall Cypres-trees doe
  sprout,

And there is Ivie blacke, and fertill Vines are al about.

Coole water there I have, distillèd of the whitest snowe,

A drinke devine, which out of wooddy Ætna mount doth
  flowe.

In these respects, who in the Sea and waves would rather
  be?

But if I seeme, as yet, too rough and savage unto thee,

Great store of Oken woode I have, and never quenchèd
  fire;

And I can well indure my soule to burne with thy desire,

With this my onely eie, then which I nothing thinke more
  trimme.

Now woe is me, my mother bore me not with finns to
  swimme,

That I might dive to thee, that I thy dainty hand might
  kisse,

If lips thou wouldst not let; then would I Lillies bring I
  wis,

And tender Poppie toe, that beares a top like rattells red.

And these in summer time, but other are in winter bred,

So that I cannot bring them all at once. Now certainlie,

Ile learne to swimme of some or other stranger passing bie,

That I maie knowe what pleasure tis in waters deepe to
  dwell.

Come forth, faire Galatê, and once got out, forget thee
  well

(As I doe sitting on this rocke) home to returne againe.

But feede my sheepe with me, and for to milke them take
    the paine,
And cheese to presse, and in the milke, the rennet sharpe
    to straine.
My mother only wrongeth me, and her I blame, for shee
Spake never yet to thee, one good or lovelie word of me,
And that, although shee daily sees how I awaie doe pine.
But I will saie my head and feete doe ake, that shee maie
    whine
And sorrowe at the hart, because my hart with griefe is
    swolne.
O Cyclops, Cyclops, whither is thy wit and reason flowne?
If thou wouldst baskets make, and cut downe browzing
    from the tree,
And bring it to thy Lambes, a great deal wiser thou
    shouldst be!
Goe coie some present Nimphe, why dost thou follow
    flying wind?
Perhaps an other Galatê, and fairer thou shalt find.
For manie maidens in the evening tide with me will plaie,
And all doe sweetlie laugh, when I stand harkning what
    they saie,
And I some bodie seeme, and in the earth doe beare a swaie.
ANON. (1588)   (*Idyll* xi. 19–79)

502 (e)   *Hylas*

WATER the fair lad went to seek and bring
    To Hêraclês and stalwart Télamon,
(The comrades aye partook each other's fare,)
    Bearing a brazen pitcher. And anon,
Where the ground dipt, a fountain he espied,
And rushes growing green about its side.

There rose the sea-blue swallow-wort, and there
   The pale-hued maidenhair, with parsley green
And vagrant marsh-flowers; and a revel rare
   In the pool's midst the water-nymphs were seen
To hold, those maidens of unslumbrous eyes
Whom the belated peasant sees and flies.

And fast did Mâlis and Eunîca cling,
   And young Nychêa with her April face,
To the lad's hand, as stooping o'er the spring
   He dipt his pitcher. For the young Greek's grace
Made their soft senses reel; and down he fell,
All of a sudden, into that black well.

So drops a red star suddenly from the sky
   To sea—and quoth some sailor to his mate:
'Up with the tackle, boy! the breeze is high.'
   Him the nymphs pillowed, all disconsolate,
On their sweet laps, and with soft words beguiled;
But Hêraclês was troubled for the child.

Forth went he; Scythian-wise his bow he bore
   And the great club that never quits his side;
And thrice cried 'Hylas'—ne'er came lustier roar
   From that deep chest. Thrice Hylas heard and tried
To answer, but in tones you scarce might hear;
The water made them distant though so near.

C. S. CALVERLEY   (*Idyll* xiii. 36–60)

502 (f)   *Gorgo and Praxínoa*

GORGO. Praxínoa at home?

PRAXÍNOA.   Of course she is.
    Dear Gorgo, what a long time since we met,
    I'm quite surprised to see you. A chair, Eunóa,
    and throw a cushion on it.

GORGO.   O, no thank you,
    it's quite nice as it is.

PRAXÍNOA.   Then do sit down.

GORGO. It really was a madness to come out—
    I don't know how I'm here alive, my dear!
    There's such a crush, and horses everywhere:
    nothing but boots and men in uniform—
    the street went on for ever. Really, dear,
    this house you've taken is a long way out.

PRAXÍNOA. O, all my idiot's fault! He would come here,
    right at the world's end, and a den at that,
    not a human habitation: all for spite!
    to get me as far away as he could from you—
    he's made up of pure jealousy: always the same—

GORGO. My dear, don't talk so harshly of your Dînon
    before the baby. How he's staring at you!
    Never mind, little Zôpyrus, honey-pet—
    it's not your daddy that she's speaking of.

PRAXÍNOA. O, by our Lady, the child understands.

GORGO. Pretty daddy!

PRAXÍNOA.   Yes, that pretty fellow
    the other day—I said to him—the other day:
    'Dad, please buy mother here some soap and rouge,'
    and would you credit it? the great big boob
    came back and handed me a packet of salt.

GORGO. O, men are all the same, my Diocleidas
simply flings money away. He paid seven shillings
just yesterday, for what's nothing but dog's combings,
five fleeces, he said! the shreddings of old bags,
all utter trash—O, trouble upon trouble—
But come now and put on your cloak and gown,
we're going to pay a visit to the King,
our bountiful Ptolemaios, with a peep
at the *Adônis*. I've been told the Queen
is doing things most gorgeously this year.

PRAXÍNOA. Fine folks can do fine things.

GORGO.   And those who see them
have something that's worth talking of to those
who didn't go and see. Come on, it's time
we made a start.

PRAXÍNOA.   All days are holidays
for people with no work to do. . . .

                                          Eunóa,
you slut there, come and take this spinning, put it
with all the rest. Cats always will lie snugly.
Hurry now, get some water, hurry now—
I want the water first and she brings soap—
never mind, give it to me—not so much,
you wasteful thing! There now, pour out the
        water. . . .
You fool! look out, you're wetting all my bodice—
Now that will do.

                        O well, I'm washt at last
as well as heaven would let me. Where's the key
of that big cupboard? Bring it to me here.

GORGO. Praxínoa, the full gathering of that dress
does suit you well. Please tell me the stuff's cost.

PRAXÍNOA. O, don't remind me—I'd to pay for it
    more than eight pounds in silver. I assure you,
    I put my soul in every single stitch.
GORGO. Well, I must say, you couldn't wish for better.
PRAXÍNOA. How sweet of you to say so.

                          Now my cloak,
    come, put it on me—and my hat too—mind!
    the stylish angle.

                 As for you, my boy,
    you are not coming with us. Big horse bitey,
    bogey-horse. Well, bawl then, if you must,
    I certainly won't have you maimed for life.
    Come along—you, Phrygia, take the child,
    play with him for a bit—and for the rest,
    call in the dog and see the front door's locked.

O heavens, what a mob! I can't imagine
how we're to squeeze through, or how long it'll take—
An ant-heap's nothing to this hurly-burly.
Though, Ptolemaios, I admit you've made
things better since your father went to heaven.
We have no brigands padding up behind,
nowadays, to murder us in the streets
in true Egyptian style. Men now don't play
such dreadful games, though underneath of course
they're still the same old lying rogues, all rotters.

O, Gorgo darling, look! what will we do?
The Royal Cavalry! Don't ride me down,
please, my good man. That bay is rearing up.
How vicious. You excitable young fool,

Eunóa, get out of the way. I'm sure that horse
will end by killing him—O, what a blessing
it is that I have left the child at home.

GORGO. There, there, Praxínoa, nothing now to fear!
they're well ahead, assembling where they're bidden.

PRAXÍNOA. So are my wits now. Two things frighten me,
ever since I was young it's been the same:
nasty cold-blooded snakes, and horses. Come,
we'd better hurry. The crowd's thickening.

GORGO. From the palace, mother?

OLD WOMAN.   Yes, my child.

GORGO.   Then we
can get in too all right?

OLD WOMAN.   My dear young lady,
the Achaians got into Troy by trying hard—
Where there's a will, there's a way.

GORGO.   Well, the old lady
left us some oracles to ponder, eh?

PRAXÍNOA. We women, we know everything, we know
how Zeus got Hêra for wife.

GORGO.   Praxínoa,
O, look at all that crowd before the door.

PRAXÍNOA. Incredible. Here, Gorgo, take my arm,
and you catch hold of Eútychis there, Eunóa,
or you'll be separated—now let's try
to push in altogether. Mind, Eunóa,
keep hold of me—O, Gorgo, what a shame,
my summer cloak is torn from top to bottom.
Here, sir, if you'd have any hope of heaven,
take care of my cloak.

MAN.   I'll do my very best,
but one can't help being pusht.

PRAXÍNOA. The crowd's tremendous:
pushing like a mob of pigs.

MAN. Don't worry, ladies,
we're not so badly off.

PRAXÍNOA. Well, I hope, dear sir,
you'll always be able to say that of yourself—
you've taken such good care of us: good-bye.
What a kind, thoughtful man—

O, look at Eunóa!
she's being squasht. Push, weakling, can't you?

At last.
All in: as the bridegroom said when he shut the door.

GORGO. O, do come here, Praxínoa. First of all,
you really must see these embroideries:
so delicate, and charming . . . why, they're robes
fit for the wear of gods.

PRAXÍNOA. By the Lady Athâna!
whoever the weavers were that made those stuffs
and the embroiderers who could produce
such detailed work and so minutely too—
well, they're beyond me! And how very lifelike:
the figures stand and move like real people.
Man really is a wonderful creature, you know:
the things he does. And there, the Sacred Boy!
stretched out so sweetly on his couch of silver
and youth so faintly downy on his cheeks—
O, thrice-beloved Adônis, whom they love
even in Ácheron. . . .

MAN. O, god help you, stop—
cooing and cooing like doves! We're bored to death
with all your drawling Doric.

PRAXÍNOA. Goodness gracious!

where does this person come from? and please tell us
what right have you to be rude if we do coo?
Buy your slaves before you try to boss them.
You're trying to boss Syracusans, let me tell you;
though, if you really want to know the facts,
we both come from Corinthian families,
as did Bellerophon—and so our accent
is Peloponnesian, and I should suppose
Dorians may be allowed to speak in Doric—
Persephonê! one husband is enough—
not that I take the slightest notice anyway,
so don't waste breath on me.

GORGO.   Now that will do.
Listen, Praxínoa, she's about to sing,
the daughter of that Argive, you know who—
that versatile young vocalist, what's the phrase—
the prize-singer of the dirge last year. She's sure
to give us something well worth listening to.
There now, she's preening ready for the song.

JACK LINDSAY   (*Idyll* xv. 1–99)

502 (g)   *The Fishermen's Hut*

POVERTY, Diophantus, wakes the Arts
  Alone, and skill to handicraft imparts,
Teacher of toil. There's little time to sleep
For any workman. Cares about him creep
And evil worries. When he starts to snore
They set upon him with a loud uproar.
  Now two old salts, who knew the fisher's trade,
Of dry sea-moss a lowly bed had made

Under a wattled hut, hard by a wall
Of leaves. Their tackle lay to hand withal,
Scattered about them: rods and creels of reeds,
And nets and hooks and lines all stiff with weeds,
And horsehair leaders, and full many a snare
For crayfish plaited, and a weathered pair
Of oars and cords all tangled in a maze,
And an old skiff drawn high upon the ways.
Under their heads were rolled thin cloaks of frieze;
Thick jackets were their coverlids; for these
Were all their substance and their property;
All else for them were superfluity.
Key, dog, or door they needed not for guard;
Over them Poverty kept watch and ward.
No neighbour near their cabin would abide,
Only the soft encroachment of the tide.

H. H. CHAMBERLIN   (*Idyll* xxi. 1–18)

502 (*h*)   *Amycus*

                              They found
Hard by a slab of rock a bubbling spring
Brimful of purest water. In the depths
Below, like crystal or like silver gleamed
The pebbles: high above it pine and plane
And poplar rose, and cypress tipt with green;
With all rich flowers that throng the mead, when
        wanes
The Spring, sweet workshops of the furry bee.
There sat and sunned him one of giant bulk
And grisly mien: hard knocks had stov'n his ears:
Broad were his shoulders, vast his orbèd chest:
Like a wrought statue rose his iron frame:

568

And nigh the shoulder on each brawny arm
Stood out the muscles, huge as rolling stones
Caught by some rain-swoln river and shapen smooth
By its wild eddyings: and o'er nape and spine
Hung, balanced by the claws, a lion's skin.

C. S. CALVERLEY   (*Idyll* xxii. 37–52)

503   *The Dogs at the Homestead*

THE dogs perceived their coming, yet far off:
    They scented flesh, they heard the thud of feet:
And with wild gallop, baying furiously,
Ran at Amphítryon's son: but feebly whined
And fawned upon the old man at his side.
Then the old man, just lifting from the ground
A pebble, scared them home, and with hard words
Cursed the whole pack; and having stopped their din
(Inly rejoiced, nathless, to see them guard
So well an absent master's house) he spake:

'Lo! what a friend the royal gods have given
Man in the dog! A trusty servant he!
Had he withal an understanding heart,
To teach him when to rage and when forbear,
What brute could claim like praise? But, lacking wit,
'Tis but a passionate random-raving thing.'
    He spake: and quickly to the byre they came.

After C. S. CALVERLEY   (*Idyll* xxv. 68–84)

569

504 Lines written to accompany the Gift of a Distaff to Theugenis

DISTAFF, the spinner's friend, gift of Athêna,
the grey-eyed goddess, to women thrifty-minded,
housekeepers of skill in profitable ways,
come with good heart to the splendour of Nêleus' city,
where Kypris in soft reed-covert is greenly enshrined.
There, pray Zeus, may a fair wind carry our sail,
for joy of a friend to befriend me, for sight of my Nîkias,
a slip of divinity nursed by the musical Graces.

You, my creature of ivory, child of much travail,
I'll bring to the hands of Nîkias' wife, my gift.
Many fleeces of wool you shall spin with her,—cloaks for
    men
she'll make, and the billowing flow of women's dresses.
Lamb'd ewes at grass might double the year's soft load
of shearings, and light-foot Theugenis not demur,
so quickly she works, her heart never set upon vanities.

Not on a thriftless house, not on a slattern's
would I choose to bestow you; for one land fathered us
    both,
one city, that Árchias out of Éphyra founded,
the very marrow of Sicily's three-tipt island,
Syracuse, city of honourable men.

You shall house with a Doctor of Medicine, rich in skill
to physic away the murderous pains of disease.
In pleasant Mîlêtus, among Iônian people,

570

your new home waits, that there, when townswomen
    gather,
Theugenis may be renowned for a Distaff of Quality,
and handling you, remember through all her days
the poet, her visitor once, the singer of songs.

And looking upon you, some one shall speak and say:
'Surely great loving-kindness yet may go
with a little gift: all's dear that comes from friends.'

T. F. HIGHAM   (*Idyll* xxviii)

ARÂTUS

(C. 315–240 B.C.)

505
Proem

FROM Zeus begin we, never nameless we
    May leave him. All the streets are full of Zeus,
And market-places: full also the sea
    And harbours. Ever in the need of Zeus
We stand, for we are also his offspring,
And mild to men he gives signs favouring.

Wakening the folk to work for livelihood,
    He tells when ground is best for ox and spade,
And when the trenching season is most good
    For trees, when seed to sow. Himself arrayed
The signs in heaven, the stars and constellations
That best may mark the season's alternations.

571

He watched year through, that all might grow unceasing;
　　Wherefore do men him first and last revere.
Hail Father! Great thy wonder, man's great blessing
　　Thou and the Elder Race! And Muses dear
Hail each and all! I tell the stars, and pray
You keep my song from trespass all the way.

GEORGE ALLEN   (*Phænomena*, 1–18)

506   *When Justice dwelt on Earth*

THE hurt of strife they knew not in their day,
　　Nor yet sharp quarrel and the noise of war.
Simply they lived, the rude sea far away,
　　No ships to bring their living from afar;
But cows and ploughs and Justice in her rule
Freely gave all, of just gifts bountiful.

So lived she while the age earth nursed was gold,
　　But with the silver little and less free
She mingled, yearning for men's ways of old;
　　Though yet in silver age on earth was she,
Who from the sounding hills would come alone
At evening, with a cheerful word for none.

But when she filled the high hills with mankind,
　　Then would she threaten, their base lives condemn,
Declare she would not come for eyes to find
　　When they should call. 'Behold the race of them!
What sons of golden sires! and baser yet,
—Degenerate stock!—you too shall misbeget!'

572

'Now surely wars and wicked lust to kill
        Shall be with men, and trouble press them hard!'
She spoke, and to the mountains made; and still
        The folk she left there all towards her stared.
But even others came at their decease,
The race of bronze, more dangerous men than these.

Now first they forged the highwayman a sword,
        And now first ate the ox from the ploughshare;
Then truly Justice all that race abhorred,
        And fled to heaven to make her dwelling there,
Where still at night the Virgin star do men
Discover near Boôtes the far-seen.

GEORGE ALLEN   (*Phænomena*, 108–36)

CALLIMACHUS
                                        (310–c. 240 B.C.)
507   *The Epiphany of Apollo*

HOW the branch trembles of Apollo's bay!
        How the whole shrine! Hence, sinners all, away!
Now Phœbus with his beautiful feet assails
The threshold. Look! on a sudden gently vails
The Delian palm her crest, while heavenward soars
The swan singing. Lift up your bolts, ye doors,
And be ye turned, ye keys! The God is near.
Prepare you, lads, for song and dance, prepare!

    Apollo doth not unto all appear,
But to the good: who seeth him is great;
Who hath not seen him is of low estate.

573

We shall behold thee, Archer, and not be base.
Boys, when Apollo visiteth his place,
Not mute your lyre nor pulseless be your tread,
If you'd be wived, and crop a silvered head,
And stedfast on their old foundations keep
Your walls! Well done! the lyre is not asleep.

Hush, listeners, at the Apolline melody!
Hushed are the waves when minstrels magnify
The Lycoreian emblems, lyre or bow:
Thetis will intermit the dirge of woe
Over her son Achilles when she hears
'Hiê Pæêon'; and the Rock of Tears,
That dripping stone, that marble woman set
Wide-mouthed in Phrygia mourning, will forget.

R. A. FURNESS   (*Hymn* ii. 1–24)

508   *Artemis visits the Cyclopës*

AT once, she went, and found the Cyclopës
in Lípara's island—not called Lípara then,
but Meligûnis, as of old. They stood
each to his anvil in Hêphæstos' forge
around a mass new-molten, hard at work
on a huge horse-trough to Poseidon's order.
    Fear took the Nymphs, seeing those shapes of horror
like scaurs on Ossa, giants every one,
each with a single brow, and single eye
big as a targe of four bulls' hides, that shot
a lowering glance; fear took them as they heard
loud-ringing anvils and the roaring blast
of bellows, and from Cyclopës themselves

a deep-fetcht groaning. Ætna's echoes rang,
rang all Trinácria, home of Sican folk,
Italy rang, their neighbour; and all Cyrnus
answered with clamour to the smiths at work—
so hard they laboured, swinging hammers down
from high over the shoulder, turn by turn,
on furnaced bronze or iron hissing-hot.

If Ocean's daughters not without dismay
looked on them, face to face, and heard that din,
let none condemn. Not even girls full-grown,
children of gods, can meet them unafraid.
When some young goddess disobeys her mother,
then for the Cyclopës her mother calls—
'Argês' or 'Steropês', she cries, 'will catch you!'
—and out comes Hermês from an inner room,
fouled with burnt ashes. At his fee-faw-fum
the child dives for her mother's lap, eyes covered.

T. F. HIGHAM   (*Hymn* iii. 46–71)

509   *Delos*

WINDY and waste and battered by the sea,
        More apt for speed of gull than horse, stands she
Fast in the waves, and from the surge that brims
Around her of Îcarian water skims
The clotted foam: wherefore upon her ground
Homes of seafaring fishermen are found.
No grudging matter if the poet styles
Her eminent, whene'er the assembled isles
To Ocean and to Tîtan Têthys take
Their way: she marches foremost. In her wake

Follow Phœnician Cyrnus, land of fame,
Abantian Macris, heir of Ellops' name,
Sardinia, island of delight, and she
Whom Cypris swam to, rising from the sea,
And gave protection as her landing-fee.
Strong in their sheltering watch-towers are they all,
But Delos in Apollo; and what wall
Can be more stedfast? Battlement and rock
Beneath Strŷmônian Bóreas' tempest-shock
May tumble down. A God can never yield.
Such is your champion, Delos, and your shield.

So many a wreath of circling song you wear,
What shall I weave you, welcome to your ear?
How a great god in the beginning swayed
His weapon triple-pronged, Telchînian-made,
And split the mountains, causing isles to be,
Levered them up, and rolled them out to sea?
He rooted their foundations in the deep,
No memory of the continent to keep;
But you, by no necessity controlled,
Floated the waters freely, and of old
Were named Astéria,—Star that would not wed
With Zeus, but leapt gulfward from heaven and fled.
Still unto you no golden Lêto came;
Astéria still, not Delos, was your name.
Sailors from holy Trœzên, on the way
To Éphyra, in the Sarônic bay
Would often sight you, and from Éphyra back
Sailing they saw you not, nor marked your track
Up the loud rapid of Eurîpus' Strait.
Nor there in Chalcian waters did you wait
Daylong, but swimming or to Sûnium's crest

576

Athenian, or to Chios, or the breast,
Lapped by the billows, of the Maiden Isle,
(For Samos yet it was not,) there awhile
Over against Ancæus' shore, the guest
Of Mycalessid Nymphs, you chose to rest.
But when for Phœbus' birth you gave your ground,
Your altered name by mariners was found,
Because no longer dimly did you fleet
But rooted in the Ægean waves your feet.

R. A. FURNESS   (*Hymn* iv. 11–54)

510   *The Blinding of Tîresias*

ONE single Nymph all other Nymphs above
   In olden Thebes enjoyed Athêna's love,
The mother, maidens, of Tîresias;
And they were never parted: but whenas
Athêna crossed Bœotia's toilèd lea
Driving her team to ancient Thespiæ,
Or Corônêa, or Haliartus,—drove
To Corônêa, to where her incensed grove
And altars lie, upon Cûralius-side,
Oft in the Goddess' chariot she would ride;
Nor met the Nymphs for converse or for show
Of merry dance but led by Chariclo.
Yet many a tear in store for her there lay,
Even her, Athêna's bosom-friend, the day
They loosed their buckles, put their robes away,
On Helicon, by the clear Horsefoot Rill,
And bathed. A noontide stillness held the hill.
They two were bathing: it was full noontide;
And a deep stillness reigned on that hill-side.

Tîresias yet, alone with hounds, (his face
Shading to manhood) ranged that holy place;
And greatly thirsting to the stream came he,
And saw, unpurposed, what he might not see.
Pallas, enraged, yet spoke: 'What Fate, O thou
Not to take hence thine eyes, has led thee now,
Son of Euêrês, this rough road?' And night,
Even as she spoke, settled upon his sight.
He stood there speechless; for the torment wrung
And gripped his knees, and palsy tied his tongue.
But the Nymph cried out 'Lady, what hast thou done?
Is this a Goddess' friendship? Alas! my son!
Thou hast taken away his sight. O child unblest!
Thou that hast seen Athêna's thighs and breast
But shalt not see the sun again. Ay me!
O mountain never revisited to be!
O Helicon! how heavy is thy price,
That those few fawns should cost my child his eyes!
Both arms about her darling son she bent,
And raised the mournful nightingale's lament,
Heavily wailing. And Athêna took
Compassion on her friend, and thus she spoke:
'Lady, all words uttered in wrath unkind
Unsay: it was not I who struck him blind.
Athêna has no wish to pluck away
Eyes from a child. 'Tis Cronus' laws that say
"Who seeth any Immortal whatsoe'er,
The God unwilling, it shall cost him dear".
Irrevocably what is done is done,
For so the fatal threads were early spun
The day thou barest him. But now attend,
Son of Euêrês, to the appointed end.

578

What offerings will Cadmus' daughter burn,
What offerings Aristæus, but to earn
Blindness for their one son, Actæon! Mate
Though he shall be of Artemis the Great
In hunting, he shall profit from that skill
And common archery upon the hill
Naught, when he sees, although he purpose not,
Her beauteous bath. His own hounds on the spot
Shall eat their master, and his mother rove
Gathering his bones through every upland grove.
Thy fate she'll call most fortunate and kind
To get back thy son from the mountains, blind.
So weep not, comrade: for thy sake remain
Manifold honours for thy son to gain.
Seer I will make him, sung of ages hence,
Having above all seers pre-eminence.
He shall discern all birds of good portent
In flight, and evil, and indifferent.
Much sooth for Thebans, Cadmus, and the line
Of later Lábdacus, he shall divine.
A staff I'll give him, in his need to guide
His feet; and years lastingly multiplied.
He only, dead, shall walk among the ghosts
Conscious, and honoured of the Lord of Hosts.'

R. A. FURNESS   (*Hymn* v. 57–130)

511   *Erysichthon*

THERE was a grove Pelasgian men had planted,—
        Dêmêter's ground of beautiful trees wide-flung,
Whose length a bow-shot scarce had travelled through.
Pines grew within, and giant elms, and pears,

And rarest sweeting apples. Runnels leapt
With liquid amber; and she loved the place,—
Never Eleusis, Tríopum, or Enna
Had moved the goddess to a madder love.
But when the House of Tríopas fell from grace,
By will of Fortune came a wicked thought
On Erysichthon, and the worse prevailed.
Hot-foot he went with twenty serving-men,
All in the sap of youth, gigantic all,
—A force to uproot a city. Armed they were
With double-axe and hatchet, making speed
Incontinently to Dêmêter's grove.

A poplar stood, a huge tree, heaven-reaching,
Where nymphs would often play towards the noon.
Stricken the first, a boding note it sang
Of death to others; and Dêmêter knew
The agony of that hallowed forester,
And cried in wrath 'Who cuts my beautiful trees?'
With that she vanished, hastening in disguise
Of one Nîcippê, whom the people made
Her public votaress. Fillets and poppy-head
She bore, with temple-key from shoulder hung;
Then to that evil-doer lost to shame
Spoke gently: 'You, my child, who cut the trees
Given to god,—I bid you, child, forbear.
Child of your parents' many prayers, have done,
And turn your men, fearing Dêmêter's wrath.
The grove you plunder is Our Lady's ground.'
He glowered down, with gaze unkinder yet
Than hunter meets on Tmarus' mountain-wold
When the cubbed lioness glares; than whom, men say,
No creature living has more terrible eyes.

'Begone,' he cried, 'or flesh this mighty axe!
These timbers build my house; and there, all weathers,
We'll feast to our hearts' content, my friends and I.'
      The lad spoke ill: and Nemesis took note.

What tongue can tell Dêmêter's wrath? No more
She cloaked her godhead. Still on earth she trod,
But towered to heaven, touching Olympus' height.
And they, in deathly fear, left axe in tree,
Scattering on a sudden before her face.
The rest she suffered,—underlings constrained
By sullen master. Him she answered back:
'So be it, dog, so be it! Go you and build!
Build, dog, and eat! There's many a feast to come.'
No more she said, but worked her grievous will,
And burning pains on Erysichthon came,—
A rampant fury of hunger ruled within,
Scruzing his vitals, making him sick to death.
O miserable man, no bite he took
But craved another, and as much again.
A score of cooks his table set; his wine
Twelve butlers drew; and double scourge he bore,—
For Dionŷsus with Dêmêter paired,
Sharing her anger, as her grove he shared.

      From wake and festival for very shame
His parents kept him, fertile of excuse.
Came sons of Órmenus, to Pallas' games
Bidding him, at Itônê. 'Sirs,' replied
His mother, 'he's but yesterday gone out;
For Krannon owes us cattle—a hundred head.'
Polyxo, mother to Actórion,

Would have him with old Tríopas attend
Against the day that saw Actórion wed.
The other wept,—'Ay, Tríopas will come;
But Erysichthon, wounded by a boar
Over on Pindus, in the valley covers,
Is keeping to his bed, these nine days gone.'
Unhappy mother, for your darling son
What lie was left unspoken? Never came
A feast, but—'Erysichthon's gone abroad';
No wedding came, but—'Erysichthon 's wounded—
Hit by a quoit', or 'from his chariot fallen',
Or 'gone to count the flocks on Othrys hill'.

Then privily at daylong feast he sat,
Eating and eating. Rank as a weed outgrown
His belly thrusted, fed on more and more;
And all the meats down to a bottomless gulf
Huge as the sea, in thankless bounty poured.
Snow on Mount Mîmas, waxen doll in the sun,
More slowly waste than fell his flesh away
Down to the sinews burning. Nothing remained
Of that unfortunate but fibre and bone.
His mother wept, two sisters deeply wailing
Mourned with his wet-nurse and the slave-girls ten;
And Tríopas himself, his grey hair clutching,
Called on Poseidon, deaf to hear his call:
'This generation of thy sons behold
False father!—if indeed thy son am I,
Born to thy Æolid Cánacê; and if
This most unfortunate child is child of mine.
Would that Apollo's arrow had shot him down
And I might bury him! For now he sits

582

The Curse of Famine incarnate in my sight.
Either remove his torment, or thyself
Take him and feed. My groaning board is bare,
My folds are stript, empty my cattle-yards,
Butcher and cook already say me no.'

But the great wains gave up their mules; and next
His mother's ox went down, the fatted ox
She kept for Hestia; down the horses went,
Winner and war-horse both; and last of all
The cat, whom little creatures shook to see.
    Now while the house of Tríopas could provide,
Only its chambers knew the plague within;
But when it failed of plenty, gnawed bone-dry,
The king's son at the cross-road sat and begged,
Craving his orts and scullions' table-scraps.

T. F. HIGHAM   (*Hymn* vi. 25–115)

512   *Daybreak in the City*

HER tale was told, the other's listening done,
    And both birds slept. After a little while
There came a frosted neighbour, breaking sleep:
'Up, for the night is gone, and home from hunting
Night thieves return; the morning lamps are lit.
Now sing the drawers of water about the well,
And loaded wagon grates on axle-tree
Waking the road-side dweller; herded slaves
Sweat in the smithies, vext with deafening din.

T. F. HIGHAM   (*Hécalê*)

513 *Hêraclîtus*

THEY told me, Hêraclîtus, they told me you were
    dead;
They brought me bitter news to hear and bitter tears to
    shed.
I wept, as I remember'd, how often you and I
Had tired the sun with talking and sent him down the sky.

And now that thou art lying, my dear old Carian guest,
A handful of grey ashes, long, long ago at rest,
Still are thy pleasant voices, thy nightingales, awake,
For Death, he taketh all away, but them he cannot take.

WILLIAM CORY   (*Epigr.* ii)

514 *The Good live for ever*

SAÔN, the Acanthian, son of Dicôn, lies
    Here, fast asleep; say not the good man dies.

H. MACNAGHTEN   (*Epigr.* ix)

515 *Dialogue with the Dead*

'ART thou the grave of Cháridas?' 'If for Arimmas'
    son,
The Cyrênæan, you inquire, I am the very one.'
'How goes it, Cháridas, below?' 'Much gloom.' 'And
    the way back?'
'A lie, there is none.' 'Pluto, then?' 'Pluto's a myth.'
    'Alack!'
'I'm telling you the truth. If you want fairy tales instead,
The market price of oxen here is half a crown a head.'

G. M. YOUNG   (*Epigr.* xiii)

516   *Nîcotelês*

PHILIP'S Nîcotelês, a twelve-year lad,
   Lies buried here: the hope his father had.

R. C. K. Ensor   (*Epigr.* xix)

517   *The Poet's Father*

WHOEVER you are who wander near
   My monument, I'd have you hear
From whom I sprang, who sprang from me:
Callimachus of Cyrênê.
You'd know them both: leader, the one,
Of his town army years agone:
The other, poet; songs he sung
Beyond the reach of envy's tongue;
Deservedly, for if the glance
Of Muses does not fall askance
On boyhood, then, when heads are grey
They will not cast their friends away.

R. A. Furness
                        (*Epigr.* xxi)

518   *To Arâtus*

HESIOD'S the theme, and style. But I surmise
   The bard of Soli did not utilise
The whole, only the sweetest part. All hail
Tense vigil of Arâtus! subtle tale!

R. A. Furness
                   (*Epigr.* xxvii)

519   *Odi profanum vulgus*

I HATE your hackneyed epic; have no taste
  For roads where crowds hither and thither haste;
Loathe vagrant loves; and from the public springs
I drink not; I detest all common things.

R. A. FURNESS   (*Epigr.* xxviii. 1–4)

520   *Love's Capriciousness*

THE hunters, Epicŷdês, go
   Among the hills in frost and snow,
And follow every hare, and mind
Keenly the slot of every hind;
But if they're told 'That beast is hit;
Look! lying there', they'll none of it.
And so my love is; for it gives
Incessant chase to fugitives,
But hurries heedless past the prize
That ready for the taking lies.

R. A. FURNESS   (*Epigr.* xxxi)

521   *The Poet's Own Epitaph*

HERE lies the son of Battus. He
   Knew well the art of poesy,
And how in season to combine
Friendly laughter with his wine.

R. A. FURNESS   (*Epigr.* xxxv)

522   *The Battle of the Books*

GO learn, O green-eyed monster's fatal brood,
  By Art, not parasangs, to judge what's good.
Look not to me for lofty sounding song;
The thunder-claps to father Zeus belong.
When first a tablet on my knees reclined,
Apollo, lord of Lycia, spoke his mind:
'Give me, good bard, for sacrificial fare
A victim fat: but let your Muse be spare.
And listen,—when your chariot skims the road,
Avoid the route that takes a wagon's load;
Leave open ways and trodden tracks alone,
And go the gate that's narrow, but your own.'
I tuned my quill, nor let the warning pass,—
A sweet cicala, not a raucous ass.
Long ears and all, another bard shall bray;
Let me go light, and flit my dainty way.

T. F. HIGHAM   (*Ætia, Prologue*)

HERMOCLÊS

                                    (fl. 290 B.C.)
523   *Dêmêtrius enters Athens*

SEE how the mightiest gods, and best-beloved,
  Towards our town are winging!
For lo! Dêmêter and Dêmêtrius
    This glad day is bringing!
She to perform her Daughter's solemn rites;
    Mystic pomps attend her:
He, joyous as a god should be, and blithe,
    Comes with laughing splendour.

Show forth your triumph! Friends all, troop around:
    Let him shine above you!
Be you the stars to circle him with love;
    He's the sun to love you.
Hail, offspring of Poseidon, powerful god,
    Child of Aphrodîtê!
The other deities keep far from earth;
    Have no ears, though mighty;
They are not, or they will not hear us wail:
    Thee our eye beholdeth;
Not wood, not stone, but living, breathing, real,
    Thee our prayer enfoldeth.
First give us peace! Give, dearest, for Thou canst;
    Thou art Lord and Master!
The Sphinx, who not on Thebes, but on all Greece
    Swoops to gloat and pasture;
The Ætolian, he who sits upon his rock,
    Like that old disaster;
He feeds upon our flesh and blood, and we
    Can no longer labour;
For it was ever thus the Ætolian thief
    Preyed upon his neighbour;
Him punish Thou, or if not Thou, then send
    Œdipus to harm him,
Who'll cast this Sphinx down from his cliff of pride
    Or to stone will charm him.

J. A. SYMONDS

ASCLÊPIADÊS

524 *Zeus too is a Victim*

GREAT God! snow, hail! make darkness! thunder!
    burn!
On earth thy store of purpling storm-clouds turn!
Slay me, and I will cease; but while I live,
I revel on, though worse than this thou give.
The god that mastered thee leads me; he drove
Thee through the brazen bower in gold, O Jove.

WALTER LEAF

525 *There is no Loving after Death*

WHY hoard your maidenhood? There'll not be
    found
A lad to love you, girl, under the ground.
Love's joys are for the quick; but when we're dead
It's dust and ashes, girl, will go to bed.

R. A. FURNESS

526 *Preface to Êrinna's Poems*

THIS sweet work is Êrinna's: no great sum—
    It is a girl's of only nineteen years—
But strong as many another's. Hadst thou come
    Not quickly, Death, whose name had equalled hers?

R. A. FURNESS

527   *A Tomb by the Sea*

EIGHT fathoms from me stay, unquiet seas,
    And boil and bluster noisy as you please.
Rend not my tomb; there lies beneath these stones
No treasure—just a heap of dust and bones.

WALTER LEAF

528   *Archëanassa*

ARCHËANASSA lieth here
    The courtesan from Colophôn,
Whose wrinkled cheeks and sere
    Were still sweet Erôs' throne.

Ah! lovers who in bygone time
    Gathered the buds unfolding fast
Of that fresh vernal prime,
    Through what a fire you passed!

R. A. FURNESS

529   *Why plague me, Loves?*

ALTHOUGH my years be not yet two-and-twenty,
    I'm sick of life as any man can be.
O Loves, with work to do elsewhere and plenty,
    Why must you make your bonfires out of me?
Nay, little Loves, where will you find employment
    When this poor soul you've teased so long decamps?
Ah, sure enough, fall to your old enjoyment
    And play at dice together, idle scamps!

J. S. PHILLIMORE

590

POSEIDIPPUS

(fl. 280 B.C.)

530 *A Statue by Lysippus*

THE sculptor's country? *Sicyon.* His name?
Lysippus. You? *Time, that all things can tame.*
Why thus a-tiptoe? *I have halted never.*
Why ankle-winged? *I fly like wind for ever.*
But in your hand that razor? *'Tis a pledge*
That I am keener than the keenest edge.
Why falls your hair in front? *For him to bind*
Who meets me. True: but when you're bald behind?
Yes, because when with winged feet I have passed
'Tis vain upon my back your hands to cast.
Why did the sculptor carve you? *For your sake*
Here in the porch I stand; my lesson take.

J. A. SYMONDS

NÎCÆNETUS

(fl. 280 B.C.)

531 *Wine and Song*

'WINE, to a gifted bard,
  Is a mount that merrily races;
From watered wits
No good has ever grown.'

Truly Cratînus spoke;
O Wine-giver, he to our faces
A caskful breathed,
Not one quart's breath alone.

Wherefor his house with crowns
Was a-flower; his head the embraces
Of ivied wreaths
Made saffron as thine own.

T. F. HIGHAM

APOLLONIUS RHODIUS

(295–215 B.C.)

532   *The Sailing of the Argo*

AS boys begin their dancing to Apollo
     At Pŷtho or Quail Island or the fount
Ismênus; there to the sound
Of lyre's concent around his hearth they follow
Their rapid measure, the feet stamping the ground;
So now to Orpheus' lute the oarsmen urge
The rushing water with oars, until the surge
Covers their blades awash.
All ways the dark salt sea boils in an eddy
Of roaring foam that oarsmen's strength pulls steady.
Like flames their weapons in the sunshine flash
As the ship moves, her wake a long bright line
As white as path seen cutting the greensward.
This day the gods in heaven all regard
The ship and strength of heroes half divine,
Men in their time the best that sailed the sea.
And there upon the mountain tops amazed
The nymphs of Pêlion gazed
At this, Athênê's work in Thessaly,
The ship, the heroes plying hand to oar;
And Chîron son of Phillyra descends
From his high peak to where the sea inshore
Breaks in white foam; he wades in it, and tarries
Often waving his sturdy hand, invoking
Godspeed and good returning for his friends;
And with him Pêleus' wife; held high she carries
Achilles in her arms, to the father showing.

GEORGE ALLEN   (I. 536–58)

533 *Hylas*

Now to the spring he came,
To Pêgæ Fountain (in the native name),
Where nymphs were set to dancing—the delight
Of nymphs for ever on that lovely mountain,
Who sing the song of Artemis by night.
All those who haunted mountain tops and streams
Remotely ranged their forest; but she rose,
The water nymph, out of her tumbling fountain,
To see him coming close.
With gallant mien, flushed beautiful he goes
By the enskied full moon lit with moon beams.
Then Cypris thrilled her heart with loving tremble,
The nymph might scarce her very wits assemble;
But when he put his pitcher on the brim,
Leaning along, while all the water splashed
Loudly into the urn, she came on him,
Her left arm round about his neck she flung,
Ardent to kiss his lips; her right hand clung
To his bent arm, and him in the lasher pool she dashed.

GEORGE ALLEN   (I. 1221–39)

534 *Erôs and his Mother*

WITH that she rose, Athênê at her side,
  Both hurrying back; but Cypris made her way
Along the Olympus valleys. There she tried
To find him, and there she found him, far removed
In the deep garden of Zeus, not lonely, at play
With Ganymede, whose beauty Zeus so loved
He enskied him in the Immortals' house for ever.

And there the same as any other boys
Like-minded in their joys
They played with golden knucklebones; the greedy
Erôs his left hand holding full already,
The palm just under his breast; erect he stood,
His bright cheeks blushing in a happy fever.
The other dumbly knelt and sulked beside him,
Had two bones left, threw one, the other next,
Angry at Erôs shouting to deride him,
And lost them like the rest; he went perplexed
And empty-handed away, blind as he went
To Cypris coming. But she touched the chin
Of her child, stopping by him: 'And why grin,
You utter rogue?' she asked, 'and have you cheated
Like that? it wasn't fairly you defeated
The little innocent!
But come and do the work that I want done,
And I will give you Zeus's favourite toy,
The one dear Adrasteia made, his nanny
In Ida cave, and him a tiny boy,—
A nice round ball, nicer you'd not get any,
Even if old Hêphæstus gave you one.'

GEORGE ALLEN

(III. 111–36)

535   *Mêdêa's Dream*

THERE as she lay, a deep sleep brought relieving
    Out of her griefs; but horrid dreams deceiving
Vexed her, the nightmares of a woman's pain.
She thought that why the stranger dared this task
Was not for any passion of achieving
The ram's fleece: not that prize he came to ask

In the city of Æêtês, but to carry
Herself back home, the bride he came to marry.
She dreamed that she contested with each bull
Herself, and easily the task she met.
But then her parents made their promise null,
Claiming it was not her but him they set
To yoke the bulls—from that a quarrel broke,
Father and strangers wrangling; but both sides
Agreed to leave it to her heart's directing;
And suddenly, her parents both neglecting,
She chose the stranger.
But they were bitterly hurt, and cried in anger,
And with the cry sleep left her; she awoke.

GEORGE ALLEN   (III. 616–32)

536   *Mêdêa's Hesitation*

SHE spoke, and rose, and opened the room-door,
  Unslippered, a single cloak about her put;
Eager to see her sister, forth she came
And crossed the threshold floor.
A long time in the impediment of her shame
She waited at the porchway, irresolute;
And then she turned again upon her track,
Again she came outside, again slipped back;
This way and that her fear bore her in vain;
When she ran out, shame tethered her again
Fast in her room, by passion of her will
Still driven, by her shame impeded still.
Three times she tried, three times herself she stayed,
But fell upon her pillow the fourth time

595

Face downward, like a bride within her room
Mourning the lusty groom
Brothers and parents had given her in troth,
And still her women, for shame and thought of him,
She dare not join, but sits and cries in a corner;
For him some doom laid low, before they both
Came each in other's blisses to exult.
With burning heart she sits, a silent mourner
Watching the bed unslept,
Afraid the other women will insult
And mock at her; like her Mêdêa wept.

GEORGE ALLEN   (III. 645–64)

537   *Remorse*

NIGHT mantled earth in gloom, while mariners
        Orion and the Bear watched on the deep
Sailing, and now the wish of wayfarers
And keepers of the gate was all for sleep;
Now mothers lay in trance, though sons were dead,
And through the city not a dog would bark,
No chattering rose: the night was hushed and dark.
Nor yet Mêdêa slept,
Watching for love of Jason, dreading still
The field of Arês, set for grim mischancing
When the great bulls should kill.
Rapid the heart within her bosom leapt,
As troubled as reflected sunbeam glancing
Indoors off water pouring into vat
Or pail,—this way and that
With twist and turn and glitter

596

Flutters the shining dart:
So in her breast quivered the troubled heart.
Her pitiful eyes ran tears, the grief within
Hurting her, smouldering in the flesh the thin
Sinews, and deep through the neck's nape inuring,
Where sorrow is most bitter
When love visits the heart with pain enduring.
Now she would give her charm, the bulls allaying,
Now would not give, and now herself was slaying,
Now would not die herself, nor the charm give,
But wait in patience, bear her doom alive.
Doubting she sat, and cried:
'Alas, where stand I in the path of sorrows?
My mood avails me not, and no relief
Comes in my woe, but always burning grief.
Would Artemis had pierced me with sharp arrows
Before my eyes might see!
Before the two sons of Chalciopê
Came to Achæan country, heaven-sent
Or by a fury sent, our hurt and harm!
If death in the ploughland waits him, let him die
There striving! How shall I
Deceive my parents as I mix the charm?
What plea, what scheme will serve for my defending?
What cunning trick? And shall I in some place
Hold him, when none is there for company?
Not that I think his death will be the ending
Of these my woes—ill-fated, I must face
Calamity, the day his life is severed.
But honour let me lose!
Lose royalty! By impulse mine delivered
Let him go scatheless, whither he may choose!

597

Yet I, the day that he achieves the labour,
Would kill myself, neck hanging from a rafter,
Or mingle drugs that make an end of living.
Dead also they will mock me ever after,—
Cities far off will ring with me, reviling
My evil fate, and each one to her neighbour
Women of Colchis then shall talk me over
Despitefully, "she who loved a foreign lover
So much and died, her parents' house defiling,
Whom passion overcame" . . .
Mine shall be every shame, woe for my plight!
Were it not better done this very night
To die by some dark death, and to be freed
Here in this house from all their taunted shame,
Before I do the hateful nameless deed?'

She stopped, and to the casket moved away,
Where many potions good and deadly lay.
She took it on her knees and wept; her gown
Was wet with her tears falling
In torrents: she her doom bewailed, in haste
To choose out venomous potions and to taste.
Now she began to slip the fastenings down,
Unhappy maiden, eager to take out;
But a fierce terror came of Death appalling,
Moved sudden in her heart.
Long time she waited in a dumb misgiving,
Thronged by the little cares that make life gay,
Dreaming of all the joys among the living,
Of happy playmates,—as a maiden may.
And now the sun, the truer that she weighed
Her thoughts, appeared more lovely than before;

Then from her knees the casket down she laid,
By will of Hêra changed; nor ever more
Doubted, but wished the dayspring to be swift,
That she might give the charm, her promised gift,
And look upon his eyes.
Often she drew the door bolts back in grooving,
Looking for light; then welcome the sunrise
Lit her, and men in town were moving.

GEORGE ALLEN   (III. 744–824)

538   *The Meeting*

WISELY he spoke, a plan for both to accept,
    And even now Mêdêa could not alter
Her mood for all her singing, and no song
Of those she tried to play with pleased her long,
    But she would fail and falter;
And not among her maids her gaze she kept
At rest, but scanning every distant road
She turned her cheeks abroad,
With heart that broke each time she seemed to hear
A sound of wind or footfall running near.
But soon he showed before her waiting eyes
High striding, much like Sîrius ascending
From Ocean: loveliest he, far-seen to rise,
But dismal ruin to the flocks impending.
So lovely to her sight came Æson's son.
But when she saw, he hurt her with desire,
The heart sank from her breast, a mist drew on
Over her eyes, her cheeks went hot as fire.
Too weak to move her knees forward or back,
She felt her feet rooted to earth; and now,

Her women drawing back from her, they two
Without a single sound, without a word,
Stood there like oaks or lofty firs that grow
Upon the mountain side and close together
Are quiet in calm weather.
Then the wind blows again and stirs the grove
Incessant whispering; so they two were stirred
To talk their fill, now that the wind was Love.

GEORGE ALLEN   (III. 948–72)

539   *Amor Omnipotens*

                              Hearing his courtesies
Blissfully smiling did she her eyes abash.
By his praise in a confusion of her heart
Raised up, she lifted up her eyes to his,
But found no single word to make a start,
Striving all to express in one packed voicing.
Out of her scented sash
The charm she took, unsparing, and he rejoicing
Received it in his hands: at his desire
She would have plucked the very life from her breast
And given it him, such bright and beautiful fire
On Jason's yellow hair, Love's influence, played.
The flashings of her eyes he captive made,
And all her heart its secret warmth discloses,
Melting like morning dew upon the roses
That warm day melts; and now
Shyly they to the ground their eyes abase,
And now gaze at each other face to face,
Each smiling love under a shining brow.

GEORGE ALLEN   (III. 1008–24)

540   *Mêdêa's Parting Words*

THEN to keep covenant in Greece is well!
      Yet among men Æêtês is not such
As Mînos, husband of Pasiphaê,
You tell of, nor do I myself avouch
To be like Ariadnê—do not tell
Of guest or host; do but remember me,
Once in Iolcos you are safely home.
And still, although my parents interfere,
You I'll remember: but may rumours come
Or tell-tale bird from Greece, when you forget me;
Or let swift storm winds snatching me from here
Over the sea down on Iolcos set me
Myself, that with reproaches face to face
I may remind you how you owed your flight
To my good will. May I then take my place
There as your guest, though you should not invite!

GEORGE ALLEN   (III. 1105-17)

541   *Jason's Sowing and Reaping*

WITH the third part of day's diminishing
      Still to be run from dawn, what time their lull
The ploughmen swinked invoke
Loosing their beasts from yoke,
The tireless ploughman ploughed his fallow full,
All the four roods of it, and finishing
Released the bulls from plough; them to the plain
He scared, and then returned to ship again,
Seeing the furrows free of the Earthborn still;
And there his mates' assembly

601

Spoke cheerfully to him, while he went to fill
His helmet with stream-water, quenching thirst.
And now he flexed his knees to move more nimbly
Swelling his heart with strength; his rage he rehearsed,
As savage as the boar that whets its tusks
Against the hunters, and to earthward drips
The seething froth down from its raging lips.
But now the Earthborn rose within their husks
On all that ground, and the grim Martial field
Bristled with horrid growth of sturdy shield,
And spear-shafts held two-handed,
And lightnings through the air of glittering helms;
The glitter reached Olympus from below,
As when deep snow the whole earth overwhelms,
And then the clouds in the dark night are disbanded
By a blowing wind, and all the packed stars show
Shining in the dark together; so they shone
Arisen from earth. But Jason, yet recalling
The wit of wise Mêdêa, lifted a stone
Round and huge from the plain, the quoit appalling
Of Arês, god of war,
And four men's strength could never have raised it clear
An inch from the ground; but Jason in his hand
Took it, and with a run he heaved it far
Into their midst—himself crouched happily under
His shield unseen; and the Colchians all gave tongue,
As the sea roars when it breaks on the reefs in thunder.
But dumb surprise to see the quoit so flung
Came on Æêtês, while like eager hounds
The Earthborn men were falling by leaps and bounds
Howling upon each other, and slew each other
On their own spears; down on the earth their mother

They fell, like pines or oaks that the winds break
In storms; and like a star that fiery
Shoots out of heaven, leaving a burning wake,
To men a portent in the darkened sky
Visible flashing,—so fell Æson's son
On the Earthborn men. Bare sword from sheath he drew
Smiting pell-mell, mowing them many down,
Some sidelong belly-high to air still pushing
Half up, some shoulder high, some standing new
Upon their feet, some now to battle rushing.
And as a fight for a boundary is begun,
So that the farmer fears they'll waste his lands,
And gripping a bent sickle in his hands
New whetted, goes and cuts the green corn down;
He never waits for the timely rays of the sun
To come and turn it brown—
So now the Earthborn harvest Jason cuts.
The furrows fill with blood like fountain ruts
Running with water, and still the dead were dropping
Some on their faces, clods of turned earth bitten
In teeth, some on their backs, and others flopping,
Looking like sea beasts, down on arm or flank;
And many of them were smitten
With not a footstep out of the earth; repressed
As far as they had risen in air, they sank
To earth, and clammy-faced took up their rest.
And so sometimes new planted vineyard-shoots
Droop to the ground, when Zeus has sent a squall
Immeasurable that broke them from their roots,
The drudgery of all the garden's men,
And sullenness and killing sorrows hit
The nursery owner, for he nursed them all;

So to the king Æêtês entered then
Resentment, heavy on his heart to sit.

GEORGE ALLEN   (III. 1340–1404)

542   *Mêdêa betrayed*

'JASON, what scheme is framed, what's laid in store
      For me, between you? Have old glories won
Steeped your remembrance, banishing all regard
For speech you made when the strait clutch of need
Gripped you, and when by the Suppliants' God you swore?
Where are your pledges now? Where is there gone
That honey of promises, by which deceived
Unruly, lost to all shame and modesty,
I have put away from me land and famous home,
My very parents, all of my all at once,
To drift with the melancholy halcyons
For your work's sake, alone over the water;
That safe, my friend, you still should overcome,
First with the bulls contesting and men earthborn,
And last, when all was known, winning the fleece
All through my blindness!
On the name of woman I have poured foul scorn.
You are all my kin: I must ship with you as daughter,
As the wife of you, as sister, back to Greece.
Then stand and guard me, show me your loving kindness;
Do not desert me when you visit the kings
For judgement, leaving me alone, but still
Deliver me. So either do you fulfil
What's just for god and man, the plight of our plighting,
Or shear my neck with a sword, giving requiting
Justly agreeable with my passionate follies.

      604

O horror, if the king you both entrust
With unkind pact to judge me, shall decide
I am in my brother's keeping! With what grace
Am I to come before my father's face?
In what brave triumph? What shall I not be given
Of painful vengeance from the ponderous stroke
Of fate's requital, doing the thing I did?
And you meanwhile would happily make for home?
Then may the queen of queens, the lady of Heaven
In whom you glory, never grant this thing!
Some time may all the pains that sap you tell you
To think of me! Into the nether dark
May the fleece vanish, empty as the wind!
May my Avenging Spirits at once expel you
Out of your land, as pitilessly unkind
As I have found you stubborn to my hurt.
God's doom will never let my curses fall
Down to the ground before they find their mark.
Unfeeling! a great oath you broke; but not
For long shall you and your friends sit safe, for all
Your winking scorn, all covenants you plot!'

GEORGE ALLEN, T. F. HIGHAM   (IV. 356–90)

543   *The Moving Rocks*

AS dolphins coming up to take the sun
    Curvet about a vessel on the run
In their schools frolicking,
And sailors like to see them, whether now
Astern, amidships, or beneath the bow;
So Nêreïds from below to surface fling

And circle swimming in their crowds at play
About the ship, while Thetis steered the way.
And now when Argo seemed on point of drifting
Upon the Moving Rocks, their shining knees
They bared, the gathered skirts for work uplifting;
High on the very rocks and breaking seas
On either side and separately they hastened,
As the tide hit the ship and sidelong raised,
And all around, the raging climbing wave
Kept shattering on the Rocks. Now the Rocks grazed
High heaven like precipices, now they were fastened
Deep down at the sea bottom; but high above
The full fierce wave still drove.

There went the Nêreïds, like some girls together
On a sandy beach; their skirts waist high they gather
And play with a round ball, and each girl there
Catches from other, flinging it high in air
Never to earthward dropping.

And so the Nêreïds catching each from other
The running ship, then sent it aery on
Still from the rocks away over the flood,
The waves still gurgling round them in a smother.
And king Hêphæstus watched from where he stood
Upon a polished crag high overtopping,
His mighty shoulder on hammer handle propping;
And the lady of Zeus gazed down from where she was
High on the brightness of heaven to see them pass.
She clung to Athênê with both arms, so strong
The fear that seized her watching.
And still the Nêreïds toiled for time as long
As a spring day gets longer; clear they heaved
The ship from the echoing Rocks; and once more catching

The wind, away again the Heroes run.
Quickly they passed beside the field three-tipped
Sicilian, grazed by the cattle of the Sun.
And there the Nymphs like so many sea-mews dipped
Into the sea deep down, with all achieved
That the great queen of Zeus had ordered done.

GEORGE ALLEN, C. M. BOWRA   (IV. 933–67)

ALEXANDER ÆTÔLUS

(fl. 276? B.C.)

544   Euripidês

ANAXÁGORAS' ward was as true as his lord, but to
talk to a little austere.
Jokes were not in his line, and not even in wine had he
learned how to jape or to jeer;
But whatever he wrote, from his honey-sweet throat a
Siren-song came to the ear.

C. M. BOWRA

LEÔNIDAS OF TARENTUM

(fl. 274 B.C.)

545   An Only Son

O MY poor son, O Anticlês, and poor me, who beheld
The body I bare, the only one, amid the leaping
fires!
But eighteen years, life at the full! and now in lonely eld
I sit and think on good things gone and empty old
desires.

607

Would I might go to Hades' house, where all is dark and
    still!
    No joy have I of dawn, no joy to see the travelling
      sun.
O Anticlês, my poor, poor bairn, thy weird was woven
    for ill;
    Come quickly and take me out of life: let this long
      day be done!

EDWYN BEVAN

546   *Time*

MEASURELESS time or ever thy years, O man,
    were reckon'd;
    Measureless time shall run over thee low in the
      ground.
And thy life between is—what? The flick of a flying
    second,
    A flash, a point—or less, if a lesser thing can be found.

EDWYN BEVAN

547   *Shepherd*

SHEPHERDS, ye who wander with your white flocks
    feeding,
    Your white flocks and your goats, on this airy brow,
A little thing Clîtágoras entreats, but dear exceeding,
    By Earth, by the Queen to whom dead men bow:

Let the sheep bleat near me still, the lad their warder,
    As soft they feed, sit piping on his rude rock-seat;
Then, when spring comes, let a fellow set in order
    A flower or two, and so make my gravestone sweet;

And with milk let one bedew it from a ewe late-deliver'd,
    Holding up the udder, that the warm stream jet
Just a little on the base: in the land dark-river'd
    I shall know, shall repay it. Do the dead forget?

EDWYN BEVAN

548   *A Wayside Grave*

WHO *art* thou? Whose relics, I wonder,
    In a plot that the roadway runs through,
The coffin half-starting asunder,
    Lie bare to the traveller's view?

Alas, by unceasing attrition
    The axles and wheels of the wains
Have worn out of all recognition
    The stone that once marked thy remains.

The wheels very soon in foul fashion
    Will be grinding thy breast-bone, I fear,
Poor devil, and no man's compassion
    Afford thee so much as a tear.

EDWYN BEVAN

MŒRO

(3rd cent. B.C.)

549   *The Childhood of Zeus*

SO Zeus in Crete throve mightily, unespied
    Of all the Blessed Ones. In power and pride
Within that holy cavern his body grew,
    Now fed with ambrosy shy pigeons drew

From Ocean, now with nectar the eagle caught
From rock-born springs, and in his talons brought,
A mighty minister to Zeus the All-wise.
So, at the end, when Kronos lost the skies,
Fallen to his son, whose eye beholds afar,
Zeus lifted the eagle up, to shine a star
And live for ever. And, with like intent,
Set the shy pigeons in the firmament,—
His starry Pleïadës, who make a Sign
To herald summer and the year's decline.

T. F. HIGHAM

NÎCIAS

(fl. 260 B.C.)

550   *Hermês of the Playground*

MINE is Cyllênê's mountain steep
    Whose tossing forests hang above
The plain whereon my watch I keep
    To guard the playing fields I love.

And hither children often bring
    The garlands that they weave for me,
Fresh violets for offering,
    With hyacinth and rosemary.

J. A. POTT

CÉRCIDAS

551   *The Voyage of Love*

APHRODÎTÊ has a son
   with azure wings:
he breathes a gentle breath on one
   (so the poet sings)
on others he blows harsh and strong—
Dêmónomus, you know the song.

When he sends a happy breeze
   from friendly lip,
Love voyages in tranquil ease
   and the prudent ship
letting safe Obedience steer
finds the ocean mild and clear.

But whenever he unbinds
   the hurricane
of fierce Desire, its wanton winds
   infuriate the main:
then Love must sail on perilous seas
   —Truly said, Euripidês!

Choose the favourable wind;
   call to the wheel
Obedience, let the temperate mind
   keep us on steady keel.
So shall we voyage fair and far
setting our course by Love's high star.

GILBERT HIGHET

THEODÔRIDÊS

(fl. 240 B.C.)

552　　　*Pass on*

TOMB of a shipwrecked mariner am I,
　　But sail thou on, and never stay for me;
Yea, for when death to us was drawing nigh
　　The other ships were sailing on the sea.

W. H. D. ROUSE

MNASALCAS

(fl. 240 B.C.)

553　　*The Dead Fowler*

HERE too the birds, god's children, that lightly come
　　　and go
　　Shall find sweet haven, perch'd upon the plane.
Dead is the man of Mêlos, Pœmander their old foe;
　　With reed and lime he'll never come again.

T. F. HIGHAM

554　　　*A Mare*

BRED on the dry land with the winds to race
　　The good mare Seagull here lies sepulchr'd.
Light as a ship she'd coast from place to place,
　　And take her leagues of travel like a bird.

T. F. HIGHAM

555　　　*A Temple*

UPON the low brine-sprinkled shore stand we,
　　Beside the shrine of Cypris of the sea,
And poplar-shaded spring, whence, piping shrill,
The kingfisher draws water with his bill.

W. H. D. ROUSE

HERÔDAS

556   *A Low Trade*

PERHAPS he'll tell you 'Once I brought a cargo
   of wheat from Acre, stopped the dreadful famine'—
I bring soft goods from Tyre; and what's the difference
in the eyes of the public? he don't give his cargo
and I don't give my girl, to grind for nothing.
What if he sails the seas or wears a topcoat
worth twenty guineas, while I stay ashore and
trail bauchly slippers and a threadbare jacket?
Is he to kidnap wenches without paying,
burglariously? Then farewell to our Civic
Security!—and what you pride yourselves on,
your Independence, is destroyed by Thalês!
Who he is, and from what clay he's moulded—
he should remember that, and live like me, sirs,
quailing before the least important burgher.
But actually the pillars of the city,
the highborn bloodstock, are far less highhanded
about the law than Thalês: me, an alien,
no citizen has thrashed me, or attacked my
front door at night, or come with burning torches
to fire my house, or carried off my wenches
kicking, and bolted—but this man from Phrygia
(the sometime Shabrach, now the good Greek Thalês)
committed all that, sirs, without respecting
the statutes, or his patron, or the mayor!

GILBERT HIGHET   (*Mime*, ii. 16-40)

ALCÆUS OF MESSÊNÊ

(fl. 197 B.C.)

557 *Philip, King of Macedon*

UNWEPT, unburied, traveller, we lie here
Three myriad men, on this Thessalian hill,
A grief to Macedon. Fast runs a deer,
But Philip, that brave soul, ran quicker still.

SIR WILLIAM MARRIS

PHILIP V, KING OF MACEDON

(238–179 B.C.)

558 *Alcæus of Messênê*

UNBARK'D and leafless, passenger, you see
Fixed in this mound Alcæus' gallows-tree.

J. H. MERIVALE

DIOTÎMUS

(fl. 200 B.C. ?)

559 *The Cow Herd*

UNCALLED the cattle did at evening go
From fell to farmstead through the falling snow.
Alas! Therímachus beside an oak
Sleeps the long sleep, hushed by a lightning-stroke.

R. A. FURNESS

DÂMÂGÊTUS

560   *A Wife's Grave*

THESE words, Phôcæa, were Theâno's last
    When into the night where no man reaps she passed:
'Woe's me, Apéllichus! How wide, how wide,
Husband, the gulf whereo'er your ship must ride!
But Death stands close to me. Ah, would that I
Might put my hand in your hand as I die!'

R. A. FURNESS

ANONYMOUS

561   *A Mountain Glen*

SWIFTLY through the forest brake
    Piping birds their journeys take;
Comes a jangle of bird-speech
From the pine-boughs' utmost reach,—
Here a rueful miserere,
There a twitter glib and cheery;
These in prelude, those abating,
Or a descant meditating;
Shrilling others, open-throated;
Till the mountain-walls without
Find a voice to sing and shout,
And lone Echo where she dwells
Flings a chatter, backward-floated,
To the music of the dells.

    On brisk wing, with murmur low,
Ground-bees traffic to and fro,

Born to toil, a snub-faced brood,
Summer's faithful harvesters.
Moulded cells of earth are theirs,
Theirs an austere sisterhood:
Harmless creatures, strange to hiving,
That no carnal love ensue,
But in wells of nectar diving
Draw delicious honey-dew.

T. F. HIGHAM

562 *A Nile Chantey*

COME, you seamen, deepwater mariners,
mermen bred on the sea waves hoary,
and come, you Nilemen, freshwater mariners,
sailors over the waves that smile,
come now, friends, and sing me the story
of the sea's meeting with Father Nile.

GILBERT HIGHET

DIOSCORIDÊS

(fl. 180 B.C.)

563 *A Young Mother*

I WAS Polýxenê in life,
Archelaüs' wedded wife,
Child whom Theodectês had
And Dêmáretê the sad:
And I, though death removed my son
Before his twentieth day was run,

616

Am mother, birth pangs me entitle;
But my life was all too little,
Newly mother and newly bride
I was aged eighteen and died.

GEORGE ALLEN

564 *A Faithful Servant*

A LYDIAN, yes, a Lydian I;
But though I was a slave,
My master let his tutor lie
In this, a free man's grave.

Good years and happy be thy share!
And when, with life's decline
Thou comest, master, even there
Tîmanthês will be thine.

R. A. FURNESS

PAMPHILUS

(fl. 180 B.C.)

565 *The Swallow*

A LL day I heard your high heart-broken laughter,
swallow, and, hearing, cried, 'Is there no place
or time when you forget, Pandîon's daughter,
your maidenhood, and Têreus, King of Thrace?

HUMBERT WOLFE

ANTIPATER OF SIDON

(fl. 120 B.C.)

566 *Orpheus*

NO more with rocks and trees shalt thou prevail,
  Or tameless beasts of prey draw after thee,
Nor hush the roar of clanging wind and hail
  Or storm of snow or thunder of the sea.
O lost one! how the Maids of Song lament,
  And most thy mother, sad Calliopê:
Yet wherefore mourn our sons? Can God relent
  Or grant deliverance from the death to be?

A. J. BUTLER

567 *Preface to Erinna's Poems*

THOUGH short her strain nor sung with mighty
    boast,
  Yet there the power of song had dwelling-room;
So lives her name for ever, nor lies lost
  Beneath the shadow of the wings of gloom,
While bards of after days, in countless host,
  Slumber and fade forgotten in the tomb.
Better the swan's brief note than thousand cries
Of rooks in springtime blown about the skies.

A. J. BUTLER

568 *Greater Love . . .*

AMYNTOR, son of Philip, lies
  Entombed in Lydian land;
In battle's iron exercise
  He proved his stubborn hand.

618

No sickness dragged the veteran here,
    Where Night is journey's end;
He lived and died a targeteer,
    He died to shield a friend.

T. F. HIGHAM

569   *The Ruins of Corinth*

WHERE, Corinth, is the glory of thy keep,
    The ancient wealth, the turret-circled steep?
    Where are thy fanes, thy homes? Where all thy
        wives?
Where do the myriads of thy people sleep?

Of all thy pride no sign is left to-day:
All has war taken, all consumed away.
        Only the halcyons, Ocean's Nêreïd brood,
Unravished yet, to weep thy downfall stay.

WALTER LEAF

MOSCHUS
                                        (fl. 150 B.C.)

570   *Eurôpa and the Bull*

SHE spoke and laughed, his back she sat upon;
    The rest made ready, but the bull was gone.
Away with prize he leapt to the sea side,
But she turned round and to her playmates cried
With outstretched hands; yet none of them could reach.
Lithe as a dolphin, seaward from the beach
He skims the wide waves, plunging with dry hooves,
And all the sea grows calmer as he moves.
Sea monsters at the feet of Zeus now gambol,
Dolphin leaves deep for jolly surface tumble,

619

And from the sea there rise in order due,
Perched on the monsters' backs, the Nêreïd crew.
Himself, earth-shaker loud and ocean's lord,
Levelled the wave and for his brother scored
The salt sea path; and Trîtons, round him clustered,
Gruff hautboy music of the ocean blustered.
On conches long they wedding strain produce,
While she, still riding the bull's back of Zeus,
Holds in one hand the taper horn, and holds
Her bright robe in the other by the folds,
Lest in the grey sea waters wet they trail.
From shoulders' height deep-bellying fly the folds,
Lifting the maiden like a ship in sail.

GEORGE ALLEN

571 *The Landsman*

WHEN winds that move not its calm surface sweep
The azure sea, I love the land no more;
The smiles of the serene and tranquil deep
Tempt my unquiet mind.—But when the roar
Of Ocean's gray abyss resounds, and foam
Gathers upon the sea, and vast waves burst,
I turn from the drear aspect to the home
Of Earth and its deep woods, where, interspersed,
When winds blow loud, pines make sweet melody.
Whose house is some lone bark, whose toil the sea,
Whose prey the wandering fish, an evil lot
Has chosen.—But I my languid limbs will fling
Beneath the plane, where the brook's murmuring
Moves the calm spirit, but disturbs it not.

P. B. SHELLEY

MOSCHUS

572   *A Lesson to Lovers*

PAN loved his neighbour Echo—but that child
  Of Earth and Air pined for the Satyr leaping;
The Satyr loved with wasting madness wild
  The bright nymph Lŷda,—and so three went weeping.
As Pan loved Echo, Echo loved the Satyr,
  The Satyr, Lŷda; and so love consumed them.—
And thus to each—which was a woful matter—
  To bear what they inflicted Justice doomed them;
For, inasmuch as each might hate the lover,
  Each, loving, so was hated.—Ye that love not
Be warned—in thought turn this example over,
  That when ye love, the like return ye prove not.

P. B. SHELLEY

BION

(fl. 120 B.C.)

573   *Lament for Adônis*

FOR Adônis I am crying, for Adônis' beauty dead.
  'Adônis' beauty dead'—the Loves return my cry.
  Sleep no more, Cypris, on couch of purple spread;
Wake you, unhappy; put on you the dark panoply,
Beating your breasts, and cry 'Adônis' beauty dead.'
For Adônis I am crying: the Loves return my cry.
  Beautiful Adônis on the hills is lying gashed,
White the tusk and white his flank. For Cypris to lament
Faintly ebbs the breath, and dark the blood is splashed
Down his skin of snow, and his eyes are browed in mist.
The roses vanish from his lips, the kiss is lent
And dies; no more from Cypris may lips their debt recover.

For Cypris there is kissing comfort, dead though her lover,
But little knows Adônis that dying he was kissed.
For Adônis I am crying: the Loves return my cry.
   Bitter bitter wound in Adônis' thigh driven!
But to Cytherêa's heart a greater wound is given.
And now all around the lad his dearest hounds went
      whining,
And mountain nymphs are mourning him; and uncon-
      fining
All her tresses, through the oak shaws Aphrodîtê rushes
Distraught, with streaming hair, unshod, and the bramble
      bushes
Graze her in her going and pluck her holy blood.
But lifting up her wailing far through the mountain wood
She hurries, crying to her darling, calling her Assyrian lord.
The dark blood spirts round him, is past the navel poured
Crimson up from thigh, and discolours from below
The breasts of Adônis that once were white as snow.
'Woe for Cytherêa!' The Loves return my cry.

   She has lost her lord, the beautiful, and lost are her looks,
For beautiful was Cypris while Adônis had breath;
But dead is Adônis, and her beauty suffers death.
The hills mourn for Cypris, 'woe for Adônis' cry the oaks,
Rivers run sobbing for Aphrodîtê in her woe.
In tears for Adônis the upland fountains flow,
Flowers redden sorrowful, and Cythêra sends her keening
High in the hillside valleys and the ridges intervening,—
'Woe for Cytherêa, for Adônis' beauty dead!'
And Echo sounded answer 'Adônis' beauty dead.'
Who would not weep for Cypris, too passionate in love?

   When she found, when she marked Adônis wounded
      sore,

When scarlet she found the blood upon his wasting hip,
She cried 'O wait, Adônis,' with her arms outstretched
      above,
'O wait ill-starred Adônis, that now though nevermore
I may have thee and enfold thee, and lip wed with lip.
Wake a little, kiss me for the last time, Adônis,
Kiss me no longer than the lifetime of a kiss,
That ebbed from thy soul thy breath upon my lips may
      light,
From lip to heart, sweet potion, thy love will I drain deep
And drink in thy love, thy kiss for me to keep
As though it were Adônis: for from me is thy flight.
Thou dost flee far, Adônis,—away to Ácheron,
To a rude king relentless. But I forlorn live on,
I who am a goddess and cannot follow thee.

                    (*She invokes the goddess of the dead.*)

Then, Queen, receive my lord. For thou, Persephonê,
Art stronger far: to thee sink all things beautiful.
I am utterly cast down, my sorrow shall not dull,
I mourn Adônis dead to me—and for thy thought fear I.
O thrice desired, thou diest, my desire is dreamlike flown;
Bereft is Cytherêa, and her Loves keep house alone.
Now is dissolved my magic girdle: tell me, madman, why
Have beauty and go hunting, to beastly grapple fled?'

      Thus lamented Cypris, and the Loves return her cry,
'Woe for Cytherêa, for Adônis' beauty dead!'

GEORGE ALLEN   (I. 1-63)

623

ANONYMOUS

574   *Nox est perpetua una dormienda*

AY me, ay me, the mallow in the mead,
     The parsley green, the anise-tendril's ring,
Fade all and die, but in due season freed
Grow yet again and greet another spring:

But we, we men, the mighty and the strong,
Wise-witted men, when our one life is o'er,
Low laid in earth sleep silently and long
A sleep that wins no waking evermore.

E. J. MYERS   (*Lament for Bion*, 98–104)

ARISTÓDICUS

(2nd cent. B.C. ?)

575   *A Dead Locust*

WHERE Alcis keeps her state, shrill grasshopper,
     no more shall sun invest thy tiny glee.
Now only Pluto hears thy music stir
     the dew-rich flowers of gold Persephonê.

HUMBERT WOLFE

HERMÓCREON

(2nd cent. B.C. ?)

576   *Water-nymphs*

HAIL, water-nymphs, to whom Hermócreon paid
     These offerings, where he met your fountain
          welling.
Good drinking to you always, as you tread
     A lovely dance in this your watery dwelling!

SIR WILLIAM MARRIS

624

TYMNÊS

(2nd cent. B.C.?)

577   *A Maltese Dog*

HE came from Malta; and Eumêlus says
  He had no better dog in all his days.
We called him Bull; he went into the dark.
Along those roads we cannot hear him bark.

EDMUND BLUNDEN

MELEÂGER

(fl. 90 B.C.)

578   *His Anthology*

FOR whom, sweet Muse, this harvest do you ravish
  Of various song? who lyric wreath composes?
  This Meleâger in remembrance laboured
For Dioclês renowned, and wove the lavish
Lilies of Ánytê, with lilies neighboured
Of Moiro many; of Sappho few, but roses;
Of Melanippidês, narcissus big
With song; Simonidês—a young vine twig;
And in and out the scented orrice weaving
Of Nossis (Love himself moulded her waxen tables).
Of dulcet Rhíanus he wove marjoram;
Tender soft crocus to Êrinna's name;
And poet's bluebell where Alcæus babbles,
With Sámius' laurel darkly interleaving.

GEORGE ALLEN

579   *The Cup-bearer*

FILL up, and say, 'To Heliodore!'
      Once more, once more
Say it, and mix with liquor neat
      That name so sweet.

About my brow the garland set,
      With perfume wet;
Garland of yestereven, her
      Remembrancer.

It weeps, you see, the true-love rose;
      Because it knows
She is not in my arms to-day,
      But far away.

R. A. FURNESS

580   *Love in Spring*

NOW the violet blooms again;
      Blooms the lover of the rain,
The jonquil; blooms on every hill
The upland-roaming daffodil.
And now the favourite flower of Love,
Flower of spring, all flowers above,
In bloom perfected sweetly blows—
Zênophilê, Persuasion's rose.
Meadows of your tresses fain,
You brightly laugh, but laugh in vain;
How sweet soe'er your posies be,
Far more excellent is she.

R. A. FURNESS

581   *Hêliodôra's Wreath*

I WILL weave the violet white,
  Mid the myrtle weave the light
Jonquil, and therewith I will
Weave the laughing daffodil.
Then the saffron, sweet of smell,
Weave I will, and weave as well
Purple iris, and with those
Interweave the true-love rose.
So, on the brow where clusters fair
Hêliodôra's fragrant hair,
This my coronal will fling
Every flower of the spring.

R. A. FURNESS

582   *The Mosquito turned Messenger*

MOSQUITO, fly away, and be
  My herald to Zênophilê;
And swiftly with a skimming kiss
Close in her ear you'll whisper this:
'There's one who waits, awake; but you,
Forgetful of your lover true,
Slumber.' Up, you musical thing!
Up and away! To wing! To wing!
But whist! See you say it low,
Lest you arouse her bedfellow
As well, and in his breast excite
A jealous pang, to my despite.

And if you bring me back the girl,
I'll give you a great club to twirl
In your hand, and a lion-skin,
Mosquito mine, to wrap you in.

R. A. FURNESS

583   *Love the Rascal*

NOW hue and cry I make for Love!—wild Love, the
    runaway,
Now, even now he's left his bed and flown at dawn of day:
A boy of April tears who runs and brags and talks for ever,
And laughs and sneers; and on his back has wings and
        wears a quiver.
Whose son he is I cannot say, for earth and skies above
And seas, they one and all disown a Gascon like this Love:
By everyone and everywhere he's hated; but beware,
He may be setting for your hearts some new and secret
        snare:
There, there I spy him near his nest! you've not eluded me,
Small archer, ambushed in the eyes of my Zênophilê.

SIR WILLIAM MARRIS

584   *A Child for Sale*

SELL him! though snuggled at his mother's breast.
    Sell him! why should I rear the little pest?
Snub-nosed, half-fledged, and, scratching all the while
he weeps the better to display his smile.
How can I rear a lynx-eyed chatterbox,
whose venom at his mother's guidance mocks?

The thing's a monster. Find a pedlar! Maybe
one leaving town at once will buy this baby!
But look! love pleads, he weeps. Nay! cease I tell you!
Stay with Zênophila and I'll not sell you.

HUMBERT WOLFE

585   *A Bride*

BRIDEGROOM none but death alone
    Has my Clëarista won,
So to loose her virgin zone.

Yester eve the flutes blew sweet,
Bridegroom and the bride to greet,
And the bridal doors were beat.

Now at dawn they sound again,
But another sadder strain,
Hymen's song is hushed in pain;

And the torch that flared so gay,
Lighting up her bride's array,
Lit the dead her downward way.

H. C. BEECHING

586   *On Himself*

MY birthplace was of Syria,
    The Attic haunt of Gadara;
My foster-nurse was island Tyre,
And Eucratês I own for sire.
By Muses' help the first to vie
With Menippêan Graces, I

Am Meleâger. Yes, and what
If Syrian? Stranger, marvel not.
Own we not all one common earth?
One chaos brought us all to birth.
Now full of years these lines I trace,
Here with my burial face to face:
In House of Eld who sojourneth
Hath for his next-door neighbour Death.
Bid an old garrulous man 'good-bye';
Such garrulous age mayest thou enjoy.

WALTER LEAF

587   *A Cicada*

CHIRRUPING grasshopper, drunken with dew-
       drops,
Lonely thou tunest a shrill meadow-lay,
Perched upon petals, with legs that are saw-like,
Swarthy one, as on a cithern to play.

Friend, sing anew for delight of the tree-nymphs,
Answer to Pan with a rivalling strain,
That I, fleeing Love, may get sleep in the noon-tide
Here, lying under the shade of the plane.

WALTER HEADLAM

588   *Hêliodôra*

TEARS for my lady dead,
    Hêliodore!
Salt tears and ill to shed,
    Over and o'er.

630

Tears for my lady dead,
 Sighs do we send,
Long love rememberèd,
 Mistress and friend.
Sad are the songs we sing,
 Tears that we shed,
Empty the gifts we bring,
 Gifts to the dead.
Go tears, and go lament!
 Fare from her tomb,
Wend where my lady went,
 Down through the gloom.
Ah, for my flower, my love,
 Hades hath taken!
Ah for the dust above
 Scattered and shaken!
Mother of all things born,
 Earth, in thy breast,
Lull her that all men mourn
 Gently to rest!

ANDREW LANG

PHILODÊMUS OF GADARA
(fl. 58 B.C.)

589   *Moonlight*

SHINE out, O hornèd Moon, O festal night's befriender,
 Shine through the latticed window with thy silver light;
My golden fair illume, gaze forth in all thy splendour,—
 Immortal eyes are free to look on love's delight:—
Thy conscious heart, I know, is kind to us and tender,—
 Endymion, O Selênê, set thine own heart's flame alight!

WALTER HEADLAM

ANTIPATER OF THESSALONÎCA

(fl. 15 B.C.)

590 *Drowned in Harbour*

ALL sea is still the sea: why vainly blame
  The Needles, Cycladës, or Hellê's jaws?
Them I escaped for all their empty fame,
  And Scarphê's haven sank me—for what cause?
Who will, may pray safe passage home; but I
Know well that seas be seas, as here I lie.

SIR WILLIAM MARRIS

591 *Amphipolis*

ON Strŷmon built and Hellespontus wide
  Amphipolis, Êdônian Phyllis' mound!
The wrecks of Dian's temple still abide;
  The waters run that armies fought around;
But thou, for whom Athenians strove so sore
Art as a rag of purple, flung on either shore.

SIR WILLIAM MARRIS

592 *A Water Mill*

CEASE from grinding, O ye toilers; women, slumber
  still,
  Even if the crowing roosters call the morning star;
For Dêmêter has appointed Nymphs to turn your mill,
  And upon the water-wheel alighting here they are.
See, how quick they twirl the axle whose revolving rays
  Spin the heavy hollow rollers quarried overseas;
So again we savour the delights of ancient days,
  Taught to eat the fruits of Mother Earth in idle ease.

SIR WILLIAM MARRIS

POMPEIUS

(1st cent. B.C.)

593   *Mycênæ*

WHERE I, Mycênæ, stood in state
            Is left alone
A heap of dust, more desolate
            Than desert stone.

Yet look on Troy, whose famous wall
            I trod to naught,
The house of Priam, and the fall
            My havoc wrought.

So may you guess my ancient weal;
            If wreckful age
Has brought me low, yet I appeal
            To Homer's page.

WALTER LEAF

APOLLÔNIDÊS

(fl. 6 B.C.)

594   *The Poor Farmer's Offering*

I AM old Euphron, with no broad array
    Of arable, nor vineyards rich in wine;
My ploughshare scrapes a bit of shallow clay,
        The juices of a grape or two are mine:
Mite can but yield its mite. God, give me more,
And take the first-fruits of my ampler store.

SIR WILLIAM MARRIS

EUÊNUS

595   *The Vine to the Goat*

AY, gnaw me to my root
  And yet will I bear fruit
For a libation, goat,
 When priests shall cut thy throat.

SIR WILLIAM MARRIS

596   *A Swallow*

ATTIC maid! with honey fed,
  Bear'st thou to thy callow brood
Yonder locust from the mead,
  Destined their delicious food?

Ye have kindred voices clear,
  Ye alike unfold the wing,
Migrate hither, sojourn here,
  Both attendant on the spring.

Ah! for pity drop the prize;
  Let it not with truth be said,
That a songster gasps and dies,
  That a songster may be fed.

WILLIAM COWPER

STATYLLIUS FLACCUS

597   *An Exchange of Fortune*

WHO sought for death, some gold espying,
  Slipped off the noose that he was tying.
Who sought the gold, and found it gone,
Espied the noose, and slipped it on.

T. F. HIGHAM

BIANOR

(fl. A.D. 17)

598 *Unseen Riches*

THIS household drudge, a slave whom all despise,
   Is loved, and royal to one pair of eyes.

WALTER LEAF

ÎSIDÔRUS

(1st cent. A.D.)

599 *Sea Trade*

ETEOCLÊS was I, whom hope of gain
   In ocean trade lured from a farmer's home;
I crossed the ridges of the Tyrrhene main
      And, ship and all, plunged headlong to my doom,
Crushed by a sudden squall; for different gales
Blow on the threshing-floor, and on the sails.

SIR WILLIAM MARRIS

ANTÍPHILUS OF BYZANTIUM

(fl. A.D. 53)

600 *Noontide Rest*

TALL oak, who spread on high your shady boughs
   Above men sheltering from the naked sun,
Close as a roof of tiles—wood-pigeons' house,
   Home of cicadas, canopy at noon—
Here as I lie beneath your leafy sprays
Protect me also from the hot sun's blaze.

SIR WILLIAM MARRIS

635

601   *The Old Ferryman*

GLAUCUS, the islander, whose ferry crossing
  Brought travellers to Thasos from the land,
Skilled ploughman of the sea, who even a-dozing
  Guided his rudder with unfailing hand,
Grown old, a torn sea-tatter, near the mark
  Of death, yet would not quit his ancient wherry;
With him, his shell they burned, that his own bark
  Across the Styx the veteran might ferry.

SIR WILLIAM MARRIS

602   *A Freshet*

O HOTSPUR torrent, crested high in air,
  Why do you cut in twain a traveller's road?
No lucent wave fit for the Nymphs you bear,
  Drunk with your drawings from a thunder-cloud;
I'll see you shrivel yet—the sun can tell
A bastard from a lawful stream full well.

SIR WILLIAM MARRIS

603   *Once in a Way*

ON a ship's poop I'd like to lie, if I could have my way,
  With over it the weather-cloths, thumped loudly by
    the spray;
A sputtering fire between two stones, edging it like a
    mound,
A pot perched on them, boiling brisk, with bubbling
    empty sound;
An unwashed cabin-boy to serve; for table I would make
Use of some handy plank; maybe a game of give and take

636

With sailors gossiping around . . . Lately this chanced
    to me,
Who always find myself at home in simple company.
J. E. B.

JULIUS POLYÆNUS

(fl. A.D. 60)

604 *Prayer for Home-coming*

THOUGH myriad voices ever fill thine ear,
    Prayers of the faithful, thanks for answered vow,
Zeus, holy Scheria's guardian, me too hear,
    And in unfailing promise bend thy brow.
Grant me an end to exile, grant repose
In mine own land from all my weary woes.
WALTER LEAF

605 *Deceitful Hope*

LIFE is the fool of hope, till one last morning
    Sweeps all our schemes away, without a warning.
H. MACNAGHTEN

LÛCÎLIUS

(fl. A.D. 60)

606 *A Dead Song-writer*

EUTÝCHIDÊS is dead, and what is worse
    (fly wretched shades!) he's coming with his verse.
And listen! they have burned upon his pyre
two tons of music, and a ton of lyre.
You're caught, poor ghosts. But what I want to know
is where in Hell, now he's in hell, to go.
HUMBERT WOLFE

MARCUS ARGENTARIUS

(fl. A.D. 60?)

607 *The Poor Man is not loved*

YES, you were loved, Sôsicratês, when rich; but now
in her
Love's dead: the drug of poverty's to blame;
She called you 'dear Adônis' once; she found you very
myrrh,
And now she dares to ask you—'what's your name,
And whence you come and where you live?' O don't you
know, good Sir,
That 'penniless' and 'loveless' are the same?

SIR WILLIAM MARRIS

608 *A Blackbird*

NO longer by the oak, O blackbird, sing
Nor whistle, resting on its topmost spray:
Oaks are your foe: come, where the vineyards spring
And spread the shadow of their green and grey:
Upon the branches plant your feet and so
Pour forth your throaty music shrill and strong;
For oak-trees bear the murderous mistletoe,
But vines bear grapes—and Bacchus loves a song.

SIR WILLIAM MARRIS

609 *Reading Hesiod*

I on Hesiod idly browsing,
when I saw where Pyrrha trod,
dumped the volume with a rousing
'So much for old Hêsiod!'

HUMBERT WOLFE

638

610   *The Lyre and the Crown*

MY revelry is this: to scan
 The evening sky o'er head,
The golden dance of starry quires;
 No human dance I tread.

My lyre rings music; on my brow
 Rose-wreaths rain petals down;
So is my life to heaven attuned;
 Heaven has its Lyre and Crown.

WALTER LEAF

AMMIANUS
                                        (fl. A.D. 120)
611   *Omnes eodem cogimur*

DAWN upon dawn goes by,—one day there'll come
 The Black One on us, while we heed no whit:
And some he'll rot, and some he'll roast, and some
 He'll swell; but all he'll lead into the pit.

SIR WILLIAM MARRIS

P. ÆLIUS HADRIANUS IMPERATOR
                                        (A.D. 76–138)
612   *Troy restored*

O HECTOR, blood of Arês, can you hear beneath
 the ground?
 Rejoice, and get your breath awhile on this your
  country's day!
For Îlion, famous city, is re-peopled: she has found
 Men, not as brave as you were, but still lovers of the fray.
Go near and tell Achilles: 'Dead are all your Myrmidons,
And all your Thessaly subdued beneath Æneas' sons.'

SIR WILLIAM MARRIS

ARCHIAS

(fl. A.D. 120)

613   *A Dedication to Athênê*

SÁTYRÊ, Hêracleia, Euphro, three
   Samians, to Xouthos born and Melitê:
One brings a rod and distaff long with her,
Swift servant of the threaded gossamer;
The next her comb, whose murmuring ministerings
Make raiment rich; the last a wool-tray brings.
These tools Athênê queen, by which have lived
Poorly and long thy servants, are their gift.

GEORGE ALLEN

614   *A Tomb by the Sea*

I'M dead, and yet must thole the sleepless surge.
   When billows threw me battered on the sands,
By spouting reefs I found, beside the verge
   Of mine old foe, a grave at strangers' hands;
But still among the dead am I distressed
   To hear the boom and thunder of the seas:
Not even Hades couches me to rest;
   Alone of ghosts I cannot lie at ease.

SIR WILLIAM MARRIS

615   *Imitatrix ales*

I WAS a jay-bird, screeching back the noise
   Of fishermen or foresters or herds;
Often with Echo's iterative voice
   My mocking beak would caw a string of words:
Now dumb and tongueless here in earth I lie,
Having renounced my taste for mimicry.

SIR WILLIAM MARRIS

616   *Echo*

I'M voluble; I'm voiceless; I am Echo: I reply
   To all I hear; so heed your talk as you are passing by.
Whatever word you say I shall return to you, reflung:
But if you're silent, so am I. How well I mind my tongue!
SIR WILLIAM MARRIS

ANONYMOUS
                       (1st or 2nd cent. A.D.)
617   *Flute Song*

WINTER days and spring and summer still the yearly
   round renew;
And the Sun himself goes under, giving lady Night her
   due.
Weary not your soul with asking whence the sunshine,
   whence the showers,
But where sweetest myrrh is selling, where the lover's
   crown of flowers.
               Piper, play on.

O for living streams of honey from a triple fountain
   spilling!
Five of milk, of wine ten other, and a dozen myrrh-
   distilling!
Add me two of fresh spring-water, three of snowy coldness
   add,
With a lad to every fountain and a lass to every lad.
               Piper, play on.

Lydian pipe and lyre of Lydia work to make my holiday,
Phrygia's reed is never idle, timbrels tap their hides away.
Dear to me in life their music, and when death comes, I
 entreat,
Set the pipes above for headstone and a lyre to mark my
 feet.

                              Piper, play on.

T. F. HIGHAM

LUCIAN

                                        (A.D. 120–200)

618   *A Dead Child*

THE frowning fates have taken hence
     Callimachus, a childe
Five years of age: ah well is he
     From cruell care exilde.
What though he lived but little tyme,
     Waile nought for that at all:
For as his yeres not many were,
     So were his troubles small.

TIMOTHE KENDALL (1577)

619   *A Rule of Life*

USE up thy store, for thou must die;
     Thou hast to live, therefore put by.
Herein lies wisdom's rule, to pair
Expense and thrift in balance fair.

WALTER LEAF

620   *Passing away*

THE world is fleeting; all things pass away;
    Or is it we that pass and they that stay?

WALTER LEAF

PTOLEMÆUS

(fl. A.D. 180)

621   *Starry Heavens without*

MORTAL though I be, yea ephemeral, if but a
    moment
  I gaze up to the night's starry domain of heaven,
Then no longer on earth I stand; I touch the Creator,
  And my lively spirit drinketh immortality.

ROBERT BRIDGES

GLAUCUS

(2nd cent. A.D.)

622   *Cenotaph*

NO heap of dust and petty stones
      Marks Erasippus' grave;
His tomb spreads wide before thine eye,
    The illimitable wave.
Lost with his ship, somewhere his bones
    Are mouldering below,
Whelmed in the deep; but where they lie
    Only the sea-mews know.

WALTER LEAF

623 *Pan and Daphnis*

PAN. Tell me, ye nymphs, and tell me right,
　　　　Has Daphnis passed this way?
　　　　Rested he here his kidlings white?

NYMPHS. Yea, Pan the Piper, yea:
　　　　He passed, and on yon poplar's bark
　　　　He carved a line for thee to mark:
　　　　'To Málea come, O Pan, my Pan,
　　　　To Mount Psôphîdion;
　　　　Thither go I.'

PAN.　　　　　　　　Ye Nymphs, good-bye,
　　　　For I must hasten on.

WALTER LEAF

OPPIAN

(fl. A.D. 200)

624 *The Ichneumon*

WELL worthy the mongoose, though wanting in size,
　　as much as monsters to be made a hero,
being brave and bold in a niddering body.
With cunning and care two tribes it killeth—
the sliding snakes, and crocodiles savage,
a bloodthirsty brood born in the Nile.
When such a beast sleepeth and in his slumbering
throweth open his throat and his threebarred teeth
that glitter in his gape ghastly to see,
then maketh the mongoose a maze of cunning.
With sidelong sight he spies on the monster
till he be sure that slumber has sunk him deeply.
Then in sand and slime swiftly he swathes him

and lightly leaps down the long throat,
through the door of death with heart of daring.
Woe worth the beast when from sleep he waketh!
He beareth in his belly unlooked-for bane,
and far he fareth, helpless in fury:
down he dives to the river's depths,
now walloweth wildly on the water edge,
in the pains panting and pitching wildly.
The mongoose marks it not, but joys in his meal:
by the liver he layeth him, and leaves not his feasting,
and hardly doth he quit the hollow carcass.
Mongoose, thou art a marvel for cunning and might!
Brave art thou and bold! how dost thou bear
to set thyself in the shadow of death?

GILBERT HIGHET   (*Cynêgetica*, iii. 407–32)

625   *Temptation*

SOON now Sir Mullet, when the scent reacheth him,
cometh forward, and far off flinching from the hook
with sidelong sight looks on the snare.
As sometimes a stranger standeth pondering
when to crowded crossroads he chanceth to come:
the righthand road now moves his resolve,
now will he wend by the way on the left;
this way and that he throws keen glances,
while his soul sways like the seawave,
and he pitches not on a path till much time pass.
So wavers and wonders Sir Mullet warily,
looking for a lure, but loving harmless food.
His desire draweth him at last towards death—
but straightway he starts back shivering with fright.

Full often fear takes him as he feels at the bait,
his lust lessens, he leaveth it again.
As it might be a little maid, whose mother is away,
who fain would fill herself with food or other thing:
she trembleth to touch it, in terror of her mother,
but she cannot contain her, for the craving is sore.
Stealthily she steps to it and sidles away again,
as cruel fear constrains her, or her courage grows;
and sharp stare her eyes, straining always to the door.
So retreats and returns that ruthful fish.

GILBERT HIGHET   (*Halieutica*, iii. 499–519)

FLAVIUS CLAUDIUS JULIANUS IMPERATOR
(A.D. 332–63)

626   *Beer*

CAN *this* be Dionŷsus? How the deuce!
   Now, by the very Bacchus, in this guise
      We do not recognize
         The son of Zeus.

How came this goat-reek? *Wine* is nectar-scented.
The Celt from barley-tops, so We suppose,
      For want of grapes and nose,
         This brew invented.

Beer is no scion of the God etherial,
No son of Sémelê to the lightning born,
      But plain John Barleycorn,
         In fact, a Cereal.

T. F. HIGHAM

646

DELPHIC ORACLE

(c. A.D. 360)

627   *The Fallen Shrine*

TELL ye the king: the carven hall is fallen in decay:
   Apollo hath no chapel left, no prophesying bay,
No talking spring. The stream is dry that had so much to
      say.

SIR WILLIAM MARRIS

QUINTUS SMYRNÆUS

(4th cent. A.D.)

628   *Paris is dead*

SHE spoke, and sadly from Œnônê's eyes
   Fell tears. Remembering the young man's doom,
Like wax in fire she faded, secretly,
Awed by her father and trim serving-maids;
Till from broad Ocean over the bright land
Night poured, and brought mankind release from toil.
   Then, when her father and his household slept,
Out through the gateway opening on the hall
She broke tempestuously, and swiftly ran.
As goes some heifer of the hills, bull-mad,
Whose heart within her drives her flying hooves
Hotly, and in the strong itch of desire
Fears not the herdsman—nothing holds her back
If she may see her bull among the brakes—
So ran she swiftly over the long roads
Hoping to climb soon on the dreadful pyre.
No faintness took her knees; ever more lightly
Her feet bore onward; hellish Doom and Love

647

Urged her; and shaggy beasts whom once she feared
She met in night's encounter unafraid.
Each rock and crag among the brushwood hills
She trod, and all the gullies left behind.
Surely the bright Moon marked her in that hour,
Mindful of pure Endymion, and for pity
Of that sad haste, bending from heaven's top
Illumined with full splendour the long ways.

Œnônê crossed to where the other Nymphs
Around the corpse of Paris made lament.
The strong flame wrapped him yet; for shepherds came,
Gathered from many places in the hills,
Who piled great mass of timber, giving tears
And this last office to their lord and friend.
Sadly they mourned around him. But Œnônê
Who saw him clearly, wept not in her grief.
With mantle drawn over her lovely face
She leapt upon the pyre; and Nymphs around
Wondered to see her fallen on her man.

ANON.   (X. 432–69)

629   *The Return from Troy*

GONE was all hope of life. The night was dark,
    Heavy the storm; and dreadful the gods' wrath
Arose. Poseidon stirred the brute sea-waves
To please his brother's noble child, who now
Ravened insatiably on high, and stormed
Among the lightnings. Gladly Zeus, her sire,
With honourable thunder shook the skies,
Till isle and continent were drenched with sea

Towards Eubœa, where to most effect
The goddess used her latest cruelties
To plague the Argives yet. Their fleet was loud
With cries and groaning and continual crash
Of stoven vessels, one upon other driven,
And all was pain and labour and despair.
Some strained with oars, pushing to keep away
The imminent collision. Oars and all
The deep gulph took them, piteously fallen
And done to death between the long ship-beams
That tossed this way and that, crushing their limbs
With hideous grinding. Some were felled aboard
And lay like dead men. Others, forced to swim,
Fell down a-straddle on the smooth-planed oars,
Or rode upon the wreckage. Still the sea
Roared from its depth, till water, sky, and land
Seemed caught together in a single whole.

ANON.   (XIV. 505–29)

NONNUS

(fl. A.D. 400 ?)

630   *Chalcómedê prays to be saved from Love*

SO vainly through the night prayed Morreus, sick for
love.
Nor did the sweet wing of Sleep, who driveth cares away,
Lull wakeful, wandering Chalcómedê. She longed
For death in her fear of mad Morreus, lest he seize
And, heated with love, force her to a violent bed
Far from the succour of Bacchus. To the Red Sea
She turned her steps through the night and cried to the
    deaf wave:

649

'Mêlis, I call you happy. Once, not knowing love,
You cast yourself down spinning into the sea below,
And fled Damnámeneus, your lover woman-mad.
I bless the passionate purity of your doom; against you
Aphrodîtê, the sea's daughter, aroused a mad lover:
The sea saved you, though she was the Paphian's mother,
And you died in the combing surges a maiden. May the
    sea
Cover Chalcómedê, who comes of her own free will
Virginal from the embrace of Morreus' lecherous arms.
Call her a new Britomartis fleeing from wedlock:
—Her once the waves welcomed and gave back to the land:
She pitied not Mînos' love sent by the Cyprian.—
The Earth-Shaker's loving madness flutters me not
Like innocent Astériê, whom in the sea
He followed as she ran doubling off, until Apollo,
The while she drove her way unstopping with changing
    winds,
Rooted her fast and unshakably fixt in the waves.
Take me, take me, O sea, in thy hospitable bosom,
Take Chalcómedê after Mêlis, O take her too,
A younger Britomartis who refuses wedlock,
That I may flee from Morreus and your Aphrodîtê:
Pity Chalcómedê, O succourer of maidens!'
She spoke, and her mind was whirling by the neighbouring
    sea.

C. M. BOWRA   (*Dionŷsiaca*, xxxiii. 317–46)

631　*Chalcómedê wards off her Lover*

A STORY of passion's conflict that the laughter-lover
　told,—
The smiling Aphrodîtê, with a jest at the marriage-rite
And at its sponsor Arês,—a tale of Morreus' love.

　By the sea-shore stood Morreus, and he bathed in his
　　nakedness
With his clothes put aside untended, and the dear distress
　of love
Was warm and sweet within him, and washed in cold sea
　he shone,
While the Paphian's small sharp arrow fired him and
　fanned the flames.
As he stood in the eddying shallows, he prayed as a
　suppliant
To the goddess Aphrodîtê, the Queen of the Indian Sea,
Waiting for her to give answer as the daughter of the
　waves.

　But he kept his outward seeming as Nature gave it him;
For he rose again from his bathing with his blackness still
　unchanged,
And the spray from that Sea called Red could not alter
　his colouring.
But in vain he bathed; vain hope was his longing to
　appear
Snow-white and awaking desire in the heart of the virgin-
　maid.
Then he clad his form in a mantle of linen, shining white
As the linen within the breastplate that warriors always
　wear.

　But silent upon the sea-shore stood the wise Chalcómedê.

And she spoke no word but she turned from Morreus'
    nakedness,

While she took her virgin glance from his unclothed limbs
    in shame

And in fear that a maid behold a man's body bathed in
    the sea.

  But seeing the shore deserted as though for his passion's
    will,

He stretched out his shameless hand on the maiden's
    shrinking form,

And would have torn her mantle that none yet had loosed.

Then in truth he would have seized her, and held her in
    his embrace

In a hold of might, and have burnt with his fire the
    Bacchic maid.

But sudden at that a serpent sprang forth from her virgin
    breast,

The protector of that chaste maiden. On the scarf that
    was round her waist

With the guardian coils of its body it encircled her all
    about,

And it hissed forth shrill and sharp and its maws never
    ceased the sound,

So that all the rocks re-echoed; and in fear did Morreus
    start

When he heard as from some trumpet this noise of a
    serpent's throat,

Cowering to see the protector of a maid's virginity.

MICHAEL BALKWILL   (*Dionysiaca*, xxxv. 184–215)

MUSÆUS

632   *Leander's Death*

THE time was night, when most the violent breathing
   winds
Hurl forth their cries in stormy blasts, while with one
      strength
They fall in headlong force upon the shores of the sea.
On such a night Leander, moved by his heart's desire
For the maid he knew in love, was borne on the shrieking
      waste,
On the mighty back of the sea while wave was rolled on
      wave,
While the waters in tumult gathered and sky was merged
      with sea,
While on all sides the rising whine of striving winds
As East with West contended, as South to North pro-
      claimed
Its mighty menace, was heard with the sea's unending
      thunder.
Leander sore distressed amid the eddying waters
Found them inexorable, though many a time he prayed
To Aphrodîtê the ocean goddess, and many a time
To lord Poseidon himself, the ruler of the sea;
Yet no help came, nor even Love could stay Fate's hand.
But dragged and buffeted by the deadly swirling waves
He was carried hither and thither until his thrusting limbs
Faltered and failed, and the restless strokes of his hands
Availed him nothing. Then by its own huge strength the
      sea
Poured down his throat; and of the constraining surge he
      drank,

653

Quenching no thirst—but life; and as the cruel wind
Stole from the unsteadfast lamp its light, so from Leander
In this distress it took the warmth of life and love. . . .

Hero with fierce reproach upbraided the heartless winds
As now in vision she saw Leander tarrying still
In the long delay of death; and yet with unwavering watch
She kept in storm of sorrow her troubled vigil,
And saw the morning break—and still saw not her lover.
Everywhere over the sea's wide plains with straining eyes
She searched for sight of him, lest perchance his way was
    lost
When the light of her lamp was gone. And when she saw
    him dead,
Torn by the rocks and lying at her tower's foundation,
About her breast she tore the wondrous woven mantle
And from the sheer crag plunged in hurtling headlong
    fall
To find with her dead love a death among the waves,
And the joy of love together in life's last separation.

MICHAEL BALKWILL   (*Hero and Leander*, 309–43)

PALLADAS
(c. A.D. 360–430)
633   *Freedom*

I'M done with hope and chance. O never again
    I'll fear those cheats. I am to haven come.
    A poor man I, yet freedom shares my home,
And wealth that mocks the poor man I disdain.

GEORGE ALLEN

634   *A Question of Gender*

THE dominie's daughter eloped with a suitor,
And the baby was masculine, feminine, neuter.

SIR WILLIAM MARRIS

635   *God's Concern*

IF caring profits, then for care take thought;
But if God cares for thee, what need to care?
Thoughtful or thoughtless art thou, as God wrought;
And if thou carest, God's care worketh there.

A. J. BUTLER

636   *What is Man?*

REMEMBER, O man, how your father made you,
his son!
Then you will cease from your boasting and put it by.
In Plato's dreams was this idle fancy begun—
He called you immortal, a creature sprung from the sky.
You are made of dust. Are you proud of that? So a man
Might deceitfully dress up the truth in a lordlier name.
But if you would know what you are, why then, you began
Your life in unquenchable lust and a drop of shame.

C. M. BOWRA

637   *Naked I came*

NAKED I reached the world at birth;
Naked I pass beneath the earth:
Why toil I, then, in vain distress,
Seeing the end is nakedness?

A. J. BUTLER

638 *Life a Voyage*

LIFE is a perilous voyage. Tempest-tossed,
By worse than shipwreck we are often crossed.
Like men at sea uncertainly we sail,
Chance at the helm to steer us through the gale.
Some well, some ill, we fare; but all are bound
For one sole harbour, underneath the ground.
R. A. FURNESS

639 *All the World's a Stage*

THIS life a theatre we well may call,
Where every actor must perform with art;
Or laugh it thro' and make a farce of all,
Or learn to bear with grace his tragic part.
ROBERT BLAND

640 *Sail with the Wind*

THE stream that carries you doth carry all;
Bear and forbear, however fortune fall.
'Tis vain to strive and cry, whate'er you do;
The stream that carries all will carry you!
J. A. POTT

641 *We are born Every Day*

FROM day to day we are born, as each night wanes,
And nothing of our former life remains.
The alien course of yesterday is run;
What life we have this morning is begun.
Say not, old man, that you are rich in age:
Of years gone by you keep no heritage.
R. A. FURNESS

642   *Lacrimæ rerum*

WEEPING I came to life, weeping I go;
  All life I found one weeping tale of woe.
 Ah piteous weeping race of feeble men,
 Swept under earth to lie and rot below!

WALTER LEAF

643   *Sentence of Death*

DEATH'S herd are we, and all the world a sty.
  For Death we're primed and butchered,—god
  knows why!

T. F. HIGHAM

644   *The Rest is Silence*

SOON wilt thou pass to earth; waste not thy breath;
  Hush, man! and while thou livest ponder death.

WALTER LEAF

645   *Eremites*

HERE 'solitaries', two-a-penny,
  By multitude their name belie.
 If 'solitaries',—why so many?
  If many,—'solitaries' why?

ANON.

ÆSÔPUS

(c. A.D. 400?)

646 *The Way of Life*

HOW, save only by death, from thee, O life, can I flee?
　　Thousand evils are thine, grievous to bear or shun.
What though the beauties of earth be sweet, the land and
　　the sea,
　　Lovely the stars in heaven, lovely the moon and sun,
All is fear and sorrow besides; or if good there be,
　　Balance and vengeance of ill maketh it all undone.

A. J. BUTLER

GLYCON

(c. A.D. 400?)

647 *Futility*

ALL is dust, and a mocking dream,
　　'All' and 'Nothing' are just the same,
For nothing is, and the things that seem
　　Out of a mindless chaos came.

J. A. POTT

DAMASCIUS

(fl. A.D. 529)

648 *A Slave Girl*

O Zôzima, your soul was ever free,
　　And now your body too hath liberty.

J. A. POTT

658

JULIANUS

(fl. A.D. 532)

649   *An Old Fishing Net*

SHORN of his strength by time, these worn-out nets
  Old Cínyras offers for the Nymphs as spoil.
His quivering hand the mesh no longer sets
  To shoot and belly as the lines uncoil.
Take them, ye Nymphs, and though the gift be small,
Reproach him not—for 'tis his all in all.

A. J. BUTLER

LEONTIUS

(fl. A.D. 550)

650   *Plato, a Musician*

WHEN Orpheus died, some Muse the lyre still
  fingered:
  But Plato passed, and mute the viol lies:
For in his heart and in his hand there lingered
  Some remnant of the ancient melodies.

A. J. BUTLER

651   *Picture of a Physician*

OLD was Iámblichus, the whole world's friend,
  Yet innocent of ways that lovers use.
Mending our health, and teaching how to mend,
  All fees, with modest hand, he would refuse.

T. F. HIGHAM

MACEDONIUS

(fl. A.D. 550)

652 *The Sailor's Dedication*

BRACED to the temple-foot by Krantas' hand
His boat, an offering to Poseidon made,
Laughs at the winds. The old rover, too, on land
    Spreads a broad shoulder, sleeping unafraid.

T. F. HIGHAM

653 *Statue of a Dog*

THIS hound (no chase too stern for such a creature!)
    Was carved by Leucon for Alcímenês.
Alcímenês, beholding pose and feature
    True to the life,—there's nothing disagrees—
Collar in hand said, 'Leucon, bid him come!
He's barking, I'll be bound,—good dog, go home!'

T. F. HIGHAM

RUFÎNUS

(fl. A.D. 550?)

654 *Grey Hair*

HER eyes are gold, her cheek is hyalite,
    Her mouth delicious as a dark red rose;
Her bosom gleams, her neck is marbly bright,
    And white as silvery Thetis' are her toes:
In those dark locks some thistle-down she hath?
I take no heed of that white aftermath!

SIR WILLIAM MARRIS

655 *The Rosy Wreath*

RHODOCLEIA, flowers of spring
    I have woven in a ring;
Take this wreath, my offering.
Here's the lily, here the rose
Her full chalice shall disclose;
Frail narcissus; wet with dew,
Wind-flower, and the violet blue.
Wear the garland I have made;
Crowned with it, put pride away;
This wreath that blooms to-day must fade;
Thou thyself must fade some day.

MAURICE BARING

656 *Love the Archer*

CUPID, when you shoot your darts,
    Aim alike at both our hearts.
Gods must never partial be,
Else they lose divinity.

F. A. WRIGHT

657 *Her only Flaw*

ALL else I love, but this abhor,—
    Your eye, so fondly turning
On men I have no stomach for
    A look so undiscerning.

T. F. HIGHAM

JOHANNÊS BARBUCALLUS

(fl. A.D. 551)

658   *A Ruined Harbour*

STAY not your course, nor, shipman, drop your sail
    Because of me: see you, my harbour's dry;
I am a tomb: some gladder place may hail
    The thud of rowlocks as your bark draws nigh:
Poseidon and the guesting gods decree it.
    So fare ye well, by land or water be it!

SIR WILLIAM MARRIS

PAULUS SILENTIARIUS

(fl. A.D. 563)

659   *Love or Death*

SHALL we for ever stealing looks of fire
    Fling covert glances thus with bated breath?
Nay, tell aloud our loves: and if we fail
    Of those soft claspings, where pain vanisheth,
The sword shall bring deliverance. Better far
    One lot together, be it life or death.

A. J. BUTLER

660   *The Vain Farewell*

THE last farewell is on my tongue,
    But fierce I draw the rein:
The word recoils as backward flung,—
    And I remain.

For bitter as the stream of death
    In everlasting night
Is that fell hour that sundereth
    Me from thy sight.

The light of thee is like the day;
    Yet daylight is but dumb,
But when thou comest in the way,
    Sweet voices come:—

Tones sweeter than the Sirens' song
    That on the waters rang;
And there with all its hopes in throng
    My heart doth hang.

A. J. BUTLER

661   *The Tears of Fear*

SWEET is my Laïs' smile, and sweet the tide
    Of tears that floods her eyes alive with meaning:
Now yesterday without a cause she sighed,
    Her head a long time on my shoulder leaning:
I kissed her as she wept, but tear on tear
    Fell on our meeting lips like fountain dew:
I asked her why she cried. She said, 'For fear
    You will desert me: men are never true.'

SIR WILLIAM MARRIS

662   *Vanities*

MY name—my country—what are they to thee?
    What—whether base or proud my pedigree?
Perhaps I far surpass'd all other men—
Perhaps I fell below them all—what then?
Suffice it, stranger! that thou seest a tomb—
Thou know'st its use—it hides—no matter whom.

WILLIAM COWPER

AGATHIAS SCHOLASTICUS

(C. A.D. 536–82)

663   *The Best Memorial*

COLUMNS and graven monuments, these can give
    Great joy of owning—while you live.
Not very far can men's vain praise help on
    The spirits of the dead and gone.
'Tis skill and grace of art that follow there,
    Yet live, winning remembrance here.
Plato and Homer the assurance have
    Only of art, not painted grave.
Happy, whose fame, secure in books' enshrining,
    Need in no vain tomb be pining.

GEORGE ALLEN

664   *The Swallows*

NIGHT long I sigh, and soon as comes the day
    To grant me rest a little, in mine ears
The swallows' twittering sounds, and hunts away
    Sweet sleep and drives me back again to tears:
Tight-shut I keep my eyes, and yet the thought
    Of dear Rhodanthê haunts my heart once more.
Peace, peace, ye jealous prattlers! it was not
    My hand the tongue of Philomêla shore;
Wail o'er the hills for Itylus, or from
    The hoopoe's craggy nest cry your alarms;
So may I drowse awhile: maybe will come
    A dream and fold me in Rhodanthê's arms.

SIR WILLIAM MARRIS

665   *Leave a Kiss within the Cup*

I LOVE not wine; yet if thou'ldst make
    A sad man merry, sip first sup,
    And when thou giv'st I'll take the cup:
If thy lip touch it, for thy sake
    No more may I be stiff and staid
    And the luscious jug evade:
The cup convoys thy kiss to me,
And tells the joy it had of thee.

J. M. EDMONDS

666   *The Girls' Lot*

YOUNG men have all the luck! They do not know
    How hard is life for each soft-hearted maid:
They've friends of their own age to whom they go
    And tell their cares and worries unafraid;
They've games to play at, and can freely roam
    The streets and roll their eyes at paintings bright;
While victims of our own dull thoughts at home
    We're kept indoors and cut off from the light.

SIR WILLIAM MARRIS

667   *Dicing*

IT'S sport for gentlemen, but rage and pain
    And loss self-sought for them who fail in poise;
If you come last, from blasphemy refrain
    And don't boil over with a snorting noise;
Toil not o'er toys nor with your duty jest,
But learn to give each hour what fits it best.

SIR WILLIAM MARRIS

ANONYMOUS

668   *Land and Sea*

DEAR Cypris, if thou savest those at sea,
    I perish wrecked ashore; save also me.

SIR WILLIAM MARRIS

669   *Love in her Hair*

WHETHER I find thee bright with fair,
    Or still as bright with raven hair,
With equal grace thy tresses shine,
Ah, Queen, and Love will dwell divine
In these thy locks, on that far day
When gold or sable turns to grey.

ANDREW LANG

670   *Would I were the Wind*

O WOULD I were the salt sea-wind
    And you upon the beach
Would bare your breast and let me blow
    Until your heart I reach.

F. A. WRIGHT

671   *Would I were a Rose*

I WOULD I were a damask rose
    For thee to pluck, thy hand embrace,
That so thy bosom I might grace
    And blush amid the snows.

F. E. GARRETT

666

672 *Anacreon's Tomb*

POUR a libation, stranger, as you pass.
It is Anacreon's tomb. He loved his glass.

EARL OF CROMER

673 *A Child*

O HADES, death's inexorable king,
Wilt never turn aside from plundering?
Now is Callæschrus of his life bereft.
And what avails to know the child shall be
A plaything in thy halls, Persephonê,
When sorrow broods above the home he left?

J. A. POTT

674 *A Joyful Mother of Children*

OF children nine and twenty that I bore,
Nor son nor daughter but remains alive:
No staff mine agèd hand hath trembled o'er:
I ended well my fivescore years and five.

A. J. BUTLER

675 *An Unhappy Man*

I, DENYS of Tarsus, lie dead
At the age of three-score,
Unwed,—and better unwed
My father before.

T. F. HIGHAM

676   *Waiting*

HERE I lie dead, and here I wait for thee:
      So thou shalt wait
Soon for some other; since all mortals be
      Bound to one fate.

W. H. D. ROUSE

677   *A Gardener*

DEAR mother Earth, within your breast
      Take old Amyntichus to rest,
Remembering the years, not few,
Spent in various toil for you.
Many's the time in you he'd plant
Olive-trees, that never want
For foliage, and array you fine
In livery of branching vine;
With fields of corn he'd make you rich,
And lead through many a channelled ditch
The waterbrooks, letting your ground
Abound with fruits, with herbs abound.
Lay, in return, a gentle, light
Burden upon his temples white,
And, for his grave's adornment, bring
Flowers and verdure in the spring.

R. A. FURNESS

678   *A Bee-keeper*

WHEN bees come hither in the fair springtide,
    Tell them, ye nymphs and cattle-pastures chill,
How on a wintry night Leucippus died
    While snaring scampering hares upon the hill;
    The hives no more shall feel his fostering skill,
But the sad hollows where the flocks are fed,
    For very grief are sighing for him still;
The neighbour of the mountain-peak is dead.

J. A. POTT

679   *Plato's Tomb*

EAGLE! why soarest thou above that tomb?
    To what sublime and star-ypaven home
      Floatest thou?—
I am the image of swift Plato's spirit,
Ascending heaven; Athens doth inherit
      His corpse below.

P. B. SHELLEY

680   *The Tomb of Sardanapalus*

ASSURED that you are doomed to die, do as your
    passions crave,
Rejoicing in good cheer: you'll find no profit in the grave:
For I am ash who once was king of Nineveh the brave:
All that I ate or drank or learned of love's delights, I have:
But of my rich possessions no penny could I save.

SIR WILLIAM MARRIS

681   *A Stalker of Geese*

ARISTON had a sling, wherewith he got
    A scanty living: for wild geese he shot,
Stalking them very softly, to surprise
The pack that fed with sideways-glancing eyes:
Now he's in Hades; and his sling is dumb
And lorn: but o'er his grave the wild geese hum.

SIR WILLIAM MARRIS

682   *Après moi le Déluge*

NOW I am dead, be earth devoured of hell:
    I reck it not: with me the world is well.

A. J. BUTLER

683   *Lacedæmon*

SPARTA, the proud inviolate city, sees
    Corinthian smoke across her river sweep:
Birds nest on earth and mourn for their lost trees,
    And wolves can hear no bleat of any sheep.

H. MACNAGHTEN

684   *Tenancy*

ONCE Achæménidês, Menippus now
    Calls me his field and dreams me all his own:
But tenant follows tenant: I allow
    No claim but Fortune's, I am her's alone.

H. MACNAGHTEN

685   *To Pan*

TWY-HORN Pan, the ridgy hills
      Walking and the maiden rills
    Leading in thy rocky haunt,
Favour us the stony way
Travelling, who have drunk to-day
    Of thine ever-springing fount.

A. LOTHIAN

686   *The Cicada*

WHY, ruthless shepherds, from my dewy spray
      In my lone haunt, why tear me thus away?
Me, the Nymphs' wayside minstrel, whose sweet note
O'er sultry hill is heard and shady grove to float?
Lo! when the blackbird, thrush, and greedy host
Of starlings fatten at the farmer's cost,
  With just revenge those ravagers pursue:
But grudge not my poor leaf and sip of grassy dew.

FRANCIS WRANGHAM

687   *Rome*

ROME, from thy queenly walls lest glory die,
    A pinioned Victory wants the means to fly.

R. A. KNOX

688   *The Way to Hades*

STRAIGHT is the downward journey, tho' it be
    From Athens we descend, or Meroê.
If far from home I perished, make no moan.
One breeze blows fair to Hades, one alone.

W. C. LAWTON

689 *A Very Ancient Proverb*

THERE'S many a slip
'tween the cup and the lip.

D. M. MOIR

690 *Hours*

WE spend six hours
on work and strife;
the rest is life
more truly ours.

GILBERT HIGHET

691 *Prison-house of Flesh*

OUR body is our doom, a place of death,
A binding chain that holds us here beneath,
A sickness of the soul, a burden sent
By Fate to be our test and punishment.
But when it leaves the limbs, death's bondage riven
The soul escapes to God and reaches heaven.

F. A. WRIGHT

692 *Few there be . . .*

MANY the Bacchi that brandish the rod:
Few that be filled with the fire of the God.

RICHARD GARNETT

693 *The Way to Poverty*

KEEP open house; dabble in bricks and mortar.
Of all the roads to ruin none is shorter.

H. WELLESLEY

694   *When the Rose is dead*

THE rose's bloom is short; and when it goes
   You'll seek, and find a thorn and not a rose.
R. A. FURNESS

695   *Quid sit futurum*

DRINK and be merry: there is no man knows
   To-morrow, or thereafter, how it goes:
         Run not nor strive;
Give, share, and eat; be kindly as you can;
Think only thoughts that do befit a man;
         Dead or alive,
   Between the two's not much to choose:
Life is just that, a dip of weighing-pans;
      Quick, and you take the lot,
But if you die, 'tis all another man's,
         And you have not.
SIR WILLIAM MARRIS

696   *Expectation of Death*

FAR happier are the dead, methinks, than they
   Who look for death, and fear it ev'ry day.
WILLIAM COWPER

697   *In Praise of Hunting*

THE hunter learns a soldier's trade;
   He learns to scotch an ambuscade,
To meet the attacker face to face,
And when a back is turned, give chase.
T. F. HIGHAM

698   *On a Stone at Salonîca*

W HEN Marathônis in this chest of stone
    Laid his Nîcopolis, vain tears he shed:
How vain! for what is left a man alone
    On earth but sorrow, when his wife is dead?

SIR WILLIAM MARRIS

699   *On a Stone at Corinth*

S O this, my good Sabînus, is the one
    Record of our great love, this little stone.
I'll miss you always: you, if so it may be,
O drink not there oblivion of me!

R. A. FURNESS

700   *A Statue of Pan*

C OME, sit beneath
    The pine that bendeth to the kind
Western wind,
And sweetly murmureth.
Watch how the sweet drops leap
In the waterfall,
While lonely reeds melodious call
Hither gentle sleep.

R. A. FURNESS

701   *A Painting of Dido*

O N Dido's famous image, friend, you stare,
    I am her portrait shining heavenly fair;
And fair was I, yet schemed not to allure
As you hear sung; the fame I got was pure.

674

I never saw Æneas, neither came
To Africa while Troy went up in flame;
But fleeing fierce Iarbas for my lord
Into my breast I plunged the two-edged sword.
Why gird me, Muse, with Virgil? the chaste saint
Levelling his lies against my self-restraint!

GEORGE ALLEN

702   *The Aphrodîtê of Praxítelês*

'SHAME!' Cypris cries her statue when she sees,
   'You saw me naked! When, Praxítelês?'

HUMBERT WOLFE

703   *Hermês of the Lonely Hill*

NOT of my choosing, traveller, this desert eminence;
   Archélochus so willed it, who set my vigil here.
To set me by the high-road had shown a better sense,—
   No hill-top, Sir, for Hermês: he is no mountaineer.
Archélochus is happy unneighboured and alone;
My solitude, wayfarer, does but reflect his own.

T. F. HIGHAM

704   *A Charioteer*

MY Constantine, why sleep in bronze? Awaken.
   Now on the track the people mourn your bridle,
And charioteers, like orphan boys, sit idle,—
Fatherless, by your master hand forsaken.

GEORGE ALLEN

705   *A Pythian Oracle*

COME pure in heart before this hallowed fane,
   Your hands fresh sprinkled with the fountain spray:
Few drops the good need; but a foul soul's stain
   All ocean's water shall not wash away.

A. J. BUTLER

COMÊTAS

(fl. A.D. 950?)

706   *Country Gods*

A. Tell me, shepherd, tell me, pray,
   Whose the trees set all a-row?
B. Olives,—Pallas' care are they;
   Vines around for Brómius grow.
A. Whose the corn? the flowers whose?
   Name a God to each demesne.
B. This Dêmêter loves: and those
   Hêra, with the Paphian Queen,
   Aphrodîtê, called The Rose.
A. Pan, dear Pan, with me remain;
   Touch the pipes and run them over;
   Somewhere in this sunny plain
   Echo waits upon her lover.

T. F. HIGHAM

NOTES

These Notes are a supplement to both parts of the Introduction. They give brief information about most of the authors not mentioned in Part I; and explain the context of each piece when it is known, or else indicate that the piece is a fragment only. In the main they are intended for those who cannot read the Greek.

Some acquaintance with the outlines of Greek mythology is assumed; but most allusions that may prove obscure have been explained, either where they occur, or by means of cross-reference.

Notes about the translations usually follow those on the subject-matter. Where several translations of one Greek author are by the same hand, any such notes attach to the first of the series.

Occasional references and comments have been added which scholars also may sometimes find useful. Most are concerned with textual points or points of interpretation. But neither space nor leisure have permitted the recording of every minor mistranslation, or of every translation based on a different text.

The frequent citations of printed works serve partly as acknowledgements. Still more they are intended as guides to fuller information, contained in books that the general reader can consult with profit. More especially thanks are due to Professor H. J. Rose for his Handbooks of Greek Literature and Greek Mythology, both serviceable to scholars and to general readers alike. These Notes confine themselves to the mere externals of Greek myth—complex enough in themselves. All who seek to explore the origin and meaning of the myths will find in Professor Rose's book not only learned guidance but much good reading.

The references in the left-hand margin are to the numbers of the pieces.

1. In the opening lines of the *Iliad* Homer has announced the wrath of Achilles as his subject, and here he explains its origin; for Agamemnon, obliged eventually to restore Chrŷsês' daughter, took Brîsêis from Achilles. *The son of Zeus and*

677

Lêto is Apollo.   *Atrîdæ*: the sons of Atreus, Agamemnon and Menelâus.

Of his translation Sir William Marris writes: 'I aimed directly at catching Homer's simplicity and pace, and less studiously at reproducing his dignity—hoping none the less that enough of this would manifest itself if one could keep a firm grip on ordinary words and make them carry their full weight. I tried for simplicity by avoiding mannerisms and bombast, and for pace by using short sharp words, co-ordinated non-complex sentences, and giving the measure a trochaic flow. Sometimes I sought realism by risking an unusual but vivid word where it seemed true; also in adapting the pitch, especially in dialogue, to what seemed the needs of the occasion.'

2. Agamemnon has summoned an assembly of Achæans, at which Thersîtes, a commoner, reviles him.

Maurice Hewlett's translation of *Iliad* i–x was published after his death. The text, by all the signs, was ready for press, but lacked his final revision. Among the rough notes left for his Preface is the following: 'Grand manner—I don't find. I find idiom—racy language—great directness and simplicity —much seriousness and much humour.' Professor Lascelles Abercrombie, whose Introduction puts together the available evidence of Hewlett's intentions, finds this denial of the grand manner 'an astonishing opinion', adding 'but it is just here that we get the peculiarity of Hewlett's individual response to Homer; it is just where we find this defect that we find the qualities which make his version so remarkably alive'. He writes also: 'The adventurous modulations of his verse make it more dramatic in its movement than narrative. . . . Its extreme freedom is simply another aspect of his refusal to see the grand manner in Homer. . . . It is the same with his metre as with his diction.'

3. These lines precede the first fighting described in the *Iliad*.

4. Îris has told Helen that her former husband, Menelâus, and her present husband, Paris, are about to engage in single combat.

NOTES

5. Helen on the wall of Troy has pointed out the chief Achæan leaders to Antênor.

6. After an inconclusive fight between Menelâus and Paris a general battle ensues. On this translation see F. W. Newman's *Reply to Matthew Arnold* (printed with *Essays Literary and Critical*, Everyman's Library Edition, pp. 290–3): 'Now if any fool ask, Why does not Mr. Gladstone translate *all* Homer ? any fool can reply with me, Because he is Chancellor of the Exchequer.' The last four lines of the translation are supplied by T. F. Higham.

7. Sarpêdon, a Lycian prince, fights on the Trojan side, and helps to stop the Achæan advance.

8. Glaucus and Diomêdês, though fighting on opposite sides, exchange courtesies, and Glaucus (the second of that name—see No. 277, note) tells the story of his ancestor, Bellerophon. Hallam Tennyson states: 'My father often expressed a wish that he could find time to translate the *Iliad* into rhythmical prose. Not long after the publication in 1877 of *Achilles over the Trench* [see No. 26] I made this experimental translation of the Sixth Book, . . . and, when in print, it was finally revised by him from the point of view of rhythm, and by my uncle, Professor Lushington, from the point of view of scholarship' (*The Works of Tennyson*, ed. by Hallam, Lord Tennyson, vol. vi, p. 351). One passage, not in this piece, was specially contributed by Alfred Tennyson himself. It begins 'Nor did Paris linger' and ends 'his swift feet bare him'. See also Introduction, p. xcvii. *And he bad him show them* . . . (p. 10): Prœtus bad Bellerophon show the tablet to Anteia's father, in the hope that Bellerophon might perish.

9. Hector has come back to Troy in an interval of the fighting and meets his wife. See further Nos. 32, 33, 157. The fall of Troy and the captivity which Andrómachê anticipates are treated in Nos. 363–6, 373–4 by Euripidês. *Astyanax*: 'Lord of the citadel', 'Keeper of the city'. When Troy fell, he was hurled from the battlements by the Greeks. *Aiantës* is the plural of Aias (Ajax) and refers to Ajax the son of Télamon and Ajax the son of Oileus.

NOTES

10. Zeus decides that for the moment the Trojans shall get the better of the fighting.

11. The Trojans are encamped outside the Achæan lines. Pope's translation of these lines was much admired; but Wordsworth (with Coleridge and Southey) regarded it rather as showing 'to what a low state knowledge of the most obvious and important phenomena had sunk'. Byron, writing to Leigh Hunt, 30 Oct. 1815, decried Wordsworth and remarked that 'there is a burst and a lightness . . . about the night in the Troad which makes the "planets vivid" and the "pole glowing" '. (See his letters, ed. Prothero, vol. iii, p. 239 f. and reff.; and cf. 'Christopher North' in *Blackwood's*, July 1831, where the points at issue are discussed in some detail.) Tennyson (*A Memoir*, by his son, vol. ii, p. 419) agreed with Walter Leaf that lines 557–8 are more appropriate in another passage (*Il.* xvi. 299 f.) where they recur. Cf. Ap. Rhod. iii. 1359 ff. (No. 541, p. 602).

12. Odysseus and Diomêdês have asked Achilles to end his anger against Agamemnon, and here he answers them.

13. *Phoenix*: an old friend of Achilles' father.   *Achileus*: another form of Achilles' name.   *Crónidês* or *Cronión*: a name for Zeus as being the son of Kronos, who is sometimes (e.g. in No. 23) latinized as 'Saturn'. On the quantitative hexameters here used see Introduction, p. lvi.

14. Ajax is the last of the Achæans to retreat.

15. The wall is built by the Achæans to protect their camp.   *Menœtius' son*: Patroclus.

16. The two Ajaxes have been encouraging the Achæans to resist. The translation is in the metre of R. Bridges's *The Testament of Beauty*.

17. The Trojan attack on the Achæan camp reaches its crisis.

18. For the wall cf. No. 15.

19. Ajax leads the resistance to the Trojan attack on the Achæan ships. On the translation see Introduction, pp. lxxvi, xcvii ff.

NOTES

20. Patroclus has stayed with Achilles away from the fighting, but now asks that he may join in it.

21. Achilles prays before sending Patroclus to the battle.

22. Patroclus is killed by Hector.   *Croniôn*: cf. No. 13, note.   *Lêto's son*: Apollo.

23. Achilles had lent his horses to Patroclus.   *Son of Saturn*: cf. No. 13, note.

24. After a long fight the body of Patroclus is saved from the Trojans, but Hector has already taken Achilles' armour from the dead body.   *Aiantês*: see No. 9, note.

The translation (cf. No. 504) is in 'sprung rhythm', i.e. the line is 'divided into musical bars, each bar containing one stress, either alone or followed by a varying number of "slack" syllables'. (So defined by 'Critic' in *The New Statesman and Nation*, 5 Dec. 1936, p. 882; see also W. B. Yeats, *The Oxford Book of Modern Verse*, 1936, pp. xxxix ff.; and G. M. Young, *The London Mercury and Bookman*, Dec. 1936, pp. 112–22, for its history and some comments.) It is probable that the metre is better suited to short extracts, such as this, than to Homer *in extenso*.

25. Thetis, a sea-goddess and mother of Achilles, comes up from the sea to comfort him on the loss of Patroclus.

26. Îris has promised Achilles that he shall have a new set of armour in place of that taken by Hector. While waiting for it, Achilles appears on the rampart.   *Pêleion*: a name for Achilles, as being the son of Pêleus. The last eight lines of the translation are supplied by C. M. Bowra.

27. Thetis visits Hêphæstus and asks him to make new armour for Achilles.   *My fearful fall*: he was born lame, to the disgust of his mother Hêra, who flung him from Olympus.

28. Details of the new armour.   p. 43. *Now all at once . . . revel end*. A more literal rendering is given by Lang, Leaf, and Myers: 'And now would they run round with deft feet exceeding lightly, as when a potter sitting by his wheel that fitteth between his hands maketh trial of it whether it run:

and now anon they would run in lines to meet each other. And a great company stood round the lovely dance in joy; and through the midst of them, leading the measure, two tumblers whirled.'

29. Lycâon, son of Priam, has been caught by Achilles.

30. The river-god, Scamander, is angry with Achilles because of the dead bodies thrown by him into the water.

31. Hector has been waiting for the approach of Achilles.

32. Hector, left with nothing but a sword, has decided to face Achilles' spear and die fighting.

33. Hector's wife, Andrómachê (cf. No. 9) has not heard of his death. On the translation see Introduction, pp. xcviii ff.

34. Achilles has kept Patroclus' body from burial.

35. The chariot-race is an event at the funeral-games of Patroclus. Antílochus, son of Nestor, has won from Menelâus, by sharp practice, the prize of a mare. Here he replies to Menelâus' rebuke.

36. Hermês has guided Priam to the tent of Achilles to ransom the body of Hector. On Bridges's quantitative hexameters see Introduction, pp. lvi ff.

37. Hector's body has been brought back to Troy for burial.   p. 61. *Alexander* is another name for Paris.

38. Penelope, wife of Odysseus, has had no news of her husband for ten years. She is embarrassed by suitors, one of whom tells her son Têlémachus of her artfulness.   *Lâertês*: Odysseus' father.

39. Têlémachus is on a visit to Nestor at Pylos, searching for news of Odysseus. Athênê, in the likeness of Mentor, a friend of Odysseus' house, accompanies him. Nestor's reminiscences of Troy form a link with the *Iliad*. In the second piece he tells of Agamemnon's homecoming, on which see Nos. 250-3. p. 66. *A false tale is his return*: the reference is to possibilities of Odysseus' survival.

In the Preface to his translation Dr. Mackail writes: 'Technically the metre is that of FitzGerald's *Rubaiyat*; it may be of some interest, though of no importance, to mention that it was chosen by me more than fifty years ago, before I had read FitzGerald's then little-known masterpiece. . . . The first requirement in any translation of Homer is that it should carry the reader on, to some degree at least, as he is carried on by Homer himself. The metre of the translation must therefore be capable of the largest variation of pause and elasticity of musical phrasing that can be brought within the bounds of accurately patterned structure. . . . Its aim throughout must be to suggest . . . the combination of leisureness and rapidity, of swift motion with the stateliness in which, as Aristotle observes, the Homeric hexameter is unequalled. It is not 'the surge and thunder of the Odyssey' which is the final impression left by long acquaintance, but rather its quiet magnificence.'

40 (i). From Pylos Têlémachus goes, on the same quest, to visit Menelâus at Sparta. Helen and Menelâus, in their reminiscences, characterize both themselves and Odysseus. Another story of the wooden horse occurs in No. 45.

40 (ii). Menelâus here tells of his voyage from Troy, and how he was weather-bound off the Nile. Eidótheê (*the fair goddess*) advises him to learn the cause of his misfortune by questioning her father, the old sea-god Prôteus; and tells him how to do so. On the translation see Introduction, pp. lxxvii, xcvii ff.

41. Têlémachus had said nothing to his mother about going on his voyage. On the characterization of Penelope see J. W. Mackail, *Penelope in the Odyssey*, Cambridge University Press, 1916.

42. Hermês is sent to Ôgýgia, the island where Calypso has kept Odysseus for seven years. He reached this island after the adventures he describes in No. 46.

43 (i). Odysseus has left Ôgýgia on a raft of his own making. p. 76. *So spake he*: the reference is to Poseidon.

43 (ii). His raft has been destroyed and he has to swim, upheld by a magic veil with which Îno, a friendly sea-deity, has supplied him.

44 (i). Nausícaä is daughter of Alcinoüs, king of Phæacia,

where Odysseus has landed. Athênê has just appeared to her in a dream. On the translation see Introduction, pp. c–ci.

44 (ii). Nausícaä and her maidens arrive at the place where Odysseus has been sleeping in some bushes.

On the accentual hexameters here used see Introduction, pp. lii ff. Edward Carpenter, in *My Days and Dreams*, claims that Cotterill, while devoting himself to the suppression of slave-traffic in Africa, gained a knowledge of tribal life and custom invaluable to a translator of the *Odyssey*. (Cf. E. Stuart Bates, *Modern Translation*, 1936, p. 108.)

45. The blind bard Dêmódocus is present at the court of Alcinoüs. Cf. No. 40 (i) on the wooden horse.

46 (i–ii). Odysseus tells his adventures to Alcinoüs and his court. At an early stage of his wanderings he and his men had visited an island-cave in search of hospitality. But its owner the Cyclops, a one-eyed giant, shut them in and devoured some of their number. Here Odysseus tells how he and the rest escaped. See Nos. 350, 501, note, and 502 (d).

46 (iii). The adventure which left Odysseus with a single ship and crew—afterwards lost in the storm that drove him to Calypso's island (No. 42).

46 (iv). They next visit Ææa, Circê's island. Odysseus, with Hermês' help, forced her to restore his men to human shape, and stayed with her for a year. She then tells him that before returning home he must journey to Hades and seek advice from the ghost of Tîrésias, the Theban seer (cf. No. 510).

46 (v–vii). Other ghosts evoked by Odysseus while in Hades. Draughts of sacrificial blood enable them to communicate with him.

47. Having concluded the story of his adventures, Odysseus is conveyed to his own island of Ithaca by a magic ship of the Phæacians.

48 (i). The first man met by Odysseus in Ithaca is his faithful swineherd Eumæus, who gives him shelter. Athênê has altered Odysseus' looks to those of an old beggar-man, so that he goes unrecognized.

NOTES

48 (ii). Eumæus tells how first he came to Ithaca and was purchased by Odysseus' father. Lines 2–3: more literally, 'Ortýgia, where are the turning-places of the sun'. Some identify Ortýgia with Delos (as in later poetry) and find in the expression an observation of the solstice. But see T. D. Seymour, *Life in the Homeric Age*, p. 46, and Edd. *ad loc.*

49. Têlémachus, brought back from his voyage by Pallas Athênê (whom Cowper latinizes into 'Minerva'), finds his father in Eumæus' hut. They next make plans to overcome the wooers.

50. Odysseus, disguised again as a beggar, has come from Eumæus' hut to his own palace. The dog's name 'Argos' means 'swift'.

51 (i). Penelope does not recognize the beggar-man as her husband. *The crone*: Eurycleia, an old nurse, has recognized Odysseus from a scar (cf. No. **56** (ii)) while washing his feet, but swears to keep his secret. *Itylus*: see No. **565**, note. *Twelve in a row*: some suppose that the helves of the axes were crossed and that the arrow was shot between them. Others assume a form of axe in which the lower point of the blade was returned towards the helve, leaving a semicircular opening. See illustrations in Butcher and Lang's translation, p. 419.

51 (ii). The same night. Penelope lies sleepless.

52. Theoclýmenus, a seer, has been brought to Ithaca by Têlémachus from Pylos.

53 (i). The suitors are unarmed in the hall of the palace, and Odysseus prepares to kill them. Philœtius, a faithful cowherd, has been taken into his confidence.

53 (ii). The killing is over.

54. During the killing Athênê has kept Penelope fast asleep. Now she is told the news, but is careful to prove the identity of Odysseus.

55. Hermês (latinized as 'Mercury') is the usual conductor of the dead; cf. No. **313**, p. 350.

NOTES

56. Odysseus' reunion with his father Lâertês. Cf. No. 46 (v), pp. 100–1.

57. *The Slayer of Argos*: Zeus loved Io, but changed her into a white cow in order to conceal his love from Hêra (but cf. No. **238**, note). Argos was the hundred-eyed keeper set by Hêra to watch Io and killed by Hermês at Zeus' request. p. 132, l. 3: *Pandôra* should mean 'the all-giver', but Hesiod twists it to mean 'gifted by all the gods'. The myth is obscure. See H. J. Rose, *A Handbook of Greek Literature*, p. 59, and T. A. Sinclair's edition *ad loc*. *Epimêtheus*: the brother of Promêtheus. *Only Hope remained*: T. A. Sinclair concludes that Hope was kept imprisoned because she was a good denied to man, whose condition is *hopeless*. Man must expect only to earn his bread by the sweat of his brow—that is Hesiod's lesson. But here again the meaning of the myth is much disputed.

Of his translation Mr. Lindsay writes: 'I have trusted to ear while building on a five-beat—hoping to transport some of the variety of the original line.'

58. The last line of the paragraph on the top of p. 114 in the Greek text is regarded as spurious and is omitted in the translation. It runs: 'Far from the gods, for Kronos is king of the blest' (Jack Lindsay). With the ending of this piece cf. Aratus, No. **506**.

59–65, 68–9, 73–6. Hesiod uses hexameters throughout. But as these short pieces are excerpted for their own interest without any context, the translator has used such metres as the subject-matter (proverbial wisdom, &c.) suggests.

66. Girls were sometimes married in Greece at 14, 13, or even 12 years. Hesiod puts the best age at 16, Plato at 20. (Cf. T. A. Sinclair, *ad loc*.)

67 (i–vi). *The Farmer's Year*: see the excellent discussion in A. W. Mair's translation (Oxford University Press, 1908, pp. 104 ff.) to which the Editors are deeply indebted.

67 (i). *The Pleiads*: cf. Nos. **266, 549**. Hesiod refers to their heliacal rising (towards the end of April) as the signal for grain-harvest; and to their cosmical setting (towards the end of Oct. or the beginning of Nov.) as the signal for ploughing, i.e. the ploughing that is part of the work of sowing. These dates assume that Hesiod wrote in Bœotia about 800 B.C. *They are hidden*: i.e. owing to the proximity of the sun. *Appear once more*: they now arrive sufficiently in front of the sun to appear on the eastern horizon before dawn, i.e. they rise heliacally. On the translation see Introduction, p. lxxxix.

67 (ii). *The crane*: cf. Nos. 3, 199, 423, 425, 502 (*b*). A passenger in Greece; for it nested in adjacent countries to the N. and NW. Its migration to the African continent about October marks the time for 'ploughing', which here again implies sowing. Later (p. 141 f.) Hesiod says that, if sowing is delayed until the winter solstice, the crop will be poor—unless a heavy rain chances to fall on the third day after the cuckoo's arrival, i.e. sometime in March. *Plough in the spring*: this ploughing means only the first turning of fallow ground. The land was worked on a two-shift system. One field, after being harvested, lay fallow till the following spring, when it was turned, sometimes more than once, preparatory to re-sowing in the autumn. Meanwhile a second field provided a crop—and so on, alternately. *With criss-cross sheaves*: see T. A. Sinclair's note. To lay the heads and butts of the corn alternately one way and the other, is a practice found in parts of France when the harvest is bad ('*Bêcheveter les avoines*', Mazon). *Grey-husked spring*: the Greek epithet is simply 'grey'. Another interpretation refers it to the mists of early spring.

67 (iii). *The month of Lênaion*: corresponds to part of December and part of January. This is the first occurrence of the name of a month in Greek poetry. *Bóreas*: the North wind. p. 142, last line: alternatively, 'But the old man he sets a-running.' *The Boneless One*: there was a popular belief that the polypus or cuttle-fish lived through the winter by eating its own suckers. For similar descriptive expressions cf. Nos. 67 (iv), where the snail (literally) is 'The house-carrier'; 68 (i) 'The Wise One'; 73 'The Hairless One'. Some may reflect local parlance, some may be invented, in hieratic manner, to heighten the effect. But A. B. Cook would also regard them as survivals from the time 'when certain animals were never referred to by their proper names

lest they should hear and take notice' (see T. A. Sinclair's note and reff.). On the translation see Introduction, p. xcviii.

67 (iv). The time is April, before the heat marked by the Pleiads' rising.

67 (v). The *Skólymus*, an artichoke or cardoon, flowers in June. The dog-days follow, especially with the rising of Sîrius, *c.* 12 July. *Biblis*: possibly a place-name which came to denote a type of wine independently of local origin. T. A. Sinclair compares the phrase 'Australian Burgundy'. Alcæus (No. **135** (iv)) imitates this piece. On the translation see Introduction, p. lxxxix.

67 (vi). *The fifty days*: say July–August. *The new wine*: vintaging took place in September.

68 (ii). Cf. No. **423**, which has many reminiscences of Hesiod.

69. Of *The Precepts of Chîron* 'we know three things; That it contained the advice "first of all, when thou comest to thine house, make sacrifice to the gods"; that it said a child should not learn to read till he was seven years old; and that it states the life of Nymphs to be $9 \times 4 \times 3 \times 9 \times 10$ times as long as man's'. (Cf. H. J. Rose, *A Handbook of Greek Literature*, pp. 66–7.)

70 (i). The last line is a proverbial expression for irrelevance.

70 (ii). *The daughters of Zeus*: the Muses were born to Zeus by Mnêmósynê (Memory) in Hesiod's account.

71. *The Titans* were the offspring of Gaia (Earth) and Uranus (Heaven). There were six males, the youngest being Kronos, and six females, among them Rheä. Three Cyclopës —divine smiths (cf. No. **508**) very different in conception from Homer's Cyclopës (No. **46** (i), (ii))—were also born to Gaia; so too the hundred-handed giants *Kottos, Briareus,* and *Gyês* (p. 151). All these last six were hated by Uranus, who thrust them down within the earth. Later he was mutilated, at Gaia's instigation, by Kronos.

Kronos in his turn submitted to Zeus, his child by Rheä. No. **71** describes the final stage in the ten years' war which led to this result. With Kronos were ranged the Titans (except Promêtheus and Themis); and with Zeus, among others, the

NOTES

Cyclopës and the hundred-handed trio liberated by him from their prison below. Zeus fought from Olympus, Kronos from Mt. Orthrys. The Titans are nature-powers, mostly not Greek. The legend of their overthrow by Zeus and the Olympians seems to reflect the victory of Greek invaders over the indigenous population and their gods. See further H. J. Rose, *A Handbook of Greek Mythology*, chapters i, ii.

72. Cycnus, son of the war-god Arês, used to plunder the cattle brought for sacrifice to Apollo at Delphi.

73. From a papyrus fragment. Zeus sends a cataclysm to destroy mankind. Cf. No. 67 (iii), note.

74. Cf. Virgil, on Camilla, *Aen.* vii. 808.

75. The Greek name *Parthenios* means 'maiden' or 'virginal'. Cf. No. 78, line 3.

77–91. *Homeric Hymns.* For many of the following notes the Editors are much indebted to the edition by T. W. Allen, W. R. Halliday, and E. E. Sikes (Oxford, Clarendon Press, 1936), who are subsequently referred to as Edd. (1936).

77. Aïdôneus is another name for Hades or Pluto, the 'many-titled'. Sometimes the Greeks preferred to talk of him obliquely as '*The god who houses many*' or '*The Ready Host*'—euphemisms due to superstitious fear.

The hymn seems to date from the 7th cent. B.C. It is the earliest document relating to the Eleusinian mysteries. (Cf. Edd. (1936).)

78. Line 1. *She*: i.e. Dêmêter, in her search for the ravished Persephonê.

77–8. W. M. W. Call, of St. John's College, Cambridge, translated many of the Homeric Hymns in *Lyra Hellenica* (G. Bell, 1842). His translation of the *Hymn to Dêmêter* was probably written about the same time, but not published till 1871. He was clearly influenced by Shelley (cf. Nos. 82–4), and with good effect; but in general is over-free and somewhat careless in execution. Adaptation of his work, short of re-writing it in the same metre, was usually prevented by the rhyme-system. In No. 77 lines 12–19, 22–30 are substantially his, and in No. 78 lines 15–16, 18, 31–2, 43, 70, 106, together with parts of 19, 53–5, 72, 85, 95. The rest is by T. F. Higham. See also Walter Pater, *Greek Studies* (Macmillan's Library Ed., 1910, pp. 83 ff.), where parts of both pieces are translated, rather loosely, into prose. Pater omits most of the ornamental epithets; cf. Introduction, pp. lxxxiv, xcviii.

79. The Assembly of Ionians at Delos was famous as early as the 8th century B.C.; and the hymn (or part of it) may belong to the later years of that century. The chorus of Delian maidens were accomplished in dialects. Edd. (1936) compare the mimetic powers of Helen—cf. No. 40 (i). They add that religious centres appear to have been polyglot, and that Apollo answered pilgrims in their own dialect and with their own music. On the translation of Nos. 79–81 see Introduction, p. lxxxix.

80. In the Greek text inverted commas should close line 173, not line 175.

81. Cf. No. 95.

82. Line 2. *He*: i.e. Hermês, the son of Zeus and Maia. Shelley latinizes Hermês into *Mercury*, and Zeus into *Jove* or *The Saturnian*. Maia he calls *May*, p. 163. The tortoise-shell lyre serves (No. 84) as a peace-offering to Apollo.

83. As hinted at the end of No. 82, the baby Hermês has now stolen Apollo's cattle—no less than fifty of them. Like Cacus in Vergil, *Aen.* viii. 210, he backed them away from their pasture, so as to leave misleading prints. His own tracks were disguised by large brushwood sandals and led the reverse way to theirs.

Edd. (1936) describe the *Hymn to Hermês* as 'excellent racy literature of an early period'—not later than the 7th century—and 'unique in its free cynical style'.

85–6. Both the date and the place of composition of this hymn remain obscure. 'Aphrodîtê is mistress of the animal world; but there is no hint of a deity who inspires the whole Cosmos'—an Eastern conception not found in Greek literature till the 5th century (cf. Edd. (1936), p. 350).

86. Spoken by Aphrodîtê to Anchîsês, after the union

from which Æneas was born. The passage on p. 172 'is the first to contain a definite statement that the life of tree-nymphs is bound up with the tree'. In later poetry, from Pindar onwards, the belief is common (Edd. (1936) *ad loc.*). See also No. 69.

87. Perhaps written in Naxos, 6th or 7th century B.C. The Greek style is 'direct and rather rough'. *Tuscans*: the Greek word *Tyrsênoi* may refer only to the pre-Hellenic inhabitants of the Balkan peninsula. See further Edd. (1936), pp. 376 ff. on the origin of the myth and its place in art.

88. Pan, the shepherd god of Arcadia, is little recognized in literature before the Persian wars. The hymn may belong to the 5th century. The name *Pan* is more scientifically explained as coming from the same root as the Lat. *pa-sco*—he is the Feeder of flocks. (Cf. H. J. Rose, *A Handbook of Greek Mythology*, p. 167.)

89. Some of the minor hymns were preludes to the recitations of Homeric rhapsodes. No. 91 is also of this kind.

90. Hestia 'represents the religious focus of family life at meals'. She received the last as well as the first libation except at bedtime, when the last libation went to Hermês, who is associated with her in subsequent lines of this poem—apparently 'as protector of the sleep of the family'. (So Edd. (1936).) To 'eat the ox that was fatted for Hestia' (No. 511, p. 583) was a desperate resource.

91. Later than the *Hymn to Dêmêter* (see No. 77, note), but the date and place of origin are unknown.

92. See No. 209, a contradiction of this poem. George Chapman's translation of No. 92 is characteristic:

> A maid of brass I am, infixed here
> T'eternize honest Midus' sepulchre;
> And while the stream her fluent seed receives,
> And steep trees curl their verdant brows with leaves,
> While Phœbus rais'd above the earth gives sight,
> And th' humorous Moon takes lustre from his light,
> While floods bear waves, and seas shall wash the shore,
> At this his sepulchre, whom all deplore,
> I'll constantly abide; all passers by
> Informing, 'Here doth honest Midus lie.'

NOTES

93. The *Margítês* was a poem of unknown authorship describing a dunce. It stood to Epic in much the same relation as Comedy to Tragedy.

95. The *Títanomáchia*, of unknown authorship, had the same subject as No. 71.

96. The *Cypria* (variously attributed) told of events from the Judgement of Paris to the early stages of the Trojan war.

97. On the translation see Introduction, p. lxiv.

100. *Memory's daughters*: see 70 (ii), note.

102. The fifth line of the Greek is lost. On the translation see Introduction, p. lxiv.

103–13. For a new discussion of the date of Archilochus see A. Blakeway in *Greek Poetry and Life: Essays presented to Gilbert Murray*, 1936, pp. 34–55.

103. Cf. Hybrias, No. 237.

104–5. Like his great grandfather, the poet went to Thasos, a colony of Paros, his native place. No. 104, a deliberately shocking confession, records an affair with the Thracians of the mainland.

108. *Cape of Gyræ*: off the SE. promontory of Eubœa.

110. Line 2. Read ἀνάδυ.

111. The eclipse which inspired these lines is placed by some at 6 April 648 B.C., and by Blakeway at 14 March 711 B.C. Cf. No. 292.

114. The song is sung by a choir of ten maidens just before the dawn. They are competing against a rival choir called the Pleiads (or Doves) and describe playfully the charms of their two leaders, Hâgêsíchora and Agido. On p. 158, line 12 of the Greek text, read αὐτεῖ: 'is here present'.

115. The Greek author who preserves this fragment connects it with the legend that when the male birds are grown too old to fly, their females carry them.

116. The reference is probably to some Bacchic revel on the mountains, when the Bacchants were filled with superhuman

692

powers. In line 2 read πολύφανον, 'with many torches', for πολύφαμον.

122. This curious poem 'related in substance to the beast-fable' (H. J. Rose, *A Handbook of Greek Literature*, p. 92) has been often translated from the time of George Buchanan (1506–82) onwards. The latest version is in Chaucerian style by J. M. Edmonds: see *The Classical Review*, Dec. 1936, p. 210.

123. Herodotus (i. 24) tells how Arîon was saved by a dolphin after leaping overboard to escape robbery and violence. Nothing of Arîon's work survives. These lines are probably from an Athenian dithyramb of the 5th century. On dolphin-legends see Allen, Halliday, and Sikes, *The Homeric Hymns*, 1936, p. 378.

125 (i). Sung by reapers.

125 (ii). Sung by women over the mill-stone in Lesbos, where Pittacus was tyrant 590–580 B.C.

126 (i). A children's game called 'Flowers'.

126 (ii). A game in which the speaker of the first line was blindfolded and tried to catch the other children, who struck at him with stalks of papyrus.

126 (iii). A girls' game. 'Tortoise' sat in the middle and the others ran round her, exchanging these verses, till one was caught and took her place.

127. From Locris in South Italy.

129. *Linos* was some kind of year-spirit, whose death was lamented at harvest or vintage. Cf. No. 28 (iii), p. 42. In one form of the legend he is a son of the Muse Urania, and is killed by Apollo as a rival in music.

130. Sung in the spring at Rhodes by children who went begging round the town. See No. 664, note.

131. There was a famous shrine of Athêna at Corônêa in Bœotia. Cf. No. 510, p. 577.

133. Both these poems are probably allegorical, referring to the political struggles of Alcæus' time in Mytilênê. They represent different fragments.

693

NOTES

134. Alcæus' brother was a soldier of fortune under the king of Babylon.

135 (iv). Cf. No. 67 (v).

137. Sîsyphus directed his wife to cast out his dead body unburied, and so got leave from Hades to return to life for long enough to punish her impiety. Once returned, he enjoyed the joke with her and stayed on until he died a second time of sheer old age. (See H. J. Rose, *A Handbook of Greek Mythology*, p. 294.)

138. Thetis, the good wife, is contrasted with the bad wife, Helen.

139. Towards the end of a tempest Castor and Polydeucês were thought to appear in the form of lights—the electric phenomenon known as 'fuoco di Sant' Elmo'. They indicated that the danger was passing. See also No. 287.

140–2. The metre used by Sappho in these three poems has often been imitated. Swinburne's *Sapphics* (*Poems and Ballads*, i, p. 234), which are 'true-timed' on the whole (see Introduction, p. lv), are certainly the most successful experiment. Cf. also Bridges's quantitative sapphics (*The Poetical Works*, Oxford ed., 1914, p. 442). Canning's much-quoted 'Needy knife-grinder, whither art thou going ?' &c. (a parody of Southey's experiments) suffers from the perverse influence of Horatian sapphics as read aloud by English readers in times not wholly past. Cf. J. P. Postgate, *Flaws in Classical Research*, 1908, p. 22. Echoes of No. 140 occur in Swinburne's *On the Cliffs* and *Anactoria*.

141. See No. 146, note. Line 7: read φώναισ', i.e. φώναισαι (infin.).

142. 'Silver' is not a translator's 'embellishment'. The epithet belongs to this fragment, though not printed in the Greek text. See E. Lobel, *The Fragments of the Lyrical Poems of Sappho*, p. 18.

143. On imitations of Sappho's metre in this poem, see No. 504, note.

145. About a girl who has gone to Lydia, leaving Atthis, whose name recurs in No. 154.

NOTES

146. A. E. Housman in *Epithalamium* (*Last Poems*, p. 48) adapts this fragment. Sappho's lines, if we may judge by similarities in Catullus lxii, were composed for the wedding feast which took place before a bride was conducted home. No. **141** (cf. Catullus li) may well have been suggested by a similar occasion, when the bride would be seated next the bridegroom. Hesperus marks the time for leaving the feast.

147. Sappho recalls those hours with a friend which she had thought most pleasant. The poem has neither beginning nor end, and many of its lines are fragmentary.

148. Like No. 146, Hymeneal. No. (i) probably leads to the conclusion that a girl, after all, is better married, and No. (ii) laments the loss which marriage means to her—cf. Catullus, lxii. 38–44.

149. From a love-song. Cf. No. **156**.

150 (i). Traditional in character. Usener quotes a good parallel from Moravia, translated in Bowra, *Greek Lyric Poetry*, p. 226 f.

151. As reported in *The Times* of 16 July 1937 (while this book was in the press), a potsherd of the 2nd century B.C. has supplied a new version of this fragment together with the remains of one preceding and two succeeding stanzas—the last of them previously known. See *Annali della R. Scuola Normale Superiore di Pisa*, Serie ii, vol. vi, 1937, pp. 8–15, where the new find was first published by Medea Norsa; and *Philologus*, vol. xcii, 1937, pp. 117–25 for comments by Rudolf Pfeiffer. The title 'Rain' in the Greek text of this book had been altered to 'Garden of the Nymphs' (which is nearer the mark) before the new find was reported. After 'appled boughs' a revised translation would run 'everywhere is the shade of roses, and slumber falling from the rustle of leaves'. But the new text is doubtful in two places.

153. On her daughter Cleïs.

154–5. See Swinburne, *On the Cliffs*, for echoes of these fragments; and Maurice Baring, *Have you anything to declare?*, 1936, p. 141, on Swinburne.

NOTES

156. The authorship is not certain. It seems to be a folk-song.

157. This poem is attributed by good authority to Sappho, but has been thought to be the work of an Athenian imitator. See No. 9, where Andrómachê tells her story.

158–60. Solon is best known for his political and economic reforms at Athens. His elegiac verse is competent, with occasional touches of poetry.

160. *Pæôn*: The Healer, i.e. Apollo.

161. From an account of Hêraclês' journey in the Sun's boat to the West in search of the cattle of Gêrÿon. Cf. No. 296, note.

162. Stêsíchorus was said to have been blinded by Helen for speaking ill of her, and here he recants what he said. Euripidês in his *Helena* adopts this recantation, which made the real Helen go to Egypt and a phantom Helen to Troy. Cf. No. 379 and note.

163. Given to Glaucus of Sparta. See Herodotus, vi. 86. 3, for the story. On the accentual hexameters cf. Introduction, pp. lii ff.

164. The natural ripening of young love, symbolically expressed in lines 1–7, is contrasted with the unseasonable gusts of passion that vex Ibycus, presumably late in life.

166. Written for the young Polÿcratês, son of the tyrant of Samos.

167. Given by Amphílytus of Acarnania to Peisístratus before his third entry into Athens. Cf. Herodotus, i. 62, 4.

168. Compare the lines of R. Porson:

> The Germans in Greek
> Are still much to seek;
> Not five in five score
> But ninety-five more;
> Excepting friend Hermann—
> And He is—a German.

171. Artemis, as worshipped in her famous temple at Mag-nêsia, had acquired many qualities of the Asiatic Cybêlê, and the city itself was the seat of a Persian satrap. Anacreon implies tactfully that the Magnêsians are Greeks after all.

172. Sung in the spring, when the blue anemones are on the hills and Anacreon over his wine turns to thoughts of love. (Cf. Wilamowitz, *Sappho u. Simonides*, pp. 114 ff.)

174. Anacreon fancies that Erôs summons him to a song and to love by throwing a ball at him. An older fashion would have been to throw an apple. (Wilamowitz, *op. cit.*, p. 116.)

175 (*a*). *Amalthêa's horn* provided its owner with a magical supply of meat and drink in unlimited quantities. *Tarshish*: Herodotus, i. 163, says that Arganthonius lived to be a hundred and twenty years old and was king of Tartessus for eighty years. Anacreon gives round figures.

178–80. The Anacreontea are imitations of Anacreon written by different hands in the Hellenistic and Greco-Roman periods. One sign of late writing in No. 179 is the treatment of Love as a small boy—the sportive Cupid of our own literature. This treatment began with the Samian epigrammatists, *c.* 300 B.C. To Anacreon Erôs is a youth.

181–3. The meagre fragments of Hippônax have chiefly a metrical interest. He invented the *chôliambus*, i.e. *limping iambic*—a 6-ft. line with spondaic close, imitated in the (5-ft.) translation of No. 181. A. D. Knox (*Herôdês*, &c., Loeb ed., pp. xi–xii and 13) explains that the basis of the metre is essentially different from that of the tragic iambus and also from that of Herôdês' chôliambi, for which see No. 556. The last line of No. 181 should probably be excised (ibid., p. 43). Nos. 182 (in Hippônax's metre) and 183 (in plain iambics of a later type) are generally agreed to be by other hands. The former is sometimes taken to mean 'Two days in life of woman are sweetest, when she is wed, and when she is buried' (ibid., p. 6). With No. 181 cf. No. 304 and No. 437, note.

184. Xenóphanês mocks the Pythagorean doctrine of metempsychosis.

185–99. It is not certain that all the poems attributed to Theognis were written by him. But most belong to the 6th and early 5th centuries. His advice, essentially aristocratic and conservative, is bestowed on a young friend Kyrnos. Nos. 191, 194, 199 seem to reflect a period of revolution in Megara and, as far as we can tell, the fortunes of Theognis himself. In lines 7–8 of No. 191 there is reference to a proverb or fable the exact meaning of which is lost. See also No. 204, note.

203. The Spartan dead were buried at Thermopylæ, but seem to have had a cenotaph and shrine at Sparta, where annual rites were paid to them. These lines would, then, form part of a hymn composed for such an occasion. Leonidas, like all Spartan kings, was accorded some divine honour after death. He had a shrine to himself, which enables him here to be cited as an impartial witness. Cf. Bowra, *Greek Lyric Poetry*, pp. 361 ff.

204. Written for a patron, Scopas of Thessaly. In Pittacus' saying, 'excellence' implies every advantage of birth, physique, and property. Moral excellence, according to the old aristocratic notions which we find e.g. in Theognis, was inseparably bound up with these; and possibly Simonidês was expected to say that Scopas was possessed of them all. Instead, he criticizes the old notions; for, as Theognis had seen, a new monied class had arisen and property was now separated from the other patents of excellence. 'The old code', he says, 'is impossible in this world, and it leaves too much outside a man's control; a man's willing actions are the only test of his excellence.' To-day this conclusion may seem trite; but at the time it was novel, if not revolutionary. Cf. Bowra, op. cit., pp. 341 ff.

205. Written when the whole house of Scopas was destroyed by their home collapsing on them.

206. A famous fragment from some kind of choral song. King Acrísius, warned by prophecy that his grandson by Danaê will slay him, has put them both to sea in a wooden chest, borne eventually to the island of Serîphos. Cf. No. 283, note.

209. An answer to No. 92. Cleobûlus was one of the seven sages—a native of Caria resident for a time in Lindus. *A*

NOTES

stone: the corresponding Greek word is given contemptuous emphasis by means of a metrical device.

210. Develops a theme in Hesiod, *Works and Days*, lines 289–92. Cf. also No. 459.

211. In 506 B.C. the Athenians defeated the men of Chalcis in Eubœa. *Narrow Waters*: the straits called 'Eurîpus', between Eubœa and Bœotia.

212. See Introduction, pp. lix–lxv

213. Privately written by Simonidês for his Spartan friend and inscribed at Thermopylæ, some time after the battle had become a story (see H. T. Wade-Gery, *Journal of Hellenic Studies*, 1933, pp. 71 ff.).

214. Written for those who fell fighting the Persians in 479 B.C.

215 (i). Probably written about 476 B.C., when Tégëa rebelled against Sparta.

215 (ii). Seems to be a later imitation.

216. Hippias, tyrant of Athens, was expelled in 511 B.C. Archédikê was the wife of Hippoklos, tyrant of Lampsakos.

217 (i). *To Apollo*: i.e. to Delphi. The translation assumes that the bodies were recovered and buried. But it is possible that the inscription, if not merely 'literary', was cut on a cenotaph bearing the names of the dead, and that the sea is thought of as being their tomb. Cf. No. 622 and Propertius' line 'nunc tibi pro tumulo Carpathium omne mare est'.

217 (ii). *Geraneia*: a mountain range on the west coast of Megaris, abutting on the Isthmus of Corinth. The Skîrônian Rocks were named after the robber Skîrôn killed by Thêseus (No. 309 (ii)).

222. A mock-epitaph. Tîmócreon (cf. No. 305) was an enemy of Themístoclês and Simonidês. J. M. Edmonds (*Lyra Græca*, ii, 1924, p. 419) by a coincidence uses the same play on words:

> Thy guttling o'er, thy tippling done,
> Thou'rt lying still, Tîmócreon.

NOTES

H. W. Garrod modernizes:

> Here lies Timócreon: Lord, what a mess
> Of beer and beef and bitterness.

(*Worms and Epitaphs*, Oxford, Basil Blackwell, 1919, p. 17.)

224–5. The translations are in accentual elegiacs; cf. Introduction, pp. lii–lvi.

226–36. These verses were convivial songs ('skólia') sung by Athenian nobles in the period 525–480 B.C. Cf. Bowra, *Greek Lyric Poetry*, pp. 402 ff.

229. Attributed by some ancient authorities to Simonidês.

230. The four stanzas preserved probably represent a longer series. They celebrate the murder in 514 B.C. of Hipparchus, brother of the tyrant Hippias, at the Panathenaic procession. The murderers were heroized and their descendants had special privileges. The swords they used are said to have been concealed in myrtle-sprays. This story and the song may account for the custom by which a myrtle-spray was held by the singer of a skolion and perhaps passed on to successive singers at the end of each stanza.

231. Written in memory of the Athenian rebels killed at Leipsýdrion *c.* 514 B.C. when fighting against Hippias.

233. Cf. Nos. 670–1.

237. A Cretan song, of obscure origin and authorship. Cf. Bowra, *Greek Lyric Poetry*, pp. 437 ff. The sentiments in No. 103 are similar. Thomas Campbell's lines were written at the age of sixteen. Gilbert Murray has kindly provided a rather closer version:

> I have great riches, spear and sword
> And raw-hide fluttering at my breast:
> My land is ploughed, my harvest stored,
> My sweet wine from the vintage pressed,
> The Mnoan trash hath learnt its Lord,
> By spear and sword.
>
> And all who dare not walk with spear
> And sword and raw-hide fluttering,
> They needs must kiss my knees and cling,
> And hail me, cowering in their fear,
> Lord and Great King!

NOTES

Raw-hide: a skin, tied by its feet round the wearer's neck, and held out in front of the body by the left arm, formed the kind of shield indicated. *Mnoan trash*: a class of publicly owned serfs who tilled state-lands in Crete.

238. The Chorus of fifty daughters of Dánaüs tell of their descent from Io. Æschylus follows a story in which Hêra, not Zeus, changed Io into a cow; see No. 57, note. *Wingèd herd*: a gadfly sent by Hêra to keep Io moving. *Épaphus*: this name was thought by the Greeks to mean that Zeus impregnated Io by a mere *touch* of his hand.

239. The daughters of Dánaüs are pursued from Egypt to Argos by fifty lovers, from whom they ask deliverance.

240. A Messenger tells Atossa, the Persian Queen-mother, of the defeat of King Xerxês at Salamis. Æschylus himself was a combatant at this battle, as at Marathon (cf. No. 269).

Mr. G. M. Cookson states his views on translation in *The Classical Review*, vol. xxxvii, 1923, pp. 146–8. His main thesis is that 'the translator, if it be possible, must feel as the poet felt and rouse the same feelings in those who read his translation. . . . No mind can make itself an absolutely transparent medium through which the mind of another shall be discerned. . . . The psychological effect must be produced by this or that bias natural to the genius of the translator, and wherever niceties of resemblance stand in the way they must be sacrificed to the supreme end. It must be said of the translator, as it is said of the inspired teacher, that the mind of the master dwells in him.' As to method: 'Sensuously you cannot hope to compete with the rich effects of Greek poetry if you throw away the indigenous wealth of your own.'

241. The Chorus of Persian Elders lament the defeat.

242. Polynîcês, at variance with his brother Éteoclês, has come from Argos with six other chieftains to attack him in Thebes. In return for some unfilial action, their father Oedipus, some time after his blinding (cf. No. 319), had pronounced a curse upon the brothers—'that they should divide their inheritance with the sword'; cf. p. 256, last line.

243. Promêtheus has just been nailed to a rock in the

NOTES

Caucasus for giving fire to mankind. Cf. No. 57, and see also No. 71, note.

244–5. Addressed to the Chorus of Oceanids.

245. *He plots a marriage*: any son born of Thetis was fated to be stronger than his sire. Promêtheus knew this secret, from his mother Themis. Zeus, who desired Thetis, did not. Cf. No. 290, p. 324.

246. Promêtheus refuses to yield to Zeus and is punished for this by being engulfed in the earth.

247. The Chorus of Argive Elders sing of Agamemnon, who sacrificed his daughter Îphigeneia at the advice of the seer Calchas. Agamemnon had offended the goddess Artemis, and hence the Greek fleet, on its way to Troy, lay weatherbound at Aulis. Cf. Nos. 284, 386.

248. Clytæmêstra, wife of Agamemnon, tells the Chorus how a chain of beacons has announced to her the fall of Troy.

249. A lesson on sin and its retribution, with special reference to the origin, and cost in lives, of the Trojan war.

250. Clytæmêstra's welcome to Agamemnon, whom she intends to murder, having taken a paramour, Ægisthus, during his ten years' absence at Troy. Cf. Nos. 39 (ii), 284.

251. She invites Agamemnon to walk on a purple carpet spread in his honour, but he hesitates, in fear of presumptuous sin.

252. Cassandra, a daughter of Priam, has come with Agamemnon as a captive. A prophetess, she knows the fate that awaits them both, and also that Clytæmêstra and Ægisthus will in their turn be killed by Orestês. Mr. MacNeice's translation was 'written primarily for the stage' and purposely 'sacrifices certain things in the original' including 'the liturgical flavour of the diction'.

253. Orestês and his sister call upon the ghost of their murdered father Agamemnon while preparing to avenge his death.

254. After killing his mother at the bidding of Apollo ('Loxias'), Orestês is tormented by avenging Furies. *The*

NOTES

links that bound my father: a bath-robe which served to impede Agamemnon while the murderers cut him down. *Nombril-precincts*: Apollo's oracle at Delphi was thought of as the centre or navel ('nombril') of the earth. With this piece compare No. 381.

255. The Furies sing of their duties. *Lêto's Lion-cub*: Apollo, who sanctioned Orestês' matricide.

256. The Furies, transformed into Euménidês or Kindly Ones, wish good things for Athens. Orestês has there been tried by the ancient court of the Areópagus and acquitted by the casting-vote of Athênê (the 'Unmarried Maiden', p. 285), who calms the Furies and domiciles them under their new title.

257–67. Fragments from lost plays.

257. Aphrodîtê is the speaker.

258. Lycurgus, king of the Êdôni, a Thracian people, opposed the worship of Dionŷsus with results fatal to himself. The fragment is doubtfully restored, but seems to refer rather to Bacchic orgies of Phrygian origin than to the worship of Cotys (Kotytto), a Thracian goddess. Between lines 1 and 2 some others, describing her orgiasts, are probably missing. Strabo says that lines 2 ff. refer to Bacchants.

259. A well-known fragment. Cf. No. 404.

260. A source of frequent similes, e.g. Aristophanês, *Birds*, 808; Byron, *English Bards*, &c., 841 ff.

261. Cf. Swinburne, *Phædra*, 97 ff.:

> For of all gods Death only loves not gifts,
> Nor with burnt-offering nor blood-sacrifice
> Shalt thou do aught to get thee grace of him;
> He will have nought of altar and altar-song,
> And from him only of all the lords in heaven
> Persuasion turns a sweet averted mouth.

262. Quoted by Plato, *Republic*, 391 E.

264. On *Philoctêtês* see No. 328 and note.

265. The subject of this play was the ransom of Hector Cf. No. 36.

266. Atlas was punished for fighting with the Titans against Zeus. Cf. No. 71, note.

268. Perhaps in memory of the few Thessalians who tried to oppose Xerxês' invasion in 480 B.C. Cf. H. T. Wade-Gery, *Journal of Hellenic Studies*, 1933, p. 75.

269. Æschylus died in Sicily. *Braided hair*: see A. S. F. Gow, *Journal of Hellenic Studies*, 1928, pp. 133 ff.

270. The Proem to Parménidês' poem on the nature of reality. An allegory of the passage from ignorance to knowledge. Cf. J. Burnet, *Early Greek Philosophy*, 2nd ed., 1908, pp. 215 ff.

271–3. Fragments, in Bœotian dialect.

271. Myrtis was a Bœotian poetess who competed unsuccessfully against Pindar. Corinna, another Bœotian, gave him the famous advice 'to sow with the hand and not with the whole sack', and had the luck to defeat him five times. To which he is said to have retorted by calling her 'a sow'. See J. M. Edmonds, *Lyra Græca*, iii, p. 644 and reff.

272. The eponymous heroes of two mountains, Helicon and Cithæron, have a contest in song.

273. The nine daughters of the river-god Asôpus were all carried off by deities and became the mothers of famous cities. See H. J. Rose, *A Handbook of Greek Mythology*, pp. 115–16, for the Bœotian legends of Hýrieus, Orion, and Orion's daughters.

274. Written for Híeron of Syracuse in 476 B.C. Line 1, *He*: i.e. Pelops, 'whose chariot-race for the hand of Hippodameia was the true beginning of Olympian contests' (Gildersleeve, *ad loc.*). She rode beside her suitors. Oinomáos, her father, pursued, and speared the slow-paced from behind. *A busy tomb*: Pelops' tomb was beside the great altar of Zeus at Olympia. On the translation see Introduction, pp. civ ff.

275. Written for Thêron of Acragas in 476 B.C. Cronos, as dynast of the Golden Age, is made to preside over the Islands of the Blest. Cf. No. 58, note. *Cycnus*: a son of Poseidon, who opposed the Greek landing at Troy. Invulnerable, but strangled by Achilles.   *Morning's son*: Memnon; cf. No. 286, end.

L. R. Farnell, in an obituary notice of C. J. Billson (*The Times*, 14 Nov. 1932), wrote: 'He had the advantage of belonging in his prime to the age of the best Victorian tradition, but he always had a strong sympathy with new aims and younger writers. . . . When we were discussing together the best method of rendering Pindar, he told me that he had come to the opinion that his own was too luscious.'

276. Written in 468 B.C. for Hâgêsias of Syracuse, who was also steward of an oracle at Olympia and connected with the prophetic clan descended from Evadnê.   p. 296, line 1: *Æpytus* is 'Eilatus' wise son' of the first stanza.   *She*: Evadnê.   p. 297, *An all-embracing festival*: the festival of Zeus at Olympia.

277. Written for Xenophon of Corinth in 464 B.C.   Line 1, *His father*: i.e. Glaucus' father, Bellerophon (a Corinthian hero). The full genealogy is: Poseidon—Æolus—Sîsyphus—Glaucus—Bellerophon—Hippólochus (omitted by Pindar)—Glaucus (on whom see No. 8). In line 1, p. 298, the title 'Æolian king' refers to Bellerophon's descent from Æolus; and in the next line by the words 'thy father' is meant Poseidon, later called 'the Earth Enfolder'. See also No. 289, end.

278. Written for Híeron of Syracuse in 470 B.C.   *Týphôs*: son of Earth and Tartarus, and father of winds whose subterranean action was thought to cause volcanic eruptions and earthquakes. Cf. H. J. Rose, *A Handbook of Greek Mythology*, pp. 58–60. He had a long war with Zeus, but was finally thrust into prison under Mt. Etna.

279. Written for Híeron of Syracuse *c.* 472 B.C.   *Phlé-gÿas' daughter*: Corônis. While with child by Apollo (*the Loxian watcher*) of Delphi (*Pytho*), she formed an irregular union with *Ischys* (p. 302) instead of waiting for a marriage of her father's choice. Apollo in anger requested his sister, the *Huntress Maid* Artemis, to kill her with the shafts of pestilence; but saved her child Asclêpius—the god of healing imported into Rome (293 B.C.) as 'Æsculapius'.

280. Written for Arcésilas of Cyrênê in 462 B.C. On their return voyage the Argonauts had formed unions in *Lemnos* (p. 312) with the daughters of Dánaüs (cf. No. 239) who had slain their husbands. From one such union sprung the stock of Euphâmus, founders of Cyrênê; and hence the excuse for introducing the story of Argo into this ode—a notable treatment in lyric of an epic theme. Cf. Nos. 532–43.

p. 304. *Æolus' proud sons*: Jason was a grandson, in the male line, of *Crêtheus*, the eldest son of Æolus. *Pélias*, of the same generation but older, was the son of *Poseidon* and *Tyro*, the daughter of *Salmôneus*, Æolus' second son. *Phrixus* was the child of a third son, Athamas. Pélias contrived to oust *Æson*, Jason's father, from the kingship before Jason was born. It was given out that Jason had died at birth, but he was secretly put in charge of the centaur *Chîron*, whose mother was *Philyra* and wife *Chariclo*.

p. 306. *Both his uncles*: brothers of Æson, viz. *Pherês* (father of *Admêtus*), and *Amythâon* (father of *Melampus*).

p. 308. *Phrixus* and Hellê escaped from their stepmother Ino on a golden-fleeced ram which bore them overseas. Hellê fell off and gave her name to the Hellespont (Dardanelles). Phrixus deposited the fleece with *Aêtês*, king of Colchis, where he died. His spirit required kinsmen from Greece to lay it at rest.

p. 310. *Wryneck*: tied by legs and wings to the four spokes of a wheel, this bird was used as a love charm. But incantations were often made over small revolving wheels without the bird. See No. 499 and note.

281. Written for Aristómenês of Ægina in 446 B.C. The gods and heroes at the close are the traditional protectors of Ægina.

282. Written for Telesícratês of Cyrênê in 474 B.C.   p. 314, *An island people*: Cyrênê was founded from Thêra by Battus, a descendant of Euphâmus the Argonaut (cf. No. 280, note).

283. From Pindar's earliest known poem, written for Hippoclês of Thessaly in 498 B.C. *The Hyperboreans* lived in the far north—a people favoured by Apollo and semi-

mythical, yet real enough to send him offerings at Delos (cf. Herodotus, iv. 33). *Ransomed . . . ire*: i.e. they had no fear of Nemesis. *Danaê's son*: see No. 206 and note. Polydectês, king of Serîphus, pursued Danaê with unwelcome attentions and hoped to get rid of Perseus by sending him on the quest of the Gorgon's head.

284. Written for Thrasydæus of Thebes in 454 B.C. See Notes on Nos. 247, 252. *Amyklai*: the scene of Agamemnon's murder in Stêsíchorus and Pindar. Homer places it at Mycênæ, Æschylus at Argos.

285. Written probably in 476 B.C. for Chrómius of Syracuse, who claimed descent from Hêraclês.

286. Written for Aristocleidês of Ægina, the island of Achilles' Myrmidons. Date unknown. *Phílyra*: the mother of Chîron. *Jason*: cf. No. 280. *Asclêpius*: cf. No. 279. *Nêreus' daughter*: Thetis. *Their great son*: Achilles. *Memnon*: cf. No. 275, end.

287. Written for Theæus of Argos, probably in Pindar's old age. On Castor and Polydeucês cf. No. 139. Like Clytæmêstra and Helen, they were sons of Lêda. In Pindar's account Polydeucês was her son by Zeus, Castor her son by Tyndareus, king of Sparta, her husband (p. 321). *Îdas* and *Lynceus*, whose cattle the twins had raided, were the two *sons of Aphareus*. p. 320. *Lêda's son*: Polydeucês.

288. Written for Phylácidês of Ægina, c. 474 B.C. *Her warrior sons*: i.e. Ægina's. *Œneus' sons*: Týdeus and Meleâger; on the latter cf. No. 308. *Œnône*: the old name of Ægina. *Cycnus*: No. 275, note; exploits of Achilles follow, cf. Nos. 275, 286. *Ajax' isle*: Salamis.

289. Written for Strepsiadês of Thebes after the defeat of the Thebans by Athens at Œnóphyta, 457/456 B.C. Strepsiadês' uncle (line 2), the *son of Diódotus*, fell in this battle. *Holder of the Earth*: Poseidon, who as Lord of the Isthmus granted this victory at the Isthmian games. *Bellerophon*: cf. No. 277.

290. Written for Cleandrus of Ægina, c. 478 B.C. *Thetis* ('*Nêreus' child*'): see No. 245, note. *Æacus*: married

NOTES

Ægina, one of the daughters of Asôpus, cf. No. 273. *Chîron*: cf. No. 286.

291–4. Fragments only.

291. Probably composed for the Great Dionysia held at the beginning of spring. Hence Pindar speaks of himself as again approaching '*The Ivy wreathed*', &c., i.e. Dionŷsus or Brómius son of Zeus and Sémelê. Cf. No. 418, end.

A. S. Way, who was born in 1847 and died at the age of 83, was a prolific translator. His works include all the chief Greek poets from Homer to Quintus Smyrnæus; Vergil and part of Horace; the Nibelung Lay; selections from the Song of Roland; and a versification of the Psalms. He is best represented by this piece.

292. Cf. No. 111.

293. Written late in life.

294. Thrasybûlus succeeded for a short period to the tyranny of Syracuse after the death of his brother Híeron in 466 B.C. Compare with this poem No. 311.

295. From a dirge, with flute accompaniment. Walter Headlam writes: 'With the Greeks it was initiation in the Eleusinian Mysteries that gave hope of life hereafter and admission into Paradise. The Mysteries displayed it to the eye, and also the other place, where the uninitiated were seen "lying in the mire". Paradise is many times described, e.g. in the 2nd Olympian (No. 275). . . . It is always a flowery Meadow, radiant with Light—symbolical of spiritual light—wherein the blessed walk amid celestial harpings and with wreaths upon their heads. But it is pretty here to notice how with all this Oriental happiness the Greek is not content to be without his games.'

296. A much-quoted fragment. Herodotus in a famous chapter (iii. 38) is authority for the translation 'custom'. See also Plato, *Gorgias*, 484 *b*. But Pindar may have meant by the Greek word νόμος *the law of civilization* which Hêraclês was chartered to impose: cf. E. B. Clapp, *The Classical Quarterly*, 1914, pp. 226–8. In his 10th labour Hêraclês sailed the stream of Oceanus in the golden cup of the Sun (cf. No. 161)

NOTES

and looted the cattle of Gêrÿon, a three-headed and/or three-bodied monster, Oriental in conception, whom he shot after killing his dog Orthrus (a brother to Cerberus) and his herdsman Eurÿtion.

297. Interesting chiefly as part of a *Pæan*—a name derived from the cry Iêpaiaôn (probably non-Hellenic) which sometimes forms a refrain. In general the pæan was used to invoke Apollo, or some other deity, as healer or averter of evil. In the worship of Apollo, as here, it represents a special type of choric song, or song-dance, of prayer or thanksgiving, used in procession (or at stopping-places) after sacrifice and libations were over. Cf. J. M. Edmonds, *Lyra Græca*, iii, pp. 650 ff., who enumerates pæans of other kinds, e.g. as sung before battle (cf. No. **240**, p. 252, line 10). It was from the pæan sung after victory that the modern notion of praise accrued to the word. *Their portion*: i.e. the Ionians' portion. *Astéria*: a name for Delos; for Astéria, the sister of Lêto, was transformed into that island. Cf. No. **630**, note.

298. A topical joke from Comedy. Periclês, who was sensitive about his elongated head, habitually wore a great helmet to conceal it. Here he is introduced wearing a model of the *Ôdêum*, a domed concert-hall built in imitation of Xerxês' state-marquee to commemorate the repulse of the Persian invaders. Further, a political storm had lately (444 B.C.) blown over, in which he was lucky enough to escape ostracism—a name derived from the *ostraka* or *tiles* on which votes were written. The city was stripped, as it were, of its tiles, and hardly a sound roof remained. Hence the use of a public building for head-cover. (Cf. Gilbert Norwood, *Greek Comedy*, p. 134.) The old slang use of *Tile* for *Hat* helps the translation.

299. Cf. Nos. **415**, **531**, and Horace, *Epistles*, I. xix.

300–2. Given during Xerxês' invasion of Greece in 480–79 B.C. Cf. Herodotus, vii. 140–1, 148. On the accentual hexameters see Introduction, pp. lii ff.

301. *Cecrops*: a legendary ancestor of the Athenians, born from the soil, his lower half a snake; cf. No. **418**. *The*

709

NOTES

Triton born: Athênê. An obscure title, see H. J. Rose, *A Hand-book of Greek Mythology*, p. 108.

302. *Thy head*: i.e. those with full citizenship, the nucleus of the population; *body* being the remainder (A. D. Godley).

304. On Tîmócreon cf. No. 222. When the Persians occupied Rhodes he sold himself to them and was taken to Sûsa. After their defeat he was debarred from return to Rhodes and wrote this drinking-song deploring the effects of wealth. It had a great vogue and was sung even in the 4th century A.D. His use of the Greek word translated 'continents' may refer especially to Persia. *Blind god*: cf. Nos. 181, 437.

305. Probably a drinking-song. It is also a hymn of hate. After Salamis Themístoclês failed to restore Tîmócreon to Rhodes, and is taunted in return with missing the prize for valour, voted for at the Isthmus of Corinth (Herodotus, viii. 123). Themístoclês' influence declined in the winter 478–477 B.C. See further, Bowra, *Greek Lyric Poetry*, pp. 371–8.

306. Written for Híeron of Syracuse in 468 B.C. The first two lines describe the rejoicings at Syracuse; 3–6 the offerings of Híeron and his brother Gelon at Delphi. Then follows the story of the Lydian king Crœsus, himself a generous donor to the Delphian Apollo (cf. p. 336, top). Bacchylides differs from Herodotus (i. 86 ff.) at several points, notably in making Crœsus resolve on his own destruction and that of his family, and in treating the Hyperborean paradise (cf. Nos. 283, 343) as a refuge for the living. These features are unique. On the translation see Introduction, p. xcv f.

307–8. Written for Híeron of Syracuse in 468 B.C., and sent to him from Bacchylidês' island-home in Ceos.

307. *A friend*: Simonidês may have introduced the poet, his nephew, to Híeron while travelling in Sicily 478–476 B.C. The plural *your* in line 4 couples Híeron with his brother.

308. The different names for the same persons used in this piece may cause confusion. There are only two speakers, viz. (1) *Hêraclês*, son of Zeus (line 2) and Alcmêna (line 13); also

NOTES

twice called the son of Amphítryon, Alcmêna's ostensible husband. (2) *Meleâger*, the *grand*son (strictly) of Porthâon (line 12) and the son of Œneus (line 35). His mother was Althæa, daughter of Thestius.

Althæa was told at Meleâger's birth that he should live only so long as a brand, then on the fire, remained unconsumed. She snatched it off and locked it away. Meleâger grew up to love Atalanta, and after the slaying of the boar, awarded her the spoils. A fight for the spoils ensued, in which he killed the brothers of Althæa, who then allowed the brand to burn. It took effect as he was pursuing a rival claimant of the spoils to Pleurôn, a town of the *Cûrêtës* (an Ætolian tribe) some eight miles NWN. of Calydon. *Dêianîra*: cf. No. 327.

309 (i). From a pæan (cf. No. 297, note) to Apollo written for a chorus of Ceans to sing at Delos. Thêseus has just rebuked Mînos for laying hands on one of the Athenian maidens who are sailing to Crete as an offering to the Mînotaur. p. 341. *Son-in-law of the Sun*: Mînos, whose wife Pasíphaê was daughter to Hêlios, the Sun. Mînos was the son of Zeus by Eurôpa (*the Tyrian*, p. 342), on whom see No. 570. *Amphitrîtê* (anglicized on p. 343 to a trisyllable) was the divine consort of Thêseus' father Poseidon. Thêseus was Poseidon's child by *Æthra* (p. 342); see next note.

309 (ii). A dithyramb, peculiar in its dialogue form. Æthra of Trœzên bore Thêseus to Poseidon, but Ægeus of Athens was the ostensible father. Thêseus was left at Trœzên till strong enough to lift a rock, under which Ægeus had left sandals and a sword, and make his way to Athens, where Ægeus lived in fear of the fifty Pallantidæ, his designing cousins. Thêseus deliberately chose an overland route, beset with perils, viz. *Sinis*, at the Isthmus, who tied his victims by the arms to bent pine-saplings, which sprang apart and rent them; the *Sow* called Phaia ('grey') of Cremmÿon, *c.* 12 miles E. of Corinth (cf. No. 367, where it is called 'a boar'); *Scîron* (cf. No. 217 (ii)) who compelled travellers to wash his feet and meanwhile kicked them into the sea; *Cércyon* the wrestler, who killed his defeated opponents; and *Procoptês*, better known as Procrustês, who lopped his guests to fit their beds.

NOTES

310. Fragment of a pæan (cf. No. 297, note). *Webs of the spider*: an idea much imitated, from Euripidês (No. 394) to Tennyson's *Maud*, 'And the cobweb woven across the cannon's throat / Shall shake its threaded tears in the wind no more.' (Cf. Walter Headlam's note.)

311. From a drinking-song, written for Alexander, son of Amyntas, king of Macedon. Cf. No. 294.

312. Ajax, restored to sanity, and bent on death, makes a last address to the Chorus of Salaminian sailors. His words are chosen to veil his intention, for he wishes to die in solitude; but they nowhere belie him. *Teucer*: his stepbrother, son of Telamon and Hêsionê.

313. Ajax, on a lonely beach, soliloquizes before falling on his sword. *Hermês*: cf. No. 55 and note. *Erînyês*: cf. No. 255.

314. Clytæmêstra has had a dream which seems to portend that she and her paramour Ægisthus, the murderers of Agamemnon, will be overcome by one of the latter's stock. The Chorus of Mycênæan women adopt this interpretation. They address Chrysóthemis, who has reported the dream, and her sister Êlectra, daughters of Agamemnon.

315. At the time of Agamemnon's murder, his son Orestês was secretly removed to Crîsa by an old servant. Orestês (aged about 20) has now returned, directed by Apollo to take vengeance on the murderers by stealth. The old servant, disguised as a Messenger from friends of the Palace, tells a brilliantly circumstantial lie, to the effect that Orestês has been killed in a chariot-race.

316. Êlectra too has been deceived by the lie (No. 315). Here, in the presence of the disguised Orestês, she holds the urn believed to contain his ashes. Some fifty years after Sophoclês' death, the actor Pôlus, in playing this scene, used the funeral urn of his own son, recently dead.

317. About sixteen years before the action of the play begins, Lâïus, king of Thebes, had been killed on the road to Delphi in a chance encounter. After a short reign by Creon, brother of Lâïus' widow Jocasta, the throne passed to Œdipus, a stranger who rescued Thebes from the Sphinx and after his accession married Jocasta. A plague has now descended on Thebes, and Creon, sent by Œdipus to Delphi (Pytho), has brought back the oracular response that the city still harbours an unclean thing, the slayer of Lâïus. Here the Chorus of Theban elders have been assembled to hear this news.

318. Against his will the seer Tîrésias has denounced Œdipus himself as the slayer. Œdipus, in a stormy scene, accuses Creon of plotting with Tîrésias to oust him from the throne; and Jocasta, in calming him, expresses her distrust of oracles. Both have shown some presumption, giving further cause for these uneasy reflections of the Chorus.

319. Œdipus has been proved not only the slayer of Lâïus but also his son, born to Jocasta—thus fulfilling an oracular prediction at which Jocasta had scoffed. Œdipus, ignorant of his own early history and of the identity of the man he had slain, was slower to divine the truth than Jocasta, who stole away and hung herself.

320. Œdipus is led forth blind and addresses the Chorus. *Cithæron*: the mountain on which at birth he was exposed, from fear of the oracle that he should kill his father. The slave to whom his exposure was entrusted gave him instead to a herdsman of *Pólybus*, king of Corinth, who brought him up as his own son. *Three roads*: the junction of the Thebes–Delphi road with that from Daulia and a third running South. It was here he slew Lâïus in a brawl about right of way.

321. Antígonê is a daughter of Œdipus and sister of Éteoclês and Polynîcês, on whom see No. 242, note. On the day before the action of the play begins her brothers had killed each other in single combat; six other chieftains of the besieging force were dead, and their troops dispersed. Creon, once again ruler of Thebes, has decreed that Éteoclês shall be honourably buried, but that Polynîcês shall be left to the dogs and birds. Antígonê, on pain of death, has stolen out from Thebes and defied this edict. This choral ode, sung by Theban elders, is suggested by the discovery that burial rites have been paid to

NOTES

Polynîcês by the boldness and resource of some person unknown. (Jebb's punctuation is preferred by the translator in lines 370 ff.)

322. Antígonê, convicted of the deed, gives her reasons to Creon.

323. Creon's son, Hæmon, who is betrothed to Antígonê, has faced his angry father and pleaded ineffectually for her life, hinting, as he withdraws, that he does not mean to survive her. Creon then declares to the Chorus his verdict—Antígonê shall be buried alive, i.e. immured in a rock-tomb with a formal dole of food. This ode follows. Cf. No. 342.

324. Antígonê addresses the Chorus on her way to the tomb. *Tales of doom*: the Chorus have said 'No mortal's fate was ever like yours'. *A daughter of Tantalus*: Niobê, wife of Amphîon, king of Thebes, boasted of her fourteen children as against Lêto's two. Those two, Apollo and Artemis, then slew the whole fourteen. Niobê went back to her old home and was turned to stone on Mt. Sipylus, a branch of the Tmôlus range. Cf. No. 507, end. On the translation see Introduction p. ciii.

325. Antígonê's last speech.

326. Dêianîra (cf. No. 308, end) is living in Trâchis. Her husband Hêraclês has been away for fifteen months and is reported to be warring against King Eurytus of Œchália in Eubœa. Both the time and the place, as she knows from oracles, are of fateful importance. Now Lichas, a herald, has arrived, with news of the fall of Œchália. He brings with him some captive maidens, among them Iolê, Eurytus' daughter, who excites Dêianîra's interest. Lichas has professed no knowledge of her, but a messenger has informed Dêianîra that Hêraclês' love for Iolê was the true cause of his campaign. Here Dêianîra asks Lichas for the truth. (See further No. 328, note.)

327. The Chorus of Trâchinian women celebrate the power of Love, which in past days brought Hêraclês to fight for Dêianîra with the river-god Achelôus, a rival suitor. On the translation see Introduction, p. ciii.

328. When Hêraclês was tortured by the poisoned robe sent by Dêianîra (in all innocence) as a love-charm, Philoctêtês, at his urgent prayer, kindled the pyre on which he was consumed, and was given in return the bow and arrows received by Hêraclês from Apollo. On the way to Troy Philoctêtês, suffering from a noisome snake-bite in the foot, was abandoned by the Greeks at Lemnos. Here he describes their treachery and his lonely life for ten years on the island.

329. A seer had informed the Greeks that Troy would stand until Philoctêtês and his bow were brought against it. Odysseus, who undertook his marooning, has now undertaken with young Neoptólemus, the son of Achilles, to fetch him to Troy. Neoptólemus gains Philoctêtês' confidence (and his bow) on the pretence of taking him home, but is honest enough to confess the deceit. This outburst follows.

330. Some years after his blinding (Nos. 319–20), Œdipus was expelled from his seclusion in Thebes. His sons Éteoclês and Polynîcês did not intervene; but his daughters were loyal— Antígonê shared his exile and Ismênê watched his interests at home. When this play opens, Œdipus, led by Antígonê, has reached a grove sacred to the Euménidës (cf. No. 256, note) at Colônos, about 1¼ miles NW. of Athens. He knows from certain predictions that he has found his last resting-place; but the citizens force him in horror from the holy ground pending the arrival of Thêseus, king of Athens. Meanwhile, Ismênê brings news that her brothers are about to dispute the kingship of Thebes, and that Creon (lately regent, now supporting Éteoclês) hopes to remove Œdipus to a place within his control; for both parties have learnt from an oracle that on Œdipus, alive or dead, their welfare must depend. Œdipus resolves that his blessing shall fall upon Athens, his curse upon his sons. When Thêseus has promised to guard him, as well in death as in life, he is warned in this speech that a breach between Athens and Thebes may result. (The second line of the translation is by Edward Fitzgerald.)

331. The Chorus of Attic elders praise the land which has granted Œdipus a home. Cicero and others tell a story (probably fictitious—see Jebb, 3rd ed., pp. xxxix ff.) that Sophoclês, sued by his sons for neglecting his property, secured acquittal by reciting part of this famous ode, a work he was then

composing.   p. 377.   *The Great Queens*: Dêmêter and Perse-phonê. The narcissus was connected with their cult, cf. No. 77.   *Self-engendering*: an allusion to the miraculous sprouting of the sacred olives the day after Xerxês had burnt the Acropolis.   *Her Mother's portion*: i.e. Athens' portion. The *Child* is Colônus.   p. 378.   *Her throne*: in apposition to 'the waves'. Horses were the gift of Poseidon to Attica.

332. Creon, after a violent scene with Œdipus, has removed Antígonê and Ismênê as hostages. Hardly have they been rescued by Thêseus, when the arrival of Polynícês is announced, whom Œdipus unwillingly consents to see. The Chorus then sing this ode.

Walter Headlam, in reviewing A. W. Pollard's *Odes from the Greek Dramatists* (translated into lyric metres by various hands), gave the highest place to A. E. Housman's versions, which included two others (Æsch. *Sept.* 848–60, Eur. *Alc.* 962–1005) besides this. He was writing in *The Cambridge Review*, vol. xii, p. 274, 12 March 1891, about five years before the appearance of *A Shropshire Lad*. This version is rather Swinburnian in manner. Housman, his brother records, once said 'that when at Oxford (1877–81) he found he could imitate Swinburne quite well'—sometimes bettering his model, in his own opinion—'but even then he thought the Swinburnian method wrong' (*Memories of A. E. Housman*, by Laurence Housman, *John o' London's Weekly*, 23 Oct. 1936, p. 148). Perhaps for this reason he was not particularly proud of these translations. Of Swinburne as a critic he had a very poor opinion (ibid., 16 Oct. 1936, p. 110).

333. Œdipus has heard Polynícês and sent him to his doom with a curse upon both brothers. During a choral ode thunder is heard, which warns Œdipus that his end is near. Thêseus and his heirs alone must know the place of his death, a secret whose guarding will keep Attica safe from her enemies. Here a Messenger tells what he can of the final scene.

334–44. Fragments of lost plays.

334. A disputed text. The sense given to πτερόν, translated 'leafy pinions', is doubtful. See Jebb-Pearson, *ad loc.*

NOTES

336. *Hécatê*: here the Moon-goddess, but her underworld power is also recognized; for crossways were haunted.

337. *Made a traffic of*: i.e. by means of dowries.

338. Besides Lucr. ii. 1 ff., cf. Tibullus I. i. 45 ff.

341. The Greek text is very uncertain in lines 6–7.

342. Cf. No. 323.

343. The land of the Hyperboreans. Cf. Nos. 283, 306.

344. Apart from Euripidês' *Cyclops* (No. 350) and the large fragment of Sophoclês' *Ichneutæ* ('Trackers') from which this piece is taken, no Satyr-plays have been preserved. In them we see the Tragedians at play, providing release after tension. The subject of the *Ichneutæ* is the same as that of Nos. 82–4, Hermês' first adventure. The Satyr-chorus are tracking the lost cattle of Apollo. They hear a strange sound, which has been explained to them as 'the voice of a dead beast'. The Latin poet Pacuvius transplanted the scene to a tragedy (*Antíopa*, fr. 4), whether from this source or another.

345. According to Empédoclês, 'perception is due to the meeting of an element in us with the same element outside. This takes place when the pores of the organ of sense are neither too large nor too small for the "effluences" which all things are constantly giving forth' (J. Burnet, *Early Greek Philosophy*, 2nd ed., London, A. & C. Black, 1908, p. 286).

347. A rhymed version by Sir J. G. Frazer will be found in *The Magic Art*, vol. i, p. 390 (ed. of 1911).

349. The last two lines of a poem by Frances Cornford on Transmigration.

350. From a Satyr-play, see No. 344, note. The plot is taken from the *Odyssey*, cf. No. 46 (i) and (ii). The three characters are Odysseus, the Cyclops, and Sîlênus. Here the Cyclops is addressing Odysseus. p. 390. *The inner god*: we should say 'the inner man'. The last two lines, omitted by Shelley, are supplied by T. F. Higham.

351. The *Alcêstis* (438 B.C.) is the earliest surviving play of Euripidês. It is said to have been acted as the fourth play of

NOTES

a tetralogy instead of a Satyr-play; see H. J. Rose, *A Handbook of Greek Literature*, p. 180 and reff. Apollo, in return for past kindness, secures that Admêtus, king of Pheræ, need not die at his destined hour, provided that some one else will die instead of him. All refuse, except his wife Alcêstis. Death (Thánatos) calls for her, vainly besought and threatened by Apollo. This ode, sung by the Chorus of Pheræan elders, follows her death and the lamentations of her son. *The month Carneius*: approximately August.

The translation is in the Imagist manner (Introduction, pp. lxx, ciii) brought to notice by the translator and others (e.g. H. D. in *Choruses from the Iphigenia in Aulis*) about 1912–16. In line 8 'far, far the best of women' would be the true rendering, but the author prefers not to alter what he has printed elsewhere.

352. While the funeral is being prepared, Hêraclês arrives and is entertained by Admêtus, who conceals the truth, telling him that a stranger has died (cf. p. 392, *'grief that's out-of-door'*). Hêraclês drinks well, to the surprise and disgust of a servant, who is here addressed. On Browning's theory of translation cf. Introduction, p. lxvi.

353. Having learnt the truth, Hêraclês prepares to rescue Alcêstis from Death. *Korê*: Persephonê.

354. Admêtus has returned in sorrow from the funeral. Here the Chorus try to console him.

355. Mêdêa has been brought by Jason from Colchis (cf. Nos. 535–42) and borne him two sons. He now intends to marry Glaucê, daughter of Creon, king of Corinth. Creon, who knows the magical arts of Mêdêa and the threats she has made, has ordered her to leave Corinth, together with her children, but gives one day's grace. Mêdêa has expressed to the Chorus of Corinthian women her resolve to destroy her enemies. They sympathize (at this point) and have promised secrecy. Here they declare that honour is coming at last to their sex.

356. Mêdêa has just arranged for a place of refuge. She has told Ægeus, a chance visitor, about her banishment, and after promising to cure his childlessness, has won in return a sworn promise of protection. Now she has formed her full plans for revenge, and acquaints the Chorus with them.

357. The poisoned robe has done its work. Glaucê is dead, and so is Creon, who embraced her corpse. It remains only to complete her spite on Jason.

358. After Hêraclês' death, his mother Alcmênê, his old comrade and nephew Iolâus, and his children have been expelled by Eurystheus from Argolis and from any other city within his power to coerce. Dêmophon, king of Athens, protects them, at the cost of war. He learns from an oracle that victory must depend on the sacrifice to Persephonê of a maiden nobly born. Macária, daughter of Hêraclês, offers herself.

359. Hippólytus is the stepson of Phædra, who is living at Trœzên in the absence of her husband Thêseus, king of Athens. Hippólytus scorns Aphrodîtê and consorts always with Artemis, the Virgin Huntress, a goddess of tastes in keeping with his own. Here he makes her an offering.

360. By spite of Aphrodîtê, Phædra is afflicted with a wasting passion for Hippólytus. Though intending to die with her secret, she tells it at the last to an old nurse, who betrays her to her stepson, but under oath of silence. He rages at Phædra, and women in general, yet means to keep his oath. Phædra resolves on death, with obscure threats against Hippólytus. The Chorus of Trœzênian women, who hear her resolve, are bound to secrecy. They sing this ode, a yearning for escape. *Phäethon*: when he drove the chariot of the Sun and was destroyed, his mourning sisters became poplar trees, and their tears amber.

361. Thêseus returns, to find that Phædra has hanged herself. A letter clutched in her hand accuses Hippólytus of violence done to her. Hippólytus cannot clear himself, being bound by his oath of silence; and Thêseus, disbelieving his protestations, not only condemns him to exile, but invokes Poseidon to destroy him. Here this invocation takes effect— it is one of three wishes that Thêseus' father Poseidon has promised to fulfil.

NOTES

362. From the last scene of the play. Artemis has appeared and told Thêseus the truth. Hippólytus is brought in dying.

363. A choric ode sung by women of Phthia in Thessaly, the home of Neoptólemus (Pyrrhus), son of Achilles. The play deals with the perilous fortunes of Andrómachê, mother of a child by Neoptólemus and deserted by him for marriage with Hermíonê, daughter of Helen and Menelâus. The latter part of the ode is suggested by the entrance of Orestês, who removes Hermíonê and instigates the murder of Neoptólemus.

364. Troy has fallen. The Greeks and their captives are encamped in Thrace. Polýxena, the youngest daughter of Hécuba, Priam's widow, is now to be sacrificed at Achilles' tomb. Odysseus has come to fetch her.

365. Sung by the Chorus of captive Trojan women after the parting of Polýxena and her mother.   *Thessalia*: the home of Achilles.   *Delos*: here Zeus caused the bay-tree and the date-palm to spring up and shelter the birth by Lêto (Lâtôna) of his children Apollo and Artemis (The Maiden).

366. A new grief comes to Hécuba, foretold by a dream at the opening of the play. Her youngest son, Polydôrus, has been murdered by the Thracian ally to whom he had been given in trust. Agamemnon connives at her vengeance and allows her to send for the murderer and his children. Meanwhile this ode is sung.   p. 412, line 2: Helen is the *sister of the sons of Zeus*, viz. Castor and Polydeucês, cf. No. 287, note.

367. The Suppliant Women who give a name to this play and form its Chorus are the mothers (with their attendants) of the Chieftains who followed Adrastus, king of Argos, against Éteoclês in Thebes, and now, by edict of Creon, lie unburied upon the field: cf. Nos. 242, 321, notes. Æthra, mother of Thêseus, king of Athens, has been approached by the Suppliants, and Adrastus himself, in the hope of winning from the Thebans permission to bury the dead. Here Æthra prevails upon Thêseus to champion their cause.   *Boar*: cf. No. 309 (ii), note.

368. Thêseus has conquered the Thebans, and the obse-

quies have taken place. Here the ashes of dead chiefs are brought in by their sons.

369. While Hêraclês was fetching Cerberus and Thêseus from Hades, he left his wife Mégara and three sons in the charge of old Amphítryon, his father, at Thebes. He returns just in time to save them from Lycus, who has seized the throne and intends to burn their house about them. He hears their plight, relates his exploits, and promises to destroy Lycus. This ode follows, sung by the Chorus of Theban elders, but expressing also (so it seems) the thoughts of Euripidês on his own old age.

370. Soon after the slaying of Lycus madness is sent upon Hêraclês by his old enemy Hêra. He himself murders Mégara and his sons. Restored to sanity, he is saved from self-destruction by Thêseus, who takes him to Athens.

371–2. Creûsa is the wife of Xuthus, an ally of the Athenian king Erectheus. Before this marriage she had secretly borne and abandoned a child by Apollo, as she tells in No. 372. Her marriage with Xuthus is childless, and now the pair have come to Delphi to seek guidance and a remedy from the god. Ion, the young temple-servant here shown at his morning tasks, proves in the end to be the child of Creûsa and Apollo, and becomes the founder of the Ionian race. Xuthus, by a ruse of the god, is led to accept him as his own.

373. This play had a moral for the times, showing the Athenians the dark side of conquest and hinting at Nemesis. As in the *Hécuba* (Nos. 364–6), captive Trojan women form the Chorus, and Hécuba again is a central figure. The scene is the Greek camp outside Troy at the time when the Greeks are about to burn the city and sail away—many of them, as Poseidon threatens, to their doom. Horror follows horror— the women are allotted to their captors; Cassandra sings the frenzied parody of a bridal song; Polýxena is sacrificed; and now Ástyanax, the child of Hector and Andrómachê, is to be flung from the walls. This choral ode follows, recalling a former capture of Troy. *In wrath for the Steeds*: Hêsionê, daughter of Lâómedon, king of Troy, had been rescued from a sea-monster by Hêraclês. His promised reward was a

pair of horses presented by Zeus to the father of Ganymede—
the beautiful Trojan youth who became Heaven's cup-bearer,
cf. No. 534. When the promise was broken, Hêraclês sacked
Troy and gave Hêsionê to his ally Télamon, the father of
Ajax. *Tîthonus*, for whom his lover Eos (Dawn) obtained the
gift of immortality, but not of eternal youth, was a son of
Lâómedon and brother of Priam.

374. From the end of the play, after the mangled body of
Ástyanax has been brought to Hécuba.

375. The same story as in Nos. 253, 314–16, but with
differences of plot and characterization. Ægisthus has been
killed (cf. line 1) without the knowledge of Clytæmêstra, who
now approaches her doom.

376. All men believed that Îphigenîa was sacrificed at
Aulis (cf. No. 247). But in truth she was rescued by Artemis,
and now conducts in her honour the sacrifice of others, serving
as priestess in the Crimea, among the barbarous Taurians. Her
brother Orestês and Pyladês his friend have come in quest of
the image of Taurian Artemis, which Apollo has named as
the price of Orestês' return to sanity (cf. Nos. 254, 381). They
are captured, and she is charged to prepare them for the altar.
Here she questions them, as ignorant of their identity as they
are of hers.

377. In the same mutual ignorance she offers to spare
Orestês if only he will carry a letter to Argos. Orestês insists
that Pyladês shall go.

378. Pyladês insists that the letter be read. It is addressed
to Orestês, and so recognition ensues. The three arrange to
escape, taking the image with them. Here the Chorus of
Greek captive maidens express their own longing for home.

379. See No. 162, note. The scene is Pharos, off Egypt,
where the true Helen is waiting faithfully for Menelâus and
taking sanctuary from the amorous pursuit of the Egyptian
king. Teucer (No. 312, note), a chance visitor, has brought
her sad news. Menelâus is reported lost at sea; her mother
Lêda is dead; and her brothers, Castor and Polydeucês, by one
account, have killed themselves for shame at (the phantom)

NOTES

Helen's disgrace. Here Helen laments, and the Chorus of captive Greek women are drawn to her cry.

380. See No. 242, note, for the general situation. In this version of the story Œdipus, after his blinding, is kept in seclusion by his sons; their mother Jocasta lives on; and the kingship of Thebes is divided by annual turns, a compact which Éteoclês has broken. Jocasta here brings the brothers together and hopes for a peaceful settlement before Polynîcês attacks. Phœnician maidens, dedicated to Apollo, form the Chorus. The war has detained them on their way to Delphi. (In the Greek text the first speaker should be Jocasta.)

381. After murdering their mother, Orestês and Êlectra are awaiting trial by the Argive court. The Chorus of friendly Argive women has entered, waking Orestês from sleep that ensued on a fit of madness (cf. Nos. 254–5). An adverse verdict by the court will mean death by stoning. Menelâus' arrival holds out some hope.   p. 442, *Tyndareus' daughters*: Clytæmêstra and Helen are meant, cf. No. 287, note.

382. Occasioned by the madness into which Orestês has lapsed.   *Royallest goddesses*: the Avenging Furies who madden him, cf. No. 255.

383. This play was written in Macedonia, where the cult of Dionŷsus retained much of its primitive wildness and vigour. Dionŷsus was the child by Zeus of Sémelê, a Theban. Her sisters Autónoê, Îno, and Agâvê (No. 384) denied this divine parentage. Now, after conquest of Asia, Dionŷsus, disguised as a prophet, has come to punish their disbelief and destroy the son of Agâvê, young Pentheus, king of Thebes, by whom his cult is opposed. Already the women of Thebes are converted and revelling on Mt. Cithæron. Old Cadmus and old Tîrésias, bent on joining them, are rudely treated by Pentheus, who intends to imprison the prophet and all the converts he can find. The Chorus of Phrygian Bacchantes rebuke his presumption and sing these verses.

384. Pentheus, deluded by phantoms, has vainly tried to imprison Dionŷsus. Earthquake and flame have destroyed his palace. Here a messenger brings him news from Cithæron.

385. Pentheus has been persuaded by Dionŷsus to spy on the revels in woman's dress. The Chorus know that death awaits him, and here rejoice in their coming freedom and the mastering of Pentheus whose hate has restrained them. On the translation see Introduction, p. xciii.

386. See No. 247, note. Agamemnon had written to Argos bidding Clytæmêstra bring Îphigenîa to Aulis, nominally for marriage to Achilles, but actually for sacrifice. Here he summons an attendant to take a second letter countermanding the first.

387. The true authorship and date of this play are unknown. Its plot comes from the tenth *Iliad*, and the scene is laid in the Trojan camp. During the day the Greeks have been defeated. Now it is night, and Dolôn, a spy, has been sent by Hector to watch their intentions. Meanwhile, the Thracian prince Rhêsus, a long-expected ally of Troy, arrives with his force and is shown by Hector to some forward lines. This ode is sung by a Chorus of sentinels who rouse their reliefs to take fifth watch.

388. Odysseus and Diomede, having seized Dolôn and learned the password, surprise the sleeping Thracians, kill Rhêsus, and capture his famous chariot-horses. A wounded charioteer brings word to Hector.

389–403. Fragments of lost plays. 390. The *Andrómeda* was the play which led Dionŷsus, as represented in Aristophanes' *Frogs*, to contemplate bringing Euripidês back from death. It is parodied by Aristophanes in No. 429. Here No. (i), which conflates two fragments, opens the prologue spoken by Andrómeda. She is chained to the rock, a sacrifice to the Beast of the Sea, and Echo repeats her laments at every close. Perseus, flying home with the Gorgon's head, thinks her at first a statue of marble (Frag. 125, Nauck). After making terms (Nos. iii–v), he goes to the fight, invoking Love (No. vi) to his aid. The last three lines of No. vi belong to another fragment. 394. Cf. No. 310, note. Swinburne's *Erectheus* has the same theme as this fragmentary play. 395. The name Theseus (ΘΗCΕΥC) is described by a herdsman who has seen it somewhere inscribed. **397.** From a marching song of the Cûrêtës (cf. No. 496), priests of Cretan Zeus. On the Orphic tale of Zagreus, see H. J. Rose, *A Handbook of Greek Mythology*, pp. 51, 96, and reff. He is sometimes identified with Dionŷsus. Initiates were called 'Bacchi'. Cf. No. **692.** **403.** On the *Phäethon* see *New Chapters in Greek Literature*, 3rd Series, p. 145.

404–7. Tragic fragments of unknown or disputed authorship. **404.** Falsely attributed to Æschylus. Perhaps an 'improvement' on No. 259. **405.** Among the 'fragmenta dubia et spuria' of Sophoclês. **406–7.** No author cited. The two lines of No. 407 were spoken by Hêraclês in some lost play, and quoted by Brutus at his death, according to Dion Cassius, xlvii. 49.

408. Also attributed to Tîmotheus (446–357 B.C.), but possibly of Alexandrian date.

409–10. Fragments. **409.** From Praxilla's *Hymn to Adônis*, which the Greeks, according to Zenobius, thought very ridiculous. But regrets which couple gourds and the sun are not inappropriate to the year-god Adônis. **410.** The metre of the original took its name from Praxilla. The English represents it by simple substitution of stressed for long syllables, i.e. it is accentual but not true-timed. Cf. Introduction, p. lv.

411. Another fragment; possibly by Pindar.

412. The *Acharnians* was produced in 425 B.C., after six years or so of war with Sparta. Acharnæ is a hamlet of Attica much ravaged by invasion. The Acharnian charcoal-burners, who form the Chorus, firmly support a war of revenge; Dicæópolis of Acharnæ, a farmer of the old type, does not. Long service, poor rations, and mistrust of popular leaders have induced him to conclude with Sparta a separate peace for himself and his family. Interrupted by the Chorus while celebrating a long-suspended rustic festival, he narrowly escapes a traitor's death. Here he speaks with his head on a block, after borrowing, to excite compassion, the rags and tatters kept by Euripidês for staging the tragic prince

Têlephus. Dicæópolis pleads that the war arose from a muddle, and that Sparta is not wholly to blame. Such a scene, as Gilbert Murray notices (*Aristophanes*, p. 31), would not have been possible in any average European theatre during the late war. It illustrates the high level of tolerance reached by Athens and extended especially to her comic poets.

Lênæa: the more domestic feast of Dionŷsus, held in February, as opposed to the Great Dionysia (about March) when 'strangers', i.e. Athenian subject-allies, were present. Aristophanês had lately been prosecuted by Cleon for attacking him on behalf of these allies in the *Babylonians*, shown at the Great Dionysia in 426.

Mégara's little coats: a principal article of export from the Megarid. Just before the war a strict embargo was placed by Athens on Megarian goods, and informers were active in denouncing contraband.

p. 467, *Gilding Pallases*: figure-heads, representing Pallas Athênê. *Têlephus*: here means Sparta, whose case Dicæópolis is pleading in the words and character of Euripidês' Têlephus.

413. Dicæópolis has now won over the whole Chorus to the side of peace. These lines come from the parábasis, a regular (and very primitive) part of Old Comedy, in which the Chorus frequently speak in the name of the poet or 'chorus-instructor', as happens here. Aristophanês had a profound distrust of the new oratory, and especially of foreign envoys who betrayed the Assembly into rash decisions by using flattery. *Violet crown . . . shiny*: Pindaric epithets for Athens. *Ægina*: the home of Aristophanês. Its conquest by Athens in 457 B.C. was among the causes of the war.

414. The *Knights* (424 B.C.) is a bold attack on Cleon, owner of tan-yards, a 'friend of the people' (or *arriviste*) now at the height of his power. Aided by luck and effrontery he had captured at Pylos a Spartan garrison already brought to extremities by Dêmosthenês (cf. p. 471, line 2) and prevailed on the people to reject all offers of peace. The two generals Dêmosthenês and Nîkias, both of good birth and moderate views, are here represented as the slaves of Dêmos (an im-

NOTES

personation of the Athenian people). Dêmos has entrusted the care of his household to a Paphlagonian slave, i.e. Cleon. The Chorus of Knights (Nos. 415–16) would share the aristocratic prejudices of the two generals and embody the old ideal of unselfish patriotism.

415. This again is from a parábasis (cf. No. 413, note). The Chorus speak for the poet himself, who reviews the fortunes of older comic playwrights.   p. 472, His *Wings* and his *Flies*: comedy developed partly from the old Animal Masquerade; hence Choruses of Birds, Wasps, Gall-flies, Frogs, &c., were not uncommon.   *Cratînus*: cf. Nos. 298–9, 531. He retorted to these remarks by producing in his 96th year a play called *The Flagon*, which won first prize over Aristophanês' *Clouds*.   *Connas*: a famous musician. *Lênêan salute*: cf. No. 412, note.

416. Nîkias and Dêmosthenês have secured the services of an Offal-monger or Sausage-seller, fully qualified to outdo the Paphlagonian in virtue of his low birth and calling, his lies, impudence, glibness, and brutal vulgarity. In a series of contests, first before the Senate and then before Dêmos himself, every pretension of the Paphlagonian has been shattered. Here, in a final 'Transformation Scene', the Offal-monger appears as a gentleman of the old school. Like Mêdêa with her magical brew, he has boiled and rejuvenated Dêmos, who is now The Athenian People of Marathonian Days, untainted by the corruptions of democracy.   *The grass-hopper*: buckled hair-slides of this design were worn by an older generation.

417. The *Clouds* (423 B.C.) is concerned with the new philosophic movement, typified by Socratês, and especially with its effects upon education. Strepsíadês, a country gentleman, has been ruined by the expensive tastes of his wife and son. By learning the new Sophistic art of argument he hopes to outface his creditors in the courts. Here he applies to the Thinking-shop or Reflectory of Socratês for admission as a pupil. *Chærephon*: a disciple of Socratês.

418. Current philosophies treated the soul as a vapour-like essence. Hence Socratês finds in the Clouds a congenial atmosphere, and later explains them as 'Great goddesses to all

men of leisure, contributing sententiousness, logic, intelligence, humbug, circumlocution, chicanery', &c., and enjoying the worship of every kind of quack. Here they appear in answer to his invocation, looking 'like great wool-packs, but with noses', and singing one of the best of Aristophanês' choral lyrics. *Cecrops*: cf. No. 301, note. On the translation see Introduction, p. xcv. It follows the metre of the Greek by substitution of stress- for quantitative-rhythm.

419. From the *Agôn* or *Debate*, which, like the parábasis, is a well-recognized and very primitive feature in the structure of Old Comedy. Strepsíadês has been superannuated from the Reflectory, and Socratês has agreed to teach his son instead. First he introduces him to the *Just* and *Unjust Arguments*, personifying respectively the Old and the New Education and shown on the stage (by one account) like fighting-cocks in cages. The *Just Argument*, who speaks first, is here represented. He pleads for a simple life, respectful ways, and sound physique: his opponent for self-indulgence, scepticism, and forensic skill. As Gilbert Norwood puts it, 'The Unjust Argument produced Alcibiadês, who ruined his country by his counsels to Sparta; the Just Argument produced Nîkias, who ruined his country because he did not understand eclipses' (*Greek Comedy*, p. 216). See further Gilbert Murray, *Aristophanes*, ch. iv. *Phrŷnis*: a poet and musician of Mytilênê (*fl. c.* 445 B.C.), whose innovations were considered decadent by the older school; cf. Nos. 438–9, note. *Hippócratês*: a general, whose sons, as the Greek conveys by a pun, were swinishly stupid.

420. The *Wasps* (422 B.C.) is a satire on the jury-system at Athens. In Cleon's time citizens were paid a small sum for service in the courts, where their functions, roughly speaking, combined those of a modern judge and jury. They jealously guarded their democracy, and sometimes were inclined to argue that the more a rich man was 'bled' the better it would be for the State. The leading characters in this play are Philocleon and his son Bdelycleon, i.e. 'Bless-Cleon' and 'Blast-Cleon' respectively (cf. H. J. Rose, *A Handbook of Greek Literature*, p. 234). Jury-service is the main passion of Philocleon's life,

NOTES

but his son forcibly keeps him at home, and the other jurors (who form a Chorus of Wasps) have to go to the courts without him. To give his father something to do, Bdelycleon stages a domestic mock-trial of the dog Labês, accused by a servant of stealing some Sicilian cheese. The dog's name suggests 'Grab' and also 'Lachês'—an Athenian politician suspected of misconduct in Sicily; which was, incidentally, the goal of the more aggressive Athenian imperialists. The usual court properties are reproduced at Philocleon's house; but he also enjoys his home-comforts, a bowl of soup and the presence of his pet cock. *Thucydidês*: not the historian, but probably the leader of the aristocratic party, ostracized in 444 B.C. *His pups*: produced *in misericordiam*, like the children of defendants in Attic courts.

421. The *Peace* was produced about March 421 B.C. Cleon had died in the preceding autumn, and the Peace of Nîkias was now in sight. Trygæus, a country man of the favourite Aristophanic type, has heard from Euripidês' play how Bellerophon mounted to heaven on Pegasus and questioned Zeus on the wrongs of the world. Having no Pegasus, he breeds a huge Sicilian dung-beetle. On this he now takes flight, in a passage delightful for its rhythm. Later, with the help of a Chorus of farmers, the maiden Peace is restored to the world.

422. The *Birds* was produced in 414 B.C., some eight months after the sailing of the Sicilian expedition. It is a fantasy, or 'Play of Escape', with an undercurrent of wholesome satire. Pisthetairos and a friend leave Athens in disgust and go to consult the king of the birds, once the Thracian prince Têreus, now transformed to a hoopoe. Their first desire is to find with his help some city less litigious than Athens—a place of quiet and *laissez-faire*. But soon Pisthetairos conceives the idea of a vast bird-empire, strategically placed between heaven and earth. This appeals to the Hoopoe, who here calls his subjects together for discussion. His wife Procnê, the nightingale, is the piper to whose notes the Chorus of birds sings and dances. See also No. 565, note.

On the translation see Introduction, p. xcv. As far as possible it follows the Greek metre, substituting stress- for quantitative-rhythms. The rhythm of (i) is anapæstic, with occasional $- \cup \cup$ and $- -$ in place of $\cup \cup -$. In (ii) the rhythm varies with the class of bird summoned, and is not too easy to analyse in the Greek. In representing it one may at least catch the bawling sound of the Hoopoe's opening (*Come . . . over*), where the Greek iambic feet are closed five times out of six with long *ō*. Other points worth noticing are: The '*smaller folk about the clods*' must hop in trochaics. '*Hurry over . . . gardens*' represents $\cup \cup - -$ three times repeated, not $- \cup - \cup$. A flurry of short syllables in the Greek follows, giving an idea of garden- and hill-birds on the wing. The English approximates; it should be read *prestissimo*. Then come the cretics (*Marshy dyke . . . francolin*) which recall (so Eduard Fraenkel suggests) the deliberate gait of long-legged water-birds. Sometimes for $- \cup -$ a 'resolved' ($\cup \cup \cup -$) form of the cretic is substituted, e.g. *speckled and splashed*. Finally sea-birds are called in dactylics—a reminiscence of Alcman (No. 115).

The pipe-solo after (i) is attested by a stage-direction in the Greek. In (ii) some scholars would attribute all the bird-notes to the Hoopoe. He would then be imitating the calls of other birds.

423. From the parábasis. Pisthetairos has persuaded the birds that once, in the beginning of things, they were lords of the universe, and that now their power may be regained. They must build a great city in mid-air, claiming back their former worship from men below and intercepting the smoke of sacrifice from gods above. Zeus will then restore their sovranty. Here the birds celebrate their lineage in a style which parodies the Orphic theogonies and the works of Hesiod. p. 488, *Prodicus*: a famous sophist of the day. p. 489, *Winged fame*, &c.: more literally, 'A chance saying is an omen'. From the practice of augury, one word did duty in Greek for 'bird' and for 'omen'. *All tokens*: better, 'chance meetings', e.g. with a 'lackey'. *Donkeys*: their bray was considered ominous.

In *The Athenæum*, No. 2766, 30 Oct. 1880, p. 568, Swinburne explains that he 'was allured into the audacity of this experiment' by consideration of a fact hitherto apparently neglected by all previous translators, viz. that the anapæstic heptameter is 'almost exactly reproducible in a language to which all variations and combinations of anapæstic, iambic, or trochaic metre are as natural and pliable as all dactylic and spondaic forms of verse are unnatural and abhorrent'. He claims to differ from 'the verbal pattern of the original' only in two metrical points: first, in using rhymes and double rhymes, 'as necessary makeweights for the imperfection of an otherwise inadequate language'; and secondly, 'in not reproducing the rare exceptional effect of a line overcharged on purpose with a preponderance of heavy-footed spondees'. His main desire 'was to renew as far as possible for English ears the music of this resonant and triumphant metre, which goes ringing at full gallop as of horses who

> dance as 'twere to the music
> Their own hoofs make'.

(Swinburne's free verse in classical metres is far more successful than this experiment, which is, however, interesting historically. B. B. Rogers's translations of Aristophanês render anapæsts, and other metres, on much the same principles. They were written from 1902 to 1915; the Gilbert and Sullivan Operas, to which they are also indebted, from 1875 to 1896.) See further, Introduction, pp. xciii ff., and No. 332, note.

424. The projected city has been named; heralds have been sent to heaven and earth; and Pisthetairos, after several interruptions by pests from Athens, has retired to complete sacrifice to the new gods. This is part of the choric song which follows. The English has been adapted by T. F. Higham from that of H. F. Cary, best known as the translator of Dante. His version has been shortened by six lines and brought closer to the Greek, but its general character has been maintained. He lived 1772–1844.

425. Pisthetairos has just returned to announce the omens favourable, when this Messenger arrives. *Proxénidês* is a shadowy figure. *Theógenês* helped Cleon to fulfil his boast and capture the Spartan garrison off Pylos (cf. No. **414**, note). In line 1149 the translator reads ἐπλινθοβόλουν. See *The Classical Quarterly*, vol. xxvi (April 1932), pp. 108 ff.

NOTES

426. Zeus has been brought to terms and has given his daughter 'Sovranty' to Pisthetairos. The comedy ends, like many others, with triumphant marriage celebrations. This ode is sung while the hero and his bride depart in a blaze of glory. *The child, &c.*: a child with both parents living was a regular attendant at weddings to bring good luck.

427. In the *Lysístrata* (411 B.C.) the women stop the war. They seize the Acropolis, assume control of the public funds, and declare a sexual strike which extends through their agency to all the belligerent States. Here a Commissioner of the Public Safety (appointed after the Sicilian disaster) has been threatening to force the Treasury. Lysístrata, the prime mover of the women's plan, has checked his design and states her case.

428. The plan has succeeded. The men of Sparta treat for peace and find the Athenians equally willing. Lysístrata befriends (and lectures) the plenipotentiaries of both sides. Here they feast with song and dance as her guests in the Acropolis. The Scots does duty for the Spartan vernacular. *Brassin-dome*: a bronze temple of Athêna stood on the Acropolis at Sparta.

429. '*Thesmophoriazusae*' means 'celebrants of the Thesmophoria', a festival of Dêmêter and Persephonê observed by women. Euripidês has learned that the celebrants, angered by his treatment of their sex on the tragic stage, intend to meet and discuss his fate. His old relative Mnêsílochus acts as a spy in woman's disguise. Here he has been detected and trussed to a board by a Scythian policeman. Euripidês (after previous attempts at rescue) now joins the prisoner in a parody of his own *Andrómeda* (see No. 390 and note), vainly hoping that the illiterate Scythian will allow 'Andrómeda' to be released. *I'se fetch de mad*: i.e. a *mat* to lie on. The play was produced in 410 B.C.

430. During 406 B.C. both Euripidês and Sophoclês died. In the *Frogs* (405 B.C.) Dionŷsus, finding a lack of creative genius, descends into Hades for the sake of retrieving Euripidês (cf. No. 390, note). Here he is rowing across the Styx, while Frogs (they are not the Chorus) call the time.

The comic effect of this scene depended as much on the

732

music and metre as on the spectacle of Dionŷsus (who probably carried a pot-belly) attempting to row. Wilamowitz (*Griechische Verskunst*, 1921, pp. 592–4) pointed out the metrical joke, explaining that *brekekekex koax koax* is trochaic (͝ ∪ ∪ ⏑ ∪ ⏑ ∪ ⏑) and demands a short, sharp stroke which Dionŷsus attempts the whole time to acquire. There is conflict between this trochaic rhythm, which the Frogs adopt also in their songs (except the first), and the slow iambic interjections of Dionŷsus. Finally, he gets the swing of the Frogs' metre and claims to outdo them.

According to Wilamowitz, the iambics of Dionŷsus, wherever they occur, are spoken, not sung. They are, as it were, 'asides', and their rhythm does not correspond to that of his rowing, which aims at being trochaic throughout. Others prefer the view (adopted in the translation) that Dionŷsus both rowed and spoke, or sang, in the slower iambic rhythm, and relapsed into it even after the trochaic spurts to which the croak had stung him when nearing shore.

The translation attempts to represent the Greek metres, but resolved trochees (∪ ∪ ∪ for — ∪) almost inevitably become dactyls in English. See also Introduction, p. xcv.

Nŷsa's lord: Dionŷsus. An old temple of his stood in the *Marshlands*, a district of SE. Athens. The *Feast of Pots* was the third day of the spring festival called Anthestêria.

Reeds, of a wood . . . : Reeds were used to make sounding-boards for string instruments, cf. No. 82, p. 163, line 3.

(Read Διώννσον in 216; and insert the croak (with many MSS.) after 222.)

431. Disembarked in a region of darkness and mud and legendary terrors, the god is relieved to hear the sound of flutes. Now the Chorus enter—Initiates, men and women, who enjoy in Hades their promised happiness and here re-enact the processional solemnities and merry-making of Athenian Mysteries.

432. Meanwhile all Hades is excited at the approaching contest for the throne of tragedy. Æschylus, the holder, has accommodated Sophoclês, who does not wish, at the moment, to compete. Now Euripidês intends to dispute the claim of

NOTES

Æschylus. Here the Chorus anticipate the tactics of the rivals—Æschylus, the leonine, the heavy dragoon, the titanic; Euripidês, the wild-boar, the skirmisher, the logic-chopper.

433–5 are all scenes from this same contest.

433. Æschylus makes fun of Euripidês' prologues (all from lost plays). It is doubtful whether serious criticism is intended. A well-known game, then as now, was to end some passage of serious poetry by affixing a ridiculous tag.

434. Euripidês parodies the music and rhythms and diction of Æschylus. Scraps are strung together from the *Agamemnon* and other plays, scarcely yielding continuous sense.

435. Æschylus parodies his rival. Here there is no option for a translator but to parody the best-known English versions of Euripidês.

Euripidês is criticized for his secularization of tragedy. It is intimated that the theft of a barn-door fowl by one goodwife from another might find a place in his plays. The diction takes sudden drops from the mystical and romantic to a flat colloquial plane; and the music, which employs roulades (*spindle-indle-indle*) and senseless repetitions (cf. *sorrow, sorrow* and *drip-drop*), has become more important than the language and thought.

436. The *Ecclesiazusæ* (Women in Parliament) was produced in 392 B.C. Praxágora has induced other Athenian women to gather before dawn dressed in their husbands' clothes and further disguised by false beards. They intend to pack the Assembly (*Ecclêsia*) and support a proposal that the government be entrusted to women. Here they rehearse, and after various attempts by speakers who betray their femininity, Praxágora shows how best to move the proposal. Plato, in writing of communism (*Republic*, bk. v), seems to have had parts of this play in mind. Line 2, *The chaplet*: this was worn by speakers addressing the Assembly. Line 21, *By Aphrodîte*: a *woman's* oath. It would at once betray the speaker. p. 511, *Æsimus*: a lame man, otherwise unknown.

437. The *Plûtus* (388 B.C.) belongs really to the Middle Comedy, in which the Choral part is negligible, the fun sobered, the slaves uppish, and the style disintegrating (cf. Gilbert Norwood, *Greek Comedy*, pp. 272 ff.). Chrémylus, being honest but poor, asks an oracle how best to guide his son—shall he make him a rogue and rich? Told to follow the first person he meets, he encounters Plûtus, the God of Riches, blinded by Zeus for preferring wise men and good, and now invariably falling in with their opposites (cf. Nos. 181, 304). He takes Plûtus to the temple of Asclêpius (cf. No. 279, note), hoping to restore his sight. Meanwhile Poverty appears and states her case. Her expulsion from Greece, she urges, will be disastrous, for she is the source of all that is good. Here is part of the debate. *Furmety*: i.e. Frumenty, husked wheat boiled in milk and seasoned. *Crutch*: the word so translated should mean a cask or a crock.

Fielding, when he left Eton, was said to be 'uncommonly versed in the Greek authors'. His collaborator, 'The Rev. Mr. Young', was the model from which Parson Adams in *Joseph Andrews* is drawn—'his veneration for Æschylus was as passionate, the overflowings of his benevolence as strong, and his fits of reverie as frequent'. Once, while serving as Chaplain with a regiment in Flanders, he strolled 'in a deep fit of absence' as far as the enemy's camp. But recognizing 'the undesigning simplicity of his heart' his captors 'very politely gave him leave to pursue his contemplations home again' (Arthur Murphy, *Essay on the Life and Genius of Henry Fielding*, 1762; pp. 68–9 in vol. i of Fielding's Works as published in 1784). Samuel Johnson, in distinguishing him from Edward Young, the author of *Night Thoughts*, gives his Christian name as William and adds: 'He supported an uncomfortable existence by translating for the booksellers from Greek; and, if he did not seem to be his own friend, was at least no man's enemy' (*Lives of the Poets*, Everyman Edn., pp. 359–60).

438–9. Tîmotheus, 'a red-haired man from Milêtus', was a pupil of Phrŷnis (No. 419, note) and friend of Euripidês, another modernist (No. 435, note). His musical innovations were at first unpopular. 'Music', in a comic fragment, complains of his 'titillating ant-runs' and his 'filling her with flourishes, thick as caterpillars in greens'. But he reached a

735

leading position in his day and his works were long current. No. **439**, from a 4th-century papyrus, revives an old but not obsolete form of lyric called the *nome*; but is crossed with the extravagances of dithyramb, especially in the use of strange compounds. It begins by describing the death-struggles of a drowning Persian at Salamis. The true grand style of Æschylus in Nos. **240–1** is worth comparing. On the translation, which suggests a distant affinity with Gerald Manley Hopkins, see Introduction, p. lxxxvii f.

440–1. Fragments of lost comedies. **440.** Gilbert Norwood (*Greek Comedy*, p. 184) writes: 'Curiously enough it is precisely this power that Alcibiadês in Plato's *Symposium* (215 *e*) denies to Periclês and assigns to Socratês. It is commonly thought that Periclês left his "sting" in Thucydidês—that the Funeral Speech (ii. 35–46) contains real Periclean phrases.'

442–50. The authenticity of the Platonic epigrams has been much disputed. It is unlikely that all were written by Plato. Doubt attaches especially to Nos. **442, 449–50.**

442. *Laïs*: There were two famous courtesans of this name, separated by a generation or more. The elder was well known at the time of the Peloponnesian war. Matthew Prior's quatrain—

> Venus! take this votive glass,
> Since I am not what I was:
> What I shall hereafter be,
> Venus! let me never see—

probably derives from Ausonius, *Epigr*. lv. Sir Edward Cook in *More Literary Recreations* (1919), pp. 345 ff., collects several versions.

443. These Eretrian captives were brought to Sûsa in 490 and settled by Darius at Ardericca in Kissia (Herodotus, vi. 119).

445 (i). First translated into English by George Turberville, *Epitaphs, Epigrams, Songs, and Sonnets*, 1567:

> My girl, thou gazest much
> Upon the golden skies:
> Would I were heaven! I would behold
> Thee then with all mine eyes.

The Greek name *Aster* means a star.

NOTES

447. Dio(n) of Syracuse was assassinated in 353 B.C. after a short and embittered rule. His ideals of statesmanship were largely formed by Plato, whom he joined at Athens during exile, renewing a friendship begun in Sicily about 388.

448. Wilamowitz on Euripidês, *Hercules Furens*, 664–9, deals with the distinction between αἰών and χρόνος in this epigram.

451–3. Fragments of lost comedies.

454. Moschiôn is interesting because his tragedies dealt (like Æschylus' *Persæ*) with historical as opposed to legendary themes. This was exceptional. Only a few fragments survive and next to nothing is known of their author. The title of the play from which this fragment comes has not been preserved.

455. Chæremôn wrote tragedies for readers, not for the stage. Œneus, father of Meleâger, gave a title to the play from which this fragment comes. In its studied prettiness of detail the picture is almost Alexandrian, as comparison with a similar scene from Euripides' *Bacchæ* (No. 384, p. 446) will show. But the colour effects and sensuous images are hard to match even among the Alexandrians.

456. Êrinna wrote a poem called *Distaff* in memory of her dead friend Baucis. She herself died young, cf. Nos. 526, 567, 578. No. (i) seems to come not from the *Distaff* but from a poem wishing Baucis good luck on a voyage. In (ii) read Πραϋλόγοι for Παυρολόγοι; and in (iii) Τουτόθεν for Τηλία.

457. In line 7 read Τηλία for Τηνία.

458. Probably also comes from Êrinna's *Distaff*.

459. Written in memory of Hermeias, ruler of Atarneus in Mysia, Aristotle's friend and patron from 347 to 344 B.C. He was put to death by the Persians. The Greek text followed in the translation is disputable, especially in lines 6–8.   *Lêda's pair*: Castor and Polydeucês.

460–5. Fragments of lost comedies.

466–77. Apart from Latin adaptations Menander survived only in one-line maxims, or in chance quotations of no great length, until the Cairo papyrus, discovered in 1905, restored substantial portions of five plays. Two of these five plays are represented in Nos. 478–9.

467. Cf. Herodotus, i. 31 (the story of Cleobis and Biton); and No. 196.

469. Quoted by St. Paul, 1 Cor. xv. 33.

470. The translator reads καταλύσεις βελτίονας in line 11.

477. In line 3 the translation is a compromise between the printed text and Meineke's conjecture παραινέσας πέπωκεν.

478. Pámphilê, while still unmarried, suffered violence from a stranger at a night-festival, and shortly after marriage to Charîsius secretly bore and exposed the child of her former union. Charîsius, when the secret was betrayed, showed himself 'high and mighty' and moved to a separate house. There, while still loving Pámphilê, he lived (innocently enough) with a slave-girl, Habrótonon, and attempted to drown his cares. He himself has now been proved (or so he thinks) the father by Habrótonon of a foundling child, for she claims to have suffered the same violence as Pámphilê, and Charîsius has memories which point, with other tokens, to his own guilt. Pámphilê, in spite of his riotous living and new disgrace, has now rejected her father's advice to break off the marriage, and Charîsius is overcome by remorse. It is striking that in his self-rebuke he postulates a single code of sexual morality for men and women. In this he is several centuries ahead of his time.

The foundling is identified, in the end, as Pámphilê's child, and Charîsius as her unknown assailant. Disputed possession of the tokens found with it provides a name for the play— 'The Arbitrants'.

479. The *Shorn Woman* is a tale of twins—Glýcera and her brother Moschiôn—exposed at birth by their father Patæcus and adopted by different households. They grow up unknown to each other, till Glýcera, now bestowed upon a soldier Pólemo, learns from her foster-mother that the putative son of Mýrrhinê, a rich neighbour, is really her own twin-brother. This knowledge she keeps to herself, for fear of spoiling his social position. Moschiôn snatches a kiss, accepted (but not intended) as fraternal. Pólemo surprises the couple, cuts off Glýcera's hair, and retires to a house in the country. Glýcera then takes refuge with Mýrrhinê, whose household includes Patæcus. Pólemo wishes to storm the house, but is here persuaded by Patæcus to adopt a gentler course. The scene is laid in Corinth.

480–1. Philêtas of Cos is very poorly represented by the fragments that survive. Roman love-elegy owes him a certain debt; so, too, the pastoral poetry of his friend Theocritus. He was tutor to Ptolemy II.

482. This reply was given by the oracle of Serâpis in Egypt to Nicócreon, King of Cyprus, who asked what god Serâpis was.

483. Cleanthês succeeded Zeno, the founder of Stoicism, and presided over the Stoa for some thirty years. E. H. Blakeney (*The Hymn of Cleanthês*, translated with brief Introduction and Notes, London, S.P.C.K., 1921, p. 9) summarizes the argument as follows: (1) Cleanthês feels himself akin to the divine, and therefore worthy to hold communion with it; (2) he expresses his admiration for, and submission to, the divine order of the world; (3) he recognizes that moral evil in the world is the result not of fate but of man's freewill; (4) he prays God to free human souls from ignorance; and (5) closes with an apostrophe in praise of God's law. Line 4: cf. *Acts of the Apostles*, xvii. 28, and No. 505, line 5, note.

The translation is in the metre of R. Bridges's *Testament of Beauty*. See also the translation and comments of J. Adam, *The Vitality of Platonism*, pp. 108 ff. Another good translation (in rhymed quatrains) was written for *The Oxford Magazine*, 27 Apr. 1933, by Edwyn Bevan.

485. Little is known of Phanoclês or of his poem Ἔρωτες ἢ Καλοί from which this fragment survives. *Phorcys*: a sea-deity. On *Orpheus* cf. Nos. 207, 566.

486. From a lost comedy.

487–90. In their style, and sometimes also in their feeling for Nature, Ánytê's epigrams recall the early lyric poetry of

Greece. Meleâger (No. 578) calls them 'lilies', while Sîmias (Nos. 491–2) reminds him of 'a tall wild-pear'. Eleven of Ánytê's twenty-one surviving epigrams are collected and translated into verse by B. Farrington in *Samuel Butler and the Odyssey* (London, Jonathan Cape, 1929, pp. 87–90).

491. Robert Bland (cf. No. 639, note) in the *Monthly Magazine*, 1805, No. 19, p. 137, records that a version of this piece, printed in Addison's *Spectator*, 2 Dec. 1712, 'excited a sensation so strong, that music was adapted to the words and it is sung and admired by the beautiful and the gay'. It runs:

> Winde, gentle Ever-green, to form a Shade
> Around the tomb where Sophocles is laid;
> Sweet Ivy winde thy Boughs, and intertwine
> With blushing Roses and the clust'ring Vine:
> Thus will thy lasting Leaves with Beauties hung
> Prove grateful Emblems of the Lays he sung;
> Whose Soul exalted like a God of Wit,
> Among the Muses and the Graces writ.

493. This Addæus was a Macedonian. His epigrams 'give a picture of the simple and refined life of the Greek country gentleman' (J. W. Mackail, *Select Epigrams from the Greek Anthology*, 3rd edn., 1911, p. 311).

494. For a variation on this theme see *Anth. Pal.* ix. 627, xvi. 201, and Shakespeare's *Sonnets*, 153, 154.

495. Compare with this fragmentary lyric poem some lines from Menander (Fragg. 482–3, Kock), translated by Gilbert Norwood, *Greek Comedy*, p. 320: 'All our thoughts, words and acts are Chance, and we are sealed as hers. Chance governs all: unless we delight in empty names, this goddess alone must we call Mind and Providence.'

496. From an inscription discovered (1903) near Mt. Dictê in Crete, on the site of the temple of Zeus Diktaios. The singers marched or danced towards an altar, addressing their Megistos Kouros ('Boy, Mighty One') who is Zeus; while they themselves, the Kourêtës, i.e. young full-fledged warriors with priestly functions, form his retinue, just as Sîlênoi, &c., attend Dionŷsus. The story ran that when Zeus was an infant, his mother Rheä concealed him from his child-eating father

Kronos by help of the Kourêtës, who danced round him in panoply, clashing their weapons so as to drown the noise of his cries. Cf. Gilbert Murray, *New Chapters in Greek Literature*, 1st Series, 1921, pp. 50–3 and reff., who adds that the story was no doubt invented to explain the rite. Leaping is a common ritual act—cf. the Salii at Rome, and the Arval hymn. See also Lucretius, ii. 629 ff.

497. Thyrsis and a goatherd are seated at noonday under the shade of an elm. The goatherd, by offer of this cup and another gift, persuades Thyrsis to sing 'The sad tale of Daphnis'. On the probable design of the cup see A. S. F. Gow, *The Journal of Hellenic Studies*, 1913, pp. 207 ff.

498. Part of Thyrsis' song. Daphnis was born to Hermês by a nymph, and learnt his shepherd-craft and music from Pan, his half-brother. In the story here followed by Theocritus he rejects the love of woman and so is wasted by Aphrodîtê with a hopeless passion, unreturned and unconfessed. *Callisto*: one of Artemis' attendant nymphs, was loved by Zeus and bore a son Arcas, ancestor of the Arcadians. Either Artemis or Hêra changed her into a bear; and Zeus enskied her as the constellation *Hélicê* (Ursa Major). On the translation given in line 9 see A. S. F. Gow, *The Panpipes of Daphnis*, in *The Classical Review*, vol. xlviii (1934), p. 121.

499. Simætha, deserted by her lover Delphis, employs against him magic both of attraction and destruction. Hécatê (cf. No. **336**, note) is invoked, now by that name, and now as the Moon-goddess (Selênê) or as Artemis. A serving-maid, Théstylis, attends; and prayer, spoken or implied, accompanies each magic act.

Meanwhile a bird-wheel (cf. No. **280**, p. 310, note) is spun, with recurrent incantation. This object is a spoked wheel (sometimes a disk) pierced with two holes opposite each other and equidistant from the centre. By increasing and relaxing the tension of a cord, whose ends pass through the holes and are tied together, it is made to revolve. The *Magic bronze* (p. 545) is a different object, a 'bull roarer', i.e. a flattish piece of metal, oval or diamond-shaped, swung round on the end of a cord. See A. S. F. Gow, *The Journal of Hellenic Studies*, 1934,

NOTES

pp. 1–13.   p. 545, *The mammet melts*: cf. D. G. Rossetti, *Sister Helen*:

> Oh the waxen man was plump to-day,
> Sister Helen,
> How like dead folk he has dropped away.

500. A rustic serenade. In line 18 Mr. Trevelyan reads τὸ πᾶν λίθος.

501. A singing-match between Daphnis and Dâmœtas. Daphnis is perhaps the same figure as in No. **498.** He addresses the giant; whom Dâmœtas impersonates in reply. Even in the *Odyssey* the Cyclops Polyphêmus showed a tenderer side while handling his ram. Later poets, from Philóxenus in the 4th century onwards, domesticate him still further (a common Hellenistic habit) and delight in the contrast between the monster and his love Galatêa, a sea-nymph: cf. No. **502** (*d*). *Moves her last piece*, p. 552: a metaphor taken from an ancient game, somewhat resembling draughts.   *Têlemos*: he prophesied that Polyphêmus would be blinded by Odysseus (Nos. **46,** i, ii). *This one beauty of mine*: the eye in the middle of Cyclops' forehead. In line 22 Mr. Trevelyan reads ποθόρημαι.

500–1. Of his metre Mr. Trevelyan writes: 'I have used an unrimed verse of seven accents, the same in structure as the normal half-stanza of the English ballad. In the form of rimed couplets it is used by Chapman in his translation of the *Iliad* and by other Elizabethan poets and translators. Blake in the Book of Thel, was the first to dispense with rime and vary the position of the cæsura.'

502. A tradition survives that this poem is autobiographical, containing a mixture of real and pet-names.   *Lycidas* is thought to be Leônidas of Tarentum (Nos. **545–8**), *Sîmíchidas* to be Theocritus himself. *Sîcélidas* is almost certainly Asclêpiadês of Samos (Nos. **524–9**). On *Philêtas* see Nos. **480–1,** note; *Amyntas* may be the young Ptolemy, his pupil. In lines 9–12 on p. 555 a reference is seen to Apollonius Rhodius and his quarrel with Callimachus (cf. No. **522**), whom Theocritus supports. The translator reads λαιοῖο in line 15. On Pater's translation of **502** (*a*), see Introduction, pp. lxxxiv, xcviii.

NOTES

502 (*b*) and (*c*). Sung by the reapers Bucæus and Mîlon respectively. Bucæus is amusingly gauche. Some of his couplets resemble those of rude love-songs that circulate in Greece to-day. Mîlon's verses represent the traditional popular reaping-songs of Theocritus' time. *Corn-flag's lettered crest*: the flower that sprang from the blood of Hyacinthus; cf. Virgil, *Ecl.* iii. 106, and J. Sargeaunt, *The Trees, Shrubs, and Plants of Virgil*, 1920, pp. 56–60. It was marked with Hyacinthus' initial (*Y*); or with αἲ αἲ (*woe, woe*), cf. Milton, *Lycidas*, 'The sanguine flower inscribed with woe'. Another legend connected the flower and its marking (αἲ αἲ) with Ajax. See R. J. Cholmeley's *Theocritus*, ad loc., and H. J. Rose, *A Handbook of Greek Mythology*, pp. 140, 160 and reff. The flower is variously identified.

502 (*d*). Cf. No. 501, note. This translation comes from the Bodleian copy of *Sixe Idillia*, which is unique. Its authorship, in spite of conjectures, remains unknown; see the Introduction by Sir Stephen Gaselee to Duckworth's reprint of 1922. On the whole it keeps very close to the Greek and hardly exaggerates that impression of *naïveté* which Theocritus (a highly sophisticated artist) yet managed to convey. There is also a translation to be found in the works of Mrs. Browning.

502 (*e*). Cf. No. 533. Hêraclês had broken an oar and caused the Argonauts to put in at Kios. While he looked for timber the rest prepared supper, and Hylas, his young page and favourite, went to draw water. Such are the antecedent events as given by Apollonius Rhodius; Theocritus is less detailed. F. T. Palgrave records that Tennyson (about 1857) dwelt particularly on the last four lines of the Greek here translated and said 'I should be content to die if I had written anything equal to this [Idyll]' (*Tennyson, A Memoir*, by his son, vol. ii, p. 495).

502 (*f*). From a 'mime' or scene from common life, in which Theocritus plays amusing tricks with the hexameter. Gorgo and Praxínoa (like Theocritus) are Syracusans, who speak a broad Doric. They live in Alexandria, where Ptolemy II is making festival to Adônis. Gorgo persuades Praxínoa to visit

the show and hear the dirge for Adônis (cf. No. 573). Eúnoa (Praxínoa's maid) and Eútychis (Gorgo's) accompany them. See also Matthew Arnold's comments and translation in *Pagan and Medieval Religious Sentiment* among the *Essays in Criticism*. There is also a translation by Leigh Hunt in *A Jar of Honey from Mt. Hybla* (1848). Anstey's *Voces Populi* is in this tradition and so, too, Harry Grattan's *Emma and 'Erb*, duologues for male and female in Cockney dialect.

502 (*g*). Probably not by Theocritus. The list of fishing-tackle suggests Leônidas of Tarentum or an imitator. The moral of lines 1–4 is pointed by a dream related by one of the pair. He caught in his sleep a golden fish and swore (so he dreamt) to pursue his trade no more. His friend's comment may be quoted from an anonymous manuscript of the 17th century, a transcript of which has kindly been allowed by Mr. P. J. Dobell of The Antiquarian Bookstore, Tunbridge Wells:

> Feare not at all, for neither didst thou sweare,
> Nor saw'st or hook'st a Golden Fish, but such
> Visions of Night Day-lies resemble much;
> For if not sleeping but awake thou all
> These places search, thy dreaming hopes then shall
> Look for a common Fish, lest the extremes
> Of hunger kill thee, midst thy Golden Dreames.

This appears to be the earliest English translation of this Idyll. It is among a collection of poems and translations (by various hands) 'plac'd as they were done by J. F.'.

In lines 13–14 of the Greek Mr. Chamberlin uses a different text.

502 (*h*). From a hymn to Castor and Polydeucês. Theocritus goes on to describe a boxing-match between Polydeucês and Ámycus, a churl encountered on the Bithynian coast, where the Argonauts had landed. With lines 13–16 cf. Tennyson, *The Marriage of Geraint*:

> Arms on which the standing muscle sloped
> As slopes a wild brook o'er a little stone,
> Running too vehemently to break upon it.

503. From an epyllion (i.e. short treatment, in hexameters, of an epic subject; cf. Nos. 512, 570, notes) on Hêraclês. He

744

is visiting King Augêas in Elis, whose stables he was later to clean, and is being put on his way by an old ploughman. In lines 11–12 of the translation the meaning more probably is: 'How wild a creature the royal gods have given | Man in the dog! How tardy in reflection!' See R. J. Cholmeley, *ad loc*. (The modern Greek dog still responds, as a rule, to a lifted stone.)

504. A poem described by Louis XIV (so Andrew Lang records) as 'a model of honourable gallantry'. It is written in Æolic dialect and Asclêpiad metre. Theocritus is about to sail from Syracuse, a colony of Corinth, to Mîlêtus, a city founded by Neileus or Nêleus, son of Codrus. The old name of Corinth was *Éphyra*. Nîkias was a poet as well as a doctor.

On the metre used in translation, see No. 24, note. The Greek metre ('Greater Asclepiad') is used by Sappho in No. 143. Horace's Latinization of it—'Tu ne quaesieris, scire nefas, quem mihi, quem tibi . . .' is imitated in Swinburne's choriambics:—

Large red lilies of love, sceptral and tall, lovely for eyes to see;
Thornless blossom of love, full of the sun, fruits that were
    reared for thee.

Gilbert Murray, quoted by J. W. White, *The Verse of Greek Comedy*, Macmillan and Co., Ltd., 1912, pp. xx–xxi, arranges the metre differently, writing by way of illustration:

An old eagle, a blind eagle, who waits hungry and cold and
    still;
He seeks nothing, he fears nothing: he stands alone on a lonely
    hill.

505–6. Arâtus of Soli in Cilicia enjoyed great fame not only in Greece (cf. No. 518) but also among the Romans. Virgil owes him a debt; and the long fragments of Cicero's Aratea are only one of three Latin verse translations. The *Phænómena* is an astronomical treatise based on the work of Eudoxus of Cnidus. 505. *For we are also his offspring*: St. Paul (Acts xvii. 28) *may* have derived these words from Arâtus; but perhaps they had proverbial currency. Cf. No. 483, note. *The Elder Race*: a reference which puzzled even the ancient commentators. **506.** For this account of the Golden Age cf. No. **58.** *Justice* becomes the constellation *Virgo*.

507–10. The Hymns of Callimachus are written ostensibly for recitation at religious festivals, in the manner of the Homeric Hymns, but are commonly regarded as literary *jeux d'esprit* with no religious intention. In the Notes that follow, those appended by Mr. Furness to his own translations are distinguished by the initials R. A. F.

507. Written as if for the feast of Apollo Carneius at Cyrênê. This is the proem. Beneath the figure of Apollo that of Ptolemy III may here and there be traced. See No. **282** for the myth of Apollo and Cyrênê. On the *bay* and the *palm* cf. No. **365,** note. The *swan* was also an Apolline emblem. *Lycoreian*: Lycorêa was a town on Mt. Parnassus, near Delphi, where the refrain 'Hië Pæëon' of the Apolline melody originated (R. A. F.). *Rock of Tears*: Niobë. Cf. No. **324,** note.

508. From a Hymn to Artemis. It opens with a picture of the goddess in childhood, seated on the knees of her father Zeus and begging for the gifts that later became her attributes. Among these were a bow and arrows to be fashioned by the Cyclopës (see No. **71,** note); a choir of sixty Oceanids, all nine years old; and a retinue of nymphs from Cretan rivers. Here she goes to get the promised weapons.   *Trinacria*: Sicily. *Cyrnus*: Corsica.   *Argês* and *Steropês*: i.e. The Flasher and The Lightning Man.

509. From the Hymn to Delos—once, so the story went, a floating island, cf. **630–1,** note. When Lêto was driven from land to land by Hêra's jealousy, Delos (Asteria) gave her a resting-place for the birth of Apollo and Artemis. Cf. No. **365,** and Ovid, *Metamorphoses*, vi. 189 ff.:

> Miserata vagantem
> 'hospita tu terris erras, ego' dixit 'in undis'
> instabilemque locum Delos dedit.

The island itself was then given rest.   *Têthys*: wife of Oceanus.   *Cyrnus*: Corsica was colonized by Phœnicians. *Macris*: Eubœa, also called Ellópia, after Ellops, son of Ion,

NOTES

on whom cf. Nos. 371–2. *She whom Cypris swam to*: Cyprus. *Telchînian-made*: the Telchînes were legendary metal-workers; the *Great god* is Poseidon. *Éphyra*: Corinth. *Maiden Isle*: Parthénia, the old name of Samos. *Ancæus*: King of Samos (Strabo, xiv. 1. 3). *Mýcalê*: a town on the mainland opposite Samos.

510. The Palladium, i.e. the image of Pallas Athêna seized by Diomed and Odysseus at Troy, was conveyed once a year from the old citadel at Argos and bathed by maidens in the River Înachus. This ceremony provides the fictitious occasion of the *Hymn for the Bath of Pallas*. For the poet the image becomes Pallas herself. No man may see her naked:

> Whoso the Keeper of the Town shall view
> Naked, shall look his last on Argos too.

Then follows this story of Tîrésias, the son of Euêres and Chariclo (cf. R. A. F.). p. 577, *Cûrálius-side*: at Corônêa, where the Pan-Bœotian festival was held; cf. No. 131. (In this passage the translator does not adopt Ernesti's transposition of lines 63–4 to precede 61–2.) *Horsefoot Rill*: Hippocrene; a kick from the hoof of Pegasus (No. 277) caused it to spring. p. 579, *Much sooth for Thebans*: cf. No. 318, note. *Among the ghosts*: No. 46 (iv), note.

511. The *Hymn to Dêmêter* is written as if for a ritual procession—the Carrying of the Sacred Basket—established at Alexandria by Ptolemy II in imitation of the Thesmophória (No. 429, note) at Athens. After references to the ceremony, to Dêmêter's wanderings (cf. No. 78), and her gifts to mankind, this story is introduced 'as a warning to avoid transgression'. See H. J. Rose, *A Handbook of Greek Mythology*, pp. 94 ff. and reff., for the history and variants of this myth. Callimachus is the first extant author to treat it in full. Ovid's version (*Metam.* viii. 738 ff.) is worth comparing.

Erysíchthon is the son of Tríopas, who gives his own descent on p. 582. The scene is Dótium in Thessaly. In the same country are: Orménium, ruled by *Ormenus* (p. 581), and *Itônê* (ib.), with its cult of Pallas Athênê. p. 580, *Tríopum*: in Caria. *Enna*: in Sicily. *Tmarus*: near Dôdôna, in

747

NOTES

Epîrus.   p. 582, *Mount Mimas*: on the coast of Ionia.   p. 583, *Hestia*: cf. No. 90, note.

512. This part of the *Hécalê* is preserved on a wooden tablet found in Egypt. Hécalê, old and poor, entertained Thêseus on the way to his fight with the Bull of Marathon (Plutarch, *Theseus*, xiv). But though she provides the ostensible theme, her story, so it seems, becomes subordinate to incidental narrative and description. This is the way with Hellenistic epyllia, on which cf. Nos. 503, 570, notes, and H. J. Rose, *A Handbook of Greek Literature*, p. 321. Here Callimachus is digressing on early Attic legends. A crow has just explained to another bird (perhaps an owl) why Athênê banished crows from the Acropolis, and prophesies that the raven, for telling on Corônis (cf. No. 279), will be turned by Apollo from white to black. This passage follows, and apparently refers in the opening lines to the two birds. So, too, the 'frosted neighbour' is a bird. Alfred Körte writes: 'The custom was for birds to report the new day to mankind. Callimachus now turns the tables and has the birds deduce the coming of day from the restless activity of men. This bold somersault of the imagination is very characteristic' (*Hellenistic Poetry*, Eng. trans. by J. Hammer and M. Hadas, Columbia University Press, 1929, p. 156).

513. *Hêraclîtus*: only one of his poems is known, viz. *Anth. Pal.* vii. 465. But it justifies the verdict of Callimachus. It is a 'nightingale'—and 'still awake'. Some have supposed that 'Nightingales' was the title of a book of Hêracleitus' poems. But cf. Nossis, in *Anth. Pal.* vii. 415; and see Wilamowitz, *Hellenistische Dichtung*, ii, pp. 122–3. On the translation, cf. Introduction, pp. lxix f.. No one has produced a convincing substitute.

514. W. Rhys Roberts (*Eleven Words of Simonides*, p. 23) notes that both in No. 212 and here 'the ill-omened word *dies* is, in the Greek, kept from the end and placed emphatically elsewhere'. But translators find this difficult to arrange in English rhymed verse.

515. Mr. G. M. Young writes: 'An attack on popular

748

NOTES

superstitions concerning Hades. Cháridas may have been a philosopher, as Legrand assumes (*La Poésie alexandrine*, 1924, p. 54). Here, at any rate, he is in agreement with Callimachus, who was very sceptical about Hades.' Line 6: the cheapness of commodities in Hades was proverbial. See also A. W. Mair and R. A. Furness, *ad loc*. If coins of Pella were called 'Pellæan oxen'—they had an ox as type—Callimachus is saying, as it were, 'You can buy a crown for five shillings' (R. A. F.). For the dialogue-form, cf. No. 662.

517. The line of descent was: Callimachus the General, Battus, Callimachus the Poet. Though Battus, the poet's father, is the subject of this poem, his name is not even mentioned; and nothing is said of him except that his father and son gained distinction in their respective professions. Mr. G. M. Young (*The Epigrams of Callimachus*, Oxford, 1934, p. 129) notices this point and suggests an interpretation that would make the poet appear not unfilial. But the last two lines of the Greek may well be interpolated. They occur (with an initial gap of 7 letters and the form ὄθματι) in the Prologue to the *Aitia*, soon after the lines translated in No. 522 of this book. See E. Lobel in *Hermes*, vol. lxx, p. 33. The name Battus is that of the mythical founder of Cyrênê; cf. No. 282, note.

518. Refers to the *Phænomena* of Aratus, on whom see Nos. 505–6, notes. Hesiod appealed especially to Callimachus; cf. No. 522, note. In lines 1–2 the text is not quite certain, but the meaning more probably is that Aratus did not copy Homer (τὸν ἀοιδῶν ἔσχατον); he took his model, rather, from Hesiodic poetry—a sweet second-best. See E. Reitzenstein in *Festschrift Richard Reitzenstein*, 1931, pp. 42 ff. At the end of the poem the translator reads σύντονος ἀγρυπνίη.

519. 'Hackneyed' is probably the best translation of κυκλικόν. Callimachus is thinking of contemporary treatments of stale themes, not of the early 'cyclic' poets who supplemented Homer's Tale of Troy. With line 2 cf. No. 522, lines 9–12.

520. Cf. Horace, *Satires*, i. 2. 105 ff.; Ovid, *Amores*, ii. 9. 9 and 19. 36.

NOTES

521. *Son of Battus*: cf. No. 517, note.

522. Callimachus is conducting the famous quarrel with his critics, including Apollonius Rhodius, whose *Argonautica* (Nos. 532–43) sustained that unity of theme which, as Callimachus puts it, 'makes a big book a big bore'. The *Ætia*, from which this fragment has lately been recovered, was Callimachus' most considerable work—an elegiac poem in four books dealing with the *Origins* of rites and customs and the foundations of cities and shrines, &c. Its aim and methods are reflected in Propertius, Bk. IV, and in Ovid's *Fasti*, or, with change of metre, in Ovid's *Metamorphoses*. Callimachus drew very largely on folk-lore, preferring the obscurer local legends that others had left untouched, as this Prologue intimates. His model, as he states elsewhere, is Hesiod, whose Helicon (cf. No. 70, i) he has visited in a dream, there to receive instruction from the Muses themselves. Like Hesiod, he keeps in contact with Nature, asserts his own personality, and avoids the tedium of a single subject long sustained. He also relies on a novel conversational tone with popular touches, on clever joinery of diverse material, and constant charm and surprise. Wilamowitz compares Byron's *Don Juan*; cf. A. Körte (ref. as in No. 512, note, pp. 108, 120–1).

523. In the summer of 290 B.C. Dêmêtrius Poliorcêtês entered Athens with Lanassa, who had been the wife of Pyrrhus of Epîrus. They came as the divine pair Dêmêter and Dêmêtrius, and were invoked as deliverers who would save Athens from the Ætolian League (cf. W. W. Tarn, *Antigonos Gonatas*, Clarendon Press, 1913, p. 49). The metre of the original is suggested in the translation, which substitutes stress- for quantitative-rhythm.

526. Cf. Nos. 456–7, 567. It is possible that Asclêpiadês edited Êrinna's poetry after her death.

527. *Fathoms*: 'cubits' in the Greek.

531. Cf. No. 299. The translation suggests the metre of the original. The crowns in the third verse are the trophies of victory gained by Cratînus' comedies in the Dionysiac Festivals.

NOTES

532–43. Apollonius Rhodius. Mr. George Allen writes:
'Apollonius tells the old story of Jason and Mêdêa in an old
epic style, but with a new and sophisticated enjoyment. He
carries off his archaism with a gusto which never fails and allows
him without embarrassment to indulge a later-born taste for
psychology. The motives and hesitation of Mêdêa, and the
similes which refer to states of mind, are drawn by him with a
sharp and modern lucidity. These excite him; while the story
itself he treats as an entertaining and vivid affair with great
opportunities for pictorial effect. This combination of archaic
style with a new accuracy of picture and motive produces a
fascinating result which is better not criticized until the reader
is fully conscious of Apollonius' deliberate aim.

'A translator may well despair of rendering so effective a
piece of sophistication into English. It is occasionally possible
to suggest that something great and old was being followed
with delight, but in a world and in a way very different from
those of the old Epic. The metre used in the translation seemed
appropriate for narrative. It is inspired by Milton's *Lycidas*;
and there are occasionally other unconcealed allusions to the
Miltonic style. But the result is not meant to be a copy of anything Miltonic—only to suggest a faint flavour of the archaic.
A little of that goes a long way in English; and as a rule
respect has been paid to the rapidity and directness with which
Apollonius always comes to the point.'

532. For Pindar's account of Jason, see No. 280.   *Pytho*:
Delphi.   *Quail Island*: translates Ortýgia, the old name
for Delos (cf. Nos. 630–1, note).   *Ismênus*: in Bœotia.
Pêlion: a mountain in Thessaly.   *Chíron*: the Centaur (cf.
No. 280, note).   *Pêleus' wife*: Thetis.

533. Cf. 502 (*e*), note.

534. Aphrodîtê is in search of her child Erôs, the god of
love.   *Ganymede*: cf. No. 373, note.

535. Æêtês, Mêdêa's father and king of Colchis, purposes
to set dangerous tasks to Jason, including the yoking of fire-
breathing bulls. Mêdêa is asked to help him, and at first she
does not see how to.

751

NOTES

536. On waking from her sleep Mêdêa decides to leave her parents and join Jason.

537. Her sister, Chalcíopê, who married Phrixus (No. 280, note), has suggested that Mêdêa should find some means to tame the bulls. Chalcíopê's sons are among the Argonauts, and she fears for their safety.

538. Mopsus, the seer, has just told Jason to go to a temple where he will find Mêdêa. *Æson's son*: Jason.

539. Jason has just reminded Mêdêa of the glorious destiny of Ariadnê, who rescued Thêseus; adding that Mêdêa's good looks promise a spirit as gentle as hers.

540. Jason has answered Mêdêa's questions about his home, and expressed a wish that her father Æêtês would recognize ties of friendship as readily as Minos had done when Thêseus paired with Ariadnê.

541. Jason has yoked the fire-breathing bulls and sown the dragon's teeth in the furrows. *The packed stars show*: cf. No. 11, and note.

542. Mêdêa's brother Apsyrtus has cut off the Argonauts' retreat. They have bargained with him that the fleece shall be kept, as justly won, but that Mêdêa shall be given in ward to Artemis. Some neutral king shall decide her fate—whether to return to her home, or follow Jason to Greece.

543. For the Moving Rocks cf. No. 280, p. 310.

544. Euripidês is referred to as the ward or pupil of Anaxágoras, a physicist friendly with Periclês.

545–8. Leônidas has much in common with Ánytê. No. 547 best illustrates this side of his work, and also his sympathetic interest in humble folk.

549. A fragment. Mœro was a poetess of Byzantium, of whom little is known. On lines 1–2 see No. 496, note.

551. The reference in this fragment is to a passage of Euripidês (Nauck, *Trag. Frag. Adesp.* 187), where he said 'Love, you blow with two winds'. Cércidas was a Cynic, who popularized philosophy.

752

NOTES

554. Cf. No. 509, lines 1–2. The mare travelled from port to port by land as fast as a coasting-vessel would do the same journey.

556. Báttarus, the keeper of a low establishment, pleads his case against Thalês who has broken into it. The translation suggests the metre of the Greek, on which see Nos. 181–3, note.

557–8. Alcæus mocks Philip for his defeat by the Roman general Flamininus at the battle of Cynoscéphalæ in 197 B.C. and Philip answers him. Alcæus' use of epigram as a political weapon is unique in the Anthology (cf. A. Körte, ref. as in No. 512, note, pp. 397–400).

561. From a papyrus of which the date is about A.D. 100: the piece itself may be earlier. The epithets which describe the bees show knowledge of a particular species, probably *Chalicodoma Sicula*, common in S. Europe and N. Africa. These mason-bees, 'which visibly collect, prepare, transport, and mould into shape their building materials', are not mentioned by any other ancient writer. Aristctle is probably responsible for the notion that the worker bees are non-mating (cf. Virgil, *G.* iv. 198 f. 'nec corpora segnes | in Venerem solvunt'). (See Powell and Barber, *New Chapters in Greek Literature*, 1st Series (1921), p. 56 f.; 2nd Series (1929), p. 62 f.)

562. From a papyrus of the 2nd or 3rd century A.D. Here, as in No. 617, the accent on the penultimate syllable of each line is regulated and plays a part in the scansion. See *Greek Poetry and Life*, Oxford, 1936, p. 313, and cf. Nos. 630–1, note.

565. In Greek legend, Têreus, King of Thrace, married Procnê, daughter of Pandîon, King of Athens, and had by her a son Itys or Itylus. He then violated her sister Philomêla, cut out her tongue, and hid her away. Procnê, informed by means of a picture in needlework, secretly killed and cooked Itys and beguiled Têreus into eating him. Têreus then became a hoopoe; Procnê a nightingale, mourning ever for Itys; and Philomêla a swallow, twittering of her wrorgs with clipped tongue. Latin authors, far less suitably, make Procnê the swallow and Philomêla the nightingale (cf. No. 664).

NOTES

566. Cf. No. 485.

567. Cf. No. 526.

569. Corinth was sacked in 146 B.C. by the Roman general Mummius.

570. Zeus fell in love with Eurôpa and, disguised as a friendly bull, carried her off on his back. The poem is a late but good example of the Hellenistic epyllion (cf. Nos. 503, 512, notes). Catullus' *Marriage of Peleus and Thetis* has many similar characteristics.

571. Also well translated by Richard Garnett, *Idylls and Epigrams* (Macmillan and Co., 1869), p. 1.

572. Also well translated by E. J. Myers, *Gathered Poems* (Macmillan and Co., 1904), p. 39.

573. Cf. No. 409, note; 502 (*f*), note. This poem is a development of the dirge as found in Theocritus xv. 100 ff., and the use of a refrain is also Theocritean. But its passion has the tints and the taint of the Orient. *Cypris*, *Cytherêa*, and *Cythêra* are all names for Aphroditê. There are several translations, including one by Mrs. Browning.

574. Gilbert Murray kindly contributes:

> Alas, when mallow in the garden dies,
> Or parsley green or crinkled anise dear,
> They live again, they rise another year:
> But we, the tall, the mighty and the wise,
> Once dead, beneath the hollow ground must keep
> A long dumb changeless unawakening sleep.

Cf. W. Wordsworth, *Valedictory Sonnet to the River Duddon*:

> Still glides the Stream, and shall for ever glide;
> The Form remains, the Function never dies:
> While we, the brave, the mighty, and the wise,
> We Men, who in our morn of youth defied
> The elements, must vanish: be it so!

The first line of the Greek is omitted by both translators. It runs: 'Begin, Sicilian Muses, begin your mournful song.' Cf. the refrain in No. 498.

577. E. Blunden, *Halfway House*. R. Cobden-Sanderson, Ltd., 1932.

NOTES

578. These lines come from the Preface to the Anthology or Garland of poems made by Meleâger, which forms the basis of the Palatine Anthology. Forty-one poets are named, and the work of each is characterized by the name of some flower or plant.　*Dioclês* was a philosopher, and younger contemporary of Meleâger.　*Anytê*: cf. Nos. 487–90. *Moiro (Mœro)*: cf. No. 549.　*Melanippidês*: a writer of Dithyrambs in the 5th century B.C.　*Nossis*: a poetess of Locri in South Italy; wrote epigrams.　*Rhiânus*: a writer of epics on historical subjects in the 3rd century B.C.

585. Cf. R. Herrick, *Hesperides*, No. 271 (Muses Library Edition).

586. *Menippêan Graces*: Meleâger's early work included satirical prose dialogues in the manner of Menippus of Gadara, who is best known to us through his imitator Lucian. The book was called 'The Graces'. See, further, F. A. Wright, *The Poets of the Greek Anthology*, 1924, p. 121.

589. Philodêmus is an important figure in the history of Latin poetry and of æsthetic theory generally. See L. P. Wilkinson in *Greece and Rome*, vol. ii, No. 6, May 1933.

590. *Hellê's jaws*: the Hellespont or Dardanelles.　*Scarphê's haven*: on the Corinthian Gulf.

591. *Phyllis*: a Thracian princess. Loved and deserted by Dêmophon, son of Thêseus, she hung herself. See Ovid, *Heroides*, ii. The Athenians fought disastrously for Amphipolis in 465 B.C., but with more success in 437. The site was familiar to British troops 1915–18.

595. Cf. Leônidas (*Anth. Pal.* ix. 99) and E. R. Bevan's note in *The Poems of Leonidas*, p. 104.

597. Sir Edward Cook, *More Literary Recreations* (Macmillan and Co., 1919), pp. 343–5, collects many previous versions of this *jeu d'esprit*, viz. by Ausonius (*Epigr.* 22) and Dr. Johnson in Latin; by Sir Thomas Wyatt, Wordsworth, Coleridge, Shelley, and W. J. Courthope in English.

599. *The Tyrrhene main*: on the western coast of Italy.

604. *Schéria*: probably Corcyra.

NOTES

607–10. The date of Marcus Argentarius is uncertain. He may belong to the last years of the 1st century B.C.

612. *Æneas' sons*: the Romans. Troy was re-established by Julius Cæsar among others. This epigram is also attributed to Germanicus.

613–16. There are three epigrammatists named Archias. One was Cicero's friend—to whom Nos. 613 and 615 may perhaps be ascribed.

615. Cf. Norman Douglas, *Birds and Beasts of the Greek Anthology* (Chapman and Hall, 1928), pp. 74–5, who summarizes Plutarch's excellent story of the Roman barber's jay (*Sol. Anim.* 973 c).

617. See *Greek Poetry and Life* (Oxford, 1936), where this papyrus fragment is fully discussed in connexion with other examples of the same rare metre—dactylic hexameters in which the 1st syllable of the last, and sometimes of the fifth, foot is short instead of long. The three quatrains here translated are the first which survive intact from a longer series arranged alphabetically according to the initial letter of each quatrain. Here we have ι (for so ει is written in the papyrus), κ, and λ. A complete text and translation will be found *op. sup. cit.*, pp. 308, 324. The attribution of the fragment to Mesomêdês in the *Oxford Book of Greek Verse* lacks authority. See also No. 562, note.

The song, or collection of quatrains, was made for convivial use. One of a party would sing to the accompaniment of a piper ('flute-girl'), while another drained off a long drink. The refrain, 'Piper, play on' is perhaps the injunction given by each of the party in turn when called upon to take up the singing.

618. *From cruell care exilde*: The correct translation would be 'with carefree heart'. For a modern version, cf. H. Macnaghten, *Little Masterpieces from the Anthology* (Gowans and Gray, Glasgow, 1924), p. 77:

> Death unrelenting snatched me, light of heart,
> Callimachus, a child of five; but you
> Weep not for me. I had but little part
> In life, and in life's sorrow little too.

621. Ptolemæus is Claudius Ptolemæus of Alexandria, the

mathematician, astronomer, and geographer who gave his name to the Ptolemaic System. On the translation (in quantitative elegiacs) see Introduction, p. lvi f.

622–3. The date of Glaucus is very uncertain. He may be much later.

622. See No. **217**, note; and cf. Tennyson, *The Captain*:

> There the sunlit ocean tosses
> O'er them mouldering,
> And the lonely sea-bird crosses
> With one waft of wing.

623. *Málea*: a town in Arcadia.

624. 'The *Herpêstês Ichneumon*, or Pharaoh's Cat, is a species of Mongoose still domesticated in Egypt as a destroyer of rats and mice' (A. W. Mair, Loeb Library Edn., *ad loc*.). On the translation of Nos. **624–5** see Introduction, p. lxxxix.

625. From an account of the Cestreus or Grey Mullet.

626. In the last line of the Greek there is a play upon words between *Bromos* meaning 'oats' and *Brómios*, a name of Dionŷsus: so too between πῡρογενῆ, *wheat-born*, and πῡρογενῆ, *fire-born*. Grotius' version 'non satus ex Semele matre sed ex simila' is very neat. (Quoted by Shane Leslie, *The Greek Anthology, Selected and Translated*, Ernest Benn, 1929, p. 171.)

627. Written at a time when the term 'Hellenes' denoted pagans in distinction from Christians. Some one with a sentimental attachment to the old religion composed for the emissaries of the Emperor Julian (361–3, born A.D. 331) what was said to have been the last oracle delivered at Delphi. (Cf. E. R. Bevan, *Christianity*, Home University Library, 1932, pp. 106–7.)

628–9. The *Posthomerica* of Quintus Smyrnæus, in fourteen books, continued the history of the Trojan war from the death of Hector to the return of the Greeks, drawing on earlier poets of the Epic Cycle.

628. The nymph Œnônê has heard from Helen of Paris' death.

629. The storm falls on the Greeks returning home from the sack of Troy.

NOTES

630–1. Nonnus, of Panopolis and Alexandria, has left an epic of forty-eight books recounting every possible story of Dionŷsus from his pre-natal days to his Assumption. His conquest of India occupies Books XIII–XL. It represents the struggle of civilization against barbarism, and makes the supreme test of his qualifications for divinity. Greeks and other converts follow in his train.

Nonnus' hexameter has a character of its own. It avoids consecutive spondees; prefers cæsura (trochaic) in the 3rd foot, and regulates the accent in the 6th (cf. No. 562, note). Later he made a paraphrase in hexameters of the Gospel of St. John.

Chalcómedê is a Bacchic maid; *Morreus* an Indian chieftain. *Damnámeneus*: apparently one of the Idæan Dactyls, gigantic smiths, whether of the Cretan or the Phrygian Mt. Ida (Strabo, 493 (x. 22)). The myth is as obscure as the identity of *Mêlis*. *Britomartis*: Cretan for 'Sweet Maid'. She was one of Artemis' attendant nymphs. When she leapt from a cliff to escape the amorous pursuit of Minos she was saved by fishers' nets (*dictya*), and hence is sometimes called *Dictynna*. Very probably she is simply Artemis, called by her Cretan title. The name Dictynna is common to both. (Cf. H. J. Rose, *A Handbook of Greek Mythology*, p. 117.) *Astériê*: Lêto's sister. By other accounts she took the form of a quail and plunged into the sea to escape Zeus, not, as here, Poseidon. She then became the floating island of Delos, on which see No. 509, note. (Cf. H. J. Rose, ibid., p. 130, note 50.)

The translations of Nos. 630–2 are all in the metre of R. Bridges's *Testament of Beauty*.

632. Also well translated in rhymed decasyllabic verse by E. E. Sikes, *Hero and Leander* (Methuen, 1920).

633–45. On Palladas the pessimist see F. A. Wright, *The Poets of the Greek Anthology*, pp. 201 ff. One of his poems is addressed to Hypatia, the heroine of Kingsley's novel.

633. The four lines in the original are probably a conflation of two distinct couplets, the first on a dead man, the second on poverty. J. A. Pott, *Greek Love Songs and Epigrams* (Kegan Paul, 1911), vol. i, p. 105, quotes a version taken,

NOTES

apparently, from John Lyly (1554?–1606) by Robert Burton (1577–1640):

> Mine haven's found: fortune and hope adieu,
> Mock others now, for I have done with you.

639. Robert Bland first popularized the Greek Anthology in England by his articles in *The Monthly Magazine*, 1805–6. These were afterwards published in book form and had a great success. Byron refers to the book in *English Bards and Scotch Reviewers*, 'And you associate bards . . .'. He wrote to Francis Hodgson on 29 June 1811: 'I regret very much in Greece having omitted to carry the Anthology with me—I mean Bland and Merivale's' (*Letters*, ed. Prothero, vol. i, p. 272).

645. The *Solitaries* are the Christian hermits of the Thebaid.

650. This Plato was a Byzantine musician of whom next to nothing is known.

659–62. The author was one of the eighty *Silentiarii* or Ushers who kept order in the palace of Justinian. He has also left a poem on the Church of St. Sophia.

662. Cf. No. 515, note.

664. The swallows (or house-martins) would very probably be nested *within* the bedroom if (like peasant quarters in modern Greece) it was raftered and unceiled. Towards dawn they would grow restless and flit about twittering until the shutters were opened. See (Sir) J. G. Frazer in *The Classical Review*, vol. v, Feb. 1891, pp. 1–3, who discusses the reception of the swallow by peoples as diverse as Lancashiremen and the Votyaks of E. Russia; Westphalians, and the Minahassa of Celebes. D'Arcy W. Thompson replies, ibid., pp. 230–1; for further refs. see his *Glossary of Greek Birds*, 1936, p. 316. *Philomêla*: cf. No. 565, note.

670–1. Cf. No. 233.

675. A. W. Mair, *Poems* (Edinburgh, Oliver and Boyd, 1929, p. 52), modernizes:

> Here I, Jock Scott frae Peterheid,
> At saxty year lie dour and deid,
>   A bachelor—for wed I wadna:
>   And och! I wish my father hadna!

NOTES

Cf. Thomas Hardy, *Human Shows, Far Phantasies* (Macmillan and Co., 1925, p. 219):

> I'm Smith of Stoke, aged sixty-odd,
> I've lived without a dame
> From youth time on: and would to God
> My dad had done the same.

678. Cf. Mark Twain, *Huckleberry Finn*, ch. viii: 'And he said if a man owned a beehive, and that man died, the bees must be told about it before sun-up next morning, or else the bees would all weaken down and quit work and die.'

683. In 188 B.C. Philopœmen and the Achæan League dismantled the walls of Sparta.

687. Rome here means Constantinople (so W. R. Paton, Loeb Library Edn., *ad loc.*). 'Pinioned' is used in two senses.

688. *Meroê*: in Ethiopia. A proverbial 'end of the world'.

690. The letters of the alphabet were used as figures, and the seventh, eighth, ninth, and tenth letters spell ζῆθι, meaning 'live'. This idea cannot be closely reproduced in English. (In line 1 read *aí* for *ai*.)

692. Initiates in the Bacchic cult were called Bacchi; cf. No. 397.

701. Refers to Vergil's treatment of Dido (*Aeneid*, Book IV) as both unfair and unhistoric.

706. Comêtas Chartularius (Keeper of the Records) 'wrote also some epigrams on a revised text of Homer which he edited, and a poem in hexameters on the raising of Lazarus'—J. W. Mackail (*Select Epigrams*, 3rd edn., p. 335), who adds that in the last couplet of the poem here translated 'we seem to hear the very voice of ancient poetry bidding the world a lingering and reluctant farewell'.

INDEX OF GREEK AUTHORS

[The figures refer to the numbers of the pieces.]

INDEX OF GREEK AUTHORS

INDEX OF GREEK AUTHORS

INDEX OF TRANSLATORS

[The references are to the numbers of the pieces.]

INDEX OF TRANSLATORS

INDEX OF TRANSLATORS

REFERENCES

[*Where no reference is given, the translation appears for the first time in this book.*]

1. Sir William Marris, *The Iliad of Homer*. Oxford University Press, 1934, pp. 1–3. Revised by the translator.
2. Maurice Hewlett, *The Iliad of Homer*. Cresset Press, Ltd., 1928, pp. 23–4.
3. William Cowper, *Homer's Iliad*: 1st ed., 1791; 2nd ed., 1802. The 2nd ed. had considerable alterations. Text from 1st ed.
4. As No. 3: text from 1st ed.
5. As No. 3: text from 2nd ed.
6. Lord Lyttleton and W. E. Gladstone, *Translations*. Bernard Quaritch, Ltd., 1861, pp. 79–81. The last four lines by T. F. Higham.
7. As No. 1: p. 108.
8. *The Works of Tennyson*, annotated. Edited by Hallam, Lord Tennyson. Macmillan & Co., Ltd., 1908, vol. vi, pp. 357–9. See Notes.
9. As No. 2: pp. 111–14.
10. As No. 3: text from 2nd ed.
11. Tennyson; in *Cornhill Magazine*, Dec. 1863; reprinted in *Enoch Arden*, 1864, pp. 177–8.
12. As No. 2: pp. 157–9.
13. George Ernle, *The Wrath of Achilleus: translated from the Iliad into Quantitative Hexameters*. Oxford University Press, 1922, pp. 75–6.
14. As No. 3: text from 2nd ed.
15. As No. 3: text from 1st ed.; slight alterations in punctuation.
17. As No. 2: pp. 233–4.
18. The Earl of Derby, *The Iliad of Homer*. John Murray, 1864, pp. 91–2.
19. Andrew Lang, Walter Leaf, and Ernest Myers, *The Iliad of Homer done into English Prose*. Macmillan & Co., Ltd., 1901, pp. 311–12.
20. As No. 1: pp. 352–3.   21. As No. 18: vol. ii, pp. 124–6.
22. As No. 1: pp. 380–2; revised by the translator.

23. As No. 18: vol. ii, pp. 180–2.

25. As No. 1: pp. 412–14; revised by the translator.

26. Tennyson; in *The Nineteenth Century*, Aug. 1877; reprinted in *Ballads and other Poems*, Macmillan & Co., Ltd., 1880, pp. 179–81. The last eight lines (from 'The Achæans' . . .) by C. M. Bowra.

27. As No. 1: pp. 423–4.

28 (i), 28 (ii), 28 (iii). Alexander Pope, *The Iliad of Homer*, 1718, vol. iv, pp. 92–3, 94, 97–9.

30. As No. 1: pp. 473–4.   31. As No. 3: text from 1st ed.

32. As No. 19: pp. 443–5.

33. Samuel Butler, *The Iliad of Homer, Rendered into English Prose for the Use of those who cannot read the Original*, 1898. Jonathan Cape, Ltd., 1921, reissue, corrected, pp. 373–5.

34. As No. 3: text from 1st ed.

35. As No. 28: vol. vi, 1720, pp. 92–3.

36. Robert Bridges, *Ibant Obscuri: an Experiment in the Classical Hexameter*. Clarendon Press, 1916, pp. 99–111.

37. As No. 1: pp. 564–6; revised by the translator.

38. Sir William Marris, *The Odyssey of Homer*. Oxford University Press, 1935, pp. 21–3; revised by the translator.

39 (i), 39 (ii). J. W. Mackail, *The Odyssey*. Methuen & Co., Ltd., 1903; Clarendon Press, 1932, new ed., revised, pp. 42–3, 48–9, 50–1.

40 (i). Samuel Butler, *The Odyssey rendered into English Prose*. Fifield, 1900, pp. 45–6 (Jonathan Cape, Ltd., 1923).

40 (ii). S. H. Butcher and Andrew Lang, *The Odyssey of Homer*. Macmillan & Co., Ltd., 1879.

41. As No. 39: pp. 88–9. (Revised by the translator.)

42. George Chapman, *Homer's Odyssey*, 1614–16.

43 (i), 43 (ii). As No. 39: pp. 108–9, 111–14.

44 (i). *The Odyssey of Homer, newly translated into English Prose*, by T. E. Shaw (Col. T. E. Lawrence). Oxford University Press, New York, 1932 (Emery Walker, Ltd., London), pp. 85–6.

44 (ii). H. B. Cotterill, *Homer's Odyssey*. Harrap & Co., Ltd., 1911, pp. 85–8.

45. As No. 44 (i): pp. 117–18.

REFERENCES

46 (i), **46** (ii). William Morris, *The Odyssey of Homer*. Reeves & Turner, 1887, pp. 159–61, 162–3. By permission of the Executors.

46 (iii). As No. 38: pp. 164–5; revised by the translator.

46 (iv). As No. 46 (i): pp. 176–7.

46 (v). As No. 39: pp. 223–5; revised by the translator.

46 (vi). William Cowper, *Homer's Odyssey*. Text from 1st ed., 1791.

47. As No. 39: pp. 268–9.

48 (i), **48** (ii). As No. 40 (i): pp. 191–3, 203–6.

49. As No. 46 (vi).

50. As No. 44 (i): pp. 239–40.

51 (i). As No. 39: pp. 414–18.

51 (ii). As No. 38: pp. 356–7; revised by the translator.

52. As No. 44 (i): pp. 279–80.

53 (i), **53** (ii). As No. 46 (i): pp. 394–7, 411–12.

54. As No. 40 (i): pp. 304–6.   **55.** As No. 46 (vi).

56 (i), **56** (ii). As No. 38: pp. 426, 429–30.

67 (iv), **67** (vi). Samuel Butler, *Hesiod, Works and Days*. L.C.C. Central School of Arts and Crafts, 1924, pp. 17–18, 22–3 (Jonathan Cape, Ltd., 1923).

77, 78. W. M. W. Call, *Golden Histories*. Smith, Elder & Co., 1871. Revised throughout by T. F. Higham. (See Notes.)

82, 83, 84. P. B. Shelley; first published by Mrs. Shelley in *Posthumous Poems*, 1824.

91. P. B. Shelley; written in 1818; first published by Mrs. Shelley in *Posthumous Poems*, 2nd ed., 1839.

104. Revised by the translator (Sir William Marris) from *Translations from the Greek Anthology*, privately printed at the Bharat Bandhu Press, Aligarh, U.P., India, 1919, p. 137.

107. J. A. Symonds, *Studies of the Greek Poets*, 1873–6; 3rd ed., 1893, A. & C. Black, Ltd., vol. i, p. 263.

109. A. Watson Bain, *The Times*, 25 Sept. 1934, p. 15.

111. After J. H. Merivale; as adapted by G. B. Grundy, *Ancient Gems in Modern Settings*, Basil Blackwell & Mott, Ltd., 1913, p. 2, from the version in *Collections from the Greek Anthology* (see No. 161), p. 8.

REFERENCES

240, 241. G. M. Cookson, *Four Plays of Æschylus*. Basil Blackwell & Mott, Ltd., 1922, pp. 74–7, 81–3.

242. E. R. Bevan, *The Seven against Thebes of Æschylus*. Edward Arnold & Co., 1912, pp. 15–18.

243–6. As No. 240: pp. 166–7, 181–2 (No. 244 revised by the translator), 203–4, 210–12.

248; 250, 251. Walter Headlam, *The Agamemnon of Æschylus*. Cambridge University Press, 1910, pp. 65–9, 111–13 (supplemented by C. M. Bowra), 117–19.

252. Louis MacNeice, *The Agamemnon of Æschylus*. Faber & Faber, Ltd., 1936, pp. 57–8.

253–6. G. M. Cookson, *Æschylus' Agamemnon, Choephoræ, Eumenides*. Chapman & Hall, Ltd., 1924, pp. 85–7, 112–15, 131–3, 156–9.

275–7. C. J. Billson, *Pindar's Odes of Victory: The Olympian and Pythian Odes*. Basil Blackwell & Mott, Ltd., 1928, pp. 23–5, 55–9, 137–9.

278. H. T. Wade-Gery and C. M. Bowra, *Pindar: The Pythian Odes*. Nonesuch Press, 1928, pp. 79–81.

279–80. As No. 275: pp. 177–81, 197–213.

281–2. As No. 278: pp. 50–3, 152–3.

283. As No. 275: p. 279.   **284.** As No. 278: pp. 42–3.

285–90. C. J. Billson, *Pindar's Odes of Victory: The Nemean and Isthmian Odes*. Basil Blackwell & Mott, Ltd., 1930, pp. 7, 25–7, 107–11, 161–3, 181–3, 189–93.

291. A. S. Way; in W. Rhys Roberts, *Dionysius of Halicarnassus on Literary Criticism*. Macmillan & Co., Ltd., 1910, pp. 215–17 (see ibid., p. x).

295. As No. 141: p. 53.

299. Thomas Moore, *Odes of Anacreon*, 1803, p. 45.

300–2. As No. 163: vol. iii, pp. 445, 447, 457.

309 (i). J. S. Phillimore, *Poems*, Maclehose, 1902, pp. 113–16 (now published by Jackson, Son & Co., Glasgow).

310. As No. 141: p. 67.

312. C. S. Calverley, *Verses and Translations*, 1861; *Complete Works*, G. Bell & Sons, Ltd., 1901, pp. 273–4.

313. R. Whitelaw, *Sophocles*. Rivingtons, 1883, pp. 342–4.

314–16. J. T. Sheppard, *The Electra of Sophocles*. Bowes & Bowes, Cambridge, 1927, pp. 35–7, 49–53, 79–83.

REFERENCES

317. J. T. Sheppard, *The Œdipus of Sophocles*. Cambridge University Press, 1920, pp. 11–15.

318. As No. 313: pp. 37–8 (text slightly altered).

319–20. As No. 317: pp. 77–9, 85–7.

321. As No. 221: p. 116.

323. J. S. Phillimore, *The Athenian Drama*: vol. ii, Sophocles. George Allen & Unwin, Ltd., 1902, p. 169.

325–6. As No. 313: pp. 175–7, 274–6.

327. Gilbert Murray, *ΆΡΙΣΤΟΣ ’ΑΝΔΡΩΝ, A Study of Heracles*. An (unpublished) paper read to the Oxford Branch of the Classical Association, 14 May 1936.

331. As No. 141: pp. 123–9.

332. A. E. Housman, in *Odes from the Greek Dramatists*, by various hands, edited by A. W. Pollard. David Stott, 1890, pp. 85–7.

334–5. As No. 107: vol. ii, pp. 67, 72.

338. Walter Headlam; quoted by A. C. Pearson, *Sophocles, Fragments*. Cambridge University Press, 1917, vol. ii, p. 264.

340. Gilbert Murray; in *The Pageant of Greece*, edited by Sir R. W. Livingstone. Clarendon Press, 1928, p. 118.

341. As No. 323: p. lxi (adapted to suit the Greek text by T. F. Higham).

342. Sir R. W. Livingstone, *The Greek Genius and Its Meaning to Us*. Clarendon Press, 2nd ed., 1915, pp. 80–1; completed by C. M. Bowra.

343. As No. 340: p. 118.

347. W. E. Leonard, *The Fragments of Empedocles translated into English Verse*. Kegan Paul, Trench, Trübner & Co., Ltd., 1908, p. 53. Completed by the editors to suit the Greek text.

349. Frances Cornford, *Different Days*. Hogarth Press, 1928, p. 43.

350. P. B. Shelley; written in 1819; published by Mrs. Shelley in *Posthumous Poems*, 1824; completed by T. F. Higham.

351. Richard Aldington, *Euripides, Alcestis*. Chatto & Windus, 1930, pp. 27–9.

REFERENCES

352–3. Robert Browning, *Balaustion's Adventure*. Smith, Elder & Co., 1871, pp. 112–14, 119–20.

355–7. F. L. Lucas, *Euripides, Medea*. Clarendon Press, 1924, pp. 42–3, 53–5, 68–9.

360. Gilbert Murray, *The Hippolytus of Euripides*. George Allen & Unwin, Ltd., 1902, p. 39.

366. J. T. Sheppard, *Euripides' Hecuba*. Clarendon Press, 1924, pp. 49–50.

373–4. Gilbert Murray, *The Trojan Women of Euripides*. George Allen & Unwin, Ltd., 1905, pp. 51–3, 74–9.

376–8. Gilbert Murray, *The Iphigenia in Tauris of Euripides*. George Allen & Unwin, Ltd., 1910, pp. 23–32, 37–9, 64–6.

379. J. T. Sheppard, *The Helen of Euripides*. Cambridge University Press, 1925, pp. 5–6.

381. As No. 107: vol. ii, pp. 43–5; with minor alterations by the editors.

384–5. Gilbert Murray, *The Bacchæ of Euripides*. George Allen & Unwin, Ltd., 1902, pp. 42–5, 53–4.

386. F. M. Stawell, *Euripides, Iphigenia in Aulis*. G. Bell & Sons, Ltd., 1929, pp. 33–5.

387–8. Gilbert Murray, *The Rhesus of Euripides*. George Allen & Unwin, Ltd., 1913, pp. 28–30, 43–5.

390 (vi). As No. 107: lines 1–7, vol. ii, p. 79; lines 8–10, ibid., p. 78; adapted by the editors to suit the Greek text.

391. As No. 107: p. 87; completed by C. M. Bowra.

397. Gilbert Murray; quoted by J. E. Harrison, *Prolegomena to the Study of Greek Religion*. Cambridge University Press, 1908, p. 479.

399 (ii). As No. 107: vol. ii, p. 84.

400. *The Life and Poems of Walter Headlam*, with a Memoir by Cecil Headlam. Gerald Duckworth & Co., Ltd., 1910, *Poems*, p. 100; completed by the editors.

02. As No. 107: vol. ii, pp. 80–1.

08. As No. 216: vol. i, p. 25.

12–13. B. B. Rogers, *The Acharnians of Aristophanes*. G. Bell & Sons, Ltd., 1910, pp. 75–85, 97–103.

14. T. Mitchell, *The Comedies of Aristophanes*. John Murray, 1820, vol. i, pp. 161–4.

REFERENCES

415–16. Gilbert Murray, *Aristophanes, A Study*. Clarendon Press, 1933, pp. 16–18 (revised and completed by the translator), pp. 55–6.

417. As No. 414: vol. ii, pp. 25–7; with minor changes.

423. A. C. Swinburne; in *The Athenæum*, 30 Oct. 1880.

424. H. F. Cary, *The Birds of Aristophanes*, 1824, p. 99; revised by T. F. Higham.

427–8. B. B. Rogers, *The Lysistrata of Aristophanes*, 1878. New ed., 1911, G. Bell & Sons, Ltd., pp. 183–5, 207–8.

429. B. B. Rogers, *The Thesmophoriazusæ of Aristophanes*. G. Bell & Sons, Ltd., 1904, pp. 171–4.

431. Lines 399–416 from Gilbert Murray, *The Frogs of Aristophanes* (George Allen & Unwin, Ltd., 1908, pp. 34–5), the rest from *The Frogs of Aristophanes*, by D. W. Lucas and F. J. A. Cruso (Bowes & Bowes, 1936, pp. 30–40), with a few revisions by the latter, who contributed this portion.

432–3. Marshall MacGregor, *Aristophanes, The Birds and the Frogs*. Edward Arnold & Co., 1927, pp. 97–8.

436. B. B. Rogers, *The Ecclesiazusæ of Aristophanes*. G. Bell & Sons, Ltd., 1902, pp. 29–41.

437. *Plutus, the God of Riches, a Comedy translated from the Original Greek of Aristophanes, with large Notes, Explanatory and Critical*, by Henry Fielding, Esq., and the Rev. Mr. Young, 1742.

442. As No. 233: p. 60.

443 (i). H. K. St. J. Sanderson; in *Nineteen Echoes and a Song*. Cambridge: G. M. Lee, Trinity College, 1935, p. 8.

445 (i). Quoted by F. A. Wright, *The Girdle of Aphrodite*. George Routledge & Sons, Ltd., 2nd ed., 1926, p. xxxvi. The translation is believed to have been written during the period 1914–18, but its authorship is uncertain.

445 (ii). P. B. Shelley; published by Mrs. Shelley in *Poetical Works*, 1839.

447. As No. 161: p. 105; the last line of Merivale's version has been revised by the editors.

449. As No. 216: vol. i, pp. 22–3.

450. Robert Bridges; in *The Spirit of Man*. Longmans, Green & Co., 1916, No. 28.

REFERENCES

464. Robert Browning, *Aristophanes' Apology*; in *Poetical Works*. Smith, Elder & Co., 1910, vol. i, p. 748.

467. Lord Byron, *Don Juan*, 1821, Canto IV, stanza xii.

468. As No. 104: p. 32; revised by the translator.

469. Anglo-Rhemish New Testament, 1582: 1 Cor. xv. 33.

470, 473. As No. 415: p. 223 (completed by the translator), pp. 223–4.

481. As No. 214 (i): p. 61.

484. C. C. Martindale, *The Goddess of Ghosts*. Burns, Oates, & Washbourne, Ltd., 2nd ed., 1925, p. 68; revised by the translator.

487. W. H. D. Rouse, *An Echo of Greek Song*. J. M. Dent & Sons, Ltd., 1899, p. 57.

489. As No. 104: p. 125; revised by the translator.

490. R. A. Furness, *Translations from the Greek Anthology*. Jonathan Cape, Ltd., 1931, p. 38.

491–3. As No. 216: vol. i, pp. 32 and 28.

494. H. Wellesley; quoted by G. B. Grundy; see No. 111, p. 298.

499. Jack Lindsay, *Theocritus, The Complete Poems*, Fanfrolico Press, 1930, pp. 9–16; revised by the translator. With acknowledgements to J. M. Edmonds, *The Greek Bucolic Poets* (Heinemann, Ltd., 1912) in the rendering of lines 2, 20, and 166.

500–1. R. C. Trevelyan, *The Idylls of Theocritus*. Casanova Society, 1925, pp. 11, 22–3.

502. As No. 141: pp. 193–201.

502 (a). The first eight words are supplied by the editors; the rest is from Walter Pater, *Demeter and Persephone*, in *Greek Studies*, library edition, Macmillan & Co., Ltd., 1910, pp. 126–7. The Essay was first published in *The Fortnightly Review*, Jan. and Feb. 1876, and was revised by Pater in 1878.

502 (d). From the anonymous translation entitled *Sixe Idillia, that is, Sixe Small or Pretty Poems, or Æglogues. Chosen out of the right famous Sicilian Poet Theocritus and translated into English Verse*. Printed at Oxford, by Joseph Barnes, 1588.

502 (e). As No. 312: pp. 357 ff.

REFERENCES

502 (f). As No. 499: pp. 70–5; revised by the translator. With acknowledgements to J. M. Edmonds, op. cit., in the rendering of lines 34, 62, and 97.

502 (g). H. H. Chamberlin, *Late Spring, a Translation of Theocritus*. Harvard University Press, 1936, p. 138.

502 (h), 503. As No. 312: pp. 386 f., 402 f. (with minor changes in lines 6 and 17 of No. 503).

507, 509, 510. R. A. Furness, *Poems of Callimachus*. Jonathan Cape, Ltd., 1931, pp. 69, 35–7, 9–13.

513. William Cory, *Ionica*. Smith, Elder & Co., 1858, p. 7.

514. As No. 214 (i): p. 89.

515. G. M. Young, *Epigrams of Callimachus*. Oxford University Press, 1934, p. 41.

516. R. C. K. Ensor, *Odes and Other Poems*. Sidgwick & Jackson, Ltd., 1917, p. 101.

517–21. As No. 507: pp. 91, 95, 97, 99.

523. As No. 107: vol. i, p. 278.

524. As No. 216: vol. i, p. 33.

525–6. As No. 490: pp. 45, 48.

527. As No. 216: vol. i, p. 33. 528. As No. 490: p. 49.

529. J. S. Phillimore; in *The Dublin Review* (Burns, Oates, & Washbourne, Ltd.), Apr. 1907 (in an article on Asclepiades).

530. As No. 107: vol. ii, p. 340.

545–8. Edwyn Bevan, *The Poems of Leonidas of Tarentum*. Clarendon Press, 1931, pp. 80, 2, 38, 8.

550. As No. 119: 2nd ser., p. 25.

552, 555. As No. 487: pp. 39, 50.

558. As No. 161: p. 188.

559, 560, 564. As No. 490: pp. 85, 69, 74.

565. Humbert Wolfe, *Others Abide*. Ernest Benn, Ltd., 1927, p. 81.

566–7. A. J. Butler, *Amaranth and Asphodel*. Basil Blackwell & Mott, Ltd., 1922, pp. 205, 211.

569. Walter Leaf, *Quatrains from the Greek*. R. & R. Clark, Ltd., 1919, p. 12. (Privately printed.)

571. P. B. Shelley, *Alastor*, 1816.

572. P. B. Shelley; published by Mrs. Shelley in *Posthumous Poems*, 1824.

REFERENCES

574. E. J. Myers, *Gathered Poems*. Macmillan & Co., Ltd., 1904, p. 40.

575. As No. 565: p. 62.

577. E. Blunden, *Halfway House*. R. Cobden Sanderson, Ltd., 1932.

579–82. As No. 490: pp. 104, 105, 106, 108.

583. As No. 104: p. 63; revised by the translator.

584. As No. 565: p. 28.   [Lane, 1895, p. 100.

585. H. C. Beeching, *In a Garden and other Poems*. John

586. As No. 216: vol. i, p. 77.

587. Walter Headlam, *Fifty Poems of Meleager*. Macmillan & Co., Ltd., 1890, p. 19.

588. Andrew Lang, *Grass of Parnassus*. Longmans, Green & Co., Ltd., 1892, p. 189.

589. As No. 141: p. 253.   [translator).

590–1. As No. 104: pp. 114, 125 (No. 591 revised by the

593. As No. 216: vol. ii, p. 32.   595. As No. 104: p. 118.

596. William Cowper; first published in 1803.

598. As No. 216: vol. ii, p. 26.

599, 601, 602. As No. 104: pp. 111 (revised by the translator), 19 (revised by the translator), 126.

603. Quoted by Norman Douglas, *Birds and Beasts of the Greek Anthology*. Chapman & Hall, Ltd., 1928, p. 148 (now published by Chatto & Windus). The book is dedicated to his friend J. E. B., 'whose verses have enlivened' it.

604. As No. 216: vol. ii, p. 43.

605. As No. 214 (i): p. 19.   606. As No. 565: p. 105.

607. As No. 104: p. 66 (revised by the translator).

609. As No. 565: p. 83.   610. As No. 216: vol. ii, p. 34.

611, 614. As No. 104: pp. 144 and 115 (No. 614 revised by the translator).

617. T. F. Higham; in *Greek Poetry and Life: Essays Presented to Gilbert Murray on his Seventieth Birthday*. Clarendon Press, 1936, p. 324.

618. Timothe Kendall; in *Flowers of Epigrammes . . .*, 1577.

619–20. As No. 216: vol. ii, pp. 59, 58.

621. As No. 450: No. 160.

622–3. As No. 216: vol. ii, pp. 60–1.

779

REFERENCES

635, 637. As No. 566: pp. 87, 98.

638. As No. 490: p. 133.

639. Robert Bland; in *The Monthly Magazine*, vol. xix, 1805; reprinted in *Translations chiefly from the Greek Anthology*, 1806, p. 70.

640. As No. 119: 1st ser., p. 105.

641. As No. 490: p. 134.

642. As No. 569: p. 27.   **644.** As No. 216: vol. ii, p. 65.

646. As No. 566: p. 99.

647-8. As No. 119: 1st ser., pp. 110, 134.

649-50. As No. 566: pp. 121, 255.

655. Maurice Baring, *Half a Minute's Silence and other Stories*. Heinemann, Ltd., 1925, p. 146.

656. As No. 445 (i): p. 65.

658. As No. 104: p. 109 (revised by the translator).

659-60. As No. 566: pp. 13, 55.

662. William Cowper; first published in 1803.

664. As No. 104: p. 75 (revised by the translator).

665. As No. 190: p. 39 a.

667. As No. 104: p. 140; revised by the translator.

669. Andrew Lang, *First and Last Rhymes*. Longmans, Green & Co., Ltd., 1892, p. 163.

670. As No. 445 (i), p. 57.   **671.** As No. 233: p. 58.

672. Earl of Cromer, *Paraphrases and Translations from the Greek*. Macmillan & Co., Ltd., 1902, p. 66.

673. As No. 119: 1st ser., p. 152.

674. As No. 566: p. 263.

676. As No. 487: p. 41.   **677.** As No. 490: p. 199.

678. As No. 119: 2nd ser., p. 151.

679. P. B. Shelley; published by Mrs. Shelley in *Poetical Works*, 1839.

682. As No. 566: p. 113.   **683-4.** As No. 214, i: pp. 17, 19.

685. A. Lothian, *The Golden Treasury of the Greeks*. Basil Blackwell & Mott, Ltd., 1920, no. cvii.

686. Francis Wrangham; quoted by G. B. Grundy: see No. 111: p. 312.

688. As No. 214 (ii): p. 120.

689. D. M. Moir, *Mansie Wauch*, 1824, xxii.

691. As No. 130: p. 219.

REFERENCES

692. Richard Garnett, *The Twilight of the Gods*. John Lane, 1927, p. 124.

693. H. Wellesley; quoted by G. B. Grundy: see No. 111, p. 362.

694. As No. 490: p. 203.

696. William Cowper; first published in 1803.

699–700. As No. 490: pp. 199, 205.

702. As No. 565: p. 115.   **705.** As No. 566: p. 101.

PRINTED IN
GREAT BRITAIN
AT THE
UNIVERSITY PRESS
OXFORD
BY
JOHN JOHNSON
PRINTER
TO THE
UNIVERSITY